KU-570-519

About the Authors

Alfred E. Friedl is Emeritus Professor of Education at Kent State University. He was born on a farm in rural Minnesota and obtained his elementary education in a one-room school house. He attended high school in Albany, and received an undergraduate degree from Saint Cloud State College, both in Minnesota.

He began his teaching career as an elementary school teacher in Minnesota and California. After receiving his doctorate in Education from Colorado State University, he served as a curriculum coordinator for the San Diego County Department of Education. He also taught extension classes for San Diego State University and UCLA. He later moved to Kent State University where he taught for twenty-five years.

In addition to winning an "oustanding teacher" award from Kent State, he also won a national teaching award for writing and presenting a 13-week television series entitled, "Teaching Children about Space Science." Professor Friedl has written extensively for more than three decades—authoring or co-authoring more than twenty books. He co-authored his first book, *Your Science Fair*, while still a sixth-grade teacher.

Trish Yourst Koontz is a professor of Mathematics and Science Education at Kent State State University in the College of Education. She received her Ph.D. in education from Kent State University where she has been on the faculty since 1983. A former elementary, middle, and high school teacher, she has authored or co-authored several chapters and articles dealing with her special interests in the teaching and learning of mathematics and science as well as gender equity issues in education. She recently co-authored a book titled, *Science and Society in the Twentieth Century*. She has received several teaching awards, including Kent State University's 2003 Distinquished Teaching Award and a Best Practices award from the state of Ohio.

Brief Contents

Contents

Preface

❈ An Inquiry Approach

The vision of school science in the *National Science Educational Standards (NSES)* (NRC, 1995) is predicated on students' learning science with understanding. All students deserve and must have the opportunity to become scientifically literate. Students' understanding of science, their ability to use it to solve science-related personal and societal challenges, and their confidence in and disposition toward science are all shaped by the teaching they encounter in school.

The NSES states that science teaching should change ". . . with the classroom becoming a community in which students learn science through inquiry." They contend that science teaching should move away from ". . . teachers presenting information and covering science topics to students learning science through active involvement."

Again and again, the focus of the standards is on inquiry. And so it should be. Inquiry has been the focus of this book from its inception in 1972. You will find that each chapter (except the first three, which are introductory) uses an inquiry-based method to teach and learn science.

The first chapter clearly introduces teachers to how they can implement inquiry lessons using appropiate questioning, classroom environments, and alternative/authentic assessments. Chapter one supports the rest of the book; it is not separate from it.

❈ Revised Coverage

The sixth edition of *Teaching Science to Children an Inquiry Approach* preserves all of the features of the previous edition in addition to providing material you will find as valuable resources in the teaching of science to children. The major additions include a new content chapter on simple machines and a major revision of chapter one that more carefully details the scientific process skills. These process skill activities should be engaging and help teachers and students better understand a general feel for the process skills before the skills are applied to real world applications and situations.

A new chapter two introduces students to the NSES and a constructivist approach to teaching *all* children science. The diversity of students is one reason teaching is an exciting profession. By understanding constructivist teaching in general and research-based teaching strategies for specific learners, teachers learn to appreciate and celebrate the diversity of students. New features such as using WebQuests and technology updates were added to chapter three.

The remaining chapters, 4 through 21, were changed to provided a more useful format that includes in each chapter: an alignment between each of the events in the chapter and the national standards, an historical introduction, key terms, updated sites and software, and a sample alternative assessment. Each of these features should make the book a more valuable textbook and resource.

✴ Practical Instruction and Resources

Another focus of this book is "simplicity." We need not tell prospective teachers how hard it is to teach science. Instead, we need to tell them how easy it is; and that they will be able to teach it effectively. Instead of many steps, there are only three. Instead of focusing mostly on theory, the book focuses on practical exercises that work in the classroom.

Not only are the methods simple, but so are the activities. Most of the activities in the book can be presented by a typical elementary school teacher without a strong science background, special in-service work, or extra courses.

We feel that methods, in isolation, are of limited value. That is why the methods (actual inquiry activities) and content are combined throughout the text. This combining of method and content is often touted, but rarely achieved. In fact, most methods books in science education are divided into two parts; the methods in the front of the book, and the content in the back. Although the reader is told to combine the two, the authors cannot seem to do it themselves.

The NSES strongly supports the use of technologies to help teachers create a classroom environment that enables children to learn in an inquiry setting. Integrating computers into the science curriculum provides powerful new ways to help children become active learners. This book promotes children's use of computers as scientists use them: as tools for gathering data and analyzing information, as vehicles for communications, and for simulations. Chapter three gives an overview of the importance and use of technology in the teaching and learning of science. To further support teachers in implementing technology into science lessons, we use an icon 🖳 to clearly point out computer/calculator activities in each of the subsequent chapters.

This book is different. The methods in this text have been used with thousands of teachers for many years. The events and steps have been tested and retested. We hope you will find this book to be a real help in teaching science to children.

✴ New Online Resources

A Web site now accompanies the text at **www.mhhe.com/friedl6e.** The site includes a **student study guide with quizzes** and review material, and **links to sites** listed in the text. Resources for the instructor are also accessible from this site.

✴ New Instructor's Resource CD-ROM

The new Instructor's Resource CD-ROM contains the text's instructor's manual and test bank. Contact your local representative to receive your copy.

⚹ Acknowledgments

We would like to thank the following for permission to reproduce material for this book:

>   **Tom Snyder Productions, Inc.** For figure 3.1, sample screens taken from The Graph Club, copyright Tom Snyder Productions, Inc. All rights reserved. Reprinted with permission.
>
>   **The Learning Company.** For figure 3.3, sample screen taken from Super Solvers: Gizmos & Gadgets, copyright TM-Mattel, Inc. All rights reserved. Reprinted with permission.
>
>   **Wendi Koontz,** illustrator of figures 3.4, 21.9, and the disk icon used to indicate computer and calculator activities. All rights reserved. Printed with permission.

In addition, we would like to thank the following reviewers for their feedback during the development of the 6th edition:

William M. Brown, Piedmont College
Mary W. Funderburk, University of Mobile
Albert G. Hayward, South Carolina State University
Darci L. Houser, Cleveland State University
Teresa B. Jayroe, Mississippi State University
Amy L. Kavanaugh, Western Michigan University
Richard Krustchinsky, University of St. Thomas
LaVerne Logan, Western Illinois University
Nadine Meyer, Kent State University
Frank L. Misti, Bloomsburg University
Stanley S. Shimer, Indiana State University
Robin Ward, University of Louisiana, Layfayette

Finally, we'd like to thank the Editorial, Design, and Production staff at McGraw-Hill for their assistance with the sixth edition.

Alfred E. Friedl
Trish Y. Koontz

Introduction
SAFETY IN THE CLASSROOM

You can work safely in the classroom. But any time you have a classroom full of elementary school children, there is potential for danger. This is especially true in some of the science activities. Even simple activities, using generally safe materials may lead to problems if the teacher does not plan ahead. Here is a list of some possible dangers and how to plan for safety.

❄ Fire and/or Heat

In some activities, fire and/or heat are needed. It is assumed that most elementary classrooms will not have natural gas outlets. If this is the case, teachers should be instructed on how to use Bunsen burners and gas appliances safely. Ask the high school science teacher or other qualified person to do the training. The following items apply in most elementary classrooms even if gas heat is not available.

> If hot liquids are to be stored in glassware, use only heat-resistant glassware.
> Tie back long hair and confine loose clothing.
> Know the location of the fire extinguisher and know how to operate it.
> Know the fire drill procedures and the locations of the fire exits.
> When heating a liquid in a test tube, do not heat any one spot, but move the test tube in a circular or swirling motion above the flame.
> Always hold the test tube so that the opening is aimed away from people.
> Allow heated materials to cool before handling. Never leave them unattended.
> Wear safety goggles.
> Keep flammable liquids away from open flames.

❄ Hand and Skin Safety

(Although corrosive and caustic materials are not used in this book, special care is still needed.)

> If children spill any chemical on their hands or other skin area, they should wash quickly and thoroughly with cool water.
> Students should wash their hands at the end of any science period in which chemicals are used.
> Use test-tube holders when heating contents of test tubes.
> Allow heated materials to cool before handling them.
> Keep hands away from face, eyes, and mouth.

Eye Safety

Protection is needed any time any liquid or other matter can be splashed or propelled to the eyes.

Wear approved safety goggles whenever a potential danger might be present.

Electrical Safety

Make sure that all electrical equipment is properly grounded.

Do not string electrical cords where people might accidentally trip on them or where doing so could knock equipment from tables.

Work areas and hands must be dry when working with electrical appliances.

Never make "home made" electrical science equipment without careful supervision by a qualified electrician.

Never use equipment in which any live wires or terminals are capable of being touched. Note: Some science books in years past contained activities, such as the infamous "hot dog cooker," which had live wires that could easily be touched. These were extremely dangerous and could even be lethal if the person touching the wire was properly grounded (such as on a sink, faucet, refrigerator, or other appliance).

Other Safety Concerns

Never taste or ingest anything in the classroom for any reason. *(Note: Years ago, it was common practice to ask students to taste substances to determine if they were acids or bases. That should not be done.)*

Do not eat or drink from glassware that is used in science activities. *(Years ago, it was common practice for teachers to borrow glassware from the school kitchen to perform experiments. That should not be done.)* If glassware is used for science, it should be used only for science.

Dispose of materials and substances when the activity is completed.

Even the use of cool water can cause problems. How? By being spilled on the floor. Unless promptly wiped up, it may cause someone to slip and fall.

The Methods

It is useful to know that instead of spending much time discussing methods or inquiry in isolation, it is better to combine them with the content (as is done in the remaining chapters). However, some basic information is needed to set the stage for the methods that are used in this book.

For example, it is useful to know what is meant by *process* and *content* and how some early national science programs affected the balance between these two factors. It is also important to know the advantages inherent in *discrepant events* (that is, events that are unexpected or surprising to the viewer), and how these events promote *inquiry* learning by pupils. Finally, the simple three-step approach used throughout the book is clearly explained.

Process-Content

Science teaching in the elementary school has changed greatly during the past 50 years. At one time most of the science teaching focused on the *content* of science. Then, after the launching of the *Sputnik* satellite by the former Soviet Union in 1957, America took a new look at science education.

Federal funds were authorized to support a number of major national programs in science education. These programs shifted the emphasis away from content and toward *process.*

What is process? It is how a scientist works, thinks, and studies problems. In other words, it is a method of investigating. The process approach includes many specific skills including, for example, the following:

analyzing	experimenting
classifying	forming theories
collecting data	generalizing
communicating	graphing (a way of recording data)
comparing	identifying
contrasting	inferring
controlling variables	interpreting
defining operationally	measuring
demonstrating	observing
describing	predicting outcomes
drawing conclusions	questioning
estimating	recording data
evaluating	verifying

Federal funds were used to promote the "new science" for many years. What were the results? Most educators concede that the results were somewhat disappointing. The bright hopes evoked by the new programs were, too often, not realized.

Why the disappointing results? There are many likely reasons. It is generally believed that most teachers found the new programs too demanding, too complex, too costly, and too time-consuming. In addition some programs virtually ignored science content. Process had taken over completely. Many teachers found that process without content did not produce results. Consequently, most of the programs disappeared.

Overall, those programs tended to be too difficult to use in the classroom. The typical elementary teacher is, after all, responsible for many different subjects. To make matters worse, science is often the teacher's greatest weakness. As a result, success in elementary science is not easy to achieve.

In this book we try to make it easier to teach science well. We try to take away the complexity that so often surrounds science teaching. In this book you need not worry about how to teach the process approach: it is built right into the content chapters. (It is step 2 of the three-step approach.). Similarly, inquiry-based science teaching is also built right in. If lessons are begun with discrepant events, the inquiry will follow as a natural consequence of pupil interest and enthusiasm.

Nor will you need to worry about combining the methods with the content. That is done for you in every chapter. The book provides teachers with many simple, concrete, and easy-to-use examples of events or situations that encourage good teaching practices. First we will investigate several of the process skills important for elementary and middle school students to experience and understand. By understanding the process skills yourself, you will be better able to teach inquiry-based lessons.

The six process skills stressed in this chapter are: observing, inferring, communicating, classifying, measuring, and experimenting. Spending a few days at the beginning of the school year acquainting children with each skill makes it easier for students to understand the new science vocabulary and what actions are expected of them as they investigate the discrepant events of each unit studied.

1. Observing and **2. Inferring.** When students use their senses (hearing, seeing, smelling, tasting, and touching) directly to gain information about objects or occurrences, they are observing. The more senses students use, the more accurate information they can obtain about the object or occurrence. For instance, seeing a large, gray, rough object might have children conclude that it is a "rock;" but by touching the "rock" students might discover that it is a stage prop or fake rock made of foam.

For practice make four observation boxes, one for each sense excluding taste. See figure 1.1. Take this opportunity to stress that for safety reasons there is not an observation box for taste. Emphasize to the students that they not taste anything in the science lab unless directly instructed to do so by the teacher.

One box (shoe-box size) is needed for each sense. Make up the following boxes. "Seeing box": Place three or four items in the bottom of the first box with plastic wrap taped over the top opening. Sample items that can be included are: a small, bottled water container partially filled with white vinegar and laid on its side, a leaf, a foam or real rock; and an empty mini box of M&Ms, glued shut. Make a note card for this box that says, "Look at the items in the box but do not touch the box. Write your observations in your lab book."

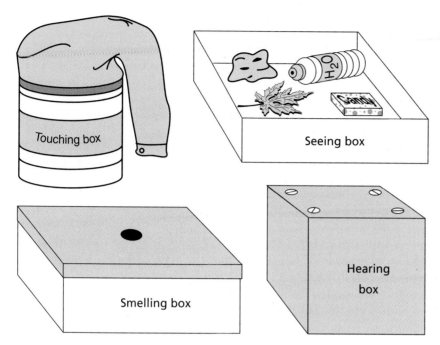

FIGURE 1.1   Four observation boxes: touching, seeing, smelling, and hearing.

"Hearing box": (*Note:* a wooden or tin box works best since it amplifies the sound of objects inside more than a cardboard shoe box: however, a shoe box can be used.) Inside the box include a few objects such as a wooden cube (something that slides), marble and/or golf ball (something that rolls), and a feather or small piece of foam (something that is so light that it is inaudible). Tape or nail the box closed so that it cannot be easily opened. Make a note card for this box that says, "You may pick up the box and move it around or shake it but do not open it. Write your observations in your lab book."

"Smelling boxes": use one or more shoe boxes with several small holes in each lid. On the bottom of the box tape a strong smelling object such as fragrant flowers, cotton balls sprayed with flower-scented perfume, an onion slice, a cinnamon stick, or a lemon slice. Tape the lid to the box. Make a note card for this box that says. "You may pick up the box and gently squeeze it to smell what is inside. Do not open it. Write your observations in your lab book."

"Touching box": Cut a sleeve from a man's long sleeve shirt and tape it to a large coffee can (tape the shoulder or upper part of sleeve to the can so that students put their hands into the can through the cuff of the sleeve). Inside the can place two or three objects such as a buckeye, walnut, peanut, small rock, peeled grape, small sponge, or rubber worm. Make a note card for this box that says, "You may place your hand inside the cuff of the sleeve and feel what is inside the can. Do not shake the can and do not look inside. Write your observations in your lab book."

The activity for understanding observation skills also teaches about inferences at the same time. An **inference** is a conclusion based on past knowledge, facts, and/or something taken for granted or assumed. For example, in the "seeing box" activities a student might infer that the clear substance in the water bottle is water since he could not use his sense of smell to inform him that it smells like vinegar and is not water. A student may also infer that the M&M box has candy in it. After students have written their observations, emphasize the difference between observation and inference by giving an empty mini box of M&Ms to each student in the class. They will be very disappointed but the empty M&M box can be used as a reference each time you want to emphasize the concept of inference. These sense observation boxes create many other opportunities to discuss inferences including: inferring that the perfume is a real flower or vice versa, and inferring that there are only two objects (ball and block) in the "hearing box" since they may assume they can hear everything placed in the box, not knowing a feather is also in the box. Can you think of other assumptions or inferences that may be made?

Students need to understand that saying, "It smells like a rose" (observation) is different from saying, "It's a rose" (inference). The more senses (observations) that can be used to observe in any given situation, the less assumptions or inferences are made. However, scientists do not always have the opportunity to use all of their senses and therefore explore unknown objects and occurrences based on inferences. Knowing the difference between observation and inference is important to making accurate conclusions.

Students often include in their observations properties such as size, color, sounds like, looks like, feels like, and texture; but students seldom use measuring tools as part of their observations. When possible students should be encouraged to measure mass, quantity, length, surface area, temperature, and volume among other measurements. This gives students the much-needed practice to develop measuring skills. Students need to go beyond word descriptions in observations. Observations should be recorded using numbers (measurements), words (describing properties,) and drawings whenever possible. Observations are both qualitative and quantitative data.

3. Communications. Communicating scientific concepts is an important skill. Students should be able to talk about, describe, explain, and write about science by using a variety of forms such as pictures, words, numbers, tracings, models, tables charts, photographs, measurements, and reports. Opportunities to communicate push students to further clarify their ideas in an effort to articulate it to others. Communicating is therefore a way to help students make meaning of scientific concepts and not an end in and of itself.

Here is a simple activity to promote the importance of thorough communications. Pass out a leaf to each student. (Shelled peanuts, rocks, or shells can also be used instead of leaves.) The leaves should be from a collection of two different types of leaves (oak and maple, for example) that have a variety of sizes for each type. Students are to write a letter to a friend about their "pet" leaf. Suggest they name the leaf and describe their leaf as completely as possible. Now place the students into groups of seven or eight. From each group collect the seven or eight leaves and letters and place them in a box. Exchange the box of letters and leaves with another group. Have each group spread out its new set of leaves. Each student should read a letter and try to pair the letter with a leaf given to his group. Students who have no problem making the pair can be asked, "What in the letter that you were assigned helped you correctly pair it to a specific leaf?" Students who successfully pair the letter to the leaf often reply that a given mark was described by color, shape, or size; the leaf was traced; or measurements of the leaf were given such as "12 cm long and 9 cm wide and the stem is 7cm long." Letters that are difficult to pair with a leaf often describe the *general* properties of the leaf that match all of the leaves of any given type. Encourage the importance of accompanying word descriptions with measurements, tracings, and /or drawings.

4. Classifying. Classifying or sorting objects or events relies on the individual's ability to determine likes and differences among a set of objects or events. To determine questions, compare and contrast objects or happenings, make sense of the real world, and see relationships, students need a way of organizing their world. Classifying activities help students develop flexibility in thinking, especially when deciding how to record, analyze, and display data. A particularly useful sorting process is the **binary sort.** In a binary sort a given characteristic is used to sort objects or events into two groups, one group *having* a given characteristic or property and the other group *not having* that characteristic or property. (This avoids the situation where an object or event belongs to two groups at the same time.) This "have, have not" binary process continues with each subgroup until identical objects or only one object remains in each subgroup. Each subset is labeled with the characteristic by which it was sorted. An example of a binary sort is shown in figure 1.2. Each butterfly has it's own unique set of properties. For instance the first butterfly in the set of butterflies can be described by following the subsets in which it belongs. It has curved wings, no dots, and stripes on its body. No other butterfly has this description.

5. Measuring. Measuring involves comparing a property/attribute of one object to a standard or nonstandard unit of the same property/attribute (weight, volume, force, area, time, length, etc.). Measuring also involves understanding how many units an object has compared to the selected unit of measure. For example, how many meters long is the swimming pool? A student must first understand what property/attribute is being measured. Length can be thought of as how far from one point to another and includes such ideas as height, width, circumference, and depth. Volume can be thought of as how much to fill an object and includes such ideas as capacity, filling, amount of stuff inside an object. Volume, like area, is derived from length (length × width × height).

When students are ready to measure they need to determine an appropriate unit to use for their comparison. The selected unit should have the same attribute as what is being measured. Grams and square meters would not be used to measure volume. Also the selected unit should not be too large or too small compared to the object being measured. For example, to measure the amount of water in a bathtub, liters or gallons would be more appropriate than milliliters or cups. The more familiar students are with the relative size of standard units, the easier it is for them to select an appropriate unit in which to measure.

Measurement instruments are tools that make measuring faster and more accurate. Students should have an opportunity to make measurement models such as rulers and balance scales. Lining up paperclips or toothpicks to measure the length of an object will help children understand the concept of length but should later be replaced with a ruler to measure length. Learning

Set of Butterflies

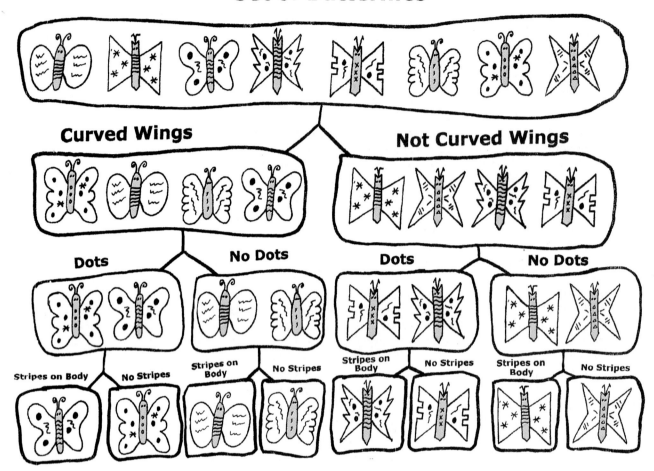

FIGURE 1.2   Binary sort for a set of butterfiles.

how to use measurement instruments is a vital part of the science process skills. In summary, to measure an object or event one must decide on the attribute to measure, select an appropriate unit, and compare the unit to the object being measured by using measurement instruments when appropriate.

Measurement in particular takes much practice for students to become familiar with the process. Children need to learn visual approximations or benchmarks for each of the standard units (that is, height from floor to door knob is about 1 meter, width of small finger is about 1 centimeter). Students need continual practice using measurement instruments correctly (line up the zero mark of the ruler and not the end of the ruler to measure an object). As stated earlier, when students are asked to write down observations they seldom think to measure the object or event. Always encourage pictures, words, and numbers (measurements) when students communicate about science.

6. Experimenting. Oftentimes students hold the misconception that any activity in science is an experiment. It is important to distinguish between an activity and an experiment. An **experiment** has specific characteristic processes:

a. Present a problem and ask a question.
b. Form a hypothesis based on that problem or question.
c. Design a study identifying the independent and dependent variables and controls.
d. Collect, record, and analyze the data.
e. State a conclusion.

An activity, however, may integrate only a few or none of the above processes. For example, students can explore electromagnets in *Event 7-M, Stop and Go Magnets,* by wrapping an insulated wire around a nail and attaching the ends of the wire to a dry cell battery. They can observe that the electromagnet can pick up paper clips and other magnetic materials. However, up until this point it is just an activity. The students might ask if there is a way to make the electromagnet stronger, to pick up more paper clips. If students don't ask questions the teacher might pose the question to model inquiry. To answer the question the students should brainstorm what can be changed in the design of the activity to make the electromagnet stronger. The students might suggest longer or shorter wire, thinner or thicker wire, more batteries, a thicker or longer nail, etc. Now the activity becomes an experiment as the students hypothesize a solution and design a process to systematically determine which of the changes if any will strengthen the electromagnet. Asking a question, forming a hypothesis, devising an experimental design by identifying the variable to be studied, and collecting and analyzing the data gives students experience with experimenting in the true sense of the word. Certainly many of the events in this book will motivate students to ask questions about the activities that should/could be further developed into experiments. A blend of activities and experiments makes for an effective learning environment considering time constraints in most science classrooms.

Students need plenty of opportunity to brainstorm and share their ideas before they can design an experiment on their own and understand the integrated processes of an experiment. Young children (third grade and up) can be guided through designing an experiment. Once children start to do an experiment, resist telling them what they are doing right or wrong. Wait until each group has had a chance to explore and then let each group present its designs, data, and conclusions. At this point the teacher and children can discuss what worked and what needed changes and why. This inquiry format takes more time, but avoids cookbook-type activities. The most important feature is that the responsibility of learning is placed on the students.

A simple investigation to teach the process of experimenting involves exploring what will happen when water droplets fall on a penny. Students can give their thoughts and then try the activity given a penny, eyedropper, and a small amount of water. Many students are surprised how many drops stay on the penny and ask, "How many drops will fit on the penny before it overflows?" The activity becomes an experiment when students hypothesize and limit the number of variables to one.

Since the students have already done some exploring with the activity the teacher should ask, "Why do you think different students have different numbers of drops staying on the penny?" Typical answers are that some pennies are old and dirty while others are clean, different droppers are being used, some students press harder on the bulb of the dropper, the distance between the penny and dropper is different and may make the water splash more, some people used the head side while others used the tail side. Using this as a start they are ready to follow the steps or format to an experiment.

a. **Consider appropriate questions:** Have each group think about what question they are investigating about the penny and drops of water.

b. **Formulate a hypothesis:** Encourage students to write a hypothesis using an If . . . then . . . statement. For example, "If the water is dropped from a distance of 1 centimeter above the penny, then it will hold more drops than if the water is dropped from 5 centimeters above." Another example might be, "If I drop water on the head side of a penny, then it will hold more water than the tail side of the penny." A third example hypothesis might be, "If I drop plain water on my penny, then the penny will hold more drops than if I used soapy water."

c. **Create an experimental design:** The groups should each describe their investigation by including the materials needed, the **independent variable** (the variable that is purposely changed), the **dependent variable** (the variable that changes as a result of the independent variable), the **controlled variable** (all other variables you keep the same or constant so as to only change one variable at a time). To keep all but one variable constant, students need to tell what they did, that is, operationally define the conditions of what was kept constant or didn't change so others can reproduce the experiment. For example, if students are investigating using clear versus soapy water, then the side of the penny, the height the dropper is held, and the person squeezing the dropper should be the same each time the experiment is performed. We can operationally define that the head side be used; the dropper be held 2 cm from the penny; and that the same dropper, penny, and person squeezing the dropper be used each time to hold as many variables constant as possible.

d. **Collect data as you experiment:** Students should be encouraged to collect the data and immediately record it in a systematic format. Use of a chart that labels the columns and includes units helps students make sense of what they are doing. Numbers without units, 2 and 17, can be confusing, but 2 cm and 17 drops will help the students make sense of the data they are collecting. Repeating the experiment more than once allows students to become comfortable with the fact that measurements are estimations and that experimental procedures are seldom exact.

e. **Display data using charts and graphs:** This is a good time to integrate the science lesson with the mathematics lesson. What type of graph would best represent the data? Bar graph, line graph, stem and leaf plot, or box and whisker plot? Do the graphs include appropriate labels, titles, units, and scaling?

f. **Analyze the data:** Look for patterns and relationships between the independent and dependent variables. Are the variables inversely or directly related? Does one value increase as the other decreases?

Predict what value might be measured if the experiment was to go one step further. Predictions are based on past knowledge and use data to give us the best "guess."

g. **Write a conclusion:** Ask students to compare their results to their hypothesis. Did their results match what they thought would happen? If the results matched the hypothesis, students should explain the relationship and why they thought it happened. If the results countered the hypothesis, students can give alternative ideas as to why by rethinking what they observed as they performed the experiment. A sample conclusion might be, "The penny did hold more drops of plain water than soapy water because we saw the water didn't pile up as high with the soapy water. It appears that the soap weakens the surface tension or cohesive forces of the water."

Inquiry

According to the National Research Council, inquiry is the "Shifting (of) emphasis from teachers presenting information . . . to students learning science through active involvement." Inquiry is not new. There has been wide agreement among science educators that inquiry is a desired goal in science teaching. The National Science Teachers (NSTA) stresses the importance of inquiry skills in their publication *NSTA Pathways to the Science Standards*. Students should develop the inquiry skills that enable them to ask questions, plan investigations, gather data using appropriate tools, reasonably explain relationships among the collected data, and communicate the results. The problem, as is so often the case with good practices, is "how to achieve it in the classroom," given the fact that so many elementary teachers have difficulty with science.

We believe that an inquiry-based science program can be achieved by using the methods employed in this book. The book is set up so that it is easy for teachers to follow methods that will bring about a natural use of inquiry. The key is to use the discrepant events to introduce the concepts and lesson, and to let students' curiosity initiate the inquiry.

The Role of the Textbook in the Classroom

The national programs discouraged the use of a textbook in the classroom. After all, the weaknesses of the typical textbook were well known. For example, a text is normally too content-oriented. In fact, content is often the *only* goal when using a text. In lesson after lesson, pupils are asked to memorize facts.

Another weakness of the typical textbook approach is that pupils are often asked to read about science when they should be *doing* science. Reading about science surely does not promote inquiry or hands-on investigation. Instead, science can become nothing more than a succession of reading lessons. To further complicate matters, science books often contain words that are difficult to read and concepts that are difficult to understand. Thus, even good readers may find the content to be abstract and beyond comprehension. For poor readers, of course, this approach is a disaster.

In summary, because the textbook approach often tends to focus too much on content while ignoring activities, processes, and inquiry it is often restricting and inflexible.

Despite all the weaknesses of texts, and despite the major attempts to replace them with the national programs, textbooks still prevail. In most classrooms it was the national programs that disappeared, not the books. Why does the text survive? The answer is probably quite simple: teachers find it easier to teach with a text than without it.

How should the problem be viewed now? The view offered in this book is threefold: (1) Recognize the fact that the basic text will continue to be used in many classrooms. It is not realistic to suggest otherwise. (2) Make it possible to teach an inquiry-based science program, with *or without* a textbook. (3) Simplify good teaching. In other words, make "good teaching" easier to achieve by typical elementary teachers.

Perhaps we should also recognize that the text approach is not all bad. One of its greatest values is that it relieves teachers of the task of organizing the body of scientific knowledge. There is really nothing wrong with that particular benefit. It is easier to work from such a base and expand it to bring in supplementary materials than to expect teachers to do the original organizing themselves.

Another benefit of a text is that it provides a common source of data for all pupils. We know that supplementary materials should be provided for your classes. However, there is really nothing wrong with having at least one common source of information for all pupils. It helps in organizing the lessons and provides a stable base from which to prepare the lessons.

The major focus of this book, however, is not to argue for or against the merits of a text or nontext approach. It is to help teachers *regardless of what approach they use in their classrooms.* If a text is used, the limitations that are often associated with texts can be overcome by adding events that stimulate inquiry.

How that inquiry is promoted is outlined in detail in a later section of this chapter ("How to Use Discrepant Events to Promote Process and Inquiry"). For now it is sufficient to say that the textbook approach can be improved by selecting appropriate activities for pupils to investigate.

Finally, the inquiry method advocated in this book is not limited to the upgrading of the text approach. The method stands alone. It can be used with *or without* a textbook. It can be used to improve a course of study or to improve teacher-made units. The teacher needs only to look over the chapters of this book and to select those activities that fit his or her classroom.

What Is a Discrepant Event?

Everyone has seen water run downhill. That fact is hardly surprising or unusual. However, if you were to see water run *uphill,* it would be an entirely different matter! Water flowing *against* the force of gravity is a discrepancy. (To see just such an event, refer to *Event 11-L. Antigravity Fountain.*)

Most people know that water freezes at 0° Celsius (32° F). But, what if you were to see ice *melt* at 10 or 15 degrees *below* the freezing point? What would you think? Again, there would be feelings of surprise and curiosity.

The surprise is even greater when, upon closer inspection, frost is seen forming on the *outside* of the beaker while ice is melting on the *inside!* (See *Event 5-C. Melt Ice Below Its Freezing Point.*)

Water is expected to run downhill, not uphill; ice is expected to melt at 0° C, not 10 or 15 degrees below zero. These are examples of discrepant events. Such events are best described as being unexpected, surprising, or paradoxical.

A good discrepant event tends to create a strong feeling in the observer. Generally, there will be an inner feeling of "wanting to know." As children stare in disbelief at some of the events, they simply *have* to know "how it works."

When pupils are strongly motivated, conditions are favorable for inquiry learning. Therefore, special emphasis was placed on selecting discrepant events whenever possible throughout this book. Such events capitalize on the curiosity of pupils and lead them to gain a better understanding of science.

Although there is much value in the use of discrepant events, it is obvious that these cannot be developed for every conceivable topic or scientific principle. In the absence of an appropriate discrepant event, it is quite acceptable to present an event that is not discrepant. The pupils will still have a chance to observe or perform some kind of investigation. The main point to remember is that the event is used as an incentive to get pupils involved. That is the essence of inquiry.

The various lessons in this text contain a carefully chosen selection of discrepant and nondiscrepant events. Discrepant events are used whenever possible, supplemented with nondiscrepant events whenever needed.

How to Use Discrepant Events to Promote Process and Inquiry

Discrepant events become quite useful when care is taken to initiate a lesson properly and time is allowed for student investigation. The teaching lessons can become effective when the following three general steps are employed:

1. **SET UP A DISCREPANT EVENT.** In this step the event (or events) are presented to gain attention, increase motivation, and encourage pupils to seek ways of solving the discrepancy. The stage is set for learning because pupils are confronted with questions or problems that they will want to resolve. They will *want to know* the answer to a good discrepant event.
2. **ASK PUPILS TO INVESTIGATE TO SOLVE THE DISCREPANCY.** After the event is properly introduced, the pupils will be anxious to seek an answer. In attempting to resolve the discrepancy, pupils will often engage in meaningful inquiry.
    They will be active in observing, recording data, classifying, predicting, experimenting, and doing whatever tasks are needed to solve the problem. (Notice that these tasks are the processes that were discussed earlier in this chapter in the section on "Process-Content") In addition, it is likely that they will learn much of the real scientific content of the lesson.
3. **RESOLVE THE DISCREPANCY.** With some luck, pupils will resolve the events themselves as a result of their own investigations. In other words, by their own direct activities and experiences they will find the answers to many of the questions posed by the discrepant event. And again, they will have learned something about how to observe, experiment, gather data, and perform other related processes of science.

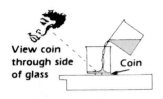

View coin
through side   Coin
of glass

FIGURE 1.3 Why does the coin "disappear" when water is poured into the beaker?

If pupils are not successful in finding all the answers, they will still be ready to benefit from a more traditional treatment of the topic at this time. Even if the teacher now merely explains the answer, the explanations will no longer be abstract. By this time pupils will have put so much effort into the event that have a vested interest in the outcome. That is far better than merely listening to an explanation of some abstract principle found in a book.

To help you understand how the three steps are used, we will use and explain them more thoroughly in the following examples:

1. **SET UP A DISCREPANT EVENT.** Place a coin under a clear beaker or jar and tell the children to watch the coin closely. It is easily visible when viewed through the side of the glass. Now pour water into the tumbler and "presto" the coin disappears! Repeat several times to be sure that all can see. (See figure 1.3.)

   An event such as this has great value in motivating children. Even adults who see this activity are generally quite surprised to see the coin disappear and will want to know how it works. As a result, such an activity is ideal for introducing a science lesson. From this point on, the inquiry, or "wanting to know" comes from the pupils.

2. **ASK PUPILS TO INVESTIGATE TO SOLVE THE DISCREPANCY.** At what better point can we involve the children! They are self-motivated and are eager to find out "how it works."

   Their involvement at this stage of a lesson is true inquiry and is likely to be quite purposeful. It will include questioning, recording data, graphing, predicting, experimenting, reading, theorizing, and many of the processes of science so strongly advocated by the national science programs.

   In this particular event the pupils will observe that the coin disappears from view when the tumbler is filled with water but only if viewed through the side of the tumbler. The coin is still visible if viewed from above.

   They will find that it makes no difference whether the water is poured quickly or slowly. (Although if poured slowly, the coin seems to move upward slightly before it vanishes.)

3. **RESOLVE THE DISCREPANCY.** Under an ideal setting pupils will gradually resolve the questions as they work on step 2. Their findings should then be placed into the proper context in step 3. They should be led to see how the event relates to a broader scientific framework.

   The event with the disappearing coin is taken from chapter 9 (*Event 9-P. The Disappearing Coin*) and pertains to the refraction (or bending) of light. Refraction occurs when light moves at an angle from one medium (a substance that allows light to pass through it) to another.

   When viewed through the side of the glass, the light travels through several different mediums (glass, water, and glass again) and is bent inwardly so much that the light from the coin never reaches the outside of the glass.

   When viewed from the top, however, the coin is still visible because there are only two mediums. Also, since the light travels from one medium to another at only a slight angle, there is not as much bending as when it passes through at a sharp angle.

In this sample lesson we used only a single event to keep things simple. In a typical classroom setting we would probably present several related events at the same time, as long as they all pertained to the same topic of refraction.

Let's trace the method through a second example.

1. **SET UP A DISCREPANT EVENT.** Select two identical bottles (such as soft-drink bottles). Fill one about one-half to two-thirds full of water. Leave the other empty. Blow across the mouth of the empty bottle and listen to the tone that is created. (See fig. 1.4.)

    Now ask the pupils to predict the tone that will be created when you blow across the other bottle. Will the tone be higher, lower, or the same? Confirm their prediction by blowing across the partially filled bottle. The tone is higher.

    Ask the pupils to generalize. Why is the sound higher in the bottle containing water? They will probably say that the higher the water, the higher the pitch.

    Repeat the event several times so that everyone is sure of the results. Then tell the pupils that we need to check the results just once more, but in a slightly different way.

    This time, instead of blowing across the tops of the bottles, tap them with a small object such as a pen or the handle of a spoon. Surprisingly, this time the results will be just the opposite of what they were earlier! Now, the higher the water, the *lower* the pitch.

2. **ASK PUPILS TO INVESTIGATE TO SOLVE THE DISCREPANCY.** At first glance the discrepancy is baffling to pupils. They will want to repeat the event themselves to check the results. They probably will want to try various bottles filled with different amounts of water. In summary, they will be using inquiry and many of the processes of science while searching for a solution.

3. **RESOLVE THE DISCREPANCY.** This event is taken from chapter 8 (*Event 8-Z. The Baffling Bottles*). A single scientific principle explains both the first and second set of sounds from the bottles. The basic principle is that the greater the mass, the lower the sound; or, the smaller the mass, the higher the sound.

    That principle is verified, not contradicted, by this event. By blowing across the top, the air produces the sound. When striking the bottles, the bottles themselves, plus the contents, produce the sounds.

    In each case, the more there was of a given substance, the lower the sound; the less there was of a substance, the higher the sound. When blowing across the bottle, the "more" was the air; when striking the bottle, the "more" was the bottle-plus-water.

As in the first sample lesson, this event should be used along with other events that also relate to the same basic concept of sound. The explanation would then receive a more thorough treatment and be better related to a continuous discourse of science content.

Let us try a third example.

1. **SET UP A DISCREPANT EVENT.** This discrepancy is set up in problem form. Give a set of two tumblers each to several committees and ask them to pour *air* (not water) from one tumbler to another. Have available an aquarium or large glass container filled with water.

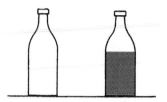

FIGURE 1.4   Strike the bottles and the left one gives the higher note. Blow across the tops and the right one gives the higher note. Why the paradox?

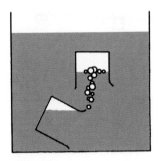

FIGURE 1.5 Pour air from one beaker to another underwater.

2. **ASK PUPILS TO INVESTIGATE TO SOLVE THE DISCREPANCY.** Pupils are likely to say that it cannot be done. Some will make pouring motions with the tumblers but will concede that they are not pouring anything. Tell them that it really can be done. In fact, if they do it right, there will be no doubt that air is actually being poured.

3. **RESOLVE THE DISCREPANCY.** The solution is very simple. Merely invert one tumbler and lower it into the water, leaving it filled with air. Lower the other tumbler underwater and invert it, filling it with water. Then tilt the tumbler that is full of air so that bubbles of air rise from it. Hold the other tumbler so that it catches the rising bubbles. (See figure 1.5.) In this way it is quite apparent that air is transferred (or poured) from one tumbler to another. (This example is taken from chapter 11 *Event 11-C. Pouring Air.*)

This activity is related to one of the important properties of air. When this event is solved, the children will readily know that *air is a real substance and occupies space.*

Again, as stated in the first two examples, the lesson may include other related events, as long as those events all pertain to the same topic.

One final comment is necessary. The three steps are important only insofar as they are useful in permitting teachers to acquire techniques that promote good instructional practices. The steps are really only generalized procedures for setting up the beginning, middle, and end of a good lesson. The steps should not be regarded as restrictive in any way. Within the three steps, teachers should feel free to use a wide range of variations in teaching any given lesson.

Questioning Skills

It is useful to understand the role of questioning in inquiry lessons. The role of the teacher is to provide students opportunities to think, reflect, and question their own thinking. A teacher should be a facilitator of learning, not the source of the "right" answer.

A discrepant event may be used to introduce an inquiry lesson. The teacher may ask questions such as "What do you know about. . . ?" or "What might we need to know more about. . . ?". These open-ended questions give the teacher a snapshot of the students' past knowledge and current interest on the topic being presented.

During the investigation teachers need to encourage reflective discussions *among the students.* Student to student discussion is much more important than student to teacher discussion. This can be accomplished in many ways.

Provide "wait time" for students to be able to collect their thoughts. This encourages more student discussion and less teacher explanation.

Ask other students questions such as:

Who agrees (disagrees) with that explanation?
How can you rephrase that answer?
Who has another idea?
How does your answer differ from his answer?

Try hard not to give body language cues as to whether an answer is correct. Your comments should be nonjudgmental such as "go on, "or" uh-huh."

Immediate feedback whether verbal or otherwise, ends many would-be fruit-ful discussions.

Ask questions that promote thinking about strategies and relationships.

What is the experiment about?
Do you need to define or set limits?
How did you organize the information?
Would a diagram or sketch help?
What if. . . ?
Why do you think so?
What's wrong with. . . ?
Is there a pattern?
Would another method work as well?
How would you restate that in simpler terms?
Which words are most important?
How is this alike (different from). . . ?
Is that conclusion reasonable?
How do you know you're finished?
What are the variables (constants)?

Above all, a teacher should be a good listener.

Alternative Assessment

How teachers assess pupils and what they include in their assessments often divulges what they value. If a teacher values a pupil's understanding and a pupil's ability to communicate scientifically, then tests and assessments must capture this valued goal.

This book contains several discrepant events for each "big idea" in science. Pupils could be presented with a few new discrepant events as an assessment alternative. Teachers could observe behaviors either individually or in small groups that demonstrate a pupil's understanding of the concepts studied. Short interviews are also possible as pupils investigate each discrepant event used during the assessment mode.

Teachers should be looking for some or several of the following pupil behaviors as pupils perform experiments either individually or collaboratively. This is only a partial list of behaviors that demonstrate scientific literacy.

Process Behaviors

- Organizes and interprets data
- Uses appropriate measurement instruments
- Recognizes the importance of patterns
- Uses estimating skills
- Asks appropriate questions
- Classifies and sorts when necessary
- Controls one variable at a time
- Observes carefully without confusing inferences as observations

I.M. MARSH LIBRARY LIVERPOOL L17 6BD
TEL. 0151 231 5216/5299

Communication Behaviors

- Communicates using appropriate scientific terms
- Synthesizes and summarizes his/her own or the group's thinking

- Uses graphs and tables appropriately
- Makes diagrams to communicate ideas clearly
- Communicates a process so that it is replicable
- Supports arguments with evidence
- Records all data

Positive Disposition toward Learning Behaviors

- Accepts being questioned by others
- Stays actively on task
- Willing to try another approach
- Asks probing questions
- Works well with others
- Uses time productively

Teachers may want to make a selected checklist of these behaviors and record when they observe these behaviors for individual pupils. By keeping records, a teacher can discover trends that suggest for which behaviors pupils need more direction and experience.

At the end of each chapter a sample alternative assessment is given. By reading the sample assessments from each chapter a teacher will have a collection of general ideas for which to assess their students beyond traditional paper and pencil tests. For example, the sample assessment for Chapter 4, "Teaching Children about the Characteristics of Matter," suggests giving an individual or group of students a list of words such as molecule, element, compound and nucleus. Ask which word doesn't belong. Students must identify which word doesn't belong and state why.

A longer list of words can be given so that students separate them into two groups, label each group with a title, and then justify why each word belongs to a particular group. For example, if the list consisted of cutting, rusting, burning, melting, dissolving, folding, changing color, and forming a precipitate; a student may put cutting, melting, dissolving, folding, and color change together under the group title, "Physical Changes." The teacher may question why the student placed changing color under physical change. If the student describes the color change as resulting from papering a wall or painting a window with tempera paint, the student is correct. However, another student may think of changing colors as a chemical change, stating that two clear liquids were poured together and a different color resulted as they combined. Sometimes there is no one correct answer. It depends upon the student's justification.

This type of assessment, grouping vocabulary words, can be used with any of the chapters. This flexibility is true of all end-of-chapter sample assessments. It is important to understand the general format of each type of assessment to have a variety of assessment strategies by which a teacher can assess student learning.

How to Use This Book

The steps of teaching a lesson are found, not only in this chapter, but are also built into all of the content chapters of this book. You will find that the first two steps are incorporated in the "Discrepant Events and Pupil Investigations" sections. The third step is built into "Events Explained in Contexts" sections of each chapter.

Teachers who depend mostly on science textbooks in their classrooms will find this book helpful in supplying challenging classroom activities in which children use the inquiry approach to science. For example, suppose a textbook lesson pertains to a topic on sound. The teacher can refer to Chapter 8 of this book ("Teaching Children About Sound") and select activities to introduce the topic, to heighten interest, and to get pupils directly involved in inquiry.

Their involvement in solving the problems will enable pupils to experience some of the processes of science. Furthermore, they will be in a much better position to understand what they read in the text.

Similarly, teachers who devise their own units or rely on courses of study may find that this book can supply them with a variety of useful activities that will help pupils to learn the process skills. In addition, the events are carefully explained in an appropriate context.

Finally, teachers who are actively working with one of the national programs in elementary science may find that the events and explanations are a useful supplement to the regular project materials.

Key Terms

binary sort, *5*

classifying, *5*

communications, *4*

controlled variable, *8*

dependent variable, *8*

experiment, *7*

hypothesis, *8*

independent variable, *8*

inference, *3*

measuring, *5*

observing, *2*

Teaching Science to All Children

National Goals

National Science Education Standards

The *National Science Education Standards (NSES)* by the National Research Council are designed to promote and enable scientific literacy for **all** in the 21st century. The *NSES* provide a road map for educators, care givers, businesspeople, and society in general to foster scientific literacy in our nation. Implementing the *standards* will require major changes in most of our schools' science programs. The *NSES* provide criteria for these changes. The six overarching standards are for

1. Teaching science.
2. Professional development for teachers of science.
3. Assessment in science education.
4. Science content.
5. Science education programs.
6. Science education systems.

Three of the above standards that affect new teachers the most are expanded below. College students should recognize that during field experiences and student teaching these standards should be the basis for evaluating and reflecting upon their own teaching.

The **science teaching standards** describe what teachers should know and be able to do as science teachers. There are six major subdivisions in this standard.

1. The planning of inquiry-based science programs.
2. The actions taken to guide and facilitate student learning.
3. The assessments made of teaching and student learning.
4. The development of environments that enable students to learn science.
5. The creation of communities of science learners.
6. The planning and development of the school science program.

The **science content standards** summarize what students should know, understand, and be able to do in the natural sciences over their K–12 education. There are eight subdivisions in this standard.

1. Unifying concepts and processes in science.
2. Science as inquiry.
3. Physical science.
4. Life science.
5. Earth and space science.
6. Science and technology.
7. Science in personal and social perspective.
8. History and nature of science.

The **assessment standards** suggest criteria for judging the quality of assessment practices. There are five subdivisions in this standard.

1. The consistency of assessments with the decisions they are designed to inform.
2. The assessment of both achievement and the opportunity to learn.
3. The match between the technical quality of the data collected and the consequences of the actions taken on the basis of those data.
4. The fairness of assessment practices.
5. The soundness of inferences made from assessments about student achievement and opportunities to learn.

For more detailed information about the standards, read *NSTA Pathways to the Science Standards: Guidelines for Moving the Vision into Practice*, Elementary edition (1997) or Middle School Edition (1998), or go to http://www.nsta.org/standards. The correlation between each discrepant event described in this book and the K–4 and 5–8 content standard are included at the beginning of each chapter of this text. This new feature will help in standards-based lesson planning.

Inquiry is suggested in three of the six overarching standards. This book provides extensive suggestions to promote inquiry in the spirit of the NSES, recognizing that using inquiry as a major teaching strategy emphasizes learning for understanding.

Fostering Excellence

A Constructivist Approach

There are no methods of teaching science to females, minorities, gifted or special needs students that are fundamentally different from those that should be used for all children. All learners use concepts, beliefs, and perceptions they currently hold to make sense of new information. Students refine and combine their present knowledge with the new information. It is the teacher's role to create a learning environment that actively engages students to investigate and reflect on concepts so that students can refine their present understanding and blend it with the new information. Such a constructivist, approach encourages students to gather information through hands-on activities, think about their thinking (metacognition), communicate (written and oral), and discuss their thoughts about findings.

One of the best ways to know whether you as a teacher are creating this rich learning environment is to videotape yourself teaching. View the tape and observe whether your teaching reflects the appropriate teacher behaviors listed below. The list is adapted from John Barell's "Self-Reflection on Your Teaching: A Checklist" and S. Lee Winocur's "Classroom Observation Checklist." Both appear in *ASCD: Developing Minds, A Resource Book for Teaching Thinking* (Costa, 1985).

Specifically, do you as a teacher

1. Foster a climate of openness by
   a. calling students by name
   b. moving around the classroom

2. Encourage student interaction and cooperation by having students
   a. work in small groups using varied roles (reporter, recorder)
   b. respond to other students
   c. explore others' points of view
   d. listen to explanations by many students
   e. use materials cooperatively
3. demonstrate attitude of acceptance by
   a. accepting all valid student responses
   b. giving supportive comments to incorrect answers
   c. probing further the "I don't know" responses
4. Encourage students to gather and organize information by
   a. having students classify and categorize data
   b. having reference materials readily available
   c. having students record data and conceptual understanding in journals
5. Provide visual cues to develop cognitive strategies by using appropriate charts, pictures, materials and models
6. Make connections to past concepts and applications
7. Elicit oral and written verbalization of students' reasoning by
   a. posing "if . . . then," "what if . . .", and "Why do you think so" questions
   b. posing questions at different levels of Bloom's Taxonomy
   c. calling on both sexes and minority students equitably at each question level
   d. providing prompts such as "compare and contrast" for students to respond to as journal entries
8. Promote silent reflection by
   a. giving appropriate "wait time"
   b. withholding "correct" response to consider alternative points of view
   c. requesting more responses even after "correct" response is given
9. Use a variety of teaching modalities simultaneously to reach varying student learning modalities by providing
   a. visual cues such as models, charts, pictures, and videos
   b. auditory cues through discussions, debates, audiotapes, poems and stories
   c. tactile materials to pass around, investigate, and build models
   d. a variety of working arrangements with self, pairs, groups, and teacher
10. Encourages equity by
    a. referring to women and minority scientists and mathematicians
    b. reflecting on your own teaching to ensure equitable instruction
    c. encouraging females to perform traditional male tasks (download a program from the Internet, move desks)
    d. using gender-fair language (scientist, she; doctor, she)
    e. holding high expectations for *all* students while respecting individual needs

Although all of the sections are important, section three demonstrates attitude of acceptance, particularly critical in an environment of inquiry. By listening to several answers or student explanations, listing them on the board, and having students discuss the pros and cons of each, several positive outcomes are accomplished. First, the teacher has a better pulse on what the students know—including possible misconceptions. Second, students feel their thinking is valued and not immediately dismissed if it is incorrect. This motivates students to clarify their own thinking and to refine concepts. Third, students hear many different approaches and concepts needed to solve problems.

These 10 general instructional strategies promote thinking and are not easily adapted by most teachers unless they themselves have experience with this type of instruction in their own pre K–12 science classrooms. Teachers can learn appropriate strategies by attending professional development sessions. If teacher-centered instruction is to move toward a more student-centered instruction, effort must be taken to incorporate as many of these strategies as possible. Teachers may need to try a few strategies at a time until they can comfortably use several in concert.

Equal versus Equitable Education

Excellent teachers incorporate more specific instructional strategies as they consider their students on a more individual basis. Teachers who value individual differences such as culture, gender, race, language, learning style, physical limitations, and intellectual differences provide specific opportunities for the unique needs of individual students. Some students may need more time to complete tests or activities. Other students may need to have someone in class assigned to take notes for them. There may need to be different rules for different students. Is this fair?

There is a difference between equal treatment of students and equitable treatment. The first is based on balance or sameness whereas the latter has a proportional basis. For example, does it make sense to feed the same amount of dog food to a small Terrier as you would to a large Saint Bernard? No. The large Saint Bernard needs proportionally more food to sustain its growth and health. This is the same with educational practices. Some children need different amounts and types of educational nourishment than other children. Equity means that all children receive reasonable and appropriate accommodations to promote access to effective instruction. The following sections discuss teaching strategies to promote effective science education for all students.

Multicultural Considerations

Multicultural education promotes curriculum and instruction that is centered around the contributions, strengths, and high standards of the many diverse groups of peoples who have contributed to the scientific knowledge base and to the nature of science throughout history. Scientists are influenced by societal, cultural, and personal beliefs. Science and society are not separate entities but are interrelated in such a way that one influences the other. Understanding that each culture has advanced science is necessary for students to respect diversity and celebrate the contributions of each individual's heritage. When students know the scientific contribution of their ancestors, it invites them to participate more fully in the study of science.

Teaching science with respect to diverse cultures helps individual students relate to science based on their own identity and a familiarity with their heritage. When this connection of science and their own culture isn't made, students often think of science in obscure terms. To promote the connection, have students write biographies of scientists from their own culture. Students may also want to develop a historical time line of contributions made by several different scientists all working toward a common end. Building models of inventions developed centuries ago in many parts of the world also promotes multicultural science education. These activities help students understand the contributions of many cultures and also promote the idea that science occurs in small incremental advances spanning years, decades, and even centuries. For example, computing devices started with using fingers and stones thousands of years ago and advanced to what we now know as the computer. The computer is based on the contributions of many scientists, inventors, and mathematicians from many different cultures working over a duration of time centuries long.

Communities have a wealth of resources to tap. Parents and grandparents could possibly contribute in some unique way to classroom activities about science. For example, they can explain or demonstrate how to winter temperature-fragile plants or how to dye cloth using common flowers. Invite community members into the classroom to demonstrate a process and to serve as positive role models for students of similar cultural backgrounds.

At-Risk Students

At-risk students come to school deprived socially, physically, and/or emotionally, oftentimes as a result of low socioeconomic status. The resulting low self-esteem and low motivation put them at risk to learning what otherwise would have come easily to them. Generational poverty perpetuates the lack of experiential background that adds to their perception that education is not important or relevant to their future. At-risk students are intellectually capable and need teachers that are committed to the philosophy that all children can learn.

Teachers can instill a love of science through a positive attitude. At-risk students are in need of teachers who encourage them to believe that they can learn and deserve the best instruction. When taught through a constructivist approach, at-risk children thrive as learners. By employing the following strategies, you can reach students otherwise doomed to fail:

- Have high expectations for students. Let them know you expect them to succeed and to make wise behavioral choices.
- Teach "big ideas" in terms to which students relate. When they are actively engaged in the lessons, students make substantial strides. Worthwhile, challenging activities strengthen their engagement.
- Use as many modalities as possible to connect concepts to vocabulary. Use models, vocabulary word-cards placed where all students can see them, and journals to promote writing about new concepts; introduce new science vocabulary as you give directions and ask questions; and discuss everyday real-world applications about the concepts being studied.
- Show concern for students beyond their classroom experiences. Ask about their lives outside school. Talk about their individual interests. Share your interests with them. Show you care!

Special Needs

There are several definitions describing learning disabilities in the literature and most of them consider the following components. First, the learning disabled (LD) student has difficulty achieving compared to his potential. Second, the LD student can be gifted in one area while very unsuccessful in another. Third, there seems to be no physical (paralysis, visual or auditory impairment, etc.) or environmental reason (poverty; lack of parental guidance; physical, emotional, and mental abuse; limited background experiences; English as a second language; etc.) for the difficulties in achievement. Mental and emotional limitations do not account for the lack of academic success in the learning disabled student.

There are several common factors that LD children experience as they attempt to learn in and outside the classroom. The LD child may experience some but not usually all of the following difficulties, although this list is not all inclusive:

- Problems with reasoning and logic that create difficulty in sequencing, finding a pattern, making decisions, relating consequences to behaviors, and making connections from one concept to another. This makes laboratory work and group explorations more difficult when a sequenced procedure is needed or laboratory safety is an issue. LD students may be easily swayed by peers to demonstrate inappropriate behaviors. Because their organizational skills are lacking, LD students may appear lazy and ambivalent, which is usually far from the truth.
- Lack of reliable long- and short-term memory. LD students often have difficulty with the concept of time, remembering instructions, and moving from one activity to the next. They seem distracted and unable to focus on the task at hand. Not being able to remember connections between and among concepts and not being able to apply ideas from one day to the next generates continual frustrations for both the student and the teacher.
- Delayed language development and language processing problems. Processing problems make it difficult for students to keep up with the pace of regular classroom discussions and instructions. LD students find it difficult to retrieve and express ideas, making it troublesome to contribute to classroom discussion. Poor reading comprehension increases the challenge of understanding scientific concepts.
- Delayed mathematical understanding and computational skills. The need to understand and apply proportional reasoning may make scaling the axis of a graph in a lab report, for example, difficult for the LD student.

Whatever the cause, there are teaching strategies that can help LD students learn science. The following strategies can help provide the support and structure the learning disabled child needs to succeed.

1. Use as many routines as possible in the classroom setting so that the LD child knows what to anticipate. Change is difficult so a change in plans may need to be announced by the teacher more than once.
2. Walk over to an LD child to subtly get his attention rather than call his name several times in a negative tone.

3. Be firm but kind with behavioral requests. Agree with the child that he may not want to stop an exciting activity to move on to the next. Try to include a win-win solution in the request. For example, say, "Billy, you may try to pick up one more object with the magnet and then I need you to put all of the materials in the box assigned to your group."

4. Post weekly assignments on the Web and classroom bulletin board so that students always know what is due. Give assignments to parents and keep them informed as much as possible.

5. Try to substitute a less annoying behavior for the distracting one. For example, when a student has a nervous habit such as tapping their pencil on the desk, give the student a small piece of play dough to squeeze.

6. Use a signal to quiet the students down when laboratory activities get too loud. Try turning the lights off and on to get students' attention and then have students close their eyes to focus on what you have to say.

7. Give extra time for assignments, provide wait-time for questioning during class, and eliminate any busy work that will waste precious time the LD student may need to catch up.

8. Allow the LD child to work in an accepting group. Carefully select mature students that will guide rather than purposely mislead the LD child.

9. Assign another student to take notes for the LD child who has difficulties with fine motor skills or written organization. Use a computer and print two copies or use carbon paper.

10. Team students to read and reread directions to LD students when necessary.

11. Stress vocabulary. Use as many modalities as possible to connect concepts to vocabulary. Use models, vocabulary word-cards placed where all students can see them, and journals to promote writing about new concepts; introduce new science vocabulary as you give directions and ask questions; and discuss everyday, real-world applications about the concepts being studied.

12. Work *with* the student, instead of doing work *for* the LD child.

13. Keep high expectations while considering appropriate modifications, as with all children.

Two useful websites address modifications for special students: www.as.wvu.edu~scidis and the online version of the Eisenhower National Clearinghouse (ENC) *Focus* magazine (vol. 2, 2003) dedicated to *mathematics and science for students with special needs,* www.enc.org.

Gender Equity

Over 10 years ago *The AAUW Report: How Schools Shortchange Girls* (1992) summarized research that focused on many components of today's classrooms that overtly—but usually unintentionally—discourage females from fully participating in learning mathematics and science. These components include, among others, language, curriculum, teacher behaviors, assessment, physical environment, administrative policies, and student support. Although there are many reasons for gender differences in science performance, most researchers agree any biological differences are far outweighed by sex-role stereotyping practices girls experience daily at home, in school, and in society.

To create a learning environment that is gender-inclusive and actively engages all students:

- Encourage group problem-solving projects.
- Increase career awareness in technical fields to all students.
- Consciously call on both sexes equitably at each question level.
- Provide hands-on activities, especially those that are unfamiliar to females such as gears and electronics.
- Discuss openly gender and minority biases in our society by providing female and minority role models as guest speakers, by researching the lives of female and minority scientists, and by honoring the contribution of all societies and cultures to scientific knowledge.
- Hold high expectations for all students.

In class and during science club (clubs that especially encourage female and minority membership) students should have the chance to explore activities such as building rockets to examine the effects of each variable on the rocket's stability, solving spatial puzzles and logic games, and using computer probes and databases to study scientific relationships. These type of activities are not traditionally taught to females and minorities unless state standards require them in the curriculum. Often teachers justify the lack of this type of class work by stating that there is no time to go beyond the "basics," that girls would not be interested in such activities, or that students would not behave if given hands-on activities. However, inquiry-based activities in which students can relate motivate students to enjoy and appreciate science. Unlike traditional "book science" which has students passively reading about concepts and inventions, these activities build on students' strengths and motivate them to ask questions, to show curiosity, and to more fully participate in learning science. Educational changes that invite all students to participate in learning the beauty and usefulness of science is crucial.

As teachers encourage cooperative group work it is important to note that especially in middle grades it is common for students to engage in "small-talk" during group work. The teacher may think the conversations seems disruptive but female groups do successfully complete projects on time even as they carry on these conversations. Cooperative groups should often consist of all-female groups to promote self-reliance and increased learning for females. Mixed gender groups do not work as well as single-sex groups for girls.

Gifted Students

Gifted students can be recognized as those students who possess a high level of academic ability and creativity, are motivated to delve deep into topics, are self-initiating, and can work independently in one or more academic areas. By this description many students never reach their full potential when opportunity and access to a rich learning environment are denied. Gifted students need settings that challenge their interests and extend their curiosity.

Early childhood and middle school teachers traditionally do not have the scientific background necessary to challenge scientifically gifted students. Teachers seldom suggest a more in-depth study of a topic knowing that they may not be able to answer questions or give direction to gifted students. Teachers need to feel comfortable as lifelong learners and perhaps team with the student and study the new information together. Modeling how to learn is as important, if not more important, than what to learn. Another alternative for providing rich opportunities for gifted and highly motivated science students is to team a community resource person to work on projects with them.

You may find that the following suggestions are particularly helpful when teaching gifted and highly motivated students:

- Challenge gifted students by providing additional resources such as websites, WebQuests, books, and scientific magazines to enrich their ideas.
- Suggest experiments that can be attempted at home with household supplies.
- Promote after school or community activities such as science clubs, fairs, and national competitions such as Science Olympiad, Odyssey of the Mind, or Problem Solvers of America.
- Research the life of a famous scientist and present a report using period dress and constructing a model of her invention or contribution. Teachers should include female, minority, and scientists of non-Western descent in their list of suggested scientists to investigate.
- Involve students in local issues concerning science concepts, for example, environmental issues.
- Create a time line that traces the roots of a common technology used today. Examples might include development of the car, the computer, the polio vaccine, or a DVD player.

All children deserve excellent science teachers and rich learning environments. Remember, children's needs are fundamentally the same. Children need teachers who have in-depth knowledge of both the learner and the subject matter, who respect diversity, and who care about children as individual learners.

Key Terms

assessment standards *19*   **science content standards** *18*   **science teaching standards** *18*

Technology in the Science Classroom

This chapter will present an overview of how computers and calculators might be used in elementary and middle school science classrooms. A general approach is used in this chapter because some background is needed to understand the computer/calculator activities in the remaining chapters. The 📷 icon will be used throughout the remainder of this book to indicate when a calculator or computer might be used in place of a more traditional instrument such as a thermometer.

It is the philosophy of the authors of this book that learning about and with computers/calculators must be an inherent part of the science curriculum. This learning is needed to provide children with the fundamental knowledge of how to solve problems, handle information, communicate with diverse populations, and learn lifelong skills necessary to understand our changing society and to adapt to the **Information Age.**

Computer/calculator activities will provide teachers with another pedagogical tool for enriching the knowledge base of their pupils. Children learn by doing and reflecting on what they are doing. Computer activities must be chosen carefully so that children gain a better sense of applied knowledge.

The interactive power of the computer is far greater than when it was just used for drill and practice. New technologies should help teachers replace the passive "book science" with interactive real-science pedagogy.

The National Science Teachers Association (NSTA), National Research Council (NRC), and American Association for the Advancement of Science (AAAS) all support the use of new technologies. New technologies help teachers create a classroom environment that enables pupils to learn in an inquiry setting.

Integrating computers into the science curriculum provides powerful new ways to help pupils become active learners. Promoting active participation implies using computers as scientists use them: as tools for gathering data, as a vehicle for communications, as tools for analyzing information, and for simulations and instructional uses.

This chapter organizes the instructional use of computers into seven areas: simulations, graphing packages, Internet/websites/E-mail, database, spreadsheet, general science software (puzzles, problem solving, tutorials, etc.) and Microcomputer/Calculator-Based Laboratories (MBLs, CBLs) for data collection.

Simulations

Simulations allow pupils opportunities to explore, manipulate ideas, and actively participate in problem solving in artificial environments that minimize real-world distractions and make it easier to note the "what if" interactions among variables. Simulations provide well-planned experiences for complex situations that might be too time-consuming, too dangerous, or too expensive.

The computer simulation packages that seem to be most effective are those that emphasize inquiry and cooperative learning, as well as those that motivate through curiosity and encourage the scientific process.

Simulations, like other programs, come in many different formats: disc, CD-ROM, and videodisc. If you have a videodisc or CD-ROM player, full advantage can be taken of the multi-path nature of simulations. Both the CD-ROM and videodisc present video just like your VCR, with one advantage. Each frame of the video is individually coded with a distinct location so that you are able to jump to any location almost instantaneously.

This coding permits pupils to proceed through a unique simulation experience. Each time pupils run the simulation and make a different decision for variables, the simulation changes.

Simulations are excellent for large group interaction as well as small group and individual experiences. A good format to follow first allows time for individual pupils to think about the challenges in the simulation. Then sufficient time is given for small groups to discuss and justify their plan of action. Finally, each small group compares and contrasts their thoughts and actions with other groups. This addition of large group interaction usually results in the greatest educational gain. When pupils experience teamwork, the interdependence of shared knowledge gives them the opportunity to reflect on the multiple perspectives of the team members. One major benefit of teamwork is that pupils are compelled to reflect and better organize their thoughts so they may articulate their ideas to others.

The strengths of simulation packages include motivation, interactivity with subject matter, and work with real-world settings. Simulations also remove extraneous distractions that may interfere with a child's focus. This enables children to view social interactions from multiple perspectives. Finally, simulations can be easily used in a one-computer classroom.

Each of the following simulations encourages students to become scientists as they experience interactive roles in the programs: *The Great Solar System Rescue, The Great Ocean Rescue, Rainforest Researchers* (Tom Snyder Productions); *A Field Trip to the Sea, Rainforest, Earth or Sky, Island Survivors with the Voyage of the Mimi,* and *Thinkin' Science ZAP!*. Most of the above-mentioned come with print material to accompany the problem-solving scenarios.

As with all software, you must make sure it matches both your educational goals as well as your computer hardware capabilities. Carefully read the section that deals with evaluating software, found later in this chapter.

Another word of caution, although worthwhile, simulations do not fulfill the physical action or sensory impressions necessary for more complete understanding of many scientific concepts. When possible and appropriate, students should perform hands-on activities in concert with the simulations.

Graphing Packages

Graphing programs give students the opportunity to collect, organize, and describe data as the computer quickly and easily creates graphs. Pupils should have many manual graphing experiences in earlier grades before using the graphing programs.

After pupils have made graphs manually, they should start to understand the parts of a graph (e.g., title, labels, and scaling). Once these basics are understood, the computer can be used to generate graphs quickly. This gives pupils more time to interpret the data and explore mathematical relationships.

Figure 3.1 shows sample computer-generated graphs. (Some forms are, of course, better than others for the data presented.)

When selecting a graphing package you might look for the following features and decide which are needed for the level of your students:

- Types of graphs and tables the package supports—bar, line, circle, histogram, stem and leaf, box plot, scatter plot, table, or Venn diagram.
- Statistical features—three measures of central tendency (mean, median, and mode), and percent table.
- Movable lines, and ability to easily change scaling.
- Data collected over time so multiple graphs can be displayed.
- Notebook feature to write about graphs or prepare a report.
- Ease of saving, printing, and editing graphs.
- The ability for data to be imported from sources other than a keyboard, such as a database or spreadsheet.

Some graphing/data analysis packages to consider for primary grades are *Graphers* (Sunburst) and *Graph Club* (Tom Snyder Production). In addition, you might critique *Data Explorer* (Sunburst) and *Graph Action Plus* (Tom Snyder Production) for the middle grade levels. All of these open-ended graphing tools encourage pupils to understand how to analyze data and how to select the best visual presentation for organizing data.

Graphing is a process skill closely linked with communication skills. Selecting the best way to show relationships among data in a visual way is an important process skill. The ease and speed of changing one type of graph to another encourages students to explore each of the formats. With practice, pupils will be better able to decide which is the best type of graph for the given situation.

Computers and graphing calculators easily take real-time data and instantly graph the relationship for the pupil. Information from a database, spreadsheet, or MBL/CBL is automatically reformatted into the graph format of their choice. This makes it important for pupils to understand why one graph format (figure 3.1) may be better suited for the situation than another (e.g., pie graph versus line graph).

Internet, Websites, and Electronic Mail (E-Mail)

The Internet is like a spider web capable of connecting all parts of the world electronically. Developed in the late 1960s for military purposes, the intercontinental telephone and fiber-optic lines extend under the ocean floor linking the world far beyond its original use of some 40 years ago. This World Wide Web of access points allows for information exchange at a rate never conceived possible a generation ago.

Information in the form of text, still and moving images, graphics, data, and sound can be routed thousands of miles away at near the speed of light. This electronic technology makes it possible for classrooms everywhere in the world to communicate and share with one another.

Daily Weather in March

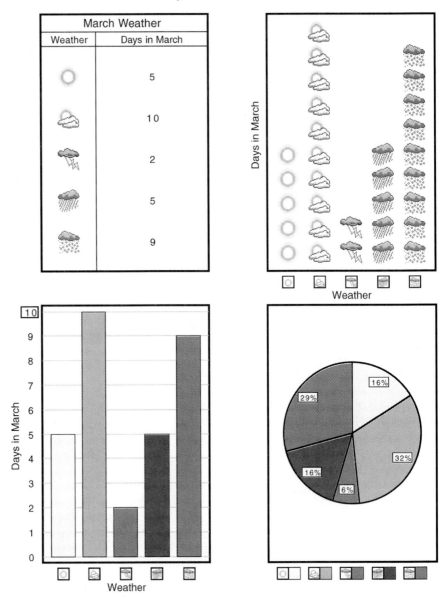

March Weather	
Weather	Days in March
○	5
☁	10
⛈	2
🌧	5
🌨	9

FIGURE 3.1   Sample computer-generated graphs using *Graph Club Jr.*

Anyone with a computer, modem, appropriate communications software, telephone and network services can get access to the Internet. With your own unique address you can exchange information immediately. You can lay out your own **site** to offer information to others by setting up your own **homepage.**

Your site will have a unique address called the URL (Uniform Resource Locator) usually starting with http:// (HyperText Transfer Protocol). It will usually end in a suffix-like ending such as one of the following: **org** (professional organization site), **com** (commercial site), **edu** (educational/institutional site, such as a university), **mil** (military site), **gov** (government agency site), **int** (international association site), or **net** (network organization site). As with other identification systems, such as zip codes, social security numbers, or telephone numbers, your site location is unique.

Searching the Internet, or "surfing," is not without some problems. Finding too much information or too many sites often makes locating the exact information you are seeking overwhelming. The best way to overcome this problem is to understand the power of a search engine. There are several search engines available, such as Alta Vista, Dogpile, Excite, Hotbot, Infoseek, Magellan, Webcrawler, and Yahoo, that are helpful in science information searches.

The solution to a successful search is narrowing your search by keywords. You can quickly become proficient at using the Internet and World Wide Web (WWW) with assistance from a tutorial or resources handbook. Several are available on the Web itself, such as:

Online Resources Handbook	http://home.eunet.no/~presno
Ask Dr. Internet	http://promo.net/drnet
NSTA Online Resources	http://www.nsta.org/ onlineresources/links
Reference Desk	http://www.refdesk.com

The Internet is an incredible tool for use in the science classroom for many reasons. With it pupils have an almost unlimited source of information literally from all over the world. The quality of research projects can vastly improve due to the amount of information available on the Internet.

The process of completing a research report using the Internet is an important endeavor for students. The first encounter could be done as a class project, small group, or individually but the basic procedure is still the same.

- Define your topic.
- Develop your questions and hypothesis.
- Identify the subtopics or keywords.
- Use the search function on the Internet.
- "Bookmark" or record the address of any site that is promising for information and links to other interesting sites.
- Evaluate each site for the "expertness" of the information.
- Take notes on paper or, better yet, use the word processor.
- Gather extra information from other sources (library, texts, local experts).
- Conduct any in-class or field experiments suitable for the topic.
- Rethink or perhaps narrow the questions.
- Complete more searches if necessary.
- Analyze and synthesize all of the information.
- Write the draft of your research report.
- Receive teacher or other group feedback.
- Rewrite final copy to share with others, perhaps as a multimedia presentation.

Software is also available to download Internet sites to your hard drive— eliminating the full accessibility pupils have to the Internet. Discussing responsible use of the Internet with the class might be the best way to handle the issue if we are trying to teach pupils responsibility. As you discuss the problem, let the pupils generate consequences for unacceptable Internet use.

Not only can pupils download information on virtually any topic, but they can use some sites to ask specific questions of the experts in any given field of science. One such site is MAD Scientist Network, http://www .madsci.org. The scientists and teachers that are members of this site volunteer to help pupils with a variety of questions about homework and projects.

Perhaps the most motivating element of using the Internet in the science classroom is its real-time data collection capability. Many long-term studies or studies that must collect data in multiple locations are impractical to accomplish in a single school framework. However, by participating in a scientific monitoring project pupils observe and record data on current scientific issues of interest to them.

For example, the Global Learning and Observations to Benefit the Environment program (GLOBE) is a worldwide network of pupils (K–12), teachers (GLOBE training required), and researchers working collaboratively to observe, study, and understand the environment. Given the responsibility of collecting accurate data such as precipitation, air and water temperature, and pH, pupils are often curious about the concepts behind the measurements. As a result they strive to collect accurate information knowing the data will be sent to a central data processing facility via the Internet. By being in contact with mentoring scientists, pupils receive feedback about the value of their data sets in world-class scientific research. GLOBE creates a format for pupils to communicate with peers around the world.

Real-world data grant pupils a more complete picture of the concepts they are studying. The multitude of data points shows pupils that a single sample does not tell the whole story. This type of collaborative effort is certainly a win-win situation, especially when the responsibility for learning is restored to the learner. Some sites for collaboration are:

Collaborative Projects CIESE	http://k12science.ati.stevens-tech.edu/ collabprojs.html
Journey North	http://www.learner.org/jnorth
GLOBE Program	http://www.globe.gov/

There are numerous additional Internet sites that are helpful to elementary and middle school science teachers and pupils. A few in particular are designed to assist educators to locate and utilize technology resources in the teaching and learning of science. Make sure you visit the following sites for professional links to research, software evaluations, and activities for teaching science:

National Science Digital Library	http://www.nsdl.org
Eisenhower National Clearinghouse for Mathematics & Science Education (ENC)	http://www.enc.org
National Science Teachers Association (NSTA)	http://www.nsta.org
Third International Mathematics Science Study (TIMSS)	http://www.ed.gov/NCES/timss
Discovery Channel School	http://school.discovery.com/students

How do you evaluate a website? Since anyone can open a homepage and profess knowledge about any subject, and because there are far too many sites to visit on any given topic, how do you evaluate the credibility and usefulness of a site? The following list of questions might be useful.

1. Is the information at the appropriate readability level?
2. Does the main focus of the site match the topic you are researching?
3. Does the author give educational credentials or employment data?
4. Does the site link to other sites or resources of experts in the field?
5. Are references provided for the information and data presented?

One note of caution, never give your or your school's name and address unless you are completely sure of the site's credibility. You may be put on many unwanted list serves.

Just as the GLOBE program has an e-mail exchange, there should be many opportunities for pupils to exchange ideas over the Internet. Pre-service science teachers could mentor a small group of elementary or middle school pupils via the Internet about a science fair project. Regular e-mail might occur during the research process as a science fair project is being developed. This is invaluable for both the pupils and the pre-service mentor as pupils are afforded another avenue for reflection and information, while pre-service teachers are given the opportunity to perfect questioning skills, to experience the successes and failures that pupils deal with in completing a science fair project, and to develop an understanding of the developmental concerns, learning styles, and expectations working with young people.

E-mail exchanges could be used to help with homework concerns. However, there is a difference between giving answers and helping students view a concept from a different vantage point.

Uniting pupils who have common science interests is another strength of e-mail. Students interested in hobbies such as robotics, rocketry, or astronomy could find other pupils interested in the same topic. This common scientific interest might develop into a friendship that not only increases the understanding of their hobby but also heightens the understanding of other cultures and their sense of a global community. For example, if you live in the northern hemisphere it would be interesting to communicate with someone from the southern hemisphere while studying astronomy and the constellations.

Database

In this information age, newspaper, magazine, and television reports clearly demonstrate how data and statistics affect our thinking about every aspect of our lives. Weather, health, educational, financial, and political data are just a few of the areas in which immense amounts of data are organized, analyzed, and synthesized as we study ourselves and our world.

A computer database is the tool that helps us to arrange and rearrange information in meaningful ways. Information can be in the form of either numerical data or alpha data (letters/words).

A database management program is like an electronic filing cabinet that helps organize, store, manipulate and retrieve information. Databases can help pupils find and analyze data when using a database as a retrieval system. When pupils create their own database, they are provided with needed inquiry practice. Pupils brainstorm and define a topic, develop questions, collect and record information, analyze the information, and generate conclusions.

Pupils usually have sufficient understanding of making a hypothesis, designing an experiment with at least one variable, and collecting data, but seldom are pupils comfortable or confident in interpreting data. Because they lack confidence and experience, pupils will sometimes change their hypothesis to fit their data or simply conclude that the data are wrong. Working with databases gives pupils excellent opportunities and motivation to analyze and interpret information of interest to them.

All database programs contain three basic elements: field, record, and file. **Field** is a category of information. Using a consumer report database on facial tissues as an example, softness, cost per 100, amount of tissues per box, strength, and aesthetics of box design might be some of the fields.

Record is a collection or listing of related fields. In our tissue example, a record would be all of the information about one brand, such as Kleenex or Puffs. Two or more records, a collection of records, form a **file.**

To summarize, **file** is like the file drawer, **record** is like the manila folder, and **field** is all of the information categories kept in each folder.

Earlier in this chapter the GLOBE program was mentioned as an example of how pupils can collect data in their community and submit it to a national database for use by scientists to analyze and draw conclusions. When pupils create and are involved in their own database, responsibility for learning is shifted to them and away from the teacher. Pupils' natural curiosity motivates them to explore numbers and relationships among information in meaningful ways. This is one advantage to creating a database in your classroom.

The information entered into a database can be easily transformed by the computer into a variety of graph formats. Interpreting data from different formats is a skill pupils need to experience often.

There are several chapters that give suggestions for creating simple databases to help pupils better understand a particular science topic (e.g., periodic table, animal classification, or nutrition concepts).

The following consumer research project, *Sneeze Please Tissue Test*, will demonstrate the process of creating database research projects used by one class. Each group of four pupils selected and designed their own consumer research project.

Pupils first selected an interesting topic to research and decided on a question. In one case a group of pupils asked, What is the best tissue for a cold? Pupils hypothesized that "Sniffers" would be the best brand since it felt thick and soft.

Pupils designed their experiment to contain the following tests and data collection: sneeze resistance (based on performance with "marbles and pump sneezer"), amount of tissues per box, cost per box, cost per 100 tissues, softness (mean rating by panel of three judges against their cheek, 1 = rough to 3 = very soft), and box appeal (mean rating by panel of three judges, 1 = not appealing to 3 = aesthetically pleasing).

Sneeze resistance was tested by fastening each type of tissue to the top of a small margarine container with a rubber band. Each tissue was then "shot" five times with water from a pump sprayer 5 centimeters away. Pupils then measured the number of marbles that could be gently placed, one at a time, on each tissue before it would tear.

Pupils collected data on nine different brands of tissues, three having more than one type per brand. Data from 14 different tissues was entered into a database. The students used the database to answer many of their questions;

TABLE 3.1

Sneeze Please Tissue Test **Database Table**

Tissue Name	Sneeze (#M)	Tissues/ box	Cost/ box ($)	Cost/ 100 ($)	Softness, 1–3	Box Appeal
Sneezi-EX	46	180	1.99	1.1	2.66	2
Generic	36	100	0.79	0.79	1.66	1
Sneezi-L	34	150	1.99	1.32	3	2.66
Muffs-EX	34	180	1.79	1	2.33	2
Kerchoo-L	33	150	2.09	1.39	3	3
Muffs-L	30	150	1.79	1.19	2.66	2
Breeze	30	180	0.99	0.55	2	2
Muffs-R	28	200	1.79	0.89	2	2
Sneezi-R	26	200	1.99	1	2	2.33
ValuPak	25	200	1.49	0.75	2.33	1.33
Kerchoo-R	24	200	2.09	1.04	2.33	2.66
Softeeze	21	140	1.29	0.92	2.33	2
Sniffles	20	200	1.49	0.75	2.33	1.66
ColdAid	16	200	1.19	0.59	1.33	1.33

TABLE 3.2

Data Arranged to Determine Softest Tissue for the Cost

The database program automatically rearranges the data to your specifications.

Tissue Name	Sneeze (#M)	Tissues/ box	Cost/ box ($)	Cost/ 100 ($)	Softness, 1–3	Box Appeal
Sneezi-L	34	150	1.99	1.32	3	2.66
Kerchoo-L	33	150	2.09	1.39	3	3
Sneezi-EX	46	180	1.99	1.1	2.66	2
Muffs-L	30	150	1.79	1.19	2.66	2
Sniffles	20	200	1.49	0.75	2.33	1.66
ValuPak	25	200	1.49	0.75	2.33	1.33
Softeeze	21	140	1.29	0.92	2.33	2
Muffs-EX	34	180	1.79	1	2.33	2
Kerchoo-R	24	200	2.09	1.04	2.33	2.66
Breeze	30	180	0.99	0.55	2	2
Muffs-R	28	200	1.79	0.89	2	2
Sneezi-R	26	200	1.99	1	2	2.33
Generic	36	100	0.79	0.79	1.66	1
ColdAid	16	200	1.19	0.59	1.33	1.33

for example, What is your recommendation for best sneeze resistance and softest tissue in that order? (see table 3.1) and What is the softest tissue for the cost? (see table 3.2).

Pupils realized that there were more questions and variables to consider in answering their original question than they originally thought at the hypothesis stage. Revisions were made to their design, more analysis was

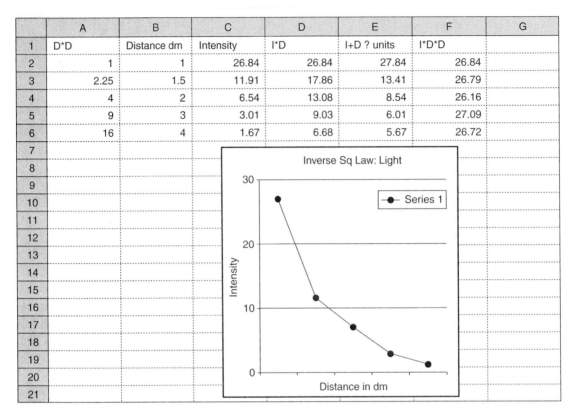

	A	B	C	D	E	F	G
1	D*D	Distance dm	Intensity	I*D	I+D ? units	I*D*D	
2	1	1	26.84	26.84	27.84	26.84	
3	2.25	1.5	11.91	17.86	13.41	26.79	
4	4	2	6.54	13.08	8.54	26.16	
5	9	3	3.01	9.03	6.01	27.09	
6	16	4	1.67	6.68	5.67	26.72	
7							
8							
9							
10							
11							
12							
13							
14							
15							
16							
17							
18							
19							
20							
21							

FIGURE 3.2   Investigation of intensity versus distance to discover the relationship between the two.

conducted, and then each group of pupils submitted a final consumer report for their "Class Consumer Report Journal."

Spreadsheet

A spreadsheet is an application tool designed in the format of a matrix—that is, consisting of rows and columns. The primary strength of the spreadsheet is its ability to calculate and make predictions based on numerical data.

Generally the rows are designated by numbers and the columns labeled by letters. The intersection of a row and column is called a cell. The cell would be named by its row and column, for example, B3 (column B, row 3).

A cell can contain one of three items: labels, values, or functions. Labels are titles and names. Values can be numbers or formulas, for example, +A2 +A3. Using a + sign in front of a letter tells the computer to treat the entry as a value. Functions are built-in formulas such as a summation of a given number of columns. Spreadsheets are particularly valuable because we have the ability to interchange variables. This makes it easier to show multiple relationships. Spreadsheets can help pupils discover what a formula is, then test their hypothesis. For example, have pupils record in column A the intensity of light on a wall as the distance between the wall and light source varies. Record the corresponding distance in column B. Subsequent columns could perform operations (B + A, B − A, B * A, B/A, etc.) on the first two columns looking for a direct or inverse relationship.

Spreadsheets are easy for middle school pupils to set up with the exception of the formulas that define a column. It is advisable to collaborate with the mathematics teacher on relationships and patterns that are being studied in both classes. These are the relationships that should be explored with the spreadsheet.

Like a database, spreadsheets can also be transformed by the computer into a variety of graph formats. (See figure 3.2.)

WebQuest

A WebQuest is an interdisciplinary, inquiry-based unit in which most or all of the information originates from the Web. The teacher selects pertinent information and links to include in the unit, saving students time from wandering the Net for information. The teacher locates several websites that would be most valuable to her diverse learners, providing students more time to analyze, question, and explore the concepts in question. Many WebQuests can be thought of as problem-based learning units since most WebQuests center around a scenario filled with real-world concerns and issues to be solved.

The format of a WebQuest provides a practical way for students to attain information, problem solve, role-play, engage in simulations and debates, and to participate in an active, collaborative manner. All of these features are important in an inquiry-based learning environment. The elements and process of creating a WebQuest as described by the WebQuest creator, Bernie Dodge, are summarized below (see also http://webquest .sdsu.edu/ click on Overview & Frequently Asked Questions (FAQ) and Training Materials):

- *Introduction* to the activity or unit, role, and scenario. Includes the guiding question to be investigated and answered.
- *Task* (or final product) that requires the learner to transform information and knowledge through analysis, synthesis, and evaluation by solving a problem or mystery, formulating and defending a position, designing a product, creating something, or delivering a persuasive message, and so on.
- *Process* (or steps) needed to accomplish the task, including resources (links to the Internet, hands-on materials, print materials, etc.).
- *Evaluation* described in terms of a rubric to guide performance.
- *Conclusion* (summary, question, extensions).

An excellent website to visit for sample WebQuests is http://www .bestwebquests.com. This site was created by Tom March and provides WebQuests that are highly rated as valuable units/lesson plans. You can submit for review a WebQuest you designed to this Best WebQuest site. *Weather Watchers* (http://www.itdc.k12.ca.us/curriculum/weather.html) and *Paper or Plastic* (http://oncampus.richmond.edu/education/projects/webquests/paper/index.html) are two sites designed for primary children that encourage the decision-making process in a very appropriate manner. In *Paper or Plastic,* children research the advantages and disadvantages of selecting either paper or plastic bags at the grocery store. Teachers can expand on this unit by having children design a strenth test experiment with the bags as one feature to consider.

For intermediate- and middle-level students, *Discovering Bats!* (http://www.webmonkeyplus.com/bats/index.htm), *The King of Tides* (http://www.bestwebquests.com), and *Paper Airplane Exploration* (http://www.geocities.com/paperplane_quest/index.html) are three samples of WebQuests that are designed to teach students how to use resources to answer such questions as, Is the Moon responsible for tides? or Are bats a benefit or a threat to humans, and why? Learning *how* to find answers is more important than the answer itself. WebQuests provide students with the opportunity to experience this process.

General Science Software

There are many science software programs in the form of puzzles, problem solving, tutorials, and information resources. As with any additional curriculum material you must critique the software first and then decide if it has a valuable place in your curriculum.

Games take away from the finite time pupils have to investigate concepts. Instruction should be focused on the question, Does the classroom environment promote construction of concepts by children in a variety of ways? This environment must provide opportunities for a balance among exploration, reflection, discussions, and practice of concepts.

If a computer program meets these needs in a timely fashion, then consider its use. There are many software evaluation forms available. You may want to use the one published in the ENC *Focus: Special SchoolNet Issue, 1998* periodical. The website address for the Eisenhower National Clearinghouse (ENC) is given in the Internet section of this chapter.

In general, you may ask yourself the following questions when critiquing science software:

- Does the software fit my curriculum goal?
- Does the software reflect the instructional format needed?
- Is the software format compatible with my hardware?
- Is the software appropriate for the age of my students?
- What group size is the software designed for?
- Does the software encourage group interaction and discussion?
- To what extent does the software support the scientific processes?
- To what extent does the software promote applications and connections within and between subject matter?
- Does the software place more emphasis on learning and thinking than rewards and praise?
- Does it give appropriate feedback? (i.e., Does it move on quickly if the answer is correct and does it redirect the student if the answer is not correct?)
- Is the science information up-to-date?

A sample list of science software follows. Figure 3.3 shows a sample screen from a problem-solving program for elementary children called *Gizmos & Gadgets*. The majority of the software can be ordered in disc or CD-ROM formats. The list is in order of suggested grade levels.

Zurk's Learning Safari (Soleil Software), Grades preK–1
Sammy's Science House (Edmark), Grades preK–2

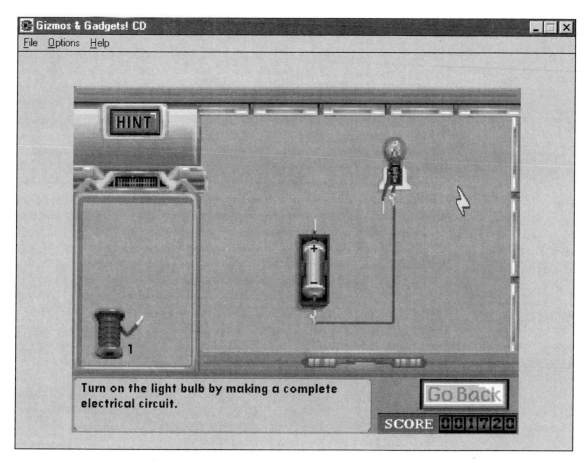

FIGURE 3.3   Sample screen of *Gizmos & Gadgets*.

Thinkin' Science (Edmark), Grades preK–2

Zurk's Rainforest Lab (Soleil Software), Grades K–3

Learn About . . . Collection: The Human Body, Animals, Plants, Dinosaurs, Astronomy, Simple Machines, Senses, Weather, and Matter, Measurement & Mixtures, sold separately (Sunburst), Grades K–3

Scholastic's The Magic School Bus Explores Inside the Earth (Microsoft Home), Grades 1–4

Scholastic's The Magic School Bus Explores the Human Body (Microsoft Home), Grades 1–4

Scholastic's The Magic School Bus Explores the Ocean (Microsoft Home), Grades 1–4

Zurk's Alaskan Trek (Soleil Software), Grades 1–4

Science Court Explorations: Flight, Heat Absorption, Rockets, Pendulums, Magnets, and Friction, sold separately (Tom Snyder Productions), Grades 2–4

Gizmos & Gadgets (The Learning Company), Grades 2–6

The New Way Things Work (DK Multimedia), Grades 3–5

Grossology (Segasoft), Grades 3–5

Thinkin Science ZAP! (Edmark), Grades 3–6

Bill Nye the Science Guy: Stop the Rock (Disney), Grades 3–6

Tabletop Jr. (Sunburst and TERC Inc.), Grades 3–6

Microscope: Nature Explorer (New Media Schoolhouse), Grades 4–6
Space Academy GX-1 (Sunburst) Grades 3–6
Science Court Explorations: Living Things, Work & Simple Machines, Soil, Seasons, Statistics, Electric Current, Water Cycle, Particles in Motion, Sound, Gravity, Inertia, and Fossils, sold separately (Tom Snyder Productions), Grades 4–6
Logical Journey of the Zoombinis (Broderbund), Grades 4–6
Operation: Weather Disaster (Discovery Communications, Inc.), Grades 4–6
A.D.A.M. The Inside Story 1997 (Mindscape), Grades 4–8
A Field Trip to the . . . Sea, . . . Rainforest, . . . Earth or . . . Sky, sold separately (Sunburst), Grades 4–8
Ecosystems simulation, (Sunburst), Grades 4–8
Everything Weather (The Weather Channel and Sunburst), Grades 4–8
Rainforest Researchers (Tom Snyder Productions), Grades 5–8
Great Solar System Rescue (Tom Snyder Productions), Grades 5–8
The Great Ocean Rescue (Tom Snyder Productions), Grades 5–8
Virtual Labs Bundle: Electricity & Light, sold separately (Sunburst), Grades 6–12

Microcomputer and/or Calculator-Based Laboratory

Both microcomputers and designated calculators can be used to collect real-time data and almost instantly display the data as a graph or table. These systems are typically known as Microcomputer-Based Laboratories (MBLs) and Calculator-Based Laboratories (CBLs).

The unique and key part of these systems is the sensory probes that interface with the computer and/or calculator. Probes or sensors help pupils to quickly and easily collect data over long or short periods of time. The computer/calculator software supplies readouts and graphs of data in formats specified by the user.

The software also presents the flexibility to manipulate the data (e.g., change the scale, zoom in on a part of the graph) and use statistical functions on the data (e.g., mean, median, mode, summations, standard deviation). The probes and sensors read both continuous data (analog) and discrete data like on/off (digital data) and give very accurate readings when calibrated.

The use of MBLs and CBLs greatly increases the ability for pupils to explore the world around them. By decreasing the necessary time to complete lessons, CBLs and MBLs help provide inquiry experiences through motivating, real-world applications.

When teachers provide a chance for pupils to explore, discuss, reflect, and practice process skills through real-world explorations, the lesson then mirrors the type of instruction that helps pupils gain in-depth conceptual understanding.

There are many types of probes or sensors, including temperature, light, sound, pH, pressure, magnetic field, conductivity, voltage, force, and motion. Temperature, light, and sound are the probes used generally for elementary grades (3–5), whereas all of the probes listed above are suitable for middle school (5–8) use because concepts like pH are more developmentally appropriate at a middle level. As with any hands-on activity, it is important to also discuss and reflect on concepts than to just "do" the lab work. "Minds-on" must accompany the exploration. Figure 3.4 displays a sample of the probes.

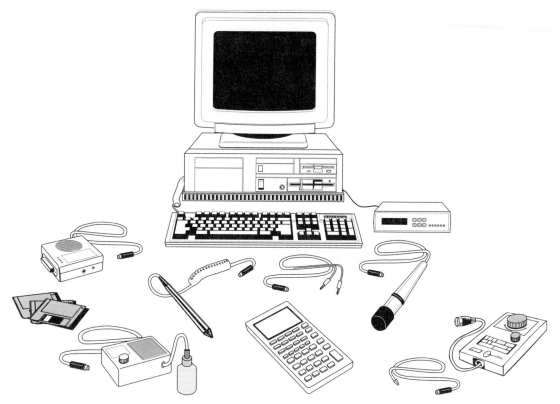

FIGURE 3.4   Sample probes.

Temperature probes usually have a range of –10° to 110° Celsius. However, some are only meant to measure air temperatures from 0° to 40° Celsius. Temperature probes react to changes in temperature by changes in electrical resistance. The computer can sense electrical changes and convert that into a change in the temperature.

Readings in temperature changes take anywhere from nearly zero to a few seconds for the computer to respond. The manual that comes with your specific probe will give more details.

The photocell or light probe is made with a light-sensitive material that changes electrical resistance in response to changes in light. The light sensor response time is usually very quick. Note that in low light levels, some probes work better than others. The sound sensor responds best to continuous background sounds. Some sensors do not register quick changes in sound levels as well as others. However, at an elementary level this may not matter.

With all of the sensors, whatever is being measured must somehow be changed into electrical data in order for the computer to measure the changes. In the case of sound, pressure differences on a diaphragm are changed into electrical impulses very similar to how the brain interprets sound at the eardrum.

The pH sensors have a range of 0 to 14 pH. The pH sensors need to be stored in water or a buffered solution when not in the long-term storage bottle. Their life span is usually about 12 to 18 months.

By using CBL and MBL activities, pupils become scientists. Activities using the pH sensor allow pupils to collect data about acid rain and to explore the acidic or basic nature of household chemicals. Understanding the acid/base nature of household chemicals may help pupils decide what action needs to be taken in the case of an accidental poisoning.

The temperature probes can be used extensively and more safely than a mercury- or alcohol-filled thermometer. Recording the fingertip temperature of a pupil before and after he eats a chocolate bar and drinks a can of cola can lead to a wonderful discussion and debate as to the effects of sugar and caffeine on the body. Health issue investigations need to begin in elementary school and progress to lifelong learning.

There are literally more than a hundred different experiments that take advantage of the CBLs and MBLs. They are very easy to use and come with well-tested lesson plans and pupil handouts for both the elementary and middle school levels. Actually, the MBL probes have been used in the elementary and middle school levels since the mid-1980s. Therefore, there are many published ideas available.

Listed in the following text are some of the sources for MBLs or CBLs and related resource materials: Vernier Software (CBLs and MBLs): phone (888) 837-6437, fax (503) 277-2440, e-mail info@vernier.com; PASCO Scientific (Science Workshops MBL): phone (800) 772-7800, fax (916) 786-8905, e-mail www.pasco.com; Texas Instruments (CBL-2) & CBRs): phone (972) 917-6411, fax (972) 917-7103, e-mail http://education.ti.com; Casio Inc. (CBLs): phone (800) 582-2763, e-mail http://www.casio-usa.com.

The Calculator-Based Laboratories have an advantage in that they can be used outside of the classroom. Calculators can measure and store data connected to or disconnected from a computer.

Each subsequent chapter in this text will give suggestions on how to use probe technology in your classrooms to help motivate pupils to become lifelong learners of science. Use of new technologies is certainly recommended but of course not mandatory. The majority of the experiments still could be performed using traditional equipment, but the probeware has the advantage of recording and graphing the data instantaneously. Data can also be collected over a period of time even when pupils are not in school (i.e., temperature can be recorded at regular intervals for 48 hours if necessary).

Teachers who relinquish "teaching book-science" to provide an environment where *pupils* take the responsibility to learn concepts, skills, and applications in an inquiry mode are following the guidelines issued by the National Science Education Standards (NSES).

Key Terms

field, *34*   **file,** *34*   **Information age,** *27*   **record,** *34*

Teaching Children about the Characteristics of Matter

NATIONAL SCIENCE EDUCATION STANDARDS ALIGNMENT TO EVENTS

The events in this chapter help accomplish several of the NSES for content. The event(s) that align with a given content standard are listed below that standard.

LEVELS K–4

UNIFYING CONCEPTS AND PROCESSES
- Systems, order and organization
  4-A
  4-C
- Change, consistency, measurement
  4-D through 4-G
  4-H through 4-J
  4-O through 4-U
- Evidence, models and explanation
  4-B
  4-O
- Evolution and equilibrium
  4-B
  4-D through 4-G
  4-K through 4-N
  4-S through 4-BB
- Form and function
  4-K through 4-N

SCIENCE AS INQUIRY
- Abilities necessary to do and understand scientific inquiry
  4-A through 4-BB

PHYSICAL SCIENCE
- Properties of objects and materials
  4-A through 4-C
  4-D through 4-G
  4-H and 4-J
  4-K through 4-N
  4-O through 4-R
  4-S through 4-BB

HISTORY AND NATURE OF SCIENCE
- Science as a human endeavor
  historical introduction
  4-B and 4-C

LEVELS 5–8

UNIFYING CONCEPTS AND PROCESSES
- Systems, order and organization
  4-A
  4-C
- Change, consistency, measurement
  4-D and 4-G
  4-H through 4-J
  4-O through 4-U
- Evidence, models and explanation
  4-B
  4-O
- Evolution and equilibrium
  4-B
  4-D through 4-G
  4-K through 4-N
  4-S through 4-BB
- Form and function
  4-A through 4-N

SCIENCE AS INQUIRY
- Abilities necessary to do and understand scientific inquiry
  4-A through 4-BB

PHYSICAL SCIENCE
- Properties and changes of properties of matter
  4-A through 4-C
  4-D through 4-G
  4-H and 4-J
  4-K through 4-N
  4-O through 4-R
  4-S through 4-BB
- Motion and forces
  4-H and 4-J
  4-S through 4-BB

SCIENCE AND TECHNOLOGY
- Understanding science and technology
  4-C

SCIENCE IN PERSONAL AND SOCIAL PERSPECTIVES
- Risks and benefits
  4-I
  4-M
- Science and technology in society
  4-C

HISTORY AND NATURE OF SCIENCE
- Science as a human endeavor
  historical introduction
  4-B and 4-C

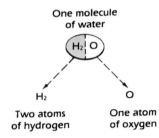

One molecule
of water

Two atoms   One atom
of hydrogen   of oxygen

FIGURE 4.1 When one
molecule of water is divided,
it ceases to be water. Instead,
it becomes two atoms of
hydrogen and one atom of
oxygen.

Democritus and the Atom

During the Golden Age of Greece, a philosopher named Democritus gave us the first look at the smallness of "matter." He wondered how small a bit of matter could be. Can something be so tiny that it could not be divided? Suppose, for example, that we had a bucket of water and that it could be divided and redivided until the amounts would be too small to be seen.

If we had a magic knife, could those tiny bits be divided further, or is there a limit to how small something can be? Democritus thought that, yes, there must be a limit. Beyond a certain point, he reasoned, it could not be divided further. For this smallest of all parts he gave the name *atom*.

Today we know that from one point of view, Democritus was right. There is, indeed, a limit to smallness. In the case of water, for example, the smallest part is called a *molecule*. It contains two atoms of hydrogen and one atom of oxygen (H_2O). If it is divided any further, it is no longer water. Thus, there *is a limit to how tiny a substance can be and still retain the properties of that substance.* When molecules and atoms are divided still further, the divided parts no longer have the characteristics of the original substance. (See figure 4.1.)

Until the mid-1800s, scientists believed that the *atom* was the smallest possible particle. They then discovered that the atom was made of even tinier parts. Today, scientists are aware of dozens of subatomic particles, and they continue to find ever smaller bits of matter.

Will we ever discover the elusive "smallest of all possible parts"? The subject calls to mind a poem by an unknown poet:

> Do fleas have little fleas
> Upon their backs to bite 'em.
> And these little fleas have littler fleas
> In ad infinitum?

Classifying Matter (Event 4-A)

Discrepant Event and Pupil Investigations

Event 4-A. Where Does It Belong?

Display pictures of things such as a rock, river, baseball, balloon, cloud, fire, cup, ocean, and plowed field. Ask pupils to classify the objects into as many groups as they feel is appropriate. Sometimes it is best to organize the class into committees of three to accomplish this task. (Why three pupils instead of four or more? It is more difficult to maintain reasonable order. With three pupils, if A talks to B, C has to listen. But if there are four or more pupils, there can be two or more sets of discussions going on at the same time.)

Pupil Investigations (may include the following processes):

1. Identifying similarities and differences among the items shown in the pictures.
2. Making a rule about the characteristics that are valid for the various groups.
3. Classifying objects into two or more groups.

Event 4-A Explained in Context (Classifying Matter)

Why Classify Matter?

There are so many thousands of "things" in the universe and it is impossible to memorize each of them as a discrete item. Without a way of grouping, the things in the universe would become a massive jumble, or chaos, in our minds. If a way can be found to put things into related groups, it becomes easier not only to remember the discrete items but also how they interact with each other. A system of classification can bring order out of chaos.

An example of how classifying can make things simpler is the alphabet. Twenty-six letters can be used to form tens of thousands of words. These letters can be used to describe and transmit ideas that would be impossible to do without such simplification. Some societies do not have an alphabet, so each object in the universe must be shown with a different written symbol. It is extremely difficult to learn how to read and write in such a system.

Thousands of years ago Greek philosophers studied the concept of matter in the physical world. (Animal life and plant life were separate from physical matter.) Aristotle decided that all matter in the universe could be divided into just four groups: air, water, fire, and earth. This was his attempt to make order out of chaos. As time went on, however, it became apparent that many substances would not fit very well into those groups. Scientists found that better order could be achieved if additional groups were formed. After 2500 years, scientists had organized the physical universe into 23 groups. These groups were called elements.

Additional discoveries have been made so that there are now more than 100 of these elements. Further study has shown that these elements are related to each other and can all be shown in a comprehensive chart called the *Periodic Table of the Elements.*

Event 4A, Where Does it Belong? is an event that can be used even in lower grades to give pupils practice in simple grouping. The purpose of the exercise is to have pupils recognize that groups exist and to give them practice in deciding how to place objects or items into those groups. Pupils generally will not agree on the number or types of groups.

On the one extreme, pupils could put all items into just two groups, such as solids and liquids. Others will have many groups based on characteristics such as size, shape, color, and weight. It is not important that they agree. Discussion about which system is better is generally beneficial for all pupils. In addition, it prepares them for the many types of groupings that they will see as they continue their studies in science.

Inside the Atom (Events 4-B and (4-C)

Discrepant Events and Pupil Investigations

Event 4-B. What Is It?

Divide the class into groups of about three pupils each. Each group should be supplied with modeling clay or Play-Doh about the size of a baseball. Prior to class, imbed inside each sample of clay a small object such as a marble, a coin, or a die (from a pair of dice), or a more complex object like a thimble.

Each committee should have several dozen toothpicks. Ask each group to try to determine what is inside the clay by carefully inserting the toothpicks. (**Caution:** Be sure to monitor this activity carefully, so no pupil will cause injury. Pupils should insert the toothpicks slowly and carefully and once inserted leave them there.) After all toothpicks have been inserted, ask the committees to decide what they think is inside.

Pupil Investigations (may include the following processes):

1. Observing how far the toothpicks enter the clay before hitting something inside.
2. Feeling how much resistance there is to the toothpicks when they touch an object inside.
3. Predicting what the object is on the basis of the position of the toothpicks.
4. Appreciating the work of scientists who find out what is inside an atom even though they cannot see it.

Event 4-C. Database of Elements

Give each pupil a common element to investigate. After each pupil has completed his/her investigation, have the class brainstorm to form a list of important information needed for each element. Information might include atomic number, atomic mass, symbol, uses, state of matter, and common combinations with other elements. Let pupils search for any characteristic they may not have found during the first search. Encourage the use of the Internet as part of the search process. Have the class again identify the list of important characteristics about each element. This will be the *field* names for a database on elements, Have pupils enter the information for their selected element into the *file*, "Element Database." This assignment should be extended by having pupils make a brochure to sell their element.

Pupil Investigations (may include the following processes):

1. Collecting information known about common elements.
2. Sorting for a given *field* or characteristic of the elements using a database.
3. Relating the periodic table to the outcomes of a database sort or search function.
4. Recognizing patterns in the periodic table through the database sort.

Events 4-B and 4-C Explained in Context (Inside the Atom)

The problems faced by the pupils are somewhat like the problems faced by scientists when they explore the inside of an atom. Scientists determine what the atom is like even though they cannot see it. In the classroom, pupils try to determine what is inside the ball of clay. Some pupils will be able to judge that the hidden object has a round or flat surface, but most will have great difficulty in being more specific.

Although it is too small to be seen, scientists have learned much about an atom's structure. For example, we know that an atom is mostly space. Even dense materials like iron, lead, bricks, and stone contain atoms made up mostly of space.

How do we know this? Many of the explanations about the structure of an atom are too complex to discuss here. However, there was one important experiment performed by an English physicist in 1901 that gives us a clue to how scientists "looked" inside the atom. Earnest Rutherford designed an experiment as shown in figure 4.2. He decided to test a sample target by shooting it with atomic "bullets," The target was a piece of gold foil, the gun a bit of radium, and the bullets were alpha particles from the radium.

He drilled a hole into the center of a block of lead and dropped a bit of radium inside. Lead is a shield against radiation, so no alpha particles came out except through the drilled hole. The hole was like the barrel of a rifle, and the atomic particles came out like bullets from a gun.

He aimed the atomic bullets toward a screen coated with a phosphorescent material that glowed when struck by radiation. In this way it was easy to see where the atomic bullets were hitting.

Rutherford then placed the thin piece of gold foil between the barrel and the screen to see what might happen. To his surprise, the screen continued to glow as if the foil did not even exist! The atomic particles went right through the foil.

He observed the event for a long time. Then he noticed that from time to time a tiny fleck of light appeared on the phosphorescent screen *outside* the target area. This meant that on rare occasions an atomic particle hit something inside the foil and was deflected.

Careful study showed that only about twenty out of every million bullets were deflected. He concluded that (1) since most bullets went right through the foil, the atoms of gold must consist mostly of space; (2) an atom must have a very small nucleus, since it was seldom hit; and (3) since the nucleus was able to deflect the bullets, the nucleus must be very heavy compared to the rest of the atom.

Rutherford's experiment can be compared to firing rifle bullets through a bale of straw with a cannon ball inside it. Most of the bullets go right through the straw, but a few will hit the cannon ball and be deflected. By studying the pattern of deflected bullets, it is possible to estimate the size and shape of the unseen metal.

The comparison, to be accurate, would require a huge bale with a mass of 1000 kilograms. Of that total, the cannon ball would have a mass of 999.5 kg while the rest of the bale would have only 0.5 kg. Most surprising of all, the heavy cannon ball nucleus would be so tiny that it could hardly be seen.

If the nucleus of an atom were 1 centimeter in diameter, the outer part of that atom would be about 120 meters away, or farther than the length of a football field. These figures show that an atom is made up mostly of space. Only about one part in fifty thousand is actually solid.

It is easy to see from the figures that it is very difficult to make an accurate classroom model of an atom. Still, diagrams can be used if we are careful to stress the limitations. In other words, a diagram or model of an atom such as shown in figure 4.3 is quite inaccurate with respect to scale, and it gives a poor representation of motion. However, the diagram can be helpful in showing some relationships.

In Event 4-C, *Database of Elements,* the use of a database gives pupils a chance to discover patterns in the periodic chart based on the characteristics *(fields)* of the elements. For example, all of the elements (except hydrogen) in a gaseous state are located on the right-hand side of the table. The atomic numbers ascend in order just as the atomic mass does. Elements found in the first

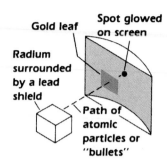

FIGURE 4.2   Rutherford's experiments gave evidence that atoms contained mostly space.

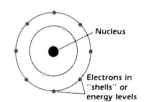

FIGURE 4.3   A two-dimensional model of an atom may be helpful in showing some relationships.

column tend to combine with elements found in the seventeenth column. Elements in the eighteenth column do not react with other elements. It is meaningful for students to discuss what information is significant to know about each element. It is important for students to develop an appreciation for the ease and speed at which a database can sort information. By having students construct an "element sales brochure" and then present it to the class, pupils get a chance to use different learning modes.

Terms

Two terms can be used to describe every substance in the universe. All matter is made up either of *elements* or *compounds.*

ELEMENT: A substance made up of only one kind of atom. It cannot be separated by ordinary chemical means into anything other than a sample of that element. There are 103 known elements. Some well-known examples are iron, carbon, uranium, hydrogen, oxygen, gold, and silver.

COMPOUND: A substance made up of two or more kinds of atoms. There are countless numbers of compounds. Some well-known examples are water, made up of two atoms of hydrogen and one atom of oxygen (H_2O); carbon dioxide (CO_2); and sugar, made up of atoms of carbon, hydrogen, and oxygen. Some complex compounds (such as synthetics) contain thousands of atoms.

Two additional terms can be used to describe the smallest parts of elements and compounds. They are atoms and molecules. They are not the smallest particles in the universe, but they are the smallest parts of matter that can exist alone or in combinations.

ATOM: The smallest part of an element. For example, you can have a single atom of the elements of hydrogen and oxygen, but not of the compound water (H_20).

MOLECULE: The smallest part of a compound. For example, the smallest part of water is a single molecule (H_2O) containing two atoms of hydrogen and one atom of oxygen. Some complex molecules contain thousands of atoms.

Another way to describe the structure of matter is to look at the order of size from the largest to the smallest.

COMPOUND: Made up of molecules.
MOLECULE: Made up of atoms.
ATOM: Made up of electrons and nucleus (of many parts).
NUCLEUS: Made up of protons and neutrons (plus many other parts).

Spaces between Molecules (Events 4-D through 4-G)

Discrepant Events and Pupil Investigations

Event 4-D. Does 2 + 2 = 3½?

Before the class begins, pour about 50 milliliters of rubbing alcohol (or you can use spirit duplicator "ditto" fluid if your school still has it) into a graduate cylinder. This should be an "unknown" liquid as far as the pupils are concerned.

Later, while the class is observing, pour about 50 milliliters of "known" liquid, identified as water, into another cylinder. Measure the volumes carefully and write the number on the chalkboard. Add a drop or two of food coloring to the containers to make the liquids easier to see. (It is not necessary to have exactly 50 ml in each container. But read the values carefully and add them together.)

Now pour the contents of one cylinder into the other and mix well. Check the volume of the combined liquids. Surprisingly, the sum will be about 2 to 4 milliliters *less* than the total of the two liquids measured separately. What happened to the missing liquid?

Pupil Investigations (may include the following processes):

1. Identifying by smell the "unknown" liquid as alcohol.
2. Discovering that traces of liquid remain inside the emptied cylinder and theorizing (incorrectly) that this accounts for the loss in volume.
3. Devising a method to check that theory—by pouring together two volumes of a known liquid (water) and observing that there is no measurable loss of volume.
4. Graphing the volume of the combined liquids at 5-minute intervals for 30 minutes to see if the liquid is lost by evaporation. (Students will find that there is no measurable loss of volume after the initial mixing of the two liquids.)
5. Detecting the correct level of the liquid; take this opportunity to teach pupils how to read the level of a liquid. (See figure 4.4.)

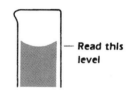

FIGURE 4.4   The level of liquid in the container should be read at its lowest point in the curve.

Event 4-E. Where Does the Water Go?

Fill a narrow-necked flask about one-fourth to one-half full of water-softener salt pellets. Then add warm water to nearly fill the flask. Mark the water level with a grease pencil or with tape. (See figure 4.5.)

After a few minutes the level will have dropped noticeably. Why? (**Note:** You can use table salt for this activity, but it tends to cake together if you let it stand for a few days.)

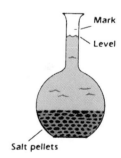

FIGURE 4.5   Why does the water level go down? Use a grease pencil to mark the original level.

Pupil Investigations (may include the following processes):

1. Feeling that the flask is warm to the touch. (Some pupils may conclude incorrectly that the heat is produced by a chemical reaction. However, other pupils will have noticed that the water was added from the hot water faucet.)
2. Measuring the level of the water at periodic intervals for 40 to 60 minutes. (Pupils will notice that most of the decline in the level occurs in the first 10 to 20 minutes and then stabilizes.)
3. Discovering that the pellets become smaller. (Pupils may conclude—correctly—that the pellets are dissolving.)
4. Forming a theory (incorrectly) that the loss in volume is due to the fact that the pellets are absorbing the water. (Have pupils check this theory. Empty the liquid from the flask and refill with warm water. The water level drops again, even when you start with saturated salt pellets.)
5. Forming a theory (incorrectly) that the water level drops because of evaporation. (Pupils can check this theory by measuring the water level

every 5 minutes for 40 to 60 minutes. Evaporation would cause a uniform rate of decline during the entire period.)

Safety Note: Some pupils may want to taste the liquid. Be sure to impress upon the pupils that unknown liquids should *never* be tasted. An unknown liquid could be poisonous.

Event 4-F. Pour Salt into a "Full" Tumbler

Fill a tumbler level-full with warm water. Then slowly add a measured amount of table salt. How much can be added without causing the tumbler to overflow? (See figure 4.6.)

Pupil Investigations (may include the following processes):

1. Measuring the amount of salt that can be poured into the tumbler before it overflows.
2. Observing that the top surface of the water will stand above the rim of the tumbler after enough salt is added to the water.
3. Generalizing (incorrectly) that the amount of salt is equal to the amount of water standing above the rim of the tumbler.

FIGURE 4.6   How much salt can you pour into a "full" tumbler?

4.   Devising a method to check this theory by using a second tumbler and adding water instead of salt. (They can add more salt than water before the tumbler overflows.)

Event 4-G. The Shrinking Balloon

Fill a balloon and tie it shut. Measure the distances around its length and width with a string. Put the balloon aside for a few days. Then measure again. The balloon will get smaller each day. Where does the air go?

Pupil Investigations (may include the following processes):

1.   Predicting that the balloon will get smaller each day.
2.   Measuring to confirm the predictions.
3.   Inferring that the loss of size is due to a loss of air.
4.   Controlling variables: avoiding air loss at the neck by sealing the balloon securely.

Events 4-D through 4-G Explained in Context (Spaces between Molecules)

It is difficult to show the size and shape of atoms and molecules in the classroom. Those particles are too small to be seen with ordinary lab equipment. Yet, surprising as it may seem, the previous four events in this chapter show us something about the makeup of molecules.

Event 4-D, Does 2 + 2 = 3½? shows that the two volumes do not add up. Some volume is lost when alcohol and water are mixed. When 50 ml of water are added to 50 ml of alcohol, we are surprised to find that the total adds up only to about 96 to 98 ml.

What happened to the missing liquid? It went into the spaces *between* the molecules. When mixed, the combined molecules fit together better than when they were alone, so they take up less space. It is similar to mixing 50 ml of marbles and 50 ml of fine sand. When mixed, the volume will be much less than 100 ml because some of the sand will fill in the spaces between the marbles.

In *Event 4-E, Where Does the Water Go?*, volume is lost again. The salt dissolves and the ions of sodium and chloride find room in the spaces *between* the molecules of water. If a narrow-necked flask is used, it is possible to see the level drop by as much as 3 centimeters in 30 minutes.

Sometimes pupils will say that the water is absorbed by the pellets. To test this theory, pour out the water after the level has dropped and refill the container with fresh warm water. This time the pellets are already saturated, but the water level drops again. (You can also use cold water, but it takes longer for the level to go down.)

In *Event 4-F, Pour Salt into a "Full" Tumbler,* the dissolving salt, again, fills the spaces between molecules of water. That is part of the reason why you can add salt to a "full" tumbler. However, it is not the entire reason. Another factor, cohesion (to be discussed in more detail later in this chapter), is also responsible. Cohesion is a force that causes water to "heap up" somewhat over the rim of a tumbler before it overflows.

Thus, because of these two factors—spaces between molecules and cohesion—a surprising amount of salt can be added to a "full" tumbler before it overflows. Pupils should be cautioned to add the salt slowly. Also, they will

LIVERPOOL JOHN MOORES UNIVERSITY
LEARNING SERVICES

have better success with this activity, if the water is warm so that the salt dissolves more quickly.

Event 4-G, The Shrinking Balloon, is an activity, that almost all pupils will predict correctly. They seem to know instinctively that the balloon will be smaller after a few days. Yet many will not know why. The main reason for the loss of size is the loss of air. Molecules of air slowly escape through the spaces between the molecules of rubber or plastic.

All four of the events give evidence that there are spaces between molecules.

Molecular Motion (Events 4-H through 4-J)

Discrepant Events and Pupil Investigations

Event 4-H. The "Smell" Box

Place a cut onion into a small cardboard box. Cut a hole in the box and place a barrier inside it so that the onion cannot be seen. Do not tell pupils what is in the box. Ask them to identify the object by using the sense of smell. (You can use other substances such as mothballs or a vinegar-soaked cloth in place of the onion.)

Pupil Investigations (may include the following processes):

1. Identifying the object in the box by smelling it. (Most pupils will be able to identify an onion by its odor.)
2. Experimenting to see how far away the onion can be detected.
3. Forming a theory that unseen particles are escaping from the onion and are mixing with the air.

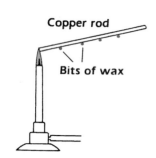

FIGURE 4.7   What happens to the little blobs of wax as the heat moves along the rod?

Event 4-I. The "Hot" Rod

Place small bits of wax at 1-centimeter intervals along a copper or other metal rod. Heat one end of the rod and observe what happens. (See figure 4.7) **Caution:** Guard against burns: The rod should be held in place with a clamp and holder.

Pupil Investigations (may include the following processes):

1. Observing that the wax bits melt, first close to the heat source and then progressively along the rod.
2. Inferring that the heat travels along the rod to melt the wax.
3. Comparing the rate of heat travel among different metals.

Event 4-J. How Does the Ink Spread?

Place a drop of ink into a still glass of water. Do not stir the water. After a day or so the jar is uniformly colored. Why? (You can use food coloring in place of ink.)

Pupil Investigations (may include the following processes):

1. Recording data describing how much of the ink has dispersed through the liquid at periodic intervals. (Hourly data for one school day is often enough.)

2.   Forming a theory (incorrectly) that the ink mixes because of very slow currents in the water.
3.   Generalizing that some other force spreads the ink throughout the water.

Events 4-H through 4-J Explained in Context (Molecular Motion)

Molecules are in constant motion. This motion is generally undetected by most of us because the molecules are too small to be seen. However. we have all seen and heard certain effects of random molecular motion without being aware of it. Random molecular motion causes electronic interference on television and radio receivers. The interference is seen as "snow" on television and is heard as "hiss" on radio.

Molecular motion increases when the temperature rises, and decreases when the temperature falls. As a result, electronic interference can be reduced by cooling down the equipment. Such cooling is not practical in home TV or radio equipment. However, liquid helium is used to cool some very costly equipment used in satellite communication systems. At that very cold temperature, the motion of molecules is so slow that "hiss" is almost totally eliminated.

Evidence of molecular motion is shown in *Event 4-H, The "Smell" Box.* Many pupils will be able to identify an onion by smell alone. Almost all will be able to smell something, even if they cannot tell what it is. The event almost seems too simple.

The point of the event, however, is not to see if you can detect the onion. Instead, it is to find out *how the onion travels from the box to your nose.* Are there little bits of the onion that jump from the box and go to your nose? (Pupils usually laugh when you ask that question.) Yet, in a way, the answer is yes!

The event is meant to show that *molecules travel through gases.* The molecules are too small to be identified by sight but, in the case of onions, can be identified by smell. Molecules of the onion evaporate. That is, the liquid parts of the onion change to a gas and escape into the air. The gaseous onion molecules can then be detected by smell.

In *Event 4-I, The "Hot" Rod,* we see that heat is sent from molecule to molecule along the rod. This movement of heat through a substance is called *conduction.* This topic will be studied in greater detail in chapter 5. At this point we are concerned only with the evidence that molecules move in solids.

Finally, we see evidence that molecules move in liquids in *Event 4-J, How Does the Ink Spread?* The molecules of ink are bumped by the molecules of water and gradually spread evenly throughout the container. The random motion of the ink and water molecules is called **Brownian Movement** and is named for Robert Brown, the scientist who discovered it.

Note: Care must be taken to avoid heating the liquid because then the liquid will begin to develop a slow movement (or convection current). That current will obviously mix the liquids. In this event, you want to see whether the mixing will occur even if the water remains totally still. It does. Molecular motion will eventually disperse the ink evenly throughout the water. It will take from several hours to several days for the mixing to occur.

The Phases (or States) of Matter (Events 4-K through 4-N)

Discrepant Events and Pupil Investigations

Event 4-K, Make Ice Disappear

Put some crushed ice into a Pyrex beaker. Connect the temperature probe to the interface box of one of the recording devices. Set the device to record the temperature every 20 seconds. Place the temperature probe into the ice. Press start and slowly heat the beaker. Stir the ice gently every minute for a few seconds and record your observations during the process. Graph the results on your computer or calculator. At what point does the ice melt? What is the temperature as it boils? Why does the temperature stay level for a long period of time?

Pupil Investigations (may include the following processes):

1. Observing the temperatures at regular intervals.
2. Recording the readings on a graph.
3. Interpreting the graph to note the effects of melting and boiling.

Event 4-L. Liquid to Gas to Liquid

Boil some water in a teakettle. Hold a cold piece of glass or small mirror over the spout and observe.

Pupil Investigations (may include the following processes):

1. Observing that a "cloud" forms above the spout of the teakettle.
2. Discovering that the pane of glass or mirror becomes fogged, and that drops of water fall from it.
3. Generalizing that water (liquid phase) is formed from steam (gaseous phase).
4. Comparing this activity with the water cycle.

Event 4-M. What Put Out the Fire?

Place a small candle inside a beaker and add a small amount of baking soda and water. Then light the candle and pour about 2 or 3 cubic centimeters of vinegar ("unknown" liquid to pupils) into the beaker, being careful not to touch the candle flame. Soon the flame goes out. Why? (See figure 4.8.)

Pupil Investigations (may include the following processes):

1. Observing a foaming action as the unknown liquid touches the baking soda solution.
2. Identifying, by smell, the unknown liquid as vinegar.
3. Inferring that there is a substance produced by the foaming action that causes the flame to go out.

Event 4-N. Solids to Liquids

Slowly melt common household solids such as petroleum jelly, vegetable shortening, crayons, margarine, and ice using a hot plate. Using a temperature probe connected to the computer, record the temperature over time.

FIGURE 4.8   Why does the flame go out when you pour the liquid into the beaker?

Pupil Investigations (may include the following processes):

1. Observing that different substances melt at different times.
2. Recording the times at which the different solids melt.
3. Generalizing that the different solids have different melting points.
4. Analyzing the temperature-time graph.

Events 4-K through 4-N Explained in Context (The Phases of Matter)

In the beginning of this chapter we discussed the importance of grouping, and that it is needed to make order out of chaos. In this section, we see an important example of grouping. Just about all matter on earth exists in one of three forms: solid, liquid, or gas. (There is a fourth state called plasma that is found in the sun and stars. It can also be formed on earth but is not commonly found outside the lab.) Some characteristics and definitions of solids, liquids, and gases are shown in table 4.1.

Event 4-K, *Make Ice Disappear*, is excellent because it shows all three states of matter. It also gives us some evidence of the melting and boiling points of water.

TABLE 4.1		
Phases of Matter		
Solid	**Liquid**	**Gas**
Definite volume and definite shape	Definite volume but no definite shape	No definite volume or shape
High cohesive force	Low cohesive force	Cohesive force almost nonexistent
Molecules tightly packed	Molecules not tightly packed	Molecules fairly far apart
Easily visible	Easily visible	Almost always invisible
Example: ice	Example: water	Example: steam

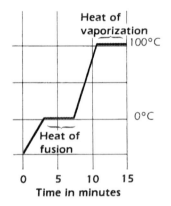

FIGURE 4.9 Study the graph. What are the effects of the heat of fusion and heat of vaporization?

FIGURE 4.10 The steam coming from the strongly boiling teakettle is invisible. The part you see is not steam but a cloud of tiny droplets of liquid that condensed when the steam is cooled by the air in the room.

Students will find that the temperature of the water will remain more or less stationary at the melting point until all the ice is melted. Then the temperature will rise rapidly until it boils. At this point the temperature will again remain stationary as the water boils away. (See figure 4.9.) All three states are evident: ice (solid), water (liquid), and steam (invisible gas).

Not all substances go through the liquid state when they change from a solid to a gas. Some materials, such as mothballs and dry ice, change directly from a solid to a gas.

Even ordinary ice can change directly from a solid to a gas. Ice and snow will gradually disappear in very cold weather, even if temperatures do not go above freezing.

This direct change from solid to gas is called **sublimation.** The reverse can also happen. A gas (such as water vapor) can change directly into solids (such as snow and frost) without going through the intermediate liquid phase.

Most Gases Are Invisible

Students are often surprised to discover that most **gases** are invisible. They commonly believe that fog, clouds, and steam are visible gases. Of course, fog and clouds are visible; but they are not gases. They are liquids. And although steam is a gas, it is not visible.

Pupils will question the invisibility of **steam.** If it is supposed to be invisible, *why can we see steam coming from a teakettle?* We have all seen the cloud that forms over the spout of a teakettle. If that cloud is not steam, what is it?

The answer is simple. The visible cloud is not steam. It's a *cloud!* The cloud above the spout is formed just like the clouds in the sky. It is mostly liquid, consisting of tiny floating drops of water. In both cases the cloud forms, not when H_2O is heated up, but when the H_2O cools down.

Just follow the path of the H_2O in the kettle as it goes from water to steam to cloud. As the water boils inside the kettle, it is changed to steam. Then as the steam travels up the spout it is chilled by the much colder room temperature, and condenses into a cloud. (See figure 4.10.) Once you are able to see it, it has already changed from steam (an invisible gas) to a cloud (a visible liquid). Outside, the clouds in the sky are formed in the same way. Water vapor rises high into the sky and is chilled. As it cools, the water vapor (a gas) is changed into tiny droplets of water to form a cloud (a liquid).

Sometimes the air is very dry and the steam will go directly to ordinary water vapor without forming a cloud and nothing will be visible. (Remember that water vapor is already in the air, and that steam only adds to it. The only difference between steam and ordinary water vapor is that steam is hot and water vapor is not.) In that case, using a mirror or pane of glass, as suggested in *Event 4-L, Liquid to Gas to Liquid,* will still show the formation of a liquid.

If you hold the glass in the steam long enough, you will see not only fog but possibly also "rain." The droplets sometimes gather and grow until they combine into drops of water. That is an example of how rain forms in nature. The tiny droplets in the clouds combine until they become large enough so that they no longer float in the air. When those drops fall, it is called rain.

Another simple experiment can be done to show that water vapor is invisible. Just wipe a chalkboard with a damp cloth. The dampness that is visible is a liquid. However, the damp spot quickly disappears. Where does it go? It evaporates into a gas (water vapor) and mixes with the air. It is still in the room but is no longer visible.

Event 4-M, What Put Out the Fire?, also shows the existence of an invisible substance—one that put out the fire. When the vinegar is poured into the dissolved baking soda, carbon dioxide is released. It fills the container, pushing out the oxygen. Thus, deprived of its oxygen, the flame goes out.

In summary, the event is an indirect way of proving the existence of a substance that you cannot see. You can tell it is there *by what it does:* it puts out the fire. (This event also can be used to show that oxygen is necessary to support combustion.)

All common gases (such as oxygen, nitrogen, hydrogen, carbon dioxide, and water vapor) are invisible. Only a few rare gases, such as iodine vapors, can be seen.

Even invisible gases can sometimes cause visible effects. For example, you may notice a shimmering effect if you look at an object through the rising air currents directly over a hot stove or above a candle flame. Also, on a very hot day you may notice that objects in the distance appear to "dance." That, too, is caused by rapidly rising air currents.

Changes of Phase

When a substance is heated, its molecular action increases. This action, in turn, weakens the forces that hold a substance together. If enough heat is applied, the molecular action becomes so strong that the substance can no longer hold itself together. It changes from a solid to a liquid. In other words, it melts.

If the substance is heated still more, it eventually becomes a gas. At that point molecular action is much greater than when the substance was a liquid or a solid. Probably the simplest example of these changes is the melting of ice and heating it to form steam. It changes from a solid (ice) to a liquid (water) and then to a gas (steam).

A change of a solid to a liquid is shown in *Event 4-N, Solids to Liquids.* Pupils will see that the solids have different melting points. It is not too important which substances you use. The event is merely intended to show that different substances have different melting points.

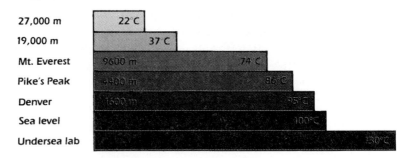

27,000 m	22°C
19,000 m	37 C
Mt. Everest	9600 m 74 C
Pike's Peak	4400 m 86 C
Denver	1600 m 95 C
Sea level	100°C
Undersea lab	130°C

FIGURE 4.11   The boiling point of water decreases as air pressure decreases (at higher altitudes).

The Boiling Point of Water

In this chapter we have discussed boiling and melting points. Normally, those terms are used as if they represent fixed points on the thermometer. In fact, those points are not fixed: they change if air pressure changes.

The boiling point, especially, is affected by pressure. At sea level pure water boils at 100° C. At higher elevations the boiling point is lower. In fact, the boiling point drops about 1 degree for every 300-meter gain in altitude. Thus, water boils at about 95° C in Denver, at 86° C on top of Pike's Peak, and at 74° C on top of Mount Everest.

At even greater heights reached by planes or spacecraft, water boils at still lower temperatures. At 19,000 meters water boils at body temperature (37° C). That means that body fluids of an unprotected astronaut will boil at that altitude. At 27,000 meters water will boil at room temperature (22° C). Astronauts are protected from those dangers by wearing pressurized suits.

The opposite effect occurs as pressure is increased: the greater the pressure, the higher the boiling point. For example, a higher boiling point can be obtained by using a pressure cooker. The effect of pressure on the boiling point has even been observed in undersea labs where the boiling point of water was raised to almost 130° C. (See figure 4.11.)

Changes in Matter (Events 4-O through 4-R)

Discrepant Events and Pupil Investigations

Event 4-O. Separate the Materials
Mix together sand, sugar, iron filings, bits of cork, and marbles. Let students separate them. Do not tell them ahead of time what the materials are or how many different ones are in the mixture.

Pupil Investigations (may include the following processes):
1. Devising a method of separating the materials.
2. Recording data of the materials separated.
3. Generalizing that the process of mixing did not change the materials.

Event 4-P. Rearrange Some Molecules

Mix together some iron filings and sulfur. Show that the two elements can be separated because each element still retains its own properties. (Use a magnet to pull out the iron filings.)

Then remix the substances and heat them in a well-ventilated area (an offensive odor will be produced). If heated enough, the mixture is changed to iron sulfide. Let it cool and check it with a magnet.

Pupil Investigations (may include the following processes):

1. Discovering that the magnet will have no effect on the substance after the mixture was heated.
2. Forming a theory (incorrectly) that the sulfur acts like glue to hold the iron particles. (The magnet would still be attracted to iron even if the iron were held in glue.)
3. Generalizing that the materials have been greatly changed.

Event 4-Q. Cooling Off

Mix together equal amounts of baking soda and water at room temperature. Record the temperature of the solution every 20 seconds using the temperature probes. Repeat this experiment replacing the water with either vinegar or lemon juice.

Pupil Investigations (may include the following processes):

1. Discovering that mixing things produces a gas.
2. Hypothesizing that forming a gas makes the solution cold.
3. Generalizing that the materials have been chemically changed when a gas is produced or the temperature changes.

Event 4-R. Let's Get Physical and Chill Out

In a pint-size freezer bag mix 1 cup whipping cream and one-fourth cup sugar (vanilla is optional). Close the bag securely and put aside. Connect the temperature probe to the computer and start to record soon after you add the following together. Place 2 cups crushed ice, 1 cup water, and one-fourth cup rock salt into a quart-size bag. Record the temperature for a few seconds, then place the closed pint-size bag into the solution. Zip the bag as securely as possible with the temperature cord sticking out one corner of the bag. Squeeze the quart bag to mix the cream inside the pint bag. Experiment by adding more salt, water, or ice (one at a time) to bring the temperature even lower than 0° C. Repeat the activity without using sugar (or vanilla) in the cream.

Pupil Investigations (may include the following processes):

1. Forming a theory about how to lower the salt water bath temperature.
2. Observing that the cream mixture hardens.
3. Questioning whether the freezing of cream is a chemical or physical change.

Events 4-O through 4-R Explained in Context (Changes in Matter)

Here again, we see the value of grouping. There are many changes that occur in matter, but they all can be placed into just three groups: physical, chemical, and nuclear. The three types are explained in table 4.2.

Two of the three types of change can be shown in the classroom. For example, *Event 4-O, Separate the Materials,* focuses on the physical differences of matter. All of the substances in this mixture can be separated by using only physical means. The marbles can be picked out by hand and the iron filings drawn out by a magnet. The bits of cork will float to the top if the mixture is dumped into a bowl of water, and the sugar that dissolves in water can be crystallized again by letting the water evaporate.

All of the substances are located in a grouping called a *mixture.* A mixture is a collection of matter in which each substance keeps its own property.

Event 4-P, Rearrange Some Molecules, represents a chemical change. Before the heat is applied, the two substances are still only a mixture and can be separated by physical means. After the mixture is heated enough, it becomes a *compound* called iron sulfide. Iron sulfide is quite different from either iron or sulfur. A magnet will no longer pull out the iron, because the iron no longer exists.

In *Event 4-Q, Cooling Off,* when baking soda (bicarbonate of soda) is mixed with water and mild acids (vinegar or lemon juice) carbon dioxide gas (CO_2) is produced. The solution becomes colder in this endothermic reaction. Endothermic reactions occur when heat energy is drawn from the surroundings to help form new chemical bonds as a new compound is being created. The "instant ice packs" in first aid kits use an endothermic reaction between two substances to produce a new substance. Exothermic reactions are a result of energy given off to the surroundings when the new substance formed has weaker bonds than the original substances. "Instant hand warmers" use chemicals that produce exothermic reactions. Water mixed with plaster of Paris, Alka-Seltzer tablets, or calcium chloride are all examples of exothermic reactions. For safety reasons use small amounts (about 2 tablespoons) of calcium chloride. It can get very hot when too much is mixed with water.

TABLE 4.2

Changes in Matter

Types of Change	Definition	Examples
Physical Change	A change in appearance only; the substance is still the same after the change takes place	Cutting paper, melting butter, dissolving salt in water, breaking glass
Chemical Change	A substance is changed into one or more different substances	Rusting, fire, overcooking food (charring)
Nuclear Change	A rearrangement of the nuclei of atoms to form new atoms	Atomic fission, nuclear fusion, energy of sun and stars

Event 4-R, Let's Get Physical and Chill Out, shows that in order to change a liquid to a solid, heat energy must be transferred from the liquid to some other place. In this case the heat energy from the liquid cream is being transferred to the salt-ice-water solution. The cream is therefore becoming a solid in the form of ice cream. Freezing the cream is a physical change. This can be easier to explain if the sugar or vanilla is not present. The sugar and vanilla only add a pleasant taste; it is not chemically reacting with the cream. See *Event 5-C* as to why the water-ice-salt temperature lowers.

Adhesion (Events 4-S through 4-V)

Discrepant Events and Pupil Investigations

Event 4-S. Why Does the Water Climb?

Place capillary tubes of varying sizes into a jar of water and observe how high the liquid climbs up the tubes. What causes the differences in height? (Mix some food coloring into the water so that the liquid is easier to see in the tiny tubes.)

Pupil Investigations (may include the following processes):

1. Observing that the water level inside each tube is above the water level in the bottle.
2. Measuring the height of the liquid in each tube.
3. Inferring a relationship between the diameter of a tube and the height of the liquid in that tube.
4. Forming a theory (incorrectly) that air pressure is causing the water to climb the tubes. (Point out that the tubes are all open on top so that the air pressure pushes down equally on all.)

Event 4-T. What Pulls Out the Water?

Drape a washcloth over the edge of a partially filled bowl of water. Leave it for about an hour. Why does the water leave the bowl?

Pupil Investigations (may include the following processes):

1. Observing that the water climbs up the cloth and over the edge of the bowl.
2. Investigating to see if water climbs other materials.
3. Measuring how high water will climb in different materials.

Event 4-U. Get a Lift

Fill a tin can with pieces of cardboard. Then add water and place a heavy weight on top of the cardboard. Observe for an hour. Soon the weight is lifted up by swelling and expanding cardboard.

Pupil Investigations (may include the following processes):

1. Measuring how much the weight is lifted at equal time intervals and plotting the readings on a graph.
2. Repeating the activity using different weights.
3. Inferring correctly that there is a relationship between the water and the swelling cardboard.

Events 4-V. Make a Cork Stay in the Middle

Place a cork into the middle of a partly filled glass of water. What happens to the cork? Ask the pupils to find a way to make the cork float in the middle.

Pupil Investigations (may include the following processes):

1. Observing that the cork moves to the side of the glass even when the cork is placed in the center.
2. Discovering that the water level in the middle of the tumbler is slightly lower than the water touching the side of the glass.
3. Testing (unsuccessfully) various ways to keep the cork in the middle (by floating it on either end, on its side, etc.)
4. Experimenting with corks and containers of varying sizes and filled to different heights.

Events 4-S through 4-V Explained in Context (Adhesion)

Why does paint stick to a wall? Why does glue hold things together? Why does a paper towel get wet (but not a sheet of waxed paper)? All the questions have the same answer: *adhesion.* **Adhesion** is the attraction between *unlike* substances.

Another way to remember this topic is to think about an old sticky piece of adhesive tape that is being pulled from the skin. Why does adhesive tape stick? Because of adhesion.

The force of adhesion varies greatly among different substances. In most of the examples given above, the adhesion is quite strong. In other cases it is quite weak. For example, water does not stick very well to other substances. It does not stick to a wall nearly as well as paint does. Indeed, the attraction between water with most other substances is so weak that most people do not think that there is any attraction at all.

Surprisingly, water *does* attract other substances. In fact, all four events in this section are related to adhesion. Go back to figure 4.4. Remember that the water in the test tube was lower in the middle and was curved up at the sides? That upward curve is caused by an attraction between glass and water.

The force of adhesion becomes more evident when tubes of smaller size are used. Hence, in *Event 4-S, Why Does the Water Climb?*, the smaller the tube, the higher the water level. Those fine hairlike tubes are called *capillary tubes,* and the upward climb of liquids in those tubes is called *capillary action.*

Capillary action also occurs in *Event 4-T, What Pulls Out the Water?* The fibers of the washcloth contain thousands of tiny hairlike passages that act as capillary tubes to attract water. Thus, the water is pulled out of the bowl, eventually draining it.

The strength that can be generated by adhesion becomes more apparent in *Event 4-U, Get a Lift.* As the water soaks into the cardboard, it swells up and lifts the weight. The force is so great that it can lift a fully grown adult standing on the cardboard. (Unfortunately, the action is so slow that few would be willing to stand on the cardboard long enough to find out.)

It is the adhesion between the water and wood that causes wood to swell. Thus, damp floors sometimes bulge, and during humid summers, windows and doors sometimes expand so that they are hard to open and close.

Event 4-V, Make a Cork Stay in the Middle, also shows the force of adhesion. Regardless of how carefully you put the cork into the middle of the tum-

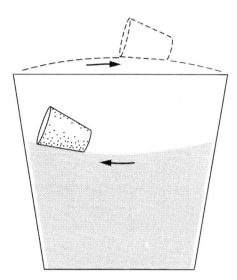

FIGURE 4.12   The cork always goes to the highest point of the water. If the tumbler is not full, the highest part is along the edges. If the glass is "heaping" full, the highest part is in the middle.

bler, the cork will slide off to the side and attach itself to the glass (unless you use a large container and a small cork).

The reason for the cork's movement is really quite simple. The cork is light and it floats to the top. If you look closely, the water is higher at the edge of the glass than at the middle. Thus, the "top" of the water is along the side where it touches the glass. As explained earlier, the water is pulled upward because of adhesion (attraction) between the glass and water.

As long as the cork is fairly large and the tumbler fairly small, it is almost impossible to keep the cork from moving to the side. However, if you have a large container then the middle becomes fairly flat; and the cork might stay there.

The "trick" in getting the cork to stay in the middle is merely to fill the tumbler "heaping" full. Now the high point of the water is in the middle, not the sides. Again, the cork just floats to the top, but in this case the top is in the middle. (See figure 4.12.)

Cohesion (Events 4-W through 4-BB)

Discrepant Events and Pupil Investigations

Event 4-W. Water at an Angle
Anyone can pour water that falls straight down, but use a string and pour water *at an angle*. Have available a full glass of water, an empty glass, some string, and some weights. Try the event over a sink or large pan to collect spills.

Pupil Investigations (may include the following processes):
1.   Observing that water does not flow along a dry string.
2.   Experimenting with ways of pouring water along the string.
3.   Discovering that water tends to "stick" to a wet string and to flow along it even at an angle.

Event 4-X. Join the Water

Punch several holes close together along the bottom of an empty milk carton. Fill the carton with water and observe how the water comes out of the holes. Under certain circumstances the streams will join together to form a single stream.

Pupil Investigations (may include the following processes):

1. Experimenting to see the effects of high and low water levels on the stream.
2. Devising a method of separating and joining the streams.
3. Experimenting to see the effects of holes farther apart and closer together.
4. Forming a theory that the streams will join together because of an inner force or attraction in water.

Event 4-Y. Suspended Drops

Mix together a combination of two thirds alcohol and one-third water. Place a few drops of salad oil into this solution. Enlarge the drops with a medicine dropper. What shape do the drops take? If the drops tend to rise, add more alcohol to the mixture. If the drops sink, add water. (See figure 4.13.)

FIGURE 4.13   Why does salad oil form spheres in the water-alcohol solution?

Pupil Investigations (may include the following processes):

1. Observing that the drops of salad oil assume a spherical shape.
2. Observing that the salad oil remains more or less suspended in the solution. (The drops do not move up or down very much.)
3. Comparing these drops to the shape of typical raindrops as described in books.
4. Inferring that a force holds the salad oil together.

Event 4-Z. Float Metal on Water

Carefully lower a metal screen onto water in a bowl. If done with care the screen will float. A needle, paper clip, tin-can lid, pepper, sawdust, feather, or string should float also. Then add a drop of soap or detergent and see how many items sink.

Pupil Investigations (may include the following processes):

1. Observing that the surface of the water is pushed down, or forms a depression, by the weight of some objects.
2. Discovering that some objects float even though they seem to be heavier than the water.
3. Inferring that the surface of the water seems to have a lifting power.
4. Observing that many of the objects sink after the soap is added.
5. Inferring that the soap reduces the lifting power of water.

Event 4-AA. What Keeps the Water In?

Fill a flask or bottle with water. Cover the container with a metal screen or piece of cloth and invert it over a sink. Initially, a few drops of water may spill, but then the water will not run out. Why not?

Pupil Investigations (may include the following processes):

1. Observing that water will not run through the screen or cloth as long as it is held tightly against the inverted flask.
2. Testing to see if the screen or cloth is clogged. (It is not.)
3. Forming a theory to explain what keeps the water in the flask and the air out of it.

Event 4-BB. Sink the Pepper

Sprinkle some pepper on the surface of a bowl of water. Then place a drop of liquid soap on the water near one edge of the bowl. What happens?

Pupil Investigations (may include the following processes):

1. Observing that most of the pepper floats on the water before the soap is added.
2. Observing that the water "explodes" away from the point where the soap is added to the water.
3. Discovering that the pepper falls like rain after the soap is added.
4. Generalizing that the soap has an effect on the water that reduces its lifting power.

Events 4-W through 4-BB Explained in Context (Cohesion)

Why does your desk stay together? Why doesn't a chunk of iron fall apart? Why can you push your hand through water but not through a board?

The answers to these questions all relate to **cohesion.** *Cohesion is the attraction of like molecules for each other.* Refer to the discussion about the phases of matter earlier in this chapter. Recall that there are differences in the cohesive forces of solids, liquids, and gases. In solids the force is strongest. *It is cohesion that holds a solid together.*

The cohesive force of liquids, however, is so weak that they have no definite shape of their own. The cohesion of a liquid is so weak that you can easily push your hand through it.

Gases have the least cohesion of all. Gas molecules have so little attraction for each other that a gas will not even stay in an open container. It just floats out.

We mentioned the effect of cohesion briefly during our discussion of adhesion; water is affected by both forces. That is, water is attracted to many substances (adhesion), while there is also an attraction of water molecules for each other (cohesion).

If you can reduce the effect of one force, then the effect of the other force is easier to observe. For example, water is not attracted to waxed paper. Thus, if you put a drop of water on waxed paper, you see only the effect of cohesion.

What is the shape of that drop? The water "beads up" because cohesive forces pull the water as close together as possible. If you put the drop on a blotter, however, adhesive forces (along with gravity) quickly spread out the water. Cohesion is not strong enough to keep the drop together in such a situation.

The events in this section pertain mostly to the cohesive forces within water. As a matter of fact, go back to the last event before this section (Event 4-V), where we saw the cork move to the middle when the tumbler was filled heaping full. What caused the water to "heap up" over the rim of the glass? Why

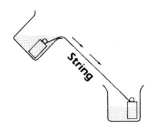

FIGURE 4.14   Water flows along a wet string. The string must touch the lip of the top beaker but not the lip of the lower one. Weights are used to hold the string in place.

FIGURE 4.15   The three streams tend to stay together because of the cohesive attraction of water molecules for each other.

didn't the water overflow? The answer: cohesion. The attraction within water is great enough to overcome (somewhat) the force of gravity.

Cohesion is also the explanation for *Event 4-W, Pour Water at an Angle.* Water can be poured along the string, but only if the string is wet. If you try to pour along a dry string there is no cohesion and the water just spills. If the string is wet, however, it works nicely because the poured water is attracted (by cohesion) to the water that is already on the string. With some care and practice you can pour water at quite an angle. (See figure 4.14.)

Note: Be sure that the string touches the lip of the top beaker but does *not* touch the lip of the bottom beaker. It is easier to do this event if you tie a weight to each end of the string.

Event 4-X, Join the Water, also shows the cohesive forces within water. The water will flow out of the holes at the bottom of the milk carton in separate streams until you use your fingers to pull the streams together. Once joined, they tend to "stick" together to form a single stream. That "sticking" is due to cohesion. (See figure 4.15.)

In *Event 4-Y, Suspended Drops,* another example of cohesion is seen. In this event the salad oil weighs just about the same as the water-alcohol mixture. Thus, the salad oil will tend to float within the mixture without either rising or settling. (If you find that the salad oil rises too quickly, add alcohol to the mixture. If the salad oil sinks too quickly, add water.)

Because the force of gravity of both the oil and the mixture are almost exactly the same, gravity exerts no net force. Cohesion is the only force that exerts itself in the drops of oil. Cohesion will pull the oil as close together as possible, and thus the drops will form into round spheres. (There is very little, if any, adhesive force between oil and water, so adhesion is no factor in this event.)

A special form of cohesion called *surface tension* occurs along the surface of a liquid. Its special effects can be noted in the three remaining events of this section. In *Event 4-Z, Float Metal on Water,* for example, the metal floats because of surface tension.

We all know that metal is heavier than water. Yet a metal screen, needle, tin-can lid, or paper clip will float if placed carefully on the surface of water. The molecules of water on the surface hold together so well that they often keep heavier objects from breaking through. In fact, the surface acts as if it has a "skin" on it.

Once the object breaks through the surface, however, the cohesive force of the water below the object is the same as the cohesive force of the water above it. The cohesive forces are equalized, leaving only gravity to act on the object. It therefore sinks to the bottom.

When soap is added, however, the floating objects sink right away. Why? Because soap lowers the cohesive forces of water. In a washing machine, soap reduces the cohesion of water. That means that water no longer "sticks together," so it can enter fibers and fabrics more easily to flush out the soil and grime.

Surface tension is an important factor in *Event 4-AA, What Keeps the Water In?* For water to flow out, it must break up into tiny streams and pass through the openings of the screen or through the openings between the fibers of the cloth. However, the cohesive force of water is strong enough to keep it from separating into the tiny streams. (Another factor, air pressure, is also involved in this event. Air tries to enter the bottle to replace the water going out, so air exerts a pressure against the water.)

Finally, *Event 4-BB, Sink the Pepper,* shows another example of surface tension. Or, more accurately, it shows what happens when the surface tension is broken.

As soon as a drop of soap hits the water, the pepper seems to "explode" away. That happens because the soap reduces cohesion (or attraction). The water no longer has any cohesion where the soap hits it, but is still attracted at all points away from the soap. This causes the "explosion."

As soon as the soap spreads out across the surface of the water, the surface tension is lost and can no longer hold up the heavier pepper. In fact, the pepper seems to "rain" down.

The events show that cohesion is a form of attraction among molecules of the same substance. Cohesion is very strong in solids—strong enough for a solid to hold its shape. Cohesion is quite weak in liquids but is still evident if shown in the right way. In summary, cohesion is molecular attraction that holds things together.

Combining Assessment with Instruction

This assessment may be a group or individual assessment. Give the student(s) a group of words such as element, compound, and atom. Ask which one doesn't belong. Students must identify which one doesn't belong and state why. There is no one correct answer. A student should be given credit for logical thinking even if it does not match the teacher's idea of which doesn't belong—unless of course the student's reasoning is incorrect.

A longer list of words can be given so that students separate them into two groups, label each group with a title, and then justify why each word belongs to a particular group. For example, cutting, rusting, burning, melting, dissolving, folding, changing color, and precipitate. A student may put cutting, melting, dissolving, folding, and changing color together under the title "Physical Changes" and rusting, burning, and precipitate in another group called "Chemical Changes." You may question why the student put "changing color" in a group she describes as being a physical change; however, if the student describes changing colors by painting a wall, then she is correct. Another student may think of changing colors as a chemical change stating that two clear liquids were poured together and a different color resulted as they combined.

Sites and Software

The following websites and software are appropriate to use with this chapter. Note that computer software and websites change rapidly. This makes it necessary to investigate the stable websites for new links and software catalogs for updates. Visit www.mhhe.com/friedl6e to link to these directly and for study resources.

Sites

Elements	www.chemicalelements.com
Chem 4 Kids	www.chem4kids.com
Mad Scientist	www.madsci.org/experiments/
Elements	www.webelements.com

Howstuffworks: "Chemistry"	www.howstuffworks.com/category.htm
Periodic Table of Elements	www.environmentalchemistry.com/ yogi/periodic
Smile Program Chemistry Index	www.iit.edu/~smile/cheminde.html
The Four States of Matter	www.fusioned.gat.com/ SlideShowFolder/FourStates.html

Software

I (Hate) Love Science! (DK Multimedia) (2–6)
All about Science Series: Matter (Carolina) (4–8)
Science Sleuths Elementary CD-ROM, Vol. 1 and 2 (Videodiscovery, Inc.) (3–6)
Learn about Matter, Measurement & Mixtures (Sunburst)(K–2)

Key Terms

adhesion, *62*
atom, *48*
Brownian Movement, *53*
cohesion, *65*
compound, *48*

element, *48*
gases, *56*
liquid, *56*
molecule, *48*
nucleus, *48*

solid, *56*
steam, *56*
sublimation, *56*

Teaching Children about Heat Energy

NATIONAL SCIENCE EDUCATION STANDARDS ALIGNMENT TO EVENTS

The events in this chapter help accomplish several of the NSES for content. The event(s) that align with a given content standard are listed below that standard.

LEVELS K–4

UNIFYING CONCEPTS AND PROCESSES
- Evidence, models and explanation
  5-A
  5-C
  5-F
  5-J through 5-M
  5-N
  5-Q

- Change, consistency, and measurement
  5-D
  5-N
  5-Q
  5-Y

- Evolution and equilibrium
  5-B and 5-C

SCIENCE AS INQUIRY
- Abilities necessary to do and understand scientific inquiry
  5-A through 5-Y

PHYSICAL SCIENCE
- Properties of objects and materials
  5-H through 5-I
  5-S
  5-V
  5-X
  5-Y

- Light, heat, electricity, and magnetism
  5-A through 5-Y

SCIENCE AND TECHNOLOGY
- Abilities of technological design
  5-G

SCIENCE IN PERSONAL AND SOCIAL PERSPECTIVES
- Changes in environment
5-B through 5-C

HISTORY AND NATURE OF SCIENCE
- Science as a human endeavor
  5-A

LEVELS 5–8

UNIFYING CONCEPTS AND PROCESSES
- Evidence, models and explanation
  5-A
  5-C
  5-F
  5-J through 5-M
  5-N
  5-Q

- Change, consistency, and measurement
  5-D
  5-N
  5-Q
  5-Y

- Evolution and equilibrium
  5-B and 5-C

SCIENCE AS INQUIRY
- Abilities to do and understand scientific inquiry
  5-A through 5-Y

PHYSICAL SCIENCE
- Properties and changes of properties of matter.
  5-H through 5-I
  5-S
  5-V
  5-X
  5-Y

- Light, heat, electricity, and magnetism
  5-A through 5-Y

SCIENCE AND TECHNOLOGY
- Abilities of technological design
  5-G

SCIENCE IN PERSONAL AND SOCIAL PERSPECTIVES
- Risks and benefits
  5-K through 5-M
  5-P
  5-R through 5-S
  5-U through 5-X

- Science and technology in society
  5-A
  5-T

HISTORY AND NATURE OF SCIENCE
- Science as a human endeavor
  5-A

How Temperature Is Measured: Historical Introduction

Temperature is a measure of how hot or cold something is. It is measured in degrees. However, the *size* of the degree varies, depending on which temperature scale is used.

A number of scales have been developed since 1714 when Gabriel Daniel **Fahrenheit** developed the first **scale** to be widely used. He decided that a scale should have three major reference points: (1) a boiling point, (2) a freezing point, and (3) a zero point.

Absolute zero could not be the zero point because in those days, nobody knew where it was. It could not be measured. The only sure reference points known at that time were the boiling and freezing points of water. The boiling point was obviously a poor reference because it would make all the temperatures of ordinary weather read in minus values (or below zero). Fahrenheit did not like the freezing point either. In the winter time, the temperature would still go below freezing and he felt that people would be confused by "below zero" numbers.

To avoid the confusion, he decided to invent a zero point that would be low enough so that minus values would not normally be needed to measure winter weather. His solution was to mix together equal amounts of salt and crushed ice. The temperature of such a mixture drops far below freezing. It became his zero point.

The next step was to choose the *size* of the degree. He could have chosen any size at all, because the degree is an arbitrary unit. If he wanted to, he could have chosen a degree so large that only 5 degrees would have fit between the boiling and freezing points. Or he could have chosen a size that would allow hundreds of degrees to fit.

He decided to use a size that permitted 180 degrees. He felt that 180 was a convenient number because it seemed to fit into the world of mathematics. After all, if you go in one direction and then turn around and go the opposite, that is a 180-degree turn. He reasoned that boiling and freezing were opposites also, so 180 degrees seemed to be just right.

Once he selected 180 degrees to measure the difference between the boiling and freezing points, it was simply a matter of arithmetic to find how many of those degrees fit between the freezing and zero points. He found that there were 32 degrees between those points. Thus, starting with the zero point, the freezing point became 32 degrees and the boiling point (180 degrees higher) became 212 degrees.

Fahrenheit's scale was certainly useful and was quickly adopted by most of the countries of the world. As useful as it was, however, it was not without problems. First of all, the zero point was not really a fixed value. It could not be accurately duplicated around the world. The temperature of an ice-salt mixture varies depending on the size of the crushed ice and the size and type of the salt. Thus, the zero point meant different temperatures in different places. It was not a fixed value.

Second, although the 180 degrees seemed to imply "opposite," it had no practical meaning in this case. It did not fit into the decimal system and scientists had to apply conversion formulas to use them.

Third, although Fahrenheit wanted to avoid the use of minus numbers in measuring winter temperatures, that problem was not avoided either. In many countries, winter temperatures often went below zero anyway.

Because of these problems it took only 28 years for another scale to be introduced. In 1742, Anders Celsius, a Swedish astronomer, invented a scale that was originally named the **Centigrade scale.** Later it was renamed *Celsius scale* in honor of its author. It used the freezing point of water as its zero point, a fixed point anywhere in the world. It used 100 degrees between boiling and freezing, a value that fit into the decimal system. Scientists all over the world quickly adopted it.

A third major scale was developed by Lord Kelvin of England. His scale became possible when scientists discovered absolute zero. Remember, that in the times of Fahrenheit and Celsius, that point was unknown.

Once absolute zero was known, Kelvin moved the zero point down to it. Thus, he had a scale in which a temperature "below zero" could not exist. Moving the zero so that no temperature could go below it was Kelvin's contribution to the temperature scales. He kept the size of the degree the same as the Celsius degree. In other words, there were 100 degrees between the freezing and boiling points.

He found that there were 273 degrees between absolute zero and the freezing point. The boiling point was 100 degrees higher, or 373 degrees. You can see that the **Kelvin scale** is the same as the Celsius, except that in the Kelvin scale, the zero point starts 273 degrees lower.

A summary of the three scales is shown in table 5.1.

As stated earlier, heat and temperature are different, so temperature scales measure temperature but not heat. The difference between heat and temperature can be seen by performing *Event 5-A, Heat or Temperature?* Both the large bolt and the small nail have the same temperature—the boiling point of water. But do they have the same heat? No, the large bolt has more heat because it is bigger. The bolt will raise the temperature of an equal amount of water more than will the nail.

Another way of showing the difference between heat and temperature is to compare a match flame with the air in the room. Which is hotter? Of course the flame is hotter. It has a higher temperature. But does the flame have much heat? No. Even if it burned for hours, it would not warm up the air in the room. There is just not enough of it.

To summarize, **temperature** refers to how hot or how cold a thing is in degrees. **Heat** refers to a quantity of energy—its total energy, measured in calories, British thermal units, or joules.

TABLE 5.1

Temperature Scales

	Fahrenheit	Celsius	Kelvin
Boiling point	212	100	373
Freezing point	32	0	273
Fahrenheit's ice-salt mixture	0	−18	255
Absolute zero	−460	−273	0

Measuring Heat and Temperature (Event 5-A)

Discrepant Event and Pupil Investigations

Event 5-A. Heat or Temperature?

For this event you will need three beakers, one large bolt, and one small nail. Fill three beakers about half full of tap water. Connect the temperature probes to the computer and measure the temperature of the tap water. Place the bolt and nail into the first beaker and heat until the water boils. Now place one of the two temperature probes in beaker 2 and the other in beaker 3. Start recording data for a few seconds. With tongs, place the bolt into the second beaker and the nail into the third beaker. (See figure 5.1.) Continue to record the temperature of the water in beakers 2 and 3 for a few more minutes. Record the temperature of the water in those beakers over a 3-minute interval every 30 seconds.

The containers should be small and have only enough water to completely cover the objects. Otherwise the temperatures will not be affected very much.

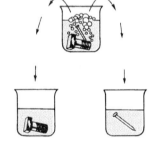

FIGURE 5.1 Does the bolt or nail contain more heat? How will they affect the temperatures of the lower containers?

Pupil Investigations (may include the following processes):

1. Recording the temperature of the water in the containers at periodic intervals.
2. Graphing the readings to show the temperature changes over time.
3. Discovering that the bolt raised the temperature of the water more than the nail did.
4. Forming a theory to explain the differences that were observed and recorded.
5. Predicting what would happen to the temperature change if two (then three) like bolts were placed in the same amount of water.

Event 5-A Explained in Context (Measuring Heat and Temperature)

Heat is a form of energy. It is the energy that a substance has because of the motion of its molecules. When a substance gains heat, the motion of its molecules becomes more vigorous. Conversely, when a substance loses heat, its molecular action decreases.

If a substance were to lose *all* of its heat, all molecular motion would stop. That point is called **absolute zero**. Absolute zero is –459.6° on the Fahrenheit scale and –273° on the Celsius scale. Absolute zero has never been reached, but scientists have gotten to within a fraction of a degree of that figure.

How Heat Is Measured

Since heat and temperature are different, they are measured differently. Heat is measured in calories, British thermal units (Btu), or joules. A **calorie** is the amount of heat needed to raise the temperature of 1 gram of water by 1 degree Celsius. A **Btu** is the heat needed to raise 1 pound of water by 1 degree Fahrenheit. The **joule**, a unit used to measure work, can also be used to measure heat. A joule is the work done by a 1 newton force or weight moving a body through 1 meter.

The calorie is a fairly common unit; the other two are not. However, the Btu is still the standard unit used to measure the heat output of home furnaces. Look at the label fixed to your home furnace. You will find the Btu rating listed. The joule is used mostly in the scientific community.

Heat of Fusion and Heat of Vaporization (Events 5-B and 5-C)

Discrepant Events and Pupil Investigations

Event 5-B. Cooling Breezes?

Place one thermometer into the breeze of a fan and another near the fan but not in the breeze. Let pupils predict which of the two thermometers will show a cooler temperature after the fan is turned on for several minutes.

Pupil Investigations (may include the following processes):

1. Predicting (incorrectly) that the breeze will cool off the one thermometer.
2. Detecting no difference in the temperatures, or, possibly, that the one in the breeze is slightly warmer.
3. Contrasting the observations with our own experience—that a breeze makes us feel cooler.

Event 5-C. Melt Ice . . . Below Its Freezing Point

Fill a beaker about one-third full of crushed ice. Carefully pour 4 to 8 tablespoonsful of salt onto the crushed ice. Then add another one-third beaker of crushed ice on top. Prepare the ice-salt mixture ahead of time so that pupils are not aware that salt was used. If done carefully, the salt will not be visible to the observer. (See figure 5.2.)

Show the beaker with the mixture to the pupils. Point out that liquid is collecting at the bottom of the beaker. Ask them at what temperature ice melts. Most pupils know that it melts at 0° C (32° F). Have pupils check the temperature of the melted liquid with a thermometer.

Surprisingly, the pupils will find that the temperature is well *below* the freezing point. Ask them how it is possible for ice to melt below freezing.

Pupil Investigations (may include the following processes):

1. Discovering that the temperature of the liquid in the beaker is many degrees below freezing.
2. Forming a theory (incorrectly) that the thermometer does not work and that the temperature is actually at the melting point. (Even without a thermometer, pupils can see that *frost* forms on the *outside* of the beaker!)
3. Graphing the temperatures at periodic intervals.
4. Forming a theory that the beaker might contain something other than pure ice. (If pupils suggest that salt melts ice, respond by asking, "But why is the temperature so cold?")

FIGURE 5.2   When salt is poured on crushed ice, what happens to the temperature?

Events 5-B and 5-C Explained in Context (Heat of Fusion and Heat of Vaporization)

Which contains more heat: a gram of ice at $0°$ C or a gram of water at $0°$ C? Surprisingly, they are not the same. Try another example. Which contains more heat: a gram of water or a gram of steam if both are at $100°$ C? Again they are not the same.

Why the difference? Because heat is needed to melt the ice. Thus, after it is melted, a gram of water has more heat than a gram of ice *even if the temperatures are the same in both cases ($0°$ C).* The same principle applies to the water and steam. Heat is needed to change the water into steam. Thus, once converted to steam, it has more heat energy than water *even if their temperatures are the same ($100°$ C).*

The heat that is needed to melt ice is called the **heat of fusion,** and the heat needed to change water to steam is called the **heat of vaporization.** (The terms are also used if the processes are reversed; freezing instead of melting, and condensing instead of forming steam.)

It may be easier to understand these processes if we add heat to a gram of ice and follow its path as it moves from a solid at 10 degrees *below zero* to a gas at 110 degrees. (See figure 5.3.) It takes 1 calorie of heat to raise the temperature of 1 gram of ice by 1 degree. By adding 10 calories of heat, the 1 gram of ice is raised 10 degrees, from 10 *below zero* to 0, its melting point. *But it still remains ice.* It does not change to water (at 0 degrees), unless more heat is added.

How much is needed to change it from ice to water? A large amount: 80 calories! Once the ice has changed to water, then any additional heat will again raise its temperature. As stated earlier, 1 calorie of heat raises the tem-

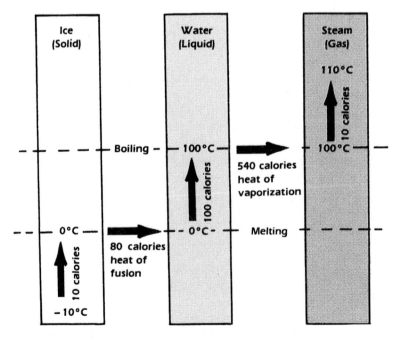

FIGURE 5.3   Heat energy is needed to raise the temperature of H_2O *and* to change it from one phase to another.

perature of 1 gram of water by 1 Celsius degree. Thus, to heat it the 100 degrees from freezing to boiling takes 100 calories.

Now, how many calories are needed to change that gram of water to steam, without any increase in temperature? An amazing 540 calories! Once the water is steam, any additional heat again raises its temperature.

Where does the heat come from that is used in the processes described above? Normally, we think of a heat source like a stove, hot plate, or burner. But the heat that melts ice can come from any source such as air or even from your body. If you put an ice cube on your hand, will it melt? Will it make your hand feel cold? Yes, because the heat from your hand is being used to melt the ice.

It should be noted that the heat of vaporization applies at any temperature, not just at the boiling point. Thus, any change of H$_2$O from a liquid to a gas requires the heat of vaporization. For example, if 1 gram of water evaporates at room temperature, it still takes 540 calories to change it from a liquid to a gas. That is why it feels cool when you step out of a shower, bath, or pool. The heat used in the evaporation process comes from your body.

Since pupils have all felt the cooling effect of evaporation, it is easy to see that *Event 5-B, Cooling Breezes?*, comes as a surprise to them. Many will predict that the thermometer in the breeze will be cooler than the thermometer in the still air. Nevertheless, the event does not work out that way. Both readings will be the same.

Why is there no change? Because there is no moisture being evaporated. The temperature of air does not change just because it is moved by the fan. In fact, if the electric motor gives off some heat, the air that it sets in motion may actually be slightly warmer.

The heat of fusion accounts for the apparent discrepancy in *Event 5-C, Melt Ice . . . Below Its Freezing Point*. Most pupils who live in cold climates know that salt is sprinkled on roads to melt ice. As a result, they are not surprised to find that salt will cause ice to melt. They assume that the ice melts because it is warmed by the salt. The surprise comes when they see that the temperature gets colder instead of warmer.

Why does the mixture get so cold? Remember the heat of fusion? Heat (80 calories) is needed to change 1 gram of ice to a liquid. Where does that heat come from? It comes from the contents of the beaker. Thus, when salt causes the ice to melt, a huge amount of heat energy is needed. That heat comes from the contents of the beaker, dropping the temperature of the salt water far below freezing. That gives us a paradox of ice melting inside the beaker while frost forms on the outside.

The forced melting of the ice has a cooling effect just like evaporation has a cooling effect. In both cases, heat is absorbed during a change of phase.

Sources of Heat (Events 5-D through 5-F)

Discrepant Events and Pupil Investigations

Event 5-D. Shake Heat into a Bottle

Take a baby-food bottle or similar container, fill it three-quarters full of sand, and wrap it with insulation. (Many layers of paper will do.) Connect the temperature probe to the computer and place the probe into the sand. Record the temperature for 10 seconds. Remove the probe and stop recording. Have students take turns shaking the contents vigorously for 4 to 5 minutes. Compare the temperature of the sand before and after the shaking.

Pupil Investigations (may include the following processes):

1. Measuring the temperature of the sand before, during, and after shaking it.
2. Graphing the data obtained above.
3. Experimenting to compare results when no insulation is used.
4. Forming a theory to account for the changes in temperature.

FIGURE 5.4 What happens to the temperature of the wire if it is bent quickly a number of times?

Event 5-E. Wire Heater

Take a short length of wire such as is used in a coat hanger. Bend it back and forth a number of times and touch it at the point where it was bent. What do you feel? (See figure 5.4.)

Pupil Investigations (may include the following processes):

1. Discovering that the point where the wire was bent becomes hot.
2. Experimenting with different wires.
3. Generalizing that some energy has been changed into heat.

Event 5-F. Slippery Friction

Freeze a block of ice in a milk carton. Connect the temperature probe to the computer/calculator and begin recording the temperature. First hold the tip of the temperature probe perpendicular to the ice and resting on the surface. Record the temperature for 25 seconds. Next, with constant pressure start rubbing the ice with the probe for another 25 seconds as the computer continues to record the temperature. Finally, holding the tip of the probe, rub other surfaces such as the desk, paper, or your jeans for another 25 seconds.

Pupil Investigations (may include the following processes):

1. Graphing the data of the different materials.
2. Inferring a relationship between the heat increase and the type of material being rubbed.
3. Experimenting with different surfaces.

Events 5-D through 5-F Explained in Context (Sources of Heat)

Where does heat come from? There are many sources of heat, but they all can be grouped into the four categories shown in table 5.2.

Most students will already be familiar with chemical and electrical sources of heat. They probably know about nuclear sources too, but that source is not practical for classroom demonstration. Mechanical sources, however, are not as well known. Fortunately, they can be shown easily.

Remind pupils that friction produces heat. Many of them will have experienced minor burns or will have felt heat that has resulted from friction. Ask them to rub their hands together firmly and briskly. It is surprising how warm the hands can become.

TABLE 5.2

Sources of Heat

Mechanical	Chemical	Electrical	Nuclear
Friction	Rearrangement of molecules	Lights	Sun and stars
Bending	Flame of any kind	Toasters	Atomic fission
Hammering	Water and plaster of Paris	Heaters	Atomic fusion
Pressure	Sulfuric acid and sugar	Stoves	Nuclear power reactor

Friction also produces the heat that is slowly developed in *Event 5-D, Shake Heat into a Bottle*. It is likely that some of the heat is also caused by the pressure of sand striking the top and bottom of the bottle during brisk shaking. To get a measurable gain in temperature, be sure that pupils shake the bottle vigorously for a long enough time. Four or five minutes should do fine, with pupils trading off after about 30 seconds each.

It is important to use insulation so that the heat from your hands does not enter the bottle. That would obscure the effect of the friction in producing the heat. Taping several layers of paper around the jars should be sufficient.

Another form of mechanical heat is produced in *Event 5-E, Wire Heater*. When the wire is bent back and forth a number of times, the point where the wire is bent becomes warm to the touch. If the wire is bent fast enough and often enough, it becomes quite hot.

Heat can be produced by other mechanical means. For example, when a nail is driven into a board, the nail head becomes warm from the blows, and the shank of the nail gets hot from the friction.

Some nails are designed to make use of this heat in a clever way. They are coated with a dry adhesive which is not active at room temperature. When driven into wood, however, the friction between the nail and wood produces enough heat to melt the adhesive. As a result, such coated nails hold very well.

In *Event 5-F, Slippery Friction*, even using a smooth block of ice, mechanical heat in the form of friction and pressure will be sufficient to melt the ice and raise the temperature slightly. The temperature on the other substances may raise even more quickly if the surfaces are not smooth and because the heat of fusion is not a factor.

Conduction (Events 5-G through 5-I)

Discrepant Events and Pupil Investigations

Event 5-G. Ice Preservation Race

Select several teams of three or four pupils each and give each team an ice cube in a tin can. Ask them to figure out a way to keep the ice from melting. Let the teams work for 5 or 10 minutes and then set the samples aside.

After a specified period of time (perhaps an hour or two), check the results. One way to determine the success of the team efforts is to pour the melted water into test tubes.

Pupil Investigations (may include the following processes):

1. Experimenting with various types of insulation.
2. Experimenting with different containers (if your rules permit that).
3. Measuring the melted water to compare results.
4. Generalizing about the conditions that keep the ice from melting (or how to keep heat from traveling).

Event 5-H. The Two-Toned Paper

FIGURE 5.5   The paper scorches more easily where it covers the wood than where it covers the copper.

Place a wooden dowel against the end of a solid copper rod of the same diameter. Wrap and tape the joint using a single thickness of paper. Apply heat from a flame to scorch the paper. Observe the pattern of the scorch marks. What caused the paper to scorch more on the wooden side of the joint than on the copper side? (See figure 5.5.)

Pupil Investigations (may include the following processes):

1. Observing that there is a sharp line of demarcation between the scorched and unscorched parts of the paper.
2. Forming a theory (incorrectly) that the heat was applied only to the part of the paper that was scorched.
3. Generalizing (correctly) that the scorching of the paper was related to the substance under the paper.

Event 5-I. Candle Snuffer

FIGURE 5.6   The copper coil puts out a small candle flame.

Place a coil of copper wire over the flame of a small birthday candle as shown in figure 5.6. Why does the flame go out? (Use a candle with only a small flame. A large flame will not work.)

Pupil Investigations (may include the following processes):

1. Verifying the activity by repeating it a number of times to see if the flame goes out each time.
2. Observing that sometimes the flame appears to be out but reappears when the coil is lifted.
3. Generalizing (incorrectly) that the flame goes out due to a lack of oxygen.
4. Inferring a relationship between the type of metal used and how heat is conducted.

Events 5-G through 5-I Explained in Context (Conduction)

How does the heat from a stove travel up through a frying pan to fry an egg? Why does smoke go up a chimney? How does the heat of the sun reach us here on earth? These and many other questions are related to a topic of how heat travels.

Heat travels in three ways: conduction, convection, and radiation. The three methods are compared in table 5.3.

The table shows how the characteristics of the three forms of heat transfer and how they are related. However, we will discuss the three methods separately as we go into more detail. The events in this section pertain only to

TABLE 5.3

How Heat Travels

	Conduction	Convection	Radiation
Definition	Transfer of heat from one molecule to another	Transfer of heat by movement of fluids	Transfer of energy by waves through space
Examples	Silver spoon, clothes iron, cookware	Winds (weather), chimney draft, boiling water	Sun's heat, heat lamp, electric heater

conduction. Convection and radiation will be treated later with events related only to those topics.

One way to introduce the topic of conduction is to perform *Event 5-G, Ice Preservation Race.* Divide the class into teams and have each team try to preserve the ice.

The event can be successful even if performed after the section has been discussed. However, if presented in the beginning, the results are likely to be more diverse. Pupils will have to "fend for themselves," and it tends to prepare them for the information about heat transfer that will follow.

It is important that a few rules are established to assure success in the activity:

1. Do not allow pupils to use refrigerators, buckets of ice, or (in the winter) the out-of-doors. All the containers should be stored inside the classroom at room temperature.
2. Teams must not lose any of the melted water (that is how the results will be measured). That means that no paper, cloth, or other materials can be wrapped directly around the ice, because they would soak up melted water.
3. An optional rule may be made about the use of the tin can. Generally, it is best to require the use of the can. However, the ice cube can first be put into a waterproof plastic bag, small glass jar, or small plastic container. Then surround the bag or jar with paper, and stuff the contents into the tin can. Some of the greatest benefits result by giving only the first two rules and nothing more.

Best results in this activity are had by focusing on two factors—size and conductivity.

First of all, reduce the area that needs to be protected. That means that the ice cube should be placed into a very small container. (Since the "melt" needs to be saved for measurement later, the container must be waterproof.) A small jar, plastic bag, or other such container will work well.

Second, get rid of good conductors. The tin can is an excellent conductor. It will bring heat to the ice quickly. Keep as much insulating material between the ice and tin can as possible.

At the end of the allotted time, have each team pour its melted water into test tubes. It is easy to compare the results of the teams in this way.

The purpose of the lesson is to learn about the movement of heat by conduction. That is the most likely way in which heat gets to the ice. The most successful teams will be those that reduced conduction the most.

The best conductors are generally metals. As stated earlier, the metal of the tin can is an excellent conductor compared to the other substances used in the event. The best metallic conductors are copper, silver, and aluminum.

Once pupils know how heat travels, they may also learn how to keep it from traveling. That is done by using materials that are poor conductors. Poor conductors are also termed *insulators*. Glass, paper, wood, plastics, and rubber are examples of insulators.

We can see the effects of good and poor conductors in *Event 5-H, The Two-Toned Paper*. The paper on the wood side of the wood-copper joint will scorch more quickly than the paper on the copper side. The paper on the copper side does not get as hot from a flame because the copper carries away the heat very quickly. Wood, however, does not conduct the heat away, so the paper quickly gets hot enough to scorch.

Event 5-I, Candle Snuffer, also demonstrates the effects of a good conductor. At first some pupils will think that the candle goes out because the flame cannot get oxygen. But, since the snuffer is a coil, air can enter between the coils as well as from above and below. Instead, the fire goes out because the copper carries away the heat so quickly.

It is important that a small candle (such as a birthday candle) be used. Large candles produce too much heat for this event to work well. Also, once the coil gets too hot, it can no longer carry away enough heat to put out even a small flame. **Caution:** Be careful not to touch the heated coil.

Convection (Events 5-J through 5-M)

Discrepant Events and Pupil Investigations

Event 5-J. The Mixed-Up Bottles

Set up four wide-mouth bottles in pairs as shown in figure 5.7. Start with two bottles of hot water and two of cold water. Mix food coloring into the lower bottle of each pair. Use an index card to keep the water from spilling while inverting each of the top two bottles.

The finished arrangement should have one pair with hot water over cold and the other pair just the opposite. Pupils should *not* be told that the water is at different temperatures.

When the arrangement is set up, carefully pull out the index cards and observe. The food coloring mixes quickly in one pair of bottles but not in the other. Ask the students to try to learn why.

Pupil Investigations (may include the following processes):

1. Observing that the water is mixing in both the top and bottom bottles of the rapidly mixing side.
2. Discovering by touching that the bottles are not all the same temperature.
3. Observing closely to see if anything is blocking the water in the side that is not mixing (Nothing is blocking it.)
4. Predicting what will happen if the unmixed side is turned over.

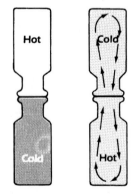

FIGURE 5.7 The food coloring mixes quickly in one pair of bottles because there are convection currents in them.

Event 5-K. The Circling Sawdust

Drop some sawdust into a beaker of water that is being heated. Set up the beaker so that it is heated at the edge as shown in figure 5.8. Observe the motion of the sawdust as the water is being heated.

Pupil Investigations (may include the following processes):

1. Observing the motion of the sawdust in the water.
2. Drawing a diagram to show the movement of the water.
3. Generalizing that water rises when it is heated.

Event 5-L. Does Air Move In or Out?

This is an activity that should be done (for a short time only) on a cool winter day. If you have windows in your room that allow it, open one of them slightly at top and bottom. Have the pupils determine how the air moves.

Pupil Investigations (may include the following processes):

1. Observing that cool air comes into the room at the bottom opening.
2. Observing that warm air escapes from the room at the top.
3. Inferring that the temperature of the air is related to its weight.
4. Generalizing that the movement of air is based on its weight and temperature.

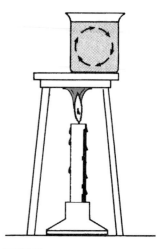

FIGURE 5.8   Heat the edge of the beaker and you can see a convection current in the water.

Event 5-M. Convection Tester #1

Draw a spiral on a sheet of paper and cut along the spiral to form a coil. Attach a thread to the inner end of the coil and suspend the coil from it. (See figure 5.9.) Hold the coil above an electric light bulb. (**Note:** If you use foil instead of paper, it is safe to use a candle flame instead of a bulb as your heat source.)

Pupil Investigations (may include the following processes):

1. Observing that the coil begins to spin when suspended over the heat source.
2. Inferring that heat causes a movement of air.
3. Generalizing that air rises when heated.

Events 5-J through 5-M Explained in Context (Convection)

Convection is the transfer of heat by the movement of fluids. (A fluid is either a gas such as air or a liquid such as water.) When a fluid is heated, it expands and becomes lighter per given volume. Being lighter, it then rises and is replaced by cooler, heavier fluid. This motion of fluids is called a *convection current.*

A convection current is shown clearly in *Event 5-J, The Mixed-Up Bottles.* In the pair of bottles where the mixing takes place, you start with the warm water in the bottom bottle and the cold water on top. When the index card is removed from between the bottles, the warm water rises and the cold water descends. In a minute or two the water is totally mixed.

In the other pair, the top bottle has warm water and the lower bottle has cold water. No mixing takes place because the warm (or light weight) water is already on top and the cold (or heavy) water is already on the bottom.

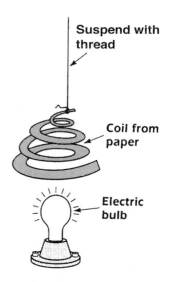

Suspend with thread

Coil from paper

Electric bulb

FIGURE 5.9   Suspend a coil from a thread and place a heat source below it. Why does the coil start to spin?

Event 5-K, The Circling Sawdust, also shows a convection current. The sawdust is so light that it is carried along by the moving water. The water rises when it is heated, and cold water descends to take its place. This action continues so that the water can be seen to move in a constant circle while the container is being heated.

Convection currents are also present in the air, as is shown in *Event 5-L, Does Air Move In or Out?* Many pupils will be able to predict that cold air will move in from the lower opening of the window. Many of them will have had experience with cold drafts coming in through doors and windows.

However, the motion at the top of the window will be another matter. Ask them to predict what will happen. Many will say that cold air will also enter there. Ask them where the air goes that is already in the room. It has to go somewhere when cold air enters. It goes out on top because warm air rises when cold air descends.

Event 5-M, Convection Tester #1, shows clearly that air rises when heated. The bulb (or candle flame if a foil is used for the coil) heats the air which then rises rapidly. The rising air causes the coil to spin.

Radiation (Events 5-N through 5-P)

Discrepant Events and Pupil Investigations
Event 5-N. Which Is the "Warmer" Color?
Obtain two cans that are alike. Paint one black and the other white. Fill with equal amounts of water and place the cans in direct sunlight. Connect two temperature probes to the computer and pass the probes through the holes in the plastic lids of the cans. Record the temperature of the water over time using the computer to measure the temperature of the water at periodic intervals for about 2 hours.

Pupil Investigations (may include the following processes):
1. Graphing the water temperature, taken at 15-minute intervals for an hour or two.
2. Observing that the water in the black can warms up more than the water in the white can.
3. Inferring that there is a relationship between sunlight, warmth, and color.

Event 5-O. Hot Car
Using two small identical shoe boxes, paint one black and one white. Paint inside and outside of both. Cut out two-thirds of each lid and replace each section with plastic wrap, plexiglass, or a glass pane. Through a small hole in the side of each "car," insert the computer/calculator temperature probe. Place the cars in direct sunlight. Record the inside temperatures of the cars every 10 minutes for a few hours.

Pupil Investigations (may include the following processes):
1. Observing the inside temperature difference between the light and dark "car".
2. Predicting what will happen if both cars have the same outside color but different interior colors.
3. Comparing this to the greenhouse effect.

Event 5-P. Heat from Light

Use a table lamp or other lamp that can be easily reached. Turn on the lamp and hold a hand close to the bulb's surface. Check to see if heat can be felt above, alongside, and below. Hold the hand to within an inch of the bulb's surface. (*But be careful. Do not touch.* Bulbs can become hot enough to burn hands!)

Pupil Investigations (may include the following processes):

1. Predicting where the most heat would be felt.
2. Feeling the heat from the bulb as the hand is held about an inch away (Careful: do not touch).
3. Generalizing about the heat rising above the bulb.
4. Generalizing about the heat that goes downward to a hand held below the bulb.

Events 5-N through 5-P Explained in Context (Radiation)

Radiation is a third method of heat transmission. In that method, energy travels at the speed of light from a source, through space, to an object. The best example is the heat from the sun.

Radiant energy does not warm up a transparent substance. It is converted to heat only when it strikes an object that is not transparent. Thus, the air high above the earth is not heated by the sun, but the ground on the earth's surface is. Likewise, on a cold winter day the sun's light warms up the inside of a windowsill, but the transparent window glass through which the energy travels is quite cold.

Substances vary in their ability to absorb and reflect radiation. We can see in *Event 5-N, Which is the "Warmer" Color?,* and *Event 5-O, Hot Car,* that black absorbs heat well but white does not. White reflects much of the energy that strikes it. As a result, the water in the black can gets warmer than the water in the white can.

Of course, the sun is not the only example of heat transmission by radiation. All objects above absolute zero actually radiate some heat, but such radiation cannot be felt until the temperatures get quite hot. Hold your hand a few inches *below* a light bulb as suggested by *Event 5-P, Heat from Light,* and you can feel the heat. The heat you feel is due to radiation. (Remember that if you hold your hand *above* the bulb, you get heat from convection currents as well as radiation. As a result, you feel more warmth above the bulb than below.) Another example of radiant heat is to hold your hand close to a car's headlight. You should be able to feel the radiant heat.

Still another example of radiant heat is the heat that you feel from a roaring fire. Have you ever stood near a hot fire in a fireplace or a huge bonfire outside? The convection currents go straight up the chimney and into the air. So the heat you feel cannot be from the rising warm air. Instead, the heat you feel comes from radiation.

Expansion and Contraction (Events 5-Q through 5-U)

Discrepant Events and Pupil Investigations

Event 5-Q. "Dancing" Dimes

Cool off some large soft-drink bottles in a refrigerator. When cooled, place them on a table and cover each with a dime or penny. Moisten the edge between the coin and bottle with a drop of water. Wait and watch. (Students should not be told that the bottles have been cooled.)

Pupil Investigations (may include the following processes):

1. Observing that again and again the coins rise slowly and then fall back with a "plink".
2. Measuring the length of time that the coins continue to dance. (They stop plinking after a while.)
3. Discovering that the bottles feel cool to the touch.
4. Generalizing about air expanding when heated.

Event 5-R. Jumping Juice

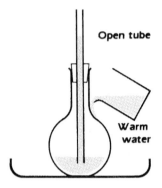

Open tube

Warm water

FIGURE 5.10 The water inside the tube rises and falls as the air inside expands or contracts.

Pour some colored water into a flask. (See figure 5.10) It appears that a single tube is pushed all the way through the one-hole stopper. It is not. *That is unsafe.* You will need to push too hard to get the glass all the way through the stopper. *If you push too hard the tube will break and the jagged end will plunge through your hand!*

Proceed safely. You must moisten the ends of the tubes with soapy water and use a *gentle* twisting motion to insert the ends into the stopper. When you are finished, one tube should extend down into the flask and the other upward about 20 to 30 centimeters. When joined this way, they act as a single tube.

Pour hot water over the outside of the flask. The colored water inside the flask will rise up the tube. Pour cold water from a different beaker and the colored water will go down. Have the pupils investigate the activity and find out what caused the colored water to rise and fall. (Do not tell the pupils that the waters are different temperatures.)

Pupil Investigations (may include the following processes):

1. Observing that one beaker of water was used to make the colored water rise up the tube and that another beaker of water was used to make it go down.
2. Checking to find out if there is a difference in the water used in the two beakers.
3. Inferring a relationship between the temperature of the water in the beakers and the action of the colored water in the tube.

Event 5-S. The Sagging Solid

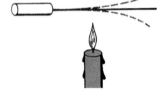

FIGURE 5.11 Does this metal strip really sag? Why does it sometimes go upward?

Everyone knows that when a metal is heated hot enough, it can become weak and sag. Tell the students that you can show how heat causes a special metallic strip to "sag," even if it is just held in a candle flame for a short time. (Do not mention at this time that the device is a *bimetallic strip*.) Then tell them that you will do it again, just to be sure it works. This time, however, turn the strip over (do not let the class notice this turn). They will be amazed to see the strip bend *upward!* (See figure 5.11)

Pupil Investigations (may include the following processes):

1. Observing whether the heat is applied to the same place on the strip with each trial.

2.   Observing how the strip is straightened between trials (The strip straightens out by itself when cooled. Water cools it quickly.)
3.   Generalizing that the metal strip is not actually sagging (losing strength) when it bends downward but that the bend is caused by something else.

Event 5-T. Expansion Meter

Attach a thin copper wire from two pegs on either side of a chalkboard. Attach a weight midway between the pegs. (See figure 5.12) Make a mark on the chalkboard to show the location of the bottom of the weight. Now connect a battery to the wires for a few seconds. Observe the weight. Does it move? (**Caution:** Do *not* leave the wires connected for more than 10 seconds. To keep them attached any longer can damage the battery.)

Pupil Investigations (may include the following processes):

1.   Observing that the weight goes below the mark on the chalkboard when the wires are connected.
2.   Observing that the weight goes back up after the wires are disconnected.
3.   Inferring that the expansion of metal is caused by something that the battery did.
4.   Generalizing that heat caused the expansion.

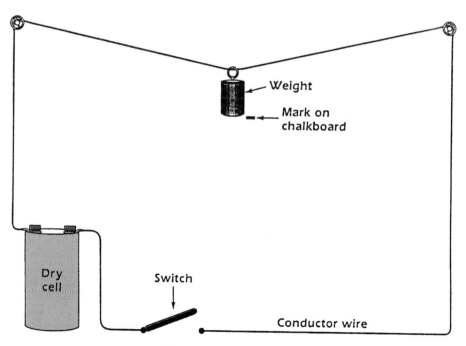

FIGURE 5.12   Suspend a weight from a wire attached to a dry cell. Mark the chalkboard to show the location of the weight. Turn on the switch for about 10 seconds. What happens to the weight?

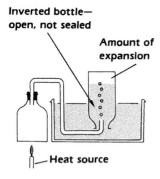

Inverted bottle—
open, not sealed

Amount of
expansion

Heat source

FIGURE 5.13   The
expanded gases move
through the tube into the
inverted bottle where they
displace the water. (*Caution:*
Bottles must not be sealed.)

Event 5-U. Expansion of Gases

This is an expansion meter for gases. Set up an arrangement as shown in figure 5.13. (**Caution:** Double check to be sure that the bottles are *not* sealed. If they are, the bottles will explode when heated.) The bottle that is placed on the heat source has a one-hole stopper and an open tube that is run into the open second container. The inverted second container is filled with water at the start of the test.

Pupil Investigations (may include the following processes):

1.   Observing bubbles rising into the second bottle when the first bottle is heated.
2.   Recording the amount of expansion of several gases.
3.   Concluding that all gases have about the same rates of expansion.

Events 5-Q through 5-U Explained in Context (Expansion and Contraction)

One characteristic of almost all substances is that they expand when heated and contract when cooled. The degree to which substances expand and contract is referred to as the **index of expansion.**

It is generally believed that expansion is caused by the increased activity of molecules when they are heated. When heated, they vibrate more vigorously and take up more space.

Water is a well-known exception to the rule. Like other substances, water expands when heated and contracts when cooled. But it does so only as long as the temperature remains above 4° C.

Below 4° C however, water reverses itself. It will then expand when *cooled.* (This oddity of water is very handy. It allows ice to form on top of a lake instead of at the bottom. If ice were to form at the bottom of a lake in winter, not only would it make for some rather tough skating, but it is not likely that heat would get down to it in the summer to melt it.)

Expansion and contraction are important factors to consider in constructing roads, buildings, and other projects. Here are a few surprising examples:

1.   The Sears Tower in Chicago (one of the tallest buildings in the world) is about 15 centimeters taller on a hot summer day than on a cold winter day.
2.   A 2-kilometer bridge may expand and contract as much as a meter between summer and winter.
3.   Concrete highways and sidewalks are built with separations or joints to allow them to expand and contract without breaking up.
4.   Electric power lines, telephone lines, and railroad tracks must be built with provisions for expansion and contraction.

Expansion is the principle that explains *Event 5-Q, "Dancing" Dimes.* To get the dimes to dance we must start with cool bottles. When the bottles are brought into a warm room, they warm up, causing the air inside to expand.

Since the air has to go somewhere, it pushes the coin aside long enough to escape. Then the coin "plinks" back down. The air in the bottle warms slowly, so the coin plinks many times before the air inside finally reaches room temperature.

For the activity to work, the coin must have an airtight seal on top of the bottle. Just moisten the edge between the coin and bottle with a drop or two of water. That provides the seal.

The answer to the mystery of *Event 5-R, Jumping Juice,* is again related to expansion and contraction of air. The air inside the bottle expands when hot water is poured over the flask. Thus, the air expands and forces the colored water up the glass tube. However, when cool water is used, the air inside contracts and the colored water in the tube drops quickly. (Be sure to do the activity without telling the pupils ahead of time that you have used hot and cold water. Let them discover that for themselves.)

In *Event 5-S, The Sagging Solid,* the metal strip does not really sag. It just bends in response to expansion and contraction. The event can be done only with a special bimetal strip—a sandwich of two metals (usually brass and iron) joined together to look like a single strip. (Such a bimetal strip can be obtained from a science supply house.)

The strip bends when heated because the metals have different rates of expansion. One of the metals expands much more than the other. To allow for the different rates of expansion, the strip must bend.

The two metals can be compared to two runners in a track meet. If one runner runs the curve in the outside lane, he or she must run farther than the runner in the inside lane. Likewise, the metal in the strip that expands more is on the "outside lane" as it bends.

To cause the strip to bend down, hold the strip one way; and to cause it to bend upward, just turn it around. A little deftness is needed in handling so that it is not obvious to pupils that you just turned the strip over. Let them discover the details in their investigations.

Another example of how heat causes a metal to expand is shown in *Event 5-T, Expansion Meter.* The battery is used to heat the wire. As soon as the wire heats up, it expands. You will see the effect of this expansion as the weight goes below the chalk mark. Then, when the switch is opened (turned off), or the battery is disconnected, the wire cools and contracts again, lifting the weight in the process.

Again, be sure to observe the warning about the need to disconnect after only 10 seconds or so. Otherwise, the battery can be easily damaged. Also, depending on the size of the wire, it is possible for the wire to become quite hot, so do not touch it.

Event 5-U, Expansion of Gases, is an event that shows how much air expands when heated. Be sure to start with an "empty" bottle. Of course it is not really empty. It is filled with air. When that air is heated, it expands. The expanded air travels through the tube and is caught inside the inverted bottle. It is easy to see how much air collects in the inverted bottle.

Fire (Events 5-V through 5-X)

Discrepant Events and Pupil Investigations

Event 5-V. Water from Fire?

Invert a cold tumbler over a candle flame for a few seconds and observe. What is seen to form on the inside of the glass? Ask the pupils to explain what they see. (See figure 5.14.)

FIGURE 5.14 What forms on the inner surface of a cold glass when it is held over a candle flame for a few seconds?

Pupil Investigations (may include the following processes):

1. Observing that the glass becomes fogged on the inside.
2. Inferring that there is a relationship between fire and the fog.
3. Forming a theory that water is an end product of fire.

Event 5-W. Boil Water in a Paper Cup

Fill a paper cup with water and set it on a screen over an open flame from a Bunsen burner. If you have no Bunsen burner, you can use some other heat source; but an open flame works the best. If you decide to try a stove or heater, use an empty iron or steel pan or tray and set the cup in it. (Do not use copper or aluminum utensils because they will melt from the intense heat.) Observe until the water boils in the cup.

Pupil Investigations (may include the following processes):

1. Observing that the water actually boils in a paper cup.
2. Observing that the cup leaks slightly after heating.
3. Inferring (incorrectly) that the cup is not really made of paper.
4. Generalizing about the factors that support combustion.

Event 5-X. Kindling Temperatures

On a large metal plate place small bits of coal, sulfur, sugar, candle wax, paper, wood, bread, and a match head. Arrange them around the outer edge of the plate so that they are all equal distances from the center. Apply heat to the center of the plate, and note the order in which they start to burn. (**Caution:** Be sure to do this event in a well-ventilated place.)

Pupil Investigations (may include the following processes):

1. Predicting the order in which the materials will ignite.
2. Recording the order in which the substances actually ignite.
3. Listing the substances according to their kindling temperatures.

Event 5-V through 5-X Explained in Context (Fire)

What Is Fire?

We have all seen fires burn. Now we will take a more scientific look at what is needed to allow a fire to burn.

We saw earlier in this chapter that fire is a common source of heat energy. You may recall that it is a chemical source of energy. Just how does it release energy? Let us look at a typical example—a candle. A candle is an example of a hydrocarbon. That is, it contains mostly hydrogen (H) and carbon (C) atoms; and when it burns, it unites with oxygen (O). Thus, you start with H plus C, and O.

The end products contain the same atoms but in different arrangements: carbon dioxide (CO_2) and water (H_2O). Surprising as it may seem to pupils, fire releases water, which becomes visible as it condenses on the tumbler in *Event 5-V, Water from Fire?*

The Fire Triangle

Three things are necessary to permit a fire to burn: (1) fuel, (2) oxygen, and (3) kindling temperature. The three factors are referred to as the **fire triangle,** and there cannot be any fire unless the triangle is complete. (See figure 5.15) (Fire is sometimes described as a form of rapid **oxidation** because it uses up oxygen quickly. Note how this is different from *slow oxidation* discussed immediately after this section.)

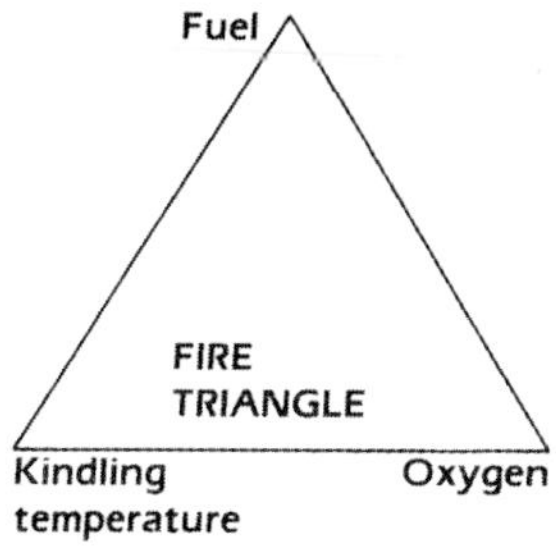

If three things are needed to sustain a fire, it means that when a fire goes out, something is missing. Pupils can easily understand that oxygen is missing when a glass jar is inverted over a burning candle. The flame goes out as soon as the oxygen is used up.

In *Event 5-W, Boil Water in a Paper Cup,* the missing factor is the kindling temperature. That surprises the students because the flame certainly seems to be hot enough. It is well above the kindling temperature of paper. However, even though the flame is hot, the paper cup is not. The water in the cup takes the heat away from the paper so quickly that the cup never reaches the kindling point. In fact, the temperature of the paper is not much higher than the temperature of water, or 100° C.

Caution: Be sure to use only paper cups, not plastic. Most thin plastic drinking cups will melt if the water is heated to the boiling point. On the other hand, the thick Styrofoam cups are such effective insulators that the water cannot take the heat away fast enough, and the outside of such a cup will burn, filling the room with acrid fumes.

Two other notes: Most paper cups have a rim around the bottom. You will see that this rim will burn away immediately because it is too far from the water to be cooled by it. The cup will still hold together, however, and the lack of a rim does not affect the experiment. Finally, paper drinking cups are coated with wax to make them waterproof. The wax melts in the boiling water, and the cup then begins to leak slowly. This also does not harm the experiment.

In *Event 5-X, Kindling Temperatures,* we saw that different substances have different **kindling temperatures.** That is, different materials will ignite at different temperatures: some, quickly at low kindling temperatures; and some, much later at high kindling temperatures. Be sure to do this activity in an area with plenty of ventilation. Some of the substances give off offensive fumes and odors.

FIGURE 5.15 All three parts of the fire triangle are needed to support a fire.

Slow Oxidation (Event 5-Y)

Discrepant Event and Pupil Investigations

Event 5-Y. Heat from Grass

Fill one waste basket with fresh grass clippings. Fill a second basket with dry grass. Connect the temperature probes to the computer and insert the probes into each basket. Record the change in temperature for a few days.

Pupil Investigations (may include the following processes):

1. Predicting (incorrectly) that the temperature will be the same in both baskets.
2. Observing that the temperature rises in the basket with the fresh grass.

3.   Observing that the fresh grass breaks down after a few days, but that the hay remains unchanged.
4.   Generalizing that there is a relationship between the breakdown of the grass and the rise in temperature.

Event 5-Y Explained in Context (Slow Oxidation)

Most children are familiar with rapid oxidation as demonstrated by fire. However, they are generally not familiar with forms of slow oxidation. When oxygen unites with materials it produces heat. With slow oxidation the heat is sometimes so slight that you cannot detect it. For example, when iron rusts (the effects of which can easily be seen on old cars), it actually produces heat. But that heat is released over a period of years and is not noticeable.

In Event 5-Y, Heat from Grass, however, measurable heat should be noticed within a day. The heat is produced by microorganisms that use the moisture in grass to break it down chemically. The moisture is not present in dried hay so it is unaffected. That is why farmers can store hay in a barn and have it remain useful for years. Moist grass, however, breaks down in a matter of a few days. (After a day or two, the clippings should be discarded, because the residue can turn into a putrid mess.)

Combining Assessment with Instruction

Working in groups of two to four students, students should discuss and explain in writing the answer to the following question: If hot air rises, then why is it so cold in the mountains? Give the students the following three words to include in their explanation: conduction, convection, and radiation. Students should be graded as a group and credit should be given for: (1) defining each word; (2) applying each word to the earth's weather and/or atmosphere; and (3) logical thinking, even if they do not answer the question completely. Tell the students that what they write will be graded but additional points will be given for a class presentation by each group. Give the students paper and a sheet of acetate to draw diagrams that might help to present their ideas to the class. The presenter from each group will be randomly selected. This strategy better insures that each person in the group contributes and tries to understand the concepts in the group discussion in case he or she is the one selected to present the group's ideas. The presenter should use the group's recording sheet and drawings during the presentation.

Sites and Software

The following websites and software are appropriate to use with this chapter. Note that computer software and websites change rapidly. This makes it necessary to investigate the stable websites for new links and software catalogs for updates. Visit www.mhhe.com/friedl6e to link to these directly and for study resources.

Sites

Science Learning Network   http://www.sln.org
Mad Scientist   http://www.madsci.org/experiments/
Howstuffworks "How Fire Works"   www.howstuffworks.com/fire.htm
About Temperature   www.unidata.ucar.edu/staff/
    blynds/tmp.html
Heat of Fusion   www.onlink.net/~bernas/fusion.htm
Convection   www.sohowww.nascom.nasa.gov/
    explore/
    lessons/convection.html
GEMS, Convection   www.lhs.berkeley.edu/GEMS/
    GEM280.html
Heat Transfer   www.buphy.bu.edu/py105/notes/
    Heattransfer.html

Software

I (Hate) Love Science! (DK Multimedia) (2–6)
Science Court Explorations: Heat Absorption (Tom Snyder Publications) (2–4)
Science Sleuths Elementary CD-ROM Vol. 1 and 2 (Videodiscovery Inc.) (3–6)
All about Science Series: Matter (Carolina) (4–8)
Science Court: Particles in Motion (Tom Snyder Publications) (4–6)
InventorsLabs: Technology (Sunburst) (5–9)

Key Terms

Teaching Children about Magnetism

NATIONAL SCIENCE EDUCATION STANDARDS ALIGNMENT TO EVENTS

The events in this chapter help accomplish several of the NSES for content. The event(s) that align with a given content standard are listed below that standard.

LEVELS K–4

UNIFYING CONCEPTS AND PROCESSES
- Systems, order and organization
  6-A
- Evidence, models and explanation
  6-B
  6-G

SCIENCE AS INQUIRY
- Abilities necessary to do and understand scientific inquiry
  6-A through 6-H

PHYSICAL SCIENCE
- Position and motion of objects
  6-C through 6-D
  6-E through 6-H
- Properties of objects and materials
  6-A through 6-B
- Light, heat, electricity and magnetism
  6-A through 6-H

SCIENCE AND TECHNOLOGY
- Abilities of technological design
  6-A
  6-B
  6-D and 6-E
- Understanding science and technology
  6-G

HISTORY AND NATURE OF SCIENCE
- Science as a human endeavor
  Historical introduction
  6-G

LEVELS 5–8

UNIFYING CONCEPTS AND PROCESSES
- Systems, order and organization
  6-A
- Evidence, models and explanation
  6-B
  6-G

SCIENCE AS INQUIRY
- Abilities necessary to do and understand scientific inquiry
  6-A through 6-H

PHYSICAL SCIENCE
- Properties and changes of properties in matter
  6-A through 6-B
- Motion and forces
  6-A through 6-B
  6-C through 6-D
  6-E and 6-H

SCIENCE AND TECHNOLOGY
- Abilities of technological design
  6-A
  6-B
  6-D and 6-E
- Understanding science and technology
  6-G

HISTORY AND NATURE OF SCIENCE
- Science as a human endeavor
  Historical introduction
  6-G

From Lodestones to Domains

Before going into some events about magnets, we will present a brief history of how they were discovered and used. The history of magnets goes back more than three thousand years. Ancient civilizations discovered that certain types of rock seemed to attract bits of natural iron. The rock was actually *magnetite* (Fe_3O_4), a mineral very rich in iron.

It is believed that magnetite was formed during the slow hardening of the earth's crust as it cooled from its molten state. The rock was magnetized by the earth's magnetic field. This magnetic action does not occur in ordinary iron or steelmaking because the metal hardens far too fast.

At first the magnetic rock was merely a curiosity. By A.D. 1200, however, it became quite important. Sailors found that, when the rock was placed on a small floating raft in a pool of water, the rock would line up in a north-south direction.

Sailors could use it to tell direction. All they had to do was mark one of the ends to always know which way they were headed, even if they were out in the high seas beyond the sight of land. Because it was used to lead a ship safely to its destination, it became known as the *lodestone* (or "lead-stone").

Prior to this discovery, they were greatly limited in navigation. They were sure of where they were going only so long as they stayed within sight of land. Once on the high seas, they could use the sun and stars to tell direction, but if obscured by clouds, they were blind! However, with this new discovery, they always knew which direction they were going.

What Causes Magnetism?

There is still much to be learned about the causes of magnetism. However, it is generally believed that magnetism comes from certain properties within the atom.

Since all materials are made up of atoms, you might think that all things are magnetic. But, that does not happen. No such properties are evident in many substances such as paper, glass, silver, wood, plastic, and ordinary rocks. Why not?

The answer is believed to be that atoms often are grouped in opposite pairs so that they cancel each other out. That is what probably happens in those substances that have no net magnetic effect. Such substances are called nonmagnetic.

In other substances, the magnetic fields of their individual atoms are not fully paired, so an excess of one type remains. In these magnetic substances, the atoms group themselves into small regions known as **magnetic domains** ranging in size from 0.01 to 0.1 centimeters across.

Nonetheless, even these substances (such as iron or steel) do not *appear* to be magnetic. For example, ordinary iron and steel do not attract each other. That is because the *domains* are scattered in a random order and cancel each other out. (Remember that in nonmagnetic objects, the *atoms*, not domains, cancel out each other.) However, when an external magnetic force is brought near, the domains line up and the substance is attracted to the magnet.

Item	Yes	No
Copper (penny)	?	?
Silver (necklace)	?	?
Nickel (Canadian nickel)	?	?
Aluminum foil	?	?
Etc.	?	?

FIGURE 6.1 Summarize class responses on a chart like this.

What Do Magnets Attract? (Events 6-A and 6-B)

Discrepant Events and Pupil Investigations

Event 6-A. What Materials Are Attracted #1?

There are many variations of this activity. Basically it is designed to test a variety of materials to see if they are attracted to a magnet. Eventually, the pupils should be able to classify objects according to whether they are attracted or not attracted by a magnet.

If you use a list such as the one in figure 6.1, ask the class to make predictions about which are and which are not attracted. Do *not* let the pupils try the items with a magnet at this point of the activity. Just ask them to predict on the basis of their past experiences. Then summarize the predictions on the chalkboard.

Of the items on the list, silver is perhaps the hardest to get. Use a dime or quarter minted in 1964 or earlier, if you can find one. It contains 90% silver. Canadian coins (except for the cent) are good sources of nickel. Those minted in 1969 or later are 100% nickel, except for the dollar coin which is 100% nickel, but coated with a thin layer of bronze. The U.S. nickel is made mostly of copper and is not magnetic.

Pupil Investigations (may include the following processes):

1. Predicting which materials are attracted by a magnet.
2. Discovering that many metals are *not* attracted by a magnet.
3. Classifying materials according to which are and which are not attracted by a magnet.

Event 6-B. What Materials Are Attracted #2?

This activity is similar to the previous one. Again, put out some materials and ask pupils to predict which will be attracted to a magnet. Include a small steel sheet and a small aluminum sheet, both of which should be labeled to indicate what they are. Also, include a small section of magnetic rubber gasket from an old refrigerator door, and hide a small steel sheet inside a note pad (even a large paper clip might do). Secure the note pad with a rubber band. Finally, include an empty "tin" can, really a juice or other can with a cardboard body, aluminum base, and steel top. (Such cans are quite common in the frozen juice section of the grocery store.)

Pupil Investigations (may include the following processes):

1. Predicting which materials are attracted by a magnet.
2. Discovering that some metals are *not* attracted by a magnet.
3. Discovering that some apparent nonmetallic objects *are* attracted to a magnet.
4. Forming a rule to explain the apparent discrepancies.

Events 6-A and 6-B Explained in Context (What Do Magnets Attract?)

There are relatively few pure substances that are attracted by a magnet. *Event 6-A, What Materials Are Attracted #1?*, calls attention to those that are. In this activity you may wish to have the students test many additional items to see if a pattern develops. They can place those items that are attracted in one pile and those that are not in another.

After a while, most pupils will see some patterns develop. For example, they will see that *nonmetallic objects are not attracted* to magnets. Even kindergarten pupils will be able to understand that. Metallic objects, however, will be more difficult. Most students believe that *all* metallic objects are attracted by magnets. Here they will discover that such is not the case.

In fact, only iron, nickel, and cobalt are attracted to a magnet. All other metals are not. However, some combinations of metals (alloys), such as iron, aluminum, nickel, and cobalt (alnico), are also magnetic.

In lower grades it may be fun to make a "fishing" game out of this activity. Use a magnet instead of a hook, a string for a line, and a ruler for the pole. Use a wide variety of common items around the classroom as the "fish."

Spread out the items on a table and allow each child to fish for one item. They should tell which item they will fish for and predict whether it will be attracted to the magnet. Then, if the item is magnetic, it is picked up by the magnet. The pupil puts the object on the magnetic pile. If it is not magnetic, the student should test with the magnet, and finally pick it up with his or her fingers and put it on the nonmagnetic pile. Eventually, all the items are checked and classified into magnetic and nonmagnetic substances.

Event 6-B, What Materials Are Attracted #2?, seems to contradict what they have just learned in Event 6-A. Although they "know" that nonmetals are not attracted to a magnet, they see that the note pad and rubber gasket are attracted. Then, if the aluminum sheet is put on top of the steel sheet, and a magnet placed on top, the aluminum and steel both seem to be attracted to the magnet.

The discrepancies can all be explained. Many pupils will guess that there is some iron hidden in the note pad. Thus, the magnet attracts only the iron not the paper. The gasket is somewhat similar. The magnet does not attract the rubber, but the magnetic iron imbedded within the rubber. In the same way, the magnet attracts the steel sheet and pins the aluminum between it and the magnet. The aluminum, itself, is not attracted.

The use of the "tin" can will prove to be surprising. Most cans contain no tin. They are made of nonmagnetic substances such as aluminum and even cardboard. However, they have a lid which contains iron to allow it to stick to the magnetic holder of a can opener.

So, if you use an empty can and check the body with a magnet you will find that it is not magnetic. If you check the aluminum base, it is not magnetic either. Finally, if you ask the pupils if the hole is magnetic, they will laugh. But the teacher has the last laugh. As you bring the magnet to the rim, the can jumps and sticks. The rim is the steel remnant of the top which is made of steel so that cans will stick to the magnetic holders of can openers, as stated earlier.

Magnetism Is a Force (Events 6-C and 6-D)

Discrepant Events and Pupil Investigations

Event 6-C. Lines of Force

Place some magnets on a flat surface as shown in figure 6.2, and cover them with a pane of glass. Then sprinkle some iron filings on the top of the glass. Observe the formation of lines between like poles and unlike poles.

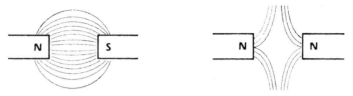

FIGURE 6.2   The lines of force show attraction between unlike poles and repulsion between like poles.

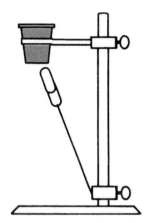

FIGURE 6.3   What is holding up the paper clip? What happens when paper, glass, and other substances are inserted between the paper clip and the cup?

Pupil Investigations (may include the following processes):

1.   Observing that lines between unlike poles connect each other.
2.   Discovering that lines do not connect between like poles.
3.   Generalizing that unlike poles attract and like poles repel.

Event 6-D. Levitation

Set up an arrangement similar to that shown in figure 6.3. Place a strong magnet inside the plastic cup, and cover the magnet with tissue, cotton, or some other material (to hide the magnet). Attach a thread to a paper clip so that the clip is held down. Do not tell the pupils that there is a strong magnet in the cup. Ask them to decide what holds up the paper clip.

Another part of this event is to insert sheets of various materials such as glass, paper, aluminum foil, plastic, copper, and iron between the paper clip and the cup. Ask pupils to predict if the paper clip will fall as each of the sheets is carefully inserted between the cup and clip, one sheet at a time.

Pupil Investigations (may include the following processes):

1.   Observing that there is nothing holding up the paper clip.
2.   Predicting which sheets will cause the clip to fall.
3.   Inferring that there is a magnet inside the cup.
4.   Generalizing that there is a relationship between sheets that cause the clip to fall and those that are attracted by a magnet.

Events 6-C and 6-D Explained in Context (Magnetism Is a Force)

Seeing Magnetic Lines of Force

In *Event 6-C, Lines of Force,* the magnetic force acts upon the iron filings to show how the **lines of force** look. This is a rather traditional activity and is quite worthwhile. Note that the lines of force show attraction between unlike poles.

However, if like poles face each other, there seems to be a wall or fence formed between them. The lines of force deflect away from the like poles and show that like poles repel each other.

The iron filings hold the shape of the lines only as long as the magnets are there. Once removed, the filings are easily disturbed and lose the pattern of the lines. A more permanent picture of the lines of force can be obtained by placing waxed paper on the top of the glass and heating the wax after the filings have formed a pattern. When the wax cools, the filings will stick well enough to hold the magnetic pattern even if the paper is moved.

Another way to obtain a permanent picture of the lines of force is to substitute a sheet of paper for the wax paper and spray the filings with a fine mist of water. If the filings are kept wet for some time, they will rust quickly, forming a stain that forms a pattern on the sheet. Try to use paper that is somewhat resistant to moisture for this variation.

Magnetism Travels through Some Materials

Magnetism is a force that acts through space. We also know that it acts through certain materials as if those materials did not exist. Some materials are, therefore, "transparent" to magnetic lines of force. This principle is shown in *Event 6-D, Levitation.*

Pupils tend to guess rather quickly that there must be a magnet inside the cup. Even primary grade pupils will come to that conclusion after a few moments. That prepares them for the lesson to follow.

The purpose of this lesson is to show that magnetism is a force that extends beyond the ends of a magnet, that is, to show that there is something called a **magnetic field.** How can the magnet affect the paper clip if it does not touch it? Because the magnet sends lines of force out through space to "grab" the paper clip.

Another purpose of the lesson is directed at middle and upper grades. We see that magnetic lines of force go through some materials and are blocked by others. Since the magnet is inside the cup, it is obvious that the lines of force go through the cup (as if it did not exist) to attract the paper clip.

Placing thin sheets of paper, glass, copper, wood, aluminum foil, and plastic between the cup and clip does not affect the magnetic force. They are all transparent to the magnetic forces. A sheet of iron, however, cuts the lines of force and the paper clip falls.

Students will find that any material that is attracted to a magnet will cut the lines of force to the paper clip. Any material that is not attracted will have no effect on those forces. Given that information, ask how an object can be shielded from magnetic forces. The answer is to surround the object with a magnetic material, such as iron or steel.

One final note is directed to the primary grade teacher who wishes to be more creative in doing this event. Replace the cup with a crepe-paper "flower" in which a magnet is hidden. Cover the paper clip with tissue paper wings to transform it into a "bee."

Ask the pupils why the bee goes to the flower. Do not be surprised to hear an automatic response, "Because the bee *likes* the flower." That comment is likely to be followed by exclamations that "it is not a real bee and it is not a real flower." They soon conclude that there must be a magnet in there.

Attraction and Repulsion (Events 6-E through 6-H)

Discrepant Events and Pupil Investigations

Event 6-E. Feel Magnetic Forces

There is no substitute for actual experience. Have the pupils experiment with two magnets. Let them hold the ends together so that they can actually feel the forces of attraction and repulsion. Be sure that the force of repulsion is not overlooked. Almost all pupils know about attraction because magnets "pick things up." Many, however, are not aware that magnets also repel.

Pupil Investigations (may include the following processes):

1. Observing that like poles of a magnet repel each other and that unlike poles attract.
2. Experimenting with and feeling the forces produced by magnets.
3. Observing that the force decreases as the distance between the poles increases.

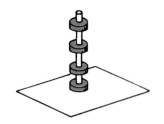

FIGURE 6.4 What causes these special rings to float when dropped on the peg?

Event 6-F. Floating Rings

Drop rings onto a peg as shown in figure 6.4. Drop them one way and they pile up neatly. Drop them another way and the rings will float. Ask the children to figure out how it is done and why the rings float.

Pupil Investigations (may include the following processes):

1. Observing and feeling the rings that float on the peg.
2. Inferring that the rings are actually magnets.
3. Analyzing the possible forces that cause the rings to float. (It is because the like poles of the magnets face and repel each other.)
4. Generalizing that when the rings do not float, it is because the unlike poles face and attract each other.

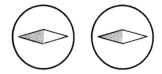

FIGURE 6.5 What rules about like and unlike poles can we discover by studying pairs of compasses?

Event 6-G. Compasses and Magnetic Forces

Let pupils observe the poles of a pair of compasses. Most compass poles are identified by color, although some have the initial N stamped on one end of the needle. Will the north pole of one compass attract the north or the south pole of another compass? (See figure 6.5.)

Pupil Investigations (may include the following processes):

1. Observing that unlike poles attract each other.
2. Verifying the initial results with other magnets and compasses.
3. Discovering that not all compasses and magnets are correctly marked.
4. Inferring that compass needles are actually floating magnets.

Event 6-H. Magnetic Mix-up

If like poles repel each other, why does the "north" magnetic pole of the compass point to the North Pole of the earth? This question produces a real dilemma. Up to this point, students have learned that like poles repel each other. In this example, however, it seems that like poles are attracting each other.

This event should be used only in the upper grades. Let students check references to see if they can solve the riddle. (See figure 6.6.)

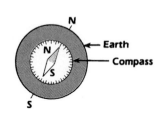

FIGURE 6.6 Is this diagram correct? Does the north pole of a compass point to the North Pole of the earth?

Pupil Investigations (may include the following processes):

1. Inferring that the north pole of a compass is really just the north-*seeking* pole (or, incorrectly, that it is really just a south pole)
2. Testing to see if a suspended bar magnet lines up the same way as the needle of a compass.
3. Verifying the results with other compasses and magnets to see if they "agree" with each other (They do not.).

Events 6-E through 6-H Explained in Context (Attraction and Repulsion)

Every magnet has a **north pole** and a **south pole.** We find that when two like poles are brought together they repel each other, but two unlike poles attract each other. This principle is presented in *Event 6-E, Feel Magnetic Forces.*

Although most pupils have handled magnets at one time or another, they probably have focused only on how two magnets "stick together" or attract each other. In this exercise they should also handle the magnets so that they experience the push or repulsion between them.

Ask if they can separate two magnets just by pulling on them, not wiggling or sliding them as they pull. Then see if they can place two like poles directly together. It will be very difficult to do so. As they try to bring the poles together, the repelling forces will push the magnets to the side.

The forces of attraction and repulsion also can be observed by suspending a bar magnet on a string and bringing other magnets close by. The results of this activity can be recorded on a table such as table 6.1. Let pupils tabulate the results of many attempts of the four possible combinations.

A sample tabulation of 24 trials is shown in table 6.1. By the time the activity is completed, it will be obvious to the pupils that *like poles repel* and *unlike poles attract.*

Event 6-F, Floating Rings, is explained by the "like poles repel" principle. The rings are really magnets with the poles on their flat surfaces. When placed over the peg with like poles facing each other, the rings repel each other and "float" in the air. If they are placed so that unlike poles face each other, the rings stick together.

Event 6-G, Compasses and Magnetic Forces, also shows the effects of attraction and repulsion. If the compasses are properly marked, we will see that unlike poles attract and like poles repel. (Compasses are not always marked correctly, so check the compasses that you plan to use for this event.)

After presenting the lessons on the poles of a magnet, a pupil may ask a question about the earth's magnetic poles. That question can be quite difficult to answer. It poses a real discrepancy: if like poles repel, why does the north pole of a compass needle point to the North Pole of the earth? (See *Event 6-H, Magnetic Mix-Up.*)

Some pupils will merely respond, "Because the compass is built to point that way." However, after spending so much time learning that like poles

TABLE 6.1

Magnetic Poles

Pole of Swinging Magnet	Pole of Hand-Held Magnet	Tabulate Numbers of Trials	
		Attract	**Repel**
North	North		⊞ (5)
North	South	⊞ II (7)	
South	South		⊞ III (8)
South	North	III (4)	

repel, the answer should be better than that. In this case it seems that like poles are attracting.

The answer is not particularly simple. You will find that the explanations vary in different textbooks. The most common explanation seems to be that the "north" pole of a compass needle is, in reality, the north-*seeking* pole. In other words, they are saying that the north pole of the compass is really a south pole!

Unfortunately, that explanation is not accurate. Just check the compass needle with a magnet. The north pole of the compass is attracted to the south pole of a magnet (if the magnet is marked correctly). To make matters worse, magnets are often incorrectly marked. In fact, you cannot rely on the accurate markings of either the magnets or compasses found in a typical elementary school.

Still, the confusion remains. What is the real answer to the question about the poles of the compass and the earth? The confusion began when compasses were originally made.

The first compasses were lodestones, or magnetic rocks. They were set on floating supports and used on ancient ships to aid in navigation. Sailors noticed that the lodestone lined up so that one end always pointed north. It was not surprising that they called that end the "north" pole. In those days they knew nothing about like poles repelling each other.

Geologists have decided that the rules of magnets can be applied accurately if the needle that points north is labeled "north," just as the early sailor had done. Then, to make all the rules agree, the point of the earth near the *north geographic* pole is, in reality, the *south magnetic* pole. (See figure 6.7.)

At any rate, it is probably just as well to avoid this discussion in the elementary school. This explanation is presented here as background information for teachers in case the question is asked by pupils.

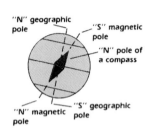

FIGURE 6.7 Strange as it may seem, the earth's south magnetic pole is located in the Northern Hemisphere. The north pole of a compass points to it, in keeping with the rule that opposite poles attract.

Temporary and Permanent Magnets

Two Kinds of Magnets

Magnets are often classified as "permanent" or "temporary." Permanent magnets retain their magnetism for long periods of time. They are used in the activities in this chapter.

A temporary magnet is one in which the magnetic force can be turned on and off by using an electric current. It is called an electromagnet and will be investigated in greater detail in the next chapter.

You can make a permanent magnet in the classroom. It requires the use of a hard steel—such as a hacksaw blade, darning needle, or a workshop file. Hold the object to be magnetized, and stroke it 20 or 30 times with a magnet. That is all it takes. The object becomes a magnet, provided it is made of the right steel.

Despite being called "permanent," such a magnet is not really permanent. It retains its magnetism only if handled with care. It can lose magnetism in several ways including (1) placing it in a powerful external magnetic field, (2) heating the magnet until it is too hot, and (3) hitting or dropping it.

How to Make a Compass

Use a magnetized needle to make a compass. Make a "raft" from a slice of cork and place the needle on it. Set the cork in a plastic or glass container and observe.

If there is no interference from magnets, metal, or electrical wires, the needle will be influenced only by the earth's field. Thus, the needle should line up in a north-south direction, just like the needle of a compass.

Combining Assessment with Instruction

Have students make a compass by using a thin sewing needle and cork as described in the last section of this chapter. Have them write a summary of why it works and how they know which end points north. What end do they label as north, and which is south? What can they say about the poles of their needle? Do they include words such as magnetic poles, domains, and field?

Sites and Software

The following websites and software are appropriate to use with this chapter. Note that computer software and websites change rapidly. This makes it necessary to investigate the stable websites for new links and software catalogs for updates. Visit www.mhhe.com/friedl6e to link to these directly and for study resources.

Sites

Mad Scientist	www.madsci.org/experiments
How Compasses Work	www.howstuffworks.com/compass.htm
SMILE Program Physics Index	www.iit.edu/~smile/physinde.html#p6
How Are Magnetic Fields Related to Sunspots?	sohowww.nascom.nasa.gov/explore/lessons/sunspots6_8.html

Software

Gizmos & Gadgets (The Learning Company) (2–6)
I (Hate) Love Science! (DK Multimedia) (2–6)
The Way Things Work: Pinball Science (DK Multimedia) (4–8)

Key Terms

lines of force, *96*   **magnetic domains,** *93*   **south magnetic pole,** *99*
magnetic field, *97*   **north magnetic pole,** *99*

Teaching Children about Static and Current Electricity

NATIONAL SCIENCE EDUCATION STANDARDS ALIGNMENT TO EVENTS

The events in this chapter help accomplish several of the NSES for content. The event(s) that align with a given content standard are listed below that standard.

LEVELS K–4

UNIFYING CONCEPTS AND PROCESSES
- Systems, order and organization
  Introduction Static versus Current

- Evidence, models and explanation
  7-N
  7-P
  7-U

- Change, consistency, measurement
  7-L through 7-M
  7-Q
  7-T through 7-V

- Evolution and equilibrium
  7-E through 7-K

SCIENCE AS INQUIRY
- Abilities necessary to do and understand scientific inquiry
  7-A and 7-X

PHYSICAL SCIENCE
- Properties of objects and materials
  7-B and 7-C

- Position and motion of objects
  7-B

- Light, heat, electricity, and magnetism
  7-A through 7-K

SCIENCE AND TECHNOLOGY
- Abilities of technological design
  7-G and 7-H
  7-K

- Understanding science and technology
  7-G and 7-H
  7-K

SCIENCE IN PERSONAL AND SOCIAL PERSPECTIVES
- Science and technology in society
  7-E

HISTORY AND NATURE OF SCIENCE
- Science as a human endeavor
  historical introduction

LEVELS 5–8

UNIFYING CONCEPTS AND PROCESSES
- Systems, order and organization
  Introduction Static versus Current to Electricity

- Evidence, models and explanation
  7-N
  7-P
  7-U
  Assessment: Things to make

- Change, consistency, measurement
  7-L through 7-M
  7-Q
  7-T through 7-V

- Evolution and equilibrium
  7-E through 7-K

- Form and function
  Build an electroscope

SCIENCE AS INQUIRY
- Abilities necessary to do and understand scientific inquiry
  7-A and 7-X

PHYSICAL SCIENCE
- Properties and changes of properties in matter
  7-B and 7-C
  7-O

- Motion and forces
  7-L through 7-X

- Transfer of energy
  7-L through 7-X

SCIENCE AND TECHNOLOGY
- Abilities of technological design
  7-M
  7-O through 7-P
  7-R through 7-V
  7-X

- Understanding science and technology
  7-V

SCIENCE IN PERSONAL AND SOCIAL PERSPECTIVES
- Risks and benefits
  7-W

- Science and technology in society
  7-N through 7-X

HISTORY AND NATURE OF SCIENCE
- Science as a human endeavor
  historical introduction

- History of science
  7-L through 7-M

From Amber to Electrons

When working with this topic, many discrepant events can be used to show pupils what static electricity is and how it works. However, let us look into some background information before beginning the activities. How did early scientists learn about static electricity?

The earliest known reference to static electricity goes back at least 2600 years. In 600 B.C. the Greeks discovered that, when rubbed, the hardened resin from a tree, called *amber,* would attract bits of lint, dust, and paper. In fact, the term **electron** comes from the Greek word *amber.*

Knowledge about static electricity did not increase very rapidly as the centuries passed. Very little new was discovered except that more and more materials were found that could be attracted to amber.

It was not until 1672 that the next real breakthrough came. Until this time it had always been necessary to charge a rod by actually rubbing it. But in that year Otto Van Guericke, a German physicist, built a machine to do the rubbing for him.

Less than 80 years later another important invention followed. Two scientists discovered the same thing at almost the same time. In 1745, E. G. Kleist, a German clergyman, and in 1746, Pieter von Musschenbroek of Holland, built devices to *store* electricity. Although Kleist's invention came earlier, it was Musschenbroek who first reported his. Thus, the invention became known as the **Leyden jar,** named for Musschenbroek's hometown in Leyden, Holland.

There is an interesting sidelight to the story of the Leyden jar. Why did scientists use a jar or bottle to store static electricity? After all, there is no reason for bottles to be used for that purpose, and today, none are used in any electronic devices.

The answer is simple. In those days, scientists thought that electricity was a form of weightless, invisible fluid. So it was natural to use a container to collect that fluid. What kinds of containers did they have? Glass jars were very common. And that is how a glass jar became the first container to store electricity.

The Leyden jar was referred to as an electrical **condenser** for much the same reason. If electricity was an invisible fluid, scientists reasoned that it might be a gas that had to be condensed. Today we still sometimes refer to tiny electronic devices that can store charges as condensers, although it is now more common to refer to them as **capacitors.**

Another leader in the field of static electricity was Benjamin Franklin. He is well known for discovering that lightning in an electrical storm is the same form of energy as the static charges that he developed in his lab.

It is important to note that Franklin was very cautious when conducting his famous kite experiment during an electrical storm. He was well aware of the danger of lightning. After all, lightning was known to kill people and start fires, so he had great respect for its power.

First of all, Franklin did not stand in the rain. He stood on dry ground under an overhanging roof. Second, the kite was attached to a thin wire, but Franklin did not touch the wire. He attached a short piece of dry string to the end of the wire, and held on to the string.

During the experiment Franklin touched an empty Leyden jar to a key that was suspended from the end of the wire. He wondered if the energy in the clouds would fill the jar with the same energy that he generated in the lab.

Was it the same as the energy he created when he rubbed amber with wool? It turned out that the charges were the same. He proved that lightning was really just a powerful form of static electricity.

Franklin was lucky that a lightning bolt did not follow the wire to where he stood. For even with his precautions, he was in great danger and could have been killed. Franklin's experiment should *never* be attempted as a school or individual project.

Franklin was responsible for perhaps the first practical use that was ever made of the research in static electricity. Scientists had worked with this form of energy for centuries, but discovered only uses that were of interest to other scientists. No practical use existed outside of the lab. What was Franklin's discovery? The *lightning rod.* He noticed that an object in the lab would quickly lose its charge if it had a pointed tip. He reasoned, therefore, that the idea might work for lightning too. He put a pointed tip on a house, connected it to a cable and anchored the cable deeply into the ground. It worked.

A lightning rod offers protection in two ways. First, electrons escape from the tip of the rod, just like they did from a pointed object in the lab. Thus, a charge that normally would form on a building will leak off instead. If the charge escapes, there is less chance that lightning will strike. Second, if lightning strikes anyway, the violent charge does not enter the building. It follows a path along a heavy copper cable straight to the ground without damaging the building.

Franklin's invention came shortly before the discovery of current electricity. Keep in mind that despite all the discoveries about static electricity, there was still no way in which it could be released in a continuous, controlled flow. Everything was still static—a charge that could be released only in a single instant. The big discoveries about current electricity were yet to come.

Charged Objects Attract Uncharged Objects (Events 7-A through 7-D)

Discrepant Events and Pupil Investigations

Event 7-A. The Balloon and Its Invisible Shelf
Rub a balloon with wool and touch the balloon to the wall. Does the balloon stay as if it were on an invisible shelf?

Pupil Investigations (may include the following processes):
1. Verifying the activity to see if pupils can also make the balloon stick to the wall.
2. Observing that the balloon does not stick unless it is rubbed.
3. Inferring a relationship between rubbing the balloon and its attraction to the wall.

Event 7-B. Make the Water Bend
Turn on a faucet so that a very thin stream of water is flowing from it. Provide a rubber or plastic comb and some wool. Ask pupils to figure out a way to get the comb to attract the water without touching it. A balloon can be used in place of the comb.

Pupil Investigations (may include the following processes):

1. Observing the water bend when the comb is held near the stream.
2. Testing to see if the experiment will work if the comb is not rubbed. (It does not.)
3. Generalizing that the rubbing does something to the comb to cause it to attract water.

Event 7-C. Pepper and Salt
Sprinkle some pepper and salt on a sheet of paper. Ask if anyone can separate the two by using just a comb (or balloon) and wool cloth.

Pupil Investigations (may include the following processes):

1. Observing that the comb attracts *both* the pepper and the salt.
2. Predicting that slight taps of the comb will cause the salt to drop off before the pepper does.
3. Comparing the heights at which the pepper and salt are attracted.

Event 7-D. Twist the Straw
Take a plastic straw and hang it from a pencil inside a wide-mouth bottle, as shown in figure 7.1. Charge a comb or balloon with wool and hold it close to the glass. Observe. What happens to the straw when you move the comb or balloon around the bottle?

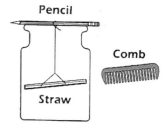

Pupil Investigations (may include the following processes):

1. Predicting that the straw will be unaffected by the comb.
2. Observing that the straw is unaffected when the comb is not charged.
3. Observing that the straw is pulled (attracted) to a charged comb.
4. Generalizing that an uncharged object (the straw) is attracted to a charged object (the comb).

FIGURE 7.1   What happens to the suspended straw when a charged comb is brought near?

Events 7-A through 7-D Explained in Context (Charged Objects Attract Uncharged Objects)

What Causes Static Charges?
A typical explanation of this event usually includes a statement that the charges are caused by rubbing. That is not the complete answer. The charges are actually caused by bringing the right substances close together. Rubbing is just a way to accomplish this task.

Some substances tend to gain electrons easily while other substances tend to lose them easily. Thus, when two such different substances are brought close to each other (by rubbing, for example), the electrons move from one to the other.

When an object has an equal number of electrons and protons, it has no static charge. It is neutral. If it gains electrons, it has a surplus of them and the object has a **negative charge.** When an object loses electrons, it has a shortage of them and has a **positive charge.**

When working with static electricity, one word of caution is needed. Weather conditions can have a major effect on experiments with such charges.

The activities work best on cold winter days. (It is easy to get shocks, on those days, just by shuffling across a rug and touching a metal object—or another person.) Warm and humid days in the summer are the very worst for such experiments.

The reason for the problems during warm weather is that moisture can carry charges. Thus, moisture in the air will discharge negative and positive charges quickly on a warm day. In winter, when the air is cold, it is very dry. On warm summer days, even when it appears to be dry, the air carries much more moisture than on any cold winter day.

Charged Objects Attract Uncharged Objects

Let us see what objects can be charged and what effects these objects have on uncharged objects. With little effort we can see that many things can be charged and attracted. In fact, almost anything will generate a charge of some sort when rubbed. Even liquids and gases can be charged; and just about anything can be attracted, including solids, liquids, and gases.

It is easy to demonstrate static charges in the elementary classroom. For example, in *Event 7-A, The Balloon and Its Invisible Shelf*, the balloon is given a strong negative charge when rubbed with wool. It is attracted to the uncharged wall. The balloon often sticks for hours because the electrons do not move very well on the balloon. (In other words, the balloon is a poor conductor.)

Eventually, however, the electrons migrate from the balloon to the wall. When this happens, the charge is lost (or neutralized) and the balloon falls to the floor. As stated earlier, the charges are lost much more quickly on warm, moist days than on cold winter days.

It should be noted that it does not matter *what* charge, negative or positive, is placed on the balloon. If it is given a positive charge (by rubbing it with silk to remove electrons) the event will also work. However, it is easier to get a strong negative charge than positive charge, so best results are obtained by using wool.

In *Event 7-B, Make the Water Bend*, we see another example of an object being attracted by a charged object. The negatively charged comb or balloon attracts the uncharged stream of water. With some practice the water can be pulled dramatically off course. (See figure 7.2.)

The purpose of *Event 7-C, Pepper and Salt*, is to show two more examples of materials that are attracted by a charged object. Both the salt and pepper are attracted, so how can they be separated? The grains of pepper are lighter than the salt so the pepper is attracted first. Also, if both substances are on the comb or balloon, the salt tends to drop off, with light tapping, before the pepper.

The final example of the attraction between a charged object and an uncharged object is shown in *Event 7-D, Twist the Straw*. When the comb or balloon is charged, the plastic straw is attracted. The reason that it is so noticeable is that the suspended straw can be moved very easily.

All the events in this section show that many different materials can be attracted by static electricity. Perhaps your pupils will discover additional examples of that principle.

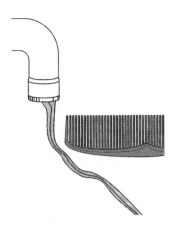

FIGURE 7.2 A charged comb will attract a stream of water.

Like Charges Repel (Events 7-E through 7-H)

Discrepant Events and Pupil Investigations

Event 7-E. Attraction or Repulsion?

Rub a comb or balloon with wool, and ask pupils to decide what will happen when the comb or balloon is brought near to (but not touching) a pith ball hanging on a thread. (A *pith ball* is very sensitive to static charges, and can be obtained from a science supply house—or from the inside of a mature stalk of corn. Another replacement for pith balls is to spray aluminum paint found in local hardware stores onto Ping-Pong balls.)

After the students make a prediction, bring the comb or balloon near the ball to show that there is an attraction. Do this several times to be sure that the attraction is seen by all. Then do the activity once more and allow the comb or balloon to touch the ball.

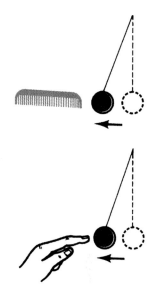

FIGURE 7.3   A charged comb will attract the pith ball. When the ball is charged, it will be attracted to your hand.

After the comb or balloon and ball touch for a moment, the ball jumps away. The two *repel* each other! The activity is quite surprising to most pupils. One additional feature can be added to this event if you wish. Show that sometimes the ball is (and sometimes is not) attracted to your hand. (See figure 7.3.)

Pupil Investigations (may include the following processes):

1. Predicting the action of the ball in various circumstances.
2. Observing that the comb attracts the pith ball as long as they do not touch each other.
3. Demonstrating that once the comb and ball touch, they repel each other.
4. Concluding that the ball is attracted to your hand only after the ball has been touched by the comb.
5. Forming a theory about the attraction and repulsion of static charges.

Event 7-F. Fill the Stocking

Let pupils decide how to fill a silk or nylon stocking *without putting anything into it*.

Then let them decide how to "empty" it. Have available a polyethylene bag.

Pupil Investigations (may include the following processes):

1. Observing that the stocking "fills out" when rubbed with the polyethylene bag.
2. Experimenting with a variety of materials.
3. Inferring that the effect is caused by the repulsion of like charges.
4. Discovering that the stocking is "emptied" by running your hand along the entire length of the stocking.

Event 7-G. Leaping Leaves

Let pupils decide how to make the leaves of an electroscope spread apart. (An **electroscope** is a device that can detect static charges.) Have a comb and a woolen cloth available for pupils to use. If pupils succeed in causing the leaves to move apart, ask them to find a way to cause them to return to normal again. (See "How to Build an Electroscope" at the end of this chapter.)

Pupil Investigations (may include the following processes):

1. Discovering that the comb influences the leaves even before the comb touches the knob on top of the electroscope.
2. Observing that when a charged comb touches the electroscope knob, the leaves spread apart.
3. Discovering that the leaves are also attracted when the comb is held near the glass side of the electroscope.
4. Demonstrating that the leaves collapse when the knob is touched with a finger.
5. Generalizing that the comb gives the leaves like charges, and that like charges repel.

Event 7-H. Newspaper Electroscope

Cut a long, thin strip of newspaper and hang it over the edge of a ruler as shown in figure 7.4. Ask pupils to see if they can make the paper act just like the leaves of the electroscope. Provide pupils with woolen cloth.

Pupil Investigations (may include the following processes):

1. Experimenting by rubbing the paper with a cloth to see if the leaves spread apart.
2. Inferring that the movement of the paper is similar to the movement of the leaves of the electroscope in Event 7-G.
3. Testing to see if other substances can be used in place of paper.

FIGURE 7.4 How can the thin strips of newspaper be made to act like the leaves of an electroscope?

Events 7-E through 7-H Explained in Context (Like Charges Repel)

We have seen that a charged object, either negative or positive, will attract an uncharged object. But what happens when two like charges are brought close together? *Event 7-E, Attraction or Repulsion?*, shows what can happen. The sequence of six steps in that activity is shown in figure 7.5. Let us go over the steps one by one:

1. When a charged comb is held near the ball, there is an attraction between them, because *a charged object (comb) attracts an uncharged object (ball).*
2. As soon as the comb touches the ball, the charge moves from the comb to the ball. Now both have the same charge.
3. Once the ball has the same charge as the comb, the ball jumps away because *like charges repel each other.*
4. If your hand is held near the ball, the ball is attracted to the hand because *a charged object (ball) is attracted to the uncharged object (hand).*
5. When the ball touches the hand, the ball is discharged (or "neutralized," or "grounded"). Your body is so large that it acts as a reservoir that is able to absorb any excess electrons on the ball. (Be sure to show that an uncharged ball is neither attracted nor repelled by the hand. The attraction occurs only when the ball is charged.)

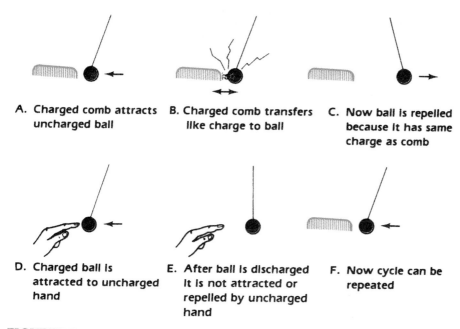

A. **Charged comb attracts uncharged ball**

B. **Charged comb transfers like charge to ball**

C. **Now ball is repelled because it has same charge as comb**

D. **Charged ball is attracted to uncharged hand**

E. **After ball is discharged it is not attracted or repelled by uncharged hand**

F. **Now cycle can be repeated**

FIGURE 7.5   The steps of the attraction-repulsion activity are explained.

6. Once the ball is discharged, the entire sequence can be repeated. The ball is again attracted to the charged comb. The conditions are again the same as they were in step 1.

The little balls can be made with a variety of materials. The best are *pith* balls (made from the inside of corn stalks). Other materials that can be used are Ping-Pong balls sprayed with aluminum paint, puffed wheat, puffed rice, bits of foam plastic, or carbon ends of burnt matches, and probably many other things. If a tiny bit of foil is wrapped around the pith ball, the responses will be very rapid.

Without the foil, the ball is a poor conductor and electrons are gained or lost slowly: the ball "hugs" the plastic comb for a moment or two before it is repelled. When it is coated with foil, however, it jumps away at once.

Event 7-F, Fill the Stocking, works best when the toe of a nylon stocking is held against a wall and the polyethylene is rubbed down along the stocking against the wall. (You can tell if a plastic bag is polyethylene by its stretch. If it stretches easily, it is probably polyethylene.)

Pull the stocking off the wall and hold it up to see if it "fills out." Since all fibers of the stocking have the same charge, all the fibers repel each other into a round shape, causing the "filling" action. The stocking can be "emptied" again by merely pulling it loosely through your fingers. Your fingers and hand will neutralize the charge on the stocking.

Event 7-G, Leaping Leaves, shows another example of how like charges repel. The leaves of the electroscope move apart when the knob on top is touched with either a positive or negative charge.

As the charge is placed on the knob, it travels down to the leaves. Since both leaves receive the same charge, they are repelled and move apart from each other. The leaves collapse again when the charge is neutralized. That can be done easily by just touching the knob with your finger.

Even strips of newspaper, as used in *Event 7-H, Newspaper Electroscope,* can be used as an electroscope. An electroscope is a device that detects a static charge. Rub the newspaper with wool and you will notice that the paper, at first, seems to stick together. However, as soon as a small space develops between the leaves, they jump apart. Again, the newspaper event shows that like charges repel each other.

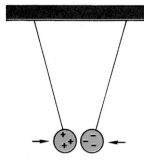

FIGURE 7.6   Unlike charges attract each other.

Unlike Charges Attract (Events 7-I and 7-J)

Discrepant Events and Pupil Investigations

Event 7-I. Unlike Charges Attract #1

Charge one pith ball with a glass rod rubbed with silk. Charge another pith ball with a plastic rod rubbed with wool or fur. Slowly bring the two suspended balls close together. What happens? (See figure 7.6.)

Pupil Investigations (may include the following processes):

1. Observing that the balls attract each other.
2. Comparing the attraction to that observed when an uncharged object was brought near a charged object.
3. Experimenting to discover that one ball is attracted and the other is repelled by a charged rod.
4. Forming a theory that the balls carry unlike charges and that such charges attract each other.
5. Discovering that after the balls touch, they are neutral.

Event 7-J. Unlike Charges Attract #2

Suspend two balloons with string about 3 inches apart. Rub one balloon with silk (to give it a positive charge) and the other balloon with wool (to give it a negative charge). When the second balloon has been charged, carefully release it and observe.

Pupil Investigations (may include the following processes):

1. Observing that the two balloons are drawn toward each other.
2. Forming a theory that the two balloons have unlike charges.
3. Discovering that after the balloons touch (and maybe stick together for a while) they separate again.

Events 7-I and 7-J Explained in Context (Unlike Charges Attract)

We have seen that (1) charged objects attract uncharged objects and (2) like charges repel each other. The third fundamental law of static electricity states that *unlike charges attract each other.* This law is shown in both events in this section.

In *Event 7-I, Unlike Charges Attract #1,* one pith ball is given a positive charge when touched by the glass rod; the other ball takes on a negative charge when touched by the plastic rod. The attraction between these two balls is greater than the attraction either ball has toward an uncharged object.

The same principle is shown in *Event 7-J, Unlike Charges Attract #2*. When the balloons are given opposite charges, they attract each other.

It is not particularly important for pupils to memorize which object receives what charge. Instead, they should focus on the three basic principles of static charges presented in this chapter.

Charging by Induction (Event 7-K)

Discrepant Event and Pupil Investigations

Event 7-K. Induce a Charge

Follow these steps to induce a static charge on an object:

1. Bring a negatively charged rod *near*, but not touching, an object.
2. Ground (neutralize) the object with your finger. Negative charges leave the object.
3. Remove the ground (your finger).
4. Remove the rod. The object now has a charge. Which charge is it?

Pupil Investigations (may include the following processes):

1. Experimenting with charged glass and plastic rods to determine what charge the object has.
2. Contrasting the charge with another object that is charged by contact instead of by induction.
3. Generalizing that charging by induction gives a charge opposite to that which is given when charging by contact.

Event 7-K Explained in Context (Charging by Induction)

Induction is usually not taught in the elementary grades. However, it is something that a gifted pupil might find challenging.

We saw earlier that when an object is charged by contact, the object receives the same charge as the rod. However, when charging an object by induction, it gets the opposite charge. This is shown in *Event 7-J, Induce a Charge*.

In this particular example the negatively charged rod is brought near to, but not touching, the ball. The negative charge on the rod repels the negative charge on the ball. Thus, when you touch the ball with your finger, the repelled electrons have a chance to escape. When these electrons have gone (which is almost instantly), you can remove your finger. Then the charged rod can also be removed. With the electrons gone, the charge that remains is positive. (See figure 7.7.)

If a positively charged rod is used instead of a negatively charged rod, the electrons will enter the ball instead of leave it. Thus, the ball would get a negative charge.

Notice that by induction we get a charge that is opposite to the charge on the rod, while by contact we get a charge that is the same as the one on the rod.

How to Build an Electroscope

An electroscope is a device that detects a static charge. You can make an electroscope by using a bottle or flask, a cork or rubber stopper, a coat hanger wire, and some foil. (See figure 7.8.)

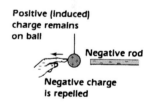

FIGURE 7.7   Charge by induction. When a negatively charged rod is brought near the grounded ball, a positive charge is induced.

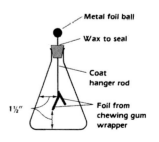

FIGURE 7.8   A simple electroscope.

Heat the bottle in an oven (on low heat) or on a radiator to be sure that it is totally dry. Otherwise it will not work. Insert the wire through the cork or one-hole stopper as shown in the diagram. Use wax to seal the wire where it passes through the cork or stopper. Be sure that you bend the wire that is inside the bottle so that two leaves can be hung alongside each other.

For the leaves, use very thin foil, such as is found on some chewing gum wrappers. It is thinner and more sensitive than regular kitchen foil (although kitchen foil will work if necessary). Be sure to peel away the paper backing from the gum foil.

To make the electroscope most sensitive, cut two leaves and hang them on separate supports (instead of making one long leaf and bending it in the middle to make two leaves). Best results are obtained when the end of each leaf is bent and hung loosely on the support. Do not fasten the end of the leaves solidly to the support. Just drape the ends loosely over the wires.

Finally, take some foil (kitchen foil is fine), form it into a ball, and press it around the top of the wire. Why? Do you remember the discovery by Benjamin Franklin? He found that charges leak away from sharp objects quickly. The wire is a sharp object and it would cause the electroscope to lose whatever charge that was put on it. You can get rid of the sharp object by merely fastening a round ball of foil to it. In that way, the charges stay inside the bottle and can be measured.

The Discovery of Current Electricity

The history of current electricity goes back to the late 1700s when two Italian scientists became involved in a great debate. Luigi Galvani, a doctor of medicine, made a startling discovery while dissecting a frog. He noticed that the frog's leg twitched while he was dissecting it.

Since the frog was dead, what caused the twitch? The leg could be made to twitch when sparks crackled from a static electricity machine nearby or during an electrical storm, so Galvani concluded that the twitch must be related to electricity.

After many further attempts, Galvani could get the frog's leg to twitch even when the weather was nice. Finally, Galvani reported his findings and advanced the theory that the electricity came from the frog. He called it "animal electricity."

Galvani was a respected scientist and his report was widely accepted by the scientific community. However, there was one notable exception—a young Italian physicist named Alessandro Giuseppe Antonio Anastasia Volta. He insisted that the source of the twitch was not in the frog, but outside it.

Volta showed that the muscular twitch could not be produced unless dissimilar metals were used in the dissecting knife and probe. He claimed that it was not the frog's leg but the dissimilar metals that caused the twitch, and he called the energy "contact electricity."

Galvani checked and double-checked his work. Eventually, he was able to get the frog's leg to twitch even when he used similar metals in the knife and probe. This appeared to overcome Volta's objections. Volta, however, countered with evidence that the similar metals had to be dissimilar in some way for the leg to twitch. He still insisted that the energy came from the dissimilarity in the metals, not the frog.

Finally, Galvani countered with a startling and convincing new discovery. He got rid of the metals altogether! He was able to get the leg to twitch by just touching the end of one nerve to the end of another. The proof seemed overwhelming: if nothing else was used, the energy *must* have come from the frog. It must be animal electricity! In the face of Galvani's discovery, what could Volta do? Amazingly, he got rid of the frog!

Volta used only dissimilar metals in a liquid, and produced an even greater discovery. In fact, it was overwhelming! It wiped away all debate. By using only dissimilar metals, a large amount of energy was produced. *He had discovered current electricity!*

Remember that scientists working with static electricity had looked for current electricity for centuries. Now Volta had found it. Keep in mind that with static electricity, the energy could be discharged only in a flash or spark. It was not a continuous current. (Even the words "static" and "current" describe the differences between the two types of electricity.)

Volta's discovery was so spectacular that it swept the scientific world by storm. First of all, it was easy for any scientist around the world to duplicate. (In comparison, Galvani's work required a surgeon's skill to duplicate.) Second, Volta produced a large amount of energy, not just something to make a frog's leg twitch.

The story of the two Italian scientists has a sad ending. Galvani admitted the greatness of Volta's discovery but suffered a personal loss of face. He felt disgraced by having led so many of his friends on a false path. He died within a year, a broken man.

However, the story does not end there. Had Galvani been able to look into the future, he would have been pleasantly surprised. Today we know that an electrical current *does* come from individual cells! For example, the *electrocardiogram* and the *electroencephalogram* are measurements of the electricity produced by the cells in the heart and brain, respectively. Also, electricity produced by our body's pacemaker regulates the ticking of the heart. It turns out that Galvani was right after all. In fact, they were *both* right!

What Is Current Electricity? (Events 7-L and 7-M)

Discrepant Events and Pupil Investigations

Event 7-L. The Mysterious Marble.

Arrange a row of marbles as shown in figure 7.9. Snap a marble against one end of the row. What happens to the other marbles? How does the activity relate to current electricity?

Pupil Investigations (may include the following processes):

1. Observing that the last marble moves away as soon as the first marble strikes the front of the row.
2. Inferring that the energy moves through the marbles instantly.
3. Comparing the movement of marbles to the movement of electrons in a conductor.

FIGURE 7.9 What happens when a marble is snapped into the row?

FIGURE 7.10 Use this device to test the conductivity of materials.

Event 7-M. Conduction Tester

Set up an arrangement as shown in figure 7.10. Place the material to be tested across the gap between the two terminals on the board. If the bulb lights up, the material is a conductor; if it does not light, the material is a nonconductor.

Pupil Investigations (may include the following processes):

1. Testing various substances to see if they are conductors.
2. Classifying materials into conductors and nonconductors.
3. Generalizing that all metals are conductors.

Events 7-L and 7-M Explained in Context (What Is Current Electricity?)

Difference between Static and Current Electricity

The work of Volta and Galvani opened up a spectacular new field in science. Prior to this time there was only static electricity with little practical value. Now there was current electricity!

In **static electricity,** the energy that accumulated in objects was stationary, moving only during the instant of discharge, often appearing as a spark or flash. Static electricity had a few interesting lab applications but provided almost no practical uses. Franklin's lightning rod was about the only exception.

By contrast, **current electricity** was a *continuous controlled flow of electrons,* kept moving by a kind of electrical "pressure" between dissimilar metals. This continuous flow was soon harnessed to do useful work. Today current electricity is used for heat, light, motors, electronics, and many other applications.

At one time electricity was believed to be an invisible, weightless fluid, so fine that it passed through the densest materials in conductors. Words expressing the early thinking can even be found today. For example, the movement of electricity is referred to as a "current" or "flow," and electricians still refer to it as "juice."

How Do Electrons Flow?

Electrical current moves along a conductor at great speed. Yet there is relatively little motion by the individual electrons within the conductor. The action is similar to pushing beans through a bean shooter. When the shooter is full, you only need to push one bean into one end of the shooter to cause another bean to immediately come out of the other end. The individual beans do not move very much, but the motion goes all the way through.

A good way to show the motion of electrons is to do *Event 7-L, The Mysterious Marble.* Place a few marbles in the groove of a ruler or between two rulers, and roll another marble so that it strikes the others in the row. As soon as the first marble strikes the row, the end marble jumps away. As with the bean shooter example, the energy moves through the row quickly, but the individual marbles do not move very much.

Some electrical currents are large, some small. Some currents have great pressure, others do not. Currents flow through some substances easily, but not through others. There are special terms used to describe the flow of current. These terms are listed in table 7.1. In the table, the electrical units are also compared to water to help us understand the meaning of the terms.

TABLE 7.1

Electrical Terms

Term	Defined	Compared to Water
Volt	Potential difference or electrical pressure (volts are equal to amps times ohms)	Water pressure in pounds per square inch
Ampere (Amp)	A unit of current flow, (one amp will light a 100-watt bulb)	Liters per second
Ohm	Resistance depends on the composition, length, thickness, and temperature of a substance	Resistance of the pipe
Coulomb	A specific quantity of charge (6 billion, billion electrons)	A specific number of gallons such as "5 liters"

What Is a Conductor?

An electrical current does not travel through all materials. Substances that are good carriers of electricity are called **conductors.** Those that are very poor carriers are called **nonconductors.** What are some good conductors? *Event 7-M, Conduction Tester,* is designed to help children find out. A substance that is a good conductor will allow the current to flow. You will know if the current flows because it lights the bulb. All metals are good enough conductors to light the bulb, but the best common conductors are copper and aluminum.

Even better conductors are uncommon gold and silver. Those precious metals are far too expensive to be widely used. They are used only in places where amounts needed are small, where extreme conductivity is required, and where the product is very expensive. Gold and silver are used in space satellites, and silver is sometimes used in computers and sophisticated electronic devices.

The atoms that allow current to flow are those with a number of free or loosely held electrons. Copper, for example, has 29 electrons. Twenty-eight are held tightly in the first three atomic shells. However, the last one is all by itself in the fourth shell. This single loose electron is the one that transmits electrical energy.

Materials that are nonconductors include paper, rubber, plastic, glass, and wood. Nonconductors are also called **insulators.**

Caution: Under no circumstances should house current be used with any of the demonstrations or explorations.

Sources of Electricity (Events 7-N through 7-P)

Discrepant Events and Pupil Investigations

Event 7-N. Current from Coins

This is a good activity if you can get an old silver dime, minted in 1964 or earlier. Clean the dime and a penny in detergent. Drop them into a dish or tray,

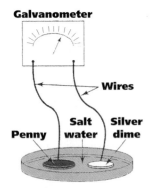

Galvanometer

Wires

Penny   **Salt water**   **Silver dime**

FIGURE 7.11 A penny and a silver dime will produce an electric current when they are soaked in salt water.

and pour in enough salt water to cover the coins. Connect alligator clips to each coin and the other ends to the voltage sensor ends. Connect the voltage sensor to the computer or calculator. A galvanometer can be used in place of the voltage sensor. (A **galvanometer** is a device that can detect very tiny electrical currents.) Observe the meter or sensor. What happens? Reverse the coins and observe the meter or sensor again. What happens? (See figure 7.11.)

Pupil Investigations (may include the following processes):

1. Observing that the meter or sensor reading changes when the coins are touched with the wires.
2. Discovering that the meter or sensor changes in the opposite direction when the coins are reversed.
3. Experimenting to see the effects of different metals and coins.
4. Forming a theory about the source of the electrical energy.
5. Comparing results when using distilled water instead of salt water.

Event 7-O. Potato Power!

Insert a copper strip and a zinc strip into a raw potato, and attach wires from the strips to a galvanometer or voltage sensor. (Zinc can be obtained by cutting up the outside shell of a dry cell; both metals can be obtained from a science supply house and from some hardware stores.) What does the galvanometer or voltage sensor read? Use different materials and observe the reaction on the meter.

Pupil Investigations (may include the following processes):

1. Observing that the meter is deflected when the strips are inserted into the potato.
2. Experimenting with different substances to see which will produce electrical current.
3. Forming a theory about the source of the current.

Event 7-P. Current from a Coil?

Wrap about 25 turns of bell wire around a tin can or box of salt, and carefully remove the wire. You now have a coil. In making the coil, leave the ends long enough to attach to a galvanometer or the MBL/CBL voltage sensor. If using the voltage sensor, attach it to the computer. (**Caution:** Remember to keep magnets away from the computer and disks.) Allow the magnet to drop through the coil without hitting the floor. Repeat several times. Push a magnet through the coil and observe the meter. Then pull out the magnet and observe the meter again. Turn the magnet around and try again. Observe the results. (See figure 7.12.)

Pupil Investigations (may include the following processes):

1. Observing that the needle of the meter moves one way when the magnet is pushed in and the other when the magnet is pulled out.
2. Discovering that when the magnet is reversed the readings are reversed.
3. Comparing the size of the meter reading with the speed of the magnet's insertion into the coil.

4. Observing that the meter shows pulses of energy instead of a continuous flow.
5. Forming a theory about the source of energy.
6. Describing the graph of one pass of the magnet through the coil.
7. Observing what happens as two bar magnets are taped together as one long magnet.
8. Predicting what will happen when both south poles are taped together end to end and then passed through the coil.
9. Comparing the readings as the number of coil turns is increased or decreased.

Events 7-N through 7-P Explained in Context (Sources of Electricity)

There are several different sources of electricity. They are listed in table 7.2. Some sources are fairly easy to duplicate, especially the chemical and electromotive sources, but others are more complex. It is generally too difficult to produce photoelectric and piezoelectric sources of electricity in the elementary classroom, although some examples can be shown. The electrothermal source is somewhat less difficult to produce but is still not easy. See figure 7.13 for details on setting up the activity.

If you do not have a CBL/MBL voltage sensor or galvanometer, it is possible to make one using a coil and a good compass. Just wrap about 20 to 30 turns of bell wire around a compass, leaving the ends about half a meter long. Attach the free ends to the metal strips in the potato. If the compass is held carefully, so that the needle is floating freely, it is often sensitive enough to detect the current that comes from the potato.

Chemical Sources of Electricity

The first kind of current electricity that was discovered was a chemical source. The energy comes mostly from dissimilar metals, but can also include some nonmetals such as carbon. The basic energy comes from atomic differences within substances.

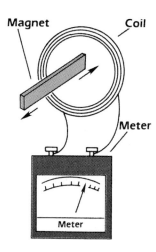

FIGURE 7.12 What happens when the magnet is inserted into the coil?

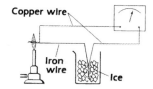

FIGURE 7.13 When dissimilar metals (wires) are heated and cooled at different points of the circuit, an electric current is produced.

TABLE 7.2

Sources of Electricity

Source	Examples
Chemical (or electrochemical)	Dry cell, potato battery, wet cell, silver dime and a penny
Mechanical (or electromotive)	Coils and magnet
Heat (or electrothermal)	Thermocouple
Light (or photoelectric)	Electric eye, photo cell, solar cell, light meter
Pressure (or piezoelectric)	Crystal detectors for radios, microphones, and headsets

Some substances tend to lose electrons easily. Other substances tend to gain electrons easily. When there is a path between the two types of substances, the electrons will move from one to the other. That movement is called an **electrical current.**

Volta produced electricity using a chemical source. *Event 7-N, Current from Coins,* is a fairly good example of Volta's original cell. If the event is done correctly, the energy from the penny and dime is quite apparent on the meter.

If the old silver dimes are not available, you can use other metals such as zinc, aluminum, brass, or tin. Experiment to see which metals produce the best currents. Another version, as shown in figure 7.14, is to use strips of copper and zinc in beakers of salt water.

The cell shown in *Event 7-O, Potato Power!,* is still another example of getting electricity from a chemical source. The moisture inside the potato conducts the current produced by the dissimilar metals.

In a sense, the potato cell is really a form of dry cell. A dry cell is not *really* dry inside. It is called "dry" because it can be tipped over and the moisture inside will not spill or leak out. The potato cell works in the same way. Regardless of how the potato is held, it does not spill.

In the place of a potato, you may use a lemon. In fact, a lemon works better in some ways. The lemon juice is a better conductor, so it produces a somewhat stronger current. Unfortunately, the juices tend to run and drip.

Electromotive Source of Electricity

The most common source of electricity today is not chemical. It is electromotive. That is the form that is generated by power stations and sent to your homes.

It is easier to understand this form of electricity by performing *Event 7-P, Current from a Coil?* In the activity, a magnet is thrust into and out of a coil of wire. When this happens, a current is produced in the coil and can be seen on the meter. The current created in the coil of wire when a magnet passes through the coil is called magnetic induction of current and was discovered in 1831 by an English scientist named Michael Faraday.

Note that the meter or voltage sensor readings move in one direction when the magnet is pushed into the coil but goes the opposite direction when the magnet is pulled out. Then, when the magnet is reversed, the readings are reversed also. This shows that polarity and direction affect the direction of the

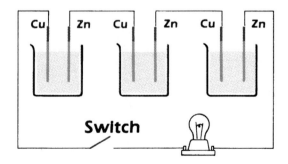

FIGURE 7.14   Wet cells, made of dissimilar metals dipped into salt water, produce an electrical current.

current. The current that is produced in this way is called *alternating current (AC)*. All other sources of electricity produce *direct current (DC)*.

Today most of our electrical energy comes from magnets and coils. Of course, the magnets and coils in a power station are so much larger and more complex that we would not recognize them as being similar to the ones in our simple experiment.

Circuits (Events 7-Q through 7-V)

Discrepant Events and Pupil Investigations

Event 7-Q. Nervousness Tester

Insert a screw eye into a board and attach it to a buzzer, battery, and probe. Set it up as shown in figure 7.15. How steady is your hand? Can you insert the probe into the screw eye without touching its sides? If you can, all is quiet. If not, the buzzer goes off to signal your error. (You can substitute a bulb for the buzzer. The buzzer provides a greater class response initially, but the noise may become annoying.) How does the device work?

Pupil Investigations (may include the following processes):

1. Experimenting with the probe to see how it works.
2. Discovering that when the probe touches the screw eye, the buzzer goes off.
3. Generalizing that when the probe touches the screw eye, it completes an electrical path.

Event 7-R. Light the Bulb

Divide the class into teams of two to four pupils. Provide each team with a dry cell, two short pieces of wire (20 to 40 centimeters long), and a 3-volt flashlight bulb. After they have the supplies, ask the pupils to "light up the bulb."

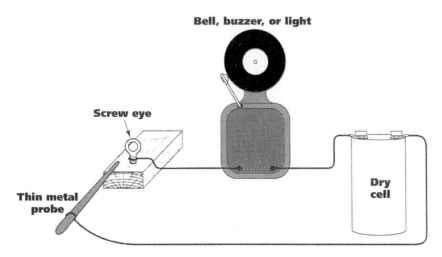

FIGURE 7.15   If you insert the probe into the screw eye and touch it, the buzzer will sound.

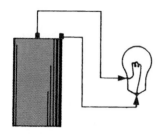

FIGURE 7.16 To light the bulb, one wire must touch the metal housing (side); the other must touch the metal tip (bottom).

Although the correct diagram is given in figure 7.16, do not show it to the pupils at this time. They will quickly learn the right way by trial and error. (**Caution:** Most pupils will probably "short out" the wires in their attempts to light up the bulb. Tell them that if a wire gets hot, to disconnect immediately and try another way.)

Pupil Investigations (may include the following processes):

1. Experimenting with wires connected in various ways.
2. Discovering that some connections cause the wires to get hot.
3. Demonstrating that when the bulb lights up the wires remain cool.
4. Visualizing the path of electrons through the circuit.

Event 7-S. Stop and Go Signals for Electricity (Switches)

Distribute strips of flexible metal. You may get them by cutting up an aluminum can, but do so only *if you can be sure that all sharp edges have been filed smooth.* Otherwise, acceptable strips can be made from folded layers of aluminum foil.

Ask students if they can find a way to make a switch that will automatically turn off the current if a person leaves it. Set up a simple circuit with bulb and battery and two wires. Ask them to place the strip between the wires so that they function as an automatic switch.

Pupil Investigations (may include the following processes):

1. Experimenting with different ways of turning the current on and off.
2. Comparing ideas with one another to see if any plan will actually work out successfully.
3. Inferring a relationship between the switch and the pathways of electricity.

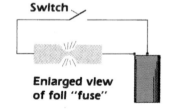

FIGURE 7.17 The gum wrapper "fuse" melts when too much energy is sent through it.

Event 7-T. Pop the Fuse

Cut a piece of foil from a used gum wrapper into the shape shown in figure 7.17. (Do not strip the paper backing from the foil.) Touch the wires from a 6-volt battery to the ends of the foil. Can you melt the foil?

Pupil Investigations (may include the following processes):

1. Experimenting with various sizes to see if they melt.
2. Observing that the foil melts if it is thin enough.
3. Generalizing that the foil acts as a fuse.

Event 7-U. Series and Parallel Circuits

Divide the class into teams of two to four pupils. Provide each team with two dry cells, four short pieces of wire (20 to 40 centimeters long), and two 3-volt flashlight bulbs. It is easy to connect the wires incorrectly. If you do, the wires will get hot and quickly drain the batteries. To avoid this, be sure to warn the pupils to disconnect at once and try another way.

This event can be used in middle and upper grades. Ask the teams to do the following activities:

1. Light one bulb with two cells. Compare series wiring with parallel wiring. Put the diagram in figure 7.18 on the chalkboard.
2. Light up two bulbs with one dry cell using series and parallel wiring. Put the diagram in figure 7.19 on the chalkboard.
3. Obtain the brightest and dimmest arrangements using two bulbs and two cells. (Do not put figure 7.20 on the chalkboard at this time. If pupils understand the first two parts of the event, they will get it right without the diagram.)

Pupil Investigations (may include the following processes):

1. Comparing series with parallel wiring of cells.
2. Comparing series with parallel wiring of bulbs.
3. Experimenting to find the brightest combinations of two cells and two bulbs.

Event 7-V. Quiz Board

Build a quiz board so that the front of it is set up as shown in figure 7.21. Ask pupils to answer the simple questions. When they answer correctly, the bulb lights up. (In place of a bulb, you can use a buzzer.) Ask pupils how the quiz board works. Have them assemble in committees to make a diagram predicting how the wires in the back of the quiz board might look. (Do not show the back of the board to the class at this time.)

Pupil Investigations (may include the following processes):

1. Discovering that when the question is matched with the correct answer, the bulb lights up.
2. Inferring that when the bulb lights up, a circuit is closed.
3. Diagramming the hidden back side of the board to explain how it works.

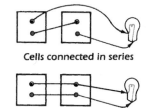

Cells connected in series

Cells connected in parallel

FIGURE 7.18   Top view of two cells connected in series and in parallel.

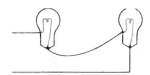

Bulbs in series

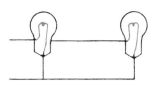

Bulbs in parallel

FIGURE 7.19   The top bulbs are connected in series; the lower in parallel.

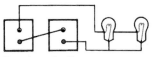

Top view of cells

FIGURE 7.20   Bulbs connected in parallel with batteries connected in series produce the most light.

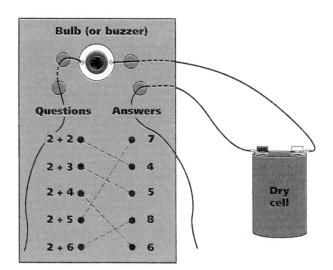

FIGURE 7.21   A quiz board. The dotted lines show how the wires are connected in back of the board.

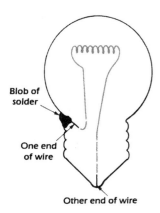

FIGURE 7.22 A bulb is a wire surrounded by glass. Connect the ends to a dry cell to get the bulb to light up.

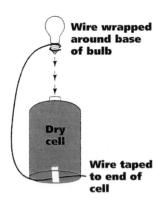

FIGURE 7.23 An example of a simple circuit to get a bulb to light up. Be sure to use a bulb that is matched to the voltage of the cell.

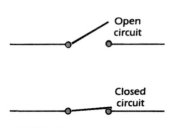

FIGURE 7.24 In which circuit is the electricity turned on?

Events 7-Q through 7-V Explained in Context (Circuits)

What Is a Circuit?

Before a current can travel anywhere, it must have a path to follow. A complete path, called a **circuit,** starts at the energy source, flows through a conductor, and returns to the energy source. *Events 7-Q, Nervousness Tester,* and *7-R, Light the Bulb,* are both designed to help pupils understand a simple circuit. In each case, when the circuit is completed, something happens. When the probe touches the screw eye, the electrical path is completed so that the buzzer goes off. When the wires between the bulb and battery are connected properly, the bulb lights up.

The event with the bulb is often a problem at first, but encourage pupils to experiment and most will get the bulb to light up. Then ask them to visualize, or mentally trace, the path taken by the current.

In their experiments, pupils will undoubtedly make incorrect connections before finally getting it right. That is permissible, of course, but needs a word of caution. An incorrect connection will cause the wires to get hot and can burn out a dry cell if left on too long. A simple remedy is to tell pupils that if the wires get hot, disconnect at once and try another way.

It helps pupils to realize that a bulb is not much more than *a piece of wire enclosed in glass.* Look closely at a bulb and you will see a small blob of solder between the glass bulb and metal base. That is where one end of the wire is attached. The other is hidden in the very bottom tip of the base. (See figure 7.22.)

To light up the bulb, the two wires from the dry cell are connected to the two ends of the wire in the bulb. Refer back to figure 7.16 for the proper connections. If you do not have the large commercial dry cells shown in the diagram, you can use ordinary flashlight cells by using tape or a large rubber band to hold the bare end of the wire against the bottom of the cell and looping the other bare end around the bulb. (See figure 7.23.)

You can use a 1.5-volt bulb instead of a 3-volt for this event. The bulb will burn quite brightly because it is matched with a 1.5-volt cell. However, you cannot use the 1.5-volt bulbs later in this chapter where two cells are connected in series. The 1.5-volt bulbs will burn out. Thus, it is probably better to use 3-volt bulbs for all activities in this chapter. They give a low, but acceptable, light in this event, and a bright light in the later event.

Open and Closed Circuits

As stated earlier, a current can travel only if it has a complete path to follow. However, often that is not enough. For convenience, there should also be an easy way to disconnect the path. Otherwise a room light, for example, would stay on all the time.

How is the light turned off? By a switch, of course. When a switch is turned off, it is called an *open circuit.* When a switch is turned on it is called a *closed circuit.* (See figure 7.24.)

In *Event 7-S, Stop and Go Signals for Electricity,* students are asked to make a switch that automatically opens the circuit when a person leaves the device. Unless you use such a switch, some pupils will leave wires hooked up to bulbs when they are finished with an activity. They forget to turn off the current, and the cells are dead in 15 to 30 minutes.

An automatic switch solves the problem, but students think it is too difficult to make. Yet the solution is simple. Just attach a metal strip to a board as shown in figure 7.25. It is just like a key of a telegraph. To turn the current on, just push down the switch. When you leave, the strip springs back. Thus, pupils cannot ruin a battery by forgetting to turn off a switch.

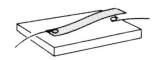

FIGURE 7.25   When the metal strip is pressed down, it turns the current on (closes the circuit). When released, it springs up and turns the current off (opens the circuit).

Short Circuits

An example of a typical circuit is an electric toaster that is plugged in. The current travels through the toaster's electrical plug-in cord (which stays cool) and through toaster wires (which become red hot). After going through the toaster, the current returns through the plug-in cord to the wall outlet, completing the path.

We know that the wires inside the toaster become red hot. Why are those wires hot while the appliance cord remains cool? After all, the same amount of electricity is going through both. The effects are different because the wires are different. The appliance cord is made of relatively large copper wires that can carry the current easily. The toaster wires are small and made of a noncopper substance (nichrome) that cannot carry the current easily. As a result, the toaster wires get hot as the nichrome resists the current.

Suppose the plug-in cord is damaged so the two wires within it touch each other. What will happen? The current will no longer go through the toaster. Instead, it will take the shorter path (making a **short circuit**) and jump across to the other wire of the cord.

As soon as the current jumps to the other wire of the appliance cord, it no longer meets the **resistance** that existed in the toaster wires. With less resistance the current increases greatly. Suddenly, instead of the toaster wires getting red hot, the plug-in cord becomes red hot! Can you guess what will happen to a house if the electric wires within its walls become red hot?

Fuses and Circuit Breakers

The scene described above would be a disaster unless protected by a safety device. Fortunately, such safety devices exist. They are called fuses and circuit breakers. A **fuse** is a protective device that cuts off the current when it is too great for the house wires. It acts like an automatic switch, turning off the current when a circuit is overloaded. Most new homes now use **circuit breakers** to perform the same function as fuses.

The operation of a fuse can be demonstrated by doing *Event 7-T, Pop the Fuse.* The center part of the fuse should be cut quite narrow to be sure that the event will work. When the current is large enough, the fuse burns out.

Foil from gum wrappers work better than kitchen foil. Gum wrapper foil is thinner and tends to melt quickly when a battery current goes through it. It is not necessary to peel the paper backing from the foil. In fact, the paper backing makes the event more visible because a tiny puff of smoke is emitted from the paper when the fuse melts.

Series and Parallel Wiring of Batteries and Bulbs

If we wish to have more light in a room, we simply turn on another lamp. How surprising it would be to find that, as we turn on another lamp, the lights become *dimmer.* Both of these results are possible in *Event 7-U, Series and Parallel Circuits.*

Refer back to figure 7.18 to check the correct way to get the brightest light from two cells and one bulb. It is a series arrangement of batteries. Refer back to figure 7.19 to check the correct way to get the brightest light from two bulbs and one cell. The parallel arrangement of bulbs gives a brighter light. In fact, the series arrangement actually gives *less* light than a single bulb.

Why does the **series** arrangement of bulbs cause a dimmer light? Think of each bulb as resistance. As the current enters the bulb, it is resisted by the fine tungsten wire inside. If two bulbs are connected so that the same current has to go through both bulbs, then the current has twice as much resistance as it originally had. Thus, less of the current can get through, and it produces less light.

In a **parallel** arrangement, however, current that goes through one bulb *does not go through the other bulb.* The current has alternate paths that it can choose. Notice that in a parallel arrangement there are always two wires between any two objects. Refer back to the diagram in figure 7.19. Suppose the current enters from the left in the lower line. The current reaches a branch where it can either go up through the first bulb, or go on to the second bulb at the right. Once through either bulb, the current goes on its way back to the cell. No electron ever goes through more than one bulb in a parallel arrangement.

You will find that when working with bulbs, it is the parallel arrangement that gives the most light, and when working with cells, it is the series arrangement that gives the most light. Thus, the brightest possible combination of batteries and bulbs is with cells in series and bulbs in parallel. (Refer back to figure 7.20.)

Why does the series arrangement of cells produce a brighter light in bulbs? Because the energy of the two cells is combined. If the cells are 1.5 volts each, two cells connected in series produce 3 volts. It is important to note that when combining cells, that the voltage rating of a bulb is not exceeded. Two cells of 1.5 volts each will produce a bright light in a cell designed for 3 volts, but will burn out a bulb designed for 1.5 volts.

When two cells are connected in parallel, the **voltage** remains the same. It is as if you added another gas tank to your car. It does not make the engine stronger, but it will run twice as long before it uses up the gas. The parallel arrangement of cells adds no brightness to the bulbs, but it doubles the time they will remain lit.

Sometimes it helps to compare electricity to water. The cells are like tanks of water. If you add one water tank on top of another, you increase the pressure. It is like connecting the cells in series. The added pressure can be compared to the added volts when batteries are connected in series. As stated earlier, two cells of 1.5 volts each produce 3 volts when connected in series.

If, instead, you place the second tank alongside the first and connect them with a pipe, the water pressure remains the same. However, it takes twice as long to use up the water supply. The increase in time can be compared to the action of cells connected in parallel. The combination still produces only 1.5 volts, but will last twice as long.

In summary, cells connected in series produce a higher voltage but no greater lifespan. Cells connected in parallel produce a longer lifespan but no additional voltage.

Finally, after practicing series and parallel wiring, pupils can try to understand how *Event 7-V, Quiz Board,* works. At first the board seems mystifying. However, it is actually easier than much of the wiring that they have already practiced. The quiz board uses only series wiring. Parallel wiring is not used. When the question on one side is matched with its correct answer on the other side to light the bulb, it merely means that a circuit has been closed.

If a quiz board is available in the classroom, it should *not* be covered in the back. By studying the back, pupils can gain an understanding of circuits. The back will show that there is a single wire running from each question to their respective correct answers.

Uses of Electricity (Events 7-W and 7-X)

Discrepant Events and Pupil Investigations

Event 7-W. Power-Packed Performer
Attach a length of bell wire to each terminal of a strong dry cell (6-volt if possible) and touch the ends to a batch of steel wool. What happens to the steel wool? (**Caution:** Do the activity as a demonstration. Avoid the hot wires, have a pan of water handy to extinguish glowing wires, and have good ventilation for possible fumes.)

Pupil Investigations (may include the following processes):

1. Demonstrating that the steel wool becomes so hot that it burns.
2. Inferring that the heat is caused by resistance in the thin strands of the steel wool.
3. Generalizing that electricity can be used to produce heat and light.

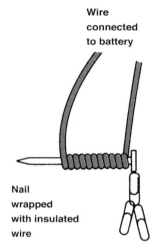

FIGURE 7.26   When an insulated wire is wrapped around a nail and connected to a battery, it becomes an electromagnet.

Event 7-X. Stop and Go Magnets
If you wrap an insulated wire around a nail and attach the ends of the wire to a dry cell, you will have made an electromagnet. See how many paper clips the electromagnet will pick up. Have pupils try arrangements of 10, 25, 50, and 100 turns of wire around the nail. Also, try arrangements of one and two cells connected in series. (See figure 7.26.)

Pupil Investigations (may include the following processes):

1. Observing that the magnetism starts and stops with the turning on and off of the electrical current.
2. Inferring that electricity produces the magnetic field.
3. Recording the results of the investigation in table 7.3.

TABLE 7.3

Electromagnets

Trial	Turns of Wire	Number of Cells	Number of Clips
1			
2			
3			
etc.			

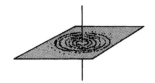

FIGURE 7.27 Iron filings sprinkled on this sheet of paper are lined up in concentric circles. This indicates the existence of a magnetic field in a current-carrying wire.

Events 7-W and 7-X Explained in Context (Uses of Electricity)

Electricity is used to produce heat in toasters, ranges, and clothes irons; to produce light in bulbs; and to do work in electromagnets and motors. Pupils should be asked to look for examples of how electricity is used around the home and in school.

In *Event 7-W, Power-Packed Performer,* electrical energy is used to burn the fine wire in steel wool. Remember to be careful. Avoid touching the red hot wires, have water handy to put out burning wires, and be sure that any possible fumes are removed by ventilation. (This activity can also be used in chapter 5, in the section on fire. The fine wire allows so much oxygen to reach the steel that it can actually burn.)

A 6-volt battery will work better than a 1.5-volt cell. (There is no danger of shock from these cells because the voltage is too low to pass through the skin.)

Electricity and magnetism are related. Just place a compass next to an electric wire and you will see the compass needle jump when the current is turned on and off. It proves that an electric current produces a magnetic field around a conductor.

Another way to see the magnetic field is shown in figure 7.27. Cut halfway through a sheet of paper or cardboard. Center the sheet around the wire and sprinkle with iron filings. The iron filings will align themselves with the magnetic field. Thus, the field will be made visible. (**Note:** If the rings are blurred or poorly formed, it helps to tap the sheet gently with a finger.)

The magnetic field of a wire can be made stronger by merely wrapping the wire around a soft-iron core, such as a nail, as is done in *Event 7-X, Stop and Go Magnets.* At first, each added turn adds to a magnet's strength. However, a point is reached when the added resistance of the additional wire reduces the current and makes the magnet weaker.

You can see if that point is reached in your class by recording the data in table 7.3. Those points will vary greatly depending on the size of wire and on the condition and quality of the cells.

Some final notes: Be sure to use insulated wire because bare wire will not work. Be sure, also, that the wire is always turned around the nail in only one direction. It makes no difference which way you wrap the wire, but do not change directions once started.

Combining Assessment with Instruction

Students need the opportunity to construct models of everyday devices. This gives them the chance to apply principles and concepts learned in this chapter. Have students select one of the following devices and build it either during class time or at home. This can also be assigned as a small group project.

Have students attach a report that includes: (1) a written description of the device, (2) a schematic, (3) advice they would give another student building this device that they wish someone had told them before they began, (4) a list of helpful suggestions they did get along the way, (5) a list of materials or designs they tried that didn't work and why, and (6) a list of uses of this device in everyday life. It is best to suggest that students keep a log as they design and build the device so that the report is easier to write.

Students may be evaluated on the following:

1. How well does the device work?
2. Neatness of construction, durability, and neatness of report.
3. Quality of report. Does it logically describe the requirement listed above?

Things to Make

A Three-Way Switch House

Suggest that students use a cardboard box to decorate as a room or house. Wire the "house" with a circuit that turns the house light on and off. In addition, have students build a three-way switch in the house.

We have all seen lights that can be turned on at one end of a hallway and turned off at the other end. What kind of switch allows the lights to be controlled from two places? Such a device is called a *three-way switch* because it needs three wires or pathways for the current to travel. (See figure 7.28.)

Rheostat (Dimmer Switch)

There are several ways of making a dimmer or rheostat. One method is shown in figure 7.29. The device works better with a 6-volt cell than with a 1.5-volt cell.

Another dimmer can be made by using salt water in place of the pencil lead. Just bring the wires close together in the salt water to make the light brighter, and move the wires away to make the light dimmer. This activity works best with somewhat higher voltage than other events. You may need to wire two 6-volt cells together in series to make a 12-volt source. However, if you accidentally touch the wires together the bulb burns out. So, be careful.

Automatic Traffic Light

The automatic traffic light is nothing more than a glorified tin can. (See figure 7.30.) Be sure that the ends of the three upright wires are cleared of insulation. The bare wire must touch the can.

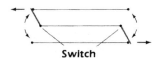

FIGURE 7.28   A three-way switch has three wires (or ways) for current to travel. The current can be turned on and off in two different places.

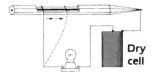

FIGURE 7.29   When the wire is moved to the right, the resistance is decreased so more current can flow through the circuit.

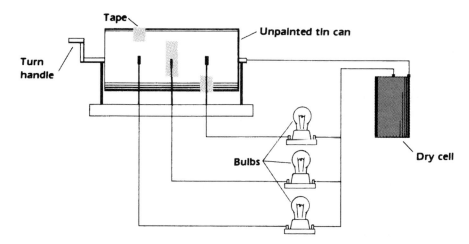

FIGURE 7.30   This tin-can timer regulates the lighting of the bulbs. The upright parts of the three wires touching the can must be bare, and the tin can must be part of the circuit.

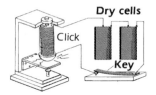

FIGURE 7.31   This is one example of a simple telegraph.

Model Telegraph

There are many ways to make a model telegraph. One example is shown in figure 7.31. Attach an iron hinge to a wooden frame. Make an electromagnet by using wire and a bolt. The bolt head must be close to the hinge but cannot touch it.

Sometimes a little latent magnetism remains in the bolt, so the hinge will stick to the bolt even when the current is turned off. A single layer of adhesive tape across the bolt head is enough to keep the hinge from sticking. Unfortunately, the tape will also deaden the sound of the "click."

An Electroscope

An electroscope can be made using a bottle or flask, a cork or rubber stopper, a coat hanger wire, and some thin foil. Refer back to figure 7.8 and the section, How to Build an Electroscope.

Sites and Software

The following websites and software are appropriate to use with this chapter. Note that computer software and websites change rapidly. This makes it necessary to investigate the stable websites for new links and software catalogs for updates. Visit www.mhhe.com/friedl6e to link to these directly and for study resources.

Sites

Franklin Institute Science Museum	www.fi.edu
Mad Scientist	www.madsci.org/experiments
How Van de Graff Generators Work	www.howstuffworks.com/vdg.htm
How Wildfires Work	www.howstuffworks.com/wildfire.htm
How Circuit Breakers Work	www.howstuffworks.com/ circuit-breaker.htm
SMILE Program Physics Index	www.iit.edu/~smile/physinde.html#p4
How Electromagnets Work	www.howstuffworks.com/ electromagnet.com

Software

Thinkin' Science ZAP! (Edmark) (3–6)
Science Court: Electric Current (Tom Snyder) (4–6)
Gizmos & Gadgets (The Learning Company) (2–6)
Virtual Labs Bundle: Electricity (Sunburst) (6–12)
Virtual Physics: Escape from Braindeath (Discovery) (7–9)

Key Terms

C H A P T E R   **8**

Teaching Children about Sound

NATIONAL SCIENCE EDUCATION STANDARDS ALIGNMENT TO EVENTS

The events in this chapter help accomplish several of the NSES for content. The event(s) that align with a given content standard are listed below that standard.

LEVELS K–4

UNIFYING CONCEPTS AND PROCESSES
- Change, consistency, measurement
  8-L
  8-N through 8-O
  8-R
  8-W through 8-X

- Evidence, models and explanation
  8-D
  8-G
  8-R
  8-V

SCIENCE AS INQUIRY
- Abilities necessary to do and understand scientific inquiry
  8-A through 8-X

PHYSICAL SCIENCE
- Position and motion of objects
  8-A through 8-X

- Properties of objects and materials
  8-E through 8-K
  8-O through 8-U
  8-V through 8-X

SCIENCE AND TECHNOLOGY
- Abilities of technological design
  8-L though 8-N
  8-R
  8-V and 8-X

HISTORY AND NATURE OF SCIENCE
- Science as a human endeavor
  Historical introduction
  8-G
  8-I

LEVELS 5–8

UNIFYING CONCEPTS AND PROCESSES
- Change, consistency, measurement
  8-L
  8-N through 8-O
  8-R
  8-W through 8-X

- Evidence, models and explanation
  8-D
  8-G
  8-R
  8-V

SCIENCE AS INQUIRY
- Abilities necessary to do and understand scientific inquiry
  8-A through 8-X

PHYSICAL SCIENCE
- Properties and changes of properties in matter
  8-A through 8-B

- Motion and forces
  8-A through 8-B
  8-C through 8-D
  8-E and 8-H

- Transfer of energy
  8-A through 8-X

SCIENCE AND TECHNOLOGY
- Abilities of technological design
  8-L through 8-N
  8-R
  8-V and 8-X

- Understanding science and technology
  8-G

HISTORY AND NATURE OF SCIENCE
- Science as a human endeavor
  Historical introduction
  8-G
  8-I

Sound Beginnings

The understanding of sound as a wave phenomenon developed from observations of water waves. Circa 350 B.C. Greek and Roman philosophers asserted that a wave is vibrating disturbance that travels large distances. Earlier, around 500 B.C., Greek philosopher Pythagoras discovered that musical instruments produced pleasant sounds when the string lengths were small whole number ratios such as 2:1, 2:3, or 3:4. Italian physicist and mathematician Galileo Galilei realized in the late 1500s that pitch was related to frequency of the wave vibrations.

Centuries later in the days of the Old West, scouts often detected the presence of wagon trains or herds of buffalo by listening for them. They did not listen for them through the air; they listened for them through solids. By holding an ear against a boulder or hard ground, a scout could detect the noises over a much greater distance than they could be detected through the air.

Today, railroad workers do somewhat the same thing when they listen for a train. A worker holds an ear against a rail. If a train is heard, they know that it is not safe to take out a section of rail for repair. They wait until no train can be heard before they remove a rail.

Another version of this activity is performed by the auto mechanic who holds one end of a stick against parts of a car engine while holding his ear against the other end. If bearings are not functioning well, the grinding noises can be heard through the stick much better than through the air.

We know that sound travels through solids, liquids, and gases. It does not travel through a vacuum. It must have some kind of material medium through which to travel. Since a vacuum is an absence of matter, it cannot conduct sound.

If sound cannot be transmitted through a vacuum, how do astronauts communicate with each other in the vacuum of the moon or space? They must use visual signals or radio.

What Is Sound? (Events 8-A through 8-D)

Discrepant Events and Pupil Investigations

Event 8-A. The Big Splash

Strike a tuning fork against the heel of your shoe, or hit it with a rubber mallet. Place the tips of the tines (the two vibrating ends of the tuning fork) into a beaker of water. What do you observe? What does this event show us about sound? (See figure 8.1.)

Pupil Investigations (may include the following processes):

1. Discovering that the water splashes out of the beaker when the tuning fork touches the water.
2. Experimenting with tuning forks of different sizes.
3. Inferring (incorrectly) that the larger the tuning fork, the bigger the splash.
4. Inferring (incorrectly) that the higher the frequency, the bigger the splash (Actually, the inference is correct up to a certain point, but then the splash decreases as the frequency increases.)
5. Forming a theory about the relationship between sound and vibration.

FIGURE 8.1 What happens when the tuning fork is dipped into the water?

Event 8-B. Ping-Pong Bounce

Strike a tuning fork and hold a tine against a suspended Ping-Pong ball. What happens to the ball when it is touched by the tine? (See figure 8.2.)

Pupil Investigations (may include the following processes):

1. Observing that the Ping-Pong ball bounces away when touched by a tine.
2. Experimenting with tuning forks of various sizes.
3. Generalizing that the tuning fork had energy that was transferred to the ball.
4. Inferring that the tuning fork was vibrating.

Event 8-C. Vibrating Voices

Ask students to hold one hand against their throat above their Adam's apple while talking or humming. What do they feel? What conclusions can be made about voice and vibrations?

Pupil Investigations (may include the following processes):

1. Feeling vibrations in their throat when talking or humming.
2. Inferring that these vibrations cause the sounds.
3. Comparing these vibrations to those produced in other events.

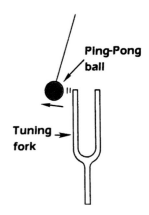

FIGURE 8.2   What happens to the Ping-Pong ball when it touches a vibrating tuning fork?

Events 8-A through 8-C Explained in Context (What Is Sound?)

This section is intended to establish the fact that **sound** *is a form of energy produced by the vibration of matter* or, to put it more simply, that *sound is caused by vibrations.*

There are many events that can be done to discover this principle. In *Event 8A, The Big Splash,* for example, it is the vibrating motion of the tuning fork that causes the water to splash. When the tuning fork is struck, the tines move back and forth (or **vibrate**) rapidly.

When the fork is dipped into the water, this vibrating motion is strong enough to cause the splash. Pupils will find that a large tuning fork of about 126 vibrations per second (vps) has a large motion that can be seen fairly easily and will produce a good splashing action.

Smaller tuning forks of 256 and 512 vps cause even greater splashes, even though their vibrating motions are much shorter and harder to see. The splashes are larger because the tines travel faster.

Tuning forks of even smaller size, however, do not work very well. Their vibrating motion becomes so small that they disturb the water less and less. By the time you use tuning forks of 2000 and 3000 vps, they do not cause any splash at all.

Event 8-B, Ping-Pong Bounce, also shows the effect of vibrations. If the tuning fork is really vibrating, then perhaps its rapid movement will cause something to happen to the Ping-Pong ball. Suspend the ball by a thread and touch it with a tine of a vibrating tuning fork. The ball will bounce away with surprising energy. The best results are obtained with tuning forks of 256 to 512 vps.

Still another activity that shows the same result is simply to hold the end of a sheet of paper lightly against the tuning fork. The vibrating sound of the tine striking the paper will be easy to hear.

Pupils may wonder if the sounds of talking, singing, and humming are also produced by vibrating matter. *Event 8-C. Vibrating Voices,* should be of great interest to them. If the pupil holds a hand on their throat, the vibrations coming from the larynx (voice box) will be felt.

In all of the events in this section, there is evidence that sound is produced by vibrations. These events make it clear that vibrations actually exist.

How Does Sound Travel? (Events 8-D through 8-K)

Discrepant Events and Pupil Investigations

Event 8-D. Slinky Waves

Stretch out a Slinky coil on top of a counter. Have one student hold one end steady while another student activates it in two ways: (1) give a series of push-pull motions to the coil, and (2) give a series of side to side motions to the coil. Observe the motion of the coils.

Pupil Investigations (may include the following processes):

1. Observing the waves as they travel from the activator to the end of the coil.
2. Discovering that the waves move from one end of the coil to the other, but that the individual coils stay in a very restricted place.
3. Inferring that there is a difference between wave motion and the motion of the individual coils.

Event 8-E. Tabletop Messages

Hold your ear against a tabletop while someone taps and scratches lightly against the other end of the table. What is heard? How do the sounds coming through the table compare to the sounds coming through the air?

Pupil Investigations (may include the following processes):

1. Listening to the sounds coming through the tabletop.
2. Controlling variables by making sure that sound is coming only through the table (plug the exposed ear).
3. Contrasting the sounds coming through the table with those coming through the air.
4. Generalizing that sounds travel through solids.

Event 8-F. Spoon Chimes

Tie two lengths of string to a spoon. Wrap one string around a finger of one hand and the other string around a finger of the other hand. Then plug the fingers into your ears. Lean forward so that the spoon strikes a desk or table. Listen to the sound. What do you hear? (See figure 8.3.)

Pupil Investigations (may include the following processes):

1. Comparing the sound heard through the string with the sound heard through the air.
2. Experimenting with spoons of different sizes and with other objects.
3. Inferring that sound travels through the string.

FIGURE 8.3   Did you ever listen to a spoon? Compare the sound as heard through the string with the sound as heard through the air.

Event 8-G. Tin-Can Telephone

Punch a tiny hole through the end of a tin can. Pull a string through the hole and fasten it to a button on the inside. (The button keeps the string from being pulled out of the can.) Do the same with the other end of the string and a second tin can. The string should be at least as long as the classroom.

Have one pupil on each end of the string, holding on to a tin can. Be sure that they pull the string tight. Then have one talk into the can while the other listens. What is heard? How does the tin-can telephone transmit sounds?

Pupil Investigations (may include the following processes):

1. Discovering that sometimes sounds can be heard quite well but at other times there are no sounds at all.
2. Experimenting to find out how the telephones must be held to produce the best results.
3. Testing with different lengths and thicknesses of string.
4. Inferring that sounds travel through the string.

FIGURE 8.4 A vibrating tuning fork causes the salt to "dance" on the stretched rubber.

Event 8-H. The "Dancing" Salt

Stretch a rubber film (from a balloon) across the open end of a tin can and sprinkle some salt on the film. Strike a tuning fork and hold it about 1 centimeter over the film. What do you observe? What does this event show us about sound? (See figure 8.4.)

Pupil Investigations (may include the following processes):

1. Discovering that the salt "dances" if the tuning fork is held a certain way.
2. Experimenting with various ways of holding the tuning fork.
3. Comparing tuning forks of different sizes.
4. Formulating a rule to explain why the tuning fork causes the salt to dance.

Event 8-I. Listening Tube

Attach a rubber hose to a funnel as shown in figure 8.5. Place the funnel against a ticking clock. Can you hear the sounds coming through the tube? Is it louder or softer than the sounds coming through the air? Use the device to listen to your heart.

Pupil Investigations (may include the following processes):

1. Comparing the sounds heard through the tube with the sounds coming through the air.
2. Experimenting with various lengths and sizes of tube.
3. Forming a theory to explain why the sounds coming through the tube are louder.

FIGURE 8.5 The ticking of the clock sounds louder through the tube than through the air.

Event 8-J. Underwater Sounds (#1)

Fill a large bowl or fish tank with water. Then place your ear against one side of the tank while holding a ticking clock against the other side. Plug your exposed ear with a finger so that you are listening only with the ear held against the tank. This activity is commonly suggested to show that sounds travel through water. *What is wrong with it?* (See figure 8.6.)

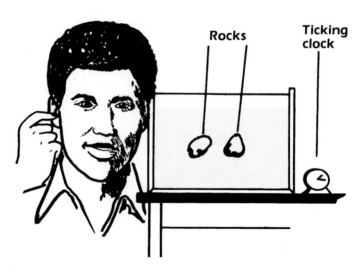

FIGURE 8.6 Can you hear the clock through the water? Can you still hear the clock if the aquarium is empty?

Pupil Investigations (may include the following processes):

1. Listening to the ticking sounds that reach the ear.
2. Inferring (incorrectly) that the event proves that sounds travel through the water.
3. Experimenting to find out if the sounds can be heard with an *empty* fish tank.
4. Devising a procedure to prove that sounds travel through the water.
5. Controlling variables. (Plug your other ear with a finger to keep sounds from reaching you through the air.)

Event 8-K. Underwater Sounds (#2)

Use a plastic food storage bag for this activity, one that can be sealed tight. Fill it partially full of water and use it in place of the glass bowl in the previous event to listen to the ticking clock. Does this event do a better job of showing how sounds are transmitted through water? (**Caution:** Take care to keep from spilling water. Wipe up any spills at once to avoid slippery floors.)

Pupil Investigations (may include the following processes):

1. Listening to the ticking sounds that reach the ear.
2. Inferring that sounds travel through the water to reach your ear.
3. Controlling variables. (Plug your other ear with a finger to keep sounds from reaching you through the air.)

Events 8-D through 8-K Explained in Context (How Does Sound Travel?)

Sounds Travel in Waves

To understand how sounds travel we need to have some background information about waves. Sounds are transmitted from one place to another in waves.

There are two types of waves: (1) **transverse** and (2) **longitudinal.** Transverse waves have a side-to-side (or up-and-down) motion similar to water waves. Longitudinal waves are push-pull waves of the type that can transmit sound. Both types can easily be shown by using a wire coil suggested in *Event 8-D, Slinky Waves.* Stretch the coil across a countertop or table and have students hold each end. Then have one student make vigorous side-to-side motions with the coil. The snakelike waves travel along the coils across the table. (See figure 8.7.)

The transverse wave can also be shown by attaching one end of a rope to a door knob or other object and snapping the other end. The snakelike wave moves quickly from your hand to the other end of the rope.

To demonstrate the longitudinal wave, again use the coil. Instead of using side-to-side motions, just make vigorous push-pull motions. The waves can easily be seen as they travel along the coil.

Sounds Travel through Solids

Many classroom activities show that sounds travel through solids. In *Event 8-E, Tabletop Messages,* pupils will notice that sounds are quite loud when heard through the table.

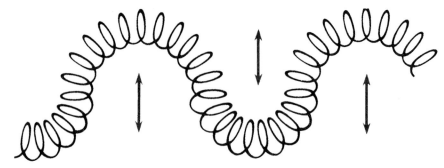

Transverse wave; side to side

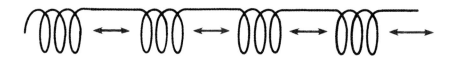

Longitudinal wave; push–pull

FIGURE 8.7   The transverse and longitudinal waves can both be demonstrated with a Slinky coiled spring.

Event 8-F, Spoon Chimes, shows how sounds travel through a solid. This event holds several surprises for pupils. First of all, most will be amazed at the rich and beautiful sounds that they hear. A tapped spoon sounds "tinny" when heard through the air, but like a chime when heard through the string.

Students are often surprised when the string is referred to as a solid. In this case "solid" is not used to refer to something like a rock or table, but a "solid" as in "solid, liquid, or gas." It is obvious that the string is neither liquid nor gas.

Generally, a string is a very poor conductor. However, when string is pulled tight by the weight of a spoon, it becomes a good conductor. You can also point out that since the pupils will plug their ears, it is proof that no sounds could reach them through the air. The sound they heard *must have* gone through the string.

You can use many other items such as forks, knives, and coat hangers in place of the spoon. Each will give a surprisingly rich sound when heard through the string.

Event 8-G, Tin-Can Telephone, also shows that a string conducts sound. If done correctly, the sounds can be carried over a distance of 50 meters or more. For it to work, the string must be tight. Otherwise no sounds will be carried by it. It is also important that the pupils place their hands on the *sides* of the can instead of the back. Holding the back will tend to smother the vibrations that are being transmitted.

Sounds Travel through Air

The fact that we can hear people talk is obvious evidence that sound travels through the air. However, there is an event that shows this characteristic of sound in a more unusual way. In *Event 8-H, The "Dancing" Salt*, a vibrating tuning fork causes the salt to dance and bounce. Since the tuning fork does not touch the salt, membrane, or tin can, it is obvious that the sound must travel through the air. (This event is also good to show that sound is related to vibrations, as was shown earlier in Events 8-A through 8-C.)

The salt will not dance if it is on another surface because most surfaces are far too massive to be affected by sound waves. However, a thin rubber membrane is so light that it works. The energy from a tuning fork is strong enough to cause the membrane to vibrate, which in turn causes the salt to dance.

Sound energy is not very great and it loses its strength rapidly as the distance increases. Thus, the salt will dance only if you hold the vibrating tuning fork no more than 1 or 2 centimeters away.

Although sound weakens rapidly through free air, it remains quite strong if trapped inside a tube. *Event 8-I, The Listening Tube,* provides this evidence. The ticking of a clock sounds much louder through the tube than through the air. It is even possible to detect your heartbeat with the tube and funnel, as long as there is no background noise to interfere with your listening.

An interesting application of the *listening tube* is found on big ships. Of course, there are telephones on big ships. But what if the electricity is shut down by an accident? How can the captain talk to the engine room? By listening tube, of course. Such tubes (called *speaking tubes*) are used as emergency lines of communication to all essential parts of the ship.

Sounds Travel through Liquids

How can you show that sounds travel through water? It is not very easy. *Event 8-J, Underwater Sounds (#1),* is sometimes suggested in some books. Unfortunately, there is a serious flaw in doing it as shown. Why? Just try the event with an *empty* container. It still works. You can still hear the ticking of the clock. Sound travels very well through the glass walls of the bowl.

The event can be modified so that it has at least a fair amount of accuracy. Just tap some rocks together underwater or open and close a scissors underwater. Even there, it is possible that the sound could travel up your arms and into the air. However, most of the sound you hear will have had to travel through some water to reach you. *Event 8-K, Underwater Sounds (#2),* is probably better. The plastic is a poor conductor so any sounds that you hear will have to travel through the water. There is one other obvious problem: the possibility that the bag will unseal and spill the water. Be cautious.

Perhaps it may be best to simply ask pupils if they have ever heard sounds while swimming underwater in a pool. Many will verify that they have heard sounds such as the filter motor and other noises.

The Speed of Sound (Events 8-L through 8-N)

Discrepant Events and Pupil Investigations

Event 8-L. Speed Detector

Make a pendulum that has a period of half a second. Shortening the string speeds up the pendulum; lengthening the string slows it down. Hang it from a support and assign a student to keep it swinging.

Have another student strike together two pieces of wood at the exact moment that the pendulum weight is at a given point in its arc. The event works just as well if the wood is struck only at every second or third swing of the pendulum. Ask the students to determine how the speed of sound can be measured.

Pupil Investigations (may include the following processes):

1. Discovering that moving away from the sound causes a delay between the time you see the pieces struck and the time that the sound is heard.
2. Inferring that sound travels more slowly than light.
3. Measuring the distance from the listener to the source.
4. Calculating the speed of sound from the data gathered in the activity.

Event 8-M. Echo Speed Computer

You can hear an echo if you hit two wooden sticks together in an open space in front of a large flat surface such as a building or even a line of trees.

Perhaps your school building is the only large surface nearby. If so, stand about 80 to 90 meters from the building and strike the sticks together. You should be able to hear an echo.

Then start walking toward the building, striking the sticks as you walk. (It is not necessary to strike the sticks in rhythm. You are merely listening for an echo.) As you approach the building, the echo will be harder and harder to detect because it is separated less and less from the original sound. Finally, it will no longer be detected as separate from the original sound. How can the speed of sound be calculated by following the instructions? (**Hint:** The ear can hear an echo following the original sound by as little as $\frac{1}{10}$ of a second.)

Pupil Investigations (may include the following processes):

1. Measuring the distance between the building and the point where the last echo was heard.
2. Forming a theory that the sound travels twice the distance to the reflecting surface because it makes a round trip to it and back again.
3. Calculating the speed of sound from the information available in the activity.

Event 8-N. Echo Range Finder

Stand in front of a large flat surface such as a building or even a line of trees. Clap your hands together repeatedly. Can you hear an echo? Clap so that your second clap is just in time with the echo from the first.

When you synchronize your claps in this way, count the number of claps in a given period of time, say 10 seconds. How can the distance to the surface be measured using this method? (**Hint:** To get the answer, you need to know that sound travels 330 meters per second.)

Pupil Investigations (may include the following processes):

1. Recording the number of claps in a given period of time.
2. Inferring a relationship between the number of claps, the speed of sound, and the distance to the surface.
3. Calculating the distance to the object with the information gained in the experiment.

Events 8-L through 8-N Explained in Context (The Speed of Sound)

Speed of Sound in Air

Scientists have discovered that sound travels at 330 meters per second at 0° C. The speed increases slightly when the air warms up and decreases slightly when it gets colder.

There are several ways of measuring the speed of sound that may be suitable for use in the upper grades. In *Event 8-L, Speed Detector,* students must combine the factors of time and distance to compute the speed of sound.

After the pendulum weight is set in motion and the pieces of wood are struck in tempo with the pendulum's swing, students begin to move away. They will soon notice that the sound is no longer in rhythm. That is, what is heard lags behind what is seen.

Finally, the lag will be a full 1/2 second and thus be exactly in tempo with the pendulum again. At this point, all that needs to be done is to measure the distance. It should be 165 meters. Thus, the sound traveled 165 meters in ½ second. That is equal to 330 meters per second, or 1200 kilometers per hour.

If there is no clear area of 165 meters on or near the school grounds, the pendulum can be set to a shorter time period. However, if the pendulum swings too fast, it becomes more difficult to time it accurately.

The speed of sound can also be found by using the method suggested in *Event 8-M, Echo Speed Computer.* Students should be able to pinpoint the distance from the last echo to the wall of the building fairly well. The point where the echo can no longer be detected should be about 16 or 17 meters from the reflecting surface.

Remember, however, that the sound makes a round trip to the wall and back, so the sound actually travels a total of about 33 meters. Given the fact that the ear can distinguish an echo that is heard 1/10 second after the original sound, it means that the sound traveled 33 meters in 1/10 second. Again, that is 330 meters per second.

Once we know that sound travels 330 meters per second, that information can be used to measure distances, as stated in *Event 8-N, Echo Range Finder.* If you clap your hands in tempo with the returning echo, you can measure the distance to the reflecting surface.

Suppose that you clapped 15 times in 10 seconds and that each clap was in tempo with the preceding echo. Thus a single clap would go to the surface and back in ⅔ second (⅔ second × 15 = 10 seconds). Sound travels 220 meters in ⅔ second. Since the sound made a round trip to the surface *and back,* the distance to the surface is one-half of 220 meters, or 110 meters.

You can also use the speed of sound to measure the distance to a lightning flash. Just count the number of seconds between the lightning and the thunder. Thus, a 3-second delay between lightning and thunder indicates that the lightning was 1 kilometer away.

Speed of Sound in Different Media

The speed of sound depends mostly on the elastic properties of a substance. Surprising as it may seem, at the molecular level, water and steel are far more elastic than air. Sound travels at 1450 meters per second in water and 4800 meters per second in steel, compared to 330 meters per second in air.

The density of a substance is also a factor in sound transmission. The more dense a substance, the worse it transmits sound. Concrete, for example, is a dense substance and a sound absorber. Although steel is also a dense substance, it is far more elastic than it is dense. Therefore, the net effect is to make it an excellent conductor of sound.

Volume (Loudness) (Events 8-O through 8-U)

Discrepant Events and Pupil Investigations

Event 8-O. Tuning Fork Amplifier

Strike a tuning fork with a mallet and press the base against a tabletop or some other surface. What happens to the sound? Explain why this occurs. Connect the sound probe to the computer. Try the experiment again but this time keep the sound probe a constant distance from the vibrating tuning fork. Measure the intensity of the sound as the type and size of the surface are varied. (**Caution:** Be sure to touch the *base* of the tuning fork to a surface, *not* the tines. The tines can damage surfaces. See figure 8.8.)

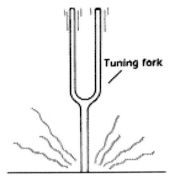

Tuning fork

FIGURE 8.8   Place the base of a tuning fork against a solid surface and listen.

Pupil Investigations (may include the following processes):

1. Discovering that the sound becomes louder.
2. Forming a theory that the object (table, desk, etc.) acts to increase the energy of the tuning fork.
3. Inferring that the tuning fork forces the object to vibrate.
4. Generalizing that there is a relationship between the size of the vibrating surface and the loudness of sound.
5. Generalizing that there is a relationship between the material vibrating and the loudness of the sound.

Event 8-P. Wastebasket Megaphone

Hold up an empty wastebasket and talk into it. What does your voice sound like? Place a battery and a buzzer or bell into the wastebasket, and listen to the bell ring. Is the sound louder?

Pupil Investigations (may include the following processes):

1. Observing that the sound becomes louder when talking into the wastebasket.
2. Contrasting the sound of the bell inside and outside the wastebasket.
3. Inferring that the wastebasket is similar to a megaphone.
4. Generalizing that there is a relationship between the size of the vibrating surface and the loudness of sound.

Event 8-Q. Make the Lion Roar

Punch a tiny hole in the bottom of an empty milk carton and insert a string. Fasten the string to a button so that it will not pull out of the hole. Hold the string tight and stroke it with a damp cloth or paper towel. What does it sound like? (You can try the same activity with a tin can to make "the rooster crow.")

Pupil Investigations (may include the following processes):

1. Estimating what sound will be heard.
2. Discovering that the sound caused by rubbing is very loud.
3. Generalizing that the size of the vibrating surface affects the loudness of sound.

Event 8-R. Vibrating Air.

Hold a vibrating tuning fork of about 520 vibrations per second about 1 or 2 centimeters above the top of an open cylinder. Hold the cylinder upright, and lower it slowly into a deep container of water so that only about 12 to 14 centimeters of the cylinder remain above the water. Then move the cylinder up and down carefully at this height to find the point of greatest effect. What do you hear? (See figure 8.9.)

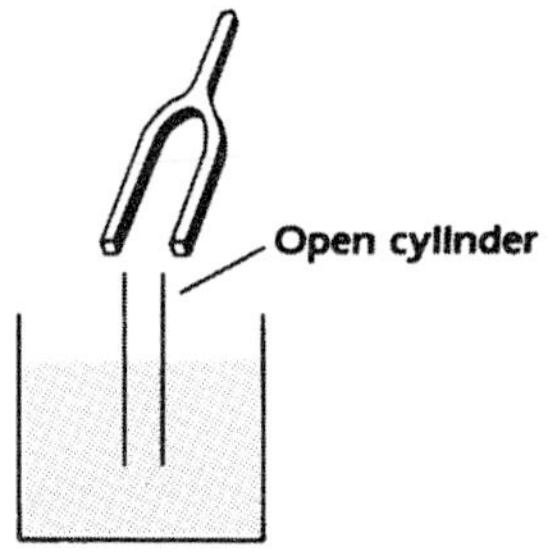

FIGURE 8.9 If the air column is made to resonate, the sound of the tuning fork will become much louder.

Pupil Investigations (may include the following processes):

1. Listening to the sound and estimating its increase in intensity.
2. Experimenting with tuning forks of different frequencies.
3. Measuring the height of best effect for each tuning fork.
4. Analyzing the relationship between the size of the tuning fork and the length of the vibrating air column.

Event 8-S. Singing Wine Glasses

Wash your hands with soap and water. Then dampen a finger with vinegar and rub it gently on the rim of a wine glass, going round and round. Keep doing this even if nothing happens immediately. (It takes practice, but it will work if you don't give up.) Vary the speed and pressure slightly, but do *not* press hard. Eventually a loud clear sound should be produced. How is the sound made? (See figure 8.10.)

Pupil Investigations (may include the following processes):

1. Experimenting to produce a loud clear sound.
2. Comparing the sounds created with different levels of water in the glass.
3. Contrasting the sound made when the glass is rubbed with the sound made by tapping the glass with a pen or pencil.
4. Generalizing that the sounds are natural vibrations of the glass.

FIGURE 8.10 Rub your finger gently along the edge of the glass goblet. Can you make it "sing"?

Event 8-T. Hurricane Huff!

Do we need to huff and puff with the force of a hurricane to blow away the heavy book? Find a way to move the book without too much puffing. (See figure 8.11.) Place a strong stick, such as a meter stick, on top of the back of two chairs, back to back, approximately a meter apart. Suspend a book on a string so that the book can swing freely between the two chairs.

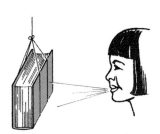

Pupil Investigations (may include the following processes):

1. Observing that the heavy book will swing slightly after it is blown.
2. Discovering that the swinging book has a natural rhythm.
3. Experimenting with puffs that are timed to coincide with the natural swing of the book.
4. Analyzing the relationship between the swinging book and the loudness of sound.

FIGURE 8.11 It will take a "hurricane holler" to blow the heavy book very far— unless you know the secret.

Event 8-U. Far Far Away

Using the sound probe connected to the computer/calculator, record the intensity of sound from a toy clicker or New Year's Eve noisemaker 1 decimeter away. Repeat for distances of 2, 3, 4, and 5 decimeters.

Pupil Investigations (may include the following processes):

1. Designing an experiment to investigate if there is a relationship between sound intensity and distance the sound source is from the receiver (probe).
2. Graphing the data of sound intensity and distance.
3. Exploring other graphic relationships such as intensity versus the inverse of the distance, intensity versus the inverse of the distance squared.
4. Generalizing the relationship found.

Events 8-O through 8-U Explained in Context (Volume or Loudness)

There are a number of factors that affect the **loudness** of sound. Most of these factors are presented in the following list:

1. The *energy* expended to make the sound. (Strike a gong harder, for example, and it makes a louder sound.)
2. The *distance* from the source to the listener. The inverse-square rule applies: If the distance increases by a factor of two, the sound is only one-fourth as loud. If the distance is three times as far away, the sound is only one-ninth as loud. What fraction results if the distance is four times as great? (one-sixteenth)
3. The *surface area* that is vibrating. The greater the area, the louder the sound. This is an important factor in the discussion of forced vibrations to follow later in this chapter.
4. The *resonance* of an object. That is, the ability of anything to vibrate by absorbing energy at its own natural frequency.
5. The *composition* of the material. Different materials absorb energy more than others; that is, steel versus cardboard of the same thickness.

The loudness of sound is measured in units called **decibels.** Common sound intensities are given in table 8.1.

Forced Vibrations

A very common means of making sounds louder is to use forced vibrations. Radio or TV speakers give off sounds because the speakers are forced to vibrate in step with the incoming source of energy. Forced vibrations can be demonstrated with *Event 8-O, Tuning Fork Amplifier.*

Strike a tuning fork and hold its base against a table or almost any solid surface. As you touch the surface, the sound becomes louder. The vibrations of the tuning fork travel into the larger surface and cause that surface to vibrate. The larger the vibrating surface, the louder the sound.

Try a variety of surfaces. Tables, desks, chalkboards, and even windows all work quite well. (But be sure to use the *stem,* or base, of the tuning fork, not the tines. Otherwise you will break the window.) Some wall surfaces will also work well if they are not built of concrete or brick. Concrete and brick absorb energy, and little if any sound will be heard.

TABLE 8.1

The Loudness of Sounds

Level of Sound	Decibels
Threshold of hearing	0
Whisper	10–20
Classroom activity	20–40
Conversation	50–60
Heavy street traffic	70–80
Loud thunder	100–110
Threshold of pain	120

Event 8-P, Wastebasket Megaphone, is another example of how forced vibrations produce a louder sound. When speaking into the empty wastebasket, the sound of your voice causes the large surface to vibrate. The larger surface produces a louder sound.

The final example of forced vibration is *Event 8-Q, Make the Lion Roar.* The string has a very small surface. So when you rub it with a damp cloth or paper, it gives off a feeble, squeaky sound. When the sound goes into the milk carton, however, a much larger surface is set in motion; and the sound is much louder. The carton will produce a lion's roar. If you use a tin can, and practice a little, you can make it produce the sound of a crowing rooster.

Natural Vibrations: Resonance

The number of times an object vibrates per second is referred to as the object's **frequency.** An object will vibrate best at only one frequency—its **natural frequency.** You can hear the natural sound of any object by striking it.

What happens when the object *is* vibrating at its natural frequency? The object is then **resonating.** When an object resonates, it becomes much louder than normal.

For example, if you sing a loud tone in front of a piano, you will hear the piano "reply" in the same tone. Only those strings with vibration rates identical to the singing tones will resonate. They will vibrate loud enough to be heard.

Resonance can be produced in an air column by doing *Event 8-R, Vibrating Air.* By raising and lowering the cylinder, we are changing the length of the air column inside the cylinder. In this way we can locate the exact height of the air column that will resonate with the sound of a tuning fork.

For example, a tuning fork with a vibrating rate of 520 vibrations per second will resonate in an air column of about 12 to 14 centimeters. A tuning fork of 260 vps will require an air column twice as high.

In *Event 8-S, Singing Wine Glasses,* the sound is produced by friction between the rim of the goblet and your finger. Actually, your finger does not move around the rim smoothly. Instead, it moves in a series of jerky motions. It slips, catches, slips, and catches, again and again. The motion is so fast that it sends out vibrations.

Those vibrations are not loud enough to produce much of a sound, until the right frequency is reached. When the natural frequency of the glass is reached, the glass resonates. Pour some water into the glass and the natural frequency changes. Note that the sound made by the finger on the rim is identical to the sound made by the glass when it is tapped.

Perhaps it is easier to understand resonance if the vibrations are slowed down. We can use a child on a swing as an example. A swing also has its own natural frequency, but that frequency is very slow. If a child tries to "pump" in a random way, the swing will not go very high. Instead, it just moves in random jerky wiggles.

Once the child learns to time the pump with the tempo of the swing, however, then each pump adds to the previous pump, and the arc of the swing builds up to go higher and higher. Thus, the same energy that earlier caused wiggles now produces a great motion.

That, in slow motion, is what happens in resonance. Input energy is reinforced so that the effect is cumulative. *Event 8-T, Hurricane Huff!*, works the same way as the swing example. Blow on the book with random huffs and the book wiggles. Time the puffs correctly, in tempo with its natural swing pattern, and the book goes into a higher and higher arc.

Event 8-U, Far Far Away, demonstrates the inverse-square rule for sound. As sound travels in all directions from the source, it covers a larger area the further it travels. As the distance from the source increases, the loudness decreases inversely by the square of the distance, as explained earlier.

Pitch (Events 8-V through 8-X)

Discrepant Events and Pupil Investigations

Event 8-V. Rubber-Band Paradox

Introduce the event by calling attention to the relationship between the size of an instrument and its tone. A big instrument has a low sound, a small instrument has a high sound. A big bass fiddle, for example, has a much lower sound than a violin. Pupils will agree that the longer the string on an instrument, the lower the sound.

Use a rubber band to represent strings of different lengths. Pluck it when slightly stretched; then stretch it and pluck again. In which position does the rubber band have the higher sound? Does the activity "agree" with the instruments? (See figure 8.12.)

Pull rubber band

FIGURE 8.12 In which position is the pitch of the rubber band higher? Lower?

Pupil Investigations (may include the following processes):

1. Testing to find that the higher pitched tones occur when the band is long instead of short.
2. Observing that there is a slight change in diameter of the band as it is stretched.
3. Analyzing the factors, other than length, that affect the pitch of the rubber band.

Movable bridge

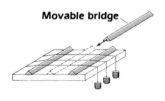

FIGURE 8.13 How do thickness, tension, and length affect the pitch of a string?

Event 8-W. Strained Strings

Set up a board with strings or wires of different sizes as shown in figure 8.13. Provide various weights and a movable triangular "bridge" under the strings. Ask students to find out what factors affect the pitch of the strings.

TABLE 8.2

Factors Affecting the Tone of a String

	High Pitch	Medium Pitch	Low Pitch
Thin wire			
Medium wire			
Thick wire			

Pupil Investigations (may include the following processes):

1. Experimenting with different weights, diameters, and lengths.
2. Recording the data in a table such as table 8.2.
3. Generalizing that the pitch of a wire depends on its length, diameter, and tension.

Event 8-X. The Baffling Bottles

Set up two bottles as shown in figure 8.14. Fill one about one-half to two-thirds full of water. Leave the other bottle empty. Blow across the tops of each and note the sounds. One bottle gives a high tone, the other a low tone. Then tap each with a pencil or pen and listen again. The tones are now reversed! What causes the paradox?

FIGURE 8.14   Blow across the top of each bottle and listen to the sounds; then strike the bottles with a pencil and compare. Why do they differ?

Pupil Investigations (may include the following processes):

1. Verifying the sounds heard during the demonstration by repeating the activity.
2. Experimenting with other bottles of varying sizes, shapes, and amounts of water.
3. Inferring (incorrectly) that the paradox is caused by factors unrelated to the principles of pitch.

Events 8-V through 8-X Explained in Context (Pitch)

What Is Pitch?

The effect of the frequency of sound on the ears is referred to as **pitch.** Put another way, it merely refers to the highness or lowness of a sound. The higher the frequency, the higher the pitch.

It is important to realize that pitch is different from volume. A sound can have a low pitch but a high volume; or, conversely, it can have a high pitch with a low volume. For example, a bass horn produces a low pitch, but it can be played loudly (high volume); and a flute has a high pitch but can be played softly (low volume).

Not all frequencies are audible to the ear. Humans with perfect hearing can detect sounds ranging from 20 to 20,000 vibrations per second. Frequencies above or below that are beyond the range of human detection. Normal conversation takes place in a frequency range of 500 to 3000 vps.

In some respects, children have an almost intuitive knowledge of pitch. They seem to know that large objects produce lower sounds than smaller objects. For example, they know that a bass drum gives a lower sound than a snare drum and that a tuba gives a lower sound than a trumpet. In all cases, the larger the object, the lower the sound.

The Pitch of a String

The pitch of an object depends on a variety of factors. For a stringed instrument, the factors are (1) length, (2) diameter (or thickness), and (3) tension (or tightness). These factors can be demonstrated with *Event 8-V, Rubber-Band Paradox.*

The event may confuse students at first. It appears to contradict the principle of length. As the rubber band becomes longer, the pitch becomes *higher,* not lower. That is just the opposite of what should be expected. Close inspection should give the pupils some clues. They will often notice that other things happen to the rubber band when it is pulled. Not only does it get longer, but (1) it gets thinner, and (2) it gets tighter.

Length, by itself, will lower the pitch, but length is *not* by itself in this activity. The effects of length are more than offset by the increased tension and reduced thickness.

This event will show the importance of controlling variables in an experiment. If there is more than one variable, it is impossible to know which variable affected the outcome of an experiment. *Event 8-W, Strained Strings,* is a way of showing how strings can be tested correctly. Only one variable is tested at any one time.

The Pitch of Other Objects

Event 8-X, The Baffling Bottles, is another surprising activity when first presented. When blowing across the bottles to produce a tone, the bottle with water in it gives the high sound. The bottle that is empty gives the low sound. When struck with a stick or pencil, the sounds are reversed!

What is the principle that governs the sounds? Do they contradict? Not at all. Just remember that *the more there is of something, the lower the sound, and the less there is of something, the higher the sound.* When blowing, the "something" is air, and the larger air column (empty bottle) gives the low sound. When struck, the is the bottle and contents, and again the larger mass (bottle with water) gives the low sound.

In each case the larger mass produced the low sound, and the smaller mass produced the high sound. It was only the mass that changed, not the principle of sound.

There are many more activities that show variations in pitch. These activities include:

1. *Stick-comb pitch-indicator.* Run a pencil or stick across the teeth of a comb. The faster the movement of the stick, the higher the pitch. You can get the same pitch differences by running your fingernail over the fibers of cloth.

2. *Saw pitch-indicator.* Use a handsaw to cut a board. The faster you saw the board (saw teeth hitting the wood), the higher the pitch. The slower you saw, the lower the pitch.

3. *Straw clarinets.* Make a straw soundmaker by cutting away the sides of one end as shown in figure 8.15. Place that end into your mouth and

15 cm to 25 cm

FIGURE 8.15 Cut one end of a paper straw as shown. Place it into your mouth and blow. It vibrates to produce a pitch that depends on the length of the straw.

blow to produce a sound. Cut a piece off the other end of the straw and notice that the sound becomes higher as the length is reduced. **Note:** A paper straw works better than a plastic straw.

4. *Variable air column.* Blow over a straw and note the pitch. Place the lower end of the straw into a beaker of water and blow again. As you lower the straw into the water, the air column becomes shorter and the pitch becomes higher.

5. *Plastic ruler pitch-indicator.* Place a plastic ruler so that it extends over the edge of your desk. Strum it and note the sound. Lengthen the part that extends over the desk and the sound becomes lower. Shorten the overhang and the sound becomes higher.

6. *Water-pouring pitch-indicator.* Pour water into a container. Notice that as the container fills up the pitch becomes higher. Also, if you pour liquid from a can with a single hole, the "glug" sounds become lower as the can empties.

Music

In a strict scientific sense, a **musical tone** is any sound produced by **regular vibrations of matter.** In an informal sense, it is usually felt that music should contain some pleasing quality.

Generally, a musical composition has (1) **melody** (also called *tune*), the effect of single notes in sequence; (2) **rhythm,** a timing pattern; and (3) **harmony,** the pleasing effect of two or more notes sounded together. (The unpleasant effect of two or more notes sounded together is called *discord.*)

The notes that fit together best for a pleasing effect (harmony) are ratios; that is, simple whole number comparisons of 1:2, 1:3, 2:3, 3:4, or 4:5:6. For example, if one note has a frequency of 100 vibrations per second (vps), it will give a pleasing sound when combined with another note of 200 vps, or of 300 vps. The frequency of the musical scale on a piano is shown in figure 8.16.

Musical Instruments

Musical instruments can be classified into three major groups: percussion, string, and wind. Percussion instruments produce sounds by being struck. Stringed instruments produce sounds by plucking or bowing. Wind instruments produce sound with vibrating air columns. This group is subdivided into three more groups: flutes, horns, and reeds. (See table 8.3 for details.)

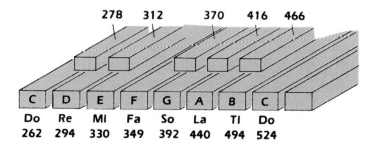

FIGURE 8.16   The musical scale is based on the frequencies shown.

TABLE 8.3

Musical Instruments

Type of Instrument	Source of Sound	Examples
Wind: Flute	Sound caused by blowing across a sharp edge, then air is amplified by instrument	Flute Piccolo Whistle
Brass horn	Sound caused by vibrating lips and amplified by air columns within the instrument	Trumpet Trombone
Reeds	Sound caused by vibrating reeds and amplified by air columns within the instrument	Clarinet Saxophone Accordion
Percussion	Sound caused by striking a membrane or other surface	Drum Cymbals
String	Sound caused by plucking or bowing a string	Violin Banjo

Musical Quality

Quality is the characteristic of music that makes it pleasing to the ear. The effect of quality in speech can be shown by asking a pupil to say "spring is coming." First of all, ask the pupil to say the words normally. Then have the child say the words while holding his or her nose. Is the quality affected?

Other ways of demonstrating the importance of the mouth, teeth, lips, tongue, and nose on the quality of speech include saying the alphabet (1) without opening one's mouth, (2) without closing one's mouth, and (3) without letting the tongue touch the teeth.

Musical Tumblers

Fill four glasses with varying amounts of water. Place a little water in glass 1, twice as much in glass 2, three times as much in glass 3, and four times as much in glass 4. Play "Mary Had a Little Lamb" by striking the glasses with a pencil, pen, or long plastic spoon. Strike them in the following sequence:

2,3,4,3,2,2,2,
3,3,3,2,1,1,
2,3,4,3,2,2,2,
2,3,3,2,3,4

Combining Assessment with Instruction

Ask students to construct an instrument. Have students write a report that includes a paragraph for each of the following:

1. Type of instrument (wind, percussion, or string). How is it classified and why?
2. What part of the design will increase the volume of the sound? Describe its function.

3. What part of the design affects its pitch? Describe its function.

    Evaluate students' projects by using the following criteria:

    - How well does the instrument sound? Can it play many notes?
    - Neatness of construction, durability, and neatness of report.
    - Quality of report. Does it logically answer the questions 1 through 3 above?

Sites and Software

The following websites and software are appropriate to use with this chapter. Note that computer software and websites change rapidly. This makes it necessary to investigate the stable websites for new links and software catalogs for updates. Visit www.mhhe.com/friedl6e to link to these directly and for study resources

Sites

Franklin Institute Science Museum	www.fi.edu
Amateur Science	www.eskimo.com/~billb/amasci.hyml
Mad Scientist	www.madsci.org/experiments
How Telephones Work	www.howstuffworks.com/telephone.htm
Smile Program Physic Index	www.iit.edu/~physinde.html#p5

Software

All about Science Series: Sound (Carolina) (4–8)

Thinkin' Science ZAP! (Edmark) (3–6)

Science Court Explorations: Sound (Tom Snyder) (4–6)

The Way Things Work (Houghton Mifflin Company) (3–9)

InventorLabs: Technology (Houghton Mifflin Interactive) (5–9)

Key Terms

decibels, *142*
frequency, *143*
harmony, *147*
longitudinal waves, *135*
loudness, *142*

melody, *147*
musical tone, *147*
natural frequency, *143*
pitch, *145*
resonance, *143*

rhythm, *147*
sound, *131*
transverse waves, *135*
vibrate, *142*

Teaching Children about Light, Lenses, and Color

NATIONAL SCIENCE EDUCATION STANDARDS ALIGNMENT TO EVENTS

The events in this chapter help accomplish several of the NSES for content standards. The event(s) that align with a given content standard are listed below that standard.

LEVELS K–4

UNIFYING CONCEPTS AND PROCESSES
- Systems, order and organization
  9-C
  9-V

- Change, consistency, measurement
  9-A
  9-C through 9-D
  9-G through 9-I
  9-M

- Evidence, models and explanation
  9-G
  9-I
  9-M through 9-N

SCIENCE AS INQUIRY
- Abilities necessary to do and understand scientific inquiry
  9-A through 9-CC

PHYSICAL SCIENCE
- Light, heat, electricity, and magnetism
  9-A through 9-CC

SCIENCE AND TECHNOLOGY
- Abilities of technological design
  9-F
  9-H through 9-M
  9-R
  9-V
  9-Z

HISTORY AND NATURE OF SCIENCE
- Science as a human endeavor
  Historical introduction
  9-A
  9-D
  9-M

LEVELS 5–8

UNIFYING CONCEPTS AND PROCESSES
- Systems, order and organization
  9-C
  9-V

- Change, consistency, measurement
  9-A
  9-C through 9-D
  9-G through 9-I
  9-M

- Evidence models and explanation
  9-G
  9-I
  9-M through 9-N

SCIENCE AS INQUIRY
- Abilities necessary to do and understand scientific inquiry
  9-A through 9-CC

PHYSICAL SCIENCE
- Light, heat, electricity, and magnetism
  9-A through 9-CC

SCIENCE AND TECHNOLOGY
- Abilities of technological design
  9-F
  9-H through 9-M
  9-R
  9-V
  9-Z

- Understanding science and technology
  9-C and 9-D
  9-G and 9-H
  9-M

HISTORY AND NATURE OF SCIENCE
- Science as a human endeavor
  Historical introduction
  9-A
  9-D
  9-M

Light Exposed

Waves or Particles?

Theories about the nature of light go back to ancient times. At one time it was believed that an object sent little images of itself to the eye and, thus, we were able to "see" it. However, the theory had a major flaw. It did not explain why those objects stopped sending those little images when it was dark.

In the fifteenth century, scientists began forming a modern theory of light, but that theory had two branches that were not in agreement. Was light made of waves or particles? By 1655 Robert Hooke and Christian Huygens were the leading exponents of the wave theory, and by 1666 Isaac Newton was the leading advocate of the particle or "corpuscular" theory.

Newton supported the particle theory. He explained that light, consisting of particles, would travel in straight lines and produce shadows and images with sharp edges. If light traveled in waves, he said, the wiggly rays would blur those edges. He showed that the images were sharp, even when magnified with lenses.

Despite the evidence by Newton, the issue remained unresolved. In fact, shortly after the 1800s began, the weight of scientific evidence shifted toward the wave theory. Augustin Jean Fresnel, with the aid of much stronger magnifying lenses, showed that the edges of shadows and images *were* slightly blurred. They had fringed edges—something that could be explained only by a wave theory.

The fringed edges limit the resolving power (useful magnification) of telescopes and microscopes. A typical telescope has a useful magnification of only about fifty times the diameter of its objective lens (the big lens). That is, if the objective lens is 2 inches in diameter (the calculations are based on the inch), the telescope has a useful power of 50 times 2, or 100 times.

The metric equivalent of the rule is two times the size of the objective lens, as measured in millimeters (mm). Thus, the same lens is about 50 mm in diameter, and when multiplied by 2 the useful maximum power of the telescope is again 100 times. When lenses are arranged so that the power is increased beyond these limits, the image becomes blurred.

An example of what Fresnel studied can be seen by performing *Event 9-A, The Multiplying Lines.* When cutting a narrow slit in a piece of tinfoil and looking through the slit at a source of light, we are surprised to find that fuzzy or fringed lines appear in the opening. It takes some practice and patience to be able to see these lines. They are caused by interference of light waves.

Interference of Waves

When two waves reach an object at the same time, the effect can be greater or less than when the waves reach the object separately. It all depends on whether the crest of one wave is in step with the crest of another.

If the wave crests arrive at the spot together, they combine to form a larger crest. This wave action is called *constructive interference.* In the other instance, when the crest of one wave is in step with the trough of another, the two waves combine to cancel each other out. That wave action is called *destructive interference.* See figure 9.1.

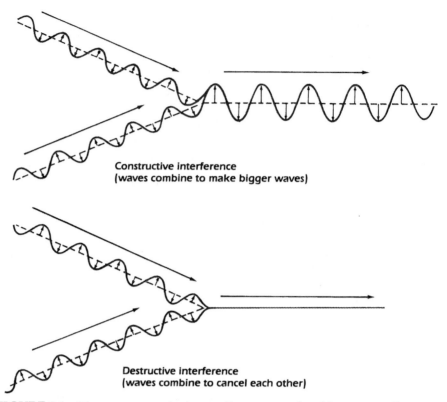

Constructive interference
(waves combine to make bigger waves)

Destructive interference
(waves combine to cancel each other)

FIGURE 9.1   Wave crests meet in the top diagram to make a bigger wave. Crest meets trough in the lower diagram to cancel the wave.

It is the destructive interference that accounts for the dark, fuzzy lines in the opening of the foil in Event 9-A. As the light passes through the slit, they are all more or less in step. However, they do not all arrive at the eye at quite the same time.

The light coming through at the edge of the slit travels farther than the light coming through the center. Thus, some waves arrive out of step with other waves and they cancel each other. Those areas show up as dark or fuzzy bands when viewing a light through the opening.

The destructive interference can be viewed in a pinhole as well as a razor cut. Begin by holding the hole near your eye as you view a light through it. Then slowly move it away. If you do it right, you should see a fuzzy spot at the center of the hole or sometimes a fuzzy, triangular-shaped "donut." Again, it should be noted that some practice is needed to observe the desired effect.

The wave theory received a boost in 1801 when Thomas Young proved that light was the result of wave action. John Jonas Angstrom went a step further. He measured the length of waves and found that the length varied according to color. Today we use a unit of length called the angstrom to honor his work. The angstrom is 0.0000001 millimeter in length (10 million angstroms in 1 meter). The visible light spectrum is 4000 to 7000 angstroms in length.

By 1865 James Maxwell found that light was a part of the electromagnetic spectrum. Thus, light is just the visible part of a much longer spectrum that includes radio waves on one side and X-rays on the other. A diagram of the electromagnetic spectrum is shown in figure 9.2.

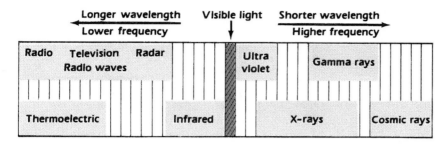

FIGURE 9.2   Visible light is only a tiny part of this electromagnetic spectrum.

Despite the evidence that mounted in the 1800s that light traveled in waves, there were still some doubts that lingered. For example, the wave theory could not explain the **photoelectric effect,** nor something as simple as a hot object.

In the photoelectric effect, electrons are knocked loose from certain substances when struck by light. According to the wave theory, the brighter the light, the greater the energy of the released electrons. However, that does not occur. Regardless of the light intensity, the freed electrons all have the same energy.

Finally, in the early 1900s the confusion was cleared up by Max Planck and Albert Einstein. They showed that light actually had the properties of both particles and waves. The two properties were considered to be an impossible contradiction. Yet, those properties were combined after all. Light exists as discrete bundles of energy called **photons.** (These photons were reminiscent of Newton's corpuscles.) Photons are emitted and absorbed as particles, but travel as waves. No wonder that it took hundreds of years to solve the puzzle.

As a particle, light is a real substance and falls of its own weight. In other words it is attracted by gravity just like any other substance. Another property of light is that when it strikes an object, it exerts a force, just as if the object were hit by a ball.

For example, it has been estimated that the pressure of the sun's light is equal to about ⅙ kilogram per square kilometer. That is not very much pressure, but it is enough to push a large tinfoil satellite out of its orbit by hundreds of kilometers per year.

What Is Light? (Events 9-A through 9-D)

Discrepant Events and Pupil Investigations

Event 9-A. The Multiplying Lines

Cut a thin slit in a piece of foil with a sharp razor blade or knife. Look through the slit at a source of light. Start by holding it close to your eye and slowly moving it away, looking *through* the slit at the light at all times. If viewed correctly, you will see multiple fuzzy lines running the length of the slit. Where do they come from? (**Caution:** Look only at a safe light source such as a fluorescent light or other soft light.)

Pupil Investigations (may include the following processes):

1. Discovering the dark bands of light in the slit.
2. Measuring the distance between the foil and the eye at a point where the bands seem the clearest.

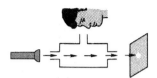

3. Inferring (incorrectly) that the bands are caused by some obstructions in the slit.
4. Generalizing that the bands are evidence of the wave characteristic of light.

Event 9-B. The Invisible Light

Darken the inside of a shoe box or similar box with black paint or dark velvet. Cut holes on the ends (to shine a light through) and a hole on top (for viewing). Shine a beam from a flashlight through the box and observe. (See figure 9.3.) The beam is not visible even though it is right below your eye. Where did it go?

FIGURE 9.3 Look at the invisible light passing through a box a few inches below your eye. What do you see? (This figure shows the box with the side removed.)

Pupil Investigations (may include the following processes):

1. Checking the opening to be sure that nothing is blocking the path of the light.
2. Measuring to see if the viewing port is located directly in line with the beam of light. (It should be.)
3. Inferring (incorrectly) that mirrors are used to divert the path around the viewing port.

Event 9-C. See Through, Shine Through

Connect the light probe to the computer/calculator. Place a light source (flashlight or lamp) and the light probe about a meter apart. Record the intensity of the light. Now place a variety of materials (for example: glass, waxed paper, aluminum foil, plastics, cardboard, writing paper, tissue paper, different colors of water in a glass) between the light and probe. Record the intensity of light read by the probe (photo cell) for each material. Make sure that each material is placed at the same spot for each reading. How would you order the degree of transparency of each material? Classify objects as transparent (see through), translucent (shine through), or opaque.

Pupil Investigations (may include the following processes):

1. Identifying materials that permit you to see objects clearly through them.
2. Identifying materials that permit light to pass through but do not allow clear images to be seen.
3. Identifying materials that block all light.
4. Classifying the materials according to light transmission.

Event 9-D. You Still Come Through for Me

Connect the light probe to the computer and place them near a window facing outside. Allow the computer to record the light intensity for a 24-hour period. Note, too, if the day was cloudy, sunny, or partial sun. Do this for several days.

Pupil Investigations (may include the following processes):

1. Calculating how long the darkness was from sunrise to sunset.
2. Calculating the percentage of sunlight that comes through the clouds on a partially cloudy day.
3. Predicting the time of sunrise and sunset for the next week.

Events 9-B through 9-D Explained in Context (What Is Light?)

Light Is Invisible

Light is visible in only two instances: (1) when it is the source of light (luminous object), and (2) when it is reflected off something (an illuminated object). Surprising as it may seem, it is invisible as it travels from the source to an object.

A good example of invisible light is to look into the sky on a clear night. The sun's light passes around the earth on all sides and fills the sky, but it is not visible unless it hits something (like the moon or a planet). The only other objects that are visible are stars, which are light sources.

Event 9-B, The Invisible Light, shows that light is invisible as it travels. The source of light is visible (flashlight), and the reflected object is visible (your hand held in the beam); but light is invisible as it passes just a few centimeters below your eyes. In fact, the box is not needed to show that light is invisible. Just lift both the flashlight and your hand up above the box and the beam is still invisible. See figure 9.4.

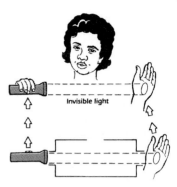

FIGURE 9.4   The box is not needed to show that light is invisible as it travels. Only the source and the object struck by light are visible.

Speed of Light

For a long time it was believed that light moved from its source to an object instantly; that there was no time lag at all. It was not until 1675 that Olaus Roemer discovered that the speed of light had limits after all.

Roemer timed the eclipses of Io, the innermost visible moon of Jupiter. Io disappeared routinely behind Jupiter every 42 hours and 28 minutes with a small, puzzling discrepancy: Io was always a little late at one time of the year and a little early 6 months later. The total difference during the 6 months was 22 minutes.

After 4 years of careful timing, he finally concluded that the difference in time was caused by a difference in distance. It took 22 minutes longer for the light to reach the earth at one time of year than the other. Look at figure 9.5 to see the positions of the earth. When the earth was at point A, the light had to travel 300,000,000 kilometers more than when the earth was at point B.

Roemer took the distance of 300,000,000 kilometers and divided it by 1000 seconds (the 22 minutes of the time lag), and he concluded that light traveled about 300,000 kilometers per second. Roemer's calculations were remarkably accurate.

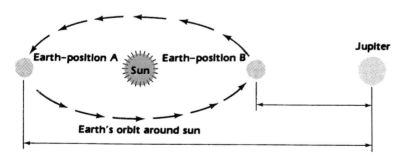

FIGURE 9.5   The earth in position A is 300 million kilometers farther away from Jupiter than when it is in position B. It takes 1000 seconds for light to travel this distance.

Materials Are Transparent, Translucent, or Opaque

Materials can be grouped into three categories depending on how well they permit light to pass through them. If light goes through a substance undistorted (as through a clear window), you can see images clearly through it. Such an object is **transparent** to light.

If a substance scatters light as it passes through, that substance is **translucent** to light. In other words, a translucent substance allows light to go through, but you cannot see images clearly through it. Frosted glass, stained glass, or waxed paper are examples of translucent substances.

A classroom exercise such as *Event 9-C, See Through, Shine Through,* is intended to show the differences between transparent (see through) and translucent (shine through) materials. If a substance blocks all light, that substance is **opaque.** Most pupils can classify according to the three groups without too much difficulty. In *Event 9-D, You Still Come Through for Me,* pupils recognize that clouds usually can be classified as translucent. Calculating the change in time from sunrise to sunset for a few days can help pupils recognize patterns, too.

Brightness of Light (Events 9-E through 9-G)

Discrepant Events and Pupil Investigations

Event 9-E. Changing Spots

Rub a bit of oil or butter into a piece of paper and hold it up to a light. Does the spot appear bright or dark? Now hold the paper down toward the floor. Does the spot still appear the same way, or has it changed? What do you observe? (See figure 9.6.)

Pupil Investigations (may include the following processes):

1. Observing that the spot appears bright when the light is behind it.
2. Observing that the spot appears dark when the light is in front of it.
3. Experimenting to find that at certain points the spot seems to disappear.
4. Forming a theory about measuring the brightness of two light sources.

FIGURE 9.6 A spot of oil or grease on a sheet of paper will appear light if it is illuminated from behind and dark if illuminated from the front.

Event 9-F. Changing Lights

Place a very weak light inside a small box. Cut a small hole in the box and turn off the room lights. Does the light in the hole appear bright or dark? Then turn on the room lights. What happens to the brightness of the light inside the box? Finally, move the box toward and away from the room lights. What do you observe?

Pupil Investigations (may include the following processes):

1. Observing that the hole appears bright when the room lights are off.
2. Observing that the hole appears dark when the room lights are on.
3. Experimenting to see the effects when the box is moved toward or away from a light source.

Event 9-G. Light Gets Lighter as It Travels

Connect the light probe to the computer/calculator. Record the intensity of light from a light source (strong flashlight or lamp) 1 decimeter away from the source. Repeat for distances of 2, 3, and 4 decimeters.

Pupil Investigations (may include the following processes):

1. Designing an experiment to investigate if there is a relationship between light intensity and distance from the source to the receiver (probe).
2. Graphing the data of light intensity and distance.
3. Exploring other graphic relationships such as intensity versus the inverse of the distance, intensity versus the inverse of the distance squared.
4. Generalizing the relationship found.

Events 9-E through 9-G Explained in Context (Brightness of Light)

The brightness of a light depends on two major factors: (1) the brightness of the light source itself, and (2) the distance from the source to the observer. The farther away the object is, the dimmer it appears. For example, a small candle held near the eyes appears brighter than a distant star in the heavens.

These factors are examined in *Event 9-E, Changing Spots*, and *Event 9-F, Changing Lights*. In each event the object being investigated is a kind of **photometer**—a device used to measure the brightness of light.

When the paper is held up to a light, the grease spot appears brighter than the surrounding paper. This means that the light is brighter behind the spot. When the paper is held down, the spot appears dark, indicating that the light is brighter in front of the spot. The spot will almost disappear when the light is equally bright on both sides of the paper.

To compare the brightness of two light sources, just move the paper with the grease spot back and forth between the two sources until the spot disappears.

The box with the hole works essentially the same way. If the room lights are on, the hole looks dark; when the room lights are off, the hole looks bright. If the box is moved toward and away from a light source, there is a point where the hole almost seems to disappear. At that point, the brightness of the lights outside and inside the box are equal.

Another photometer can be made with a piece of foil between two blocks of wax (or paraffin) held together by string or a rubber band. The wax block that receives the most light appears bright when viewed from the side. (See figure 9.7.)

Event 9-G, Light Gets Lighter as It Travels, demonstrates that the light intensity will decrease by the square of the distance. For example, at a distance of 2 decimeters the intensity of light will be one-fourth the strength it would be at 1 decimeter; at 3 decimeters, the intensity would be one-ninth the strength. This is called the **inverse square law.** The light probe is sensitive enough to be able to measure this accurately. If the experimenter is wearing white, oftentimes the light sensor will register that additional reflected light. How can the experiment be designed to avoid this problem?

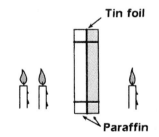

FIGURE 9.7   A paraffin (wax) photometer (side view) can be used to compare the brightness of two lights.

Light Can Be Reflected (Events 9-H through 9-M)

Discrepant Events and Pupil Investigations

Event 9-H. Light-Go-Round

Connect the light probe to the computer. Have three students each hold a mirror so that a beam of light from a laser pointer is reflected off the first

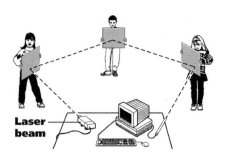

FIGURE 9.8   Three students with mirrors reflect light beam to computer.

mirror, to the second mirror, to the third mirror, and finally caught by the light probe. (See figure 9.8.) Team cooperation is needed here. Caution students about not shining the light into anyone's eyes.

Pupil Investigations (may include the following processes):

1. Investigating how the distance between each mirror affects the intensity of light.
2. Analyzing the relationship between the angle of incidence and angle of reflection.
3. Predicting the position of four mirrors and the change in angles.

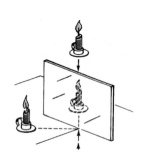

Event 9-I. Ghostly Candle

Set a mirror on a sheet of paper as shown in figure 9.9. Draw a line at right angles to the mirror, and place a candle to the left and a few centimeters in front of the mirror. Go to the right side of the paper and look just barely over the surface of the paper at the image of the candle.

Place a second candle behind the mirror to show where the image of the first candle appears to be. Measure the angles and distances from the mirror to the candle. Compare the angles and distances of the first candle with the angles and distances of the second candle.

FIGURE 9.9   Place a second candle behind the mirror to measure the distance between the image and mirror.

Pupil Investigations (may include the following processes):

1. Measuring the distance between the first candle and mirror.
2. Measuring the distance between the second candle and mirror.
3. Measuring the angles involved with both candles.
4. Making a rule about the reflection of light.

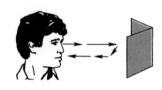

Event 9-J. Watch That Wink

Look into a plane mirror and wink your right eye. Which eye does the image in the mirror wink? Set up an arrangement of two mirrors at right angles to each other, as shown in figure 9.10. Adjust the mirrors so that you see a single image on the split halves where the mirrors join. Then wink your right eye. Which eye does your image wink now?

FIGURE 9.10   Look at a mirror and wink your right eye. Which eye does your image wink? (The two ··rors must be set at 90 :o each other.)

Pupil Investigations (may include the following processes):

1. Discovering that when you wink your right eye the image in a plane mirror winks its left eye.

2. Discovering that when you wink your right eye the image in the arrangement of two mirrors winks its right eye too.
3. Forming a theory (incorrectly) that the images in mirrors are totally reversed. (They are only reversed from left to right, not top to bottom. Otherwise the image would stand on its head.)
4. Generalizing about the principles of reflected light.

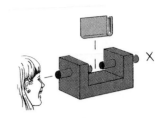

FIGURE 9.11   How does this special box allow a person to look through a book? The X is marked on paper taped to the wall.

Event 9-K. The X-Ray Box

Set up a special box as shown in figure 9.11. (Details are given later in this section.) Look through the viewer and see the *X* taped to the wall. Place a book in the opening between the two tubes and look again. Can you look right through the book to see the *X?*

Pupil Investigations (may include the following processes):

1. Observing the *X* before and after placing the book between the two tubes.
2. Inferring (incorrectly) that an *X* is located inside one of the tubes.
3. Inferring that one does not *really* look through the book but that the view is possible because of some other principle.

Event 9-L. Get-the-Kid-to-Smile Box

Set up a special box as shown in figure 9.12. Tape a picture of a smiling child against the far wall under door A, and a picture of a frowning child against the far wall under door B. Begin with door B open. Look through the viewing hole and you will see a picture of a frowning child. (Has he just been told that the school year is about to begin?) Then close door B and open door A to see the boy smile. (Has he just found out that *you* will be his teacher this year?) How can the opening and closing of the doors change the child's expression?

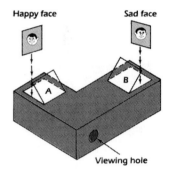

FIGURE 9.12   How does this special box change the picture?

Pupil Investigations (may include the following processes):

1. Observing that the images change when the open doors change.
2. Observing that the image seen with door A is brighter than the image seen with door B.
3. Discovering that when both doors are open, the image of door A dominates.
4. Analyzing the relationship between the images and the reflection of light.

Event 9-M. Reflecting a Colorful Personality

Attach the light sensor to the computer. Design a "wall" to reflect light from different color (include white and black) construction paper or file folders. Position a strong light source to reflect off of the "wall" using one color at a time. (See figure 9.13.)

Pupil Investigations (may include the following processes):

1. Recording the intensity of the reflective light from each color on a chart.
2. Analyzing the relationship between the color and the intensity of the reflected light.
3. Generalizing the color of clothing worn in summer or winter is related to the amount of light reflected/absorbed by each color.

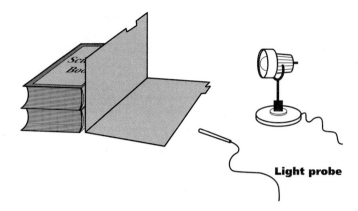

Light probe

FIGURE 9.13   Setup of reflecting "wall" and light probe attached to the computer to study reflection of light off different color surfaces.

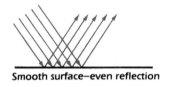

Smooth surface–even reflection

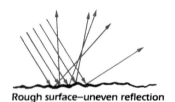

Rough surface–uneven reflection

FIGURE 9.14   Even reflection allows you to see images (as in a mirror). Uneven reflection shows only the surface from which the light is reflecting.

Events 9-H through 9-M Explained in Context (Light Can Be Reflected)

Even and Uneven Reflections

One of the major properties of light is that it can be reflected. The light reflects off mirrors and off walls. In the case of mirrors, you see images in it. In fact, if the mirror is really of good quality, you can hardly see the glass at all. You see only images that are reflected in it.

A wall also reflects the light, but there are no images visible in it; you see just the wall itself. The mirror and wall represent examples of the two ways that light can be reflected. The mirror represents **even reflection** and the wall **uneven reflection.** (See figure 9.14.)

Even reflections occur when a surface is so smooth that light rays all bounce off at the same angle. Uneven reflections occur when a surface is rough enough to scatter the rays that are striking it. Of course, the "roughness" can be so subtle that it does not appear rough to the touch, yet it scatters the light effectively. Most wall surfaces appear smooth, but when viewed through a microscope, they have a rough surface. That is why they scatter light rays.

In summary, an even reflection shows an image but no reflecting surface; an uneven reflection shows the reflecting surface but no image. The details are further summarized in table 9.1.

TABLE 9.1

Even and Uneven Reflection

	Image Visible	Reflecting Surface Visible	Examples
Even Reflection	Yes	No	Mirror; polished chrome, etc.
Uneven Reflection	No	Yes	Any visible object

Angle of Incidence Is Equal to the Angle of Reflection

How will a light ray bounce off a smooth surface? It will bounce somewhat like a basketball off a floor. If you bounce it straight down, it will come straight back. If bounced at a 45-degree angle, each will bounce away at a 45-degree angle, as shown in lines B–C in figure 9.15. Line A will bounce away as shown in line D. The angle of the incoming ray (the *incidence*) is equal to the angle of the outgoing ray (the *reflection*).

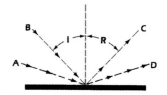

FIGURE 9.15   The angle of incidence (incoming light) is equal to the angle of reflection (outgoing light).

This principle can be demonstrated by darkening a room and shining a point source of light against a mirror. The light beam is invisible, of course, until you blow some chalk dust into the beam. Then the incident and reflecting beams become visible.

The angles of incidence and reflection can also be shown in *Event 9-H, Light-Go-Round*. Pupils may have a difficult time at first getting the three mirrors to line up to reflect back to the light probe. However, when the task is accomplished pupils have a better "feel" for reflected light. In *Event 9-I, Ghostly Candle*, if the lines are drawn carefully, the distances and angles should be identical.

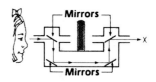

FIGURE 9.16   The inside view of the X-ray box shows the placement of mirrors and the viewing path. The *X* is attached to the wall.

Another trait of even reflection is that images are "folded over" from left to right. That is, if you stand in front of a plane mirror and wink your *right* eye, your image will wink its *left* eye. The same folding-over characteristic can be seen in reflections of printed words. However, images are not folded over top to bottom.

When two mirrors are used at right angles to each other as in *Event 9-J, Watch that Wink*, the image is reflected once by one mirror and again by the other. The double reflections make the image wink its right eye when you wink your right eye. The results are somewhat startling for most people.

The fact that light can be reflected also explains *Event 9-K, The X-Ray Box*. The box doesn't really allow us to look through a book. Instead, four mirrors are used, as shown in figure 9.16, to reflect the light around the book.

The X-Ray box is not easy to build. It takes considerable patience and trial and error to position the mirrors correctly. Even a slight misalignment of one mirror will throw off the results by a wide margin. We have found that the job is made easier by attaching small wooden blocks inside the box so that each mirror fits very loosely in its approximate position. Then they can be secured and adjusted by wedging pieces of sponge between the mirror and block. Gradually the mirrors are aligned and held securely but gently in place.

Reflection also explains *Event 9-L, Get-the-Kid-to-Smile Box*. A clear piece of glass is placed at a 45-degree angle in front of the viewing hole. When door A is closed, the darkness allows the clear glass plate to act as a mirror. Thus, you can see the frowning face at B. When door A is opened, however, you look right through the glass and see a smiling face. (See figure 9.17.)

Other activities used to demonstrate some of the principles of reflection include the following:

1. *Kaleidoscope.* Stand up two small mirrors at right angles to each other. Place bits of colored paper between them and adjust the mirrors. As the mirrors are adjusted slightly, the images are repeated many times to produce a bright kaleidoscopic effect. Then try it with three mirrors.
2. *Making money!* Stand up two small mirrors facing each other. Place a coin between the mirrors and see it multiplied endlessly in repeating images. Try various objects.

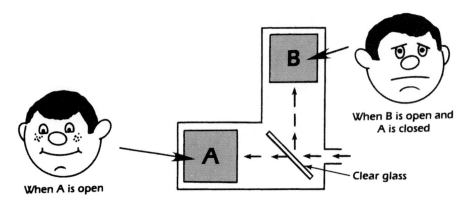

FIGURE 9.17   When door A is open, image A is visible. When door A is closed, the darkness causes the clear glass to act as a mirror showing the image at B.

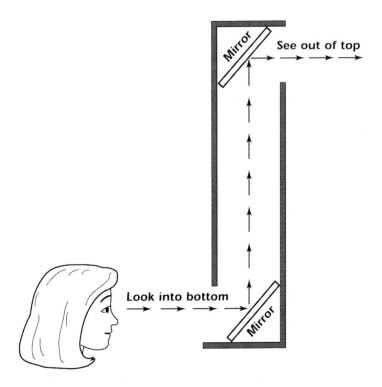

FIGURE 9.18   How does a periscope show that light can be reflected?

3.   *Periscope.* Position two mirrors inside a rectangular box as shown in figure 9.18. This is somewhat like making half of the X-ray box shown earlier. However, it is far easier to make. Although a wooden box gives the periscope some strength and permanence, it is not really needed. You can make do with a milk carton, or, if you use very small mirrors, even the cardboard tube from a roll of paper towels.

In Event 9-M, Reflecting a Colorful Personality, pupils will discover that light colors reflect most of the light and dark colors absorb most and therefore reflect little light. The absorbed light is transformed into heat energy making dark clothes warm to wear in the summertime.

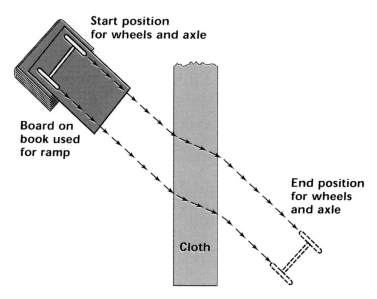

FIGURE 9.19   The wheels and axle are deflected by the cloth much like light is deflected when going from one medium to another.

Light Can Be Refracted (Events 9-N through 9-T)

Discrepant Events and Pupil Investigations

Event 9-N. Free Wheels

Use an axle and two wheels from a toy car or make a set of free wheels from Tinker Toys or other source. Make a ramp by placing one end of a wide board on a book. Attach rough fabric or felt cloth at the bottom half of the ramp. Roll the wheels down the gentle slope at various angles. (See figure 9.19.)

Pupil Investigations (may include the following processes):

1.   Observing that the wheels go straight when they do not reach the fabric at an angle.
2.   Discovering that when the wheels reach the fabric at an angle, the wheels are deflected.
3.   Comparing the path of the wheels with the path of light.
4.   Forming a theory of how light travels through various media.

Event 9-O. Pinpointing the Bolt

Place a bolt upright in an aquarium or large bowl of water. Crouch down and look at the bolt *through the front of the container.* While holding this position, estimate how far away the bolt is and hold a pencil above the bolt. However, look at the pencil *through the air* and the bolt through the water. Then, holding the pencil steady, stand up and check your results. Did you get them lined up? If you do the event right, you will get it wrong! (See figure 9.20.)

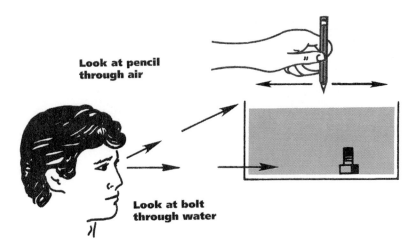

FIGURE 9.20   Estimate the position of the bolt when looking through the front of the container.

View coin through side of glass   Coin

FIGURE 9.21   Why does the coin under the beaker "disappear" when water is poured into it?

Pupil Investigations (may include the following processes):

1.   Experimenting to verify results.
2.   Discovering that the pencil is held closer to the observer than the bolt appears to be.
3.   Inferring that the water causes the light to alter the distance of the object.
4.   Forming a theory about how water causes light to bend.

Event 9-P. The Disappearing Coin

Place a coin under a beaker or clear glass tumbler. Ask pupils to view the coin *through the side of the glass.* Do not view from directly above or from desk level. Tell pupils that you have a "disappearing fluid" and pour it into the container. Watch the coin disappear. (See figure 9.21.)

Pupil Investigations (may include the following processes):

1.   Observing that the coin disappears from view when the fluid is poured into the glass.
2.   Checking to see that the coin is still under the glass. (It is.)
3.   Verifying that water works the same as the "disappearing fluid."
4.   Inferring that water makes the image of the coin disappear.

Event 9-Q. The Appearing Coin!

After losing a coin in the event above, make it appear in this one. Place a penny at the bottom of a cup (inside the cup, not under it) and stand back far enough so that the penny is just out of sight. Then have someone fill the cup with water. Why does the penny lift into view?

Pupil Investigations (may include the following processes):

1.   Observing that the coin becomes visible as the water is poured into the cup.
2.   Forming a theory that the water causes the light to bend.
3.   Generalizing that all the events in this section are related to the bending of light.

Event 9-R. Looking at Lenses

Divide students into groups of two or three pupils each. Provide each group with a convex and concave lens. (Do not describe or identify the lenses at this time.) Give them a minute or two to find out as much as possible about the lenses.

Now distribute a candle to each group and ask them to set up the candle, lens, and screen as shown in figure 9.22.

Ask the pupils to use a lens to project the candle flame onto a screen (of cardboard or notebook paper). Only one of the two lenses will work. Let them discover which one.

Candle   Screen

FIGURE 9.22   Which lens can be used as a projector? What happens to the image?

Pupil Investigations (may include the following processes):

1. Discovering that one lens is thin in the middle and the other thick.
2. Investigating to find that one lens makes images larger, the other makes them smaller.
3. Experimenting to find that the convex lens can be used to project the candle flame.
4. Discovering that the candle flame is inverted on the screen.
5. Drawing diagrams to trace the path of light from the candle to the screen.

Event 9-S. Reverse the Arrows

Place a row of many short arrows on a strip of paper. Then slowly pass the paper behind a full bottle of water. Make several passes with the paper touching the bottle. Then move the paper back about 10 to 20 cm and make several more passes. What do you see? What direction do the arrows go in each case? See figure 9.23.

Pupil Investigations (may include the following processes):

1. Observing that the arrows all appear to be moving in the same direction for the first several passes.
2. Observing that the arrows viewed through the bottle reverse direction during the later passes.

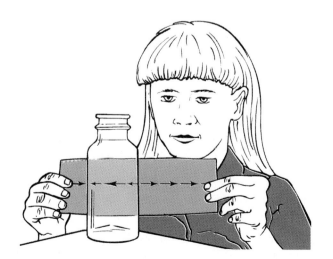

FIGURE 9.23   Why does the bottle reverse the arrows?

3. Analyzing the relationship between the movement of the arrows and the distance the arrows are held behind the bottle.
4. Generalizing from the observations that the bottle acts like a lens to invert an image.

Event 9-T. Instant Eye Test

Look carefully at the pupils in the class who are wearing eyeglasses. Look carefully *through* a lens (of the eyeglasses) to observe the edge of a pupil's face. If you look carefully you will be able to tell if the pupil is nearsighted or farsighted. (See explanation for full details.) Tell each pupil what you observe. Ask them to guess how you did it. (This event works only with those who wear eyeglasses, not contacts.)

Pupil Investigations (may include the following processes):

1. Observing that the eyes of some people appear smaller when viewed through their glasses.
2. Observing that the eyes of others appear larger when viewed through their glasses.
3. Discovering that the image through the lens is not in line with the image above and below the lens.
4. Predicting that one kind of misalignment is caused by nearsightedness and the other by farsightedness.

Events 9-N through 9-T Explained in Context (Light Can Be Refracted)

Refraction Changes the Appearance of Things

The events in this section are all related to the fact that light can be refracted. **Refraction** is the bending of light that occurs when it goes from one medium to another *at an angle.*

Refraction occurs because light travels at different speeds in different mediums. It travels fastest in a vacuum (300,000 kilometers per second). It travels more slowly through air, glass, or water. But for refraction to occur, two conditions must be met: (1) Light must go from one medium to another, and (2) light must enter or exit at an angle.

One way to understand why light bends is to think of a column of soldiers marching from hard ground into a swamp. As they enter the swamp, they slow down as their steps become shorter. If the column goes directly into the swamp, they will continue on the same direction. However, if they enter the swamp at an angle, the soldier on the side nearest to the swamp enters the ooze first, and slows down. The others, however, are still traveling at a faster pace. As each row enters the swamp, they slow down, gradually bending the column into a different direction. The same deflection can be shown by performing *Event 9-N, Free Wheels.* When the wheels are released to roll down the gradual slope, it will be deflected slightly when it goes from the smooth to the rougher fabric. It is bent the same way that the column of soldiers is bent—or as a beam of light is bent.

When light goes from one medium directly into another (not at an angle), as in *Event 9-O, Pinpointing the Bolt*, it does not bend. However, something else happens: An object appears to be closer than it really is. How much closer? Just look where you lined up the pencil. That is how close the bolt *appears* to be when viewed through the water.

Event 9-P, The Disappearing Coin, is dramatic because the coin seems to disappear right in front of your eyes. Again, refraction is the cause of the effect. When water is added to the container, the light from the coin is bent upward so much that it goes out of the top of the glass. Thus, if light from the coin does not get out of the side of the glass, it is invisible when viewed from that angle.

Refraction also occurs in *Event 9-Q, The Appearing Coin!* In this case, however, the coin appears instead of disappears. When water is added, the light is bent down so that the coin becomes visible. Again, the event shows that light is bent as it travels at an angle from one medium (air) into another (water).

Lenses

Any discussion of refraction would be incomplete without some emphasis on lenses. Lenses work because of refraction. In fact, since lenses are carefully shaped, the bending of the light is controlled. This controlled bending is shown in *Event 9-R, Looking at Lenses.*

As pupils examine the lenses they should discover that one kind of lens is thicker in the middle than at the edges. That type is called a **convex** lens. Light that shines through a convex lens comes to a focus, or *converges.* When you hold a convex lens close to the object, the object appears larger.

Another type of lens is thinner in the middle than at the edges and is called a **concave** lens. Light that shines through a concave lens spreads out, or *diverges.* When held near an object, the object appears smaller. The converging and diverging rays of the two lenses are shown in figure 9.24.

Students should also discover that only the convex lens can be used to project the candle flame onto a screen. Pupils are usually surprised to find that the image of the flame is inverted. They can see why by just following the top and bottom rays in figure 9.25. The top ray is bent downward through the focal point, and appears at the bottom of the screen. Conversely, the bottom ray is bent upward, passes through the focal point and finally appears on the top of the screen. The result is an inverted image.

Pupils can also see the reversing effect of a convex lens by doing *Event 9-S, Reversing the Arrows.* The bottle of water acts as a very thick lens. If you hold the paper strip with the arrows tight against the bottle, the arrows all point the same way. The arrows do not reverse until you hold the strip of paper back a

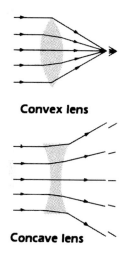

Convex lens

Concave lens

FIGURE 9.24   Light rays are brought together (converge) with a convex lens and spread apart (diverge) with a concave lens.

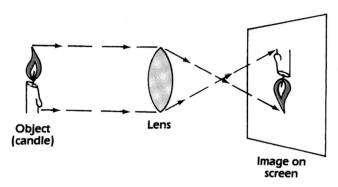

Object (candle)   **Lens**

Image on screen

FIGURE 9.25   A convex lens projects an inverted image on the screen.

few centimeters. You need to get back beyond the focal point for the image to reverse. **Note:** The focal point of a very thick lens (bottle) is very close to the lens (bottle).

A simple lens can be made by merely placing a drop of water on a pin-hole in a piece of foil. The drop of water takes on a lenslike shape and, as a result, can actually be used to magnify images. It can only be used very close to an object, so place the foil on some pencils or straws. Put the object to be viewed under the lens, and observe. (Printed matter works well.)

With this background in lenses, we can understand how *Event 9-T, Instant Eye Test,* works. Eyeglasses are really no more than very carefully made lenses. Thus, they will do just what the simple lenses did. The glasses will make objects appear larger or smaller.

Nearsighted people are those whose "near-sight" is relatively good. It is their distance vision that is bad. They wear concave lenses to correct their vision. Pupils often wonder how those lenses can help since, as stated earlier, concave lenses make objects appear smaller. The answer is that the lens corrects the user's vision by getting rid of the blur. It is not the size of the image, but how clear it is that makes for good vision.

Farsighted people have relatively good "far-sight." They wear convex lenses, which make objects appear larger. Again, it is not the change in size of the image that corrects the vision; it is the fact that the lens brings the light rays to a sharp focus on the retina.

Since lenses make objects appear smaller or larger, you can observe that change by lining up the edge of the face, *as viewed through the lens,* with the line of the face above and below the lens. If the image through the glasses is set inward, the correction is for nearsightedness. If the image is set outward, the correction is for farsightedness. (See figure 9.26.)

There are a number of other activities that can be used to show that light can be refracted:

1. *The "broken" pencil.* Fill a glass tumbler with water and stick a pencil into it. When viewed from the side, the pencil looks broken at the water line. The light reaches your eyes through different mediums (air and water), and as a result the bending of the light is different for each. (See figure 9.27.)

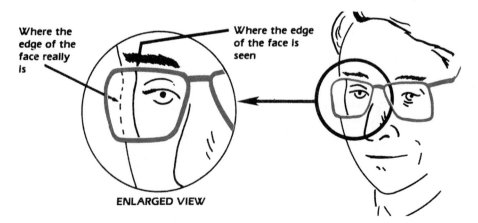

Where the edge of the face really is

Where the edge of the face is seen

ENLARGED VIEW

FIGURE 9.26   Look at the edge of the face through a lens. Compare it with the edge of the face above and below the lens. (This man is nearsighted.)

2. *Pour light.* This works only in a darkened room. Also, it does not lend itself to large groups because of limited visibility. (The bottom of the sink is not easily seen by more than a few pupils.) However, where it can be used, the event is a surprise to students.

    Shine a flashlight into the top of a tall tin can about half full of water. Observe the water pour out of the hole into the sink. If the room is dark enough, the stream should be visible from the side, and the bottom of the sink should be slightly illuminated.

3. *Silver soot.* Hard boil an egg and cover it with a thick layer of black soot from a candle flame. When completely blackened, lower the egg into a glass of water. The egg appears silvery. Why? The answer is that soot captures some air and alters the bending of light so that those rays do not leave the water. The end result is that the egg looks somewhat like a curved silver mirror. **Note:** The layer of soot must be very thick for the silvery effect to appear.

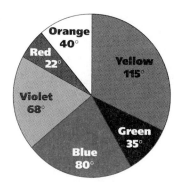

FIGURE 9.27   Can you see the "broken" pencil? It is caused by refraction.

Color (Events 9-U through 9-AA)

Discrepant Events and Pupil Investigations

Event 9-U. Color from White
Darken the room and turn on a strong light such as a projector. Hold a prism in the light beam and turn it slowly until a band of colors is visible. (**Caution:** Do not look directly into the strong light source.)

Pupil Investigations (may include the following processes):

1. Observing the formation of a band of colors on the wall.
2. Recording in their notebooks the colors that are formed.
3. Generalizing that white light consists of colors.

Event 9-V. White from Color
Cut out a disk from 10 to 25 cm in diameter. Use stiff cardboard or tagboard. Carefully divide the disk into segments and paint or color them as indicated in figure 9.28. Devise a means of spinning the disk and observe. (Smaller disks can sometimes be spun "like a top" by inserting a short pencil through the middle. Or, loop a string through two holes near the center of the disk to provide a means of spinning. Still another way is to attach the disk to the end of a hand drill.)

FIGURE 9.28   Make a color disk like this and spin it. The colors will blend to produce white.

Pupil Investigations (may include the following processes):

1. Predicting what will happen when the disk is spun.
2. Observing that the colors gradually blend to form white as the disk is spun.
3. Generalizing that white light consists of colors.

Event 9-W. Mixed-Up Lights
(**Note:** This event is quite interesting if done with good-quality color filters and projectors in a dark room. However, flashlights do not work well, and the

event should probably not be attempted with them.) Combine red and green lights so that they partially overlap on a white screen. What color results?

Pupil Investigations (may include the following processes):

1. Observing that when any two colors are combined, a lighter color is produced.
2. Recording the results in a simple table as follows:

   Red and green   = _____
   Red and blue   = _____
   Blue and yellow = _____

3. Forming a theory that the mixing of colors sometimes produces white, but never black.

Event 9-X. Lingering Images

Stare intently for about 30 seconds at a brightly colored piece of paper. Then stare steadily at a blank white sheet of paper without letting your eyes wander. What image do you see appearing on the blank surface? (It helps to make a small dot in the middle of the colored paper, as well as on the white paper. They help to hold your gaze steady.)

Pupil Investigations (may include the following processes):

1. Observing a colored fringe forming around the original color being viewed.
2. Discovering that a different color appears when the gaze is shifted to a white background.
3. Forming a theory that the original color is subtracted from white when the gaze is shifted.

Event 9-Y. Two-Toned Fluid

Mix a few drops of red food coloring into a bottle of water. View the bottle with light shining at it from your viewing position. What color is it? Then view the bottle with light shining from behind it. What color do you see now?

Pupil Investigations (may include the following processes):

1. Observing a red color when the light shines through the bottle from behind.
2. Observing a green color with the light shining on the bottle from the front.
3. Generalizing that the color changes are due to the transmission and reflection of light.

Event 9-Z. Mixing Pigments

Select chalk of various colors and grind them into powder, being careful to keep the colors separate. Mix water into the powders to produce a thin paste. Now carefully mix together various combinations of any two colors and note the results. (You can also use tempera paints, or even containers of water with food coloring added.)

Pupil Investigations (may include the following processes):

1. Observing that when two colors are mixed, a third color is formed.
2. Recording the various trials to determine which colors produce the best results.
3. Forming a theory about the fact that the colors often produce black mixtures but never white mixtures.
4. Generalizing that when paints are mixed, they tend to absorb light.

Event 9-AA. Curious Colors

Select some objects such as colored samples of cloth and Christmas foil, and ask pupils to identify the colors when viewed in colored light. Darken the room and use a colored piece of plastic (as a filter) on an overhead projector. Do not let the students see the objects in natural light until later when they can check their observations.

Pupil Investigations (may include the following processes):

1. Identifying the color of objects as seen in colored light.
2. Discovering that some of the objects have different colors when viewed in natural light.
3. Forming a theory to explain the differences observed.

Events 9-U through 9-AA Explained in Context (Color)

White Light Contains All Colors

As we look at surrounding objects, colors of all kinds can be seen. Where do the colors come from? It may be surprising to some pupils that all colors can be found in white light. If white light strikes an object, that object may absorb or reflect any or all parts of that light, resulting in anything from white to black.

The fact that white light consists of colors can be demonstrated with a prism in *Event 9-U, Color from White.* You will need to experiment with the correct position of the prism. Just hold the prism in the beam of the light and slowly turn it. The color bands will appear on the walls, ceiling, or floor, depending on how you hold the prism. You can also use sunlight as a light source if it is available in your room. Just open a curtain slightly to allow a thin ray to enter the room.

The colored band is formed by the prism because each color has a different wavelength, and each wavelength is bent differently as it passes into the prism and then out again. The result is to bend each color differently, forming a band. (See figure 9.29.) It is interesting to note that in 1704, Isaac

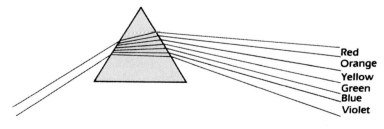

FIGURE 9.29   What happens to a beam of white light when it passes through a prism?

Newton explained that white light was made up of many colors. He started with five spectral or "real" colors. Then agreeing that orange, too, was a distinct color, he was persuaded to complete the component colors of light at seven because the number seven was firmly established in the culture of that period as a special number. Indigo was added to the light spectrum with no scientific evidence of its existence. To this day, many elementary texts incorrectly teach the seven-color composition of ROYGBIV. Scientists agree that there are only six component colors of white light and indigo is not one of them.

Additive Colors

We have seen that when white light shines through a prism, it is separated into a band of colors. Can we reverse the procedure? Can colors be added together to produce white? Yes.

Event 9-V, White from Color, shows one way to **add colors** to make white. When the disk is spun, each of the colors is by the retina for a short time. This ability to retain an image is called *persistence of vision.* Thus, one color is seen and "persists" long enough for the next color to come into view. The colors combine, one after another, so that when they are all added together, they appear white to the viewer.

Another way of mixing colors to obtain white is shown in *Event 9-W, Mixed-Up Lights.* First of all, remember that the screen is white and can reflect all light. Thus, if a blue light strikes the screen, it will, of course, reflect blue. Then if a yellow light is also shown on the screen, it will also reflect yellow. Blue and yellow contain all the wavelengths of light, so when they overlap on the screen they combine to produce white. See figure 9.30 to see the results when various colors of light are combined.

The mixing of colors is often attempted with flashlights and colored plastic films, but the results are usually disappointing. Unfortunately, it is necessary to have good quality light sources, such as projectors, and good quality filters to do this event with a reasonable chance of success.

If an object absorbs all the colors that strike it, then it can reflect none. As a result, it appears black. If it absorbs none of the colors and reflects all of them, the object appears white.

Most objects are somewhere in between. A red object, for example, absorbs all colors *except* red. It reflects red; therefore red is the only color visible to a viewer.

Complementary Colors

Most of us have seen many color combinations in homes and clothing. Often we hear that one color "complements" another. In everyday use, complementary colors are those that seem to look nice together. In science, however, the definition is more precise.

Specifically, **complementary colors** are any two that when added to each other produce white. For example, the complementary color of blue light is yellow. Other complementary colors of light are green and magenta, and red and cyan.

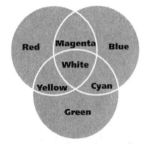

FIGURE 9.30 The primary colors of light are additive. When combined, they produce the colors shown in the overlapping areas of the circles.

Complementary colors are formed in *Event 9-X, Lingering Images*. After staring at a bright color for about 30 seconds, the eyes become tired of it. Thus, when you shift your gaze to a blank white surface (which, remember, reflects all colors), your eyes ignore the color they had just stared at (because, as we have just stated, the eyes become tired of it). As a result, you see only the remaining or complementary color. In other words, you observe the color that is "left over" after the original color is subtracted from white.

For example, suppose that you stared at a blue object for a while. The eyes become tired of that color. Then, when looking at a white surface, the blue (within the white) does not register until the eyes recover from their fatigue (15 to 30 seconds). Blue is subtracted from the colors that white reflects. The color that remains is yellow.

Complementary colors are also obtained by doing *Event 9-Y, Two-Toned Fluid*. When the light shines through the fluid, only a reddish color is transmitted. Surprisingly, the balance of the colors (the complementary color) is often scattered and will appear as green.

It may take some trial and error to get just the right kind of mixture. Also, it is important that all other lights are turned off and that only a single light source is used. Sometimes a better effect can be achieved by using Mercurochrome instead of food coloring.

Subtractive Colors

Students can experiment with colors by performing *Event 9-Z, Mixing Pigments*. When yellow and blue are mixed, for example, a green color is formed. The results of all trials should be summarized. Note that you will never get white when pigments are mixed. As more and more colors are combined, it is more and more likely that black will result.

This peculiarity can be explained by recalling that a colored object absorbs some colors and reflects other colors. Remember that a red pigment absorbs all other colors. Thus, if red is mixed with green, the red absorbs the green. The green, in turn, absorbs the red. As a result, the colors absorb each other and the mixture looks black.

When more than two pigments are mixed together, black is more likely to be produced than if only two are mixed. The subtractive primary colors of cyan, magenta, and yellow will produce black. (See figure 9.31.) Printers need only three colors of ink to produce nearly any color in the spectrum. A fourth color, black, is used for shading and depth.

In summary, when mixing pigments, many colors are absorbed, or **subtracted,** from the spectrum. That is why the mixing of pigments is sometimes referred to as the subtractive rule of colors.

Colors are also subtracted in *Event 9-AA, Curious Colors*. If you look at a red object in a green light, it looks black, because the red object reflects only red. It absorbs (or subtracts) the green light. Therefore, if there is no red light available, red cannot be reflected. Students will find it difficult to determine the actual color of objects viewed in a colored light. (**Note:** It is important that the room be darkened very well. If stray light enters the room, it will be easy to detect the colors.)

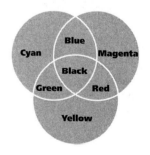

FIGURE 9.31   The primary paints are subtractive. When combined, they produce the colors shown in the overlapping areas of the circles.

FIGURE 9.32 Measure the two men. Which one is taller?

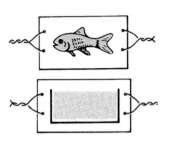

FIGURE 9.33 Put the fish into the bowl. Spin the card with the fish on one side and the bowl on the other.

Optical Illusions (Events 9-BB and 9-CC)

Discrepant Events and Pupil Investigations

Event 9-BB. Tall Man, Short Man

Look at figure 9.32 and decide which man is taller. Then take a ruler and measure the height of each. How do you account for the big difference in the *appearance* of size?

Pupil Investigations (may include the following processes):

1. Observing that the man in the back seems to be much taller than the man in the front.
2. Measuring to find that they are both the same size.
3. Experimenting with converging lines to see their effect on the appearance of size and distance.

Event 9-CC. Fish in the Bowl

Prepare a small card with a diagram of a fish on one side and a diagram of a bowl on the other. Insert strings into holes at each end of the card as shown in figure 9.33. Then twist the strings and let them unravel, causing the card to spin rapidly. What do you observe?

Pupil Investigations (may include the following processes):

1. Observing that the fish appears to be in the bowl when the card is spinning.
2. Experimenting with other diagrams and cards to verify the observations.
3. Forming a theory that both images blend together to produce the appearance of a fish in a bowl.
4. Inferring that images persist on the retina for a short time after viewing.

Events 9-BB and 9-CC Explained in Context (Optical Illusions)

Since the days of the first magician, it is likely that people had doubts about "seeing is believing." Pupils will surely doubt what they see in optical illusions. *Event 9-BB, Tall Man, Short Man,* is an example of how our eyes can be deceived.

Optical illusions work because our past experience helps us *most* of the time. For example, we know that an object in the distance looks smaller than the same object when it is closer. We make use of this experience by giving a simple two-dimensional picture the *appearance* of three dimensions by merely drawing the "distant" objects smaller.

Although the two figures in our picture take up the same height on the page, the figure on the right appears larger. Our eyes compensate for a "distance effect" by telling us that anything that far away must be quite large to appear so prominently in the scene.

Event 9-CC, Fish in the Bowl, is a simple example of another kind of optical illusion. The fish and bowl seem to merge into a single picture when the card is spun because the images linger awhile in our vision. It is another case of "persistence of vision" discussed earlier with *Event 9-U, Color from White.*

One image remains, or persists, for a fraction of a second after the picture is gone. If the card is spun rapidly, the new image appears before the old image is gone. Thus, the image of the fish and the image of the bowl merge into a single image of a fish in a bowl.

The fact that images persist allows us to see "motion" in a series of still pictures. That is what happens in a motion picture film. In one common format, 16 pictures are flashed on the screen every second. Each successive picture is slightly different so that the merged images appear to move.

Much the same thing occurs to permit us to see motion on television. On the television screen the picture is changed 30 times per second.

"Flip" pictures also produce motion. Draw a stick diagram on the last page of a notepad. Continue to make stick pictures on the pages before it, making only slight changes each time. Then flip the pages and the image appears to move!

There are many more optical illusions. Here are a few examples:

1. *Long and short lines—I.* Which line is longer in figure 9.34? Consider only the center stem of the figures, not the end lines. The upper figure appears to be longer, because the outward-angled end-lines seem to lengthen the figure. However, both center stems are of the same length.

2. *Long and short lines—II.* Which line is longer in figure 9.35, line A—B, or line B—C? Surprisingly, they are both the same length. The other lines of the parallelogram combine to make it appear that line A—B is longer.

3. *Top hat.* Look at the top hat in figure 9.36. Is it higher than it is wide? Surprisingly, no. Both dimensions are the same. The horizontal rim appears shorter because its length is divided between several vertical lines. The vertical lines, however, are unbroken, giving the appearance of greater height.

4. *The floating finger!* Touch your index fingers together, tip to tip. Hold them about ⅓ meter in front of you, and look just past them to an object on the far wall. As you look at the object on the wall, you can still see your fingers with your peripheral vision. What do you see? Your fingertips should appear to be holding a suspended double-ended finger between them. Now pull your fingers apart slightly. The double-ended finger will appear to float. (See figure 9.37.)

   The illusion is caused by **parallax.** That is, when the eyes are focused on a distant object they do not, at the same time, focus on a near object. Actually, the left eye has one image, and the right eye has another. The two images overlap to produce the appearance of a two-pointed finger in the middle. The effect works only if you focus your eyes on a distant object, and you see the near object only with peripheral vision.

5. *Hole in the hand!* Roll up a sheet of paper into a tube and hold it alongside the open palm of your hand. Look through the tube with your left eye at an object at the end of the room. Hold your right hand alongside the tube, palm open and facing you, with fingers pointing up. Keep *both* eyes open. It appears as if you are looking through a hole in your hand. Here again, your eyes see two separate images, and your brain combines them to give the illusion.

   Sometimes a pupil will have difficulty seeing the illusion. If so, ask these questions: "What do you see with your left eye?" What do you see with your right eye?The reason they fail to see the illusion is that they

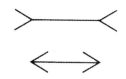

FIGURE 9.34   In which figure is the center stem longer?

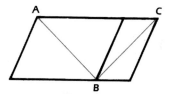

FIGURE 9.35   Is line A–B longer than line B–C?

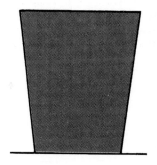

FIGURE 9.36   Is the top hat taller than it is wide?

FIGURE 9.37   The floating finger illusion appears when two fingers are held close to each other while looking past them at a distant object.

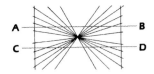

FIGURE 9.38 Hold a ruler or straight-edge alongside lines A–B and C–D. Are they curved or straight?

allow one eye to dominate. By asking the two questions, you force them to use both eyes, one at a time. (Be sure to wait for an answer to each question.)

6. *Curving parallels!* Look at figure 9.38. Do the two horizontal lines appear to be straight or curved? Place a ruler or straight edge along the horizontal lines and check. The lines are actually straight, but they appear curved because the crossed lines intersect at gradually different angles.

Combining Assessment with Instruction

Have students think about the "big ideas" or concepts in the unit on light. Using these big ideas, have students make a concept map detailing the interconnection among the ideas. This activity can be done in two ways: (1) students are supplied the list of concepts (key terms) or (2) students think of them on their own.

A concept map is a diagram or web that shows the relationships among ideas and applications. The concept map can help the teachers view students' understanding or misunderstanding about major concepts. The map also requires that students organize their thoughts.

Evaluate the concept map using the following criteria:

1. Key terms and concepts are present and organized in a logical and valid way that reflects understanding and accuracy.
2. Linking words reflect understanding of the interconnection among and between concepts.
3. Organization shows how general concepts encompass more specific ideas (a hierarchy is evident).
4. Applications and examples strengthen the evidence of understanding.

A sample of a student's concept map for light is given in figure 9.39. Can you find a concept (s)he may not understand?

Sites and Software

The following websites and software are appropriate to use with this chapter. Note that computer software and websites change rapidly. This makes it necessary to investigate the stable websites for new links and software catalogs for updates. Visit www.mhhe.com/friedl6e to link to these directly and for study resources.

Sites

Amateur Science	www.eskimo.com/~billb/amasci.html
Mad Scientist	www.madsci.org/experiments
Howstuffworks: Light	www.howstuffworks.com/category.htm?cat=Light

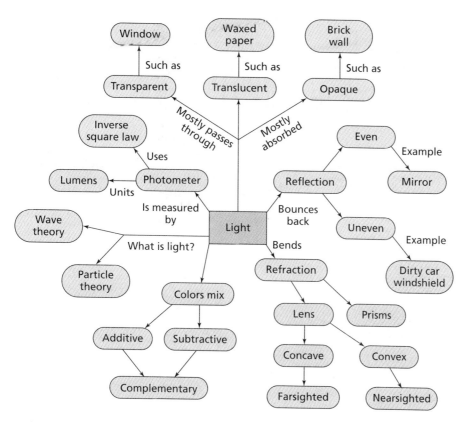

FIGURE 9.39   Sample of student's concept map for "light." Can you find a concept(s) he may not understand?

Software

Sticky Bear Science Fair: Light (Discovery) (2–5)
All about Science Series: Light (Carolina) (4–8)
Thinkin' Science ZAP! (Edmark) (3–6)
The Way Things Work (Houghton Mifflin Company) (3–9)
InventorLabs: Technology (Houghton Mifflin Interactive) (5–9)
Introduction to Science (Carolina) (2–5)
Virtual Physics: Escape from Braindeath (Discovery) (7–9)

Key Terms

additive color, *172*
complementary colors, *172*
concave, *167*
convex, *167*
even reflection, *160*
farsighted, *168*
inverse square law, *157*

nearsighted, *168*
opaque, *156*
optical illusions, *174*
parallax, *175*
photoelectric effect, *153*
photometer, *157*

photons, *153*
refraction, *166*
subtractive color, *173*
translucent, *156*
transparent, *156*
uneven reflection, *160*

Teaching Children about Simple Machines

NATIONAL SCIENCE EDUCATION STANDARDS ALIGNMENT TO EVENTS

The events in this chapter help accomplish several of the NSES for content standard. The event(s) that align with a given content standard are listed below that standard.

LEVELS K–4

UNIFYING CONCEPTS AND PROCESSES
- Systems, order and organization
  10-B
  10-D through 10-F
  10-G and 10-I
  l0-K
  10-M
  10-N

- Change, consistency, measurement
  10-B
  10-D and 10-F
  10-I
  10-K
  10-N

- Evidence, models, and explanation
  10-A through 10-0

- Evolution and equilibrium
  10-A through 10-C
  10-D through 10-F
  10-H and 10-I
  10-K
  10-N and 10-0

- Form and function
  10-A through 10-0

SCIENCE AS INQUIRY
- Abilities necessary to do and
  understand scientific inquiry
  10-A through 10-0

PHYSICAL SCIENCE
- Position and motion of objects
  10-A through 10-C
  10-D through 10-F
  10-H and 10-I
  10-J through 10-K
  10-L through 10-M
  10-N through 10-0

SCIENCE AND TECHNOLOGY
- Abilities of technological design
  10-A through 10-0

HISTORY AND NATURE OF SCIENCE
- Science as a human endeavor
  Background information

LEVELS 5–8

UNIFYING CONCEPTS AND PROCESSES
- Systems, order and organization
  10-B
  10-D throuh 10-F
  10-G and 10-I
  10-K
  10-M
  10-N

- Change, consistency, measurement
  10-B
  10-D and 10-F
  10-I
  10-K
  10-N

- Evidence, models and explanation
  10-A through 10-0

- Evolution and equilibrium
  10-A through 10-C
  10-D through 10-F
  10-H and 10-I
  10-K
  10-N and 10-0

- Form and function
  10-A through 10-0

SCIENCE AS INQUIRY
- Abilities necessary to do and
  understand scientific inquiry
  10-A through 10-0

PHYSICAL SCIENCE
- Motion and forces
  10-A through 10-C
  10-D through 10-F
  10-H and 10-I
  10-J through 10-K
  10-L through 10-M
  10-N through 10-0

SCIENCE AND TECHNOLOGY
- Abilities of technological design
  10-A through 10-0
- Understanding science and technology
  10-C

HISTORY & NATURE OF SCIENCE
- Science as a human endeavor
  Background information

Simple Machines Make Work Easier

Since earliest times man has used devices to make work easier and to do a job faster. The first tools were invented when a need arose to perform tasks too difficult for humans to accomplish. The need to dig a hole, move a boulder, catch or spear a fish, all prompted early man to invent ways to make the tasks easier. As it is often said, Necessity is the mother of invention.

The tools that our earliest ancestors invented were very primitive by today's standards but were the very first machines. These tools are excellent examples of what we call **simple machines.** Although we do not know who invented them, we do know that as with inventions of modern days, small improvements were made to these tools throughout the centuries as new materials were discovered. Earliest tools were made from wood, bone, and stone. As metals were discovered, tools greatly improved in usefulness and durability.

Even with the invention of simple machines, muscle power from both man and domesticated animals was necessary to power the machines. Levers were used to move heavy objects, and a wheel and axle afforded the movement of heavy objects over a distance by minimizing friction.

A **machine** is defined as something that makes a job easier by changing one or more of the following: the direction of the force, the amount or size of force needed, the speed or distance of the force. Simple machines first did this without an additional supply of energy such as electricity. The first simple machines used the muscle force of man.

Simple machines are classified as mechanical machines since they convert one kind of movement into another. When you pull down on the flag pole rope, you move the flag up. As you pedal your bike, your knees seem to go up and down or your feet move in small circles, but the bicycle moves forward, straight ahead.

Today we classify simple machines into six categories: lever, wheel and axle, pulley, inclined plane, screw, and wedge. Later in this chapter we will discuss how simple machines are related to one another. There are many ways to regroup the six categories. One such grouping is to sort the six into two main groups—*levers* (lever, wheel and axle, and pulley) and *inclined planes* (inclined plane, screw, and wedge).

Eventually more than one simple machine was combined with others to create more complex machines called **compound machines.** For example, the Archimedean screw, now called an auger, cleverly pumped water uphill from a water supply to a trough or pail (see Figure 10.1). A screw, inclined plane, lever, and wheel and axle together made this compound machine amazing. No one really knows if Archimedes, the Greek scientist, actually created this invention more than two thousand years ago. One thing we do know is that inventions such as the Archimedean screw and printing press helped civilizations move forward.

A **force** is a push or a pull. It is the effort made to change the motion of an object. You must apply a force to make a machine work. Force is usually measured in pounds (customary system, previously called the English system) and Newtons (Metric system). Newton's second law of motion refers to the affect of a change of speed or direction on a mass. Recall the formula, $F = ma$, where F is force, m is mass, and a is acceleration (a change in speed or direction), gravity (g) is also a form of acceleration. If an object is dropped it will fall faster and faster due to gravity pulling it toward Earth. The influence

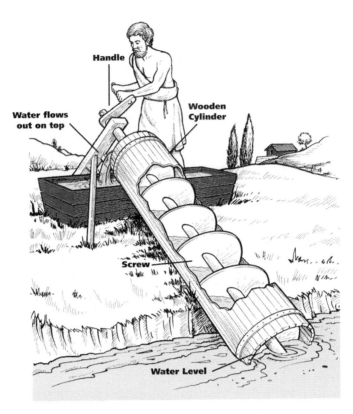

FIGURE 10.1   Archimedean screw consists of a screw, inclined plane, lever, and wheel and axle. Can you find each?

gravity has on the mass of an object makes the weight of that object a force. The force or weight of your body pushes on the area of ground on which you walk. That is why it hurts so much when you step barefooted onto a pebble. All of your weight (force) is pressing on an area of your foot as small as the size of the pebble you stepped on. When you are trying to push or pull a heavy object people often say, "Put all of your weight into it." They are referring to the force with which you are pushing.

How do we define work? To go from your house to a neighbor's house down the street, running takes more work than walking. You are going the same distance in the same amount of time but exert more force to go faster. Also consider that if you walk the same speed but go much further you also do more work. In an exercise program, to do the same amount of work you can either walk twice as fast or walk twice the distance. The two factors that affect work are force and distance. If you increase one you can decrease the other.

You can do the same amount of work if you pull a wagon full of dirt for 2 miles or pull that wagon twice as hard for 1 mile. Doing work usually involves exerting one force against another—usually a push or pull against gravity or friction.

Machines can multiply (increase) the force of your effort. But for machines to help you increase the force, you must apply that force for a longer distance. We can measure how much a machine can multiply or increase our force (strength). This is called the **Actual Mechanical Advantage** (AMA). We

FIGURE 10.2   Mechanical advantage of a screwdriver used as a lever.

say AMA is calculated as the ratio of the resistance force to the effort force. The effort force is the force you apply to get work done. An example of the resistance force is the amount of weight you need to move.

$$\text{AMA} = \frac{\text{resistance force}}{\text{effort force}} = \frac{f_r}{f_e}$$

Think about a screwdriver used to open a can of paint. As you push down on the end of the screwdriver, notice that the handle moves through a longer distance than the tip of the screwdriver. If the handle travels 3 times the distance the tip travels, then it will be 3 times easier to open than if you tried to use your fingernails. The mechanical advantage is 3 (See figure 10.2).

Work is the amount of force or weight (mass × gravity) applied over a distance. $W = f \times d$. Many middle school students confuse mass and weight. Weight is a force, mass is not. If you consider the effects of gravity on the mass of an object, then you have a force called weight. Force equals mass times gravity (acceleration).

It is important to note for upper-middle-school students that NO work is done if a person stands in one place holding a stack of bricks without moving anywhere or lifting the bricks. If no distance is moved then no work is done— even if you feel tired. Work equals force times distance. If the distance is zero then no work is done. It reminds us of the adage—Don't just stand there, do something.

Levers (Events 10-A thorough 10-C)

Discrepant Events and Pupil Investigations

Event 10-A. Uplifting Students

Ask the students how one of them can lift another student without touching him or her. After several student suggestions, select the use of a simple machine. Use a sturdy chair, table, and strong wooden broom handle. Place the straight back of the chair about 15 cm (6 inches) from the table. The back of the chair should face the table as in figure 10.3. Have one student lie on the

FIGURE 10.3   A lever can help one student easily lift another.

table holding on to the sides. The second student should kneel on the seat of the chair, placing the broom handle under the desk and over the top of the back of the chair. The second student can now press down on the end of the handle and try to lift the table and student. If necessary adjust the distance between the chair and the table.

Pupil Investigations (may include the following processes):

1.   Inferring that a slight-framed student could not lift a heavier student.
2.   Inferring that girls could not lift boys.
3.   Observing the pivot point to be the back of the chair.
4.   Generalizing that the closer the chair back is to the table, the easier it is to lift.

Event 10-B. Balancing Your Budget

Give each group of two to three students a meter stick, 15 pennies, and one 5-cm length of cardboard tube (empty paper towel roll) cut in half to act as the **fulcrum** (pivot point). Cut the paper towel roll lengthwise so that it forms two semicircles. Cut each semicircle into sections about 5 cm in length. One empty paper towel roll will be enough to make fulcrums for all of the groups in the class.

On a desk, set the 50 centimeter mark of the meter stick on top of the curved part of the cardboard tube. Adjust if necessary until it balances. Place the middle of a penny on the 30-cm mark. Where will another penny need to be placed to balance it on the other side? Keeping the first penny on the 30-cm mark, where should a stack of two pennies be placed on the other side to bal-

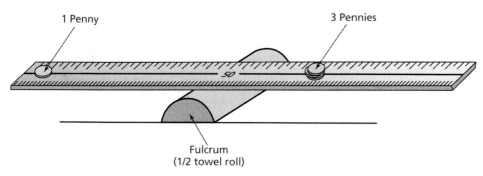

FIGURE 10.4   The pennies balance if distance and the number of pennies are considered at the same time.

ance the ruler? Try the original penny at the end of the ruler. Where will you place one penny to balance it? Two pennies? Four pennies? (See figure 10.4.)

Pupil Investigations (may include the following processes):

1. Inferring that the pennies need to be the same distance apart.
2. Inferring (incorrectly) that two pennies twice the distance will balance one penny on the other side of the fulcrum.
3. Recording the data in a table.
4. Forming a theory that the number of pennies times the distance from the pivot on one side will balance if it is equal to the number of pennies times the distance on the other side.

Event 10-C. Balancing Mobile Act

Go to http://www.vectorpark.com/levers.html to access the game. The object is to balance the mobile. Although there are no directions to this game, students quickly figure out that they need to pick items out of the water and drag them to the mobile. You can let water drip out of the faucet of the bucket and change locations of the object hanging. Each time the mobile balances a new item is introduced to the game.

Pupil Investigations (may include the following processes):

1. Observing that each time the mobile balances a new piece is introduced into the game.
2. Discovering that draining water from the bucket will help balance the mobile.
3. Discovering that the bucket can be refilled if it is dropped into the water.
4. Inferring that the mobile works like a seesaw.

Events 10-A through 10-C Explained in Context (Levers)

A **lever** is a tool that pivots on a point to change the direction and the force of a movement. It is hard to move a heavy rock or crack open a walnut without the help of a lever. A crow bar will help move the rock and a nutcracker will open the shell of the walnut.

LIVERPOOL JOHN MOORES UNIVERSITY
LEARNING SERVICES

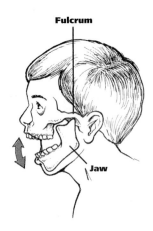

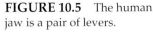

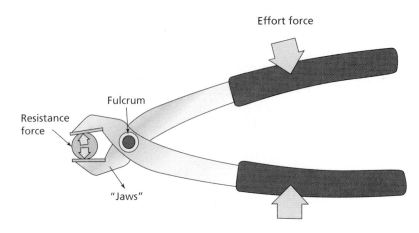
Effort force

FIGURE 10.5 The human jaw is a pair of levers.

FIGURE 10.6 Pliers act as a pair of levers.

As stated earlier, the amount of work to move something is calculated by knowing the amount of force applied, multiplied by the distance for which the force is applied ($W = f \times d$). In figure 10.4, notice that the amount of work done on one side of the fulcrum (pivot point), equals the amount of work accomplished on the other side. The side on which you apply the effort is called the *effort force*. The amount of force the lever applies on the opposite side is called the *resistance force*. We can summarize that by writing:

$W_e = W_r$ (work on effort side equals work done on resistance side)

$f_e \times d_e = f_r \times d_r$ (effort force × distance = resistance force × distance)

On either side, as the resistance force increases, the effort distance on the other side must increase. It is important for students to perform enough experiments to get a general understanding of this inverse relationship.

Levers working in pairs are common. Examples are scissors and jaws. Jaws are a lever that rotates around a hinge, the joint that serves as the fulcrum. (See figure 10.5.) When you need to bite into something hard, do you use your front or back teeth? Notice that your back teeth are closer to the pivot point, travel a shorter distance, and have a powerful bite. But your front teeth travel further, are further from the pivot point, and have less strength to bite.

Pliers are like teeth and use long handles and short jaws. (See figure 10.6.) The longer the handles, the less effort force that must be applied. The shorter the jaws are from the pivot point, the greater the pressure or force that will be applied to the object being held or crushed. Bicycle brakes are levers used to press the break pads against the wheels. Like pliers the brake handles move a great distance with little force compared to the brake pads that move a very small distance with great force to slow or stop the rotation of the wheels.

In figure 10.7, a wheelbarrow magnifies the effort force when a worker lifts the handles up 20 or so centimeters. The heavy load only moves a few centimeters since it is closer to the wheel which serves as the fulcrum.

Why is it easier for a light-weight student to lift a heavier student using a broom handle? In *Event 10-A, Uplifting Students*, the broom handle is working as a lever. The fulcrum or pivot point is the back of the chair. When the distance

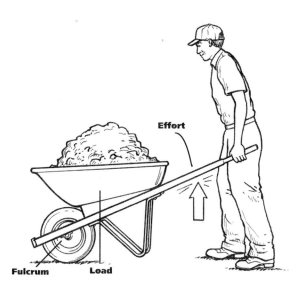

FIGURE 10.7   A wheelbarrow increases the effort force.

from the fulcrum (chair back) to the desk is much less than the distance from the fulcrum to the second student, the effort needed to lift the desk is decreased.

Event 10-B, Balancing Your Budget, also uses the same principle. The centimeter stick is acting as a lever. The longer the distance between the pivot point and the penny, the more pennies can be lifted on the other side. Effort force times distance on one side equals resistance force times distance on the other. For example, (1 penny) × (20 cm from fulcrum) = (4 pennies) × (5 cm from fulcrum). If the distances do not work out so nicely, it is due to the extra weight of the ruler that extends beyond the placement of the pennies.

Event 10-C, Balancing Mobile Act, gives students a chance to intuitively balance the levers on the mobile. Heavier objects can be placed closer to the balance point while lighter objects should be connected further away. Use the following website, http://www.vectorpark.com/levers.html (along with others listed at the end of this chapter) for students who need extra practice or were absent during the class investigations.

Not all levers work the same. The fulcrum or pivot point is not always between the effort and the resistance (load). It is not important for students to memorize in which class common objects belong but it is important that they recognize that there are three basic arrangements of the effort, fulcrum, and load. Students should be able to identify where the load, effort, and fulcrum are on common simple machines. Figure 10.8 summarizes this information.

Where are the load, fulcrum, and effort located on each of these items: bottle cap opener, spade, pan balance, hammer, tack puller, staple puller, ice tongs, tweezers, broom, shovel, and pole vault pole? Locate them for the tools listed in Figure 10.8.

Hinges are levers too. Hinges join two objects together and still allow them to move. Open a door and then close it by pushing near the door knob. Open the door again and try to push it closed pressing close to the hinge side of the door. Which is easier? Why? Other objects that use hinges include eyeglasses, jewelry boxes, toy boxes, refrigerator doors, and elbows, knees, and jaws.

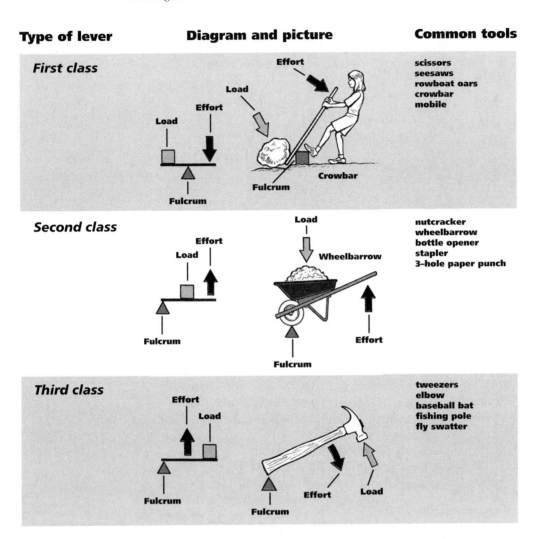

FIGURE 10.8 Three classes of levers.

Pulleys (Events 10-D through 10-F)

Discrepant Events and Pupil Investigations

Event 10-D. A Test of Strength

Place two broom handles parallel to each other, about 30–40 cm (12 to 15 inches) apart. Tie a rope around one of the broom handles and wrap it around both broom handles as shown in figure 10.9. Can the two students pull the broom handles apart while a third student is pulling the rope? Try this pulley system with only one wrap of the rope around the handles. Try two wraps, then three wraps. What do you notice about how hard it is to pull the broom handles apart?

Pupil Investigations (may include the following processes):

1. Inferring that the two students could easily pull the handles apart.

FIGURE 10.9   Pull the broom handles apart while one student holds the rope.

2.   Predicting that it is harder for them to pull the handles apart the more wraps of rope used.
3.   Inferring that friction holds the handles together.

Event 10-E. Changing Directions

Place a pencil through the center hole of an empty spool of thread. Using strong string, attach the ends of the pencil to a table or shelf so that the spool hangs down about 1 dm (4 inches). The spool should spin freely. Find a ribbon approximately as wide as the groove on the spool. Attach one end of the ribbon to the handle of an old purse or bucket. Thread the ribbon over the spool. Pull down on the free end of the ribbon. What happens to the purse? Fill the purse with light objects and lift these objects too.

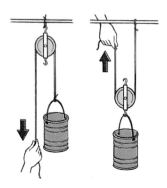

FIGURE 10.10   Fixed pulley *(a)* and movable pulley *(b)*.

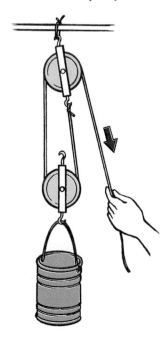

FIGURE 10.11   Block and tackle system.

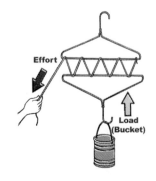

FIGURE 10.12   Use hangers to model a pulley system.

Pupil Investigations (may include the following processes):

1. Observing the bucket moves the opposite direction of the pull (effort force).
2. Observing that the spool spins around but the rope does not.
3. Predicting that the more weight that is put in the purse, the harder it will be to lift.
4. Observing that if you let the ribbon go, the purse falls down.

Event 10-F. Pulley Play

Show the students a fixed pulley and a movable pulley system as in figure 10.10. Demonstrate how each works. Encourage the students to observe the direction of the effort force and the direction the load is moving. Now attach the movable pulley to the fixed pulley as in figure 10.11.

Using a spring scale measure the weight of the load, the effort force used on the fixed pulley, the movable pulley, and now the fixed and movable pulley system (called a block and tackle). Have the students work in small groups to record what they observe with each system. Measure the distance the ribbon moves in each case. What are the advantages of each system? If time permits have the students connect more pulleys and record their observations.

Pupil Investigations (may include the following processes):

1. Observing the directions of the movements in all three systems.
2. Measuring the effort force and the load or resistance force.
3. Communicating in chart form their observations and comments about advantages and uses of each system.
4. Predicting what will happen when more pulleys are added to the system.
5. Demonstrating an alternative design for a block and tackle.

Events 10-D through 10-F Explained in Context (Pulleys)

To create a pulley, combine a grooved wheel (thread spool) with a rope (ribbon). It is much easier to lift a heavy load by using a pulley. A **pulley** is a wheel with a groove in its rim in which a rope is placed. The wheel is attached to a high surface. One end of the rope is tied to an object; the other end is threaded over the wheel and pulled down to lift an object.

The amount of effort to raise the object is equal to the weight of the object. A single fixed pulley changes the direction of the motion. You pull down on the rope as the object goes up. Using more than one pulley (wheel) in a sequence gives a mechanical advantage. Using two pulleys enables you to lift an object with half the effort. Three pulley wheels requires only one-third the effort force to lift the same object. The more wheels in the pulley arrangement, the more it magnifies the effort force.

In *Event 10-D, A Test of Strength,* the rope and broom handles model a pulley system. Each wrap of the rope acts as an additional pulley wheel to magnify the effort force. To decrease the friction, use talcum powder on the areas of the handles where the rope slides.

This above activity can be demonstrated by using two coat hangers as pictured in figure 10.12. Experiment with different numbers of wraps that you put around the hangers to pull the load up. Use a small nylon mesh bag filled with 20 pennies or marbles as the load. How many pennies or marbles are needed to lift the load with each additional wrap of the rope? How does this relate to the number of wheels on a pulley system?

In *Event 10-E, Changing Directions,* the single pulley simply changes the direction of the motion. This fixed pulley makes lifting heavy objects easier, because pulling down is easier than lifting up. Even though the effort force and the load (resistance) is equal, gravity is on your side pulling down.

An elevator is an example of a one-wheel pulley system. Think of a heavy steel rope with the elevator tied to one end and a counterweight tied to the other end. The rope is place over a pulley at the top of the elevator shaft. The counterweight balances with the elevator. The motor only lifts the weight of the passengers.

Unlike the fixed pulley in *Event 10-E, Changing Directions,* the movable pulley in *Event 10-F, Pulley Play,* moves with the rope and keeps the effort force and the load moving in the same direction. In a single movable pulley, you need to pull the rope twice as far (effort) but the load feels half as heavy. You can also think of it as pulling a much lighter load.

When the fixed and movable pulley wheels are combined, a change of direction and a gain in effort force can be accomplished at the same time. This combination is called a block and tackle. The more wheels a block and tackle has, the easier it is to lift the load. The weight is spread out over more ropes and the distance the rope is pulled is increased with every wheel added. Block and tackles are frequently used in construction equipment such as cranes and hoists. Steel cables are used in place of rope to lift extremely heavy objects like steel beams.

In a two-wheel pulley system the pulled end of the rope has to move twice the distance that the load being lifted moves. The further the effort force moves, the less force is needed to lift something. $W = f \times d$: work equals force times distance. If you double the distance, the effort force is half. This means that the force needed to lift the load is only half what it would be with only one wheel on the pulley.

Examples of uses of pulleys include clothes lines, flag poles, block and tackles, cranes, hoists, and elevators.

Wheel and Axle (Gears, too) (Events 10-G through 10-I)

Discrepant Events and Pupil Investigations

Event 10-G. Putting Teeth into Your Wheels
Show students tools having a wheel and axle. Bring in several simple machines and let the students do a binary sort starting with the categories: wheel and axle and NOT wheel and axle. Further sort the wheel and axle group into gears and not gears.

Pupil Investigations (may include the following processes):
1. Classifying tools by the type of simple machine.
2. Observing the difference between wheel and axles and special ones called gears.
3. Observing how the tools move, changing the direction of the motion.

Event 10-H. Mean Clean Bubble-Making Machine

Use two large bowls or clear plastic storage tubs (same size), liquid dishwashing detergent, water source, timer (optional), hand-rotary egg beater, and wooden mixing spoon. Which mixing tool works best, a wooden mixing spoon or an egg beater? Have the students brainstorm how to design an investigation to decide which tool is the best Mean Clean Bubble-Making Machine.

Pupil Investigations (may include the following processes):

1. Controlling a variable by using the same temperature of water.
2. Measuring the same amount of water and soap for each container.
3. Measuring the same amount of time the students mix the solution.
4. Describing the experimental design.
5. Observing how the two different tools operate and mix the solution.

Event 10-I. Gears Are Wheels Too

Turn a bicycle with a derailleur upside down. Have a student hold the bike steady. Rotate the pedals so that they are vertical (straight up and down). With a piece of chalk, mark a point on the tire that can be easily located in reference to another part of the bike.

Select either high or low gear. When the bike is in its highest gear the chain will be on the large front gear and on the small rear gear. When the bike is in its lowest gear the chain will be on the small front gear and the large rear gear.

Turn the pedal one rotation while holding the wheel very lightly. How many times did the wheel turn? Repeat the experiment using the opposite gear ratio (high or low). What generalization can the students make? Calculate the gear ratio on the bike. What does this mean?

Pupil Investigations (may include the following processes):

1. Observing how a gear is a wheel and axle.
2. Observing the difference in gear size and how the technology works.
3. Collecting data to determine gear ratios.
4. Analyzing how one size gear affects how many times other gears will rotate.

Events 10-G through 10-I Explained in Context (Wheel and Axle, and Gears)

In a **wheel and axle,** the wheel is attached to the axle so that both turn together like the sprocket and tire on the bicycle. The wheel and axle then work like a lever. The outer rim of the wheel moves a great distance with little effort, while the inner axle moves a very short distance—producing a great force. Examples of a wheel and axle requiring a greater force can be demonstrated by a steering wheel of a car or winch on a sailboat. The steering wheel of a car is turned considerably more than the wheels of the car actually turn in relation to the body of the car. Think of getting into a parked car and turning the steering wheel. The tires will turn to a different angle without the car moving. (Students may think you are describing how far the tires rotate on the road as it is moving.) The longer distance of the effort force means little effort is needed to turn the steering wheel. (See figure 10.13.)

A faucet with a large handle and thin shaft makes it easy to quickly stop the flow of water. A rolling pin and its handles also mimic the wheel and axle. How does a wrench act like a wheel and axle? (See figure 10.14.)

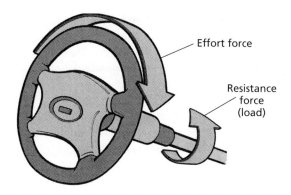

FIGURE 10.13   Forces on a steering wheel.

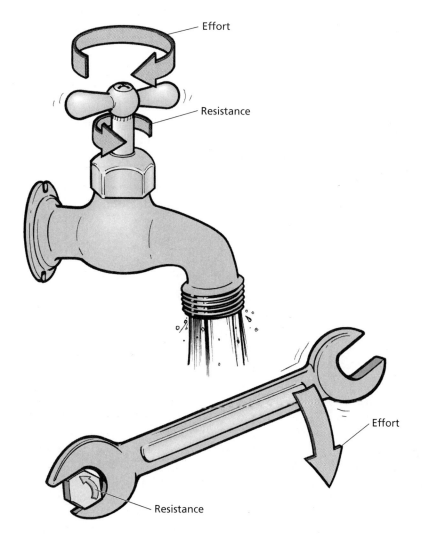

FIGURE 10.14   Faucet and wrench.

Gears are wheels with teeth that fit together to turn each other. Gears help change direction, speed, or force of the movement. In *Event 10-G, Putting Teeth into Your Wheels,* students can first observe the difference between a pulley and a wheel and axle. The axle is not attached to the wheel on a pulley, each works independently. The axle is attached to the wheel of the wheel and axle, and they rotate simultaneously.

Have the students observe that a gear is a special wheel and axle. The gear has teeth. In *Event 10-H, Mean Clean Bubble-Making Machine,* students can observe how the gears help speed up the mixing. Let them also notice that the gears are perpendicular to each other. This allows the user to spin the handle up and down (rotate vertically) while the beaters rotate horizontally. This activity demonstrates how gears change the direction and speed of the movement.

The egg beater is a wheel and axle (gears) and the mixing spoon is a third-class lever. When you turn the handle of the beater, the large gear turns the smaller gears. The small gears make the beaters rotate faster—making more bubbles quickly. Even though there is an advantage to using the mixing spoon over no tool at all, it is more difficult to move the mixing spoon through the water. The surface area of the spoon is much larger than that of the egg beater paddles. The spoon takes more effort to move a larger amount of water.

Event 10-I, Gears Are Wheels Too, demonstrates the advantage of gears in a machine in which most students have had much experience, a bicycle. Bicycle gears enable the rear wheels to turn at a different speed and with different amounts of effort compared to the pedals of the bike.

The ratio in size of the two gears determines the amount of change. Gears don't give you extra energy but they make the force or pressure needed to pedal a bike less by making you pedal a further distance. You pedal faster and therefore your feet cover more circular distance for a given amount of time to move slowly uphill with less force.

To calculate the gear ratio on the bike, first note on which rear and front gear the chain is riding. (See figure 10.15.) Count the number of teeth on both

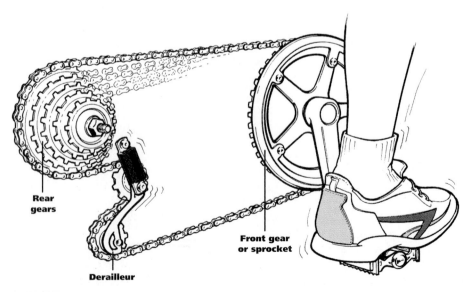

Rear gears

Derailleur

Front gear or sprocket

FIGURE 10.15   Gears in a bicycle.

of these gears. Divide the number of teeth of the rear gear by the number of teeth on the front gear to determine the gear ratio. For example, if there are 9 teeth on the rear gear and 45 teeth on the front gear then this gear ratio is 9/45, 1/5 or 1:5. In this case, the bike is in high gear and the rear wheel rotates five times as fast as the pedal but with little or one-fifth the turning force.

A cyclist is in low gear when cycling uphill. In low gear the wheels turn fewer times compared to the rate of the pedal. But in low gear there is more force to climb the hills.

Wheels were used over 5000 years ago, first as a potter's wheel before they were used vertically to roll objects along. The advantage of the wheel is its ability to have less material (surface area) in contact with the ground. This reduces the amount of friction. **Friction** is the force that opposes motion as one object slides over another.

Here are some examples of the wheel and axle: windmill, gear, wheels on a bicycle or car, screwdriver, door knob, pencil sharpener, meat grinder, and egg beater.

Inclined Plane (Events 10-J and 10-K)

Discrepant Events and Pupil Investigations

Event 10-J. Eggactly Why Do We Use a Ramp?

Tell the class that you can drop a raw egg onto a hard surface 20 cm below without breaking the egg. Show a wide empty cardboard tube from gift wrap that measures 20 cm long. Ask how you should drop the raw egg so that it falls the 20 cm onto a hard surface without breaking. You cannot wrap the egg. Drop one raw egg the 20 cm and watch it crack. Let the students experiment with a ramp that is propped up 20 cm high. (See figure 10.16.) (Use a long, narrow box 60 cm by 10 cm (2 feet by 4 inches) or 60 cm long cardboard tube from gift wrap to make the ramp).

FIGURE 10.16   Which egg ramp keeps it from cracking?

Pupil Investigations (may include the following processes):

1. Hypothesizing that if you drop it small end first then it will not break. (Inferring the small end is stronger.)
2. Justifying the use of vinegar to soften the shell before dropping it.
3. Observing that the ramp lets the egg fall a further distance without breaking.

Event 10-K. Uphill Tractor Pull

If you wanted to place a lawn tractor into a truck bed would you lift it from the driveway into the truck or would you use an inclined plane to move it onto the truck? Build a model using books to prop up a long board to lift the toy lawn tractor (block of wood) onto the truck bed (box) as shown in figure 10.17. Put an eye screw at the end of the board to hold up the string to avoid friction and to stop the tractor from falling over. On one end of a string tie the tractor and to the other end a small box or film canister to collect weights (such as paperclips). How many paperclips are needed to lift the tractor straight up?

FIGURE 10.17   Tractor ramp.

Now place the tractor on the inclined plane (be sure that the tractor can roll freely so that you are not working against too much friction). Put the string over the frame of the model with the small box or film canister tied to the other end of the string. How many paperclips are needed to pull the tractor onto the truck? Why? Change the slope of the ramp but keep the horizontal distance constant so that the distance up the incline becomes longer as the slope becomes less steep. Will the slope of the ramp affect the number of paperclips needed to move the tractor?

Pupil Investigations (may include the following processes):
1. Collecting data to compare the amount of force (number of paperclips) to move the tractor over different angles of incline.
2. Recording the data onto a chart properly labeled.
3. Measuring angles of the incline or slope.
4. Generalizing that the higher the slope, the more force (number of paperclips) is needed to move the tractor up the incline.

Events 10-J and 10-K Explained in Context (Inclined Plane)

Walking up a mountainside is hard work but imagine scaling a mountain cliff that goes straight up. An **inclined plane** is a slope like a ramp, mountainside, or set of stairs. The steeper the slope, the harder it is to climb. On a mild incline you travel further (longer distance) so less force is needed for the same amount of work. We still use the $W = f \times d$ relationship that is used for all simple machines.

In *Event 10-J, Eggactly Why Do We Use a Ramp?*, the inclined plane helps you lift or lower heavy objects by using less force. By lifting or lowering an object over a greater amount of distance the job becomes easier.

In *Event 10-K, Uphill Tractor Pull,* keep the horizontal distance constant so that the distance up the incline becomes longer as the slope becomes less steep. This demonstrates that the less steep the slope, the longer the distance the load has to move. This longer distance means less force is needed to move it. Collecting the data on the number of paperclips needed to start the tractor rolling up the ramp helps students directly see this relationship.

Examples of an inclined plane include: a plank, ramp, sloping floor in the theater, stairs, and escalator.

Wedge (Events 10-L and 10-M)

Discrepant Events and Pupil Investigations

Event 10-L. Fruit and Vegetable Challenge

Today you will be making faces with fruits and vegetables such as apples, pears, squash, cucumbers, carrot, and radishes. Give a student an apple and a circular slice of carrot (less than 1 cm thick). Ask the student to push the carrot into the apple. Ask students why it is so difficult. Is there a better way to cut the carrots so that the carrot pieces can be put into the apple to make a face? Let the students suggest that a point (wedge) on the carrot makes it easier to insert into the apple. Have students make fruit and vegetable faces from pre-cut carrot and radish pieces—some with and some without wedges. Apples, pears, squash, and cucumbers can serve as the heads. (If the food is pre-washed and the students wash their hands before the activity, the investigation makes a healthy snack.)

Pupil Investigations (may include the following processes):

1. Observing that the wedge-shaped pieces slide into the apple with ease.
2. Comparing the shape of a wedge to an inclined plane.
3. Describing other common tools as wedges.

Event 10-M. How "Aboat" That Machine

Have students make the following toy boat using half a milk carton, two pencils, two rubber bands, and a 4-by-8-cm rectangle cut from a plastic margarine lid. (See figure 10.18.) Poke two holes 6 cm apart through the bottom of the carton and place the two pencils through them. Wrap one rubber band around the pencil ends inside the boat. Wrap the second rubber band around the other end of the pencils outside the boat. Insert the plastic paddle between this rubber band and wind it about 20 times or until the band becomes tight. Wind it away from the front of the boat. Place the boat in a large plastic storage tub or plastic wallpaper tray filled halfway with water. What will happen when you let go? What direction will the boat travel? Why does the boat move? What simple machines are working to move the boat?

FIGURE 10.18   Which simple machines help the boat move?

Pupil Investigations (may include the following processes):

1. Observing that depending on how the paddle is wound, the boat may move forward or backward.
2. Inferring that the more you wind the paddle, the faster it will move.
3. Experimenting with the design of the boat, such as changing the shape of the bow (front).
4. Comparing the movement of the paddle wheel to the movement of a swimmer's feet.

Events 10-L and 10-M Explained in Context (Wedge)

Event 10-L, Fruit and Vegetable Challenge, is a fun way to introduce the wedge to younger students. A wedge is an object used to split or separate things. It is made of two or more inclined planes or has a conical shape like the point of an ice cream cone or sharpened pencil.

The **wedge** is a simple machine that changes the forward motion into a sideways motion as it pushes apart the materials it goes through. The wedge is a moving inclined plane. For example, a wedge can split wood when a hammer is used to drive it into the wood (forward motion). The wedge separates the wood fibers as it moves through (sideways motion) the log splitting it apart.

In this event the carrot could not move the apple apart until an inclined plane or wedge was cut into the carrot. The wedge made it easier for the carrot to move forward. The longer distance produced by the two inclined planes in the carrot (wedge) made the force needed to move the carrot through the apple less.

Event 10-M, How "Aboat" that Machine, demonstrates Newton's third law as well as models two simple machines. According to Newton's third law, as the paddle moves toward the front of the boat it pushes the water back, making the boat go forward. There is an equal but opposite reactive force. The paddle and rubber band are an example of a wheel (paddle) and axle (rubber band). The shape of the front of the boat serves as a wedge. It separates the water. These two simple machines make this boat a very interesting compound machine.

Common items that demonstrate the principle of the wedge include: blade on a knife, scissors, wood chisel, axe, sewing pins and needles, screwdriver, razor blades, spatula, pancake flipper, front end of a boat, nose of an airplane, nails, and screws. There are many other common uses for a wedge. Can you name a few others?

Screw (Events 10-N and 10-0)

Discrepant Events and Pupil Investigations

Event 10-N. Hardwood or Softwood?

Try to push a screw or nail directly into a piece of soft wood. Pushing it straight down makes it virtually impossible to push into the wood. The wood seems hard. Now try to put the screw into the wood by rotating the screw. You can use a screwdriver in both cases but the screwdriver doesn't help in pushing it straight down. The screwdriver helps when you use a rotating motion on the screw, making the wood seem soft. Insert two screws of different pitch. Pitch is the number of turns needed to make the screw move into the wood exactly one inch (customary screw) or one millimeter (metric screw). Use a screwdriver to put the screws halfway into the wood. Try to wind each screw further into the wood by hand. Which is easier?

Pupil Investigations (may include the following processes):

1. Inferring (incorrectly) that the screw will easily be pushed into the wood by using bare hands.
2. Comparing the force needed to push verses rotate the screw into the wood.
3. Describing the head of the screw as a type of wedge.
4. Formulating a theory relating pitch to the effort force.

Event 10-O. Screwy Pump

Ask students how they can get water to flow uphill. Inform them that they will be constructing a pump that doesn't use any fuel such as electricity to work. Give each group of students an empty Pringles potato chip can or a tall plastic drinking glass and about 1.25 meters of plastic tubing from a home improvement or pet store. The taller or larger in diameter the container the longer the piece of tubing needed.

Tape one end of the tubing to one end of the can. Follow the rim of the can at first and then wind the tubing around the can in a gentle spiral. With

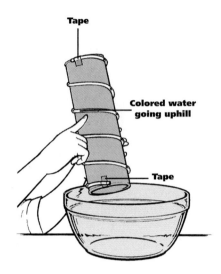

FIGURE 10.19   Screw pump model.

tape, secure the second end of the tubing along the opposite rim of the can. Adjust the tubing so that it is equally spaced along all parts of the can. The tubing should resemble threads on a screw. (See figure 10.19.) Hold the container horizontally and use an eyedropper to gently squirt in a few milliliters of colored water. Turn the container almost vertical and start to rotate the can. Watch the water move uphill.

Pupil Investigations (may include the following processes):

1. Inferring incorrectly that the tubing acts like a straw and water goes up a straw.
2. Observing that the water flows down when the can is held vertically. A slight tilt is necessary.
3. Questioning whether gravity has something to do with it.
4. Experimenting with the slope or pitch of the tubing.

Events 10-N and 10-O Explained in Context (Screw)

Circular stairs increase the distance needed, to walk to get to the second floor but reduce the effort compared to jumping from the first to second floor of a house. A screw jack is used to raise cars to change a tire by magnifying the force of the user's arm. A small force (turning the jack handle) that moves through a long distance is converted into an increased force that moves through a a very short distance (the distance the car is raised.) The jack threads are an inclined plane spiraling around the vertical shaft. Beveled gears are used in this compound machine to change the direction of the motion.

Event 10-N, Hardwood or Softwood?, can be better understood if you carefully look at a screw and compare it to an inclined plane. A **screw** is basically inclined planes wrapped around a central point. (It should be noted that a screw is also a wedge with a pointed tip.) Using the shortest side of a right triangular piece of paper, wrap it around a pencil. Notice how the paper resembles a screw pattern. (See figure 10.20.)

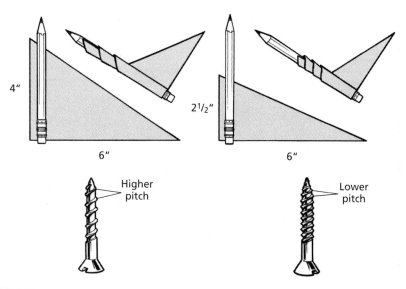

FIGURE 10.20 The screw and inclined plane are related.

Cut out two different right triangles, one with a very steep slope (pitch) and another with a very mild or low rise. Wrap each around a pencil and compare the slope or pitch of the threads. The screw with the threads closer together has a lower slope and therefore the screw travels more distance to reach the same depth into the wood, so the effort should be much less.

Show students several screws with different pitches. Pitch can be seen as the distance between the threads (lines) on a screw or the slope of the threads. Predict which screw would be easier to screw into a piece of wood. Why? The steeper the slope on an inclined plane, the harder it is to climb. Relate this to climbing up a mountain, hill, or roof.

In Event 10-O, Screwy Pump, the screwy pump is an example of an Archimedean screw. Instead of using a wheel and axle to rotate the screw your hand is doing the work. If you keep the can perfectly vertical, gravity will force the water downhill. However if you tilt the can slightly and rotate it you will see the water travel uphill. The gentle winding incline of the tubing makes the distance the water must travel to get to the top longer. The longer the distance, the less force it takes to move the water. This screw (a winding incline) enables you to move things with less force.

Examples of a screw include: wood screw, bottle top, jar lid, lightbulb base, and clamp.

Combining Assessment with Instruction

An appropriate assessment for students in grade levels 3–5 can be found at the following website: http://www.edheads.org/activities/simple-machines/index.htm, by Edheads. This animated site provides a fairly comprehensive quiz that tests student's ability to identify simple machines in everyday technology such as faucets and door knobs.

It can also be used as a review prior to a test. Students who have computers at home will probably be motivated by the site to spend a fair amount of time reviewing.

Making models is another excellent way to assess student learning. Have students make a model of a simple machine such as a pulley to raise a miniature flag. Evaluate each student on the following criteria for each of the six simple machines assigned.

1. Paragraph describing how the machine works (e.g., changes a direction or magnifies a force).
2. Design features: neatness, durability, does it move freely, etc.
3. Labeled parts, including effort force, load, and fulcrum.
4. List of everyday uses.

Sites and Software

The following websites and software are appropriate to use with this chapter. Note that computer software and websites change rapidly. This makes it necessary to investigate the stable websites for new links and software catalogs for updates. Visit www.mhhe.com/friedl6e to link to these directly and for study resources.

Sites

EdHeads	www.edheads.org/activities/simple-machines/index.htm
Enchanted Learning	www.enchantedlearning.com/physics/machines/Levers.shtml
Spice Boys	www.smartown.com/sp2000/machines2000/main.htm
Beakman & Jax	www.beakman.com/lever/lever.html
Inventors Toolbox	www.mos.org/sln/Leonardo/InventorsToolbox.html

Software

Simple and Motorized Machine Kits (Pitsco LEGO *Educational* Division) (2–9)
The Return of the Incredible Machines—Contraptions (Sierra On-Line Inc.) (6–9)
Learn about Physical Science: Simple Machines (Sunburst) (K–2)
PinPinball Science (Dorling Kindersley) (4–9)

Key Terms

Teaching Children about Air, Air Pressure, and Flight

NATIONAL SCIENCE EDUCATION STANDARDS ALIGNMENT TO EVENTS

The events in this chapter help accomplish several of the NSES for content. The event(s) that align with a given content standard are listed below that standard.

LEVELS K–4

UNIFYING CONCEPTS AND PROCESSES
- Change, consistency, measurement
  11-A
  11-G through 11-H
  11-Z

- Evidence, models, and explanation
  11-A through 11-BB

SCIENCE AS INQUIRY
- Abilities necessary to do and understand scientific inquiry
  11-A through 11-BB

PHYSICAL SCIENCE
- Properties of objects and materials
  11-A through 11-BB

- Position and motion of objects
  11-G through 11-Y

EARTH AND SPACE SCIENCE
- Properties of earth materials
  11-A through 11-R

SCIENCE AND TECHNOLOGY
- Abilities of technological design
  11-L
  11-S through 11-W
  11-Z

SCIENCE IN PERSONAL AND SOCIAL PERSPECTIVES
- Science and technology in local challenges
  11-Z through 11-BB

HISTORY AND NATURE OF SCIENCE
- Science as a human endeavor
  Historical introduction
  11-Z through 11-BB

LEVELS 5–8

UNIFYING CONCEPTS AND PROCESSES
- Change, consistency, measurement
  11-A
  11-G through 11-H
  11-Z

- Evidence, models, and explanation
  11-A through 11-BB

- Evolution and equilibrium
  11-G through 11-R
  11-S through 11-W

- Form and function
  11-S through 11-BB

SCIENCE AS INQUIRY
- Abilities necessary to do and understand scientific inquiry
  11-A through 11-BB

PHYSICAL SCIENCE
- Motion and forces
  11-G through 11-N
  11-S through 11-BB

- Transfer of energy
  11-O through 11-R

EARTH AND SPACE SCIENCE
- Structure of the earth system
  11-A through 11-R

SCIENCE AND TECHNOLOGY
- Abilities of technological design
  11-L
  11-S through 11-W
  11-Z

SCIENCE IN PERSONAL AND SOCIAL PERSPECTIVES
- Risks and benefits
  11-H
  11-O through 11-P
  11-X through 11-Y

- Science and technology in society
  11-Z through 11-BB

HISTORY AND NATURE OF SCIENCE
- Science as a human endeavor
  Historical introduction
  11-Z through 11-RB

From Experiments to Flight

Before Orville and Wilbur Wright, the possibility of a controlled, man-powered flight seemed unattainable. On December 17, 1903, Orville Wright manned the *Flyer I* for the first flight in history in which an aircraft raised itself by its own power, cruised forward without reduction of speed, and landed at a place as high as where the plane had started. The key to the Wright brothers' success was their persistence and systematic engineering that had gone beyond the trial-and-error methods of their more formally educated contemporaries.

The Wright brothers owned a custom bicycle shop in Dayton, Ohio, where their mechanical abilities and interest in aerodynamics flourished. As young men they were fascinated by gliders and kites, and studied glider data from other scientists such as Otto Lilienthan of Germany. Their first flying machine was a wood, cloth, and wire kite with a 5-foot wingspan. The construction of this machine convinced Wilbur that he could build an aircraft capable of sustaining man in the air.

Long hours and hundreds of experiments afforded the Wright brothers data that helped them invent, design and build several new parts needed to accomplish that magnificent first man-powered flight. The brothers constructed their own motor, made a carburetor out of a tomato can, and designed propellers in the form of an airfoil.

An **airfoil** is the name given to the curved shape of a propeller or wing. As the curved-shaped wing passes through the air, the air going above the wing travels further and therefore faster than the air traveling below the wing. This faster-moving air has a lower pressure than the slower-moving air below the wing. This difference in pressure forces the slower air toward the lower pressure, causing the wing to lift.

They also improvised skids similar to runners on sleds to prevent the airplane from rolling over if the plane tilted too much in one direction. The brothers determined how to move the aircraft freely up and down on a cushion of air, built a forward elevator to control the pitch of their craft, and designed a pair of rudders in back to control its tendency to sway from side to side. In addition, they assembled a pulley system that warped the shape of the wings during flight to turn the plane and to stop it from rolling in air.

Orville and Wilbur Wright left Dayton on September 23 and arrived at their camp at Kill Devil Hill to find the building they were to use to assemble the *Flyer I* had been blown over by a storm. In the subsequent months they built a new workshop, assembled the plane, calculated, experimented, and readjusted parts so that *Flyer I* was ready for trial in early December.

They tossed a coin to decide who should have the first trial. Wilbur won the toss but the trial run ended when several minor parts of the plane broke. On December 17, 1903, it was Orville's turn to attempt the flight. Several members of the Kill Devil Life Saving Station were there to witness the first flight. The wind, measured with a hand anemometer, showed velocities of 11 to 12 meters per second, or 24 to 27 miles per hour.

Years later Orville recounted the "audacity it took in attempting this flight in such high winds," but faith in their calculations and design were based on many years of careful and accurate laboratory work. With Orville at the controls, *Flyer I* lifted shakily off from Kitty Hawk and flew 120 feet for 12 seconds. By the fourth and last flight of that day Wilbur increased the flight time and distance to 59 seconds and covered 852 feet.

Air Is a Real Substance and Occupies Space (Events 11-A through 11-F)

Discrepant Events and Pupil Investigations

Event 11-A. Fill the Balloon with an Empty Bottle

This activity should be performed as a demonstration. Set up two large soft-drink bottles. Place a pencil or some other small object into one but leave the other bottle empty. Ask a pupil to "pick the empty bottle." Let several pupils verify that one is "empty."

Now attach a small balloon over the top of the empty bottle. Be sure that it lies limp. Then set the bottle into a container of water. (The water must be hot, but pupils should not be told at this time that the water is hot.) As the pupils watch, the balloon slowly fills up. How can the balloon be filled with an "empty" bottle? (For best results, use a large bottle and a small balloon. See figure 11.1.)

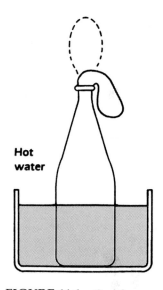

Hot water

FIGURE 11.1   Can the balloon be filled with an "empty" bottle?

Pupil Investigations (may include the following processes):

1. Verifying that the bottle seems to be empty.
2. Feeling that the water is warm.
3. Experimenting to see if the reaction is reversible when the bottle is removed from the hot water. (It is. The balloon goes limp.)
4. Generalizing that the bottle was not really empty.

Event 11-B. Squeeze-Box Candle Snuffer

Cut a 1-centimeter hole at the end of an empty shoe box. Hold up the open box so that all pupils can see it. Let them verify that the box is "empty." Cover the box with the lid and hold it so that the hole points to a candle flame. Now squeeze. The candle goes out! How did the "empty" box put out the flame? (Be sure to aim carefully. If the hole is not properly lined up, the event will not work.)

Pupil Investigations (may include the following processes):

1. Verifying that the box appears to be empty.
2. Repeating the experiment to check results.
3. Discovering that the box was not really empty.

Event 11-C. Pouring Air

Anyone can pour water from one beaker to another. But can you pour air? Provide two beakers and a large container of water. Ask pupils to find a way to pour air from one beaker to another. Tell them that the event is not only possible, but that if they do it right they will be *sure* that air is being poured. (Pupils will often make pouring motions in the air, but those motions prove nothing. Emphasize that we cannot see anything happening in such motions, so it gives no evidence about anything being poured.)

Pupil Investigations (may include the following processes):

1. Performing the pouring motions in the air.
2. Experimenting with the beakers in the water.
3. Generalizing that air takes up space and can be seen under water.

Event 11-D. Keep the Paper Dry Under Water

Fill a large container about two-thirds full of water and ask pupils to push a paper towel under water without getting it wet. Have a small, empty beaker available, but do not call attention to it.

Pupil Investigations (may include the following processes):

1. Observing that the paper gets wet when an edge is touched to the water.
2. Experimenting by pushing the paper into the bottom of a beaker, inverting it, and lowering it into the water.
3. Forming a theory that air keeps the water out of the beaker.

Event 11-E. Sink the Cork

Float a cork in a container of water and ask pupils to "sink the cork," or to make it go down, without touching it. The container should be deep enough and large enough to accept an inverted tumbler without spilling the water.

Pupil Investigations (may include the following processes):

1. Experimenting with blowing or other means of causing the cork to go down.
2. Concluding (incorrectly) that it is impossible to sink the cork without touching it.
3. Discovering that an inverted tumbler will cause the desired effect.

Event 11-F. Pour Water into an Empty Bottle

Set up a bottle with a one-hole stopper and a funnel as shown in figure 11.2. Try to pour water into the empty bottle. Be sure to use a funnel that has a narrow tubelike stem that will fit into the one-hole stopper. Or, use a short rubber hose to connect the funnel to a glass tube and (carefully) fit the tube into the stopper.

Pupil Investigations (may include the following processes):

1. Observing that the water does not run into the bottle very well. (It will sometimes dribble in a little. At other times it may "percolate" as alternately some water enters and some air bubbles leave.)
2. Inspecting the tube to see that it is not blocked.
3. Forming a theory about the invisible substance that is keeping out the water. (They will likely know that it is air.)

Events 11-A through 11-F Explained in Context (Air Is a Real Substance)

Negative Properties of Air

When discussing air, it is necessary to consider a number of factors that are *not* there. For example, air has no color, odor, or taste and cannot be seen. In a sense, we are identifying air by describing what it is *not*. These are the negative properties of air.

We can focus on the negative properties by creating a verbal discrepancy for the pupils. Begin by saying that people often believe things that are not

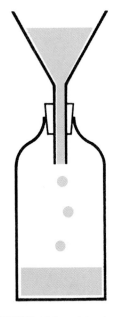

FIGURE 11.2 If the funnel and tube are fitted securely into a one-hole stopper, most of the water will not enter the bottle.

true. In fact, you might say, some people believe in superstitions. Cite examples of breaking a mirror causing 7 years of bad luck, of a black cat walking across your path, of the luck of a four-leaf clover, horseshoe, or rabbit's foot.

Then tell them that some people still believe in misconceptions and superstitions, even today. "Do you realize that even here, in this very room, there are some people who believe that there is such a thing as air!"

There will be stunned silence.

"Oh, I can see that there are some students who still believe that air exists. Well, let's check it out scientifically. If there is such a thing, where is it? Look under your desks; behind the door. Check the hallway too. Can anyone see it? Of course not. Why not? Because it does not exist!"

"Let's continue the investigation. Can you smell it?" Pupils will sniff the air but feel foolish. Then someone is likely to say, "I can smell something cooking." Some pupils will nod in relief.

"Of course you can smell cooking because 'cooking odors' really exist. They are actually there. We can also smell vinegar, mothballs, perfume, onions, and many other things because *they are really there.* But what does *air* smell like? It smells like nothing; because that's what it is: nothing! Let's investigate further. Maybe we can taste air. What does it taste like?" Pupils will stick out their tongues, again in an embarrassed way, because they know it won't do any good. Often, someone will hold an imaginary mug, scoop up imaginary air, and drink it. Pupils will laugh, and soon they are all scooping up the air with their pretend mugs.

"At last we have discovered something. I see that you are drinking air, so air must be a liquid. Right?" Well, "no," the pupils will say. They were just pretending with the mugs.

"I see. You used pretend mugs to do pretend drinking because air is a pretend thing. The mugs aren't there and neither is the air. They are just pretend."

You may continue to ask about the shape of air, its color, or other possible properties. Finally, when you have completed the various tests for air, conclude by summarizing: "Air has no smell. It has no taste. It has no shape. It has no color. It has no texture, and it cannot be seen. Why? Because *there is no such thing as air!*"

Pretend that the summary statement concludes the discussion. Tell them that tomorrow we will talk about another subject. Pupils will become quite disturbed. In the face of the so-called evidence, they will be momentarily stopped. But they *know* that air really exists. It is not just a superstition. Let them simmer and stew for a while. Then say, "O.K., if you think air really exists, how can we prove it?"

Tell them that the topic will be discussed again tomorrow. Ask them to bring in evidence that air really exists. Pupils will be highly motivated to find proof. They will discuss the topic in school, at recess, and in the lunch line. They will lean into a strong wind on their way home saying, "There just *has* to be a way we can prove that air really exists."

By the next day it is quite likely that pupils will bring in much evidence: You can feel the wind; you can see that it moves trees. You can blow on your hand and feel the air. You can fill a balloon with air. Air fills tires and holds up cars. Air fills up footballs, basketballs, and volleyballs. Many more examples are likely to be presented.

The discussion above highlights the *negative* properties of air, namely, that air is colorless, odorless, tasteless, and invisible. But it *does* exist.

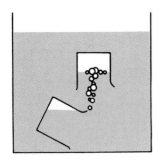

FIGURE 11.3 Pour air from one beaker to another, under water.

Paper

FIGURE 11.4 How can you keep paper dry "under water"?

Positive Properties of Air

Despite the preceding activities, air *is* a real substance and it occupies space. All of the events in this section are designed to show that air truly exists.

For example, in *Event 11-A, Fill the Balloon with an Empty Bottle,* the balloon begins to fill as soon as the air inside the bottle warms up. Obviously, if the balloon fills up, the bottle could not have been empty. (Be sure to use a large bottle and a small balloon because the expansion is not very great. The balloon will not do much more than "stand up.")

Similarly, *Event 11-B, Squeeze-Box Candle Snuffer,* also shows that the box was not really empty. When squeezed, the box pushes out a puff of air that blows out the flame. We cannot see the air itself in these events, but we can see what the air does.

Event 11-C, Pouring Air, can be achieved under water. Use two beakers. Invert the first beaker and push it under water. It is filled with air. Lower another beaker under water in an upright position. After it fills with water invert it above the first beaker. Slowly tip the first beaker (filled with air) so that bubbles stream upward into the second beaker (filled with water). You are "pouring" air. (See figure 11.3.)

When doing this event, it is a good idea to refer to the air in a positive way. The beaker with air is "full of air." The beaker with water is "empty of air" (not "full of water").

Event 11-D, Keep the Paper Dry Under Water, is somewhat similar to Event 11-C because, in both cases, the beakers trap air under water. In Event 11-D the paper towel is wadded up inside the beaker. When inverted and submerged, the air keeps the water out. As pupils often say, the water can't get in "because air is already in there." (See figure 11.4.)

The air is also inside the tumbler in *Event 11-E, Sink the Cork.* It is this air that can be used to force the water down in the bowl. As the inverted tumbler is slowly pushed down, the air inside the tumbler keeps the water from entering. Of course, as the water is pushed down, the cork goes down too.

In performing *Event 11-F, Pour Water into an Empty Bottle,* the pupils will find that the water will not enter the bottle, except for a few drops in the beginning. The reason is simply that the bottle is already full (of air). The few drops of water enter at the beginning because the air can be compressed somewhat by the weight of the water. If you use a tube that is too large, air will bubble out and water will come in, alternating back and forth until the bottle is filled with water. Even if your experiment works that way, it is still a success. It shows clear evidence that air is a real substance and that it occupies space. Point out that the water does not enter until air, a real substance, leaves.

The events in this section show that air is a real substance and occupies space. Additional activities may also be done to show the same property of air.

1. *Blow up a balloon.* When blowing up a balloon, we can see that "something" is going into it. That something is called air.
2. *Blow out a candle.* We see the effects of air when we blow out a candle, even though the air is invisible.
3. *Blow through a straw.* Blow through a straw into water. The bubbles are clear evidence that air is a real substance and occupies space.

Air Exerts Pressure (Events 11-G through 11-N)

Discrepant Events and Pupil Investigations

Event 11-G. Can Crusher # 1

Fill a gallon can with water and insert a one-hole stopper. You will need a long tube. If you do not have one, you can make it by using one-hole stoppers to connect several shorter lengths. Make a holder of strong cord or wire so that you can hang the inverted can from a high support. Let the water run down the length of the tubing into a container on the floor. As the water empties, the can is slowly crushed. (See figure 11.5. It is somewhat awkward to hang up the can because of the long tubing, so one or more helpers may be needed to accomplish the task.)

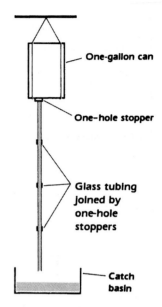

FIGURE 11.5 As water flows from the can through the tube into the catch basin, the outside air pressure crushes the can.

Pupil Investigations (may include the following processes):

1. Observing that water runs out of the can through the tubes into the container.
2. Observing that the can is slowly being crushed.
3. Forming a theory about the unseen force that is crushing the can.

Event 11-H. Can Crusher # 2

Do this event as a demonstration. Cover the bottom of a gallon can with about a cup of water. Heat the water and let it boil for a minute or two. Remove the can from the heat and immediately seal the opening with a stopper. Set the can on a high platform for all to see. Observe.

Caution: If done wrong, the event is dangerous! Do it only if you are *sure* you can do it right. Do not seal the can too quickly. The can must be removed from the heat before sealing it. Otherwise the steam quickly builds up pressure inside and the can might explode.

On the other hand, if you wait too long to seal the can, the event will not work, or work poorly. Once removed from the heat, place the stopper quickly. If done right, it is safe and exciting.

(**Note:** We have found that the best and safest method is simply to *rest* a stopper lightly in the opening of the can. If the steam is still expanding, it can easily push the stopper aside slightly as the steam escapes. However, as soon as the steam stops to form and begins to condense, it automatically pulls in the stopper at just the right time.)

Pupil Investigations (may include the following processes):

1. Observing that the can is slowly crushed.
2. Inferring that the steam drove the air out of the can.
3. Inferring that when the steam cooled, it condensed into a few drops of water.
4. Forming a theory that the condensing steam created a vacuum inside the can.
5. Generalizing that the condensing steam caused a vacuum to form inside the can, which in turn, caused the can to be crushed by air pressure.

Event 11-I. Is a Newspaper Stronger Than a Board?

This event should be performed by the teacher as a demonstration. Obtain a thin board. (A cheap wooden yardstick will do. A thin strip of plywood will

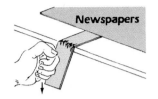

FIGURE 11.6 Air pressure on layers of newspaper is strong enough so that the stick breaks when struck.

not work.) Lay the board on a table so that one end extends over the edge by 15 to 30 centimeters.

Place sheets of newspaper over the remainder of the stick on the table. (That part should be at least 60 to 80 centimeters long.) Be sure to place extra sheets directly over the stick so that the stick does not cut through the paper when you perform the event.

Ask pupils to predict what will happen when you push slowly on the stick. Yes, the stick will push up the newspapers. Are the newspapers heavy enough to break the stick? No. After discussion, hit down on the stick sharply. What happens? Why? (See figure 11.6.)

Pupil Investigations (may include the following processes):

1. Predicting that the board will lift up the newspapers when you push down on the exposed end of the stick.
2. Discovering that the stick breaks when it is hit sharply.
3. Inferring that a force is exerted when the board is struck hard, but not when it is pushed slowly.
4. Forming a theory about the force that holds down the newspaper.

Event 11-J. Drinking Race

Ask two pupils to compete in a soft-drink race. See who can drink a small glass of the beverage fastest. See to it that one pupil has a normal straw, but give the other student a straw filled with pinholes. (Of course, the pupil should not be made aware of the pinholes. Also, the event works just as well with water as with a soft drink.)

At a given signal, they begin. The pupil with the good straw will win easily. Ask the class why there was such a difference.

Pupil Investigations (may include the following processes):

1. Inspecting the "losing" straw to see if it is defective.
2. Inferring that the pinholes caused the pupil to lose the race.
3. Experimenting by having the losing pupil try with another straw.
4. Generalizing about the force that pushes fluids up a straw.

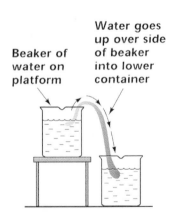

Beaker of water on platform

Water goes up over side of beaker into lower container

FIGURE 11.7 What causes the water to go up over the side of the glass to the lower container?

Event 11-K. Water Goes Up!

Set up an arrangement as shown in figure 11.7. Fill a rubber or plastic tube with water and hold the ends shut as you drape it over the walls of the container. (It is important that the tube be completely full.) Be sure that the end of the tube inside container B is lower than the other end of the tube in container A. Then the ends can be released.

Pupil Investigations (may include the following processes):

1. Observing that water flows into container B.
2. Discovering that the water level in container A gradually is reduced as the lower container fills.
3. Generalizing that the water is going from container A to container B.
4. Forming a theory to explain why the water goes up over an obstruction as it travels from one container to another.

Event 11-L. Antigravity Fountain

Set up an arrangement of containers and tubes as shown in figure 11.8. Start with 5 to 10 centimeters of water in the inverted top bottle and then open the clamps. The fountain begins to flow in the top container. Why?

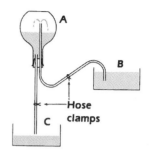

FIGURE 11.8   Why does the water run uphill from container B to A?

Pupil Investigations (may include the following processes):

1. Observing that container C fills with water.
2. Observing that container B empties out.
3. Recording with a diagram the path of the water from B, through A, into C.
4. Forming a theory to explain why water goes uphill from B to A.

Event 11-M. Weightless Water

Fill a tumbler with water, cover it with an index card or sheet of paper, and invert it. Everyone expects the water to pour out. However, it will not pour out if you use weightless water! Show the class that the water and index card remain up against the tumbler, even if the tumbler is turned upside down. (However, don't stretch your luck. Do it over a sink.) (See figure 11.9.)

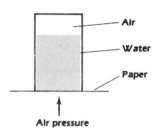

FIGURE 11.9   The water does not spill out because air pressure pushes against the paper. The tumbler does not have to have an air space for this activity to work.

Pupil Investigations (may include the following processes):

1. Observing that the card and water do not fall.
2. Inspecting the card to see that sometimes there is a slight *upward* bulge at the center of the card.
3. Experimenting with tumblers containing varying amounts of water and discovering that they all work.
4. Forming a theory about the force that holds the water in the tumbler.

Event 11-N. Stop the Leak

Punch a nail hole into the bottom and top of a tin can. Fill the container with water and securely seal the cover. The water, of course, runs out. Ask the pupils to stop the flow of water with a finger, but *without* getting it wet. **Note:** Be sure to use a can with a tight-fitting cover. A loose cover will not work. (See figure 11.10.)

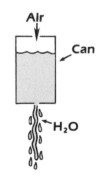

FIGURE 11.10   Can you stop the leak in the can by plugging the *top* hole?

Pupil Investigations (may include the following processes):

1. Experimenting by placing the finger on the top opening.
2. Observing that the water stops running when the top opening is closed.
3. Generalizing that some unseen force holds the water in anytime the top opening is closed.

Events 11-G through 11-N Explained in Context (Air Exerts Pressure)

The events in this section all pertain to an important principle of air: *air exerts pressure*. It will surprise most pupils to learn that air can crush a can, but that is what happens in *Events 11-G and 11-H, Can Crusher # 1 and # 2*. In Event 11-G, as the water runs out of the can, air from the outside tries to get in. However, since there is no opening for air to enter, the air tries to get in by pushing in the sides of the can. After awhile, the can is totally crushed. Where does all the **air pressure**

FIGURE 11.11 Does air exert pressure? It can easily crush a can.

come from? It comes from the weight of air. At first impression it seems unlikely that air could be that heavy. However, if you have enough of it, air begins to become a powerful force. The pressure comes from the weight of hundreds of kilometers of air pushing down from above the earth.

At sea level the pressure of air is so great that it pushes with a force of 1 kilogram per square centimeter. The total force on the can may reach more than 1800 kilograms.

If air pressure is that great, why aren't we crushed by it? Not only does it leave us uncrushed, we can't even feel it! The reason is that the air pressure pushing down on us is equaled by the pressure within our bodies pushing outward.

Only in rare cases, when pressures are not equal, do we notice it. For example, you can sometimes feel your ears "popping" when going up or down a steep road or when going up or down in an airplane. Air pressure varies with elevation, so those changes can sometimes be noticed.

If you can create a situation where the normal pressure is removed, then the existing air pressure can exert itself. That is what is done with the can crusher events. In *Event 11-G, Can Crusher # 1,* gravity removes the water from the can, leaving a vacuum. Air pressure crushes the can as it attempts to fill that vacuum.

It is important that the exit tubing be quite long. Otherwise the air will just get into the can by going up the tube. Even if the air cannot get in, the water will not get out and nothing happens.

It is also important that you use tubing with rigid or strong walls. Glass tubes are the strongest, but plastic or rubber tubing with thick walls might work also. Just be careful that the pressure does not flatten the tube. Then the water cannot get out, and the can will not be crushed.

Event 11-H, Can Crusher # 2, is similar to Event 11-G. The only difference is the method used to create the vacuum. In this event the water is brought to a boil, which quickly fills the can with steam. The steam drives out all the air, especially if you let the water boil for a minute or so.

Then, after the can is removed from the heat, quickly seal the opening. **Caution:** Do not seal the can too soon. You must wait until *after* it is removed from the heat. Otherwise, the can could explode! If you are not *sure* how to do it right, *don't do it.* Perhaps you can ask a high school science teacher to show you how to do it safely.

Then, when the can is removed from the heat, quickly seal the opening. We have found that the best and safest way is just to rest the stopper in the opening of the can. Then it is pulled into the opening at just the right time.

What happens to the steam when it cools off? It condenses into a few drops of water, leaving a vacuum in its place. The air will crush the can as it tries to get inside. (See figure 11.11.) You can speed up the event by placing the can into a pan of cold water. Then the can is crushed very quickly.

The pressure of air is also responsible for the discrepancy in *Event 11-I, Is a Newspaper Stronger Than a Board?* The newspapers should be carefully flattened out over the stick and onto the table. When the end of the stick is hit, air pressure pushes down on the newspaper with such force that the stick is broken. If the stick is pushed down slowly, air can get in from the sides to equalize the pressure, and the paper is lifted easily.

Be sure to observe a note of caution when doing this event. First, if there are too few newspapers, instead of breaking, the stick will simply cut through the paper and fly up into the air (hitting your head, if you are not careful).

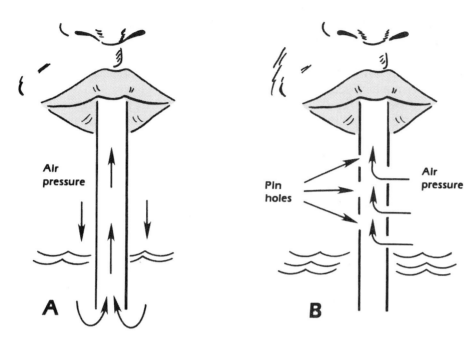

FIGURE 11.12   Why does air pressure push the liquid up straw A but not straw B?

Therefore, be sure to have enough layers of newspaper to keep them from being cut. Second, don't take chances. Keep your head out of the way in case the stick doesn't break.

Event 11-J, Drinking Race, is also designed to show how air pressure exerts itself. When you sip on a straw, you lower the air pressure inside. As a result, the outside air pressure, which is greater, pushes down on the surface of the liquid, forcing it to move up the straw.

When you sip on the straw with the holes, however, the air pressure is pulled directly inside via the holes. The pressure does not exert itself on the liquid, and the liquid does not rise. (See figure 11.12.)

Events 11-K, Water Goes Up!, and *11-L, Antigravity Fountain,* are quite baffling to pupils when they first see them. The concept of water running uphill instead of down is a true discrepancy. Let them observe the events carefully. First of all, they should determine in which direction the water is going. Ask them to find out where the water is coming from and where it is going.

The events are alike because in both cases the water goes up over an obstruction to get to a lower container. Event 11-L is more dramatic because it forms a fountain in the upward part of its journey. **Note:** If you use an ordinary glass tube for the fountain, it will drain the water in container B rather quickly. If, however, you narrow the opening of the glass tube in the flame of a Bunsen burner, or even if you just use the glass part of an eye dropper, the event will run for quite a while before container B empties.

Point out that some outside force must be causing the water to go uphill in both events. Gravity is obviously not that force, because gravity would push the water "downhill," not up. What provides that force? Air does!

It may be easier to understand what happens by starting at the top flask of Event 11-L and working backward. Open the clamp, and water flows out, leaving behind a partial vacuum in the flask. Air tries to get in to fill that vacuum but water is in the way. Since container B is higher than C, it takes less pressure to push the water in from B than from C. Thus, the path is set in which the water moves from container B to the top flask and down to the bottom container.

The force of the fountain can be increased by raising container B (so that the water does not have to be lifted as high), or by lowering the tube in container C (so that gravity pulls down with a greater force, to create a greater vacuum).

Both activities are siphons. The only difference is that the top part of a siphon does not normally contain a flask. Instead, the typical siphon is Event 11-K, in which a closed tube carried a liquid from one container, over an obstruction, to a lower container.

It is important to realize that water will flow in a siphon only as long as the outlet end of the hose is lower than the inlet. The net direction of the siphon has to be downward. There is no way that a siphon can ever raise a liquid if the outlet is higher than the inlet.

Thus, the lifting of liquid takes place only in the middle part of a siphon or antigravity device. The outlet end is always lower than the inlet.

Event 11-M, Weightless Water, again shows that air exerts pressure. It is especially good in showing that the pressure pushes in all directions, even upward. The reason that the water doesn't fall from the tumbler is that air pressure is pushing against the card, keeping the water inside.

If some air gets in along an edge, then the pressure inside the tumbler becomes equal to the pressure outside the tumbler, and everything splashes down promptly. For obvious reasons, this event should be done over a sink.

Anyone can stop the flow of water from the can in *Event 11-N, Stop the Leak,* by just putting a finger on the lower hole. However, how can we stop the leak without getting a wet finger? Just place a finger over the *top* hole.

When water runs out of the lower hole, air enters the top hole. Thus, air gets inside and makes it equal to the pressure outside the can. However, when the top hole is blocked, air pressure can no longer enter on top so it tries to enter through the lower hole. In its attempt to enter, it pushes against the water at the lower exit, keeping it from running out.

By reviewing the events in this section, it is evident that there are many ways to show that air exerts pressure.

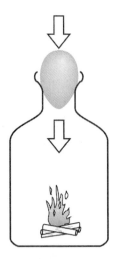

FIGURE 11.13 After the fire goes out, the air cools and shrinks (contracts). Outside air then pushes the egg into the bottle.

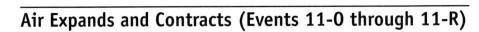

Air Expands and Contracts (Events 11-O through 11-R)

Discrepant Events and Pupil Investigations

Event 11-O. The Egg-in-the-Bottle Mystery

Take a hard-boiled egg and remove the shell. How can we put that egg into a milk bottle? Pushing it will not work.

Light a small strip of paper and drop it into the bottle. *Quickly* place the egg on the mouth of the bottle. It is important not to wait after dropping in the flaming paper. Put the egg on at once. Observe. (See figure 11.13.)

Pupil Investigations (may include the following processes):

1. Predicting what will happen to the fire. (It will burn for a while and then go out.)
2. Predicting what will happen to the egg. (It will be pushed into the bottle.)

3. Observing that the egg bounces up and down for a few seconds right after being placed on the bottle.
4. Observing that the egg goes into the bottle after the fire goes out.
5. Experimenting to find a way to get the egg out of the bottle.

Event 11-P. Oxygen in the Air

Set up an arrangement of candles on the bottom of a tray as shown in figure 11.14. Fill the tray with about 5 centimeters of water. Light one of the candles and place an inverted bottle over it. Observe and record the results. Repeat the activity, but this time with two candles. Repeat once more with three candles. What are the results?

FIGURE 11.14   Do two candles use more oxygen than one? Why does the water rise higher in the bottle when more candles are lit?

Pupil Investigations (may include the following processes):

1. Predicting what will happen to the flame. (It will go out after a short while.)
2. Predicting what will happen to the oxygen inside the bottle. (It will be used up to support the flame.)
3. Predicting that water will enter the bottle to replace the oxygen.
4. Recording the level of water that enters the bottle after each trial with one, two, and three candles.
5. Making a rule to explain the increased water levels with each additional candle.

Event 11-Q. Diving Dropper

Fill a medicine dropper with enough water so that it will either just barely float or just barely sink. Either choice will be fine. Place the dropper into a full cylinder of water. Then place the palm of your hand over the top of the cylinder. Press down, and the dropper goes down. Then carefully pull up with your palm to form a suction, and the dropper comes up. Why? (See figure 11.15.)

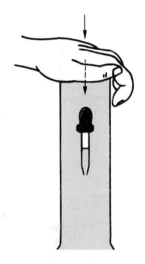

FIGURE 11.15   Push down on the cylinder and the diver goes down; pull up and the diver rises. Notice the air space *inside* the medicine dropper.

Pupil Investigations (may include the following processes):

1. Predicting what will happen when you press down (or pull up) on the water with the palm of your hand.
2. Discovering that the dropper moves up or down in response to pressures exerted by the palm of your hand.
3. Discovering that the liquid *inside the dropper* responds to the pressures by your palm.
4. Inferring that the dropper goes up (or down) because water goes out of (or into) the dropper, making it lighter (or heavier).
5. Generalizing that air can be compressed and expanded.

Event 11-R. Balloon Blowup

Set up an arrangement of bottle, tubes, and balloon as shown in figure 11.16. Blow into tube A and the balloon inflates. Release, and the balloon deflates. Now blow into A again and release, but this time hold B shut. What happens?

FIGURE 11.16
Compressed air and a partial vacuum can inflate the balloon in this activity.

Pupil Investigations (may include the following processes):

1. Predicting what will happen to the balloon if B is held shut.
2. Observing that the balloon remains inflated as long as tube B is held shut.

3. Verifying the activity—checking that air escapes from B while the balloon is being inflated.

4. Experimenting to see if the balloon can be inflated by drawing air out of the bottle through tube B. (It can.)

Events 11-O through 11-R Explained in Context (Air Expands and Contracts)

We learned in the unit on heat energy that most substances expand when heated and contract when cooled. This principle, as it applies to air, is reviewed in this section.

Event 11-O, The Egg-in-the-Bottle Mystery, is astounding to pupils who have never seen it before. Yet the explanation is fairly simple, even though the event is incorrectly presented in some books.

To get the egg into the bottle, a fire has to be dropped into the bottle and the egg placed on top at once. After the fire goes out, the egg is sucked in. (We repeat: for the event to work correctly, the egg must be placed on the bottle quickly after the fire is dropped inside. If you wait, it will be too late.)

Why does the egg go in? Some books mistakenly state that the fire uses up the oxygen, which creates a vacuum. The outside air pushes down in its attempt to get in. In reality, it is another principle that accounts for the activity: the expansion and contraction of air.

Air expands when heated and contracts when cooled. When the fire is dropped into the bottle, it heats the air inside. When the air is heated, it expands and goes out of the bottle. You will often see the egg bounce for a moment or two as the heated air escapes around it.

When the fire goes out, what happens to the hot air? It cools off. As it cools it contracts, leaving a partial vacuum inside. The air that was pushed out earlier tries to get back inside. Now, however, the egg is in the way, so it is pushed in.

There is another way to get the egg into the bottle. Instead of using fire, heat the bottle with water. Then put the egg on top. The air in the bottle slowly cools off and contracts. A vacuum is formed and the outside air gradually pushes the egg inside. Be patient, because it will take several minutes for all this to happen.

When the egg is inside, how do we get it out? Just reverse the situation. No, we do not build a fire in the room and expect the egg to pop into it. Reversing the situation means that instead of creating a vacuum inside the bottle (which brought the egg inside), we place pressure inside to force the egg out.

Of course, when the pressure is raised inside, the egg must be lodged in the opening of the bottle. Otherwise the pressure will just escape. Hold the bottle upside down so that the egg will naturally seal the opening.

You can put pressure inside by blowing past the egg into the bottle. Then when you stop blowing, the air will try to get out again. However, since the egg is in the way, it pushes the egg out instead. (A note of caution is in order. When you blow into the bottle, be on guard so that the egg is not popped into your throat. It is not likely to happen that way, but be on guard.)

Another way is to pour hot water over the inverted bottle and let the air warm up inside. As it expands, air puts enough pressure on the egg to push it out. Remember that the bottle must be inverted so that the egg is lodged in the opening when heat is applied. Otherwise the expanding air will just escape.

Event 11-P, Oxygen in the Air, is also caused by the expansion and contraction of air. It is a common misconception to state that the water rises inside the bottle because it replaces the oxygen used by the candle flame.

Based on that false theory, it should make no difference how many candles are lit. The water should rise to the same level each time because all the oxygen is used up in each case.

However, the results are quite different from those expected in the false theory. The greater the fire, the higher the water level. It is obvious that the amount of oxygen in the bottle is not the critical factor.

The key factor is that air expands when heated and contracts when cooled. The candle flame heats the air inside the bottle, forcing it to bubble out. In fact, if you listen, you can hear it bubble out during the first few seconds after the bottle is inverted. It happens so fast, however, that many people are not aware of what is happening.

Later, after the fire goes out, the air inside the bottle contracts and creates a partial vacuum. The air from the outside tries to get back inside. Since it cannot get in directly, the air pushes the water into the bottle to replace the air that was originally pushed out.

In summary, the greater the heat, the greater the expansion, and the greater the amount of air pushed out of the bottle. Then, when the fire goes out, the greater the influx of water into the bottle. Thus, the more candles you use, the higher the water level in the bottle.

Event 11-Q, Diving Dropper, also is caused by expansion and contraction of air. In this case, instead of using hot and cold to expand and contract it, you use pressure from your hand.

When you press down on the opening of the cylinder, be sure that you have an airtight fit between your palm and the rim of the cylinder. Otherwise the pressure will escape and nothing will happen. When you apply pressure, water is pushed into the dropper. With the added water, the dropper is heavier and sinks to the bottom.

When you pull up on the cylinder with the palm of your hand, you pull water out of the dropper. Then the dropper weighs less and rises to the top.

Sometimes it is easier to cover the top of the cylinder with a rubber cover taken from a balloon. Hold it firmly in place with several rubber bands. Then pull or push on the rubber to move the dropper. Use of the rubber cover allows people with small hands an easier way to operate the system.

A final example of the compression of air can be seen in *Event 11-R, Balloon Blowup.* The air inside a balloon is slightly compressed. Normally, when the balloon is opened, the compressed air rushes out quickly.

However, when tube B is closed, the balloon does not deflate. Air would have to enter the bottle through tube B to fill the space taken by the deflating balloon. If the air cannot get into the bottle directly, then it gets in indirectly. It enters through the balloon, keeping the balloon inflated.

Forces of Flight (Events 11-S through 11-W)

Discrepant Events and Pupil Investigations

Event 11-S. Lifting Forces

Anyone can lift up a sheet of paper by blowing under it. However, can you lift the paper by blowing *over* it? Hold a sheet of paper as shown in figure 11.17. If you blow into it at position A, it goes up as expected. Then blow *over* the paper, at point B, so that the air column just touches the top of the paper.

Sheet of paper

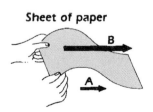

FIGURE 11.17 Blow under the sheet (A) and the paper rises. What happens when you blow over the sheet (B)?

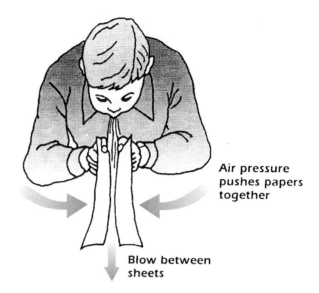

Air pressure pushes papers together

Blow between sheets

FIGURE 11.18   Blow down between two sheets of paper. Can you blow them apart?

What happens? (You will need to blow forcefully. Also, blow so that you actually hit the top-most curve of the paper.)

Pupil Investigations (may include the following processes):

1. Observing that the paper is lifted as expected by blowing against it in position A.
2. Discovering that the paper is also lifted by blowing over it at position B.
3. Inferring that a moving column of air attracts the paper upward.
4. Comparing the lift on the paper with the lift on an airplane.

Event 11-T. Blow Apart the Papers

Hold two sheets of typing paper close to your mouth. Lean over so that the paper sheets are hanging down. (See figure 11.18.) If you blow between them hard enough, will the sheets be blown apart?

Pupil Investigations (may include the following processes):

1. Discovering that instead of being blown away, the papers are drawn into the air stream.
2. Forming a theory about moving air and air pressure.
3. Comparing the forces acting on the papers with the forces that lift an airplane.

Event 11-U. The Inviting Air

Can you blow away a pair of Ping-Pong balls? Suspend two Ping-Pong balls from a support so that they are about 1 to 2 centimeters apart. Blow through a straw between the two balls. Can you blow them away? (Be sure to blow forcefully.)

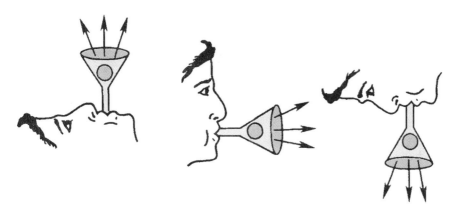

FIGURE 11.19   Can you blow a Ping-Pong ball out of a funnel?

Pupil Investigations (may include the following processes):

1. Discovering that the Ping-Pong balls seem to be pushed *into* the air column instead of away from it.
2. Forming a theory about the invisible force that seems to push into the air column instead of away from it.
3. Verifying the results by using other objects.

Event 11-V. Funnel Magic

Place a Ping-Pong ball into a funnel and ask pupils how high they can blow it into the air. Then see how far they can blow it horizontally across the room. Finally, see how forcefully they can blow the Ping-Pong ball straight down to the floor. In the horizontal and downward attempts, be sure to have pupils hold the ball in the funnel until they are blowing . . . *hard!* Who can blow the ball the farthest? (See figure 11.19.)

Pupil Investigations (may include the following processes):

1. Discovering that the ball cannot be blown out of the funnel in *any of the three positions*, if the pupil blows hard enough.
2. Forming a theory about the invisible force that holds the ball in the funnel.
3. Inferring correctly that the invisible force works best when the airflow is strongest.

Event 11-W. Straw Atomizer

Can you blow away the liquid? Or does a good blow bring the liquid *into* your puff? Set up an arrangement of two straws as shown in figure 11.20. Or better yet, take a single straw and cut almost all the way through, but let a little part remain uncut. Be sure not to hold it so that you blow downward into the lower straw. Keep it level, or better yet, angle the horizontal straw slightly upward. Observe what happens when you blow vigorously.

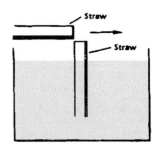

FIGURE 11.20   Blow through a straw directly across the opening of another straw in a container of water.

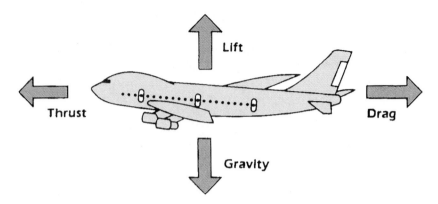

FIGURE 11.21   Four forces affect the flight of an airplane.

Pupil Investigations (may include the following processes):

1. Observing the water rise in the upright straw and being lifted *into* the air column.
2. Interferring that some unseen force is pushing the water into the moving air.
3. Generalizing that a high-speed column of air has low internal pressure.

Events 11-S through 11-W Explained in Context (Forces of Flight)

There are four basic forces that act upon an airplane in flight: *lift, gravity, thrust,* and *drag.* **Lift** is the upward force, offsetting gravity, the downward force. **Thrust** is the force that moves the plane ahead, and **drag** is the force that holds it back. (See figure 11.21.)

A number of good discrepant events can be done to show the effect of lift on an airplane. Most pupils believe that the lift on a plane is due to the *"kite effect,"* that is, the upward push of air striking the underside of the wing. Such is not the case.

The kite effect produces only a small amount of lift. Instead, most of the lift comes from the air going *over* the wing, not under it. Ask pupils to do *Event 11-S, Lifting Forces.* Blow against the underside of the sheet of paper and it rises as expected. Then blow *over* the paper and, surprisingly, it rises again *into* the air stream.

It takes a little practice with the technique to do it right. Hold the paper by the top two edges, and turn it so that it makes a rounded curve on top. Refer back to figure 11.17 and study the diagram carefully. Then blow so that the air column touches the top rounded curve of the paper. The sheet should pop upward into the air stream. Remember that you must blow sharply for the effect to occur.

The main principle of science that causes the action is air pressure. Remember that static air exerts pressure; and if a way can be found to reduce air pressure in one place (the air column), then the existing pressure around it (room air) exerts itself.

It comes as a big surprise to pupils that moving air has lower pressure than still air. So, if you can move air very fast, its pressure can be lowered greatly. That is why the static air *around it* can exert itself.

Keep the air column in mind when doing all of the other events in this section. They all work the way they do because columns of moving air have low internal pressure. (See figure 11.22.) *Events 11-T, Blow Apart the Two Papers,* demonstrates this principle quite well. The moving column of air has low internal pressure so that the still air pushes into the moving column. The two sheets cannot be blown apart. In fact, the harder you blow, the more likely it is that the sheets will be pressed together.

How does this effect work on an airplane? Air pressure pushes the wing upward just as the paper was pushed upward in Event 11-S. The top surface of the wing is curved as shown in figure 11.23, the lower surface is fairly flat. Thus, the air going over the wing has to travel farther to get to the same place.

In traveling farther, the air speeds up. It forms, in effect, a high-speed column of air above the wing, and it produces the same kind of pressure that you got when you blew above the paper. The pressure pushes upward on the underside of the wing, lifting the airplane. This relationship between the flowing air column and the change in pressure is called **Bernoulli's principle.**

The low air pressure in a moving air column is shown again in *Event 11-U, The Inviting Air.* By blowing between them, the Ping-Pong balls are not blown apart. Instead, static room air pushes the Ping-Pong balls *into* the air column. This event is like Event 11-T where two sheets of paper were used. Similar results will be obtained by using apples, baseballs, bottles, books, or just about anything else in place of the Ping-Pong balls.

Event 11-V, Funnel Magic, is also useful in showing the effects of a moving air column. The only problem, if any, is figuring out where the air column is. The air goes through the stem of the funnel and then around the ball. As it goes around the ball, the air is restricted, so it has to speed up. There it has its greatest speed and the effect is strongest. As a result, the higher pressure of the still air in the room pushes the ball *into* the funnel.

Most pupils will expect to blow the ball up to the ceiling. However, they will find that if they blow hard enough, they cannot get the ball out of the funnel, *even if they aim it toward the floor.* When aiming toward the floor, do not release the ball until you are blowing quite hard, and it will stay in. The harder you blow, the better it works. (See figure 11.24.)

The last event in this section, *Event 11-W, Straw Atomizer,* also shows how static room pressure pushes into a moving column of air. In this event the column of air is located at the top of the upright straw, so static room air pressure pushes the water up into the moving air column. When it reaches the air stream, the water is atomized (broken up into tiny droplets).

The event is a rough model of how sprayers and atomizers work. Thin straws will often give better results than larger straws because you can get higher air speeds with them.

Streamlining for Speed (Events 11-X and 11-Y)

Discrepant Events and Pupil Investigations

Event 11-X. Reverse the Flame

Light a candle, and hold a flat card (index card is fine) 10 centimeters in front of the flame. Then blow directly into the cardboard. Have others observe the flame. How does it react? (See figure 11.25.)

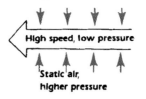

FIGURE 11.22   A high-speed column of air has low internal pressure.

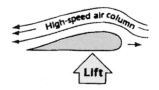

FIGURE 11.23   The upper part of an airplane wing is curved. Air flowing over the top travels farther and faster than air flowing under the wing.

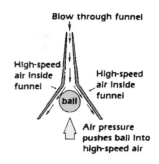

FIGURE 11.24   High-speed air has low internal pressure, so the ball is held inside the funnel.

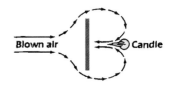

FIGURE 11.25   What happens to the flame when you blow against the flat card?

FIGURE 11.26   Can you blow through a bottle? What happens to the flame?

Pupil Investigations (may include the following processes):

1. Discovering that blowing against the flat cardboard causes the flame to move *toward* the source of air.
2. Drawing a diagram showing the path of the air currents.
3. Generalizing that some form of pressure pushes against the air stream when a flat card is used.

Event 11-Y. Blow Through a Bottle

Use an arrangement similar to the one used in Event 11-X, except that instead of using an index card, use a small bottle. Line up the bottle so that it is between the person and the candle. (See figure 11.26.)

Pupil Investigations (may include the following processes):

1. Observing that blowing into the bottle will cause the flame to move away from the source of the moving air.
2. Discovering that if you blow hard enough the flame will go out.
3. Drawing a diagram showing the path of the air currents.
4. Comparing the movement of air in this event with that of the previous event.

Events 11-X and 11-Y Explained in Context (Streamlining for Speed)

Since it is important for an airplane to travel fast, it is clear that planes need powerful engines that develop great thrust. What is not quite as clear is the need to reduce the drag on a plane, or the force that tends to hold it back.

At the high speeds attained by aircraft, drag is a far more serious problem than it is at the lower speeds involved in auto travel. As a result, aircraft engineers are constantly testing surfaces, shapes, and designs to reduce drag as much as possible.

Events 11-X, Reverse the Flow, and *11-Y, Blow Through the Bottle,* show how shapes affect drag. When the index card is used, air goes around it and actually turns back, moving *toward* the person who is blowing. With some practice the candle flame actually can be blown out that way. When using the bottle, however, the air goes around it and continues on its way. The candle flame moves in the same direction as the original air.

If you have a clear glass plate about the size of an index card, the person who does the blowing can see the results much better. An index card is very easy to use, but, unfortunately, the blower cannot see the effect very well. Likewise, a round bottle or tumbler lets the flame be visible to the person who does the blowing, but a tin can may also be used if necessary.

Ask pupils to diagram the air flow in the two trials. They will see that blunt shapes cause drag in two ways: (1) by resistance to air as the object moves, and (2) by the suction and turbulence of the air behind it.

How Airplanes Are Controlled (Event 11-Z)

Discrepant Event and Pupil Investigations

Event 11-Z. Airplane Flying Contest

Have pupils make folded paper airplanes or cardboard models that are capable of flying when tossed into the air. Have them bend the back edges of the wings on the models up or down to see the effects on flight. Let them bend the upright stabilizer left or right to see if its position affects flight.

After testing their work, let the pupils hold a paper plane flying contest. See which plane can stay in the air for the longest time, which plane flies the greatest distance, and which one flies a circular path to return nearest to its launching point.

Pupil Investigations (may include the following processes):

1. Experimenting with different weights (paper clips) on the nose of the paper plane and the effect of different launching speeds.
2. Experimenting with the control surfaces to see the effect on flight.
3. Comparing the controls to those used on full-sized aircraft.

Event 11-Z Explained in Context (How Airplanes Are Controlled)

More controls are needed to fly an airplane than are needed to drive a car. A car has two sets of controls: (1) to move ahead and back, (2) to move left and right. A plane has controls to do the same things (except move backwards). A plane has additional controls: (3) to move up and down, and (4) to tilt or roll clockwise and counterclockwise.

All of the motions of a plane can be tested with paper airplanes as suggested in *Event 11-Z, Airplane Flying Contest.* Your hand gives it its forward motion, and adjustments on the wings and other surfaces can produce all other motions.

The major control surfaces of a plane are shown in figure 11.27. The **elevators** control the up and down motion of the plane. When the elevators are angled up, the tail is pushed down and the plane climbs. Conversely, when the elevators are angled down, the tail is pushed up and the plane heads down.

The **rudder** is located on the trailing edge of the vertical tail section. When the rudder is angled toward the left, the air pushes the tail to the right. Thus, the nose of the plane is pointed toward the left. When the angle of the rudder is reversed, the plane's flight path is also reversed.

Another important control surface is the **aileron.** One is located on the trailing edge near the end of each wing. It is used to tilt the aircraft in a clockwise or counterclockwise roll. To tilt in one direction, the aileron on one wing is angled up while the aileron on the other wing is angled down. To tilt or roll the plane in the other direction, the aileron angles are reversed.

The aircraft also has **flaps.** They are located on the trailing edge of each wing. Flaps are designed to increase lift during takeoff and landing when

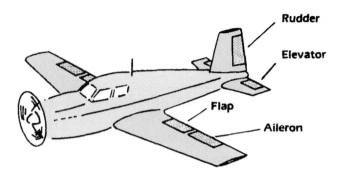

FIGURE 11.27   These are the major control surfaces of an airplane.

speeds are slow. When the flaps are extended and angled down, the air column going over the top of the wing must travel even farther than normal. This has the effect of increasing the speed of the airflow over the top of the wing, which, in turn, increases the lift. When the aircraft is flying at high speeds, the extra lift is not needed and the flaps are retracted.

Although the flaps and ailerons are both on the trailing edges of the wings, they do different things. The flaps are always used together and provide more lift when the plane is flying slowly (as in landing and taking off). The ailerons are much smaller and are always used as opposites to rotate the plane clockwise or counterclockwise.

When flying an airplane, a number of controls are often used at the same time. For example, when the pilot wants to turn the aircraft, the ailerons, elevators, and rudder are often all used at the same time.

Almost all of the controls of an airplane can be tried with the paper airplanes. Pupils will find various combinations that will permit long flights or controlled turns. In the process of flying paper airplanes, the pupils will gain a better understanding of control surfaces of real aircraft.

FIGURE 11.28   Notice how the wings angle upward. The upsweep makes the airplane more stable in flight.

The Upsweep of the Wings

Have you ever looked carefully at the front view of an airplane? Notice that the wings are *not* level with the ground. The wings are angled upward from the fuselage. (See figure 11.28.)

The upsweep serves as a very important function in the control of flight. It helps to keep the plane stable. If the plane is rolled by air currents so that one wing is pushed up, the other turns down. The wing that is turned up no longer gets as much lift as the one that is down. The added lift on the lowered wing corrects the rolling action.

The upsweep can also be tested with the paper models. It will help to produce planes that have very stable flights. Many kites are also built with the upswept design to provide more stable flight.

Supersonic Flight (Events 11-AA and 11-BB)

Discrepant Events and Pupil Investigations

Event 11-AA. Sonic Boom

Read the following description of a supersonic flight across the country: "The aircraft exceeded the speed of sound over the entire length of the country. But only the people near the start of the flight heard the sonic boom as the plane broke the sound barrier." Ask pupils to figure out what is wrong with the description.

Pupil Investigations (may include the following processes):

1. Forming a theory (incorrectly) that the boom is heard only once at the beginning of the flight when it breaks the sound barrier.
2. Forming a theory (incorrectly) that the boom is heard twice: at the beginning and again when it slows to subsonic speed at the end of the flight.
3. Discovering that a sonic boom is created all the way across the country.
4. Diagramming the sonic waves created by a supersonic aircraft.

Event 11-BB. Approaching Aircraft

Ask pupils to find the error in the following description about the approach of a supersonic aircraft: "As the plane approached, it had a high-pitched sound. After it passed by, the sound had a much lower pitch."

Pupil Investigations (may include the following processes):

1. Predicting (incorrectly) that the pitch should be the same both coming and going.
2. Discovering that the listener could hear no sound at all before the plane passed by.
3. Analyzing the relationship between the speed of sound and the cause of sound.

Events 11-AA and 11-BB Explained in Context (Supersonic Flight)

Many aircraft travel at or above the speed of sound. Just how fast is that? Refer back to *Event 8-L, Speed Detector,* in Chapter 8. Pupils will be impressed to realize that an aircraft that flies at the speed of sound will travel as fast as the sound did in their experiment. They will be even more impressed to realize that many (military) aircraft travel two and three times the speed of sound.

We saw earlier in this chapter that most of the lift of an aircraft comes from the high-speed column of air that forms above the wing. Once the plane reaches the speed of sound, however, the principle of lift changes greatly. Instead of lift, it slowly changes to a downward pressure.

The change occurs because the air going over the wing travels faster than the plane. (Remember that the air speeds up as it goes over the upper curve of the wing.) As a result, the air column reaches the speed of sound before the plane does.

In effect, the high-speed air piles up on itself as soon as it reaches the top of the wing. This "piling up" forms a higher pressure, which pushes downward, not the usual low pressure, which lifts the plane up. Thus, the wings of supersonic planes do not have the upper curved surfaces. Also, they are made as thin as possible to reduce air resistance.

As the plane goes still faster, the pressure builds up even more on all its leading edges. When strong enough, this pressure reaches the ground and is called a **sonic boom.** The pressure trails behind the aircraft much like a water wave trails a moving boat.

The faster the plane goes, the louder the boom. Of course, if the plane flies very high (as it usually does), the sound is not very loud on the ground.

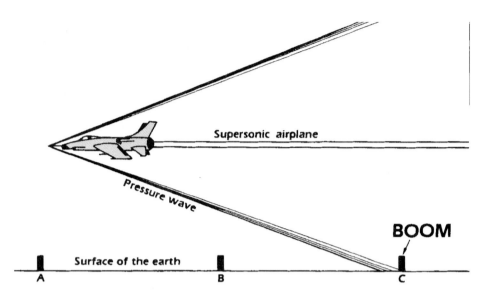

FIGURE 11.29 Why is it that people at A and B cannot hear the approach of a supersonic airplane? The "boom" is heard at C.

In fact, sometimes the boom cannot even be heard. What happens when the plane flies low enough for the boom to be heard clearly on the ground? Will it make a "boom" only when it breaks the sound barrier and then fly silently on? What is wrong with the description in *Event 11-AA, Sonic Boom?*

Some pupils will think that the boom occurs only when the plane "breaks" the sound barrier. Others will think that the boom can be heard twice: once when it enters supersonic speed, and once again when it returns to subsonic speed. They think that the boom can be heard only at both ends of the trip.

Unfortunately, the pressure wave that causes the boom is present any time the plane flies at supersonic speeds. Thus, the boom follows the plane all the way across the country.

Part of the reason for the misconception comes from a poor choice of words. For many years plane designers knew that great problems existed in attempting to reach the speed of sound. They knew that a new form of power would be needed to accomplish the task. As a result, it was regarded as a barrier. With the development of jet engines, there was finally enough power to accomplish the task. The speed of sound, which for so many years acted as a barrier, was finally "broken."

Because of the use of the terms *barrier* and *broken,* many people gained a false impression that "breaking" the sonic barrier was a single event and that, once accomplished, the plane would then fly quietly at supersonic speed.

Pupils may question the explanation because many may have heard sonic booms and they *sound* like single events. Just keep in mind that the shock wave travels as fast as the plane and it passes by so fast that we hear only a single "boom." The listener hears only a tiny instant of the continuous sound. That tiny instant is the "boom."

The "boom" is the only warning an observer would receive in *Event 11-BB, Approaching Aircraft.* An observer cannot hear the approach of a supersonic aircraft at all, because it is traveling faster than the sound it makes. By the time the sound reaches the listener, the plane *has already passed by.* Thus, all that the listener would hear is the "boom" and then the sound of the departing airplane. (See figure 11.29.)

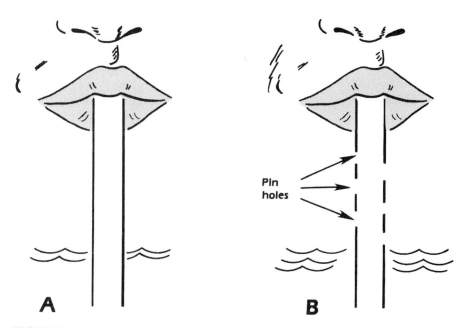

FIGURE 11.30   Why does air pressure push the liquid up straw A but not straw B?

Supersonic aircraft are designed different from subsonic aircraft. Because of the greater stress of supersonic flight, those planes are built stronger, have smaller wings, and are streamlined to offer a minimum of resistance to air.

One important design innovation is the *"Coke-bottle"* shape of the fuselage. Designers discovered that, when the fuselage is "pinched in" by an amount equal to the cross-section of the wing, drag is reduced. Look for the Coke-bottle shape in pictures of supersonic aircraft.

Combining Assessment with Instruction

After students have explored several discrepant events about air and air pressure, copy and enlarge a figure from an event that was not investigated in class. White-out any labels or arrows in the figure and copy it on a transparency. You will need one transparency for each group of three to four students.

Have students discuss how air pressure might work in the selected event. (See figure 11.30.) Each group should write an explanation and draw arrows to show understanding of air pressure in the given event. Using the transparency, a randomly selected student from each group will present the group's ideas. After each group has completed the presentation, the class should discuss which group(s) they agree has an effective and accurate explanation and why.

Sites and Software

The following websites and software are appropriate to use with this chapter. Note that computer software and websites change rapidly. This makes it necessary to investigate the stable websites for new links and software catalogs for updates. Visit www.mhhe.com/friedl6e to link to these directly and for study resources.

Sites

National Air and Space Museum	www.nasm.si.edu
NASA Rocket Activities	www.lerc.nasa.gov/WWW/K-12/TRC/rockets
Flight Activities	www.geocities.com/CapeCanaveral/1817/resource.html
Model Rocketry	www.irving.org/rocketry
How Boomerangs Work	www.howstuffworks.com/boomerang.htm
Introduction to Windows to the Universe	www.windows.ucar.edu

Software

Science Court Explorations: Flight (Tom Snyder) (2–4)
Estes Rocket Stabilization (Estes) (5–12)
The Way Things Work (Houghton Mifflin Company) (3–9)
InventorLabs: Technology (Houghton Mifflin Interactive) (5–9)

Key Terms

aileron *221*

airfoil *202*

air pressure *209*

Bernoulli's principle *219*

drag *218*

elevators *221*

flaps *221*

lift *218*

rudder *221*

sonic boom *223*

thrust *218*

Teaching Children about Weather and Climate

NATIONAL SCIENCE EDUCATION STANDARDS ALIGNMENT TO EVENTS

The events in this chapter help accomplish several of the NSES for content. The event(s) that align with a given content standard are listed below that standard.

LEVELS K–4

UNIFYING CONCEPTS AND PROCESSES
- Systems, order and organization
  12-A

- Change, consistency, measurement
  12-D
  12-H through 12-L
  12-N
  12-O

- Evidence, models and explanation
  12-B through 12-D
  12-J

SCIENCE AS INQUIRY
- Abilities necessary to do and understand scientific inquiry
  12-A through 12-O

PHYSICAL SCIENCE
- Properties of objects and materials
  12-H through 12-L

- Light, heat, electricity, and magnetism
  12-N through 12-O

EARTH AND SPACE SCIENCE
- Changes in the earth and sky
  12-A through 12-O

SCIENCE AND TECHNOLOGY
- Abilities of technological design
  12-G through 12-L

- Understanding science and technology
  12-C
  12-M

SCIENCE IN PERSONAL AND SOCIAL PERSPECTIVES
- Science and technology in local challenges
  12-M

LEVELS 5–8

UNIFYING CONCEPTS AND PROCESSES
- Systems, order and organization
  12-A

- Change, consistency, measurement
  12-D
  12-H through 12-L
  12-N
  12-O

- Evidence, models and explanation
  12-B through 12-D
  12-J

SCIENCE AS INQUIRY
- Abilities necessary to do and understand scientific inquiry
  12-A through 12-O

PHYSICAL SCIENCE
- Properties and changes in properties of matter
  12-H through 12-L

- Motion and forces
  12-G through 12-L

- Transfer of energy
  12-D through 12-G
  12-N through 12-O

EARTH AND SPACE SCIENCE
- Structure of the earth system
  12-A through 12-O

SCIENCE AND TECHNOLOGY
- Abilities of technological design
  12-G through 12-H

- Understanding science and technology
  12-C
  12-M

SCIENCE IN PERSONAL AND SOCIAL PERSPECTIVES
- Natural hazards
  12-E through 12-F

- Risks and benefits
  12-D through 12-E

- Science and technology in society
  12-C
  12-J through 12-K
  12-M

HISTORY AND NATURE OF SCIENCE
- History of science
- Historical introduction

227

From Myth to Meteorology

Think how often you listen to the radio or television, or read the newspaper to get the weather forecast for the day or week to come. So much of our daily activities and what we wear we plan according to the weather forecast.

Our ancestors used nature to forecast the weather. Some of their observations proved to be somewhat valid indicators of weather to come, yet others were nothing more than myths. About 450 B.C. Greek scientist Empedocles thought that lightning resulted from light rays being trapped in clouds.

Groundhog Day, February 2, is a popular tradition in the United States that dates back many centuries with variations from many cultures. If a groundhog (the renowned Punxsutawney Phil), sees his shadow it is a sign of six more weeks of bad weather or a "Second Winter."

Another myth takes the form of a poem you may remember:

Red sky in morning,
sailor take warning.
Red sky at night,
sailor's delight.

This saying frequently works because our weather moves most often from west to east. Clouds form because of moisture in the air and therefore a rainstorm may be headed our way. However, not all cloud formations mean storm conditions are present. The reflection of sunlight off clouds appears red. Red sky in the morning means a possible storm is coming in from the west. Red sky at night indicates clouds are moving away, toward the east, bringing in clear skies.

Through the centuries simple observations of nature gave way to collecting scientific data. In 1643, Italian physicist Evangelista Torricelli invented the barometer. A **barometer** measures air pressure. Torricelli noticed a drop in air pressure was often a sign of an upcoming storm. Shortly after, in 1664, Francesco Folli invented the **hygrometer,** an instrument used to measure the atmospheric humidity. It is noteworthy that Leonardo da Vinci built a very primitive hygrometer in the 1400s, once again showing that science evolves over long periods of time. Finally, in the 1700s, the thermometer was developed.

Even with the development of all of these instruments, it was not until the mid-1800s that weather forecasting got a break. The invention of the electric telegraph by Samuel Morse promoted rapid transmission of weather information to warn of pending storms and other weather-related disasters.

The improved communication systems of the 1900s: radio, radar, television, computers, and satellites all greatly improved weather forecasting. The science of studying the atmosphere including weather forecasting, **meteorology,** is a very complex science that depends upon understanding numerous variables. It is estimated that today's daily forecasts are about 85% accurate and weekly forecasts have an approximate 80% reliability.

What Is Weather? What Is Climate? (Events 12-A through 12-C)

Discrepant Event and Pupil Investigations

Event 12-A. Classifying Climates

List the following words and statements on the chalkboard: (1) calendar, (2) clock, (3) day, (4) month, (5) season, (6) storm, (7) it is hot today, (8) it was a hot summer, (9) it was a rainy day, (10) our summers are usually dry, (11) the wind is blowing hard, and (12) we have mild winters. Ask pupils to classify the words and statements into two groups to represent *weather* and *climate*.

Pupil Investigations (may include the following processes):

1. Comparing the words and statements to find common traits.
2. Classifying the twelve examples into two groups.
3. Inferring that time is an important factor in defining the terms.

Event 12-B. Weather-Map Bulletin Board

Cut out weather maps from the newspaper for a week and place them on a bulletin board. Using outline maps of the United States, have pupils track the "highs" and "lows."

Pupil Investigations (may include the following processes):

1. Identifying the "highs" and "lows" on the weather maps.
2. Plotting the movement of the "highs" and "lows" on an outline map of the United States.
3. Discovering a relationship between "highs" and "lows," and how they influence weather.

Event 12-C. Climate Database

Have each pupil research the climate of two different state capitals. In an average size class, most of the states would be investigated. After each pupil has completed the investigation, have the class brainstorm to form a list of important information needed to understand the climate of an area. Information might include monthly averages for temperature, rainfall, number of hurricanes/tornadoes, snowfall, and number of sunny days. Other necessary information might include location, terrain, nearby rivers, lakes, and mountains, and altitude. After class discussion, let pupils search for any characteristic they may not have found during the first search. Encourage the use of the Internet as part of the search process. Have the class again identify the list of important characteristics about climate. This will be the *field* names for the database on state climates. Have pupils enter the information for their selected states into the *file* "Climate Database."

Pupil Investigations (may include the following processes):

1. Collecting information known about climates around the United States.
2. Sorting for a given *field* or characteristic of climate using a database.
3. Recognizing patterns in climates through the database sort.

Events 12-A through 12-C Explained in Context (What Is Weather? What Is Climate?)

What is the difference between weather and climate? Time! If it is a relatively short time, the words and statements pertain to **weather.** If it covers a long time, the words or statements pertain to **climate.** The "weather" and "climate" words and statements of *Event 12-A, Classifying Climates,* are shown in the following lists:

Weather	Climate
Clock	Calendar
Day	Month
Storm	Season
It is hot today	It was a hot summer
It was a rainy day	We have mild winters

In summary, temporary or short-term conditions of the atmosphere refer to weather. Long-term conditions of the atmosphere refer to climate.

The short-term conditions can be displayed as suggested by *Event 12-B, Weather-Map Bulletin Board.* The sequence of maps can also be used by pupils to plot the path of the "highs" and "lows" on outline maps of the country.

The events can be modified to fit a fairly wide range of class levels. Upper grades will find the lessons easy but still useful. Middle grades will find it within their abilities. Lower grades may find Event 12-B too difficult, but Event 12-A can be accomplished if the list of words is shortened. If necessary, the list can be shortened to only two words, one describing weather and the other climate.

Even pupils in primary grades and kindergarten can learn about weather and climate, but by a different method. Ask them to help make a big weather calendar. Draw the calendar on a large piece of cardboard or make it out of felt board or peg board. Have available simple symbols representing the sun, clouds, wind, and rain.

Every day at a given time, perhaps an hour before dismissal, ask the class to decide which picture (symbol) best describes the "weather for today." As they focus on the daily weather for the entire month, not only do they focus on daily weather, but also a visual pattern unfolds that shows something about the long-term conditions of the atmosphere: climate. See figure 12.1 for an example of one week's weather.

Event 12-C, Climate Database, gives pupils an opportunity to understand relationships between climate fields such as terrain and rainfall. By sorting for states with the same average temperature, pupils may discover that latitude plays an important part. Pupils may also discover that states to the west of the Rocky Mountains receive more rain than those to the east of the mountains. The database can encourage inquiry about such a phenomenon as lake-effect snow. A "big idea" behind the use of a database is for students to develop an appreciation for the ease and speed at which a database can sort tremendous

Calendar

Sun	Mon	Tues	Wed	Thur	Fri	Sat
			1 ☀sun	2 ☀sun	3 ☀sun	4
5	6	7	8	9	10	11
12	13	14	15	16	17	18

FIGURE 12.1   This is an example of a weather calendar showing the weather for the first 7 days of a month.

amounts of information. A database helps scientists make sense of the overwhelming amount of data collected.

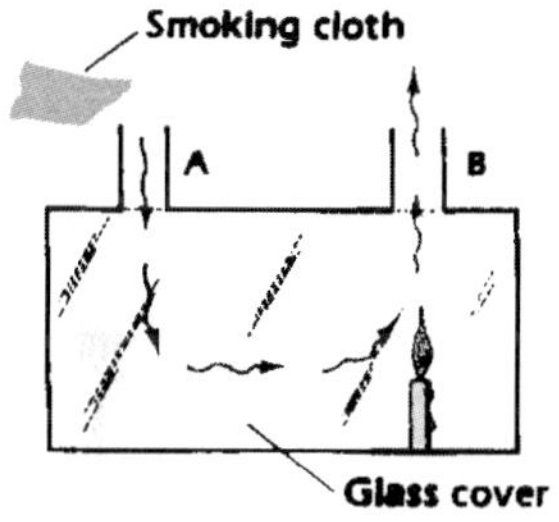

Convection Currents (Events 12-D through 12-G)

Discrepant Events and Pupil Investigations

Event 12-D. Curious Currents

Set up a convection box as illustrated in figure 12.2. A convection box is essentially a metal box with two chimneys and a sliding glass front for viewing. Light the candle and close the glass cover. Hold a smoldering piece of cloth or string that gives off lots of smoke over the top of chimney A. Then hold it above chimney B. What do you observe?

FIGURE 12.2   Smoke goes down chimney A and up chimney B in this convection box, showing that warm air rises and cool air falls.

Pupil Investigations (may include the following processes):

1. Observing that the smoke goes up at chimney B.
2. Observing that the smoke goes down at chimney A.
3. Recording data with a diagram showing the path of the air currents.
4. Inferring that warm air rises and cold air descends.

Event 12-E. Tornado Box

Select a cardboard box that is about 30 to 40 centimeters high and just slightly larger than a good square-shaped hot plate. Cut out large "windows" on two adjacent sides of the box and cover them with clear plastic. Paint the inside of the box black.

Cut a 10-centimeter hole in the ceiling of the box and insert a 1-meter chimney into it. Seal all air leaks with tape. Finally, along the four corners of the box, cut long, upright slots about 1 to 2 centimeters wide and extending to within 3 centimeters of the top and bottom. (See figure 12.3.)

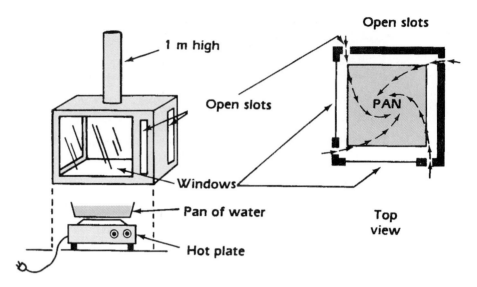

FIGURE 12.3   A specially prepared box and chimney can be used to make a miniature tornado.

Place a shallow square tray of water on the hot plate. The tray should be about the same size as the hot plate. Cover the tray and hot plate with the tornado box. Bring the water to a vigorous boil. **Note:** If the water cannot be brought to a vigorous boil, it is not likely that the tornado box will work. Vigorous boiling of the water is needed.

Caution: Be sure to exercise great care so that no pupil can be exposed to the hot plate or boiling water. Some pupils may want to crowd very close to the box, but be sure that they observe from a safe distance.

Shine a flashlight through one of the windows, and view the effect through the other window. What do you see?

Pupil Investigations (may include the following processes):

1. Observing that a cloud forms over the boiling water.
2. Observing a whirlwind over the pan, similar to a miniature tornado.
3. Generalizing that the tornado is formed because of rising air and swirling incoming air.

Event 12-F. Tornado Bottle

Obtain a large 2-liter clear plastic bottle. Those used for beverages are fine. Fill the bottle with water and swirl it for a moment or two. Then invert it over a sink and let the water run out. What is formed in the bottle? How does it compare to a tornado?

Pupil Investigations (may include the following processes):

1. Discovering that a tornado-like vortex is formed in the middle of the bottle.
2. Comparing the twisting water with the twisting air of a tornado.
3. Generalizing that the center of both the bottle and a tornado have low internal pressure.

Event 12-G. The Convection Contradiction

Present a verbal discrepancy to the class: If warm air rises and cold air descends, why is it colder at high altitudes (where the warm air goes) than at low altitudes (where the cold air goes)? (See figure 12.4.)

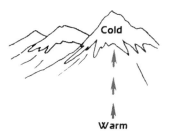

FIGURE 12.4   If warm air rises, why is it cold on top of a mountain?

Pupil Investigations (may include the following processes):

1. Checking references which show that higher altitudes are colder than lower altitudes. (Find pictures of snow on top of mountains.)
2. Discovering that the sun's energy warms the earth's surface but not the air as it passes through it.
3. Discovering that the air is warmed by the earth's surface.
4. Generalizing that air is warm at the source (earth) and gets colder as it moves away.
5. Forming a theory that something must be cooling the air as it rises and warming it as it descends.

Events 12-D through 12-G Explained in Context (Convection Currents)

The great weather patterns of the earth are caused by uneven heating and cooling of air. These air movements are called **convection currents.** There are two events used in this chapter that show how convection currents work. If more events are needed, refer back to chapter 5, Teaching Children about Heat Energy, which has a full section devoted to this same topic.

In this chapter, *Event 12-D, Curious Currents,* is an excellent activity to show those air movements. You will see that air rises when it is heated and falls when it is cooled. The candle heats the air and sends it out of chimney B, as is expected by most pupils. However, pupils are often surprised to find that air goes *down* chimney A.

Let pupils diagram the path: down chimney A, across to the candle, and up chimney B. As stated earlier, those currents are a miniature sample of how winds are formed on the surface of the earth.

On the earth's surface we find that the equator is hot and the poles are cold. Thus, the equator acts like the candle in the box and is similar to chimney B. The poles, on the other hand, act like chimney A. Cold, heavy air often comes sweeping down from polar regions, especially during the winter, to cover much of the United States.

The comparison of the earth to the convection box is not exact. The air currents do not form a single large circulating pattern from the poles to the equator and back again to the poles. The distances are too great for the air masses to make the journey undisturbed. Instead, three subcycles are formed.

Polar air pushes one of the subcycles. The air sweeps south but warms up long before it reaches the equator. The equatorial air powers another subcycle. The hot air masses of the equator rise and move north but do not reach the poles; long before, the air masses get cold and descend. The polar and equatorial currents drive an intermediate cycle between the two major cycles. The United States is mostly under the influence of the intermediate cycle. (See figure 12.5.)

In addition to the great global air patterns, which cover thousands of kilometers, there are smaller cycles covering hundreds of kilometers. These smaller areas contain the familiar "highs" and "lows" shown on weather maps.

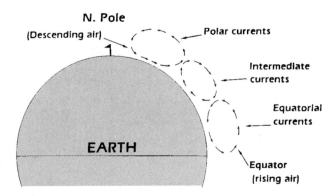

FIGURE 12.5   Rising hot air at the equator and descending cold air at the pole provide the power to move the air in great circular patterns.

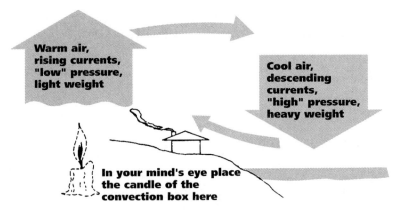

FIGURE 12.6   A sea breeze is formed when warm air rises on the land and is replaced by cooler air from the lake. The paths are similar to the currents in a convection box.

Even smaller versions of the circulation patterns, covering only a few kilometers, can form within the "highs" and "lows." The smaller patterns can form whenever the larger systems become stagnant. An example of the small, area system is the breeze that forms along a lake or seashore. The winds blowing in from the lake are called **sea breezes.**

The local sea breezes develop for the same reason that the currents formed in the convection box. Air is heated (over the land) and cooled (over the water). The cool air moves from the water to the land, just as the cooler air in the box moved to the candle. (See figure 12.6.)

What happens in the middle of the night when the land cools off and is cooler than the water? (Land gains and loses heat much faster than water, so it gets hotter in daytime but colder at night.) At that time the cycle reverses. Because the water is warmer than the land, the cool air blows from the land to the water. Those breezes are called **land breezes.**

Just remember that regardless of which way the breezes blow, they are *always relatively cool breezes* blowing into relatively warm areas. In the daytime the cool breezes come from the water; at night they come from land.

The breezes form only when there is a temperature difference. Thus, the sea breeze is strongest at mid-afternoon, during the warmest part of the day. The land breezes are strongest just before sunrise. By mid-morning and late evening, temperatures tend to equalize, and the breezes stop.

Again, it bears repeating, the land and sea breezes form only when the major weather systems are weak or stagnant. When a major weather system is moving through an area, those winds overpower any local weather patterns that might otherwise develop.

What Are Monsoons?

Monsoons are special kinds of sea breezes that cover large areas of the world. Perhaps the most famous monsoons are those that visit India each year. The winds come loaded with moisture from the warm Indian Ocean. When they reach shore, they are lifted up to go over the land and later the foothills of the Himalayan Mountains.

As the air rises, it cools. As it cools, air loses its capacity to carry the moisture. Therefore, the moisture falls in great quantities. It should be noted that the monsoon winds are not caused by local differences in heating and cooling. They are driven by much larger air masses that tend to prevail at certain times of the year in that region. In other parts of the earth, the prevailing winds will create deserts. Those drying winds will be discussed more fully later in this chapter.

Cold and Warm Fronts

You have often seen weather maps of the Northern Hemisphere on television and in the newspapers. Different air masses and temperatures are commonly shown. What happens when air masses collide?

It is often not just a simple matter of air moving in a cycle covering hundreds of kilometers. Instead, when a mass of air that large begins to move, it is hard to stop. Thus, weather masses will sometimes come out of the frigid Arctic and sweep across the entire continent.

Such an air mass forms a **cold front** as it moves south. In winter, the cold front brings with it bitter cold and strong winds. In summer, a cold front brings thunderstorms as it enters warmer air. Sometimes a cold front brings with it hail, high winds, and tornadoes.

A **tornado** is a localized violent twisting air mass that has a very low internal pressure. It causes destruction by the great force of its winds, but also by its low internal air pressure. When it hits a structure, the normal air pressure inside a building sometimes explodes the building into the low pressure of the tornado. *Event 12-E, Tornado Box,* can be used to show, in miniature, the formation of a tornado-like vortex (whirlwind). A tornado is formed from moisture and rapidly rising warm air. These conditions exist inside the box. Sometimes it helps to blow some chalk dust into the box to make the swirling winds more visible.

(It should be noted that unless the box is made correctly, the tornado will not form. There is not much room for error. However, if everything is made correctly, a powerful twisting column of steam and air is formed and will be easy to see. The most important factors are strongly boiling water, the air slots, and the careful fitting of parts.)

A much simpler form of tornado can be simulated with *Event 12-F, Tornado Bottle.* Just swirl the water in the bottle and invert it over a sink to let the

FIGURE 12.7   Heavy, cold air pushes away warmer air in a cold front (left). Warm air slides slowly over the cooler air in a warm front (right).

water run out. If the water is swirled briskly, a vortex is seen to form in the center of the twisting water that looks very much like a tornado.

As a general rule, cold air overpowers warm air because cold air is heavier. On occasion, however, a warm air mass will push into a colder area and form a **warm front.** That happens when the warm air is part of a larger weather system. Even then, the warm air does not push the heavier cold air away. Instead, the warm air slides up over the cooler air and slowly warms it. A warm front usually brings a long, gentle rain. Study the diagrams of the cold and warm fronts in figure 12.7.

This brings us to *Event 12-G, The Convection Contradiction.* Why is it that the higher the altitude, the colder the temperature? Remember that earlier we stressed that air goes up when it is heated and goes down when cooled. Why is it cold on top of a mountain (where, presumably, the warm air rises) and warm in the low lands (where, presumably, the cold air descends)?

The answer is twofold. First, although the source of the heat is the sun, the sunlight passes through the air without heating it. The sun's energy is turned into heat only when it hits something that is not transparent. Thus, the sun warms the surface of the earth. So one reason that the land is warm is that the sun heats it.

There is another factor that is just as important. Sea level air is highly compressed by the weight of all the air above it. Increasing the pressure heats the air; decreasing the pressure cools it. When air rises, the pressure on it decreases. In turn, the air expands and cools. By the time the air gets into the stratosphere it is extremely cold. As a result, the cold air of high altitudes keeps the tops of mountains cold.

Be sure to remember the cooling effect of higher altitude. This cooling effect is very important in understanding why some places have so much rain. That will be discussed later in this chapter.

The Water Cycle (Events 12-H through 12-M)

Discrepant Events and Pupil Investigations

Event 12-H. Evaporation Race

Form several teams of three or four pupils each. Give each team a small amount of water in a test tube. Hold a race to see which team can get the water to evaporate the fastest.

Rules should be set to permit any innovation as long as the team gets approval from the teacher first. (Throwing the water on the floor is not permitted, for example.) The teacher gives approval for any idea that does not cause a mess.

Another good rule is to permit only one team to use any idea. Then you can keep rules to the very minimum. Just approve or disapprove an idea when a team presents it. Otherwise it is too easy to give away solutions in the instructions (such as "be careful with the hot plate," which, of course, would give away the idea that heating the water speeds up the evaporation process). See which team wins the race and analyze the methods used.

Pupil Investigations (may include the following processes):
1. Experimenting by pouring the water from the test tube into a large tray.
2. Experimenting by heating the water.
3. Experimenting by using a fan to blow air across the water.
4. Controlling variables.
5. Generalizing that evaporation is increased by heat, surface area, and air movement.

Event 12-I. Chalkboard Evaporation
Everyone has seen windows or countertops cleaned with a damp cloth. However, most pupils take it so much for granted that they seldom notice that you can actually see the moisture disappear. Wipe a chalkboard with a damp cloth and ask the pupils to observe. What happens to the moisture?

Pupil Investigations (may include the following processes):
1. Observing the moisture disappearing from the chalkboards.
2. Forming a theory to account for the disappearing moisture.
3. Generalizing that the moisture is changing from a liquid form to a gaseous form.

Event 12-J. Two Temperatures
Connect two temperature probes to the computer/calculator. Set them side by side. Wrap one end of a short cotton cloth onto the end of one probe and place the other end of the cloth in a dish of water. The second probe is left as is. Begin measuring the temperature over time on the computer.

Pupil Investigations (may include the following processes):
1. Observing the temperatures at periodic intervals.
2. Comparing the temperature—time graphs of the two temperature probes.
3. Discovering that the wet-bulb thermometer is cooler.
4. Inferring (incorrectly) that the cool temperature is due to cool water.
5. Generalizing that evaporation has a cooling effect.
6. Inferring what would happen if alcohol were used instead of water.

Event 12-K. Discovering the Dew Point
Place a few cubes of ice into a beaker of water. Lower a thermometer into the water and carefully observe the temperature. Stir slowly, but constantly. At what point does dew form on the outside of the glass?

Pupil Investigations (may include the following processes):
1. Recording the temperature at which dew is first noticed on the outside of the beaker.
2. Repeating the activity on different days.
3. Discovering that the dew point is not at the same temperature every day.

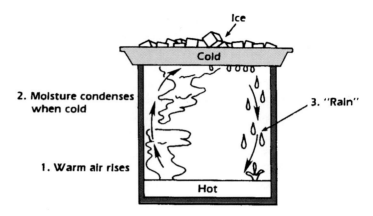

FIGURE 12.8   Can you identify the major parts of this water cycle?

Event 12-L. Water Cycle
Set up a miniature water cycle in a jar. Fill a large, wide-mouthed glass or plastic jar with one or two centimeters of hot water. (Be sure to use heat-resistant glass or plastic. Otherwise there is danger of cracking when the hot water is added.)

Cover the top of the jar with a metal pie plate filled with crushed ice. From time to time, add a small amount of smoke inside the container. See if pupils can identify miniature forms of clouds, air movement, and rain. (Allow plenty of time for the results to occur. See figure 12.8.)

Pupil Investigations (may include the following processes):
1. Observing the formation of clouds, "rain," and "wind."
2. Comparing the events inside the jar with events in the atmosphere.
3. Analyzing the factors that cause rain.

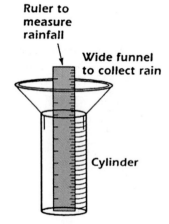

Event 12-M. Rain Gauge Mystery
Study the rain gauge shown in figure 12.9. Notice in the figure that the diameter of the funnel opening is twice the diameter of the bottom cylinder of the rain gauge and a normal ruler is used to measure the rain. What is wrong with this gauge? Divide the class into committees to study and discuss the design of the gauge. It is incorrect as shown. How can it be changed to make it accurate?

Pupil Investigations (may include the following processes):
1. Contrasting the diameter of the cylinder with the diameter of the funnel.
2. Calculating the area of the open funnel and the area of the cylinder.
3. Interpreting the differences between the two areas.
4. Generalizing that the water that collects is four times greater than what actually falls.

FIGURE 12.9   What is wrong with this rain gauge? Why will it not measure rainfall accurately?

Events 12-H through 12-M Explained in Context (The Water Cycle)

Evaporation
We have seen that air currents are essential to the formation of weather patterns. However, air does not move alone; it carries with it huge amounts of water.

Where does air get its water? It comes from oceans, lakes, and streams, as well as plants. The process whereby water changes from a liquid to a gas and goes into the air is called **evaporation.**

The speed at which evaporation occurs depends on a number of conditions, most of which the pupils can discover for themselves by doing *Event 12-H, Evaporation Race.* Initially, the teams may be unsure about what to do. However, as they discuss it among themselves, ideas soon flow. Teams typically discover the following three factors that speed the evaporation of water:

1. *Increasing the surface area.* If they keep the water in the test tube, it could take days for it to evaporate. However, spreading it out in a large pan reduces the time to minutes. Spreading it out over a counter or table could reduce the time even more. (If a cloth is used to spread the water, the cloth must be hung up to dry before the team can be considered finished.)

    Perhaps the best example of how a large surface area affects evaporation is shown by *Event 12-I, Chalkboard Evaporation.* The moisture on a chalkboard usually dries so fast that it is easy to see the drying action. It should be noted that the amount of moisture in the air greatly affects the speed of drying. On a humid day, the drying action is slow. On a dry winter day, however, the action is quite fast. (The ability of the air to accept moisture is discussed in the following text.)

2. *Increasing the heat.* Again, it could take days for the water to evaporate from the test tube if the water is kept at room temperature. However, heating the water will cause it to be boiled away in minutes. (**Caution:** Do not overheat and always point the mouth of the test tube away from people. Overheating will cause steam and boiling water to literally explode from the test tube! Supervise closely. If heat is used, it is wise to allow only a mild heat source, such as a candle; to allow only one team to use it, and to provide close supervision.)

3. *Increasing the movement of air.* When air is saturated, it cannot accept any more moisture; evaporation cannot occur. Thus, evaporation can be increased if saturated air above the water is replaced by unsaturated air. This can be accomplished by using a fan.

There is only one factor missing: the relative humidity of the air. Thus, pupils will typically discover three of the four conditions that affect the rate of evaporation. The fourth factor (relative humidity) is too technical to discover in the classroom.

Relative Humidity, Humidity, and Capacity

Relative humidity is defined as "the amount of moisture in the air compared with the amount that the air can hold." It compares capacity with the actual amount of moisture in the air. The definition is somewhat abstract.

Often it is easier to understand what the term means by comparing an air mass to a meteorologist with a water bucket. In our comparison, the meteorologist represents an air mass, the bucket represents capacity, and the water in the bucket is the humidity. (See figure 12.10.)

Relative humidity is a comparison of capacity with humidity. For example, if a 10-liter bucket contains 5 liters of water, the bucket is 50% full. Similarly, if a mass of air is able to hold 10 liters of moisture but is actually holding only 5 liters, then the air is "50% full" or, has a relative humidity of 50%.

Capacity (10 liters)
Humidity (5 liters)
Relative humidity?

Air mass

FIGURE 12.10   If an air mass has a capacity of 10 liters and humidity of 5 liters, what is the relative humidity?

TABLE 12.1

Difference between Dry- and Wet-Bulb Thermometers

Degrees—F	1	2	3	4	5	6	7	8	9	10	11	12	13	14	15
Reading of Dry-Bulb Thermometer (Degrees—F)	Percentage Relative Humidity														
63	95	89	84	79	74	69	64	60	55	51	46	42	38	33	29
64	95	89	84	79	74	70	65	60	56	51	47	43	38	34	30
65	95	90	85	80	75	70	65	61	56	52	48	44	39	35	31
66	95	90	85	80	75	71	66	61	57	53	49	45	40	36	32
67	95	90	85	80	76	71	66	62	58	53	49	45	41	37	33
68	95	90	85	81	76	71	67	63	58	54	50	46	42	38	34
69	95	90	86	81	76	72	67	63	59	55	51	47	43	39	35
70	95	90	86	81	77	72	68	64	60	55	52	48	44	41	36
71	95	91	86	81	77	72	68	64	60	56	52	48	45	41	37
72	95	91	86	82	77	73	69	65	61	57	53	49	45	42	38
73	95	91	86	82	78	73	69	65	61	57	53	50	46	42	39
74	95	91	86	82	78	74	70	66	62	58	54	50	47	43	40
75	95	91	87	82	78	74	70	66	62	58	55	51	47	44	40

Notice that (1) capacity and (2) humidity are physical quantities, but that (3) relative humidity is always a percentage. Relative humidity is a *comparison* of the first two factors.

The relative humidity of air can be found in the classroom by doing *Event 12-J, Two Temperatures*. The wet-bulb thermometer will show a cooler reading than the dry-bulb thermometer. The cooling action comes from the evaporation of water that is on the cloth on the wet-bulb thermometer.

The lower the relative humidity, the greater the rate of evaporation, and the cooler the temperature. Hence, the difference in the two readings can be used to find the relative humidity of the air. Some common relative humidity figures are shown in table 12.1. For example, what is the relative humidity if the dry-bulb temperature is 63°F and the wet-bulb reading is just 1 degree lower? Can you find the figure of 95% in the table? To use another example, what is the relative humidity if the dry-bulb temperature is 70°F and the wet-bulb temperature is 11 degrees lower? Did you get the answer of 52%?

It is important to realize that the three factors of capacity, **humidity,** and relative humidity are not fixed. They are all variables and each can change in a given air mass.

For example, evaporation increases the amount of humidity in the air, but rain decreases it. A change in temperature, in turn, affects the relative humidity. Surprising to many pupils is the fact that the capacity changes too.

Capacity is affected by temperature. The warmer the air, the greater is its capacity; the colder the air, the lower its capacity. The effect of temperature on capacity can be seen by doing *Event 12-K, Discovering the Dew Point*. We often see moisture form on the outside of a cold glass of ice water. Why does it form? Because the cold surface reduces the capacity of the air to hold mois-

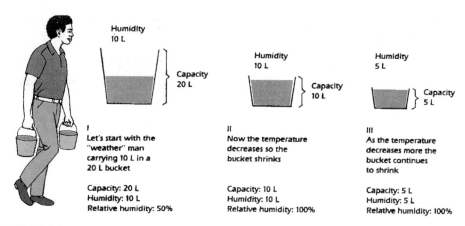

FIGURE 12.11   When air cools off, its moisture-holding capacity (the size of the bucket) decreases. How does this affect the humidity and relative humidity?

ture. If the air can no longer hold the moisture, it condenses into visible dew on the cold surface.

To use our meteorologist analogy, his bucket can stretch and shrink, depending on the temperature. If it is warm, the bucket is large; if cold, the bucket is small. Using our comparisons, if it gets very cold, the bucket is no larger than a thimble.

The analogy shows the tremendous variation in air's moisture-holding capacity. Hot summer air has a capacity hundreds of times greater than frigid winter air. And to repeat, the capacity depends entirely on temperature, nothing else.

Actual figures from the weather bureau show the following capacities: 0.02% at 0°C, 2.0% at 27°C (100 times greater), and 6.0% at 43°C (300 times greater than at 0°C).

Perhaps we can see how the three factors interrelate by looking at the diagram of the meteorologist in figure 12.11. Notice that when the capacity decreases, the relative humidity increases. In the first diagram the relative humidity is 50%; that is, the bucket is 50% full. The air would *feel* dry at that level.

When the temperature drops, however, so does the capacity. In the second example the capacity is reduced to 10 liters, equal to the humidity. At that point the bucket is 100% full (meaning that the relative humidity is 100%). The air would feel quite muggy even though there is no actual change in the amount of moisture in the air. The feeling is caused because perspiration cannot be evaporated from our bodies when the air is already "full."

In the third diagram of figure 12.11, the capacity shrinks (because the temperature drops) down to 5 liters. But remember that the air contains 10 liters of moisture in our example. How can a 5-liter bucket hold 10 liters of moisture? It can't. The excess moisture overflows the bucket. We call that overflow "rain" in summer and "snow" in winter.

Study the diagrams carefully. They contain all the factors that affect the amount of moisture in the air.

It is interesting to note that most rainfall occurs because the capacity shrinks, not because of other factors. Air gains moisture fairly slowly but can lose it quickly. All it has to do is cool off. The cooling can be caused by another air mass, by cold land surfaces, or by being lifted higher into the air.

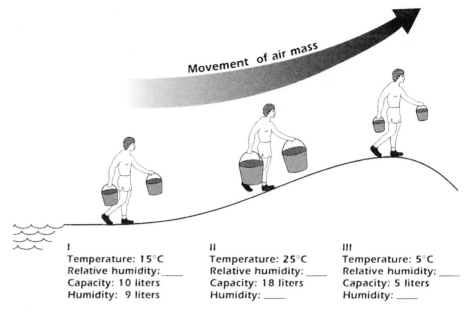

Movement of air mass

I	II	III
Temperature: 15°C	Temperature: 25°C	Temperature: 5°C
Relative humidity: ____	Relative humidity: ____	Relative humidity: ____
Capacity: 10 liters	Capacity: 18 liters	Capacity: 5 liters
Humidity: 9 liters	Humidity: ____	Humidity: ____

FIGURE 12.12   The moisture-holding capacity of air (the size of the little man's bucket) decreases as the temperature goes down. It tends to produce rain when it cools down (III) but not when it warms up (II).

Let us see how the three factors of capacity, humidity, and relative humidity are applied to an air mass that comes from an ocean and moves across a shoreline and over some inland mountains. Study the diagrams in figure 12.12.

See if you can fill in the blanks with the right answers. Is the relative humidity higher or lower in the second diagram? What happens to the humidity? Now look at the third diagram. What is the humidity? The relative humidity?

The capacity of the air mass increased in the second diagram because its temperature increased. Assuming no additional evaporation, the humidity remained the same at 9 liters. Thus, the relative humidity dropped to 50%. (The capacity increased to 18 liters, so the 9 liters filled the bucket only half full.)

The third diagram, however, shows the capacity shrinking sharply (because the temperature is lower). The capacity shrinks down to 5 liters. Can you put 9 liters into a 5-liter bucket? No! The excess moisture comes down as rain.

The example shown in the diagrams is common to many areas of the earth. When the winds reach land, they produce a dry climate.

It is different from what people often believe. There is a common misconception that an air mass moving from the ocean to the land will always produce rain. That, indeed, does happen sometimes, but only if the air mass cools down so that its capacity shrinks.

In other places, when the air warms up, the capacity increases and the air becomes drier. Some very dry lands are located right along some great oceans. Examples of such dry areas are the coastal areas of Southern California, Baja California (Mexico), Chile, and Peru. In each case the prevailing winds travel over relatively cool bodies of water but warm up when they reach shore.

In those areas there is little rain until the air masses are pushed up by hills and mountains to much colder heights. Then the capacity shrinks, and the rain falls.

All the factors of evaporation, humidity, and precipitation occur in a **water cycle.** Water moves in an endless cycle. The cycle includes water (1) evaporating and rising into the sky, (2) condensing to form clouds, and (3) coming down as rain or snow. All three elements of the cycle can be shown in miniature by doing *Event 12-L, Water Cycle.* A convection current is set up inside the jar. The hot water heats the air, so it rises. The cold metal plate cools the air, so it descends. The different temperatures power a continuous current inside the jar. If you put some smoke inside the jar, the currents become much more visible.

The moving air produces a water cycle. Warm air carries moisture up to the cold plate. The cold plate causes the water to condense into droplets. After a while enough water forms to fall down as "rain." (For best results, be sure to have the water as hot as possible. It should be understood that the "rain" forms very slowly. It may take several minutes for the first drop to form and several more minutes for each succeeding drop.)

Most pupils know that rain can be measured in a device called a rain gauge. It is not unusual to find student-made rain gauges similar to the one shown in *Event 12-M, Rain Gauge Mystery.* What is wrong with the diagram? If the opening of the funnel is twice the diameter of the cylinder, it collects much more water that would normally fall into the cylinder. In fact, if the opening is twice the size of the cylinder, it collects four times as much rain.

There are two ways to make the gauge accurate. First of all, you can remove the funnel and use only the cylinder. That gives you a straightforward reading of the rainfall. You can also keep the funnel, however. All you need to do is to measure the rainfall and divide the result by four to get the accurate reading. For example, if you measure 40 cm, the actual rainfall was 10 cm. This arrangement is a good way to measure small amounts of rain. The results are magnified.

The Seasons (Events 12-N and 12-0)

Discrepant Events and Pupil Investigations

Event 12-N. The Four Seasons
Use a lightbulb and globe to show why there are four seasons in a year. Set the light source on a table and move the globe in a path around it. Stop at four points in the path to show the four seasons. (See figure 12.13.)

Be sure to hold the globe at an angle showing the tilt of the earth on its axis. Tape two markers on the globe and label them A and B. Determine the season of the year at each of the two markers at each of the four locations.

Pupil Investigations (may include the following processes):
1. Experimenting with the globe and bulb to determine the effect of the tilt of the earth on the seasons.
2. Discovering that in June the sun (bulb) is high in the sky (more directly overhead) in the Northern Hemisphere and low in the sky in the Southern Hemisphere.
3. Observing that the sun's (bulb's) relative position changes as the globe moves around the sun.
4. Generalizing that the combination of tilt and orbital motion combines to cause the seasons.

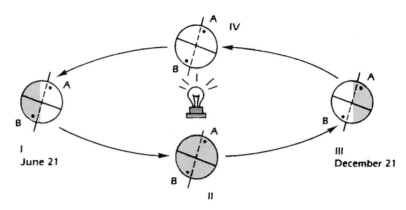

FIGURE 12.13 Use a lightbulb to represent the sun. Move a globe around the sun to show the seasons of the year. Notice that the sun is more directly overhead during summer than during winter.

Event 12-O. Direct and Slant Rays

Draw parallel lines on a sheet of cardboard to represent rays from the sun. Cut out an arc on the cardboard that corresponds to the curvature of a globe. Hold the curved end of the cardboard against the globe so that one set of five lines (sun's rays) is on the equator and the other set of lines is at the North Pole.

Note how much area is covered by the five rays at the equator, and compare with the rays at the North Pole. How does this show why polar regions are cold and the equator is warm? (See figure 12.14.)

Pupil Investigations (may include the following processes):

1. Measuring the area covered by the five rays at the equator and at the North Pole.
2. Discovering that the solar rays at the equator are high in the sky.
3. Discovering that the solar rays at the North Pole are low in the sky.
4. Generalizing that the sun's energy is high at the equator because the rays are concentrated, but low at the poles because the rays are spread out.

Events 12-N and 12-O Explained in Context (The Seasons)

Pupils may have observed that the sun is generally closer to the southern horizon during the winter than during the summer. However, they are often unaware of what causes this apparent seasonal movement of the sun.

The seasonal changes are not caused by any actual movement of the sun. The sun's change of position is caused, instead, by the movement of the earth. Perform *Event 12-N, The Four Seasons*. Tape and label some markers (points A and B) on the globe. (Refer back to figure 12.13.)

If you start at position I, labeled June 21, you will find A, located in the Northern Hemisphere, at the start of its summer season. Point B, in the Southern Hemisphere, starts its winter season. Note that the sun is high overhead at point A and low in the sky at B.

At position III, labeled December 21, the situation is just reversed. In the points in between, the fall and spring seasons trade places. In each case the sun is high overhead during its summer and low during its winter.

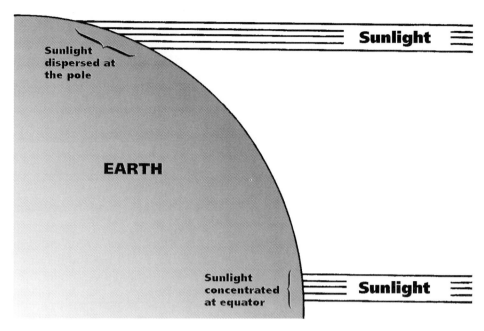

FIGURE 12.14   Can you see why sunlight at the equator produces more heat than sunlight at the poles?

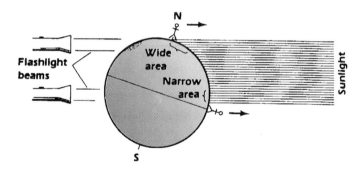

FIGURE 12.15   When sunlight strikes polar region at an angle, solar energy is spread out over a larger area at the poles than at the equator. This effect can be demonstrated with a flashlight.

Point out that the earth is tilted on its axis. That is, the North and South poles are tilted at an angle. Otherwise, the seasons would not change during the course of a full year. Experiment with a no-tilt earth in each of the positions. The angle of the sun does not change in any of those positions.

When the sun is low in the sky, a given amount of the sun's rays are spread out over a wider area of the earth than when the sun is high overhead. Perform *Event 12-O, Direct and Slant Rays*. Cut out the cardboard template and draw parallel lines on it to represent sunlight.

Pick four or five lines and see how much area is covered at the equator. Then measure the areas at the pole covered by the same number of lines. You will find that the rays are spread out and diluted at the poles, keeping the area from getting warm. (See figure 12.15.)

One final factor makes the problem even worse. The sunlight is not only diluted at the poles, but it is also filtered and weakened by the many hundreds of kilometers of atmosphere that it must pass through on its slanted path to the earth. At the equator the sun takes a much shorter and direct path to the earth.

These activities help pupils understand how some areas of the earth receive more heat energy than others. It also helps them understand why and how air currents circulate, especially if the events are related to the air movements in the convection box discussed early in the chapter.

Combining Assessment with Instruction

Weather Prediction

Using weatherchannel.com, have students collect data from several cities to sample the weather throughout the United States. Students should record temperatures, precipitation, and barometric pressure. Students should individually or in a small group record the data for the various cities on a large map. Have students analyze the data and predict the weather based on that data. Have them identify the location of possible air masses and fronts based on the temperature and precipitation information gathered. Students should determine temperature ranges for different cities on a given day and hypothesize the cause of the large and small ranges.

Students should be able to explore weather changes and have an opportunity to apply what they have learned in this chapter to have a basic understanding of how a meteorologist predicts our weather. It is helpful if heat and air pressure are studied prior to the study of weather.

Travel Brochure

To encourage students to apply what they have learned about weather and climate, ask them to construct a travel brochure. An 8.5 × 11 sheet of paper can be folded several different ways to construct the travel brochure. Students should include the following information: selected city; average temperature ranges (highs and lows) and average precipitation for each month; land features such as mountains, parks, lakes, large valleys or beaches; and the best times of the year to take advantage of these features.

Students should be evaluated on the following: how clearly they report the climate data; understanding of how seasons affect the type of recreation in which people participate; neatness, including any art work; and language arts considerations.

Sites and Software

The following websites and software are appropriate to use with this chapter. Note that computer software and websites change rapidly. This makes it necessary to investigate the stable websites for new links and software catalogs for updates. Visit www.mhhe.com/friedl6e to link to these directly and for study resources.

Sites

Weather Channel www.weatherchannel.com/education/index.html
Weather Programs nesen.unl.edu/teacher.html
Weather! www.howstuffworks.com/category.htm?cat-Wthr

Software

Science Court Explorations: Water Cycle (Tom Snyder) (4–6)
Science Court Explorations: Seasons (Tom Snyder) (4–6)
Everything Weather (The Weather Channel) (4–8)
Sammy's Science House (IBM) (1–2)
Weather Trackers (Running Press) (5–8)

Key Terms

barometer, *228*
climate, *230*
cold front, *235*
convection currents, *233*
evaporation, *239*
humidity, *240*

hygrometer, *228*
land breezes, *234*
meteorology, *228*
monsoons, *235*
relative humidity, *239*

sea breezes, *234*
tornado, *235*
warm front, *236*
water cycle, *238, 243*
weather, *230*

Teaching Children about Space Science

NATIONAL SCIENCE EDUCATION STANDARDS ALIGNMENT TO EVENTS

The events in this chapter help accomplish several of the NSES content standards. The event(s) that align with a given content standard are listed below that standard.

LEVELS K–4

UNIFYING CONCEPTS AND PROCESSES
- Systems, order and organization
  13-A through 13-E
- Change, consistency, measurement
  13-D
  13-Q
- Evidence, models and explanation
  13-C and 13-D
  13-F through 13-Q
  13-V
- Evolution and equilibrium
  13-R through 13-S
  13-V
- Form and function
  13-B and 13-C
  13-U

SCIENCE AS INQUIRY
- Abilities necessary to do and understand scientific inquiry
  13-A through 13-V

PHYSICAL SCIENCE
- Position and motion of objects
  13-C through 13-Q
  13-T

LIFE SCIENCE
- Organisms and environments
  13-V

EARTH AND SPACE SCIENCE
- Objects in the sky
  13-A through 13-U

SCIENCE AND TECHNOLOGY
- Abilities of technological design
  13-D and 13-E

- Understanding science and technology
  13-A through 13-D
  13-P

SCIENCE IN PERSONAL AND SOCIAL PERSPECTIVES
- Changes in environments
  13-V
- Science and technology in local challenges
  13-A through 13-V

HISTORY AND NATURE OF SCIENCE
- Science as a human endeavor
  13-A through 13-V

LEVELS 5–8

UNIFYING CONCEPTS AND PROCESSES
- Systems, order and organization
  13-A through 13-E
- Change, consistency, measurement
  13-D
  13-Q
- Evidence, models and explanation
  13-C and 13-D
  13-F through 13-Q
  13-V
- Evolution and equilibrium
  13-R through 13-S
  13-V
- Form and function
  13-B and 13-C
  13-U

SCIENCE AS INQUIRY
- Abilities necessary to do and understand scientific inquiry
  13-A through 13-V

PHYSICAL SCIENCE
- Motions and forces
  13-C through 13-Q
  13-T
- Transfer of energy
  13-A through 13-E

LIFE SCIENCE
- Structure and function in living systems
  13-V

SCIENCE AND TECHNOLOGY
- Abilities of technological design
  13-D and 13-E
- Understanding science and technology
  13-A through 13-D
  13-P

SCIENCE IN PERSONAL AND SOCIAL PERSPECTIVES
- Natural hazards
  13-V
- Risks and benefits
  13-C
  13-K
  13-Q
  13-V
- Science and technology in society
  13-A through 13-V

HISTORY AND NATURE OF SCIENCE
- Science as a human endeavor
  13-A through 13-V
- History of science
  13-A

From Firecrackers to Space Flight

Rockets and space travel had their beginnings in ancient China. Some 750 years ago, rockets were first used for displays of fireworks on holidays and special occasions. Not long after that they were used in warfare against Mongol invaders.

Thirty years after rockets were first used in China they were introduced in Europe. During the late 1200s and early 1300s, rockets were often used in battles. After that time, however, the use of rockets declined, because a better weapon was invented: the cannon. The cannon was superior to the rocket because it was far more accurate.

Rockets were seldom used again until the 1800s, when Sir William Congreve of England found ways to make them more effective. In fact, the British used rockets against the United States during the War of 1812. In a famous attack the British bombarded Fort McHenry throughout the night. Francis Scott Key observed that bombardment and was thrilled to see in the early dawn that the U.S. flag was still flying. He wrote a poem of his observations in which he described "the rocket's red glare." That poem later became the U.S. national anthem: "The Star-Spangled Banner."

Another great pioneer was American scientist Dr. Robert Hutchings Goddard, who conducted countless experiments from 1919 through the late 1930s. Goddard received many patents for inventions that improved the design and flight of rockets.

All his patents were purchased for a nominal fee by German scientists who later built the V-2 rockets that were used in World War II. By the end of the war, more than 1300 of the missiles had been launched against England.

During the closing days of the war, 120 of the top V-2 scientists and technicians crossed war-torn Germany to surrender to advancing American troops. Another 4000, however, were captured by Russian armies. These personnel led the development of space vehicles for *both* countries.

The USSR launched the first satellite in 1957. The United States followed in January, 1958. Since that time, rockets and space vehicles have been used for weather prediction, communication, the exploration of the moon and planets, as well as for many other scientific purposes.

Power for Flight (Events 13-A through 13-E)

Discrepant Events and Pupil Investigations

Event 13-A. Jetting to the Moon

What does the future hold? Test the pupils with the following hypothetical statement made 100 years into the future: "These new jet aircraft are so powerful that we can fly all the way to the moon." What is wrong with that statement? What is the scientific error?

Pupil Investigations (may include the following processes):

1. Predicting (incorrectly) that if made powerful enough the jet spacecraft could work.
2. Predicting that jets could never be used in space.
3. Generalizing about the kind of propulsion that must be used in space.

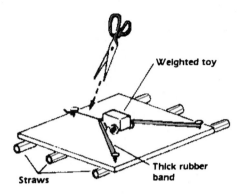

FIGURE 13.1   When the thread is cut, the toy is catapulted one way and the launching platform goes the opposite way.

Event 13-B. Balloon Rockets

Ask pupils to build rockets from balloons. If an inflated balloon is released, it flies in an uncontrolled way. Ask pupils to find ways of controlling the flight of balloon rockets.

Pupil Investigations (may include the following processes):

1. Discovering that attaching one or more straws inside the mouth of a balloon tends to stabilize its flight.
2. Experimenting with balloons attached to strings.
3. Experimenting with balloons of different shapes and sizes.
4. Comparing the flight of balloons with the flight of rockets.

Event 13-C. Rubber-Band Catapult

Build an arrangement of board, straws, rubber bands, nails, and thread, as shown in figure 13.1. Place a weight in the catapult and cut the thread. Watch the weight go in one direction and the board go in the other. Make a mark on the table to show the position of the catapult before and after the launch. What do you find?

Pupil Investigations (may include the following processes):

1. Observing that as the weight is thrown one way, the catapult goes another.
2. Experimenting with larger weights and stronger rubber bands.
3. Measuring the distance the catapult traveled and comparing it with the distance the weight was thrown.
4. Generalizing about the principles of action and reaction.

Event 13-D. Rocket-Launching Problem

Suppose that you have two large rockets ready for launching. Each has a mass of 10,000 kilograms. They are alike in every respect except for the thrust that they can produce. Rocket A can produce 2000 kg of thrust for 300 seconds, while rocket B can produce 20,000 kg of thrust for only 10 seconds. The problem: Which rocket will travel farther?

Pupil Investigations (may include the following processes):

1. Calculating the total energy of each rocket by multiplying thrust by time.
2. Predicting (incorrectly) on the basis of the calculations that Rocket A will go farther.
3. Inferring (correctly) that gravity (weight) is an important variable in this problem.

Event 13-E. Man-in-the-Desert Problem

Assume that a man is stranded in the middle of a desert, 600 kilometers from the nearest oasis. Suppose, also, that he has a truck, a jeep, and a motorcycle, each capable of traveling only 200 kilometers. He cannot transfer gas from one tank to another. How can he reach the oasis? (See figure 13.2.)

Pupil Investigations (may include the following processes):

1. Comparing ideas with each other about how to solve the problem.
2. Comparing the desert problem with space travel.
3. Generalizing that the travel-ranges of the individual vehicles must be combined to reach the destination.

FIGURE 13.2 How can this man go 600 kilometers through a desert to an oasis when each of the vehicles has a range of only 200 kilometers? (Fuel cannot be transferred in this problem.)

Events 13-A through 13-E Explained in Context (Power for Flight)

Power is one of the major ingredients of the space age. Just to place a satellite into orbit requires tremendous amounts of fuel and energy. To send a team of astronauts to the moon and back requires even more energy. For example, the Saturn moon rocket had a mass of 2,700,000 kilograms. Almost all of the mass was used up in the mission. Only 4500 kilograms remained to come back safely to earth.

What type of engine is needed to produce such great power? Only the rocket engine can do the job. **Jet engines** cannot be used in space because they *must fly through the air* to get the oxygen that is needed to burn the fuel. As a result, the error in *Event 13-A, Jetting to the Moon,* is that jet aircraft cannot operate in the vacuum of space. Because there is no oxygen in space, jet engines do not operate.

Rocket engines, however, carry with them everything that is needed to burn the fuel. With both fuel and oxidizer aboard, they can travel in the vacuum of space.

Event 13-B, Balloon Rockets, should be useful in showing some of the effects of rocket engines. Pupils will find that a long, thin balloon tends to be more stable than a short, round balloon. Also, the flight will be more stable when straws are attached to the mouth of the balloon. Still another method of stabilizing the flight of a balloon is to tie a "tail" to it.

The purpose of the event with the balloons is to show pupils how hard it is to control the flight of a rocket. Pupils will find that unless some form of control is worked out, the balloons go every which way. Such flight would be a disaster for rockets.

The Third Law of Motion

One of the principles of rocket flight that is demonstrated by a balloon is **Newton's third law of motion:** *An action produces an equal but opposite reaction.* Let's see how that law applies to the flight of a balloon.

The **action** is the escaping air; the **reaction** is the movement of the balloon. In other words, the escaping air goes one way, while the balloon goes the opposite way. The action-reaction principle works the same way in rockets. The burning gases go one way; the rocket goes the other.

Event 13-C, Rubber-Band Catapult, also shows the action-reaction principle. When the thread to the rubber band is cut, the weight is thrown one way; the catapult, on its roller platform (straws), goes another. Experiment with different weights, bands, and platforms.

There are a number of additional activities that can be done in the classroom to demonstrate action-reaction. One method that can still be found in some books is actually dangerous. It suggests suspending a bottle horizontally with two strings. Then (the dangerous part): pour vinegar and baking soda into the bottle and quickly plug it with a cork.

The vinegar and baking soda quickly react to form a powerful pressure to blow off the cork. The "action" (the exploding cork) and the "reaction" (the bottle swinging away) are demonstrated by such an activity. The activity is quite exciting for pupils. *Unfortunately, it is also dangerous. The pressure can cause the bottle to explode!* Do *not* use a glass bottle to do this activity.

The same instructional value can be achieved by using an iron pipe with a threaded cap, as shown in figure 13.3.

Once the cap is secured tightly to the pipe, the other opening can be used for the cork. The pressure of the vinegar and baking soda cannot possibly blow apart the pipe, regardless of how tightly the cork is pressed into the pipe. Of course, keep all pupils away from the exploding cork.

Getting a rocket off the launching pad requires tremendous force. As suggested in *Event 13-D, Rocket-Launching Problem,* it has a variable that is easy to overlook. The first impulse is to multiply the thrust with the time to get total energy. Unfortunately, you would get the wrong answer.

Rocket A produces three times as much thrust as rocket B. Yet, B is the winner. Why? The thrust of rocket A is not equal to the weight of the vehicle, so, regardless of how long it burned, it could not even lift off the launching pad.

Rocket B has the brute force to lift the vehicle off the pad and send it on its way. Even though it burns for only 10 seconds, it sends the vehicle farther than rocket A.

It is apparent that brute force is needed to get a rocket off the ground. Once in orbit, however, the situation changes. There, any kind of thrust affects the flight of a rocket. Thus, if the two rockets were fired from a space station in orbit around the earth, then rocket A would be the clear winner. On the ground, however, only rocket B could get off the pad.

Staging

Because of the great amount of energy needed in getting rockets into space, scientists have designed a system of "staging" to help get the job done. **Staging** is a process where one or more smaller vehicles hitch a ride, "piggy-back" style, on a large rocket vehicle. The largest section, the first stage, is the base of the vehicle. On top of it is joined the second stage. Some vehicles have a still smaller third stage on top of the first two.

Upon launch, the first stage lifts the entire vehicle off the pad and into the start of its journey. When the first stage burns out, it is simply discarded. Then the second stage ignites and pushes the rest of the vehicle on its way

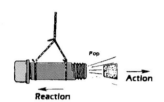

FIGURE 13.3 Baking soda and vinegar create energy to pop the cork from the pipe. The cork goes one way and the suspended pipe goes the other way.

without the heavy weight of the empty first stage. In a similar way, the third stage takes over when the second stage burns out and is discarded.

The technique of staging is somewhat similar to the question posed in *Event 13-E, Man-in-the-Desert Problem.* How can the man get out of the desert? The answer is to carry the motorcycle in the jeep, and the jeep in the truck. Then when the truck (first stage) runs out of fuel, abandon it and switch to the jeep (second stage). After the jeep's fuel is gone, the jeep is also abandoned. The motorcycle (third stage) brings the rider (the payload) to the final destination.

Using the staging method is a very expensive way to make a trip because you abandon the truck and jeep along the way. Similarly, staging is an expensive way to travel in space, but it is sometimes the only way to get to the destination.

Gravity and Inertia (Events 13-F through 13-P)

Discrepant Events and Pupil Investigations

Event 13-F. The Ascending Cones

Attach two funnels or cones as shown in figure 13.4. Also, make a triangular ramp out of cardboard or wood similar to the one shown in the diagram. First of all, set up the ramp and place a long cylinder on the top of the ramp. Ask the class to predict what will happen when you release the cylinder. The cylinder runs down the ramp. Then place the funnels at the bottom of the ramp and ask the class to predict what will happen. The cones run *up* the ramp!

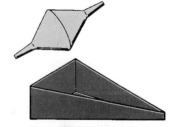

FIGURE 13.4 Tape together two funnels as shown and set them on a triangular ramp. The action may be surprising.

Pupil Investigations (may include the following processes):

1. Predicting what will happen when the cylinder and funnels are released.
2. Discovering that the funnels appear to roll uphill.
3. Measuring the height to both ends of the ramp.
4. Measuring the height of the cones (or funnels) at both ends of the ramp.
5. Demonstrating that the cones do *not* actually run "uphill," but sink down into the ramp.

Event 13-G. The Gripping Chair

Most people can get up from a chair with ease. However, by making a few rules, the task becomes impossible. Two general rules are enough: (1) Do not lean forward, and (2) keep the feet in contact with the floor *in front* of the chair. Why is it impossible to get up when following those rules?

Pupil Investigations (may include the following processes):

1. Experimenting with the simple task of standing up from a chair to notice the position of the upper body and the feet.
2. Recording data by making diagrams showing the body's center of gravity and its base of support (the feet).
3. Generalizing about the center of gravity and balance.

Event 13-H. The Balancing Ruler

Normally when you balance a ruler on the edge of a table, you can place it so that about 6 inches extend over the edge before it falls off. (That is, using the

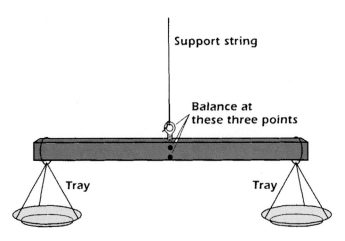

FIGURE 13.6   Suspend the scale from the screw eye and see how stable it is. Compare the stability by suspending it from the hole in the middle and then from the bottom notch.

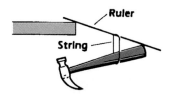

FIGURE 13.5   Hang a hammer on the end of a ruler as shown; you can suspend the ruler on the edge of a table.

old foot ruler. A metric ruler of similar size is about 30 centimeters, so you can push it to about the 15-centimeter point before it falls off.)

However, there is a way in which you can push the ruler so that only a few centimeters remain on the edge of the table and still keep it from falling off. Furthermore, you can even hang a hammer *on the long section that extends over the edge and still keep the ruler from falling off!* How is this seemingly impossible task done? (See figure 13.5.)

Pupil Investigations (may include the following processes):

1. Predicting (incorrectly) that the arrangement must surely fall.
2. Checking to see if the ruler is attached to the table in any way (It is not.)
3. Experimenting with the position of the hammer on the ruler.
4. Generalizing that when the center of gravity is below the point of support, an object is very stable.

Event 13-I. Balance Scale or Teeter-Totter?

Obtain a flat stick about the size of a wooden ruler. However, it should be thick enough so that a small eye screw can be fastened into the upper edge. Measure a distance to the middle of the stick and fasten the eye screw on top. Also, drill a hole in the middle and make a tiny notch in the bottom. These three places will be pivot points for a balance scale. Attach trays to each end of the stick. (See figure 13.6.)

Suspend the scale from the eye screw and place some paper clips in the trays. Equalize the weights so that the scale balances. Then remove the support string from the eye screw and attach it through the hole in the middle. Does the scale still stay in balance? Finally, attach the support string around the bottom of the stick. How well does the arrangement balance now?

Pupil Investigations (may include the following processes):

1. Observing that the scale balances easily when it is supported via the eye screw.
2. Discovering that the scale becomes less stable when the support point is moved to the center hole.

3.   Discovering that when the scale is supported from the bottom of the stick, that is the least stable arrangement.
4.   Generalizing about stability and the center of gravity.

Event 13-J. Fast-Falling Paper

Hold up a discarded book in one hand and a single sheet of paper in another. Ask pupils which of the two will fall faster when dropped. They will surely pick the book to drop faster than the sheet of paper.

Ask them to find a way to make the paper fall as fast as the book. It can be done; and they are not allowed to put the paper under the book, inside the book, or fasten it to the book in any way.

Pupil Investigations (may include the following processes):

1.   Experimenting with the book and paper to see which drops faster.
2.   Observing that the paper drops slowly compared to the book.
3.   Experimenting by crushing the paper to see if it falls faster. (It does, but still not as fast as the book.)
4.   Discovering that when a sheet is placed loosely on *top* of the book, they both drop at the same speed.

Event 13-K. Magic Tablecloth

Have you ever seen a magician pull a tablecloth out from under a complete setting of plates, tumblers, and dishes? We do not recommend that you try the stunt with your mother's best dishes.

Instead, a somewhat less ambitious task can be tried and still show the same principle. Use plastic or light wooden objects instead of glass and water. Even a single object on a sheet of paper will show the principle.

Pupil Investigations (may include the following processes):

1.   Experimenting with many materials and techniques to see how well the activity can be performed.
2.   Predicting what will happen when the cloth or paper is moved slowly; or when it is moved quickly.
3.   Observing that when the cloth or paper is pulled slowly, objects on it will move also.
4.   Making a rule to explain why objects remain stationary when the cloth or paper is pulled quickly.

Event 13-L. Coin in the Cup

Place a small piece of cardboard (such as an index card) on top of a cup or tumbler, and place a coin on top of the card. Find a way to get the coin into the cup without touching the coin or without tipping over the card. Essentially, then, get the card out; but do not tip the card in any way to cause the coin to slide or drop into the cup.

Pupil Investigations (may include the following processes):

1.   Experimenting with ways of moving the card to accomplish the task.
2.   Analyzing the action of the coin when the card is moved quickly.
3.   Generalizing about the effect of inertia on the coin.

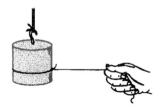

FIGURE 13.7 Pull the thread slowly and you can move the weight. Pull the thread quickly and it breaks because the weight has inertia.

Event 13-M. Strong Pull, Weak Pull

Suspend a weight from a support with a stout string or rope. (See figure 13.7.) Attach a thin thread to the weight and pull gently to make the weight swing. Repeat, but this time pull sharply. What happens?

Pupil Investigations (may include the following processes):

1. Observing that when the thread is pulled gently the weight begins to swing.
2. Observing that when the thread is pulled sharply the thread breaks.
3. Experimenting with various weights.
4. Forming a theory to explain why the weight does (or does not) move.

Event 13-N. Spin the Egg

Can you tell if an egg is raw or hard boiled by just spinning it? Yes, if you know the secret. Obtain two eggs, one hard boiled and the other raw. Spin them one at a time and observe. Touch them momentarily while they are spinning, to stop them, but release your touch quickly. How can you tell which one is hard boiled and which one is raw?

Pupil Investigations (may include the following processes):

1. Experimenting with the eggs to see if students can notice any difference when eggs are spun.
2. Discovering that one of the eggs seems harder to spin than the other.
3. Discovering that the one egg tends to restart itself after it is stopped.
4. Forming a theory about inertia and the motion of the eggs.

Event 13-O. Antigravity Pail

Pour a few centimeters of water into a bucket. Then swing the bucket in a large upright circle. Does the water pour out? (If done correctly the water does not fall out. Perhaps you should practice outside.) **Note:** This event also works well if you tie a stout cord on a tin can and then swing the can with the cord.

Pupil Investigations (may include the following processes):

1. Discovering that the water remains in the pail when the pail is swung overhead.
2. (If performed outside) experimenting with various speeds to see when the water begins to fall out.
3. Making a rule to explain why the water stays inside the pail.

Event 13-P. Parachutes Landing

Connect the motion sensor or sonic ranger to the computer. Drop a parachute from about 1 to 2 meters directly over the motion sensor. Record a distance versus time graph (velocity) of the parachute fall.

Try several designs of parachutes. Make sure the "target" of the parachute is large enough for the motion sensor to detect.

Pupil Investigations (may include the following processes):

1. Measuring the velocity of the parachute during free fall.
2. Describing the resulting graph.

3. Comparing the free fall of several different parachute designs, varying mass or surface area of chute.
4. Generalizing about variables that most influence parachute free fall.

Events 13-F through 13-P Explained in Context (Gravity and Inertia)

To a large degree the information in this section seems self-evident. Everyone knows that objects have weight and that they fall when dropped. Yet, the concept must be studied in greater detail so that its scientific principles become clear.

In several events it seems that gravity reverses itself. How can the cones roll uphill in *Event 13-F, The Ascending Cones?* The event is even more surprising if the class is "prepared" by first rolling a cylinder down the ramp. Then, the cones become a real discrepancy. Are they really rolling uphill? It takes careful observation and measuring to see that the cones are, indeed, rolling downhill.

The key to the event is the triangular ramp. The narrow end is high, and the wide end is low. Start the cones on the narrow end; they *drop down* into the ramp and *actually go downhill.* Measure the center line of the cones as shown in figure 13.8, and you will see that the **center of gravity** is actually going down as the cones sink into the ramp.

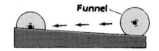

To get the activity to work correctly requires care in building the ramp correctly. Practice with different angles and different inclines to get the best effect.

FIGURE 13.8   The funnels, or cones, appear to be rolling uphill, but they do not. The funnels sink downward into the opening of the ramp.

Even such a simple task as standing up from a chair becomes impossible if done according to the rules set up in *Event 13-G, The Gripping Chair.* The action is so common that most people never think about the actions involved when getting up. However, to be able to do it, the body's center of gravity must be moved over the body's support (feet). There are two ways in which this is done. You can lean forward with the upper body so that the center of gravity moves over the feet. Another way is to just move the feet back. Most often, people use a combination of both actions. (See figure 13.9.)

Event 13-H, The Balancing Ruler, is still another example of an event that seems to defy the law of gravity. If you push the ruler so that more than half of it extends over the edge, it surely must fall. It seems impossible to push it past its midpoint, much less hang a weight on the end.

Again, careful observation will show that the arrangement is actually quite stable. The center of gravity of the hammer is located in its heaviest part, the head. The head comes to rest right under the point of balance, the table edge. Thus, the arrangement is no more than a weight resting under its point of support.

FIGURE 13.9   You cannot get out of a chair unless you move the weight of the body over the feet (by moving the upper body ahead, or the feet back).

Any time the center of gravity is located *below* the point of support, it is stable. Conversely, if the center of gravity is *above* the point of support, it becomes unstable. In fact, the higher the center of gravity, the less stable is the object. *Event 13-I, Balance Scale or Teeter-Totter,* shows this principle very well. When the scale is supported by the eye screw, the center of gravity is below its support and the balance scale is quite stable. When the scale is supported from the hole drilled in the middle, the center of gravity is near its support, making it less stable. When the support is moved to the bottom of the stick, however, it may be impossible to maintain any balance. Instead, the stick flops over to one side or another like a teeter-totter. That is because the center of gravity is above its support.

It should be noted that the results of Event 13-I will be affected by how low the trays are at each end of the stick. If the trays are relatively shallow, the results will be as described. However, if the trays are suspended far below the ends of the stick, then the center of gravity will still be below the support even when the stick is suspended from the bottom. Some practice will be needed to get the desired results.

Gravity causes all objects to fall at the same rate of speed as long as there is no air resistance. How can we prove the statement? We can see that gravity affects a book and sheet of paper the same way in *Event 13-J, Fast-Falling Paper.*

Normally a sheet of paper falls slowly because it is hindered by air resistance. The secret is to place the paper on *top* of the book. The book keeps the air from slowing the paper as it falls. Thus, the paper is affected only by gravity, not air, and it falls as fast as the book. It shows that gravity causes all things to fall at the same speed regardless of their weights as long as there is no air resistance.

In summary, the events that pertain to gravity confirm that gravity attracts objects to the earth. At first glance some of the events tend to contradict that principle, but when fully understood they actually confirm the principle involved.

Inertia

The **first law of motion,** as defined by Isaac Newton, states that *an object at rest tends to stay at rest* and *an object in motion tends to stay in motion.* The events that follow focus on that law.

No doubt, pupils have experienced the effects of inertia on the school bus. When the bus starts out, pupils, especially those who are standing, are swayed backward. The pupils tend to stay at rest, even when the bus begins to move. Later, when the bus stops, pupils tip forward because they tend to stay in motion.

The *first law of motion* is the scientific principle governing the final four events in this section. In *Event 13-K, Magic Tablecloth,* many objects will stay at rest if the cloth or paper is pulled fast enough. That is, the cloth or paper can be pulled out without disturbing the objects resting on top.

Only if the cloth or paper is pulled slowly will gravity and friction have enough time to overcome the tendency to stay at rest. Thus, if pulled slowly, the objects move along with the cloth or paper. If pulled quickly the objects stay at rest.

In *Event 13-L, Coin in the Cup,* the coin remains at rest if the card is pulled quickly. In fact, you can snap the card out with your finger, as shown in figure 13.10. The card moves so fast that the coin "stays at rest." As soon as the card is gone, of course, the coin drops into the cup.

Another example of inertia is shown in *Event 13-M, Strong Pull, Weak Pull.* The heavy weight has a tendency to stay at rest. Try to move the weight quickly and the thread breaks. If you pull gently, however, the inertia is overcome and the weight will move.

In *Event 13-N, Spin the Egg,* inertia can be used to tell which of the two eggs is raw. The hard-boiled egg will spin easily and when touched momentarily by the hand to stop it, it will remain stopped. However, when the raw egg is spun, the liquid inside tends to stay at rest. It takes several turns of the egg for the liquid center to catch up with the shell. Once it is turning, the egg spins nicely. Then, when you touch the egg momentarily to stop its move-

Snap

FIGURE 13.10 Snap the card off the tumbler and the coin drops down. The card moves too quickly to overcome the coin's inertia.

ment, the egg restarts when released. Although the shell is stopped by your hand, the liquid inside stays in motion. Thus, when released, the inertia of the liquid center tends to respin the egg for a few more turns.

In *Event 13-O, Antigravity Pail,* the effects of inertia also account for the discrepancy. In this case the swinging of the bucket puts the water in motion. Once in motion it tends to keep moving in a straight line. Since the bucket is moving in a circle, the water pushes against the bottom of the bucket in its attempt to "stay in a straight line." This "push" is strong enough to overcome the force of gravity during the part of the swing in which the bucket is upside down.

Gravity and Inertia in Space Flight

At first glance it may not appear that these events relate closely to space flight. However, they do. Gravity and inertia are essential to flight through space.

We have all experienced the effects of gravity, but only on or near the surface of the Earth. The force of gravity exists in space also, and affects rockets, satellites, and even the moon. If gravity did not extend away from Earth, satellites and even the moon would fly off into distant space.

Although gravity keeps a satellite in orbit, gravity could not do this alone. By itself, gravity would simply pull the satellite crashing into the Earth.

Another force is needed: **inertia,** the force that tends to keep it moving in a straight line. The two forces act together and cause a satellite to move in a circular path around the Earth.

Trajectories, Orbits, and Reentry (Events 13-Q through 13-U)

Discrepant Events and Pupil Investigations

Event 13-Q. Baseball Throw

Ask pupils to see how far they can throw a baseball or softball. After some warming up, have them throw several times using high, medium, and low paths. Ask them to pay special attention to the flight path of each throw. (See figure 13.11.)

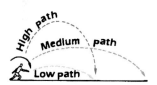

FIGURE 13.11   Throw a baseball in different arcs or trajectories. A very low or very high arc will produce less distance than an intermediate path.

Pupil Investigations (may include the following processes):

1. Experimenting to see which angle gives the best results.
2. Discovering that a ball thrown parallel to the ground does not travel as far as one thrown with an upward angle.
3. Observing that the ball follows a curved path toward the ground.
4. Generalizing that another force is acting upon the ball to bring it to the ground.

Event 13-R. High and Low Orbits

Study figure 13.12 showing two satellites orbiting the earth. Satellite A is in high orbit; satellite B is in low orbit. Which satellite is traveling faster?

Pupil Investigations (may include the following processes):

1. Generalizing (incorrectly) that the satellite in high orbit must travel faster because it has farther to go per orbit.

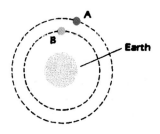

FIGURE 13.12   Does satellite A or satellite B travel faster?

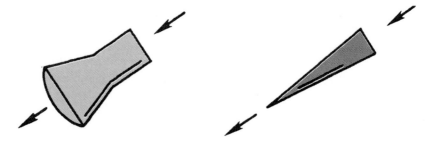

FIGURE 13.13   Assume that these space vehicles are the same weight, going at the same speed, and in the same direction. Which will get hotter during reentry to the Earth's atmosphere?

2. Generalizing (incorrectly) that both satellites may travel at the same rate of speed.
3. Concluding (incorrectly) that there is not enough information available to solve the problem.
4. Comparing the upward and downward forces acting on a satellite.
5. Generalizing that the speed needed to balance gravity varies with the altitude of the satellite.

Event 13-S. "Stationary" Satellites
There are many satellites that are in a fixed position in the sky. They are called stationary satellites. If satellites travel so fast, how can they be stationary?

Pupil Investigations (may include the following processes):
1. Generalizing (incorrectly) that a way has been found to keep them up there while not moving.
2. Inferring that although the satellite appears stationary in the sky, it is actually moving.
3. Comparing the orbit of the satellite with the rotation of the earth.

Event 13-T. Fast Friction
Rub your hands together briskly and firmly. What do you feel?

Pupil Investigations (may include the following processes):
1. Feeling the hands become warm.
2. Experimenting with different rubbing rates and speeds to see how it affects the production of heat.
3. Comparing the activity to the heat formed on a returning spacecraft.

Event 13-U. Reentry Capsules
Study the diagrams of the blunt-nosed and sharp-nosed capsules in figure 13.13. They have different shapes but are identical in weight, speed, and paths. Decide which capsule gets hotter when it returns from space and reenters the earth's atmosphere. Decide which capsule strikes the atmosphere with greater impact.

Pupil Investigations (may include the following processes):

1. Identifying what causes a reentering nose cone to get hot.
2. Predicting that the blunt-nosed capsule strikes the atmosphere with greater impact.
3. Predicting (incorrectly) that the blunt-nosed capsule gets hotter upon reentry.

Events 13-Q through 13-U Explained in Context (Trajectories, Orbits, and Reentry)

Gravity and inertia are well-known forces on the surface of the earth. However, the forces are not limited to this planet but extend out into space.

Therefore, when a spaceship goes into space, it is constantly under the influence of those two forces. In addition, the force of **friction** becomes very important when the spaceship returns from a spaceflight and reenters the atmosphere of the Earth.

Trajectory

Trajectory means "path." It refers to the path of any object in flight, from a thrown baseball to a lunar spacecraft. In *Event 13-Q, Baseball Throw,* pupils can see the trajectory, or path, of a thrown object.

Each throw is affected by gravity (which pulls the ball to Earth) and inertia (which keeps it going in a straight line). The two forces combine to form a curved path.

Even a rifle bullet is affected by gravity. Despite its speed, a shot fired parallel to the Earth is pulled down to the ground. In fact, the bullet falls to the ground just as fast as one that is not fired but merely dropped.

The forces of gravity and inertia have to be calculated very carefully in space flight. Otherwise small errors will grow into huge misses in the great vastness of space.

The distances are so great that an error of only 1 or 2 km in a 10,000-km flight near earth expands to a miss of 100 kilometers in a flight to the moon. With the same degree of accuracy, the spacecraft would miss Venus or Mars by tens of *thousands* of kilometers.

To look at it another way, a spaceship needs to reach a speed of 41,600 km per hour in order to reach Venus. If the takeoff speed is off by only 1 km, the ship would miss its target by 40,000 km.

Orbits

Imagine placing a large cannon on a mountaintop 100 km high. A cannonball fired level with the ground would be pulled to Earth by the force of gravity.

If the cannon fires the ball at one speed, it takes the path identified as A in figure 13.14. If the cannon fires the ball at greater speed, the ball travels farther before it is pulled to Earth by gravity (shown as path B).

If the cannon shoots the ball with enough force, its inertia (tendency to go straight) is great enough to balance gravity (the force pulling it to earth). At that point the cannonball will be in orbit, shown as path C. Finally, a still greater speed will send the ball out into space away from the Earth, shown as path D.

The minimum speed needed to get into orbit is 28,800 km per hour. The lowest practical orbit is at about 150 km above the Earth. Orbits lower than

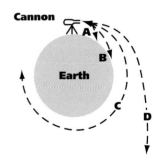

FIGURE 13.14 The imaginary cannon fires cannonballs at ever-increasing speeds, finally getting them into orbit.

150 km begin to run into the thin air of the upper atmosphere which drags satellites down to earth.

Consider the problem posed in *Event 13-R, High and Low Orbits.* Which satellite will travel faster, the one in a high orbit or the one in the low orbit? The most common response by students is to claim that there is not enough information available to make a decision.

Yet, the information is there. Assuming a circular orbit, the speed of a satellite depends on its height above the Earth. In any orbit the satellite is affected by gravity and inertia. So if the orbit is a circle (instead of an oval), the speed must be just great enough to overcome the gravity. To put it in another way, gravity pulls the satellite in, while inertia pushes the satellite out.

The force of gravity is greater as you get closer to the Earth. Thus, a satellite *must* go faster to offset that gravity. As stated earlier, a satellite 150 km from the Earth must go 28,800 km per hour to stay in orbit. On the other hand, the moon, 384,000 km from the Earth, goes at only 3500 km per hour to stay in orbit. Thus, in answer to the problem in Event 13-O, satellite B travels faster then satellite A.

If satellites are traveling at such high rates of speed, how can they appear fixed in the sky as suggested by *Event 13-S, "Stationary" Satellites?* The answer involves not just the satellite, but the Earth. All satellites, even so-called stationary satellites, travel at high rates of speed. Why do they appear stationary? Because the speed of the satellite matches exactly the rotational speed of the Earth. That means that the satellite makes one orbit around the Earth in 24 hours, precisely the time it takes for the Earth to make one turn on its axis. To a person viewing from the earth, the satellite does not appear to move.

One way to demonstrate this principle is to have a youngster sit in a swivel chair while another child walks around it. First of all, the student should just sit and not move. As viewed from the chair, the walking student is clearly moving. Then, have the sitting child turn so that he or she keeps facing the walking student. From the perspective of the sitting child, the walking child is always in plain view. This is similar to what happens when a satellite (walking student) always has the same position with respect to the Earth (sitting student).

Stationary satellites are important because they can maintain constant communication over the part of the Earth over which they are positioned. When satellites travel faster or slower than the turning rate of the Earth, they will disappear over the horizon and direct communication is lost.

Reentry

It is quite spectacular to send astronauts to the moon. Yet, as amazing as such a trip is, the mission is an obvious failure if the capsule does not return safely to Earth. The return to Earth, to reenter the Earth's atmosphere, is a dangerous part of the trip.

One of the problems of reentry is the tremendous heat that is generated when the capsule returns to the Earth's atmosphere. Much of that heat is caused by friction. Pupils can experience how friction forms heat by doing *Event 13-T, Fast Friction.* By rubbing your hands together firmly and quickly, the heat that is generated can be felt. The event also shows how one form of energy (muscular) is changed into another form of energy (heat).

The amount of heat produced by a returning satellite is enormous. There is enough energy available to vaporize the capsule many times over. Therefore, engineers have found designs that overcome the heat problems.

The most obvious design that is used to avoid the extreme heat problem is shown in *Event 13-U, Reentry Capsules.* One may think that the sharp-nosed capsule is preferred to the blunt-nosed capsule but . . . not so! The sharp nose slides through the air too easily, allowing the air to rub the sides of the capsule. The rubbing produces friction, and the friction produces heat. The sharp-nosed capsule would burn up too easily.

The blunt nose, however, hits the air and forms a shock wave. The shock wave extends out beyond the sides of the capsule and dumps off most of the heat that is formed upon reentry. The blunt-nosed capsule was the form used almost exclusively in all of our early space flights.

In recent years, the designs have gradually returned to a more pointed shape. This is done so that the reentry vehicle, which is now designed with small wings, is maneuverable enough to land safely. The problem of excess heat is overcome by entering the atmosphere very gradually. The total amount of heat that is transferred to the capsule is far greater than the early blunt shapes, but that heat is transferred very gradually over a long period of time. In this way, the excess heat can be radiated away as fast as it is absorbed.

Astronauts in Space (Event 13-V)

Discrepant Event and Student Investigations

Event 13-V. Soft-Drink Gases

Hold a bottle of a clear carbonated soft drink (one that fizzes when opened and poured). Look carefully when removing the cap. You should see bubbles form in the liquid.

If you get very poor results, shake the bottle gently once or twice *after* opening, not before. (**Caution:** It is dangerous to shake a closed bottle of pop because the pressure could cause it to explode.) How is the soft drink similar to an astronaut in space?

Pupil Investigations (may include the following processes):

1. Observing that bubbles rise to the top when the cap is removed.
2. Observing that the bubbles seem to appear out of nowhere.
3. Comparing the formation of the bubbles in the soft drink to some potential problems in the blood of astronauts.

Event 13-V Explained in Context (Astronauts in Space)

On Earth you have an environment that is friendly to human life. In space the surroundings are hazardous to life. What are the hazards? There are two kinds: (1) danger from things that *are* there and (2) danger from things that are *not* there. For example, dangers that are there include radiation and meteors. Things that are not there are oxygen and air pressure, both vital for life.

Let us take a trip out into space. On the Earth we have plenty of oxygen and air pressure. As we go up into the sky, we begin to lose both items. By the time we are 6000 meters high, there is so little oxygen that most people will lose consciousness.

At 9000 meters we run out of air pressure. Why is that a problem? Because the blood and body fluids begin to fill with bubbles from dissolved gases. It is similar to what happens in a bottle of pop when it is opened. See

Event 13-V, Soft-Drink Gases. Gases that are dissolved in the liquid suddenly form visible bubbles when the pressure is lowered (by removing the cap).

When going from sea level up to 9000 meters, air pressure decreases quickly; and we face the same condition inside our bodies that occurs in the bottle of pop. Undersea divers who come to the surface too fast, have the same problem. That condition is called "the bends."

The hazards of low pressure become still greater as the flight continues to go higher. At 19,000 meters the pressure is so low that body fluids begin to boil. The boiling point of water actually drops to 37° C, or normal body temperature.

Naturally, astronauts are protected from the absence of pressure. First of all, the capsules are usually pressurized. Second, their space suits are also pressurized. That is, the suits are filled with air, somewhat like air is pumped into a football or basketball to give them more pressure (but, of course, not that much).

By the time a spacecraft reaches a height of 150 kilometers, it faces danger from meteors and radiation. That is, the spacecraft might collide with meteors or be burned by excess radiation. However, these dangers are far less severe than was believed when the space age began. In fact, these dangers have proved to be so rare that today they are hardly ever mentioned.

Combining Assessment with Instruction

Space Poems

Have students write a poem or story about space science. Give guidelines that require students to use at least five of the key terms for this chapter in their poem or story. They may want to add an illustration too. Visit the Kid's Corner link from the home page of http://quest.arc.nasa.gov/mars/index.html to find sample poems, artwork, and stories about Mars.

Spacecraft Model

Ask students to build their own Galileo spacecraft scale model by using the instructions and printouts found at the Galileo K–12 Educator's Resources site, http://www.jpl.nasa.gov/galileo/educator.html. In addition, students should write a fictional story about what the Galileo probe and orbiter discovered about Jupiter. Have students incorporate the information and measurements that the Galileo probe gathered.

Sites and Software

The following websites and software are appropriate to use with this chapter. Note that computer software and websites change rapidly. This makes it necessary to investigate the stable websites for new links and software catalogs for updates. Visit www.mhhe.com/friedl6e to link to these directly and for study resources.

Sites

National Air and Space Museum   www.nasm.si.edu
Educational Space Simulations   riceinfo.rice.edu/armadillo/ Simulations
     Project

Galileo K-12 Educator's Resources	www.jpl.nasa.gov/galileo/ educator.html
Space	www.howstuffworks.com/ category.htm?cat=Space
Introduction to Windows to the Universe	www.windows.ucar.edu
SSDOO Education Outreach Page	ssdoo.gsfc.nasa.gov/education/ education_home.html

Software

FutureLab: Gravity for Physical Science (Discovery) (4–12)
FutureLab: Universal Gravitation for Physical Science (Discovery) (4–12)
Science Court Explorations: Flight (Tom Snyder) (2–4)
Science Court Explorations: Inertia (Tom Snyder) (4–6)
Science Court Explorations: Gravity (Tom Snyder) (4–6)
Estes Rocket Stabilization (Estes) (5–12)

Key Terms

action, *252*
center of gravity, *257*
friction, *261*
inertia, *259*

jet engines, *251*
Newton's first law of motion, *258*
Newton's third law of motion, *251*

reaction, *252*
staging, *252*
trajectory, *261*

Teaching Children about the Sun, Moon, and Stars

In with a Big Bang

How did the universe begin? With a big bang? Throughout all of history, man has wondered how existence began and life started. For thousands of years religion was the answer to these questions, but in the past few centuries science has tried to find logical proof for the beginning of life. From the invention of the telescope to the creation of the space shuttle, humans have become extremely interested and enamored by the mysteries of the sky. Many hypotheses and observations have been made about the universe, but no idea has seemed to shake up the scientific world as much as the big bang theory.

The idea of the big bang started in 1916, when Albert Einstein developed his general theory of relativity. The concept of general relativity is that gravity is no longer described by a gravitational field, but is actually a distortion of space and time. In 1919, Einstein's theory was confirmed and the theory of the big bang began. In 1922, a Soviet meteorologist and mathematician Alexandre Friedmann formed some basic ideas of the universe as a never-ending expanding space. In 1927, an unknown Belgian clergyman and physics teacher by the name of Georges Lemaitre continued Friedmann's studies and proposed that the universe began with the explosion of a primeval atom. With Lemaitre's idea, the big bang theory was born. Edwin Hubble, in 1929, found experimental evidence to help justify Lemaitre's theory. Hubble found that distant galaxies in every direction are going away from Earth with speeds proportional to their distance. Then in 1948, the Russian-American physicist George Gamow modified Lemaitre's theory of the primeval atom into the big bang theory of the origin of the universe.

The big bang theory states that between 12 and 15 billion years ago a gigantic explosion of an "atom" (smaller than a single proton) occurred, thus creating the universe. This reaction was made possible through a process called *nucleosynthesis*, which created hydrogen and helium atoms. As the explosion occurred, scientists believe that space and time itself were formed. The high temperature and density of the primeval atom caused the universe to expand rapidly. This is why all objects in space are moving away from each other. Throughout the next billion years, chemical elements, mostly hydrogen and helium, cooled and condensed into stars and galaxies.

The theory has divided much of our society on the idea of the creation of the universe. Many people are torn between the idea of the big bang and Judeo-Christian creationism. The big bang theory has become the common teaching in our public schools as the scientific creation of the universe. Science will always try to find the logic to life, while religion will always try to find the spiritual aspect of life.

The big bang theory has had a huge impact on the scientific community. Before this theory, scientists had many hypothesis of the existence of the universe. But none of these ideas had the scientific evidence and backing of the big bang theory. Undoubtedly, new ideas will refine this theory since it is the nature of science to modify present theories as new information and thoughts are investigated.

Concepts of Number, Size, and Distance (Events 14-A through 14-E)

Discrepant Events and Pupil Investigations

Event 14-A. Concept of Number
What is wrong with the following statement? "The observatory has finally completed a new star atlas that lists all the stars in the heavens."

Pupil Investigations (may include the following processes):
1. Forming a theory (incorrectly) that the stars have all been counted and listed.
2. Inferring (incorrectly) that the number of stars can be counted.
3. Generalizing that the number of stars is so great that they will never all be counted or listed.

Event 14-B. Concept of Size #1

Set up a projector and aim it at a screen or blank wall. Use a quarter and hold it in the beam of the projector so that the coin casts a sharp shadow. Then hold a dime in the beam alongside the quarter. Which casts a larger shadow? Can you move the dime or quarter so that the dime casts a larger shadow? How does this event relate to the sizes of the sun and moon? (**Note:** Instead of using coins, you can use a golf ball and baseball.)

Pupil Investigations (may include the following processes):

1. Observing the shadows cast by the coins.
2. Moving the coins so that they cast shadows of the same size.
3. Comparing the sizes of the coins to the sizes of the sun and moon.

Event 14-C. Concept of Size #2

Draw a 12-millimeter circle on the chalkboard. Assuming that the circle represents the size of the Earth, how large is the moon on that same scale? How large is the sun on that same scale?

Pupil Investigations (may include the following processes):

1. Estimating that the moon is smaller than the Earth.
2. Estimating that the sun is larger than the Earth.
3. Calculating the correct ratio using the same scale as was used to draw the Earth.
4. Applying the ratio to the moon and sun.

Event 14-D. Concept of Distance

Draw a 28-centimeter circle on the chalkboard to represent the sun. Based on that scale, how far away is the Earth? Remember, for the moment, that we are not concerned with the *size* of the earth at this time but only *how far away* it is. On the same scale, how far is the moon from the earth?

Pupil Investigations (may include the following processes):

1. Estimating the scale distance between the sun and Earth.
2. Estimating the scale distance between the moon and Earth.
3. Calculating the scale distances.

Event 14-E. Playground Solar System

Combine the concepts of size and distance in a scale model of the solar system. An area larger than a football field is needed to do this exercise. Mark out the placement of planets on a playground, athletic field, or park. Use modeling clay to make the planets and a volleyball for the sun. Use a scale of 20 centimeters equals 1 million kilometers, and make a scale model of the solar system.

Pupil Investigations (may include the following processes):

1. Calculating the scale distances from the sun to the planets.
2. Calculating the scale sizes of the planets.
3. Applying the scale of size and distance to include our Milky Way galaxy.

Events 14-A through 14-E Explained in Context (Concepts of Number, Size, and Distance)

Our Expanding Neighborhood

In ancient times a neighbor was someone who was within easy walking distance. Today, a neighbor is someone who is within easy rocket distance.

When our country was first settled, people were bound closely to their neighborhood. They seldom traveled more than a day's horseback ride from their homes. Going beyond their neighborhood was a difficult task.

As transportation improved, the distances that were traveled became greater. With the invention of trains and cars, the size of the "neighborhood" increased greatly. A day's travel covered a much greater area and was a far more comfortable journey than previously.

With the invention of the airplane, the "neighborhood" expanded again. Suddenly, whole countries and continents could be reached in a single day.

The final expansion of our neighborhood came with the space age. As a result of the gains in transportation, our concept of neighborhood has expanded to include the moon and planets and maybe someday even the stars.

Changing Concept of Number

Look into the heavens on a clear night. How many stars can you see? How many stars are there? Have they all been counted yet?

The questions call attention to a concept of number that has new meaning in the study of stars. There are so many stars that they will never all be counted and listed. The statement in *Event 14-A, Concept of Number*, is obviously false.

There are so many stars that the human mind cannot possibly comprehend the number. Perhaps a concept of number can be reached by pointing out that there are more stars in the universe than there are grains of sand on all the seashores of all the world.

Think about it the next time you are at the seashore. Look at all the sand. Then pick up a single grain and put it in the palm of your hand. That grain, according to our concept of number, represents our entire solar system of sun, planets, and moons. Our solar system is but one of many. Would that grain of sand be missed if it were lost? So, be careful. Don't lose our solar system.

Another way to think about the concept of number is to consider the possibility of another planet, somewhere in the universe, with conditions favorable for life as we know it. Does another such planet exist? If we consider only mathematical possibilities, the answer is almost surely yes.

There are so many stars that, even if only one star in a million had a set of planets, and if only one planet in a million of those sets had a planet like ours, then there would still be billions upon billions of planets with conditions just like ours.

Changing Concept of Size

How big are the planets, sun, moon, and stars? Their sizes vary so much that it is difficult for a person to comprehend their sizes by merely reading the figures in kilometers. Scale drawings give us a better idea of their sizes.

People who lived in ancient times could only guess at the sizes. When they gazed into the sky, they estimated the sun and moon were about the

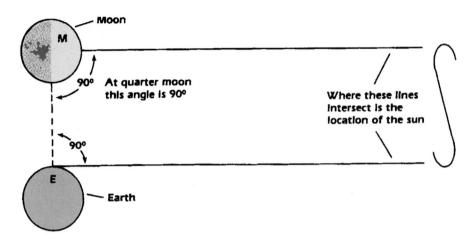

FIGURE 14.1 An early Greek astronomer, Aristarchus, found that the sun was a great distance from the Earth by observing that the sun's rays that struck the moon were parallel to the rays that struck the Earth.

same size because they "looked" the same size. Obviously, the earth appeared gigantic in comparison to the sun and moon. It is easy to see why they thought that the earth was the center of the universe.

As early as 500 B.C., however, some Greek astronomers began to believe that the sun and moon were not of equal size. They had noticed that from time to time a shadow covered (or eclipsed) the moon. They reasoned that the shadow was that of the earth. It showed that the earth was round—a shocking discovery!

In 270 B.C., Aristarchus shook the foundations of astronomy by declaring that the *sun,* not the earth, was the center of the solar system. He reached his conclusion by using his knowledge of mathematics and by following some remarkably simple logic.

First of all, it was easy to see that the moon was smaller than the earth. During an eclipse, you could see the earth's shadow on the moon's surface. The shadow showed that the earth was much larger. As a result, it was logical to conclude that the moon was a satellite of the earth.

Yet, the sun looked no larger than the moon, and it, too, seemed to circle the earth. How did Aristarchus decide that the sun was so large and that the earth was merely the sun's satellite?

This is what he did. On a day when the moon was in a *quarter moon* phase, he made careful measurements of the angles between the earth, moon, and sun. Figure 14.1 shows what he saw.

He had no difficulty with the angles from the moon because he chose the quarter moon phase to do his measuring. During the quarter moon the angle between lines MS and ME is exactly 90 degrees.

He had no difficulty in measuring the angles between EM and ES either, because those lines originated on earth. To his astonishment, that angle came to 90 degrees also!

All he had to do was add together the angles to complete a triangle. Remember that the three angles of a triangle equal 180 degrees. He was amazed to find that he already had 180 degrees using only *two* of the three angles. Thus, according to his figures, there were no degrees left when figur-

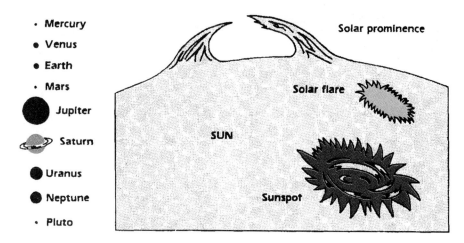

- Mercury
- Venus
- Earth
- Mars
- Jupiter
- Saturn
- Uranus
- Neptune
- Pluto

Solar prominence

Solar flare

SUN

Sunspot

FIGURE 14.2   The sizes of the sun and planets are drawn to scale. The distances between them are not shown because they would extend far beyond the pages of this book.

ing the third angle from the sun. In other words, a ray of sunlight reaching the moon was parallel to a ray of sunlight reaching the earth.

Those results could only mean that the sun is an incredible distance away. And if the sun is that far away and still looks as large as the moon, it must actually be far bigger. Given those factors, it was logical for Aristarchus to infer that the sun must be hundreds of times larger than the earth.

If the sun was so much larger than the earth, it was logical to conclude that the earth was a mere satellite and that the sun was the center of our solar system. We can get some idea of the concept of size by doing *Event 14-B, Concept of Size #1.* If the dime is moved close enough to the projector, it will cast a shadow that is as large or larger than the shadow cast by the quarter. It is easy to see that the distance the coins are from the projector will influence the size of their shadows.

Despite the published work by Aristarchus, it was almost two thousand years before the sun-centered idea was widely accepted. In fact, it wasn't until the invention of the telescope in the early 1600s that the scientific world finally accepted the seemingly incredible facts.

Today, the sun-centered solar system is universally accepted by all educated people. However, there are still some mistaken notions about size and distance. These ideas can be clarified by performing *Event 14-C, Concept of Size #2.* Using the scale of 12 millimeters to represent the size of the earth, the moon is only 4 millimeters in diameter. The sun, however, is gigantic. It is 1.382 meters in diameter. In fact, only a part of it will fit on a chalkboard or bulletin board.

The scale of the sun and planets can make an interesting bulletin board display. Draw the sun, using a string attached to a piece of chalk. Grab the string about 70 cm from the chalk and hold that point against the lower part of the bulletin board. Then draw a large arc with the chalk. You should be able to get at least the upper part of the circle on a typical bulletin board. That arc represents the surface of the sun. Then fill the area inside the circle with red construction paper. Place the planets and our moon on the bulletin board, going over the image of the sun if necessary. (See figure 14.2.)

TABLE 14.1

Bulletin Board Solar System (Scale: 1 millimeter = 1000 kilometers)

Heavenly Body	Size (kilometer)	Scale on Board (millimeter)
Mercury	5000	5
Venus	12,300	12
Earth	12,600	12
Mars	6700	7
Jupiter	138,700	139
Saturn	114,600	115
Uranus	51,200	51
Neptune	49,600	50
Pluto	5800	6
Sun	1,382,400	1382
Moon	4000	4

Note: Most educators recommend the use of metric figures. In fact, many states mandate it. However, teachers often wish to have comparisons given in inches: Mercury: ³⁄₁₆, Venus: ½, Earth: ½, Mars: ¼, Jupiter: 5½, Saturn: 4½, Uranus: 2, Neptune: 2, Pluto: ¼, Sun: 54, Moon: ⅛.

In that way, pupils will gain an accurate impression of the sizes of the sun, moon, and planets. The scale for the display is shown in table 14.1.

After impressing the pupils with the sun's huge size, see if they can gain an idea of the vast distances of space. In the bulletin board model there should be no attempt at showing distances, only size.

Changing Concept of Distance

Now, let us clarify the concept of distance. Most people, young and old, have false impressions of distances in space. Part of the reason is that it is impossible to show the correct scale of both size and distance on the pages of a book, or even on the bulletin board. Yet, in many books those scales are shown anyway. Unfortunately, they are incorrect!

Sometimes a footnote will state that the scale used to determine distances is different from the scale used for sizes. Pupils are not helped much by such notes. They are too impressed with the visual picture to notice the fine print in the footnotes.

The only scale that can be shown accurately in books is one that compares sizes only, or one that compares distances only. If the scale is reduced to show both on a single page, the planets become too small to be seen.

To find out what impressions the pupils have, do *Event 14-D, Concept of Distance*. Sometimes the event can be made more interesting by drawing the 12-centimeter circle (the sun) on one side of a long chalkboard and placing several "x's" on the board with the last being on the far side of the board. Ask them which x represents the point where the earth would be on the scale.

Most pupils will select one of the "x's" on the chalkboard. Little will they realize than none of the points on the board is even close to being accurate. The accurate distance is 30 meters away. Most pupils will be astounded!

After the concepts of size and distance have been handled separately, it is time to put the two together. Since a page of a book is obviously too small to show both size and distance, what should be used? Surprisingly, even the

TABLE 14.2

Distances from the Sun

Planet	Scale Size (millimeter)	Actual Distance (kilometer)	Scale Distance (meter)
Mercury	1	58,000	11.6
Venus	2.5	107,000	21.4
Earth	2.5	149,000	29.8
Mars	1	227,000	45.4
Jupiter	28	774,000	154.8
Saturn	23	1,419,000	283.8
Uranus	10	2,856,000	571.2
Neptune	10	4,475,000	895.0
Pluto	1	5,880,000	1176.0
Sun	276		

Note: The comparable scale sizes (in inches) and distances (in feet) are Mercury: $1/32$" and 39', Venus: $1/16$" and 70', Earth: $1/16$" and 98', Mars: $1/32$" and 149', Jupiter: $1 1/8$" and 508', Saturn: $7/8$" and 931', Uranus: $3/8$" and 1874', Neptune: $3/8$" and 2936', Pluto: $1/32$" and 3868', Sun: 11".

classroom is too small to do the job. Use an athletic field, park, or long open area on the school grounds and do *Event 14-E, Playground Solar System.*

If you use a scale that makes the planets large enough to be seen, you will need a large outdoor area just to fit in the inner planets of the solar system. A convenient scale is 1 mm = 5000 km (or, 1 m = 5,000,000 km). The sizes using that scale are given in table 14.2.

Even the playground scale is limited. It is unlikely that many playgrounds will be large enough to hold more than the first four planets. However, if you have room, build the scale out to Jupiter, 154.8 meters from the sun. The sun can be cut from construction paper and taped to a post or tree.

While standing at the outermost planet that you can fit on the playground, look back at the "sun." See how small it looks from way out there. Ask the pupils if they can understand why the outer planets are cold. Also, look at the earth, a tiny ball only 2.5 millimeters in size and see all the space between the planets.

Then, place the Earth's moon on the scale at its proper distance from the earth. On that scale the moon is only 1 mm ($1/32$") in size and is located only 48 mm ($1 7/8$") away. Thus, the Earth with its moon will fit on the palm of your hand. Compare a space trip to Jupiter with a trip to the moon.

The distances are so astounding that it is worth emphasizing them in another way. Calculate the distances by using a measuring stick of time. Assume that you had a spaceship that could travel at a constant speed of 40,000 kilometers per hour. At that speed how long will it take to make the following trips: (a) around the Earth, (b) to the moon, (c) to the sun, and (d) to the nearest star (other than our sun)? The figures are given in table 14.3.

Still another way to measure the vast distances of space is to use weight as a measuring stick. Suppose a single strand of a spider's web, long enough to go around the earth, weighed only 1 gram. According to that scale, a length needed to reach the moon would weigh about 10 grams, to the sun, 3720 grams (or 3.72 kilograms); and a length to the nearest star, an unbelievable 1,406,400 kilograms!

TABLE 14.3

Travel Times in Space

Vehicle	Around Earth	To Moon	To Sun	To Nearest Star
Jet plane	40 hours	16 days	17 years	—
Rocket ship	1 hour	9 hours 36 minutes	½ year	117,000 years

The human mind cannot fully grasp the sizes and distances in the solar system and universe. However, by using the scale models suggested in this section, pupils can begin to gain a truer impression of what space is like.

The Earth and Moon (Events 14-F through 14-J)

Discrepant Events and Pupil Investigations

Event 14-F. The Flat Earth

Common sense tells us that the Earth is flat. There are hills and valleys, of course, but other than that the land certainly *looks* flat. Yet we know that the Earth is really round. What evidence do we have to show that the Earth is round when common sense tells us it is flat?

Pupil Investigations (may include the following processes):

1. Observing the shadow of the Earth on the moon during an eclipse.
2. Observing that televised pictures from space show that the Earth is round.
3. Inferring a round Earth from observations of ships disappearing from view over the horizon.

Event 14-G. The Round Earth

Use a large globe for this event. Move close to the globe and look over the round top. Use a small toy boat and slowly move it along the top of the globe away from you. How does the boat disappear when it is moved over the "horizon" of the globe? (A large beach ball can be used to represent the globe. See figure 14.3.)

Pupil Investigations (may include the following processes):

1. Observing that the boat "sinks" below the horizon.
2. Comparing these observations with observations of actual ships that disappear over the Earth's real horizon.
3. Forming a theory about the shape of the Earth.

Event 14-H. The World at Your Fingertips

Blindfold a pupil and ask him or her to extend a finger. Guide the fingertip to touch a globe. (The student should not be told what the object is.) Ask the student to describe the object of which he or she is touching just a single spot.

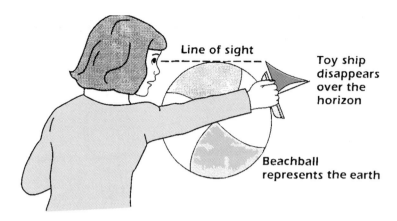

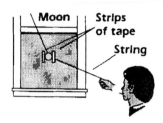

FIGURE 14.4   Sight the moon so that it fits between two pieces of tape placed 1 centimeter apart. Measure the distance from the tape to your eye. If the moon is 3500 kilometers across, how far away is it?

FIGURE 14.3   Peer over the edge of a large ball at a toy ship. How does this compare to the view of a ship that disappears over the horizon?

Pupil Investigations (may include the following processes):

1. Identifying by touch that the object is hard and smooth.
2. Identifying (incorrectly) that the object is flat.
3. Comparing the spot on the globe with a similar "spot" on the Earth.

Event 14-I. Earth-Moon Distance

This event works well at night with a full moon. However, it can also be done during the school day when the moon is in its first or third quarter. It will surprise many pupils to realize that even in the daytime, the moon is often clearly visible.

Attach two strips of tape 1 centimeter apart on a window. Look between the tapes at the moon. If you place your eye between the tapes and look out, you have a full view. The tapes will not be in the way. However, as soon as you back away slightly, the space between the tapes presents a narrower and narrower view.

Back away until the moon just fills the space between the tapes. Mark the spot and measure the distance from the tape to the eye. If you know that the moon is 3500 kilometers in diameter, determine the distance to the moon. (See figure 14.4.)

Pupil Investigations (may include the following processes):

1. Measuring the distance from the tape to the eye as 110 centimeters.
2. Comparing the distance to the tape with the distance to the moon.
3. Comparing the distance between the tapes with the size of the moon.
4. Generalizing that the distance to the moon is 110 times its width.

Event 14-J. Phases of the Moon

Demonstrate the phases of the moon as they appear to an observer on earth, and also as viewed from two points in space. Set up a projector or other strong light source in the back of the classroom as shown in figure 14.5. Observations are to be made at points A, B, and C. Hang a basketball from a support in positions 1, 2, 3, and 4 around point B. Determine the phases of the moon from each point.

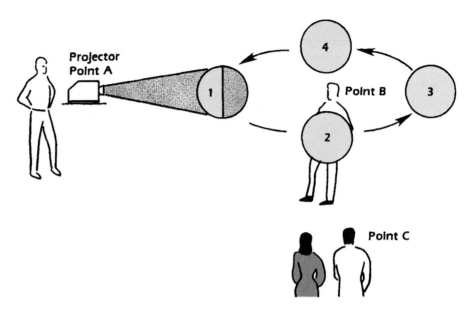

FIGURE 14.5   Gain an idea of the phases of the moon by performing the activity with a basketball and a projector. Point B is the earth and shows the moon, at position 1, in the new moon phase.

Pupil Investigations (may include the following processes):

1. Discovering that the phases of the moon change when viewed from point B.
2. Inferring that point B represents the view from Earth.
3. Discovering that the phases do not change when viewed from points A and C.
4. Demonstrating the correct phases of the moon as determined by the moon's path around the Earth.

Events 14-F through 14-J Explained in Context (The Earth and Moon)

Perhaps one of the most obvious discrepant events that confronted the early astronomers occurred when they observed an eclipse of the moon. They could see that the earth's shadow on the moon was slightly rounded. Could it be that the Earth was actually round?

Although people had seen the eclipses for thousands of years, it was not until about 500 B.C. that some Greek astronomers realized that the shadow on the moon was actually cast by the Earth. That discovery came as a great surprise because they thought the Earth was flat.

Today the concept of a round Earth is not surprising. Everyone knows that the Earth is round. Nevertheless, when suddenly confronted with the question posed in *Event 14-F, The Flat Earth*, pupils are often at a loss to give any evidence for their beliefs.

The problem for the early astronomers was much greater than for pupils. There was no equipment available in those ancient times for viewing or calculations. Everything had to be based on simple observations.

As soon as astronomers began to think in terms of a round Earth, evidence became easier to find. For example, in making long journeys (of 500 kilometers or so) in northerly or southerly directions, there were unexplained changes in the star patterns in the sky.

Those changes could be explained by the round-earth theory. As one traveled south, some stars would slowly become visible over the southern horizon. Going north, the stars would rise in the northern sky and dip below the horizon in the south. If the Earth were flat, the same stars would always be visible.

Another indication that the Earth is round is the fact that ships seem to slowly sink below the horizon as they move away from the observer. The appearance of sinking is, in reality, just the ship going over the horizon of a huge ball (the Earth). We can gain an idea of this by performing *Event 14-G, The Round Earth.* This event duplicates, in miniature, the observations of ships on the ocean.

As stated earlier, ancient people believed that the Earth was flat simply because it *looked* flat. It looks flat only because our view is too restricted. We do not get enough of the "big picture" to see that the Earth is really round.

We can show somewhat the same situation by performing *Event 14-H, The World at Your Fingertips.* A blindfolded pupil will not be able to feel the roundness of a globe by just touching it with a fingertip. It feels flat because the area touched by the fingertip is too limited for one to notice its roundness. In somewhat the same way, the piece of Earth that we look at from the ground is also too limited for us to see that the Earth is round.

Measuring the Distance around the Earth

After Greek astronomers found evidence that the Earth was round, they made other great discoveries. An astounding feat was achieved by Eratosthenes in 200 B.C. when he actually calculated the distance around the Earth.

Keep in mind that no one had ever gone around the Earth, so he had no intention of doing that to measure its size. Instead, he used two cities in Egypt, Syene and Alexandria, as points in a gigantic triangle. Those cities were known to be 789 kilometers apart.

He also knew that at Syene a festival was held every year on the one day when the sun's light reached the bottom of a well 12 meters deep. At noon of that day, upright buildings and posts cast no shadows at all. The sun was directly overhead.

In Alexandria, however, Eratosthenes noticed that at that same time (high noon) all objects *did* cast shadows (though small). What a surprise! Why were there small shadows at Alexandria but none at Syene? Why was the sun directly overhead at Syene but not at Alexandria? He realized that this was evidence that the Earth was round.

Eratosthenes also realized that he had found a way to measure the size of the earth. How? By just completing the circle. The shadows showed that at high noon in Alexandria the sun was about 7 degrees off from being directly above. Remember that at that time the sun was directly above in Syene. Since a full circle is 360 degrees, the 7 degrees amounted to about one-fiftieth of a circle. (See figure 14.6.)

Thus, if the distance between Alexandria and Syene was about one-fiftieth of the distance around the Earth, all that he needed to do was multiply by 50 the 789 kilometers between Alexandria and Syene. Eratosthenes

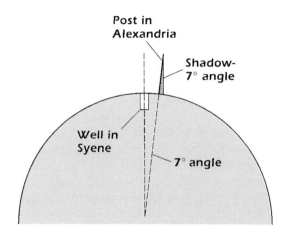

FIGURE 14.6   Eratosthenes saw that shadows at Syene and Alexandria differed by 7 degrees, or one-fiftieth of a circle. He multiplied the distance between the cities by 50 to obtain his estimate for the distance around the Earth.

obtained a figure of 39,440 km—remarkably close to the 39,728 km used today. (That figure is often rounded to 40,000 km.)

By 150 B.C. Greek astronomers had made rough calculations of the distance from the Earth to the moon. We can do the same by performing *Event 14-I, Earth-Moon Distance.*

Sight the moon through the 1-centimeter space between the tapes. Move back until the moon just fills the opening. The distance from the tapes to your eye should be about 110 centimeters. That means that the distance to the moon is 110 times greater than the moon's diameter. As long as the diameter is given (3500 km), it is easy to calculate the distance. Multiply 3500 by 110 to get 385,000 km—very close to the actual distance to the moon.

Eclipses

From time to time the Earth gets directly between the sun and the moon. When it does, it blocks the sunlight to the moon. That is called a **lunar eclipse.**

An eclipse does not occur every time the moon makes a revolution around the earth. Most of the time the Earth and moon are slightly off-line so no eclipse occurs.

On rarer occasions the moon will get directly between the sun and the Earth, causing an eclipse of the sun, called a **solar eclipse.** A solar eclipse is much less likely to occur than a lunar eclipse. Why? Because the moon is much smaller than the earth. As a result, the moon's shadow will cover only a small part of the Earth.

During a solar eclipse, the moon's shadow on the Earth is often no more than 100 kilometers wide. On the other hand, in a lunar eclipse, the Earth's shadow will often cover the entire surface of the moon.

Since a solar eclipse is so rare, people who are in the viewing path will naturally want to observe it closely. Unfortunately, the event is associated with tragedy. Thousands of people damage their eyes when there is a solar eclipse. How? They look at the sun and are partially blinded. The sun can cause partial blindness very quickly.

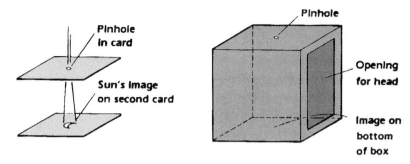

FIGURE 14.7   A safe way to view the sun. A pinhole focuses the image of the sun on a card below. The image is clearer if outside light is kept away as is done with the box at the right.

You should never look directly at a solar eclipse. Even with the use of filters such as sunglasses, smoked glass, and colored glass, direct observation is very dangerous. In fact, even welders glasses do not provide enough protection. The only safe way is to view the sun's reflected image.

The reflected image can easily be seen by using a sheet of cardboard or piece of foil with a pinhole in it. The pinhole acts as a lens and focuses the sun on a second sheet of cardboard held below the first. You view the image on the second sheet, not the sun itself.

If you wish to make a more sophisticated viewer, cut out the side of a box and use it as a viewing stage as shown in figure 14.7.

Phases of the Moon

The moon is our most impressive heavenly body next to the sun itself. All pupils have seen the moon many times. Yet it is often surprising how little they know about how the phases of the moon are formed. They generally know that the moon changes its shape—sometimes it is full, and sometimes half, and sometimes just a sliver—but they seldom understand how the phases are formed.

Event 14-J, Phases of the Moon, is helpful in finding out what the phases are and how they are formed. Refer back to figure 14.5 to see how the event is set up. It is quickly apparent that when viewed from points A and C no phases are visible at all. That means that the shadow on the moon does not change as the moon goes around point B.

Only the viewer at point B sees the changes. Point B represents how the moon appears when viewed from the surface of the Earth. When the moon is at position 1, the viewer is looking toward the projector (the sun). (**Caution:** Be careful not to look directly into the projector's light.)

Anytime the moon is that near to the sun in the sky, the moon is invisible. The blinding light of the sun makes it impossible to see the moon. That phase of the moon is called **new moon.**

Position 2 is the moon's location 7 days after new moon. This phase is called **first quarter.** When looking at the basketball, only the right side is lit up, and it looks somewhat like the capital letter *D*. During the first quarter the moon is at right angles to the sun. Thus, at 6 P.M., for example, the sun is at the horizon, and the moon is at 12 o'clock high.

Moving the moon to position 3 produces a **full moon.** The viewer must be careful not to block the light from the projector (causing an eclipse). At any rate, the sun is at the viewer's back. Thus, a full moon rises in the east when the sun sets in the west.

Finally, move the moon to position 4 to produce a **last quarter.** The lit part of the moon looks like a filled-in letter *C*. At this time the sun and moon are again at right angles to each other.

It takes 7 days to go from one position to another. The total trip of the moon around the earth takes 28 days. The 28 days were, at one time, called a "moonth." Today the length has been adjusted by a few days, and the period is known as a "month."

Do you remember the order in which the moon phases appear? Fortunately, the moon spells out a word to help you. If the moon cannot be seen, it is in new moon; but in each of the other three positions the moon formed a letter of the alphabet.

The moon looks like a *D* in first quarter, an *O* at full moon, and a filled-in *C* in the last quarter. Put them together and the moon spells *DOC*, to show the order in which the phases appear.

Why Do We Have Seasons?

The subject of the seasons of the year is sometimes presented in a unit on the sun, moon, and stars. If you choose to do so, please refer back to the last section of chapter 12 where it is presented.

Combining Assessment with Instruction

Have students keep a moon journal for at least a month to 5 weeks. At least four nights a week they should record observations of the moon. Tell them to use drawings and words to describe the shape and position of the moon in relationship to objects in their view. As they start to notice trends or patterns, they should write them down. What do they notice about the path or position of the moon? At the end of the 5 weeks they should summarize what they have learned about the phases of the moon.

Before the students start their journals, use a bright light (flash light) and spheres to simulate the movement of the sun, Earth, and moon. A darkened room is helpful. Point out the ideas of shadows on the "moon."

Have students make a journal containing at least 20 sheets of paper to keep their observations. They may decorate the cover at home. A sample observation sheet can be found on the following website: http://www.learner.org/channel/workshops/lala/moonjinstruct.html.

Point out to students that they are to use the same location each night for their observations. Look into the southern sky about the same time each night. For younger children, letters should be sent home explaining the assignment and asking for adult help with the night observations.

On the first night students should draw the horizon and any objects that will remain constant in their nightly view of the moon. This might include such structures as a tall building, water tower, or a tree. These objects should be drawn into each picture. Students should also place the time and date on each observation page.

Evaluate each moon journal for the following:

1. Number of weekly observations done over a 4- to 5-week period.
2. Time and date on each observation sheet. A relatively consistent observation time should earn more points.
3. Reference objects such as trees and buildings drawn in the same position on each observation page.
4. Attention given to both position and shape of the moon.
5. Descriptions of any trend or patterns they may notice.
6. A clear summary of their observations detailing their observations of the phases of the moon.
7. Neatness and completeness of the moon journal.

The following article may be useful for more directions. B. Brandou, "Backyard Astronomy: Observing Moon Phases," *Science and Children* 34, no. 8 (1997), pp. 18–21, 48

Sites and Software

The following websites and software are appropriate to use with this chapter. Note that computer software and websites change rapidly. This makes it necessary to investigate the stable websites for new links and software catalogs for updates. Visit www.mhhe.com/friedl6e to link to these directly and for study resources.

Sites

National Air and Space Museum	www.nasm.si.edu
Galileo K-12 Educator's Resources	www.jpl.nasa.gov/galileo/educator.html
Space Science-Berkley	cse.ssl.berkeley.edu
Astronomy	www.howstuffworks.com/category.htm?cat=Astro
Star Child: A Learning Center for Young Astronomers	starchild.gsfc.nasa.gov/docs/StarChild/StarChild.html
Imagine the Universe!	imagine.gsfc.nasa.gov
The Nine Planets	seds.lpl.arizona.edu/nineplanets/nineplanets/nineplanets.html

Software

A Field Trip to the Sky (Sunburst) (4–8)
Planetary Taxi (Discovery) (3–8)
Stars and Stories (Discovery) (2–6)
Magic School Bus Explores the Solar System (Microsoft Home) (1–4)

Key Terms

first quarter, *279*   **lunar eclipse,** *278*   **phases of the moon,** *279*
full moon, *280*   **new moon,** *279*   **solar eclipse,** *278*
last quarter, *280*

Teaching Children about the Earth (Geology)

NATIONAL SCIENCE EDUCATION STANDARDS ALIGNMENT TO EVENTS

The events in this chapter help accomplish several of the NSES for content. The event(s) that align with a given content standard are listed below that standard.

LEVELS K–4

UNIFYING CONCEPTS AND PROCESSES
- Systems, order and organization
    15-D through 15-E
    15-I
- Change, consistency, measurement
    15-C
    15-H
    15-O through 15-R
- Evidence, models and explanation
    15-A through 15-C
    15-F and 15-G
    15-J through 15-T
- Evolution and equilibrium
    15-A through 15-T

SCIENCE AS INQUIRY
- Abilities necessary to do and understand scientific inquiry
    15-A through 15-T

PHYSICAL SCIENCE
- Properties of objects and materials
    15-D through 15-I

EARTH AND SPACE SCIENCE
- Properties of earth materials
    15-A through 15-T

SCIENCE AND TECHNOLOGY
- Understanding science and technology
    15-I
    15-T

SCIENCE IN PERSONAL AND SOCIAL PERSPECTIVES
- Changes in environments
    15-J
    15-L
    15-N
    15-R through 15-T
- Science and technology in local challenges
    15-I
    15-R through 15-T

LEVELS 5–8

UNIFYING CONCEPTS AND PROCESSES
- Systems, order and organization
    15-D through 15-E
    15-I
- Change, consistency, measurement
    15-C
    15-H
    15-O through 15-R
- Evidence, models and explanation
    15-A through 15-C
    15-F and 15-G
    15-J through 15-T
- Evolution and equilibrium
    15-A through 15-T

SCIENCE AS INQUIRY
- Abilities necessary to do and understand scientific inquiry
    15-A through 15-T

PHYSICAL SCIENCE
- Properties and changes in properties of matter
    15-J through 15-T

- Motion and forces
    15-B
    15-N

EARTH AND SPACE SCIENCE
- Structure of the earth system
    15-A through 15-T
- Earth's history
    15-A and 15-B
    15-K through 15-N
    15-Q

SCIENCE AND TECHNOLOGY
- Understanding science and technology
    15-I
    15-T

SCIENCE IN PERSONAL AND SOCIAL PERSPECTIVES
- Natural hazards
    15-J
    15-L
    15-N
    15-R through 15-T
- Science and technology in society
    15-I
    15-R through 15-T
- Populations, resources and environments
    15-R through 15-T

HISTORY AND NATURE OF SCIENCE
- History of science
    15-Historical introduction

The Structure of the Earth

To understand the structure of the Earth we should begin with its formation. In its initial formation, the Earth was at one time a huge ball of molten rock. A mass as large as the Earth and hot enough to be molten rock was probably a churning, bubbling cauldron. Nevertheless, the lighter matter tended to float to the top and the heavier matter tended to settle downward.

After the planet cooled and hardened, the different rock densities were evident even on the crust of the earth. The rocks under the oceans are basalt, a very heavy rock, while the great landmasses and mountains are composed of granite, a relatively light rock.

Today, the planet is still mostly liquified, molten rock. Only the crust is solid. The solid **crust** is from 8 to 64 kilometers in thickness. Under the crust is the **mantle,** a semisolid zone about 2900 km thick. Finally, the center **core** is mostly molten and is about 3500 km in diameter. The layers of the Earth are shown in figure 15.1.

The crust is so thick that no one has ever gone below it, yet when compared to the rest of the Earth it is extremely thin. In comparison, it is thinner than the skin of a peach.

The crust "floats" on the mantle and is not of uniform thickness. It is thickest on landmasses and thinnest under oceans. In that respect, it is like ice floating on water. A larger chunk of ice will sink deeper in water than a small chunk. Likewise, a large landmass extends deeper into the mantle than the thin ocean beds. See figure 15.2.

The deeper you go into the Earth, the hotter it gets. The temperature increase is noticeable even in deep mines and oil wells. For example, a mine that is 1800 meters deep is about 55° C hotter than a mine near the surface. (The temperature increases about 1° C every 33 meters.)

How do we know so much about the mantle and the core if we have never been there? Scientists have been able to make inferences by conducting experiments, making certain observations, and using logic.

For example, the boundary line between the crust and the mantle was detected by the bending of sound waves. Scientists produced the sound waves by setting off explosions on the surface. Sound travels through the solid crust at a speed different from through the somewhat plastic mantle. In addition, sound is refracted (or bent) when it enters the mantle at an angle. In fact, it is bent somewhat like light is refracted when it goes from one medium into another. By studying the reflected echoes, scientists can tell how deep the various layers are.

We have already noted that the temperature increases as we go deeper into the earth, It is simple logic to suggest that if you keep on going deeper, it will keep on getting hotter. Finally, we know that pressure produces heat. The weight of the entire Earth is concentrated in its core, making it very hot indeed.

Scientists have also studied earthquake shock waves. An earthquake sends out several types of waves. The first wave is called a *primary wave.* It is a push-pull wave *(longitudinal wave)*—a kind of wave that travels through solids, liquids, and gases. The primary wave goes through the mantle and liquid core of the Earth to be detected all over the planet.

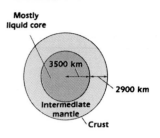

FIGURE 15.1   A cross section of the earth shows the mantle, core, and crust. At the scale shown, the crust is no thicker than the ink on the outer line.

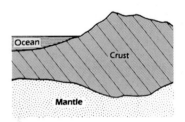

FIGURE 15.2

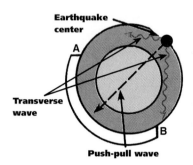

Earthquake center

A

Transverse wave

B

Push-pull wave

FIGURE 15.3   The push-pull earthquake waves go through solids and liquids and can be detected in all parts of the earth. The snakelike waves of an earthquake do not go through the earths's liquid core. Thus, the part of the earth between A and B does not receive these waves.

Another wave is a side-to-side, snakelike wave (called the *transverse wave*), which can travel only through solids, not liquids. As a result, the transverse wave does not go through the liquid core and cannot be detected in those parts of the Earth that are blocked by the core. (See figure 15.3.)

By studying the places of the earth that do not receive the transverse wave of an earthquake, geologists have found that the liquid core is about 3500 kilometers in diameter.

Surface Features of the Earth (Events 15-A through 15-C)

Discrepant Events and Pupil Investigations

Event 15-A. Geological Maps of Your Area

Obtain geological survey maps and/or aerial photos of your area. Maps and aerial photographs may be obtained from U.S. Geological Survey (USGS) http://mapping.usgs.gov/ or from Microsoft TerraServer at http://terraserver-usa.com.

If you can get maps with scales of 1:24,000 to 1:63,000, it may be possible to take a walking or riding tour of your area and compare the maps with the actual surface features of the land.

Pupil Investigations (may include the following processes):

1. Discovering that contours on the map show land shapes and elevations.
2. Analyzing the colors on the maps to distinguish between land, water, and other surface features of the Earth.
3. Interpreting the map and comparing it to on-the-spot inspections of the surface features.

Event 15-B. Folded Mountains

Flatten out several layers of clay of different colors. Place these layers, one on top of another, on a board and put two boards on each end of the clay. Press inward on the two end boards. What happens to the layers of clay? How does this activity show us something of the structure of the earth? (Look ahead to figure 15.5 if necessary.)

Pupil Investigations (may include the following processes):

1. Observing that the pressure from the sides causes the layers of clay to form folds.
2. Comparing the model to the formation of folded mountains.
3. Generalizing that many landforms are caused by pressures that formed the folded mountains.

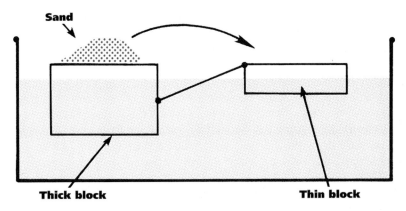

FIGURE 15.4   As the sand is transferred, the thick block rises and the thin block sinks. Thus, the elevations do not change much. This illustrates isostatic pressure.

Event 15-C. Isostatic Adjustment

Tie several strings from a thick wooden block to a thin wooden block. Arrange them so that about 15 or 20 centimeters separate the two. Float the blocks in a container of water.

Pour sand on the thick block so that it barely floats. Carefully observe the positions of the blocks in the water. (See figure 15.4.) Now take some of the sand from the thick block and place it on the thin block. What do you observe?

Pupil Investigations (may include the following processes):

1. Observing that the thick block settled deeper into the water when sand was added to it.
2. Measuring the height above the water before and after some sand was removed.
3. Discovering that the height above the water did not change much when sand was added or removed.
4. Comparing the event to isostatic adjustment in mountains.

Events 15-A through 15-C Explained in Context (Surface Features of the Earth)

Taking long trips by car or flying over expanses of land by air makes one aware of many surface features of the earth. Most land surfaces are topped with soils of various types, although bedrock is sometimes exposed in mountainous areas.

Students in the upper grades can become more familiar with their local surface features if they study geological survey maps as suggested in *Event 15-A, Geological Maps of Your Area.* Then the features on the maps can be identified by an on-the-spot tour.

By studying the maps, students will realize that a great deal of information can be placed on a flat surface. For example, the elevation of land is shown by contour lines. Certain surface features are identified by symbols, shadings, and lines called hachures.

Colors are also used on geological survey maps. Black is used to show boundary lines and the results of human effort such as roads and buildings. Blue is used for water features such as lakes, rivers, canals, and glaciers. Brown is used for land features. Red is used to emphasize built-up urban areas, boundary lines of public lands, and the importance of major roads.

Geological survey maps are usually printed in scales ranging from 1:24,000 (1 inch equals 2000 feet) to 1:1,000,000 (1 inch equals 16 miles). (Note that the dimensions are in inches and feet instead of in metric units.)

How did the surface of the earth come to look as it does? Does it always stay the same? What are the forces acting on it? Actually, the surface is in a constant state of change. Most changes usually occur far too slowly to be apparent to an observer during a lifetime, but over the span of geologic eras the changes are massive and constant.

Change is caused by both internal and external forces. The internal stresses are produced by the gradual shifting and possibly shrinking of the earth. These forces are very evident when volcanoes erupt or when strains deep below the surface are released as earthquakes.

In a more gradual way, the stresses and shifting crust form pressures that produce folded mountains, *Event 15-B, Folded Mountains,* gives us an idea of how certain mountain ranges are formed. When pressed together, the layers are humped up in the middle.

If sufficient pressure is applied, the layers will finally break apart; and some layers will slide up over other layers. (See figure 15.5.) These features are called **block mountains.**

In addition to the mountains that are formed by the stresses of the Earth, some are formed by displacement. That is, light matter floats higher than heavy matter.

Displacement mountains do not tend to become smaller. Study *Event 15-C, Isostatic Adjustment.* Notice what happens to the level of the block when sand is taken from it: it floats higher in the water.

In a similar way, when erosion wears down a mountain, it becomes lighter and tends to rise up on the Earth's crust. The net result is very little actual change in the height of the mountain.

Conversely, when sediment is washed down into the ocean, the extra weight will eventually cause the ocean floor to sink. In those places where isostatic adjustment is dominant, the elevation of the land and the depth of the ocean tend to be more or less stable.

In addition to the internal forces discussed above, other forces, external ones, are also important in causing changes on the surface of the Earth, Glaciers are examples of a visible and dramatic force that causes changes. They carve out valleys and level off mountains in their relentless advance across the Earth. Much of North America was covered by glaciers at four different occasions in geologic history.

Other important external forces that cause changes in the surface of the earth are weathering and erosion. These forces will be discussed in greater detail later in this chapter.

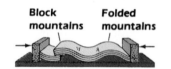

Block mountains   **Folded mountains**

FIGURE 15.5 When pushed together with movable blocks, layers of modeling clay become folded, representing folded mountains. If pushed still further, the layers may break and slide over one another to make block mountains.

Rocks and Minerals (Events 15-D through 15-I)

Discrepant Events and Pupil Investigations

Event 15-D. Classifying Rocks

Collect rocks from around your school and neighborhood. Place them in a big pile and ask pupils to identify and classify them into groups.

Pupil Investigations (may include the following processes):

1. Investigating rocks for evidence of traits or characteristics.
2. Classifying rocks according to the observed traits.
3. Comparing the classification by pupils with the official system used to identify rocks.

Event 15-E. Scale of Hardness

Divide the class into committees and ask them to compare the hardness of several common items—a penny, a piece of sandpaper, a piece of chalk—and then compare them with a fingernail.

Pupil Investigations (may include the following processes):

1. Comparing the four items.
2. Arranging the items in a "scale of hardness".
3. Comparing the activity with the official scale of hardness.

Event 15-F. Crystal Formation

Dissolve as much alum in a container of hot water as you can. Keep adding alum and stirring until no more will dissolve. Then pour equal amounts into two beakers. Place one beaker in a bed of crushed ice and insulate the other. Observe the solutions from time to time during the next several hours.

Pupil Investigations (may include the following processes):

1. Observing that large crystals form in the insulated container and small crystals form in the cooled container.
2. Inspecting the crystal formations with magnifying glasses.
3. Inferring that the size of the crystals is related to the speed of cooling.
4. Applying the results of the experiment to the size of crystals found in rock formations.

Event 15-G. "Unmix" the Soils

It is easy to mix up separate piles of sand, pebbles, loam, and clay. But can you "unmix" them once they are blended? Put enough of the mixed ingredients into a jar to fill it half to three-fourths full. Add water to fill the jar and shake vigorously for a moment. Set the jar down and observe it for a few minutes.

Pupil Investigations (may include the following processes):

1. Observing that the pebbles and larger particles settle to the bottom of the jar quickly.
2. Generalizing that the soil types settle according to the size of their grain structure (largest first).
3. Generalizing that moving water causes a layering of soils and rocks.

Event 15-H. Rock Sponges

Weigh pieces of rock such as granite, limestone, sandstone, and marble. Record the weights while dry, and then soak them in water overnight. Weigh the rocks again the next day. What has happened to their weights?

Pupil Investigations (may include the following processes):

1. Measuring and recording the weight of the rocks before and after soaking.
2. Discovering that some rocks are heavier after soaking but others do not change.
3. Inferring that those rocks that gained weight have soaked up water.

Event 15-I. Rock and Mineral Database

Pass out a collection of rocks and minerals for students to analyze. Have each pupil research the characteristics of one common rock and one common mineral. After each pupil has completed his/her investigation, have the class brainstorm a list of important information needed to classify rocks and minerals. Let pupils search for any characteristic they may not have found during the first search. Encourage the use of the Internet as part of the search process. Have the class again identify the list of important characteristics or *fields* of rocks. This will be the *field* names for the rock and mineral database. The fields may include hardness, color, streak, crystal form, texture, luster, cleavage, chemical, and density. Have pupils enter the information for their selected rock and mineral into their *file*, "Rock and Mineral Database."

Pupil Investigations (may include the following processes):

1. Collecting information known about rocks and minerals.
2. Sorting for a given *field* or characteristic of rocks and minerals by using a database.
3. Classifying rocks and minerals by using the database sort and search functions.

Events 15-D through 15-I Explained in Context (Rocks and Minerals)

What Are Rocks and Minerals?

There are so many similarities between rocks and minerals that the terms are often used to mean the same thing. However, there are some differences that should be noted.

Rocks are fairly large units of the earth's crust. They may be of organic form (made from living matter such as coal) or of inorganic form (made of nonliving matter). Rocks may include consolidated or random matter and are usually composed of two or more minerals.

Minerals are different in that they are much more limited in definition. They contain specific elements, or combinations of elements, and are entirely inorganic in composition.

Types of Rocks

Rocks are divided into three groups: igneous, sedimentary, and metamorphic. There are many subgroups within each of the three general classes. Students should be given a chance to determine some traits and characteristics of rocks by doing *Event 15-D, Classifying Rocks.*

Let the students classify rocks according to traits that they think exist. It is unimportant at this stage of the lesson for the students to select the "correct" traits. Let them classify according to their best uninformed judgments.

After they have decided on their groupings, it is useful to bring in the official classification system for comparison. Students will want to know how closely they came to the system approved by geologists. After having tried it themselves, they can often see the value of a classification system.

Characteristics of Rocks

There are eight major characteristics that are used to identify and classify rocks. They are (1) hardness, (2) color, (3) streak, (4) texture, (5) luster, (6) cleavage, (7) chemical, and (8) density.

Rocks vary greatly in **hardness.** *Event 15-E, Scale of Hardness,* calls attention to this important trait. The items in this event range in order from softest to hardest: chalk, fingernail, penny, and sandpaper. Hardness is a useful trait to help identify and classify rocks. An official scale used to measure the hardness of rocks is called **Moh's Scale of Hardness.**

The official scale is of limited value to the students until it is expanded to include examples that are more familiar to them. Table 15.1 shows Moh's scale, supplemented with many additional examples.

A second factor used to classify rocks is **color.** The color observed is sometimes different from the color seen when the rock is rubbed against something. Thus, a third test, called the **streak test,** is used to check the color when rubbed.

Another test is called **texture** and refers to the size of the grains or crystals in the rock. The grains may be coarse, fine, or nonexistent.

Rocks can also be checked for **luster**—how the sample reflects light. If it reflects no light, it is dull. If it reflects light as a coin does, it has metallic luster; and if it reflects light as glass does, it has a glassy luster.

A sixth test is **cleavage**—the way a specimen breaks when struck by a hammer. A seventh check is the **chemical test.** For example, calcium carbonate (lime) will fizz and bubble if acid is dropped on it. If sulfur is present in a specimen, it will smell like rotten eggs.

Finally, students will find that rocks have different **densities.** Weigh each sample in the air and then while immersed in water. Record the difference in the weights. Divide the "air weight" by the *difference* to get a figure that is the *specific gravity* of the sample.

When the class has learned about the tests used to classify rocks, let them classify the same samples that they had worked with earlier. How did their first tries compare with the later attempts?

TABLE 15.1

Scale of Hardness

Scale Number	Scale Example	Other Examples	Explanations
1	Talc	Soft lead pencil	Greasy flakes of the substance will be left on fingers
1½		Ice near freezing	
2	Gypsum	Chalk Lead (metal)	Can be easily scratched with fingernail
2½		Fingernail	Can be scratched by silver and by copper wire
3	Calcite	Marble	Will scratch silver Can be scratched by copper penny Can be cut easily with knife
3½		Copper penny	
4	Flourite	Yellow brass	Can be easily scratched but not easily cut with knife
4½		Ordinary nail	
5	Apatite	Steel wool	Can be scratched with difficulty with a knife
		Nail file	
5½		Knife blade Glass bottle	
6	Feldspar	Window glass	Can be scratched by a file but not a knife
6½		Steel file	
7	Quartz	Flint Sandpaper	Scratches glass easily
7½		Gamet paper	
8	Topaz		
8½		Emery paper	
9	Corundum	Silicon Carbide paper	
9½			
10	Diamond		

Igneous rocks are those that formed from molten matter. When a rock cools and hardens, it forms grains or crystals—the size of which depend on the speed of cooling. If the rock cools rapidly, it has little or no graininess. If it cools slowly, the crystals tend to be large. Examples of igneous rocks are basalt, granite, obsidian and pumice.

The crystal formation can be seen by doing *Event 15-F, Crystal Formation*. As the containers cool, alum settles out of the solutions. If the alum cools slowly, the crystals are larger than when the alum cools quickly. Alum is a substance used in pickling. It has a tart astringent taste that makes people pucker when tasting it. It is easily found in the spice section of grocery stores.

Sedimentary rocks are formed from materials carried by running water. Running water carries pebbles, rocks, and sand. As the matter is carried, pushed, and rolled, the sharp edges are ground down. As a result, most of the grains of sand, pebbles, and rocks are rounded.

The size of the grains that are deposited depends on the speed of the moving water. Fast currents move more matter than slow currents. When currents slow down, matter is dropped.

Since currents are often affected by seasonal changes, the deposited matter forms layers. Such layers are common to sedimentary rocks. To see how matter is deposited according to size and density, perform *Event 15-G, "Unmix" the Soils.* The soils in this event will be deposited in order with the largest going to the bottom and the finest soils going on top. In other words, the mixed up soils will become unmixed by the actions of the water.

Over eons of time, hundreds and even thousands of meters of sediment may be deposited. The grains of these deposits become cemented by time and pressure to form rock. Examples of sedimentary rock are limestone, sandstone, shale, chalk, and coal.

Metamorphic rock is really igneous or sedimentary rock that has been subjected to enough heat and pressure to alter its basic composition. For example, sandstone is changed to quartzite, limestone to marble, shale to slate, and bituminous coal to anthracite coal.

The location of rock layers is very important in finding water and petroleum. Sometimes water reservoirs are trapped far below the surface of the earth by a layer of impermeable rock above it. An **impermeable** rock is one through which no water can pass. When the impermeable layer is pierced, the water below can rise to the surface. Similarly, oil and gas deposits are often trapped deep below the surface in layers of **permeable** rock; a porous rock that can "soak up" fluids. Such rock layers contain vast amounts of oil and gas. Perform *Event 15-H, Rock Sponges,* to see how some stones can absorb water. Students should note that only the sedimentary rocks are capable of absorbing liquids.

Event 15-I, Rock and Mineral Database, gives pupils an opportunity to go further with their understanding of the attributes by which rocks and minerals are classified. A "big idea" behind the use of a database is for students to develop an appreciation for the ease and speed at which a database can sort tremendous amounts of information. A database helps scientists make sense of the overwhelming amount of data collected.

Weathering and Erosion (Events 15-J through 15-N)

Discrepant Events and Pupil Investigations

Event 15-J. Dissolving Stones

Place a flat piece of limestone into a glass tray. Add a few drops of dilute hydrochloric acid to the stone. (**Caution:** This should be done as a teacher demonstration. Do not get acid on hands or clothes.) After a moment or two, add a few more drops. Continue to add more acid from time to time for several minutes. What do you observe? **Note:** an alternate event safe enough for primary grades is to use chalk (made from crushed limestone) and vinegar (a mild acid called acetic acid).

Pupil Investigations (may include the following processes):

1. Observing that the acid "fizzes" on the rock.
2. Discovering that a hole is slowly being formed in the rock.

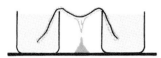

FIGURE 15.6 Tiny stalagmites and stalactites form between the two beakers containing a saturated solution of Epsom salt.

3. Inferring that the acid causes a chemical reaction.
4. Generalizing that the formation of a limestone cave may be caused by chemical action.

Event 15-K. Building Stalactites and Stalagmites

Dissolve as much Epsom salt into a jar of water as you can. Fill two smaller jars with the dissolved salt water, and drape a thick string between them as shown in figure 15.6. Let the arrangement stand for a few days and observe.

Pupil Investigations (may include the following processes):

1. Observing that water soaks the string and slowly drips from its low point.
2. Discovering that deposits slowly form on the string and on the surface below it.
3. Forming a theory that the deposits are carried in solution to the point where they appear.
4. Inferring that evaporation of the solution causes the deposits to form.
5. Generalizing to compare the deposits of Epsom salt with the formation of stalactites and stalagmites in caves.

Event 15-L. Rock Erosion

Fill a small jar half full of rock chips consisting mostly of sandstone, limestone, or shale. Have pupils take turns shaking the jar vigorously for several minutes. Observe the chips carefully under a magnifying glass. Inspect the water and the bottom of the jar for any deposits.

Pupil Investigations (may include the following processes):

1. Comparing the appearance of the chips before and after shaking the jar.
2. Observing that the chips are generally smaller and more rounded after shaking than before.
3. Inferring that the shaking ground off tiny bits of rock which clouded the water and settled to the bottom.
4. Generalizing to relate the activity to the mechanical erosion of rocks.

Event 15-M. Pebble Pinnacles

Form a mound of some nonoily clay (not modeling clay) into a level mass, about 5 or 10 centimeters across. Place the mound into a tray or pan. Press some pebbles (or coins) into the top surface of the clay. Take the mass outside and spray it with water from a hose. Direct a light spray so that it hits the clay from above. What happens?

Pupil Investigations (may include the following processes):

1. Observing that the spray slowly washes away the clay.
2. Discovering that the pebbles remain on top of pinnacles after much of the clay is washed away.
3. Inferring that the pebbles protect the clay from the erosion of water.
4. Generalizing that hard surface rock formations protect softer rock formations below from erosion.

Event 15-N. Force of Freezing

Fill a small jar brimful with water and tighten the cap securely. Place the jar into a plastic bag for safety and then, for even more safety, into a larger plastic tray. Put the tray into the freezer compartment of a refrigerator. Observe the jar after the water is frozen solidly.

Pupil Investigations (may include the following processes):

1. Discovering that the jar is broken. (**Caution:** Be careful of glass fragments, which will be inside the bag and tray.)
2. Forming a theory that water expands when it freezes.
3. Inferring that ice can do to a rock what it did to the jar.

Events 15-J through 15-N Explained in Context (Weathering and Erosion)

What Is Meant by Weathering and Erosion?

Weathering and erosion are terms often used interchangeably. However, there is a difference. **Weathering** refers to a gradual physical and chemical wearing away of rocks. Even hard rocks are slowly weathered and broken down into fine grains of sand by the action of wind, water, temperature changes, and chemical action.

Erosion is a somewhat broader term. It refers to the wearing away of the surface of the Earth. Erosion is caused mostly by running water, and to a lesser degree, wind, glaciers, and temperature changes.

Chemical action affects certain rocks. Rainwater picks up oxygen and carbon dioxide as it falls through the air. Then, by the time the rain seeps into the earth, the carbon dioxide has changed into a weak solution of carbonic acid.

Acids tend to dissolve limestone, as can be seen by doing *Event 15-J, Dissolving Stones.* When the dilute hydrochloric acid is dropped on the limestone, there is a bubbling and fizzing action as the limestone slowly dissolves. Eventually, a depression is formed in the rock where the acid has eaten away the stone.

The action of acids and other chemicals has carved out many large and beautiful caves such as Mammoth Cave in Kentucky and Carlsbad Caverns in New Mexico. The caves were formed over a period of millions of years by chemicals dissolved in groundwater. In this event the children saw a rapid simulation of dissolving rocks, an event that takes centuries to millions of years in nature.

Sometimes groundwater will deposit minerals instead of dissolve them. If the water is saturated with a mineral, some of it will change to a solid as the water evaporates. This action can be seen if water is left in a clear glass or plastic container to dry. After the water dries, a cloudy film of residue is left on the clear surface.

Another example of this depositing action can be seen by doing *Event 15-K, Building Stalactites and Stalagmites.* The Epsom salt solution travels along the string by capillary action until it reaches the low point between the two jars. There, it accumulates and drips off.

At the same time, however, air is evaporating the liquid, leaving a residue of Epsom salt on the string and on the surface below. The deposits on the string are similar to **stalactites** that hang down from the ceilings of caves.

FIGURE 15.7 The Mississippi River has dropped millions of tons of soil at its mouth, extending the delta into the Gulf of Mexico.

The deposits on the surface below the string are similar to **staglagmites** that build up from the floors of caves.

Erosion Is a Continuous Process

Running water is the chief cause of erosion. The faster the water runs, the stronger its erosive force. When a stream doubles its speed, its capacity to carry suspended matter increases by an unbelievable 64 times! In addition, the slope of the land and the depth of the stream are factors that affect the force of water erosion.

The Mississippi River carries millions of tons of suspended matter to the Gulf of Mexico every year. Some of this matter piles up around the mouth of the river, forming a delta. Study maps that show major rivers emptying into the ocean. Many of those rivers have built deltas a hundred or more kilometers into the sea. (See figure 15.7.)

Some of the most striking examples of river erosion can be found by studying the causes of some of the greatest floods of history. For example, the great flood of China's Hwang Ho River (Yellow River) in 1887 is instructive.

The Hwang Ho, like all large rivers, carries enormous amounts of suspended matter, especially as the water flows quickly down the higher elevations. When the river reaches the fairly level lowlands, it slows down, dropping great amounts of matter to the riverbed.

Year after year the riverbed is built up. To protect themselves, people built up the banks (called levees) to keep the river in its channel. Time after time, levees were raised higher and higher to keep ahead of the ever-rising riverbed. Finally, the river overflowed with disastrous results.

Sediment had built up the channel so much that even the *bed* of the river was higher than the surrounding valley. When the river finally overflowed the levees, it flooded 140,000 square kilometers of land and killed an estimated one million people.

Of course, the river did not return to its old, elevated channel. Instead, it simply cut a new channel through the lowlands and entered the ocean hundreds of kilometers from its previous mouth. Evidence shows that the Hwang Ho has changed its course in a similar manner many times during the passage of geological time. (See figure 15.8.)

Perform *Event 15-L, Rock Erosion,* to see how mechanical action can grind and erode small rock chips. This event simulates the action of running water. As the rocks are tumbled and rolled in the running water, they slide and grind over each other. Slowly they take on round shapes and get smaller and smaller.

Some of the same results can be noticed by shaking the chips in the jar. Be sure to use fairly soft sedimentary rocks for the activity. Hard samples will not show much change in any reasonable length of time.

A stream is not the only place in which water erosion takes place. Rainwater and the action of lakes and oceans also produce erosive forces.

In some of the western states there are unusual rock structures that look like tall spires or pinnacles. These were formed when relatively small layers of hard rock were deposited on top of softer rock. Over eons of time, fractures developed through the top layer and the softer underlayer eroded away

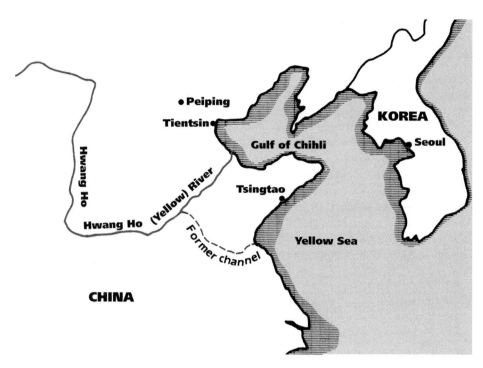

FIGURE 15.8   In 1887, the Hwang Ho (Yellow) River in China overflowed and cut a new channel to the sea. An estimated one million people died in the flood.

quickly. Now the remains of the harder rock serve as caps protecting the soft rock below it.

Event 15-M, Pebble Pinnacles, is an activity that shows how the pinnacles were formed. A fairly gentle spray from above washes away the clay, leaving the pebbles (or coins) to serve as caps on top of mounds of clay.

Sometimes water seeps into the cracks of hard rocks. Later, if the water freezes, the ice expands to break the rock apart. A simple demonstration of the action of freezing water can be seen in *Event 15-N, Force of Freezing.* The ice breaks the jar easily as it expands.

Be sure to exercise caution by placing the jar inside a plastic bag, and the bag into a larger tray or pan. In that way you protect yourself from broken glass as well as keep bits of broken glass out of the freezer.

Soils (Events 15-O through 15-T)

Discrepant Events and Pupil Investigations

Event 15-O. Permeability of Soils

Attach a screen to the bottom of a cylinder. (You can use an inverted plastic jug with the bottom removed. See figure 15.9.) Fill the container about three-fourths full of loam. Pour in some water and keep the container brimful for a minute or two. Repeat with other jars containing other soil types such as sand and clay.

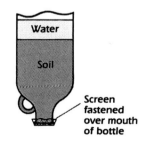

FIGURE 15.9   Use an inverted clear plastic bottle to see how quickly a measured amount of water soaks through soils.

Pupil Investigations (may include the following processes):

1. Measuring the amount of water that seeps through each of the soil types in a given period of time.
2. Observing that sandy soils allow a very large amount of water to pass through quickly.
3. Observing that clay soils restrict the passage of water.
4. Analyzing the function of a soil permeability test for a leach bed of a small home-sized septic system.

Event 15-P. Water-Holding Capacity of Soils

Fill several containers three-fourths full of different soil types as described in Event 15-O. This time, pour in a measured amount of water and no more. Allow sufficient time for the water to seep through the soils and measure again. Compare the before and after amounts for each soil type.

Pupil Investigations (may include the following processes):

1. Weighing the water before and after pouring.
2. Measuring the amounts of water to find out how much remains in the soil.
3. Appreciating the value of adding water-holding soils to croplands.

Event 15-Q. Erosion on Bare and Grassy Slopes

Fill two shallow boxes with soil. Place a layer of turf in one box, and leave the other bare. Lift the boxes so that they slope down, simulating a hillside. Then pour water on each from a sprinkler. Large basins should be used to collect the runoff. (Do not let the soil wash into the sinks. It can clog the drain. If possible, perform the activity outdoors with a hose.)

Pupil Investigations (may include the following processes):

1. Observing that the water runs off quickly from bare soil.
2. Discovering that the turf tends to "hold" the water and soil.
3. Generalizing that bare soil is easily eroded.
4. Measuring the runoff from the two boxes.
5. Generalizing about the value of grasses to reduce soil erosion.

Event 15-R. Check Dams

Select an area of ground in which a small gully has been cut by the action of running water. Build a dam in this gully using rocks, boards, and soil. Be sure that the rocks are piled on the downstream side of the dam to keep the overflowing water from washing away the dam.

Drive a stake into the stream bed a meter or two on the upstream side of the dam. Measure the stake's height carefully and inspect the site after a hard rain.

Pupil Investigations (may include the following processes):

1. Discovering that the upstream side of the dam is filled with soil after a hard rain.
2. Measuring the amount of soil deposited by the running water (by measuring the height of the stake before and after the rain).
3. Inferring that the soil was carried by rapidly moving water and then dropped as the water slowed in the lake.

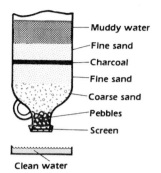

Event 15-S. Cleaning Muddy Water

Use an inverted plastic bottle with the bottom removed. Make a filter by arranging pebbles, sand, and charcoal into layers as shown in figure 15.10. Pour in muddy water and observe it as it comes out below. (**Caution:** Sometimes this process cleans up the water so well that the water is crystal clear. This does *not* make the water suitable for drinking!)

FIGURE 15.10 The layers of sand, charcoal, and pebbles are capable of filtering many impurities from muddy water.

Pupil Investigations (may include the following processes):

1. Discovering that the water is clear as it emerges from the filter.
2. Inferring that the contents of the filter removed the muddy particles in the water.
3. Comparing the demonstration with the filtering qualities of various natural soils.

Event 15-T. Chemical Cleaning of Water

Pour some muddy water into a test tube. Let it stand for a few minutes. Note how muddy the water is at that time. Then shake the test tube, and add some alum and shake again. After allowing the test tube to stand for the same length of time as earlier, compare the clarity of the water with the first sample. (**Caution:** Even though the water may clear up, it is *not* suitable for drinking.)

Pupil Investigations (may include the following processes):

1. Forming a standard for estimating the muddiness of water (perhaps by using different shadings on a sheet of paper).
2. Comparing the water before and after adding the chemical.
3. Inferring that chemicals can help to purify water.

Events 15-O through 15-T Explained in Context (Soils)

Most of the land surfaces of the Earth are covered with a layer of soil. Only the mountains have large exposed masses of rock without a soil covering. Mountain valleys, however, are filled with soil.

Fertile soils contain far more than just mineral matter. They contain organic matter as well as microscopic plant and animal life.

The size of soil particles varies greatly in different soils. Soils are classified according to the dimensions shown in table 15.2. Good soils contain a proper blend of all sizes.

TABLE 15.2

Soil Size and Type

2.0 mm or larger	Gravel
0.05 to 2.0 mm	Sand
0.002 to 0.05 mm	Silt
0.002 mm or smaller	Clay

The size of the particles influences the permeability of soils, that is, the ability of soil to allow water to pass through it. By doing *Event 15-O, Permeability of Soils,* you will find that, of the three types of soil listed in the event, sandy soil is by far the best in allowing water to pass through it quickly. Loam, if it has a good blend of soils, is next; and clay is poorest. In many states, permeability tests are required to determine the suitability of soils to drain away liquid wastes from home septic systems.

By continuing with *Event 15-P, Water-Holding Capacity of Soils,* we should find differences in how much water various soils can hold. As expected, sand does not hold much water. Clay holds more water than sand, but loam is the best "holder" of water. Loam, is a soil rich in organic matter and can hold up to 200% of its own weight in water.

Soil Conservation

Only the top 5 to 10 centimeters of soil are suitable for growing crops in most parts of the world. Much of this thin covering can be blown or washed away if it is not protected. It is easy to see why topsoil must be conserved.

One method of protecting this thin layer of fertile soil is to keep the soil covered with plant growth as much as possible. (Even croplands can now be protected from erosion by using a "no-till" method of planting, instead of the plowing and seed-bed preparation that leaves soils entirely unprotected for weeks at a time.)

The effects of plant growth can be seen by performing *Event 15-Q, Erosion on Bare and Grassy Slopes.* When water is sprinkled on both slopes, the water quickly carries away the bare soil. Small gullies are cut into the slope, and soil is washed down into the pan.

The grassy slope, on the other hand, holds much of the water and almost all of the soil. Plants provide excellent protection from the destructive effects of running water.

Once gullies are formed, pupils will see the value of building check dams to reduce erosion. When the check dam is built, as suggested in *Event 15-R, Check Dams,* pupils will find that after a hard rain a large amount of silt is dropped behind the dam.

When the running water reaches the "lake" of the dam, the water slows down and drops its silt. In fact, small check dams are often completely filled with silt after a few hard rains.

If the dams are located at strategic locations along a gully, the gully fills in with silt. Then the silt can be leveled and seeded with grasses to protect the waterway from further erosion.

Plants protect soils with their root systems. Their roots form a weblike mat that intertwines around soil particles to form a tightly knit web of soil holders. The length and number of roots and root hairs from a single plant is truly astounding.

According to a report by the U.S. Department of Agriculture, a single rye plant grown for 4 months in 1 cubic foot of loam soil developed a root system with the following statistics: 13.8 million roots, with a combined length of 616 kilometers, and a surface area of 232 square meters.

The soil also contained 14 billion root hairs with a combined length of 10,560 kilometers and a surface area in excess of 372 square meters. Figures such as these show why plants are so effective in holding soils in place.

Cleaning Muddy Water

We have seen that moving water picks up soil and dirt. It may be pointed out that scientists use the term *soil* for what we commonly call dirt. It is quite surprising for pupils to learn that some soil particles are effective in getting rid of dirt. Sandy soils are a natural filter for underground water sources. They can be used to make a classroom filter in *Event 15-S, Cleaning Muddy Water*.

Be sure that the sand is clean before using it in the filter. A classroom filter is too small to be very effective unless you use ground-up charcoal as one of the layers. It is hard for pupils to understand that charcoal, which is so messy to the touch, is so effective in cleaning up muddy water. Charcoal is a porous, black, brittle solid that is odorless and tasteless. It is denser than water, but often absorbs enough gas to make it float on water. Its ability to absorb large quantities of gas makes it a good deodorizer.

If the filter is made correctly, muddy water can come out of the filter looking crystal clear. Again, be sure to caution pupils *not* to drink it. The muddy particles are removed, but the system does not remove bacteria and harmful microscopic life.

Another way of purifying water is by using chemicals. One example of removing muddy particles is shown in *Event 15-T, Chemical Cleaning of Water*. When alum is added to the muddy water and then mixed, the muddy particles tend to settle to the bottom quickly. Alum is one of many chemicals that is used in water-purification plants.

(**Caution:** As with our earlier warnings, the water is not safe to drink. The alum just takes out the muddy particles. Invisible toxic substances remain. Other chemicals, in addition to alum, are used in water-purification plants to purify the water.)

Combining Assessment with Instruction

It is important to give students the opportunity to explore their local environment. A geological field trip is an ideal way to assess what students have learned in class as well as extend their learning about the earth's surface. Every community has local experts who can help make the most of the field trip. Consider asking the following to act as an expert on your field trip: parents; local university professors or students; local/regional educational staff from United States Geological Survey (USGS), Environmental Protection Agency (EPA), Natural Resource and Conservation Services (NRCS), and museums.

LIVERPOOL JOHN MOORES UNIVERSITY
LEARNING SERVICES

The field trip could involve any aspect of earth science that you are presently teaching. For example, students may be able to collect and learn to identify local rocks and minerals. A hike might have them finding plant fossils, while examining the geologic forces that shaped your region. A field trip gives students an intimate look at the hydrology, geology, anthropology, and biology of your unique location. Students might learn to measure stream flow and make measurements of pH, dissolved oxygen, and dissolved solids, which help to describe water quality. Young children may be asked to collect rocks of different color, texture, or other characteristics.

The actual assessment begins before you go on the field trip. As a teacher you need to be clear about your expectations and the tasks students will perform during the trip. Perhaps do related but simpler tasks in class first. Ask them to think about what they might find or see.

During the trip you can assess students' actions and conversations about their observations and the processes they perform. Observe students' organization in recording data. You should ask questions to get a better picture of their level of understanding and listen to their use of scientific vocabulary. It is a good idea to have a clipboard with each student's name and a space in which to record anecdotal notes.

After you return from the trip, have students complete a written report within a reasonable time frame. Later, students should share findings, solutions, and approaches. Ask for justifications. Students might even build models. The reports and presentations can all serve as part of the assessment.

Sites and Software

The following websites and software are appropriate to use with this chapter. Note that computer software and websites change rapidly. This makes it necessary to investigate the stable websites for new links and software catalogs for updates. Visit www.mhhe.com/friedl6e to link to these directly and for study resources.

Sites

Science Gems: Earth Science	www.sciencegems.com
Volcanos	volcano.und.edu
Earth Science	www.scicentral.com
Learning Web (USGS)	www.usgs.gov/education
How Landfills Work	www.howstuffworks.com/landfill.htm
How Sewer and Septic Systems Work	www.howstuffworks.com/sewer.htm
How Composting Works	www.howstuffworks.com/composting.htm
How Earthquakes Work	www.howstuffworks.com/earthquake.htm
How Quicksand Works	www.howstuffworks.com/quicksand.htm
Pictures of Minerals by Name	mineral.galleries.com

Software

A Field Trip to the Earth (Sunburst) (4–8)
Science Court Explorations: Soil (Tom Snyder) (4–6)
Science Court Explorations: Fossils (Tom Snyder) (4–6)
Magic School Bus Explores inside the Earth (Microsoft Home) (1–5)
Sammy's Science House (EdMARK) (1–2)
Earth Quest (DK Multimedia) (3–9)

Key Terms

block mountains, *286*
chemical test, *289*
cleavage, *289*
color, *289*
core, *283*
crust, *283*
density, *289*
displacement mountains, *286*
erosion, *293*

hardness, *289*
igneous rocks, *290*
impermeable, *291*
luster, *289*
mantle, *283*
metamorphic rock, *291*
minerals, *289*
Moh's scale of hardness, *289*
permeable, *291*

rocks, *288*
sedimentary rocks, *290*
stalactites, *293*
stalagmites, *294*
streak test, *289*
texture, *289*
weathering, *293*

Teaching Children about the Oceans

The events in this chapter help accomplish several of the NSES for content. The event(s) that align with a given content standard are listed below that standard.

LEVELS K–4

UNIFYING CONCEPTS AND PROCESSES
- Systems, order and organization
  16-A through 16-Q
- Change, Consistency, Measurement
  16-A
  16-C through 16-E
  16-J
  16-L
  16-N
- Evidence, models and explanation
  16-A through 16-D
  16-F through 16-I
  16-L through 16-P

SCIENCE AS INQUIRY
- Abilities necessary to do and understand scientific inquiry
  16-A through 16-Q

PHYSICAL SCIENCE
- Properties of objects and materials
  16-A through 16-D
- Light, Heat, Electricity, and Magnetism
  16-P and 16-Q

LIFE SCIENCE
- Characteristics of organisms
  16-C

EARTH AND SPACE SCIENCE
- Properties of earth materials
  16-A through 16-Q

SCIENCE AND TECHNOLOGY
- Abilities of technological design
  16-N

- Understanding science and technology
  16-D and 16-E
  16-L

SCIENCE IN PERSONAL AND SOCIAL PERSPECTIVES
- Science and technology in local challenges
  16-E
  16-L

HISTORY AND NATURE OF SCIENCE
- Science as a human endeavor
  16-A through 16-E

LEVELS 5–8

UNIFYING CONCEPTS AND PROCESSES
- Systems, order and organization
  16-A through 16-Q
- Change, Consistency, Measurement
  16-A
  16-C through 16-E
  16-J
  16-L
  16-N
- Evidence, models and explanation
  16-A through 16-D
  16-F through 16-I
  16-L through 16-P

SCIENCE AS INQUIRY
- Abilities necessary to do and understand scientific inquiry
  16-A through 16-Q

PHYSICAL SCIENCE
- Properties and changes in properties of matter
  16-A through 16-D
  16-I through 16-N

- Motion and Forces
  16-F
  16-0
- Transfer of energy
  16-G and 16-H

LIFE SCIENCE
- Regulation and Behavior
  16-C
- Populations and Ecosystems
  16-A through 16-Q

EARTH AND SPACE SCIENCE
- Structure of the earth system
  16-A through 16-Q

SCIENCE AND TECHNOLOGY
- Abilities of technological design
  16-N
- Understanding Science and Technology
  16-D and 16-E
  16-L

SCIENCE IN PERSONAL AND SOCIAL PERSPECTIVES
- Natural hazards
  16-0
- Science and technology in society
  16-E
  16-L

HISTORY AND NATURE OF SCIENCE
- Science as human endeavor
  16-A through 16-E
- History of science
  16-P through 16-Q

What Would They *Sea?*

Suppose that a spaceship from another galaxy happened to come upon a heavenly body that looked as though it could support life. Before trying to land, the travelers would have to make sure it was safe.

Suppose they sent down electronic probes to check the composition and environment of the unknown body. After gathering all the data they could obtain, they might give the following description of the planet:

- The unknown planet consists mostly of a liquid that is seldom found anywhere else in the universe. The molecules of the liquid contain two atoms of hydrogen (which is plentiful in the universe) and one atom of oxygen (which is scarce).
- This liquid, H_2O, covers over 70% of the surface of the planet. The rest of the surface is mostly granite, with a thin covering of organic and inorganic matter.
- Careful collection of data shows that the temperature of the liquid ranges from a low of 0°C at the poles to a high of 33°C at the equator.
- The land surfaces show much greater extremes of temperature, ranging from a low of –75°C to a high of 50°C. Not only do the temperatures vary from one place to another, but they vary even at a given spot from one day to the next.
- All in all, the sharp temperature changes on land are likely to be quite hostile to life forms. Thus, it is our belief that the higher forms of life on this planet live in the abundant and favorable liquid, and the lower forms of life are forced to live on the scarcer, more-hostile land areas.

This imaginary report describes our own planet, as seen by aliens from another galaxy. Even though humans do not live in the more "favorable" ocean, many of the other findings are correct. Certainly the oceans *are* important to this planet.

First of all, there is more water than there is land. The oceans cover most of the earth's surface. Second, the oceans are deeper than the land is high. If the highest mountain were placed in the deepest part of the ocean, the tip of the mountain would still be covered with 2 kilometers of water.

The average depth of the oceans is 3600 meters. The average elevation of land areas is only 700 meters. (See figure 16.1.) The sizes and depths of the oceans are listed in table 16.1.

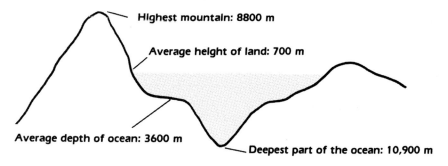

Highest mountain: 8800 m

Average height of land: 700 m

Average depth of ocean: 3600 m

Deepest part of the ocean: 10,900 m

FIGURE 16.1   A profile of the earth's surface is shown. It is clear that the oceans are a dominating feature of the globe.

TABLE 16.1

The Size and Depth of the Oceans

	Area (sq. km)	Average Depth (m)	Maximum Depth (m)
Pacific	166,000,000	4300	10,900
Atlantic	83,000,000	3900	9200
Indian	73,000,000	3960	8000
Arctic	13,000,000	1200	5000

Note: The water areas around the Antarctic are not a separate ocean. Instead, they are parts of the Pacific, Atlantic, and Indian Oceans.

Why Turn to the Ocean? (Events 16-A through 16-E)

Discrepant Events and Pupil Investigations

Event 16-A. The Appearing Salt #1

Dissolve about 35 grams of table salt in a liter of water. After it is completely dissolved (you may need to wait a while for the water to become clear), pour the contents into a shallow pan. Allow the water to evaporate, or heat gently to hasten the process. When the water is gone, inspect the pan. What do you find?

Pupil Investigations (may include the following processes):

1. Observing that the water is clear before it evaporates.
2. Discovering that a white residue forms as the liquid evaporates.
3. Identifying the residue as table salt.
4. Measuring the amount of salt that appears.
5. Generalizing that evaporation can be used to obtain salt from salt water.

Event 16-B. The Appearing Salt #2

Use the same solution of salt in water as described in the event above. Spread out a small drop of this solution on a slide and observe it under a microscope. Use a low power. What do you observe?

Pupil Investigations (may include the following processes):

1. Observing that the water is clear before it evaporates.
2. Discovering that small crystals form as the liquid evaporates.
3. Generalizing that the salt that appeared was originally in the water as an invisible solution.

Event 16-C. Seawater Gardening

Dissolve about 35 grams of table salt in a liter of water. Use this water to irrigate some young bean plants. Irrigate some additional bean plants with plain water. Compare the results after a few days.

Pupil Investigations (may include the following processes):

1. Recording the results of the experiment.
2. Observing that the salt water causes the plants to wilt and finally die.
3. Concluding that seawater is harmful to some plants.

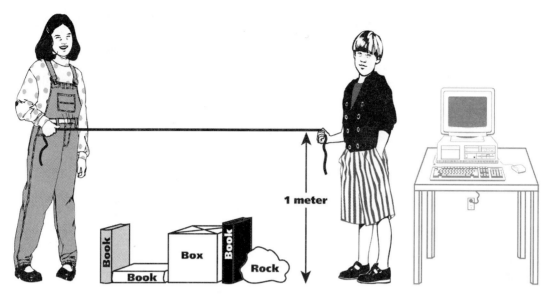

FIGURE 16.2   A setup for the imaginary ocean floor is shown.

Event 16-D. Freeze-Fresh Water

Dissolve about 35 grams of table salt in a liter of water. After it is fully dissolved, pour the clear water into an ice cube tray and place it into a freezer. Check after a few hours or the next day. What happens to the salt water?

Pupil Investigations (may include the following processes):

1. Recording the appearance of the water and ice in the ice cube tray at 30-minute intervals until the water is frozen.
2. Analyzing, by melting and evaporation, the salt content of several sections of clear ice.
3. Analyzing the unfrozen residue for its salt content.
4. Measuring the temperature of the ice.

Event 16-E. Deeper than Deep

Set up an imaginary ocean floor by using books, boxes, and other objects to simulate an irregular ocean floor. (See figure 16.2.) Have students stretch a string about 1 meter above the "ocean floor." Connect the necessary motion sensor devices to the computer and turn it on. (The motion detector is part of the CBLs or MBLs.) Move the motion detector slowly along the string to help keep the detector about the same height above the ocean. Record the data on a distance versus time graph.

Pupil Investigations (may include the following processes):

1. Interpreting the shape of the graph as corresponding to the height and shape of the objects on the floor.
2. Constructing an "ocean floor" to match a predesigned graph, then testing the match of the design.

Events 16-A through 16-E Explained in Context (Why Turn to the Ocean?)

Resources of the Oceans

The oceans are a great storehouse of resources. Not only that, their resources are constantly increasing. How? By collecting those that are draining off land areas.

Every time it rains and water runs off into a river, it carries with it some mineral resources from the land. Those resources finally reach the oceans. The oceans therefore contain all the minerals that have drained off the land since the beginning of time.

We can see that even clear water contains minerals by performing *Events 16-A and 16-B, The Appearing Salt (#1 and #2)*. The amount of salt that is mixed into the water is equal to the salt found in seawater. Seawater contains about 3.5% salt, equal to 35 grams per liter. When the water sample evaporates, the salt is left behind to be seen again. When a small drop of that water is placed on a slide and viewed through a microscope, you can see the actual formation of the salt crystals as the water evaporates.

At first, one might think that the ocean supplies only common salt. However, almost all minerals can be found as salts. Thus, just about any mineral that is found on land can also be found in the ocean.

How much does the ocean contain? The supply is almost limitless. See table 16.2 to find how many resources are contained in a cubic kilometer of ocean water.

This is truly an impressive list of resources. Of course, a cubic kilometer is a very large quantity. It would cover an area 10 kilometers long and 10 kilometers wide to a depth of 10 meters. The total resources of the ocean become even more impressive when we realize that there are about 1.4 billion cubic kilometers of water in the oceans.

Most of the resources remain untapped because it is too expensive to extract the minerals from them. Only a few substances such as common table salt (sodium chloride), magnesium, bromine, iodine, and some phosphorites are taken at the present time.

The oceans also supply some important nonmineral resources, such as food. Fish have been harvested from the ocean for centuries. In the future the

TABLE 16.2

Resources in One Cubic Kilometer of Ocean

Resource	Amount (metric tons)
Common salt	30,000,000.0
Magnesium	876,000.0
Calcium	432,000.0
Bromine	69,800.0
Carbon	28,000.0
Boron	4752.0
Fluorine	1296.0
Nitrogen	432.0
Gold	1.5

oceans are likely to take on greater and greater importance in supplying the world's supply of protein.

Another great nonmineral resource of the ocean is water—fresh water. Seawater is already being purified for use as drinking water in several parts of the world. However, it is still too costly to compete with most drinking water sources from the land. At present it is far too costly to convert seawater for use in agriculture.

Perform *Event 16-C, Seawater Gardening,* to see the effect of seawater on plants. The salt content of seawater is far too high to be used with most plant life. The salt will actually pull water *out of plants.* As a result, seawater will kill most plant life. (Of course, we are talking, about land plants. There are salt water plants ranging from plankton to seaweeds that do very well in salt water.)

One way of purifying water is to freeze it, as suggested in *Event 16-D, Freeze-Fresh Water.* When salt water freezes, it tends to form crystals of fairly pure ice. Some salt may be trapped between the crystals, but most of the salt collects as brine in unfrozen pools. So if ice is removed from the tray, melted, and evaporated, very little residue should remain. The brine, however, leaves lots of salt after it is evaporated.

Huge amounts of ice are found near the north and south poles of the earth. They represent vast quantities of freshwater. Many icebergs, several kilometers long and just as wide, float southward every year. A single iceberg—3 kilometers long, 2 kilometers wide, and 400 meters thick—contains enough pure water to supply the needs of 10 million people for a whole year.

The use of seawater for domestic and agricultural use will depend mostly on cost. At the present time, large irrigation projects supply 30 liters of freshwater at a cost that will purify only 1 liter of seawater. There are only a few places on Earth where pure water is so scarce that seawater is converted for domestic use.

Event 16-E, Deeper than Deep, demonstrates how scientists use sound to measure distances. Knowing how fast sound travels in water (adjusting for temperature), scientists measure how long it takes for sound to reflect back to the surface. The distance is calculated automatically from the speed and time. The motion sensor is based on recording reflected sound waves to determine distances.

The Motions of the Oceans (Events 16-F through 16-O)

Discrepant Events and Pupil Investigations

Event 16-F. Current Generator
Set up a fan so that it blows across across a large container of water. Sprinkle some sawdust or pepper on the water and observe.

Pupil Investigations (may include the following processes):
1. Observing that the fan blows away the surface of the water.
2. Diagramming the path of the water as traced by the sawdust or pepper. (It is a large circular path.)
3. Comparing the currents in the fan with currents in the oceans.

Event 16-G. Cold Currents

Mix some food coloring in water and freeze it in an ice cube tray. After the water is frozen, carefully lower a cube into a large, clear container of still water. Observe.

Pupil Investigations (may include the following processes):

1. Observing that colored bands flow down from the cube as it melts.
2. Diagramming the path of the flowing currents.
3. Inferring that cold water is heavier than warm water.
4. Generalizing that ocean currents can be caused by differences in temperature.

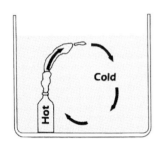

FIGURE 16.3 Hot water rises and cold water descends.

Event 16-H. Hot-Water Chimney

Fill a small bottle with hot water and some food coloring. Cover it with a one-hole stopper and slowly submerge the bottle into a large container of cold water. (See figure 16.3.)

Pupil Investigations (may include the following processes):

1. Observing that water rises from the small bottle.
2. Inferring that the warm water is lighter than the cold water.
3. Analyzing the circulation of water that takes place in the container.

Event 16-I. Floating Eggs

Lower an egg into a beaker of water. Does it sink or float? Now add several tablespoons of salt. Mix carefully and thoroughly. What happens?

Pupil Investigations (may include the following processes):

1. Observing that the egg floats after the salt is mixed into the water.
2. Inferring that salt increases the density of water.
3. Generalizing that the saltiness of ocean water is a factor in causing currents.

Event 16-J. Deep Drafts

Assume that you are the captain of a ship steaming across an ocean. Suppose that you were asked to stop at a harbor located some distance upstream on a large river and that passage was safe only for ships with a draft of no more than 6 meters. Your ship is loaded so that its draft is exactly 5.9 meters. Could you make the trip up the river?

Pupil Investigations (may include the following processes):

1. Forming a theory (incorrectly) that the ship's draft could clear the river bottom by 0.1 meter.
2. Investigating with a hydrometer to see if it sinks to different levels in freshwater and in seawater.
3. Generalizing that ships float at different levels depending on the density of water.

Event 16-K. Saline Currents

Set up an arrangement of four bottles as shown in figure 16.4. Mix food coloring into the two lower bottles. To invert a bottle without spilling, hold an index card or sheet of durable paper against the mouth of the bottle.

Be sure that the top bottle of one pair and the lower bottle of the other pair contain salt water. After the bottles are inverted, carefully slip out the index cards from between the bottles. Observe.

Pupil Investigations (may include the following processes):

1. Discovering that the colored water mixes with the clear water in one pair of bottles but not the other.
2. Investigating and finding no temperature differences between bottles.
3. Inferring that the mixing is caused by a difference in densities of the liquids.

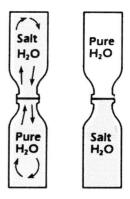

FIGURE 16.4 The colored water mixes in one pair of bottles but not in the other. How does the salt water affect the circulation in the bottles?

Event 16-L. Straw Hydrometer

Seal one end of a plastic straw with a lump of clay. Pour in enough sand so that the straw floats fairly low in a container of warm freshwater, as shown in figure 16.5. Mark the point on the straw that is exactly level with the surface of the water. Now float the straw in cold water. What do you find? Try also warm and cold salt water.

Pupil Investigations (may include the following processes):

1. Demonstrating that the hydrometer floats higher in water that is cold and salty than in water that is warm and fresh.
2. Inferring that water density increases when water becomes cold or more saline.
3. Forming a theory about the effect of salinity and temperature on the formation of currents.

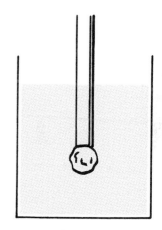

Event 16-M. Dancing Raisins

Put five or six raisins into a beaker of water. Select raisins that will sink. Mix in a small amount of baking soda and vinegar with the water. Observe.

FIGURE 16.5 A plastic straw plugged with clay makes a simple hydrometer. Compare the densities of salt water and pure water at different temperatures.

Pupil Investigations (may include the following processes):

1. Observing that the raisins sink to the bottom of the beaker when first added to the water.
2. Discovering that shortly after the vinegar and baking soda is added, the raisins rise to the top, and then abruptly sink again.
3. Discovering that the rising and sinking cycles continue again and again.
4. Forming a theory about what makes the raisins rise and sink.

Event 16-N. Penny in the Pool

Would the water level of a pool rise if you tossed a penny into it? Yes, ever so slightly. Would the level rise if you tossed the penny into a boat that was floating in the pool? Yes, again, ever so slightly.

In which of the two ways would you cause the water to rise the most: (1) tossing the penny directly into the pool or (2) tossing the penny into a boat (that is floating in the pool)?

Pupil Investigations (may include the following processes):

1. Experimenting with floating objects and weights to compare the amounts of water displaced by each of the two methods described in the problem.
2. Generalizing that the event pertains to the concepts of density and buoyancy.
3. Comparing the amount of water displaced by (1) the volume of a penny and (2) the weight of a penny.

Event 16-O. Tiny Tides

Go outside to do this event. Ask several pupils to carry a shallow tray filled with water. Ask them to carry it for 5 to 10 meters as carefully as possible without spilling. If the tray is shallow and about 30 centimeters by 20 centimeters (or more), it will be almost impossible to carry without spilling some water. How does this activity relate to the formation of tides in some parts of the world? (Note: Have pupils do this event only if they can carry the trays easily and away from their bodies. Otherwise, it is likely that some of the water will spill on their clothes.)

Pupil Investigations (may include the following processes):

1. Observing that a very small motion can produce a large effect with the water.
2. Performing the activity to find how difficult it is to walk without spilling the water.
3. Comparing the water in the tray with the water in a tidal basin.

Events 16-F through 16-O Explained in Context (Motions of the Oceans)

It is doubtful that anyone has ever seen the surface of the ocean perfectly still. Even when sailing ships of ancient times were becalmed on windless days, the ocean was covered with gentle swells that rocked the ships from side to side. It is certainly true that the oceans are in constant motion.

There are at least three types of motions: (1) **currents,** (2) **tides,** and (3) **waves.** In addition, a fourth type, a **tsunami** (or tidal wave), also occurs from time to time. We will look at these types of motion separately.

Ocean Currents

Look at a map showing the major ocean currents. You will see that almost the entire ocean surface is affected by currents of one kind or another. (See figure 16.6.)

As early as 1770 Benjamin Franklin drew charts of the Gulf Stream, which flows from the Gulf of Mexico to the northern tip of Norway. It is a broad stream that flows at speeds up to 5 and 6 kilometers per hour in some places, and carries a volume of water that is probably a thousand times greater than the Mississippi River.

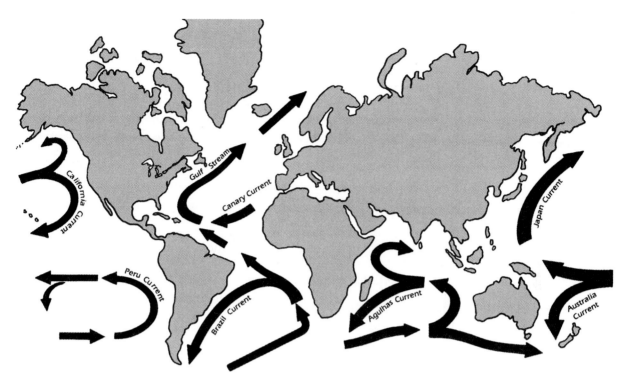

FIGURE 16.6   The major currents of the oceans.

Why is there such a current in the ocean? One of the causes is wind. A prevailing wind will tend to drive water ahead of it; and if it blows over a long enough area for a long enough time, a current will be created. A miniature wind-driven current can be seen by performing *Event 16-F, Current Generator.*

When the fan is set up to blow across the large tray, it pushes water ahead of it. The moving water begins to circulate. The current can be seen better if sawdust or pepper is sprinkled on the water.

In addition to wind, there are some other factors that cause ocean currents. Differences in temperature, for example, will cause a movement of water. *Event 16-G, Cold Currents,* and *Event 16-H, Hot-Water Chimney,* both show the effects of temperature differences. The events show that cold water descends and warm water rises. The temperature difference starts the water moving, and it gains a momentum that sets up a circulation pattern.

It should be noted that for Event 16-H to work successfully, the bottle must be small enough so that it is well below the surface of the water. Also, some care must be taken not to disturb the water too much when the bottle is placed carefully on the bottom of the larger container.

Temperatures vary widely in the oceans. The hottest water in the seas or oceans is in Elphinstone Inlet in the Persian Gulf, where surface temperatures reach 32°C. On the other extreme, the coldest temperatures are found at the poles where the saline water reaches 3°C below zero before it freezes. (Note: Pure water freezes at 0°C, but salt water does not.)

Given these temperature differences, in what parts of the world would you expect the water to rise and where would you expect it to descend? Since cold water descends, you can expect that the icy polar waters flow slowly along the ocean floor toward the equator. Even at the equator the water at the ocean floor is no more than 4°C.

The warm equatorial waters, by contrast, constantly move along the surface toward the poles. As the icy waters settle, they are replaced by the warmer currents slowly moving toward the poles.

A third important factor affects an ocean current. That factor is **salinity.** When water evaporates, it leaves behind water that is saltier than normal. And, if everything else is equal, the saltier the water, the heavier it is.

The saltiest water is located near the equator and at the poles. At the equator, hot weather speeds up evaporation so that the waters become more saline. The Red Sea has a salt content of 4% instead of the 3 1/2% that is common in the oceans.

The ocean at the poles is also more salty than average. That is because when ice freezes it takes freshwater from the ocean and leaves the salt behind. The high salt content plus the cold produces the densest waters in all the oceans.

The effect of salt on water density can be shown by doing the next three events. *Event 16-I, Floating Eggs,* shows that when salt is added to the water, its density increases to a point where it will make the egg float.

Event 16-J, Deep Drafts, is somewhat similar to the floating egg event. However, instead of the egg we have a ship. In which case will the object sink lower, in freshwater or in salt water? Even though the ship rides high enough in the salt water, the ship would sink too low in the freshwater of the river. The captain cannot take the ship up the river.

Event 16-K, Saline Currents, is the best of the activities to show how salt water can cause currents. When the index card is pulled from between the bottles, they mix on one side but not the other.

The mixing occurs on the side where the salt water is placed in the top bottle. The salt water descends because it is heavier. The water does not mix in the other pair of bottles because *the heavier salt water is already on the bottom.*

In a small way, *Event 16-L, Straw Hydrometer,* is somewhat like two earlier events. A **hydrometer** is actually an instrument that measures the density of water. However, it works just like the ship and egg. It floats high in the water when the water is salty and lower when the water is fresh.

In discussing the density of water and the floating level of a ship, we are really talking about **buoyancy,** Buoyancy refers to the upward, or lifting force, exerted on an object in the water. If the object floats, the lifting force is obviously greater than the downward force of gravity.

In the events with the hydrometer, ship, and egg, we see that freshwater has less of an upward, or lifting, force than salt water. In other words, freshwater is less buoyant than salt water.

We can see a dramatic example of buoyancy and gravity in *Event 16-M, Dancing Raisins.* If you have selected raisins that sink in freshwater (most raisins will), the addition of vinegar and baking soda will start a lifting and sinking cycle that will continue for many minutes.

The reason the raisins sink is simple: Their gravity (or downward force) is greater than buoyancy (the upward force). However, when the baking soda and vinegar are added, a chemical reaction occurs that will produce many tiny bubbles of carbon dioxide. When these bubbles form on the raisins, it increases their buoyancy, and helps lift the raisins to the surface. Once on the surface,

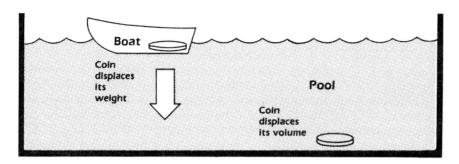

FIGURE 16.7   Toss a penny into a pool and a penny into a boat (floating in the pool). Which coin causes the water level to rise the most?

the bubbles burst, and the raisins sink to the bottom again. Then, the whole cycle starts over again. The "dancing" continues until the effect of the vinegar and baking soda is exhausted.

Think about buoyancy in *Event 16-N, Penny in the Pool.* Is there a difference in the water level depending on whether the penny is tossed directly into the pool or into the boat (floating in the pool)? The answer is yes, there is a difference. The water rises more if the penny is tossed into the boat.

Why the difference? The penny displaces very little water. It sinks and most of its weight just pushes against the bottom. The weight that pushes against the bottom does not displace any water. If the penny goes into the boat, however, its entire weight (spread out along the bottom of the boat} is offset by water that is pushed aside, thus raising the level of the water in the pool.

A way to summarize the problem is to state that when tossed into the pool, the penny displaces very little of its weight (only its volume), but when tossed into the boat; the penny displaces its entire weight. (See figure 16.7.)

Tides

A second form of motion in the ocean is caused by the influence of the sun and moon. The gravity of the sun and moon attract the water, which is pulled up by as much as a meter in the wide expanses of the ocean. This attraction or pulling of the water is called a *tide.*

If the tidal action is no greater in the middle of the ocean than 1 meter, what causes the far-greater tides that are so often seen along the shorelines of the great oceans? The answer to that question is somewhat more complex but can be partially explained by performing *Event 16-O, Tiny Tides.*

There is no tide that affects the water in the tray, but it is still hard to keep the water from spilling. What happens is that a small motion is started in the tray and, once going, is not easy to stop. The water moves against the rim and sloshes up and over.

In somewhat the same way, a rather gentle motion of ½ to 1 meter in the vast expanse of ocean starts something that does not stop abruptly when it hits the shoreline. Instead, the water "sloshes" ashore in tides that often reach 2 to 4 meters, and in the Bay of Fundy (between New Brunswick and Nova Scotia) they reach an incredible 15 meters.

Tides are greatest when the sun and moon are in line and "pull together" with their combined gravity. Those tides are called **spring tides.** When the moon and sun are at right angles, their effects are divided to produce comparatively low **neap tides.**

Air pressure also influences tides. When air pressure is low, as in a storm, water rushes in to "fill the vacuum." Tides will sometimes rise as much as a meter because of extreme changes in air pressure.

The greatest storm ever recorded in this country occurred in 1969, when Hurricane Camille hit the mainland from the Gulf of Mexico. The low pressure and 300-kilometer winds drove the water of the gulf 10 meters above its normal level, causing 256 deaths and destroying several coastal cities in Mississippi and Louisiana.

Wave Motion

Waves are caused by the action of winds. When there is a wind, the first waves are very short, steep-angled, and choppy. If the wind keeps blowing, the waves get bigger. If there is an expanse of ocean that is long enough, and if the wind keeps on blowing, the waves can keep on growing for days. During storms, ocean waves sometimes reach a height of 15 meters.

Time and distance are the two factors that influence the size of waves. As a result, waves on small lakes are almost always small and choppy. As the lake gets larger, so do the waves.

Ocean waves, once formed, keep on going for thousands of kilometers. They fan out from storms and travel far across the ocean to hit distant coastlines days later.

As the waves move across the ocean, they gradually change. The crests become smoother, and the waves move farther apart from each other.

We can actually determine how far away the waves originated by measuring the time between crests as they pass a given point. For example, when waves come ashore every 5 to 7 seconds, the storm that caused them was quite close. When they arrive every 7 to 10 seconds, the source was 300 to 400 km away. At 11 to 15 seconds, the storm was 1500 to 3000 km away, and at 13 to 20 seconds, the storm that caused them was 5000 to 7000 km away.

Tsunami (Tidal Wave)

A fourth motion of the ocean is called *tsunami* or tidal wave. (The name *tidal wave* is somewhat misleading because the motion has nothing to do with the tides.)

The tsunami, or tidal wave, is a great water wave caused by a major underwater disturbance such as an earthquake. The wave will travel across thousands of kilometers of ocean with little effect until it hits a coastline. There, it can crash ashore and cause millions of dollars of damage.

On the high seas the wave cannot even be detected except with the most sensitive of equipment. Even though the wave travels at speeds of 600 to 900 kilometers per hour, the crests are often about 500 to 600 kilometers apart. Since the size of the wave is only about 20 to 30 centimeters, it means that it will take almost an hour for the wave to lift and lower a ship by about 20 to 30 centimeters.

When the wave reaches the coast, however, it can form a breaker of gigantic proportions. Remember the activity in which you tried to walk with a shallow pan? Once the water in the pan began to move, it tended to slosh over the sides. The same is true of a tsunami, only more so. Once the water is in motion, it keeps on moving. A tsunami can cause great damage to a shoreline when it hits.

Living under the Sea (Events 16-P and 16-Q)

Discrepant Events and Pupil Investigations

Event 16-P. Underwater Distances

Tie a weight to each of several corks to hold them underwater in an aquarium. Arrange them near the side of the aquarium at various depths, as shown in figure 16.8. Be sure that all the corks are completely underwater. In fact, the corks should all be well below the surface.

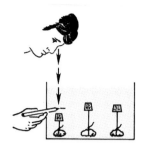

FIGURE 16.8   Look straight down into the aquarium and mark the glass where the corks appear to be. Why is the view different from the side?

Now look straight down from the top through the water at the cork. Then, without moving your head, make a mark on the glass with a grease pencil to indicate the height of the corks. To review: Look at the cork *through the water*, and make a mark on the glass by looking at the pencil *through the air*.

When completed, step to the side and compare the corks with the marks. Were they accurate?

Pupil Investigations (may include the following processes):

1. Discovering that the pencil marks are always above the actual heights of the corks.
2. Observing that the discrepancies become greater as the depth increases.
3. Forming a theory that water affects our perception of distance.

Event 16-Q. Fading Colors

Suppose a diver wearing a white swimsuit dives to a depth of 80 meters and notices that the color of his suit has changed from white to blue. How do you account for the change in color?

Pupil Investigations (may include the following processes):

1. Inferring (incorrectly) that the algae had stained the diving suit.
2. Generalizing that colors are selectively filtered out as the depth increases.
3. Comparing the color change to the changes observed in the unit on light.

Events 16-P and 16-Q Explained in Context (Living under the Sea)

Humans became interested in the underwater world many years ago. It is believed that as early as: 300 B.C. Alexander the Great viewed the wonders of the marine world from a large submerged diving bell. It was not until recent times, however, that serious attempts were made to actually live in underwater stations for days and weeks at a time.

One of the problems of diving under the ocean's surface is the pressure that builds up as you go down. It takes only a depth of 10 meters to equal the pressure of all the air pushing down on the earth.

At sea level the air pressure is referred to as *1 atmosphere.* At 10 meters the pressure is 2 atmospheres; at 20 meters, 3 atmospheres; and so on.

Because of the extreme pressures, humans are restricted mostly to fairly shallow depths. In some unusual cases, however, long-term labs have been set up at depths of 60 meters, where divers have lived for weeks at a time, inside (and outside) of living quarters that were open to the great pressures of the sea.

TABLE 16.3

Underwater Pressures

Depth (meter)	Pressure (atmosphere)	Comments
	1	
	2	No bends above 10 meters; red light limit
		Orange light limit
	3	Oxygen poisoning begins at 20 meters
30	4	
	5	Blue light limit
	6	Normal skindiving limit (50 meters)
		"Nitrogen narcosis" begins (55 meters)
60	7	Sea Lab II (62 meters)
		Yellow light limit
	8	
	9	Green light limit
90	10	Maximum momentary depth for air-breathing skindivers (100 meters)
	11	
	12	Maximum depth for hard-hat divers (125 meters)
120	13	Oxygen is only 2% of breathing mixture
	15	Depth limit for successful swim away from crippled submarine (145 meters)
150	16	
	17	
	18	
180	19	Average depth of continental shelf
	20	
	21	
210	22	
	23	
	24	
240	25	
	26	
	27	
270	28	
	29	
	30	⅔ of 1% of breathing mixture is oxygen
300	31	Keller and Small set scuba diving record (Keller died)

In general, the deeper the depth, the shorter the time that can be survived. Table 16.3 shows pressures, depths, and related information.

In addition to the great pressures there are a number of other problems that must be met when trying to function in deep water. Lack of visibility is often a major concern.

Even in clear water, vision is distorted because objects seem closer than they really are. Even using the very shallow depth of *Event 16-P, Underwater Distances,* it should be obvious that the objects seem closer when viewed through the water than when viewed through the air.

Another factor that impairs vision is the filtering effect of water on color. If you go deep enough, no light gets there at all, so everything is totally black. But even where the light is still visible, the view becomes color-distorted.

Sunlight that enters the water has light that contains all the colors of the spectrum. However, the water soon filters out the colors, one color at a time. Red light is gone within the first 5 to 10 meters. Orange light goes no deeper than 18 meters; yellow, 60 meters; and blue 75, meters.

Thus, the problem posed in *Event 16-Q, Fading Colors,* is answered by the fact that no other light reached down to the depth of the diver. Even though the diving suit was white (which reflects all colors), it could reflect only the color that it received: blue.

In many cases light will penetrate even less if water is not crystal clear. Most waters are clouded with microscopic plants and animals, which blot out the sunlight at much shallower depths.

Combining Assessment with Instruction

Have students brainstorm how the ocean serves as a resource and/or interconnects with our everyday lives. Students may mention such topics as:

- water supply,
- food supply,
- recreation,
- weather,
- storage of the sun's energy,
- "roadway" between continents,
- pollution.

After sufficient time, let students select an area either individually or as a small team so that each reasonable idea is assigned to at least one person/group. Students are to write a report or poem, build a model, or make a map or diorama that will help present their topic to the class.

Sites and Software

The following websites and software are appropriate to use with this chapter. Note that computer software and websites change rapidly. This makes it necessary to investigate the stable websites for new links and software catalogs for updates: Visit www.mhhe.com/friedl6e to link to these directly and for study resources.

Sites

Kids Corner NOAA	www.yoto98.noaa.gov
Science Gems: Earth Science	www.sciencegems.com
Learning Web (USGS)	www.usgs.gov/education/ learnweb
Earth Science	www.scicentral.com
Ocean Planet and Jason Project	seawifs.gsfc.nasa.gov
Earth's Heat Budget	www.oceansonline.com/ heat.htm
Welcome to the Remarkable Ocean World	www.oceansonline.com

Software

A Field Trip into the Sea (InView/Sunburst) (4–8)
The Great Ocean Rescue (Tom Snyder) (5–8)
Magic School Bus Explores the Ocean (Microsoft Home) (1–5)
Ocean Planet Smithsonian (Discovery) (5–15)

Key Terms

buoyancy, *312*

currents, *310*

hydrometer, *312*

neap tides, *314*

salinity, *312*

spring tides, *313*

tides, *310*

tsunami, *310*

waves, *310*

Teaching Children about Energy, Environment, and Pollution

NATIONAL SCIENCE EDUCATION STANDARDS ALIGNMENT TO EVENTS

The events in this chapter help accomplish several of the NSES for content. The event(s) that align with a given content standard are listed below that standard.

LEVELS K–4

UNIFYING CONCEPTS AND PROCESSES
- Systems, order and organization
  17-F through 17-M
  17-O through 17-Q
- Change, Consistency, Measurement
  17-C and 17-D
  17-N
  17-G through 17-I
  17-M
- Evidence, models and explanation
  17-A and 17-B
  17-F through 17-I
  17-M and 17-N

PHYSICAL SCIENCE
- Properties of objects and materials
  17-C and 17-D

LIFE SCIENCE
- Organisms and Environments
  17-C through 17-E
  17-I through 17-L

EARTH SCIENCE
- Changes in earth and sky
  17-C through 17-E

SCIENCE AND TECHNOLOGY
- Understanding science and technology
  17-A through 17-C
  17-M through 17-Q

SCIENCE IN PERSONAL AND SOCIAL PERSPECTIVES
- Personal health
  17-C through 17-E
  17-I through 17-L
- Types of resources
  17-F through 17-J
  17-M through 17-Q

- Science and technology in local challenges
  17-A and 17-B
  17-I and 17-J

HISTORY AND NATURE OF SCIENCE
- Science as a human endeavor
  17-A and 17-B
  17-J through 17-L
  17-M through 17-Q

LEVELS 5–8

UNIFYING CONCEPTS AND PROCESSES
- Systems, order and organization
  17-F through 17-M
  17-O through 17-Q
- Change, Consistency, Measurement
  17-C and 17-D
  17-N
  17-G through 17-I
  17-M
- Evidence, models and explanation
  17-A and 17-B
  17-F through 17-I
  17-M and 17-N

PHYSICAL SCIENCE
- Properties and changes in properties of matter
  17-C and 17-D
- Transfer of energy
  17-F through 17-Q

LIFE SCIENCE
- Regulation and Behavior
  17-C through 17-Q

- Populations and Ecosystems
  17-A through 17-Q

EARTH SCIENCE
- Structure of earth systems
  17-C through 17-E
- Earth's history
  17-C through 17-E

SCIENCE AND TECHNOLOGY
- Understanding science and technology
  17-A through 17-C
  17-M through 17-Q

SCIENCE IN PERSONAL AND SOCIAL PERSPECTIVES
- Personal health
  17-C through 17-E
  17-I through 17-L
- Populations, resources, and environments
  17-A through 17-Q
- Natural hazards
  17-C through 17-E
  17-I through 17-L
- Risks and Benefits
  17-A through 17-Q
- Science and technology in society
  17-A through 17-Q

HISTORY AND NATURE OF SCIENCE
- Science as a human endeavor
  17-A and 17-B
  17-J through 17-L
  17-M through 17-Q
- History of science
  17-F through 17-Q

In this chapter we look at some issues that are often discussed in the classroom. As issues, they are more than just traditional science facts. They also affect opinions and attitudes. As a result, special care should be taken to assure an unbiased presentation.

Yet, how can an unbiased presentation be accomplished? Frankly, it is difficult, especially considering the importance that is given to some of these issues in the news. Nevertheless, we will try to present some suggestions for handling the topics objectively.

One effective technique is to have students answer short surveys about some of the issues. Their responses can be compared with national figures, and the items become a basis for classroom discussion.

What Is Energy?

Most books give a definition of **energy** as "the ability to do work." Often the topic is broken down into such subtopics as heat energy, sound energy, light energy, and so on. In this chapter, however, we talk about the energy needed to produce our goods and services.

In fact, the first step is to define energy. What is energy?

Energy is *food*.
Energy is *clothing*.
Energy is *shelter*.
Energy is *heating* in winter and
cooling in summer.
Energy is *transportation*.

Let us look at each of the benefits of energy in more detail.

How Can Energy Be Defined as Food?

Have you ever tried to raise vegetables in your garden? Did you do the weeding, watering, fertilizing, and debugging of the plants? Did you dig up the soil with a spade or shovel? How big a garden can you maintain using only muscle energy?

It is unlikely that many school children have ever tilled a garden of substantial size. However, many may have raised a few carrots or radishes. They may also have dug into the turf enough times to learn that it is almost impossible to dig up an entire garden using only muscle energy.

Ask the children to check their neighborhoods. They will find that those who used only muscle energy have *very* small gardens—often no larger than the size of a table or two. Ask the children how long they could survive if they depended entirely on their own muscles for growing food. Not very long.

With a power tiller, however, the energy of gasoline is used to till a much larger area much more quickly. With even larger equipment, a farmer tills an area that is enormous in comparison. In the United States each farmer grows enough food to feed 50 or more people.

U.S. farmers are such good producers of food that only 2% of the working population is involved in growing food. That means that 98% of the population can be busy producing other things.

The situation elsewhere is quite different. Worldwide, two-thirds of the population is engaged in the full-time production of food. Thus, only one-third of the world's population is free to produce other things. As a general rule, the greater the percentage of people who produce food, the poorer the country.

Look at references such as *The World Almanac,* or the *World Factbook,* commonly sold in supermarkets. The World Bank provides an online database. You will find that the poorest countries are those with the greatest percent of the workforce in agriculture. For example, in a recent year the 10 countries with the highest percentage of workers in agriculture (84%) had an annual income of less than $300 per person. In contrast, the 10 countries with the lowest percentage (1.7%) of workers in agriculture had an annual income of more than $31,000 per person.

If we depended on our muscle energy alone to produce food, many of us would starve. With the use of energy and machines, however, food is plentiful. That is why we can say that energy is food.

How Can Energy Be Defined as Clothing?

How many people are wearing clothes made entirely by muscle energy? How many sheared the sheep, cleaned the wool, carded it, spun it into yarn, and then knitted the clothing . . . all by hand? Very few.

If you wear cotton clothing, did you plant the cotton, tend it, pick it, clean it, spin it into yarn, and weave it into cloth? Did you then make the clothes you wear? Even those who do their own sewing are using electrical energy for running the sewing machine and are using cloth spun and woven on big machines in factories. Thus, the "handwork" covers only the final "assembly" of the product, not the production of the basic materials that are needed. That is why we can say that energy is clothing.

How Can Energy Be Defined as Shelter?

How many people live in homes in which all the work was done with muscle energy? How many went into the woods to chop down trees, hauled them to the building site, and built a home? It is unlikely anyone in this country is living in a home built entirely with muscle energy. How many people would have shelter if they needed to depend only on their muscles? Very few. That is why we can say energy is shelter.

How Can Energy Be Defined as Heating or Cooling?

Can you imagine what winter would be like without heat? Most of the heat for homes is provided by fuel oil and natural gas. Before those resources were available, people used mostly coal; and prior to coal, wood. Without heat much of the world would be too cold to live in during the winter months.

To a lesser degree, we can make some of the same claims about cooling. Some parts of the countries have oppressive heat during the hottest summer months. Dallas, Texas, for example has an average July high of 97°F. In addition, it is almost always very humid, resulting in exposure that is labeled dangerous by the weather bureau. Phoenix, Arizona, has an average July high of 106°F. With its usual very low humidity, however, it is actually less dangerous than the Dallas weather.

In almost all areas with long months of oppressive heat, most commercial buildings, office buildings, churches, schools, and homes are air-conditioned. That is why we can say energy is heating and cooling.

How Can Energy Be Defined as Transportation?

Have you ever made a trip across the state or across the country? Would that trip have been possible if you had to rely on your own muscles to get you there? We are so accustomed to modern transportation that we do not appreciate how vital it really is. We cannot imagine what things would be like without it.

One way to appreciate modern transportation is to look briefly at transportation in pioneer times. For example, in the early 1800s a survey team left Connecticut for Ohio, for the purpose of surveying the land in the newly opened frontier. They left Connecticut on January 1 and arrived at their Ohio destination in mid April. Walking and carrying equipment, even with help of mules and horses is a slow process, especially if there are no roads to follow. Now, that same trip can be done comfortably by car in 1 day, or by plane in a few hours. That is why we can say energy is transportation.

In a unit on energy, the pupils should realize that muscle energy is too weak to produce many of the necessities of life. If we depended entirely on our muscles to produce food, most of us would starve. Likewise, if we depended on our muscles for clothing or shelter, most of us would freeze.

Energy is needed for the production of goods. If energy is expensive, then food, clothing, and shelter will be expensive. If energy is scarce, then food, clothing, and shelter will be scarce.

What are the major sources of energy? They are (1) petroleum (oil), (2) natural gas, (3) coal, (4) nuclear, and (5) waterpower. (All other sources combined, such as wind, solar, geothermal, and others, produce less than 1% of the energy used in this country.)

How Opinions Change (Events 17-A and 17-B)

Discrepant Events and Pupil Investigations

Event 17-A. Opinion Survey

Give pupils the survey shown in table 17.1. **Directions:** The exercises in this survey are followed by several suggested answers. Mark the space representing your choice.

Pupil Investigations (may include the following processes):

In this event, the processes are inherent in taking the survey and include comparing, analyzing, interpreting, concluding, predicting, and perhaps also suspending judgment while awaiting further data.

Event 17-B. Build a Power Plant

This event has two parts. In Part 1, pupils fill in table 17.2, Build a Power Plant. Ask pupils to act like directors of a power company. They are to build a new power plant. What energy source should they use? Assume that five sources (coal, natural gas, nuclear, oil, and waterpower) are equally available and that they should evaluate the environmental problems in making their choices. Place table 17.2 on the chalkboard and fill in responses from the class. (**Note:** 1. Mark *yes* if it is a problem and is hard to control. Mark *no* if it is not a problem or it is easy to control. Place a question mark (?) if people differ widely; you might tell them to decide in their own minds how they would consider it.)

TABLE 17.1

Opinion Survey: How Much Do You Agree or Disagree with Each of the Following Statements?

	Strongly Agree	Moderately Agree	Moderately Disagree	Strongly Disagree
1. Coal mining should be limited to the underground to protect the environment from strip mining.				
2. More dams should be built to generate electricity even if they will cover scenic wonderlands and wildlife areas.				
3. To save gasoline, the government should tax cars that do not get good gas mileage.				
4. The government should offer tax incentives to people who make their homes energy-efficient (weatherizing, insulating, etc.)				
5. You should be forced to help pay to insulate your neighbor's house.				

Source: Some items are taken from *Energy: Knowledge and Attitudes*, 1978, by the National Assessment of Education Progress [NAEP], a project of the Education Commission of the States.

TABLE 17.2

Build a Power Plant

Pollution Problems	Coal	Natural Gas	Nuclear	Oil	Waterpower
Smoke	Yes	No	No	No	No
Noxious gases	Yes	Yes	No	Yes	No
Carbon dioxide	Yes	Yes	No	Yes	No
Thermal	Yes	Yes	Yes	Yes	No
Radiation	No	No	?	No	No
To obtain	Strip mines	Pipe lines	—	Pipe lines	Lake
Other					

Note: The responses in this table are typical of most classes. Your class may be different.

When table 17.2 is filled in and the energy sources have been thoroughly discussed, ask pupils to rank their choices from 1 to 5 (with 1 being their first choice). Tabulate the votes on the chalkboard using a form such as table 17.3.

Pupil Investigations (may include the following processes):

In this event, the processes are inherent in responding to the activity. The processes include comparing, analyzing, interpreting, concluding, predicting, and perhaps also suspending judgment while awaiting further data.

TABLE 17.3

Responses to Survey

Rank	Coal	Natural Gas	Nuclear	Oil	Waterpower
1	0	1	1	0	28
2	0	15	11	2	2
3	1	10	10	9	0
4	6	4	2	18	0
5	23	0	6	1	0

Note: The responses shown in this table are typical of most classes. Your class may be different.

Events 17-A and 17-B Explained in Context (How Opinions Change)

Most elementary pupils like to "vote" on things. Thus, they are likely to enjoy the opinion survey on energy, environment, and pollution.

How should teachers treat topics like these? It is obvious that energy, environment; and pollution are not just abstract scientific concepts. They also involve opinions and attitudes. How can we respect opinions and still strive for facts?

One of the most important lessons to be taught is that opinions are surprisingly fragile. As a matter of fact, in *Event 17-A, Opinion Survey,* it is likely that pupils will contradict themselves. Their responses will often depend not so much on the issue, but on how the item is worded. Thus, the phrasing of items or questions will often *form* and *shape* opinions, instead of just gathering them.

Here are results found in typical college classes involving hundreds of prospective teachers. The items are presented with an alternative form. The first three items are essentially similar except for the endings, which give a sharply different "feel" to them. Item 4 is an alternative form of item 5.

1. Coal mining should be limited to the underground . . .
   a. to protect the environment from mining. (53% favored)
   b. even if thousands of miners will die of black-lung disease. (92% opposed)
2. More dams should be built to generate electricity . . .
   a. even if they cover scenic wonderlands and wildlife areas. (69.9% opposed)
   b. especially if they will create scenic wonderlands and wildlife areas. (72% favored)
3. To save gasoline, the government should tax cars . . .
   a. that do not get good gas mileage. (65% favored)
   b. designed for use by large families. (96% opposed)
4. The government should offer tax incentives to people who make their homes energy efficient (weatherizing, insulating, etc.). (85% favored)
5. You should be forced to help pay to insulate your neighbor's house. (91% opposed)

Compare items 4 and 5. At first glance these are two different items. However, a second look shows that they are actually alike. Note that the word "incentives" in item 4 gives the impression of voluntary action. However, it refers to taxes which are compulsory, and if not paid, will result in the same "force" as described in item 5.

Look further at item 2 of *Event 17-A, Opinion Survey,* pertaining to water-power. If the question is phrased to show that it will *cover* scenic areas, people are opposed to it. If phrased to show that it will *create* scenic areas, they favor it. Also, compare the responses of that item to those obtained in *Event 17-B, Build a Power Plant.* Typical college classes voted overwhelmingly in favor of waterpower as the first choice. Your class will very likely do the same. You can then ask them: "If you really liked waterpower that much, why didn't you vote for it in item 2 of Event 17-A?" Students will often not realize until that moment that they have contradicted themselves.

In any lessons on energy, environment, and pollution, biases can easily creep in. It is important for pupils to know how easily their opinions can be affected by the words used in the survey items. That knowledge is likely to help them reserve judgment when these issues are discussed and helps them guard against jumping to conclusions.

Acid Rain (Events 17-C through 17-E)

Discrepant Events and Pupil Investigations

Event 17-C. Investigating pH

Connect the pH probe to the computer and take the pH readings of each of the the following: baking soda, clear soda pop (7-Up), lemon juice, detergent, ammonia, drain cleaner, and vinegar. Fifty milliliters (mL) of each solution will be needed. **Note:** The teacher should demonstrate reading the pH of the drain cleaner since it is somewhat dangerous to handle. Always wear safety glasses when handling chemicals. After each reading is taken using the pH probe, use red cabbage juice as an acid-base indicator. Place 2 to 3 mL of baking soda solution into a test tube labeled #1. Place 2 to 3 mL of the remaining household solutions into one each of the #2 to #7 test tubes. Add an equal amount of red cabbage juice indicator to each.

Pupil Investigations (may include the following processes):

1. Observing and recording any color change to the solutions.
2. Generalizing that pH above 7 turns the cabbage juice shades of bluegreen to yellow-green.
3. Generalizing that pH below 7 turns the cabbage juice shades of blue-pink to red-pink.
4. Testing local pond water and rain water to determine the pH of each.
5. Comparing and contrasting the accuracy and ease of use of a pH indicator versus a pH probe.

Event 17-D. Pollution and pH

Connect the pH probe to the computer and measure, the pH of dilute sulfuric acid (H_2SO_4) and that of carbonic acid (H_2CO_3). (**Caution:** Sulfuric acid can cause burns. Do not put it in contact with skin or clothing. Avoid inhaling its vapors.) Disconnect the pH probes from the computer. Place a small amount of marble chips and limestone into each of the acid solutions (100 ml.). Observe what happens overnight.

Pupil Investigations (may include the following processes):

1. Observing what happens to the marble and limestone.
2. Inferring what might happen to buildings and statues made of these materials.

Event 17-E. Acid Rain and Soil

Keep two small identical plants like *Coleus* in the same growing conditions. Mist one with distilled water (pH = 7 and the other with "acid rain" (pH about 3) each day over several weeks.

Pupil Investigations (may include the following processes):

1. Observing the changes between the two plants.
2. Inferring what acid rain may do to certain vegetation.

Events 17-C through 17-E Explained in Context (Acid Rain)

Pupils can perform some simple experiments to understand chemically what is meant by **acid rain** and what are the consequences of it. *Event 17-C, Investigating pH,* helps pupils categorize acids and bases. Acids in water ionize to the **hydrogen ion** (H^+). This (H^+) combines with water (H_2O) to make the **hydronium ion** (H_3O). For example, hydrochloric acid (HCl) mixed in water separates into H^+ and Cl^- to become H_3O and Cl^-. Bases on the other hand form negative **hydroxide ions** (OH^-). When a base such as sodium hydroxide (NaOH) mixes with water, it separates into Na^+ and the negative hydroxide ion (OH^-). Stronger acids give up more H^- and stronger bases give up more OH^-.

Many household solutions are classified as acids and bases. Bases (pH > 7) turn an indicator like cabbage juice shades of blue-green if they are weak, and to shades of yellow-green if they are strong. Baking soda, ammonia, detergents, and drain cleaner are all bases. Acids (pH < 7) turn the red cabbage juice shades of blue-pink if they are weak, and to shades of red-pink if they are strong. Vinegar, carbonated beverages, and lemon or apple juice are all acidic.

With a beginning understanding of acids and bases pupils can begin to investigate acid rain as in *Event 17-D, Pollution and pH,* and *Event 17-E, Acid Rain and Soil.* Acid rain pollution is regularly in the news. As carbon dioxide gas, CO_2, dissolves in water droplets in unpolluted air, carbonic acid, H_2CO_3, formed. This is a weak acid and fairly harmless is small amounts.

$$H_2O + CO_2 \rightarrow H_2CO_3$$

When sulfur oxides dissolve in water droplets, stronger acids are formed. Sulfur trioxide (SO_3) and water (H_2O), form H_2SO_4, sulfuric acid. However, both acids contribute to acid rain as do other pollutants. Many people add lime (basic) to their lawns to adjust the pH in the soil to be closer to a neutral 7. If a lawn is too acidic or too basic, important nutrients such as potassium, phosphorus, and nitrogen may not be absorbed properly.

It is interesting to note that many flowers can be used as pH indicators just as red cabbage juice was used. Fuchsia and violets are just two such flowers. Red cabbage juice is very inexpensive but has a short shelf-life and an unpleasant odor. It is important that students understand that cabbage or flower juice can easily be used to identify acidic or basic substances. However, instruments such as the pH probes are necessary for ease of use and accuracy in scientific research.

Energy Use in the United States (Events 17-F through 17-H)

Discrepant Events and Pupil Investigations

Event 17-F. Total Energy Use

There are five sources of energy that provide more than 99% of all the energy used in the United States. Those sources are coal, natural gas, nuclear energy, oil, and waterpower. Ask the pupils to rank them in the order of their use.

Pupil Investigations (may include the following processes):

1. Estimating the energy sources and their use.
2. Analyzing how and where energy is used.
3. Comparing their estimates with official figures.

Event 17-G. Energy for Electrical Power

List the same five energy sources as were used in Event 17-F. This time ask pupils to think only of the energy used to generate electrical power and to rank the sources again.

Pupil Investigations (may include the following processes):

1. Estimating the energy sources used in electrical power.
2. Analyzing how and where the energy is used.
3. Comparing their estimates with official figures.

Event 17-H. Where Is Energy Used?

All the energy used in this country can be divided among four groups: industry, commercial, home (including the family car), and transportation (trains, planes, trucks, etc.). Ask pupils to rank the groups according to how much energy each group uses.

Pupil Investigations (may include the following processes):

1. Estimating the use of energy by groups.
2. Analyzing how and where energy is used.
3. Comparing their estimates with official figures.

Events 17-F through 17-H Explained in Context (Energy Use in the United States)

The three events in this section focus on the three main questions of energy use: (1) What are the total energy sources used in this country? (2) What are the energy sources used to generate electric power? (3) Where is the energy used? The answers are shown in table 17.4.

TABLE 17.4

Total Energy Used in the United States

Source	Percentage
Oil (refined into gasoline and heating oils)	39
Natural gas	24
Coal	23
Nuclear	8
Waterpower (hydroelectric)	3
Other	3

Source: Energy Information Administration Report, October 2003.

You will see that by far the greatest amount of energy comes from petroleum (oil). Natural gas and coal are second and third, and nuclear and hydroelectric energy are far behind. Most of the energy is used for two purposes—driving and heating.

Coal was widely used to heat homes a generation or two ago. Gradually, coal was replaced by oil, natural gas, and electricity. The trend away from coal is shown in the U.S. coal consumption figures. Coal consumption reached a peak in 1929 and then declined steadily for 40 years. Coal use began to increase again in the mid-1970s because of a sharp increase in number of coal-fired electric power plants. Oil, natural gas, and nuclear energy were either banned or restricted as energy sources for new power plants.

Coal is now used mostly in very large installations that can afford the cost of air pollution equipment and where coal can be burned efficiently. By far the greatest amount of coal is used to generate electrical power. Nuclear energy and waterpower are used exclusively for generating electrical power.

Energy for Electrical Power

Students sometimes get confused when comparing *all* the energy used in the United States with that portion used to generate electrical power. Be sure to point out that most of the energy in this country is used, not to generate electricity, but for motor fuel and for heating purposes.

Different energy sources are used for electrical power. It is obvious that coal, nuclear energy, and waterpower cannot be used directly as motor fuel or (except for coal) to heat homes. Those sources, however, are important in the production of electricity. The figures for 2003 are given in table 17.5.

There is some value in going back to *Event 17-B, Build a Power Plant,* in which the five sources of energy were evaluated and ranked by students. For the sake of that event, we assumed that all sources were equally available.

Unfortunately, in the real world they are *not* all equally available. Oil and natural gas cannot be used in new power plants. They were banned by Congress because it was feared that we would run out of those fuels for use in motor vehicles and heating homes.

Waterpower is not widely available either. Hydroelectric plants can be built only in mountainous river canyons. They cannot be built in the flatlands. The best waterpower sites have already been used.

That leaves only coal and nuclear power. Almost all of our future power plants will use these two sources of energy. Nothing else is available. (Sources

TABLE 17.5

Energy to Generate Electricity

Source	Percentage
Coal	56.9
Nuclear	22.4
Natural gas	9.4
Waterpower (hydroelectric)	6.7
Oil	4.2
Other (wind, tides etc.)	0.4

Source: Energy Information Administration Report, October 2003.

TABLE 17.6

Where Energy Is Used

Place	Percentage
Home and family, including family transportation	36
Industry	34
Commercial	18
Transportation (bus, truck, train, and airplane)	12

Source: Energy Information Administration Report, October 2003.

such as wind, solar, geothermal, tides, etc., are experimental and are not likely to make an impact in our lifetimes.)

We have seen where our energy comes from. Now, let us look at where the energy is used (as was asked in Event 17-H). The figures for a recent year are given in table 17.6.

Nuclear Energy (Event 17-I)

Discrepant Event and Pupil Investigations

Event 17-I. Nuclear Power Survey

Potential hazards of nuclear energy were surveyed by the National Assessment of Educational Progress. Table 17.7 lists the potential hazards in that survey. Ask the class to take the survey and then compare their results with the national figures.

Pupil Investigations (may include the following processes):

In this event, the processes are inherent in taking the survey and include comparing, analyzing, interpreting, concluding, predicting, and perhaps also suspending judgment while awaiting further data.

Event 17-I Explained in Context (Nuclear Energy)

The first commercial nuclear power plant was built in the United States in 1957. As of the turn of the century, there were approximately 440 nuclear

TABLE 17.7

Opinion Survey: How Serious Do You Consider Each of the Following Potential Hazards Associated with Nuclear Energy?

	Very Serious	Moderately Serious	Not Serious
1. Thermal pollution			
2. Radiation exposure from normal operation			
3. Explosion			
4. Theft of plutonium			
5. Disposal of radioactive waste			

Would You Be Willing to Have Each of the Following Energy Producers Built within 25 Miles of Your Home?

	Yes	Maybe	No
6. Coal-burning power plant			
7. Nuclear power plant			
8. Dam with hydroelectric plant			
9. Geothermal power plant			

Source: Taken from survey by the National Assessment of Educational Progress.

power plants in operation worldwide, 104 them in the United States. They generated about 22% of the electricity used in this country. In some countries, including France, Belgium, South Korea, Lithuania, and Sweden, nuclear energy provided more than half of all generated electricity.

Despite the wide use of nuclear power throughout the country and the world there is still much confusion about the topic. Let us explore this confusion by checking the responses to the survey items.

The responses to the items are shown in table 17.8. The figures for the national sample are those reported by the National Assessment of Educational Progress. The figures for the college sample are from 276 elementary teacher training students at Kent State University, Kent, Ohio.

At this point the opinions can be compared, and the items can serve as a good base for classroom discussion. But that does not guarantee that the opinions are based on sound information. One way to proceed is to compare the opinions of scientists with those of the general public.

Students may be surprised by the results. In a study jointly sponsored by Columbia University, Smith College, and George Washington University, scientists were asked if they would be willing to have a nuclear power plant in *their* city. (**Note:** The scientists were selected at random from "American Men and Women of Science.") The results are shown in table 17.9.

TABLE 17.8

Response to Survey: How Serious Do You Consider Each of the Following Potential Hazards Associated with Nuclear Energy?

		Very Serious %	Moderately Serious %	Not Serious %
1. Thermal pollution	College sample	37	56	7
	National sample	34	48	17
2. Radiation exposure from normal operation	College sample	56	31	13
	National sample	42	36	21
3. Explosion	College sample	69	21	10
	National sample	57	26	16
4. Theft of plutonium	College sample	41	42	17
	National sample	43	37	13
5. Disposal of radioactive waste	College sample	91	8	1
	National sample	76	19	4

Would You Be Willing to Have Each of the Following Energy Producers Build within 25 Miles of Your Home?

		Yes %	Maybe %	No %
6. Coal-burning power plant	College sample	9	39	52
	National sample	14	37	48
7. Nuclear power plant	College sample	3	20	77
	National sample	20	25	54
8. Dam with hydroelectric plant	College sample	57	30	13
	National sample	34	32	33
9. Geothermal power plant	College sample	22	57	22
	National sample	21	46	32

Source: Taken from data reported by the National Assessment of Educational Progress and from 276 elementary teacher training students at Kent State University, Kent, Ohio.

TABLE 17.9

Opinions of Scientists

Scientists	Percent Responding Yes
Random sample of all scientists	69
Energy experts	80
Nuclear experts	98

Source: Taken from study sponsored by Columbia University Smith College, and George Washington University.

Compare these figures with those obtained in the national and class surveys. It is apparent that the more people know about nuclear energy, the more they tend to support it.

Ask children to ponder why scientists favor nuclear energy so much more than nonscientists. Do they favor it because they know it is dangerous? Or, do they favor it because they know it is safe?

Sometimes a pupil will say that a scientist is willing to take risks because he or she may work at a nuclear power plant. However, if there is real danger, scientists probably do not want to be exposed to it any more than anyone else. Just remember that if there is a danger of cancer, for example, the scientist will be the first to get it. If there is a danger to his or her life, the scientist will be the first to die. It is not likely that many scientists will accept those risks.

Second, even if scientists were willing to accept hazards for themselves at their workplace, very few would be willing to accept that risk for their families where they live. That is precisely what was asked. Would they be willing to *live* near a nuclear power plant?

In any event, point out that many of the energy experts in the survey are *not* employed by power companies. Instead, they are scientists who work in universities and research labs.

What is it that scientists know that leads them to their opinions? Perhaps we can find out by looking more closely at radiation and other hazards in the following sections.

Radiation (Events 17-J through 17-L)

Discrepant Events and Pupil Investigations

Event 17-J. What Is Radiation?

Ask students to classify into two groups the following sources of radiation: (1) cosmic rays, (2) electric heater; (3) fire, (4) fluorescent bulb, (5) incandescent bulb, (6) luminous watch dial, (7) medical X-ray, (8) nuclear power plant.

Pupil Investigations (may include the following processes):

1. Classifying the examples into two groups: ionizing and nonionizing radiation.
2. Analyzing the examples to determine possible dangers.
3. Comparing their choices with scientific evidence about ionizing and nonionizing radiation.

Event 17-K. Ionizing Radiation

Ask student to rank the following sources of ionizing radiation according to amount: (1) medical uses, (2) natural background, (3) nuclear industry, (4) all other sources.

Pupil Investigations (may include the following processes):

1. Estimating and ranking the exposure from the various sources.
2. Analyzing the sources to determine possible dangers.
3. Comparing their choices with scientific evidence.

Event 17-L. Average Radiation Doses

Everyone is exposed to some radiation. Where does that radiation come from? Ask pupils to rank the following sources: (1) eating food, (2) breathing air, (3) watching television, (4) getting medical diagnosis and treatment, (5) living in homes, (6) flying in airplanes.

Pupil Investigation (may include the following processes):

1. Estimating and ranking the exposure from the various sources.
2. Analyzing the sources to determine possible dangers.
3. Comparing their ranking with scientific evidence.

Events 17-J through 17-L Explained in Context (Radiation)

How Do We Know?

Before we look at the scientific evidence, let us look at the problem of selecting the sources. Who knows about the effects of radiation? What sources are likely to be most accurate? To place the question in perspective, consider the history of radiation.

Radiation was first discovered by William Roentgen in 1895. It was soon realized that this mysterious ray could be used to take a picture *of the bones inside the body!* X-ray pictures were used to help set broken bones—a truly amazing achievement! X-ray machines were easy to build and were soon used by hospitals and doctors around the world.

Considering the poor level of medical practice at the beginning of the 1900s, it is no surprise that the X-ray became the equivalent of a medical "wonder drug." Not only was it essential for setting broken bones, but people soon regarded the X-ray as a "cure-all" for everything else.

Massive doses of radiation were used to treat many kinds of ailments. In England, for example, it was widely used to treat a severe form of arthritis called ankylosing spontelitis.

Were people afraid of radiation? Not at all. In fact, they refused to believe that it could do any harm even after evidence became clear that overdoses could be dangerous. When it became known that a place in Czechoslovakia had unusually high levels of radiation in its water, it did not scare people at all. Instead, people from all over Europe flocked to the site to bathe in "the healing waters" and drink "the healing liquids." For decades, the radioactive liquid was bottled and sold as drinking water all over Europe.

X-ray machines became so popular that they were even installed in shoe stores in this country. Many older people still remember the late 1940s, when they could go to a shoe store to see the X-ray view of the bones of their feet. Those machines were used without any controls or supervision.

Nevertheless, it became more and more apparent to scientists that uncontrolled exposure to radiation could have harmful side effects. By the 1920s an international body of scientists and medical experts was organized to study the possible problems. Other bodies were formed in this country and most other countries for similar reasons. At the present time, the major national and international groups are as follows:

IAEA	International Atomic Energy Agency
ICRP	International Commission on Radiological Protection
UNSCEAR	United Nations Scientific Committee on the Effects of Ionizing Radiation
NCRP	National Council on Radiation Protection and Measurements
BIER	The Committee on Biological Effects of Ionizing Radiation, of the National Academy of Science
EPA	The Environmental Protection Agency

In addition, every major country of the world now has its own national agency to supplement the work of the international bodies.

What Is Radiation?

Many people are confused about radiation. Do we mean the kind of radiation that comes from light and heat sources? No. The radiation of heat from a radiator or of light from a bulb is called **nonionizing radiation.** That means that the rays cannot penetrate and dislodge electrons from atoms. Thus, the examples in *Event 17-J, What Is Radiation?*, fit into two groups. Examples of **ionizing rays** are numbers 1, 6, 7, and 8. The other items produce nonionizing rays.

In summary, radiation that can penetrate an atom to knock off electrons (ionize it) is what we are concerned with when we talk about atomic or nuclear radiation. The concern is with ionizing radiation, not nonionizing radiation. Even with ionizing radiation, there are big differences among various types of rays. The three major types are:

Alpha particles—Very weak. They can be stopped by a sheet of paper or by a few centimeters of air. They are no danger unless lodged directly in the lungs or injected into the bloodstream.
Beta rays—Also weak. They can be stopped by a few centimeters of wood or a few meters of air.
Gamma rays—Powerful. These are like those used in X-rays. They can penetrate muscle and bone. Very powerful forms of these rays are even used to X-ray heavy metal casings to look for flaws.

Where Does Ionizing Radiation Come From?

Ionizing radiation comes from just about everywhere. It comes from the ground we walk on, the air we breathe, the food we eat, the homes we live in, and even (don't say this too loudly) from the person sitting next to you! The sources of ionizing radiation are shown in table 17.10. Compare it with the student list in *Event 17-K, Ionizing Radiation.*

Radiation exposure is measured with a variety of units. Some units indicate the volume of rays emitted, but not their penetrating power. Those are not particularly useful. An object might emit large quantities of radiation, but they are so weak that they can be stopped by a sheet of paper. The most useful measurements are by units that indicate the biological effects that radiation has on the body. That unit is the **millirem** (mrem).

What doses are received by people living in the United States? The exposures differ greatly, but the average is about 360 millirems per person per year. (Originally, the figure most often cited was 210 mrem, but that did not include the exposure to radon in most homes.) Compare the exposure values listed in

TABLE 17.10

Sources of Ionizing Radiation

Source	Percentage
Natural background	75.19
Medical diagnosis	24.04
All others except nuclear industry	0.37
Nuclear industry	0.40
Total	100.00

table 17.11 with the responses by pupils in *Event 17-L, Average Radiation Doses.* The exposures are those received in 1 year (except where noted otherwise).

One way to gain an understanding of the various exposures is to use a string to measure out some distances on the playground. If you use a scale of 1 meter per millirem, the total average annual exposure (360 millirems) will be longer than three football fields.

On that same scale, watching TV or wearing a watch with a luminous dial gives an exposure that measures 1 meter. However, the exposure to the general public from nuclear power plants measures only 1 *centi*meter. That means, you get one hundred times more exposure from TV or a watch than from a power plant.

Perhaps most surprising of all, a coal-fired power plant gives a radiation exposure hundreds of times greater than is obtained from the normal operation of a nuclear power plant. Since coal contains radium, uranium, and thorium, those particles are vented into the air and settle in the vicinity of those plants.

TABLE 17.11

Radiation Sources*

Sources	Doses in Millirem
	Dose per Year
Average dose in the United States	360
Radon in the home	198
Air	5
Food	25
TV watching	1
Grand Central Station	525
Cosmic rays at sea level	35
Cosmic rays at 2000 meter elevation	75
Heart pacemaker (from Plutonium-238)	5000
Coal-fired power plant (50 kilometer)	50 to 380**
Nuclear power plant (50 kilometer)	.4
	Dose per Occurence
Chest X-ray (dose to the bone-marrow)	30 to 80
Chest X-ray (dose to the skin)	1500
Fluoroscopic X ray	20,000 to 60,000
Jet airplane flight (per hour)	1

*Sources of radiation exposure include six main categories: natural radiation, occupational (radiation workers), nuclear fuel cycle, consumer products, miscellaneous environmental sources, and medical diagnosis and therapy. For each of these sources, the product of the estimated number of people exposed and the average effective dose equivalent received from that source is expressed as the collective dose from that source. The collective dose from each source is then divided by the entire U.S. population to obtain the contribution from that source to the average effective dose equivalent for a member of the United States. The average person is exposed to an approximate 360 mrem (wholebody exposure) per year from all sources.

**Depending on the kind of coal used. Coal contains uranium, thorium, and radium—all of which are vented into the air along with smoke and gases when burned. Western coal gives the higher figure.

Source: *Ionizing Radiation Exposure of the Population of the United States* (NCRP Report No. 93), National Council on Radiation Protection and Measurements, 1987.

According to measurements published by the Environmental Protection Agency (EPA), a person living within 50 kilometers of a coal-fired plant is likely to receive a dose of 50 to 380 millirems per year, depending on the type of coal that is burned in the plant. (Western coal is generally more radioactive than eastern coal.)

Explosion and Theft

The NAEP survey reveals that many people fear that nuclear power stations can blow up in a nuclear explosion. However, there is no scientific basis for that fear. The fuel rods are enriched to about 3% or 4% purity. They would have to be enriched to at least 90% to sustain an explosive reaction. Thus, the fuel rods *cannot* explode any more than a desk or chair can explode.

There is also some fear that terrorists could steal plutonium from nuclear power plants and make bombs. This fear is also unfounded. First of all, there are no commercial power plants that use plutonium as fuel, so there is no plutonium available to steal.

Some plutonium is gradually formed as a waste product in fuel cells, but that is so difficult to extract for weapons that no country in the world has done so. The fuel rods would have to be processed in a highly sophisticated plant. If thieves possessed such a plant, it would be easier and safer for them to refine the material directly from ore.

Finally, if terrorists wanted to have nuclear weapons, they could probably get them more easily by stealing some of the thousands that already exist instead of trying to build some from spent fuel rods.

Waste Disposal

The survey shows that there is great fear about the disposal of radioactive waste. Yet, even here, there is much unfounded concern. There are five important considerations that are often overlooked:

1. A nuclear plant does not add any net radioactivity to the earth. Less comes out of the plant than goes into it. Radioactive ore is dug from the ground, is concentrated into fuel, and is burned to make electricity. When spent, there is less than there was in the beginning, and it ends up deeper underground than from where the original ore came.
2. There is very little to dispose of. Processed waste from a large power plant totals only 1 to 2 cubic meters of high-level waste per year. A coal-fired plant of the same size produces waste that covers 5 cubic kilometers to a depth of 2 meters . . . plus adding thousands of tons of waste to the air.
3. Even if nuclear power were ended, the problem, if any, would be unaffected. More than 99% of the high-level waste comes from weapons produced for military uses. The total accumulated volume of all high-level wastes in the United States through 1983 was 210,000 cubic meters. Of that total, only 300 cubic meters came from power plants.
4. The radioactivity of spent fuel rods is very intense immediately after being removed from a reactor. The intensity, however, declines quickly—by a factor of 2100 in 10 years. After 30 years, no external danger remains from radiation.

5. After 30 years, wastes pose a danger only if ingested (by getting into drinking water, for example). Using drinking water standards as a guide, high-level atomic wastes decay below the toxic levels of several natural ores and wastes (such as mercury, pitchblende, chromium, lead, coal wastes, and silver ores), in about five hundred years.

Danger of a Possible Meltdown

The possibility of nuclear meltdown is another potential hazard. It was not listed in *Event 17-I, Nuclear Power Survey,* and is included now only with reservations.

It was not included in Event 17-I because the National Assessment did not include it. To remain objective, it should be added only with caution. However, the national survey was prepared prior to the accident at Three-Mile Island (3MI) and the publicity that resulted could now justify its inclusion.

What are those dangers? Let us look briefly at what happens inside a nuclear reactor. Nuclear fuel is inserted into the reactor along with control rods. The fuel produces heat, which, in turn, is used to generate electricity. Control rods absorb excess radiation and are used to keep the reactor from overheating.

Overheating is also controlled another way. The fuel rods are constantly immersed in water. This brings us to the potential danger. What would happen if an accident caused a loss of water so that the fuel rods would be exposed to air? If the control rods were fresh: nothing.

It should be noted that fresh fuel rods can be stacked like firewood and nothing would happen. It is only after fuel rods are inside the reactor and exposed to constant atomic bombardment that they begin producing undesirable secondary radiation. It is because of this secondary radiation that they are removed from the reactor after 3 years. If the rods are recycled to remove the undesirable radioactivity, they can be used again as fuel.

Why are fresh fuel rods safe when exposed to air? Because the radiation cannot be "captured" by the atoms to set up an atomic chain reaction. It is only when the radiation from the fuel rods is slowed down by a **"moderator"** that the chain reaction can begin inside the power plant. (The terms "capture" and "moderator" are commonly used to describe the atomic reaction.)

In all U.S. commercial power plants, water is used as a moderator. Thus, if there is an accident that causes a loss of water, that same accident also stops the chain reaction. In other words, without water, the reactor cannot function.

Nevertheless, there is latent heat from the natural atomic decay inside partially spent fuel rods even after the power plant is shut down. (As stated earlier, this does not occur in new fuel rods.) It is this latent heat that could cause a potential meltdown of the reactor core.

How great is that possibility? A look at the Three-Mile Island accident may be instructive. Prior to the accident, it was assumed by some that a meltdown could occur if the fuel rods would lose water for as little as a few seconds or minutes. However, the accident showed that such was not the case. The fuel rods in that accident were exposed to air for up to 8 hours. The temperatures were far lower than expected and, although the core was severely damaged, a meltdown did not occur.

Two special commissions (the Kemeny Commission appointed by the President, and the Rogovan Commission appointed by Congress) investigated the accident. They reported that: (1) there was never any danger to the public, (2) there was never any danger of a meltdown, and (3) even if there had been a meltdown, the danger to the public would have been the same: zero. They reported that greatest danger to the public was "mental stress" caused by alarmist news reporting.

Can Chernobyl Happen Here?

Ask that question and most students will "admit" that it probably can. However, scientists know that it cannot. Why not? Because of the laws of physics. Or stated another way: Water does not burn!

The Chernobyl reactor did not use water as a moderator. Instead it used graphite. At Chernobyl, when the reactor lost its coolant, the graphite was still in place to continue the chain reaction. Without the water, it got so hot that the graphite ignited. Since graphite ignites at over 6000°C, it burned with the intensity of a gigantic arc welder. It vaporized the huge inventory of radioactive fuel and spewed it high into the atmosphere.

U.S. power plants do not use graphite as a moderator. They use water. Thus, if the coolant is lost, so also is the moderator lost. Without a moderator, it cannot operate. It shuts itself down.

A final note: Students will sometimes ask if the scientists of the former Soviet Union did not know that they could use water instead of graphite. Of course, they knew. This information is no mystery to atomic scientists of either country. Graphite was used because it is especially suited to make nuclear material for weapons. They were using the Chernobyl plant not only to generate electricity but also to make bomb material. They have more than a dozen Chernobyl-type plants in operation at the present time.

Conservation (Events 17-M through 17-Q)

Discrepant Events and Pupil Investigations

Event 17-M. Energy Conservation: Home Heating

Have students rank the four items in the list below according to how much energy could be saved.

Assume that you are living in a 1210-square-foot home (equal to a five-room home or a two-bedroom home). Assume, also, that it had no insulation in the walls or ceiling, no storm windows, and poor weather-stripping.

____ Add storm windows.
____ Add 2 inches of fiberglass insulation to ceiling.
____ Close drapes at night.
____ Renew weather-stripping.

Pupil Investigations (may include the following processes):

In this event, the processes are inherent in responding to the survey. The processes may include comparing, analyzing, interpreting, concluding, and predicting.

Event 17-N. Water Coats

Connect the temperature probe to the computer/calculator. Fill a glass container with 250 mL warm water (50°C or higher). Record the temperature over time (about 21 minutes). Repeat this several times with different types of insulating "coats" for the glass container. Try fabric, newspaper, fur, feathers, foam, or plastic bubble wrap.

Pupil Investigations (may include the following processes):

1. Comparing the length of time it takes for each trial to drop 10°C.
2. Observing that some insulators feel cool to the touch during the whole time period.
3. Ordering from best to least insulation capability.
4. Comparing and contrasting insulators found in the home.

Event 17-O. Energy Conservation: Driving

Have students rank the four items in the list below according to how much energy could be saved. Assume that you own a "gas guzzler" that gets 10 miles per gallon (mpg), that is driven 15,000 miles per year.

____ Drive only 12,000 miles annually instead of 15,000 miles.
____ Get a compact car (30 mpg) and drive only 12,000 miles annually.
____ Get a compact car (30 mpg) and drive the same mileage.
____ Get a standard car (21 mpg) and drive the same mileage.

Pupil Investigations (may include the following processes):

In this event, the processes are inherent in responding to the survey. The processes may include comparing, analyzing, interpreting, concluding, and predicting.

Event 17-P. Energy Conservation: Home Appliances

Have students rank the six items in the list below according to how much energy can be saved during a full year:

____ Each member of a family of four takes a shower daily instead of a bath.
____ Fix two dripping hot water faucets.
____ Prohibit the use of outdoor Christmas lights. (Assume the use of 72 bulbs of 7 watts each, turned on for 3 hours each night for 3 weeks.)
____ Replace 400 watts of incandescent lighting, used 1 hour per day, with fluorescent bulbs of equal light-giving value.
____ Substitute a window fan for a room air conditioner about 20% of the time.
____ Shave with a blade razor instead of an electric shaver.

Pupil Investigations (may include the following processes):

In this event, the processes are inherent in responding to the survey. The processes may include comparing, analyzing, interpreting, concluding, and predicting.

Event 17-Q. Energy Use in the Home

Have students rank the 10 items below according to how much energy they use during a year.

____ blanket (electric)
____ blender
____ clock (wall)
____ clothes dryer
____ hair dryer (hand held)
____ range
____ refrigerator-freezer (14–21 cubic feet, side-by-side)
____ toaster
____ TV, color
____ washer, clothes

Pupil Investigations (may include the following processes):

In this event, the processes are inherent in responding to the survey. The processes may include comparing, analyzing, interpreting, concluding, and predicting.

Events 17-M through 17-Q Explained in Context (Conservation)

Pupils have heard about the importance of conserving energy. However, many do not know how to do so for two main reasons: (1) They don't know where energy is used in significant amounts, and (2) they don't know where it can be saved. The above events are short, simple exercises that can be used to teach pupils where energy is used and how that energy can be conserved.

Where does the typical U.S. family use its energy? About 80% is divided evenly between two major uses: (1) heating and cooling the home, and (2) transportation (the family car). So to be able to save energy, we need to focus attention on where the energy is used. That is done in the first two events in this section.

Most of the remainder of the energy is used to heat water and operate home appliances. Although not nearly as important as heating and transportation, they are the most practical for instructing children. Pupils are not likely to make any decisions about heating and transportation. However, children use appliances all the time. They can form better judgments about how to use them and how energy can be saved. That makes the last two events especially useful in the classroom.

Conserving Energy in Home Heating

The easiest way to save energy in heating a home is to add insulation above the ceiling. Heat escapes very quickly through the ceiling of an uninsulated home, so adding only 2 inches of insulation saves a great amount of energy (and money). Compare the savings in energy by each of the four practices in *Event 17-M, Energy Conservation: Home Heating.* The results are shown in table 17.12.

The second best way to save energy in this event is to add storm windows. Glass is a poor insulator; and if there is only a single pane of glass between the inside of a home and the cold outside air, the heat will escape

TABLE 17.12

Energy Saved in Home Heating

Rank	Item	Fuel Oil Saved (gal)
1	Add 5 cm of fiberglass insulation above ceiling	1044
2	Add storm windows	290
3	Renew weather-stripping	230
4	Close drapes at night	58

TABLE 17.13

Energy Saved in Driving

Rank	Items	Gas Saved (gal)
1	Get a compact car (30 mpg) and drive only 12,000 miles	1100
2	Get a compact car (30 mpg) and drive the same miles	1000
3	Get a standard car (20 mpg) and drive the same miles	750
4	Drive only 12,000 miles instead of 15,000 miles	300

quickly. In fact, heat escapes 10 times as fast through a single window pane than through a typical wall. Storm windows cut in half the heat that is lost through windows.

In third place is the renewal of weather-stripping. Weather-stripping is the lining (usually of soft plastic) around the edges of doors and windows that keeps air from leaking in or out of a home. Unless a lining is used, heat is quickly lost in cold weather; and you can feel the cold draft of air as it enters a home.

Even closing the drapes helps to conserve energy. The drapes act as another layer blocking the movement of air between the outside and inside of a home. In the daytime, however, the drapes should be opened if the sun is shining, because sunlight helps heat the home.

You can let some of the students compare the cost of the energy saved with the cost of making the improvements. In many cases the cost of the improvements is gained back within a few years. Thus, conserving energy not only saves fuel, it also saves money.

In *Event 17-N, Water Coats,* **insulators** are something that stop heat exchange. Air is a poor conductor of heat as seen with the plastic bubble wrap. The best insulators trap a lot of air. Examples of good insulators are air, wood, Styrofoam, and cloth. Knowing properties of good insulators helps to make wise decisions in home insulation selection.

Conserving Energy in Driving

Another area of energy use is driving. Two obvious factors influence the amount of energy used: (1) the amount of driving, and (2) the efficiency of the car. Both factors are critical to saving energy and are used in *Event 17-O, Energy Conservation: Driving.* The results are shown in table 17.13.

TABLE 17.14

Gallons of Gasoline Used per Year

Distance Driven (miles)	(miles per gallon)		
	10	20	30
12,000	1200	600	400
15,000	1500	750	500

TABLE 17.15

Energy Savings in Home Appliances

Rank	Item	Kilowatt-Hours Saved
1	Each member of a family of four takes a shower instead of a bath	720
2	Fix a dripping hot water faucet (one drop per second)	625
3	Substitute a window fan for a room air conditioner about 20% of the time	250
4	Replace 400 watts of incandescent lighting, used 1 hour per day with fluorescent bulbs	117
5	Prohibit the use of outdoor Christmas lights	32
6	Shave with a blade razor instead of an electric shaver	–44

The figures are obtained by dividing the number of miles driven annually by the miles per gallon. The actual amount of gasoline used for each car at each of the two distances is shown in table 17.14.

What are the major factors that influence how many miles per gallon you can get from a car? The most important factor is weight. The heavier the car, the more gasoline it needs to operate. A general rule of thumb is that 1 mile per gallon is used for each additional 180 kilograms (400 pounds of weight). Thus, to get the best mileage, a car must be light in weight.

Perhaps the next most important factor is speed. At a low speed, there is very little resistance from air, but at high speeds, wind resistance becomes very important. Beyond 55 miles per hour, wind resistance increases so much that most cars suffer substantial losses in gas mileage.

Other factors are important also. Radial tires have lower rolling friction than other types of tires. As a result, there is a small improvement in mileage. Driving habits are very important. A "jackrabbit start" will waste gasoline; a smooth start will save it. Underinflating tires will waste gasoline; proper tire pressure saves it. Keeping the engine well tuned saves gasoline, while poor maintenance wastes it.

Conserving Energy in the Home

Energy can be saved by carefully watching how much energy is used by appliances in the home. *Event 17-P, Energy Conservation: Home Appliances,* is a good exercise to draw attention to some energy conservation practices. The figures for the items in that event are given in table 17.15.

TABLE 17.16

Energy Used by Appliances

Rank	Appliance	Watts	Kilowatt-Hours*
1	Refrigerator-freezer (21 cu ft)	720	2160
2	Range	12,200	1500
3	Clothes dryer	1800–5000	1044
4	Blanket (electric)	175	504
5	Television (color)	130	576
6	Hair dryer (hand-held)	1000	120
7	Washer, clothes	500	90
8	Toaster	1100	27
9	Clock (wall)	2	17
10	Personal computer	170	100

*The rankings are based on the energy used for a full year. Energy is measured in *kilowatt-hours (Kwh)*. A kilowatt-hour is 1000 watts used for 1 hour.

After the energy needed to heat a home, the next biggest energy use in the home is for heating water. That is why the two examples about water-use rank first and second in table 17.15. Surprisingly, an average shower uses about 5 gallons less water than an average bath. The added water for an entire year adds up to a savings of 721 kilowatts.

A dripping hot water faucet wastes a surprising amount of energy. The reason for the large loss is the fact that the water drips day and night, every day of the year. The constant drip, drip, drip, uses 625 kilowatts of energy per year (to heat the lost water).

As can be seen in the table, prohibiting Christmas lights will not save much energy. The bulbs are small and use is limited to a few weeks in a year. Changing to fluorescent bulbs is better. They give much more light per watt of energy used than do incandescent bulbs. That is why the change will provide the same amount of light with much less energy.

The item in which the window fan is substituted for a room air conditioner may be misunderstood by students. They sometimes feel that if you want to be uncomfortable, you don't need to use the air conditioner at all. They miss the point of the exercise. There are times when a window fan is just as efficient as an air conditioner in keeping a house cool.

This is especially true after sunset when the outside air often cools off while the inside of a house is like an oven. At a time like this, a window fan is very effective in cooling the house. So it is possible to remain comfortable and still save energy.

The use of a blade razor will not save any energy at all. In fact, it will lose energy. Much more energy is needed to heat the water used for blade shaving than is used with an electric shaver.

Event 17-Q Energy Use in the Home, is another good exercise to let students know the energy used by the appliances. The results of that event are shown in table 17.16.

You will note that some of the appliances are of high wattage but have low Kilowatt-hour figures. That is because they are not used very many hours during the year. A toaster, for example, uses 6 times more watts but only about 1% as much total energy than does the refrigerator-freezer. The biggest users are those that are on most of the time.

Combining Assessment with Instruction

1.	Have elementary children, grades 3–6, take home an energy use survey such as the one at the following website: www.ase.org/educators/lessons/ex.4.pdf. This is an activity created by the National Wildlife Federation originally appearing in their *Animal Tracks Activity Guide for Educators* (1995). By working with family members to fill out the chart, children and families can discuss ways to better conserve energy at home. After observing and recording an estimated time any given appliance is used per day, week or month, students should calculate the cost of using a variety of appliances for the month given the information in the lesson. Each student will compare home energy use with that of other students in class and with national averages. Have each student list five ways in which she and her family can lower home energy use. Students should include a plan and rationale for implementing their reduction in home energy consumption.

2.	Middle school students should enjoy participating in a role-playing game, Energy Street. The game has students investigating the energy efficiency of technologies used in homes through websites listed in the directions of the game. The students will need to describe and defend their knowledge of specific energy-efficient technologies they choose when building homes. A scenario is given to start the game and a rubric is included to evaluate the students. Students are evaluated on the following criteria: ability to work in groups, ability to use the Web to gather information to make educated decisions, complete and clear written descriptions, clear oral presentation with compelling statements made, and effective use of mathematical information. Energy Street was created by the National Renewable Energy Laboratory (NREL) and can be found at www.nrel.gov/education/energystreet/game.html.

3.	Don't Let Smoking Take the Color Out of You could also be used as an assessment for this chapter. Refer to Chapter 21, Teaching Children about Fitness.

Sites and Software

The following websites and software are appropriate to use with this chapter. Note that computer software and websites change rapidly. This makes it necessary to investigate the stable websites for new links and software catalogs for updates. Visit www.mhhe.com/friedl6e to link to these directly and for study resources.

Sites

Recycle City	www.epa.gov/recyclecity
Energy Quest	www.nucleartourist.com/basics/why.htm
Energy Education Resources	www.eia.doe.gov/bookshelf/eer/ kiddietoc.html

Energy Information Administration	www.eia.doe.gov
Energy and Electrical Power	www.howstuffworks.com/ category.htm?cat=Powr
Nuclear!	www.howstuffworks.com/ category.htm?cat=Nucl
Utilities	www.howstuffworks.com/ category.htm?cat=Utility
Energy Use of Home Appliances	www.eren.doe.gov/consumerinfo/ refbriefs/ec7.html

Software

Earth Explorer (Interactive/Sunburst) (4–9)
Discoveries: Explore the (Desert, Forest, or Everglades) Ecosystem (Houghton
Mifflin/Sunburst) (3–6)

Key Terms

acid rain, *326*
alpha particles, *334*
beta rays, *334*
energy, *320*
gamma rays, *334*

hydrogen ion, *326*
hydronium ion, *326*
hydroxide ion, *326*
insulator, *341*
ionizing rays, *334*

millirem, *334*
moderator, *337*
nonionizing radiation, *334*
radiation, *333*

Teaching Children about the Plant and Fungi Kingdoms

National Science Education Standards Alignment to Events

The events in this chapter help accomplish several of the NSES for content. The event(s) that align with a given content standard are listed below that standard.

Levels K–4

Unifying Concepts and Processes
- Systems, order and organization
  - *18-H*

- Change, consistency, measurement
  - *18-B through 18-D*
  - *18-F and 18-G*
  - *18-J*

- Evidence, models and explanation
  - *18-B and 18-C*
  - *18-E*
  - *18-I*
  - *18-K*
  - *18-M through 18-V*

Life Science
- Characteristics of living organisms
  - *18-A*
  - *18-E and 18-F*
  - *118-I*
  - *18-L through 18-R*
  - *18-T*
  - *18-V*

- Life cycles
  - *18-A and 18-B*
  - *18-D*
  - *18-K*
  - *18-R*

- Organisms and environment
  - *18-C through 18-G*
  - *18-L*
  - *18-P through 18-R*

Science and Technology
- Abilities of technological design
  - *18-I and 18-J*
  - *18-U*

- Understanding science and technology
  - *18-R*

Science in Personal and Social Perspectives
  - Personal health
    - *18-T*

Levels 5–8

Uniting Concepts and Processes
- Systems, order and organization
  - *18-H*

- Change, consistency, measurement
  - *18-B through 18-D*
  - *18-F and 18-G*
  - *18-J*

- Evidence, models and explanation
  - *18 B and 18-C*
  - *18-E*
  - *18-I*
  - *18-K*
  - *18-M through 18-V*

Life Science
- Structure and function in living systems
  - *18-A and 18-B*
  - *18-D*

- *18-L through 18-R*
- *18-T*
- *18-U and 18-V*

- Reproduction and heredity
  - *18-A and 18-B*
  - *18-E through 18-K*
  - *18-Q*
  - *18-U and 18-V*

- Regulation and behavior
  - *18-C through 18-G*
  - *18-I through 18-L*
  - *18-T through 18-V*

- Populations and ecosystems
  - *18-A through 18-V*

Science and Technology
- Abilities of technological design
  - *18-I and 18-J*
  - *18-U*

- Understanding science and technology
  - *18-R*

Science in Personal and Social Perspectives
- Personal health
  - *18-S through 18-V*

- Risks and benefits
  - *18-S through 18-V*

- Science and technology in society
  - *18-R*

Shining Light on Food Production in Plants

Humans have always depended on plants for food and medicinal purposes. Through observation and careful seed-gathering, humans began to domesticate varieties of plants for agricultural purposes. Using carbon-14 dating, scientists have traced domesticated wheat and barley back to 9000 B.C. in the Middle East, rice and millet were traced back to 5500 B.C. in China and Southeast Asia, and squash was traced back to 6000 B.C. in Mexico. Native Americans used sap from maple trees to make maple sugar long before written history. The first documentation of maple sugar use among Europeans came in 1609 when the early European settlers met with Native Americans who shared their maple sugar with the foreign visitors. Artificial pollination of fruit trees also began long before written history, the first written accounts occurring around 700 B.C.

Theophrastus (371–290 B.C.), a pupil of Aristotle, is credited as the first botanist. He was the first to use the word *fruit* as a botanical term defined as a ripened ovary with any parts of the flower that may be attached. Only two books on plants authored by Theophrastus, *A History of Plants* and *About the Reasons of Vegetable Growth*, remain fairly intact. These works were translated into Latin in the 1400s and into German in 1822. Theophrastus also began the first system of classification by dividing plants between flowering and nonflowering. Most of his work and the work of other scholars like Saint Hildegard von Bingen (A.D. 1099–1179), Charlemagne (A.D. 771–814) and Pliny the Older (A.D. 23–79) focused on physical descriptions of plants and their practical uses.

It wasn't until 1735 when Carl Linneaus published *Systema naturae* that a classification system for plants and animals was created. Linneaus created the binomial nomenclature based on external physical characteristics of plants. His system was mainly a cataloging method to help scientists find the names of plants. The initial system Linneaus created separated plants and animals into groups organized by the *kingdom, phylum, class, order,* and *genus.* The system was modified to include *family* and eventually *species.* Science and emerging technology helped to refine Linneaus's system by dividing animals based on internal and external physical structures, sexuality, and eventually genetics.

The study of plant physiology began in the 1600s with the advent of magnification through the use of ground lenses and was enhanced by the advancement of chemistry in the late 1700s. Marcello Malphighi and Nehemiah Grew independently discovered stomates, small openings on the surface of leaves which were hypothesized to be related to plant respiration. The discovery of oxygen by Joseph Priestly followed by the correlation between oxygen and carbon dioxide in respiration by Antoine Lavoisier paved the way to Jan Ingen-Housz's discovery of assimilation (the conversion of light into food, which would be termed *photosynthesis* in 1893) and plant respiration.

Ingen-Housz was commissioned by Empress Maria Theresa of Austria to conduct experiments on plants. His book, *Experiments Upon Vegetables* (1779), described over 500 experiments he conducted, which proved that plants required light for photosynthesis and that leaves were the primary site of photosynthesis. Julius Robert Mayer discovered that all plants convert solar energy received through the leaves into chemical energy that the plant needs to survive. Glucose, the "food" produced by photosynthesis, was first discovered in 1747 by Andreas Marggraf through his experiments with beets. The term *glucose* was coined by Jean-Baptiste-Andre Dumas in 1838. The connection of photosynthesis to chlorophyll didn't occur until Richard Willsatter was able to isolate chlorophyll and discovered that its chemical composition was similar to that of hemoglobin. Hemoglobin, the red coloring of the red blood cells, carries oxygen from the lungs to the tissues and carbon dioxide from the tissues to the lungs, in animals. Emil Fischer discovered the structure of glucose, which helped determine that the chemical reaction of carbon dioxide with water in the presence of chlorophyll produced glucose and oxygen in plants.

It is important for students to understand that seldom if ever is a discovery made by a single scientist. Science builds on the networking of knowledge from many people researching the different ideas that often unknowingly build the foundation of a concept one brick at a time.

Seeds (Events 18-A through 18-H)

Discrepant Events and Pupil Investigations

Event 18-A. Soaking Seeds
Soak lima beans in water overnight. After soaking, the tough outer covering can be easily removed. Carefully separate the seed halves and study them. What are the major parts of the seed? Compare seeds with some that were not soaked.

Pupil Investigations (may include the following processes):
1. Observing that the seeds expand when soaked.
2. Discovering that the seed coating is tough when dry, but is easy to remove when wet.
3. Examining the three main parts of a seed: the covering, the "baby" plant (embryo), and the food supply.
4. Diagramming the parts of the seed.
5. Generalizing about the functions of seed parts in germinating plants.

Event 18-B. Seed Germination
Plant five radish seeds and five bean seeds in a container. Give the seeds some water and place them in the sunlight. Wait several days and then remove one seedling of each type, each day until they are all removed. Have pupils diagram what they see and chart the germination of the seeds.

Pupil Investigations (may include the following processes):
1. Examining the seeds after they are removed from the soil.
2. Drawing diagrams of their observations.
3. Generalizing about the germination rates of two types of seeds.

Event 18-C. Seed Depth
Plant several types of seeds in each of several sets. Make all conditions the same except for the planting depths. Select large seeds such as lima beans and small seeds such as radishes.

Pupil Investigations (may include the following processes):

1. Recording growth rates of emerging seeds for 2 weeks.
2. Comparing the size of seeds with their planting depths.
3. Examining the seeds after 1 week to study their development.
4. Forming a theory about the relationship between the depth of the soil and the size of the seed.

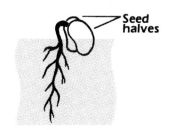

FIGURE 18.1 The developing bean plant pushes the original seed halves out of the ground.

Event 18-D. Bean Power

Plant a handful of bean seeds in several containers. As the bean germinates, the roots and stem develop and push the original bean seed up through the ground into the air.

When the beans begin to emerge, divide the seedlings into three groups. In one group, carefully remove one of the halves of the original seed. In the second group, remove both halves of the seed. Leave the third group as a control. (See figure 18.1.)

Pupil Investigations (may include the following processes):

1. Recording the growth rates of the beans.
2. Observing that the beans with no seed halves do poorly, those with one half do better, and the control group does best.
3. Inferring that the seed halves contain the energy needed to support the early growth of the plant.

Event 18-E. Upside-Down Seeds

Place several layers of absorbent paper towels against the sides of a drinking glass. Push some lima beans between the glass and towels. (The blotters or towels draw up water from the bottom of the tumbler to keep the seeds moist.)

Position the seeds so that they face various directions—up, down, and toward both sides. How does the position of the seed affect the germination and growth of the plants?

Pupil Investigations (may include the following processes):

1. Experimenting with seeds planted in various positions.
2. Observing that the leaves always go up and roots always go down.
3. Generalizing about the factors that control growth.

Event 18-F. Water for Seeds

Plant radishes in five pots and lima beans in five additional pots. Use potting soil, and plant the seeds to the depth recommended on the packages. Carefully arrange a watering program in which one pot of each gets no water, and move in increments to a point where the last pot in each is almost always standing underwater.

To achieve the last condition, seal the drain hole in the bottom of the pot, or set it, rim deep, into a large container of water.

Pupil Investigations (may include the following processes):

1. Recording the amounts and frequency of watering.
2. Observing and keeping a record of the growth of seeds.
3. Inspecting some ungerminated seeds after a week.
4. Analyzing the effects, on seeds, of various amounts of water.

Event 18-G. Growth in Light and Dark

Plant some radishes and bean seeds in two drinking glass "gardens" made of absorbent paper towels and drinking glasses. Cover one drinking glass with dark construction paper so that the seeds are in total darkness; leave another tumbler exposed to light. What happens in the two settings?

Pupil Investigations (may include the following processes):

1. Recording the germination of seeds and the rate of growth over a period of 1 or 2 weeks.
2. Discovering that seeds grow faster in the dark than those exposed to light.
3. Forming a theory to account for the growth differences in daylight and darkness.

Event 18-H. Do Seeds Travel?

This event is best done in the autumn when a wide variety of seeds is available. Have pupils collect seeds of all kinds. Ask pupils to examine and classify them and to determine how they travel.

Pupil Investigations (may include the following processes):

1. Collecting some common seeds.
2. Inspecting the outward appearances of seeds.
3. Classifying seeds into groups according to how they travel.

Events 18-A through 18-H Explained in Context (Seeds)

There are many plants that reproduce from seeds. Seeds are divided into two main groups: the flowering plants, **angiosperms;** and the nonflowering plants, **gymnosperms.** Most seed plants are of the following kind. In fact, there are some 250,000 species of flowering plants and only about 600 of the nonflowering species.

How Seeds Germinate and Grow

In *Event 18-A, Soaking Seeds,* students will have a chance to study a number of seeds. Lima beans are excellent for use in this event. They are large and fast-growing. Other large seeds such as sunflower, corn, pea, pumpkin, and even peanut seeds can be used in these activities.

Seed **germination** can be observed in a variety of ways. Small seeds, such as the radish, carrot, and onion, can be sprinkled on moist cloth or absorbant paper towels and observed. Just be sure that the cloth or paper is kept wet at all times. (See figure 18.2 for an example of how these seeds may be germinated.)

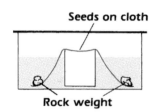

Seeds on cloth

Rock weight

FIGURE 18.2 Small seeds can be germinated on a thick piece of absorbent cloth. Drape the cloth over a container and dip the ends in water. Moisture moves up the cloth to keep the seeds wet.

The three main parts of a seed can be seen clearly in the lima bean: (1) the **embryo** (the "baby" plant), (2) the **food supply,** and (3) the protective **seed coat.** (See figure 18.3.)

The three parts can be studied if the seed is soaked overnight in water. The seed cover becomes soft and is easy to remove, thus making the other parts easy to inspect. Pupils will find that toothpicks are helpful in separating the seed parts.

After a number of observations, pupils should be able to notice that there are two major groups of seeds: some with two halves (**dicotyledons,** such as beans and peanuts) and those with single units (**monocotyledons,** such as corn, rice, and wheat). (Of course, pupils in lower grades do not have to refer to them by their scientific names.)

Let the seeds germinate for several days and have pupils study the seeds and new plants carefully. Repeated observations at periodic intervals will show that each baby plant has a growing system of leaves, stems, and roots. As it germinates, the food supply of the seed is slowly used up in the new plant's growth.

A more systematic study of seed germination can be done by performing *Event 18-B, Seed Germination.* The rapidly germinating seeds can be studied by removing one seed of each per day. Pupils can see the development of roots, stem, and finally leaves. The germination process can be recorded in individual notebooks and on the bulletin board. A drawing of each seed for each day should clearly show the germination process.

Pupils can study the germination of seeds by performing Events 18-B through 18-G. In *Event 18-C, Seed Depth,* they will notice that large seeds, like lima beans, will do well when planted fairly deep in the soil. If it is good soil, a depth of 5 centimeters is recommended. Small seeds, however, should be planted at more shallow depths. Radish, onion, and carrot seeds should go no more than about 5 or 6 millimeters deep.

After working with seeds for awhile, pupils should be able to discover a relationship between size and planting depth. Small seeds are planted " shallow"; large seeds are planted "deep."

Plants grow entirely from stored energy until they reach sunlight. As a result, large seeds, with more stored energy, can push the new growth through more soil than small seeds. The greater depth also protects the seed from drying out.

The growth energy of the bean seed's stored food can be studied by performing *Event 18-D, Bean Power.* The beans without the two seed halves will grow poorly, if at all. The seed with one half removed will grow better, but the seed with both halves in place will do best of all.

The growing beans use up the energy in the seeds after about 2 weeks. By that time the plant will have developed to the point where it can manufacture its own food supply.

By studying the development of the embryo of a seed, pupils can see that the leaves and stems always grow upward and the roots always grow down. Even when the seedling is turned around, the plant will right itself again. This up-and-down seeking of the plant parts can be seen by doing *Event 18-E, Upside-Down Seeds.*

All of the beans in this event have an equal chance of germinating. Regardless of the position of the seeds, the roots will always turn down and

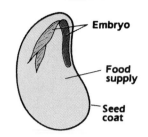

FIGURE 18.3   The lima bean has a "baby" plant (embryo), a protective seed coat (a thin outer covering), and a food supply for the new plant.

the stem will always move up. The up-and-down growth is governed by cells that are sensitive to gravity.

Another factor necessary for the proper germination of seeds is water. However, there should not be too much water. If pupils perform *Event 18-F, Water for Seeds,* they may be surprised to note that seeds that get *too much* water will not even germinate.

This event shows that while water is needed for growth, too much is harmful. The roots need oxygen as well as water, and too much water blocks the oxygen that is needed for growth. The same is true for plantings as for seeds. If there is too much water, the plants will die.

Event 18-G, Growth in Light and Dark, may also turn out to be a surprise to pupils. Most pupils believe that seeds need light to permit them to grow. Yet the seeds in this event will germinate very well in the dark. In fact, after germination, the seeds left in darkness will often grow faster than the seeds exposed to light.

Although the results will be surprising to pupils, the explanation is really quite simple. *Seeds* do not need light to grow, but *plants* do. After all, seeds are planted underground where it is dark. It is only after they reach the sunlight that they develop into little plants. At that point they begin to manufacture their own food and need the sunlight to survive.

During the first few days of germination, the seed grows because it uses its own stored energy. During those days the seed is in underground darkness. If a seed is kept in darkness after it germinates, it will grow a long "leggy" stem "searching" for the sun. Often the plant's stem will be longer than one grown in sunlight.

Some of the best examples of plants with large amounts of stored energy are potatoes, parsnips, beets, and carrots. There is so much stored energy in each of these plants that they can grow stems of amazing length in the darkness. These examples are not seeds, however. They are either roots or stems that can develop into plants. They will be discussed in more detail later.

Minerals are also needed for plant growth. These are generally obtained from the soils in which they grow. Thus, plants growing in sand or other sterile surroundings will die even when the sunlight and water conditions are ideal.

If the plant gets its minerals, sunlight, and water, it can grow even if there is no soil. In fact, there is a type of soilless gardening called **hydroponics** where the correct nutrients are supplied in the water. This type of gardening may be of interest to some pupils. Details about the correct mixture of chemical nutrients can be found in some encyclopedias and secondary science textbooks.

How Seeds Travel

Seeds travel in many ways. A partial list can be made after performing *Event 18-H, How Do Seeds Travel?* The list may include the three types detailed as follows:

1. *Seeds that fly.* Dandelion and milkweed seeds are "fliers." Individual seeds are attached to light "parachutelike" puffs of growth that are easily carried by the wind. Such seeds are scattered over a very wide area.

    Modified fliers, such as the seeds of the maple and box elder trees, have winglike attachments that permit them to drift on wind currents or "helicopter" down for some distance before they land.

2. *Seeds that stick.* Have you ever seen a dog returning from a burdock thicket? The dog is covered with burrlike seeds. These seeds have hooks

and barbs that attach themselves to the fur of animals. As a result, the animals disperse the seeds over a fairly wide area.

3. *Seeds that are eaten.* There are many seeds that are eaten. Some of them (such as nuts) are eaten for food. They are destroyed in the process and cannot germinate.

Other seeds are located inside a fruit and are discarded after the fruit is eaten. Those may germinate. Examples of such fruits are apples, oranges, avocados, pears, grapes, apricots, and peaches.

Still other seeds are eaten along with the fruit and survive the trip through the digestive tract. They can also germinate. For example, many types of berries eaten by birds survive and grow into plants. Just look at what happens along a farmer's fence line. Those fence lines become rows of berry bushes. Birds sit on the fences and excrete seeds. The seeds germinate and grow into plants.

Seedless Reproduction of Plants (Events 18-I through 18-K)

Discrepant Events and Pupil Investigations

Event 18-I. Carrot Plantings

Take several carrots and plant them in potting soil. Plant them at various depths and keep the soil moist.

Pupil Investigations (may include the following processes):

1. Discovering that a carrot grows as long as it receives enough oxygen and water. (Too much water will kill the carrots.)
2. Inferring that the new plant obtains its energy from the carrot itself.
3. Observing that the carrot begins to shrivel as the new plant grows.

Event 18-J. Grass Growing

Plant some grass in a small box of potting soil. Be sure to plant the grass sparsely. Observe the grass over a period of a month or more.

Pupil Investigations (may include the following processes):

1. Observing that the grass is thinly spaced when it emerges.
2. Discovering that new shoots keep developing, making the grass more and more dense.
3. Devising a system for measuring grass density per unit area.
4. Inferring that grass develops in other ways than from seeds.

Event 18-K. Begonia Beginnings

Cut a section of stem with leaf attached from a rex begonia plant. Place the stem in water and set it in sunlight. Observe it for several weeks.

Pupil Investigations (may include the following processes):

1. Observing that roots form on the stem after a few days.
2. Contrasting this form of propagation to other forms.
3. Generalizing about the propagation of plants by cuttings.

Events 18-I through 18-K Explained in Context (Seedless Reproduction of Plants)

Seeds are extremely important in plant reproduction. However, pupils may be surprised to discover that many types of plants can be grown without seeds. In fact there are a number of nonseed methods of plant reproduction.

Certain plants can reproduce from specially adapted roots and stems. Such plants have large amounts of stored energy that nourish the new plant. An example can be seen by performing *Event 18-I, Carrot Plantings.* The new growth of a carrot plant will receive great amounts of stored energy from the planted carrot itself. Only after a set of green leaves has developed will the plant manufacture its own food.

Similar results can be achieved by planting sweet potatoes, white potatoes, parsnips, onions, and numerous flower bulbs. (Be sure to point out that these plants can also be grown from seeds.)

It is important to stress again that a new planting needs oxygen to grow. Therefore, a carrot will grow best if it is placed only about halfway into the moist soil so that part of it will be exposed to air. A carrot will rot if it is completely buried in waterlogged soil.

Another means of plant propagation is by the formation of **runners.** Runners are special growths that develop on the stems of some plants. These runners grow away from the main stem, take root, and then form new plants. Many common grasses reproduce this way. That is why a newly seeded area looks so thin when the seeds emerge, but soon thickens into a lush lawn. The grass can be observed in *Event 18-J, Grass Growing.*

Since the thickening process is gradual, it may be difficult to notice it. As a result, pupils should find a way to measure grass density. This can be done by actually counting the blades in a sample area of, say, 1 centimeter by 1 centimeter.

Another way of measurement is to compare photographs taken at periodic intervals. Care must be taken that the measurements are not distorted by changes in the length of the grass from one period to another. Other plants that propagate by sending out runners include strawberries and some forms of ivy.

A third form of seedless reproduction is achieved with **cuttings.** This is a process in which a leaf or leaf stalk is cut from a plant and placed into moist soil where the cutting takes root. Another option is to place the leaf stalk into a container of water where it forms roots. It can then be planted in soil.

Pupils can observe this form of growth by doing *Event 18-K Begonia Beginnings.* The rex begonia, African violet, coleus, geranium, and echeveria, among others, can be propagated in this manner.

A more complex form of reproduction is **grafting,** a process in which cuttings are joined to other plants. Usually a branch or stem is cut from one plant and grafted to the stem of another plant. This practice is fairly common in nurseries. For example, the seedless orange tree can only be propagated in this way. Since it is seedless, it is obvious that it cannot grow from seeds. Instead, branches of the seedless trees are grafted to hardy roots and stems of a seed variety. Grafting is used to improve many other varieties of trees.

Parts of a Plant (Events 18-L through 18-R)

The Discrepant Events and Pupil Investigations

Event 18-L. Roaming Roots

Plant a few radish seeds in a mixture of sand and humus near the outer walls of a glass container. Give the seeds enough moisture to germinate. Then water only one end of the container and observe the growth of roots.

Pupil Investigations (may include the following processes):

1. Observing that the root hairs grow toward the water supply.
2. Comparing the root development with the roots' distance from the watered spot.
3. Generalizing that seeds need water.

Event 18-M. Carnation Waterpumps

Mix some food coloring into a bottle of water; then insert the stem of a carnation into it. Observe the carnation after several hours.

Pupil Investigations (may include the following processes):

1. Observing that the flower takes on the color of the water.
2. Inspecting the stem to find that a cut section has colored spots around the outer edge.
3. Inferring that the plant has a method of pulling liquid up the stem into the leaves and flowers.

Event 18-N. Moisture Makers

Enclose the leaves and branches of a plant with some clear plastic as shown in figure 18.4. Gather the plastic together at the base of the stem. Set the plant in the sunlight and observe it for several hours.

Pupil Investigations (may include the following processes):

1. Observing that water condenses on the inside of the plastic cover.
2. Inferring that the plant releases moisture into the air.
3. Forming a theory that plants contribute to the water cycle.

Event 18-O. Sun Block

See the effect of sunlight on plants. Enclose a leaf in an envelope of cardboard or tinfoil. Be sure that no light gets through to the leaf. Remove the cover after 3 or 4 days and observe the results. Check to see if the leaf contains any starch. Compare it with a leaf that was not covered.

Pupil Investigations (may include the following processes):

1. Observing that the covered leaf has lost most of its green color.
2. Testing with an iodine solution to see if the leaf contains starch.
3. Contrasting the covered leaf with an uncovered leaf.
4. Generalizing that sunlight is essential to the food manufacturing process of a leaf.

FIGURE 18.4 Moisture from the plant condenses on the inside of a clear plastic sheet that covers it.

FIGURE 18.5   A plant will grow around obstructions to a source of light.

Event 18-P. Light-Seekers
Place a bean plant or potato that has started to sprout into a shoe box arranged with dividers similar to those shown in figure 18.5. Keep the box covered for about a week (except for brief observations and for watering).

Pupil Investigations (may include the following processes):
1. Observing that the plant grows rapidly while enclosed in the box.
2. Discovering that the green color of the leaves begins to fade.
3. Observing that the plant moves around the dividers in the box toward the light.
4. Inferring that plants have a mechanism that causes them to seek light.

Event 18-Q. Parts of a Flower
Study the parts of a simple flower, such as a tulip or a sweet pea. Identify the parts and their functions.

Pupil Investigations (may include the following processes):
1. Identifying, with the aid of references, the main parts of a flower.
2. Inferring a relationship between the pollen and ovule.
3. Analyzing how wind, insects, and gravity affect the distribution of pollen.

Event 18-R. Free Plant "Food"
Composting is nature's way of conserving valuable nutrients plants need to be healthy. Put the five essential ingredients needed to compost in layers in a 5-gallon paint container. The ingredients are: organic matter, bacteria, nitrogen, water, and oxygen. Start with about 15 cm of organic matter such as leaves, grass clippings, weeds, vegetable trimmings, and then add another 5 cm layer of more organic matter in the form of dried animal manure (bacteria) and vegetable trimmings. The third layer consists of a light sprinkling of nitrogen-enriching matter such as fertilizer, blood meal, or cottonseed. Also include some wood ash or lime. The fourth layer should be about 5 cm of rich soil. Repeat the layers until the container is full. There should be enough water and oxygen in the mixture to start the process. Place a cover on the mixture. The lid should have a small hole in the center large enough to place the temperature probe into the middle of the compost. Start recording the temperature every 10 minutes. The computer should be set to record temperatures for 24 hours. After recording for a couple of days, open the lid and mix the compost. Record the temperature again for another 2 days.

Pupil Investigations (may include the following processes):
1. Interpreting from the graph that the temperature rises but then falls off when one of the necessary components is depleted.
2. Predicting what will happen when the mixture is turned.
3. Inferring that lack of oxygen slows decomposition and therefore lowers the temperature of the mixture.
4. Concluding that decomposition is an exothermic reaction and that a chemical change has occurred.

Events 18-L through 18-R Explained in Context (The Parts of a Plant)

What are the major parts of a plant and their functions? Pupils can usually identify these parts. Even at a very early age they seem to know that most plants have **roots,** a **stem** (or trunk), a system of **leaves,** and **flowers.** In this section these parts will be studied more carefully.

Roots

Roots serve at least two important functions: (1) they anchor the plant and (2) they gather raw materials such as water and minerals. The water-gathering function of roots can be observed in *Event 18-L, Roaming Roots.*

The roots need moisture so they grow only on the side of the container that is watered. They do not grow into the dry soil on the other side of the container. Radish seeds work well in this event (as in many others) because they germinate so quickly. Results will be seen in several days to a week.

Roots also serve to anchor the plant to the ground (which is well known to those who have tried to pull out weeds from a garden). The root systems of some weeds are so extensive that it is almost impossible to kill them by pulling them from the ground. There always seems to be enough of the root system remaining to permit them to grow back.

Study the root system with a magnifying glass. Place the roots on some black paper so that the fine white root hairs are seen more easily. Note the extensive network of root hairs.

Stems (Trunks)

The stem of a plant carries the water and nutrients to the leaves where they are used in the manufacture of food. Much of the manufactured food is then transported through the stem back to the roots as well as to all other parts of the plant.

By performing *Event 18-M, Carnation Waterpumps,* we can see that liquids actually travel up the stem of a plant. It takes only a few hours for the plant to draw up the colored water and appear on the flower. Thus, if a white carnation is placed in red-colored water, a red fringe forms on the flower.

The event can also be done by using celery instead of carnations. After the celery has been in the colored water for an hour or more, just slice open the stalk to see how high the colored water has been pumped.

The movement of liquid observed in the carnation and celery also takes place in trees. Some large trees must pump hundreds of liters of water to the leaves daily. The returning flow of sap is often seen dripping from breaks or wounds in trees, especially during the spring of the year. In some trees, V-shaped notches are cut into the bark for the purpose of collecting the sap and making it into syrup and sugar.

The cross section of a tree trunk is fascinating. The rings in the trunk are formed by variations in growth patterns during the course of each year. A tree will generally have a vigorous growth spurt during the spring and summer of each year, but will slow down and go dormant in the fall and winter.

The dark rings represent dormant or slow-growth periods. By counting the rings in the trunk of a tree, a good estimate of the tree's age can be obtained.

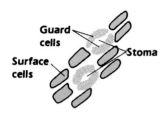

FIGURE 18.6 Under a microscope the openings, or stoma, of the underside of a leaf are visible.

Leaves

What happens to water that goes up the stem to the leaves? The water is given off. Evidence of this water loss can be seen in *Event 18-N, Moisture Makers.* The moisture that is given off by the leaves condenses on the plastic that surrounds the plant. The plastic is soon covered with a fine film of water droplets.

Caution: Watch the plant closely for signs of overheating. Sunlight speeds up the water-emitting process, but it also heats the air and plant inside the plastic cover. Too much heat will damage the plant. In that case, set the plant near a window to get plenty of light, but keep it out of the direct rays of the sun.

Pupils may be able to see how a leaf is structured by studying it under a microscope. Tear a leaf into two parts. If you look closely along the tear, a thin filmlike layer can be seen on the underside of the leaf. Remove a small section of that layer and observe it under a microscope.

Tiny openings, called **stoma,** should be visible as shown in figure 18.6. These are generally located on the underside of a leaf. If a leaf's top surface is studied, the openings cannot be seen.

The leaf is the manufacturing center of a plant. It takes carbon dioxide from the air and chemically combines it with water to produce a simple sugar that is quickly changed to starch. **Starch** is used as energy for growth or is stored for later use. **Chlorophyll,** the green coloring matter of plants, acts as a catalyst. **Oxygen** is a by-product of the manufacturing process and is released into the air.

The manufacturing process cannot take place without sunlight, which supplies the energy to "run the factory." Plants that use the sunlight have green-colored leaves. Anytime the process stops, as in the fall of the year, the leaves lose their green color. This manufacturing process is called **photosynthesis,** which means "putting together by means of light."

This process by which green plants manufacture carbohydrates (one being glucose sugar, $C_6H_{12}O_6$), oxygen, and water is seen in the following simplified reaction.

$$6\,CO_2 + 12\,H_2O \rightarrow C_6H_{12}O_6 + 6O_2 \rightarrow 6\,H_2O$$

The effects of sunlight can be seen by doing *Event 18-O, Sun Block.* When a leaf is covered, blocking out all light, it loses its green color in about 3 or 4 days. In the covered area, the starch-making process stops. As a result, the iodine test will verify that starch is absent.

In the starch test, iodine will turn deep purple if starch is present. If starch is not present, iodine does not change color.

It is somewhat more difficult to test the starch in green leaves than in foods because the green color masks the results. Therefore, the color should be removed prior to the test.

The green color can be removed by boiling the leaf in alcohol for about 15 to 20 minutes. Then the colorless leaf can be easily tested. (**Caution:** Alcohol is quite flammable. Do *not* boil alcohol over an open flame. Heat it in a double boiler, with water in the bottom section and alcohol in the top.)

Because leaves need light, a plant is quite sensitive to its light source. Houseplants will often lean toward the light of a nearby window. The leaves all seem to turn so that each gets the maximum amount of light.

An exaggerated example of this attraction is seen in *Event 18-P, Light Seekers.* A plant left for several days in the specially designed box will grow around the dividers and finally grow right through the small opening. A bean plant is good to use in this event because it grows so quickly.

In the manufacturing process, a leaf uses **carbon dioxide** and gives off oxygen. If the supply of carbon dioxide is cut off, the leaf will die. You can test this statement by coating the leaf with petroleum jelly, cold cream, or some other greasy substance. The substance will clog the tiny openings of the leaf so that carbon dioxide cannot be obtained from the air. In a few days the leaf will turn yellow.

What happens when the opposite is done, when plants get an enriched supply of carbon dioxide? It encourages rapid growth. In fact, for this reason greenhouse operators often add carbon dioxide to the greenhouse air.

Structure of a Flower

To study the structure of a flower as suggested in *Event 18-Q, Parts of a Flower,* it is recommended that a simple plant be used such as a tulip or sweet pea. Do not use a compound flower, such as the sunflower, which has hundreds of duplicate parts all crowded together. Simple flowers tend to stand out separately, usually with four or five petals.

A simple flower will generally have a number of **petals,** several **stamens,** and a **pistil.** (See figure 18.7.) **Pollen** is produced on the upper knobs of the stamen and falls down to fertilize the ovules at the base of the pistil. The base of the pistil can be opened carefully with a toothpick or other sharp object. Inside are the small round objects that later turn into seeds.

Some flowers are **self-pollinating;** that is, the pollen produced by a flower will fertilize the ovules of that same flower. Other flowers depend on insects and wind to carry the pollen from one plant to another.

In *Event 18-R, Free Plant "Food,"* pupils are surprised by the increase in temperature of the compost pile. In nature it goes unnoticed. Pupils may also be surprised how quickly materials decompose. Experiment with growing plants using the composted soil. Do plants grow better in it than in other soils found around the school? Pupils have the misconception that soil is food for plants. Plants do absorb nutrients from the soil but do not "use up" the soil itself. The decomposed materials are a source of needed nutrients.

Composting is nature's way of recycling. Leaves, vegetation, animal, and other organic materials are converted back into usable materials for future growth. The five ingredients needed for the composting process are organic matter, bacteria, nitrogen, water, and oxygen. Five parts green matter to one part nitrogenous matter, such as animal manure, is best. Because bacteria and fungi are largely responsible for the composting process, oxygen is required to keep them alive and multiplying. When air is cut off, **anaerobic** (without the use of oxygen) bacteria take over and an unpleasant odor occurs. Reintroducing oxygen by turning the layers, as well as periodically adding moisture, increases the composting process. Try *Event 18-R, Free Plant "Food,"* again, without the lid or with and without turning the layers.

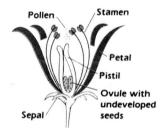

FIGURE 18.7   The major parts of a flower are shown.

Microscopic Forms of Life (Events 18-S through 18-V)

Discrepant Events and Pupil Investigations

Event 18-S. What Sours the Milk?

Pour some milk into a beaker and let it stand in a warm location. Leave it for a day or two. Observe it from time to time.

Pupil Investigations (may include the following processes):

1. Observing the milk at regular intervals and noting that it slowly changes from a liquid to a semisolid.
2. Testing the milk with litmus paper to find its acid-base level.
3. Detecting a change in the odor of the milk.
4. Inferring that there is a fundamental change occurring in the milk.

Event 18-T. Fruit-Jar Cultures

Boil several uncovered fruit jars with a thin wedge of potato in each for 20 minutes. Boil the lids as well. Remove the jars and cover them loosely with the lids. After they cool, remove all but one cover and expose each to a different condition.

    For example, touch the potato of one jar with your finger, let another jar stand in open air for several minutes, and cough into a third. Cover the jars loosely and set them in a dark place at room temperature. Observe the samples from time to time for about a week. (**Caution:** Gases might form in some of the jars, so the covers should be loose enough for the gases to escape. Otherwise, a jar might explode.)

Pupil Investigations (may include the following processes):

1. Discovering the formation of growths on the potatoes inside the jars.
2. Observing (if lucky) that the one jar that was not opened is free from any growth.
3. Generalizing that there are many sources of contamination.

Event 18-U. Mold Farming

Find the best conditions in which molds will grow. Use several slices of bread and vary the conditions. Set one in a moist warm place; another in a dry warm place; a third in a cold dry place; and so on. Observe from time to time for several days.

Pupil Investigations (may include the following processes):

1. Observing the different slices of bread at periodic intervals.
2. Recording the data found by the observations.
3. Analyzing the conditions that are most favorable for the growth of mold on bread.

Event 18-V. Yeast Plants

Mix some yeast and sugar in warm water. Let the mixture stand for several hours. Examine a drop under a microscope about every 30 minutes.

Pupil Investigations (may include the following processes):

1. Observing yeast plants under a microscope.
2. Drawing diagrams of yeast plants, especially showing the formation of buds.
3. Discovering that yeast plants grow rapidly.

Events 18-S through 18-V Explained in Context Microscopic Forms of Life)

Pupils are familiar with the visible plant world that is all around them: the trees, grasses, garden plants, weeds, and farm grains, which cover the earth. However, there are many smaller forms of life that were at one time considered parts of the plant kingdom, but are now classified as separate kingdoms on their own. They are the kingdoms of *protists, monerans, and fungi.*

Protists are one-celled forms of life that can manufacture their own food. They include paramecia and diatoms. **Monerans** are also one-celled forms of life. One example of monerans are bacteria. Some bacteria are helpful, such as those that are in yogurt, and those in the intestines that aid in the digestive process. Other bacteria are harmful, including those that cause tetanus, lyme disease, and food poisoning.

Visible or not, the *effects* of these organisms are often far easier to observe than the organisms themselves. For example, *Event 18-S, What Sours the Milk?,* shows the effects of bacteria. If left in a warm place, milk will turn sour and after a day or two will form a semisolid mass, floating on a watery liquid.

Among the changes that occur is a chemical change when lactose (a sugar) is changed to lactic acid by the action of bacteria. The change can be detected by using litmus paper. Sour milk is acidic and turns litmus paper red.

You can simulate the souring of milk by pouring some vinegar into milk. The milk will curdle (form semisolid chunks) almost at once. The acid in this mixture will turn litmus paper red, just as the acid did in the sour milk.

Microscopic organisms form colonies (or heavy growths) that are clustered together by the thousands or millions. In *Event 18-T, Fruit-Jar Cultures,* it is likely that each of the exposed cultures will develop colonies of microorganisms in a fairly short time.

In fact, even the control sample may form colonies because it is quite difficult to get a perfectly sterile environment inside a jar and to keep it that way before it is sealed. At any rate, the control bottle should at least show that the growths are not as dense as in the other jars.

Be sure to exercise caution with the boiling water and jars. Also, attach the lids loosely so that excess gas pressure inside the jars can escape. Gases are sometimes given off by the growths on the cultures. Too much pressure could cause a jar to explode.

The harmful effects of bacteria on our food supply have been greatly reduced during the past several decades. Food spoilage still occurs, of course, but it is not as severe a problem as formerly because there are now better ways of preserving foods. Some of the methods used to prevent spoilage are listed below.

1. **Refrigeration and freezing.** Bacteria do not grow well if it is too cold. Thus, refrigerated foods are safe from spoilage far longer than foods kept at room temperature. If foods are frozen, they are safe from spoilage for years.
2. **Canning.** The high temperatures used in canning kill all bacteria. If the jars are sealed, then no bacteria exist inside to spoil the foods.

3. **Salting.** Salt inhibits the growth of bacteria. Salting was a popular method of preserving food before the use of freezing and canning.

4. **Drying.** Since bacteria cannot grow without moisture, foods can be preserved by drying them. Some forms of dried meat, such as *jerky,* were popular in the Old West and are still found as snacks today.

5. **Chemical preservatives.** Certain chemicals inhibit or stop the growth of harmful bacteria. Many foods contain these chemicals, and thus a wide range of low-cost foods are made possible.

6. **Smoking.** Certain meats, when subjected to dense smoke, become permeated with it, preventing the growth of bacteria. This method of preservation was widely used along with salting before the use of refrigerators.

7. **Radiation.** High-energy radiation can kill all forms of bacteria without leaving any radiation danger in the food itself. It appears that radiation may prove to be the cheapest and safest way to preserve foods.

Fungi

Fungi make up one of the five kingdoms of life forms. They were originally considered part of the plant kingdom, but are now classified as a separate kingdom. There are many varieties, such as molds, yeasts, mushrooms, lichens, and the organisms that cause athlete's foot. They are all alike in one fundamental way: They do not produce their food with the aid of sunlight. That is, they can grow in the dark. In fact, many fungi grow best in the dark.

Some of the conditions in which molds thrive can be explored by doing *Event 18-U, Mold Farming.* The bread mold will grow best if it is kept warm, moist, and in a dark place. The bread that is allowed to dry out, is placed in direct sunlight, or is kept too cold will not produce a mold.

Mildew is another form of fungi. It is sometimes referred to as a mold that grows on nonfood items. Again, it needs warm, dark, and moist conditions. Mildew can grow rapidly in a pile of damp clothing during hot summer months.

It is important to realize that not all fungi are harmful. In fact, many are quite beneficial. They serve a useful function in speeding the decomposition of dead plant matter, breaking it down to become useful nutrients in the soil. Other useful fungi are used to produce life-saving drugs such as penicillin, streptomycin, and aureomycin.

Yeast is another useful fungus. It produces a chemical reaction that breaks down sugars and starches into simpler compounds, such as carbon dioxide or alcohol. Yeasts are used in breadmaking and in the production of alcohol. The growth of yeasts is shown in *Event 18-V, Yeast Plants.*

Yeasts grow rapidly in dark surroundings, with plenty of warmth and sugar. When viewing yeast through a microscope, the budding process of reproduction should be clearly visible. Buds, which form on a yeast stalk, develop into new plants.

Combining Assessment with Instruction

1. Many elementary students think (falsely) that plants need soil to grow. Tell the children that you want them to grow a bean in a bag. Tape a lima bean (that has soaked overnight) to the middle of the inside of a Ziploc bag. See Figure 18.8. To assess what students have already learned from

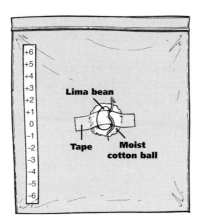

FIGURE 18.8   The stem will grow up and the root will grow down.

the plant unit they have studied, ask students which of the following will help their bean to grow in the bag.

a. Putting a moist cotton ball or paper towel in the bag? Why?
b. Leaving the bag open? closed? Why?
c. Placing the bag in the sunlight, closet, or other parts of the room? Why?
d. Placing dry soil in the bottom of the bag? Why?
   However the students answer their questions let them explore growing their plant under those conditions. (An assessment activity can help the teacher determine what the students know but also should give students another opportunity to reflect on what they know and perhaps refine their understanding of a concept.) As they collect data throughout the next 2 weeks, let each compare how his/her seed is growing compared to other students' seeds. Place a vertical centimeter number line on the side of the bag so that zero is in the middle of the bean and positive numbers go up and negative numbers go down. Each day students should use a bar graph to record the height of the stem and the length of the roots. This is an easy way to incorporate mathematics and a first introduction to integers. It is not important to talk about integers other than to relate the negative sign to growing in the down direction and the positive sign to growing in the up direction. Perhaps even relate it to temperature with above and below freezing on the Celsius scale. Assess how competent students are in collecting the daily data and recording it in a table or on graph paper.

2. Intermediate and middle-level children can be assessed as they explore what soil is, what the purpose of soil is in plant growth, and whether plants grow without soil. The University of Illinois Extension, http://www.urbanext.uiuc.edu/gpe/index.html, has developed an excellent teacher guide including activities and games for students to learn about plant life. *The Great Plant Escape: In Search of Green Life*, is a series of six mysteries students solve to better understand plant life. Detective LePlant and his two assistants, Sprout and Bud, will guide your students through the hands-on activities used to give your students first-hand experiences with growing crops such as lettuce. Assess

students' attention to detail in measuring and recording information as they grow their plants. For example, do children record the indoor temperature each day, the amount of water they add to the growing system, the amount of fertilizer added, whether their plant is in a location to get sun, is it a cloudy or sunny day, soil or water pH, etc. These plant care jobs and recordings need to be done at the start of each science lesson. Do children follow-through with their jobs, do they need to be reminded, are they careful in their measurements?

Depending upon the grade level, experiments can be designed and conducted by your students to answer many of the questions Inspector LePlant asks about plant life. At the end of the mystery cases you have chosen to explore, have groups of students report what they have discovered about growing plants and gardening. Encourage students to include in their presentations diagrams of plants they grew.

Tip: If you are going to grow rapidly sprouting seeds, put them in water on Friday to soak so they will be ready for students to prepare on Monday for growing. They will sprout early in the week, giving students more time to view the growing stage uninterrupted. Radishes and alfalfa sprout faster than beans. Lettuce is fast growing in cooler night temperatures. If it is out of season to buy garden seeds, a health food store may carry radish, alfalfa, mung beans, and wheat all year.

Sites and Software

The following websites and software are appropriate to use with this chapter. Note that computer software and websites change rapidly. This makes it necessary to investigate the stable websites for new links and software catalogs for updates. Visit www.mhhe.com/friedl6e to link to these directly and for study resources.

Sites

Learning Web (USGS)	www.usgs.gov/education
Biology Lessons (grades K–8) San Diego State U.	www.biologylessons.sdsu.edu/index.html
People and Plants	www.muohio.educ/dragonfly/ plant/index.htmlx
First Gov for Kids	www.kids.gov/k_plants.htm
How Rainforests Work	www.howstuffworks.com/rainforest.htm
Smile Program Biology Index	www.iit.edu/~smile/biolinde.html#b3
Hydroponics for Kids	www.growingedge.com/kids/ educators/links.html
Simple Hydroponic Garden	www.k12.hi.us/~ckuroda/ Start_hydroponic_garden.html
What Is Hydroponics?	www.k12.hi.us/~ckuroda/ what_is_hydroponics.html

Software

One Small Square: Backyard (Carolina) (3–7)
Science Court Explorations: Soil (Tom Snyder) (4–6)
SimPark (Discovery) (2–6)
Sammy's Science House (IBM) (K–2)
Learn about Life Science: Plants (Sunburst) (K–3)

Key Terms

anaerobic, *359*
angiosperms, *350*
carbon dioxide, *359*
chlorophyll, *358*
composting, *356*
cuttings, *354*
dicotyledons, *351*
embryo, *351*
flower, *357*
food supply, *351*
fungi, *362*
germination, *350*

grafting, *354*
gymnosperms, *350*
hydroponics, *352*
leaves, *357*
minerals, *352*
monerans, *361*
monocotyledons, *351*
oxygen, *358*
petals, *359*
photosynthesis, *358*
pistil, *359*
pollen, *359*

protists, *361*
roots, *357*
runners, *354*
seed coat, *351*
self-pollinating, *359*
stamens, *359*
starch, *358*
stem, *357*
stoma, *358*
yeast, *362*

Teaching Children about the Animal Kingdom

NATIONAL SCIENCE EDUCATION STANDARDS ALIGNMENT TO EVENTS

The events in this chapter help accomplish several of the NSES for content. The event(s) that align with a given content standard are listed below that standard.

LEVELS K–4

UNIFYING CONCEPTS AND PROCESSES

* Systems, order and organization
  19-A through 19-H
  19-M and 19-N

* Evidence, models and explanation
  19-D
  19-H
  19-O and 19-P

* Evolution and equilibrium
  19-A through 19-P

LIFE SCIENCE

* Characteristics
  19-A through 19-N
  19-P

* Life cycles
  19-B
  19-D through 19-H
  19-O and 19-P

* Organisms and environment
  19-I through 19-M
  19-P

SCIENCE AND TECHNOLOGY

* Understanding science and technology
  19-H

SCIENCE IN PERSONAL AND SOCIAL PERSPECTIVES

* Science and technology in society
  19-H

HISTORY AND NATURE OF SCIENCE

* Nature of science
  19-A through 19-H

LEVELS 5–8

UNIFYING CONCEPTS AND PROCESSES

* Systems, order and organization
  19-A through 19-H
  19-M and 19-N

* Evidence, models and explanation
  19-D
  19-H
  19-O and 19-P

* Evolution and equilibrium
  19-A through 19-P

LIFE SCIENCE

* Structure and function in living systems
  19-H through 19-M

* Reproduction and heredity
  19-A through 19-P

* Regulation and behavior
  19-O and 19-P

* Populations and ecosystems
  19-A through 19-H
  19-N
  19-P

* Diversity and adaptations
  19-A through 19-P

SCIENCE AND TECHNOLOGY

* Understanding science and technology
  19-H

SCIENCE IN PERSONAL AND SOCIAL PERSPECTIVES

* Science and technology in society
  19-H

HISTORY AND NATURE OF SCIENCE

* Nature of science
  19-A through 19-H

* History of science
  19-A through 19-H

Birth of Biology

Biological studies can be traced back to 640 B.C., when Greek philosophers Hippocrates and Alcamaeon studied animals to learn more about the human body. Three hundred years later, Aristotle, the father of biology, developed a method of studying natural phenomenon through the observation of the structure, physiology, and development of organisms. Focusing primarily on animals, Aristotle developed a classification system that looked beyond superficial characteristics. He studied the embryonic development of animals, discovering that they go through gradual stage changes as they develop, debunking the idea of pre-formation (i.e., that animals are tiny adults starting at conception and grow into full-sized adults over time).

Much of Aristotle's work was lost during the reign of the Roman Empire. What remained was used for theoretical reading and writing, but the use of the scientific method and direct observation ceased. Science became a study of transcripts. Theories were proved by reading other people's writing. Many of the nonscientific explanations for phenomena, such as pre-formation, resurfaced during this period of time and held fast in the belief systems of Western civilization for thousands of years.

Then, in the A.D. 1500s, experimentation entered into the realm of science. For example, William Harvey used experiments to demonstrate and prove the circulatory system, Andreas Vesalius perfected the use of dissection to describe the human anatomy, and Francesco Redi proved that insects are not manifested from the putrefaction of the environment around them but are born from eggs deposited in the environment most suitable for the development of the larvae. Scientists began to use carefully constructed experiments to explain phenomena within the circulatory, nervous, and reproductive systems. Tools that were not available during Aristotle's lifetime, such as microscopes, were developed during this time, creating new avenues for scientific study of living and nonliving organisms. In 1665 Robert Hooke coined the term *cell* to describe the compartments he saw within a slice of cork as he experimented with the use of ground lenses for magnification.

The term *biology* first surfaced in 1800 in a footnote of an article in an obscure journal. Four years later two scientists used the term for their research and a new form of scientific study was created. Biology, in contrast to nature study, focuses on the physiological structure of all organisms, plant and animal, to determine how the animal functions. Nature study focuses on the geographical, interspecies and intraspecies relationships of living and nonliving organisms.

During this time period scientists were making progress in the study of bacteria, cell structure, and the processes of life. In 1876 Robert Koch created the first experiment that proved disease was caused by microscopic organisms called bacteria. Through the use of microscopes Koch discovered tiny rod-shaped bodies in the blood of an animal that had died of anthrax. He began to experiment with growing cultures of the bacteria outside the host and perfected it in 1881.

As science progressed, biology began to include the study of the basis for the diversity of plants and animals. The first theory of evolution surfaced in 1800 when Jean Lanmarck described a process of evolution that accounted for variance and inheritance of physical characteristics among similar species. The premise of Lanmarck's theory stated that all species were evolving toward a perfect state and at some point in time would reach a fixed ideal. In 1859, Charles Darwin revolutionized the field of evolutionary study with his publication of the *Origin of Species.* Darwin expanded upon Lanmarck's theory, modifying the strict rules of variance and heredity, and added the influence of environment, which Darwin termed *natural selection.* Darwin rejected the idea that all species were moving toward a final form. Through his studies he discovered that species undergo change regularly; nothing in nature is fixed.

Biology has focused on the study of plant and animals with an underlying goal to improve the health and knowledge of humans. One of the most monumental discoveries in the 1900s was that of DNA. Four researchers, Rosalind Elsie Franklin, James Watson, Francis Crick, and Maurice Wilkins worked diligently using x-ray technology and experiments to describe the structure of the human genome. James Watson and Francis Crick are credited with the initial discovery but their work was greatly enhanced by the x-ray photographs taken by Rosalind Franklin and other research completed by her colleague Maurice Wilkins.

The advent of industrialization in the early 1900s lead some biologists to direct their studies on plants and animals in relation to their habitats. Rachel Carson, Jane Goodall, and E. O. Wilson studied the connection of human action together with changes in the natural world. Through careful study of natural organisms such as birds, chimpanzees, and insects, these scientists were able to prove the detrimental effects of human-introduced changes, such as pesticides and habitat destruction, on animals and plants—leading to a larger connection between humans, animals, plants, and the natural processes of the earth and the development of ecology.

Animals with Backbones (Events 19-A through 19-H)

Discrepant Events and Pupil Investigations

Event 19-A. Classifying Animals

Display 20 to 30 pictures of animals. Ask children to classify them into groups of their own choosing. (The number of pictures can be reduced to 5 or 10 for primary grades.)

Pupil Investigations (may include the following processes):

1. Classifying animals according to such traits as size, how they move, where they live, what they eat, their coats (hair, feathers, scales), and which make good pets.
2. Checking references as an aid to classifying animals.
3. Analyzing the usefulness of the groupings.
4. Comparing the groups selected by children with those selected by biologists.

Event 19-B. What Am I? (#1)

Ask pupils to classify the following mystery animal into one of five classes— mammal, reptile, bird, fish, or amphibian: "I have a backbone and lay eggs. My skin is covered with hair, and I cannot fly. What am I?"

Pupil Investigations (may include the following processes):

1. Classifying on the basis of the backbone that the animal could belong to any of the five groups.
2. Inferring (incorrectly) that, because it lays eggs, the animal could *not* be a mammal.
3. Predicting (incorrectly) that its lack of flying ability is a key to the correct placement of the animal.
4. Generalizing on the basis of having hair that the animal is a mammal.

Event 19-C. What Am I? (#2)

Ask pupils to classify this mystery animal into one of five classes—mammal, reptile, bird, fish, or amphibian: "I live in the water, I cannot survive on land. I have a backbone, and hair on my skin. My body temperature does not change very much."

Pupil Investigations (may include the following processes):

1. Predicting (incorrectly) that the animal is a fish because it lives in water and cannot survive on land.
2. Generalizing (incorrectly) that the animal is a reptile or amphibian because it lives in water.
3. Classifying the animal on the basis of its hair.

Event 19-D. What Am I? (#3)

Ask pupils to classify the following mystery animal into one of five classes—mammal, reptile, bird, fish, or amphibian: "I have a backbone and walk on two legs. I cannot fly. I am warm-blooded and have no teeth. I grow to 8 feet tall and have feathers. I lay eggs."

Pupil Investigations (may include the following processes):

1. Predicting that the animal could be either a bird or mammal because it has two legs and is warm-blooded.
2. Analyzing that factors of size, egg-laying, and lack of teeth are not valid traits used to classify animals.
3. Inferring (incorrectly) that since it cannot fly, it could *not* be a bird (thinking that all birds can fly).
4. Classifying the animal as a bird because it has feathers.

Event 19-E. What Am I? (#4)

Ask pupils to classify the following mystery animal into one of five classes—mammal, reptile, bird, fish, or amphibian: "I have a backbone and eat meat. I live in the water and on land. I lay eggs and am cold-blooded. I have an armored skin."

Pupil Investigations (may include the following processes):

1. Predicting (incorrectly) that the animal is a fish because it can live in the water.
2. Classifying the animal (incorrectly) as a mammal because it can eat meat.
3. Classifying the animal as a reptile because it is cold-blooded and has an armored skin.

Event 19-F. What Am I? (#5)

Ask pupils to classify the following mystery animal into one of five classes—mammal, reptile, bird, fish, or amphibian: "I have a backbone and lay eggs. I live on land and in the water. I have smooth skin and am cold-blooded."

Pupil Investigations (may include the following processes):

1. Classifying the animal (incorrectly) as a reptile.
2. Inferring that because it is cold-blooded it has to be a reptile, fish, or amphibian.
3. Generalizing that only amphibians meet all the characteristics of the mystery animal.

Event 19-G. What Am I? (#6)

Ask pupils to classify the following mystery animal into one of five classes—mammal, reptile, bird, fish, or amphibian: "I have a backbone and a lung. I live in water and breathe with gills. I am cold-blooded and have a scaly skin."

Pupil Investigations (may include the following processes):

1. Generalizing (incorrectly) on the basis of its having a lung that the animal would have to be a bird, mammal, or amphibian.
2. Inferring that the animal is either fish, amphibian, or reptile because it has gills.
3. Identifying that the animal is either a fish or reptile because it has scaly skin.
4. Classifying the animal as either amphibian or reptile because it is cold-blooded.
5. Generalizing that a lung is not a distinctive trait for the purposes of classifying animals.

Event 19-H. Chordata Database

Collect pictures of about 50 animals belonging to the Chordata phylum. The collection should include about 10 pictures from each of the five classes: mammals, reptiles, birds, fish, and amphibians. Have each pupil research the characteristics of two animals. After pupils have completed their investigations, have the class brainstorm a list of important information *(fields)* needed to classify the Chordata phylum. Let pupils search for any characteristic they may not have found during their first search. Encourage the use of the Internet as part of the search process. Have the class again identify the list of important characteristics or fields of animals. This will be the field names for the Chordata database. The fields may include: size; animals that make good pets; body covering (fur, feathers, hair, armored skin, etc.); habitat (land, water, both, etc); and birth of young (live birth or egg). Many of the fields the pupils select will be part of the official grouping system, others will not. Try to encourage both. Have pupils enter the information about their selected animals into the *file,* "Animals with Backbones Database."

Pupil Investigations (may include the following processes):

1. Collecting information known about animals with backbones.
2. Sorting for a given *field* or characteristic of animals using a database.
3. Classifying animals by using the database sort and search functions.

Events 19-A through 19-H Explained in Context (Animals with Backbones)

There are thousands of different forms of animal life. One of the best ways to understand the animal kingdom is to classify them into related groups. In that way we can understand the characteristics of a group instead of trying to memorize the animals one at a time.

Before going into any classroom exercises that focus on animal groupings, it may be helpful to see how biologists have classified the animals. They have grouped animals into levels of greater and greater specialization. These groupings are presented briefly, beginning with the most general and ending with the most specific.

1. **Kingdom.** All living things are divided into five main groups: Monerans, Protists, Fungi, Plants, and Animals. In this chapter, we focus on the animal kingdom.

    Animals have the following characteristics: (a) they are capable of independent movement; (b) they contain no cellulose (or woody) material; (c) their cells contain no chlorophyll (the substance that colors plants green); and (d) they are capable of feeling and sensation.

2. **Phylum.** The animal kingdom is divided into a number of large divisions or phyla. These phyla include *Protozoa* (the one-celled animals) and **Chordata** (animals with with a backbone).

3. **Class.** The phyla are further divided into classes. For example, the phylum *Chordata* is divided into mammals, reptiles, birds, fish, and amphibians.

4. **Order.** Each class is divided into orders. The class of mammals, for example, is divided into 16 orders that include *Carnivora* (the meat-eating animals), *Marsupialia* (the pouched animals), and *Probosciden* (the long-nosed animals).

5. **Family.** Each order is divided into families. The order *Carnivora,* for example, is divided into families that include felines (the cats) and canines (the dogs).

6. **Genus.** Each family is divided into genera. For example, the family of felines is divided into a number of genera that includes lions and tigers.

7. **Species.** Each genus is divided into species. For example, the lions are divided into a number of species that include *Felis concolor* (the mountain lion).

8. **Subspecies.** Sometimes the species are divided still further into subspecies.

It is impossible to present all of these groups in elementary school science lessons. Instead, relatively few animals should be presented to help children understand how the classification system works.

In this chapter, we will focus on the five classes of *Chordata.* In other words, we will study the five groups of animals that have backbones. They include the mammals, reptiles, birds, fish, and amphibians. In addition, insects will be discussed.

Placing pictures of animals into groups will help pupils to become familiar with factors that distinguish one group of animals from another. In intermediate or higher grades, you should use a group of 20 to 30 familiar animal pictures. For primary grades, the number should be reduced. Be sure that you have examples of all the groups that you want to teach about. Display them on a bulletin board or in any way that makes them all visible at the same time.

Ask pupils to classify them according to any system that seems to make sense to them, as suggested in *Event 19-A, Classifying Animals*. In the beginning of this exercise it is not important if they follow any guidelines about official grouping systems. Let them select characteristics on their own. They may choose groupings based on size or even "animals that make good pets."

After they have worked with their groups for some time, go back over the traits that they have chosen with a more critical eye. Ask, "Why is the trait good or weak?" Do all people agree about the animals that are listed as "pets"? If a dog is grouped as a pet, ask if a vicious dog is a pet? If size is selected, does a puppy change its classification just by growing up?

The pupils should be led to realize that any characteristic that is too vague is not of much help in classifying. Neither is a system helpful if it means different things to different people.

It is quite likely that the pupils will select at least some characteristics that are used in the official classification system. For example, "animals with feathers" is not too uncommon, or "animals with hair."

Some of the basic factors in the classification system can be highlighted by presenting a series of "What am I?" exercises from Events 19-B through 19-G. These six events focus on the five classes of animals that have backbones.

Mammals

Mammals are a class of warm-blooded animals that possesses hair at some stage of their development and nourish their young by means of milk glands. Most, but not all, mammals give live birth to their young (instead of incubating an egg).

Event 19-B, What Am I? (#1), describes one of the rare egg-laying mammals: the duck-billed platypus. After the eggs hatch, they are nourished by milk glands just like other mammals.

Of course, we should not expect children to be able to identify the animal by name. The purpose of the exercise is to focus on the characteristics that are relevant in selecting a group. Egg-laying is not a relevant consideration among animal classes. The reason that it is not a helpful characteristic is that there are egg-layers among all five groups.

Event 19-C, What Am I? (#2), is somewhat easier for most pupils. In this event pupils can often name the correct animal. Examples of the mystery animal are the whale, dolphin, sea lion, and porpoise. All of these are mammals that must live in water. Each is a lung-breather, has hair on its skin, has a constant body temperature, and gives milk to its young. Those characteristics are quite different from fish, which are cold-blooded, lay eggs, obtain oxygen with gills, and have a scaly skin.

Animals are referred to as warm-blooded or cold-blooded. By this reference we mean that some animals have a near constant body temperature, while others have temperatures that vary with the environment. Humans, for example, have a normal body temperature of $37°$ C. This value changes only slightly depending on rate of body activity and conditions of health. Even hibernating animals do not have a big change in their body temperature.

Cold-blooded animals are quite different. They generally undergo wide swings in temperature, depending on the temperature of their surroundings. A fish, for example, has a body temperature that is identical to the water in which it swims.

When the temperature warms up, cold-blooded animals become more active; when it cools down, they become less active. If it gets too cold, they cease activities altogether. Many such animals will remain inactive all winter.

Cold-blooded animals survive long winters because they use negligible energy to maintain body temperature. Furthermore, if it is cold, they do nothing, so little if any energy is used. Thus, they wait for the return of warm weather to become active again.

Warm-blooded animals, by contrast, use a great amount of energy just to maintain body temperature. Therefore, warm-blooded animals must eat much more food than cold-blooded animals.

Birds

Birds are distinguished by their feathers. The most common misconception people have is that all birds can fly. That is not true. There are several kinds of flightless birds, including the ostrich, kiwi, emu, cassowary, and penguin.

In *Event 19-D, What Am I? (#3)*, the characteristic of feathers is what identifies the animal as a bird. The event describes an ostrich. In addition, all birds are warm-blooded and have two legs. (All birds also have two wings, but that does not necessarily mean that the birds can fly.)

Birds have huge appetites. Many smaller birds eat their weight in food every day. They need these great amounts of food because flying uses up a lot of energy. In addition, much food is needed just to maintain body temperature.

A smaller bird needs more energy per gram to keep warm than does a larger bird. The smaller the bird, the greater the relative skin area through which heat is lost. This statement may seem vague, at first, but should become clear by doing a simple experiment.

Compare the surface area of one milk carton of ½-gallon size, with two cartons, each of 1-quart size. Their volumes are the same; but the surface area of the two smaller cartons, when added together, is greater than that of the larger carton.

Just cut the three cartons apart carefully at the seams so that they can be laid flat. Then measure the surface areas and compare. The same figures can be gained by simply measuring the boxes and doing the calculations. The two smaller cartons, when combined, should have 57% more surface area than the large carton.

In like manner, large animals have less surface area per unit of volume than small animals have. As a result, the larger animals need less energy per unit of volume to maintain body temperature than do smaller animals.

Can you guess the diet of birds that live in cold, snowy climates in the winter? Are they likely to be those that live on insects? No, because there are no insects available when it gets cold. Only birds that can survive on seeds live in cold winter climates.

Those that need insects fly south. Some winter birds eat both insects and seeds, but in the winter they eat only the seeds that are available.

One easy way to observe birds is to build a birdfeeder. (See figure 19.1 to see how to make a birdfeeder from a tin can and pie plate.)

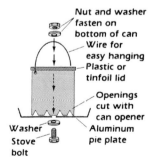

FIGURE 19.1 A simple birdfeeder can be built with a tin can and a pie plate. A wire can be attached to hang the feeder on the limb of a tree.

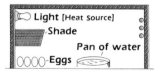

FIGURE 19.2 A cross section of an egg incubator. A thermostat is needed to keep the temperature accurate.

Hatching Eggs

One activity that is a real hit in the classroom is the incubation and hatching of eggs. Fertilized eggs will hatch if they are properly cared for in an incubator.

The temperature and humidity must be carefully controlled for the incubation to be a success. As a result, it is not likely that a "homemade" incubator will be successful. Most homemade incubators will either broil or freeze the eggs.

If it is well made, however, a homemade incubator might work. It must have a source of heat (usually a lightbulb) and a thermostat wired into the electrical circuit to maintain an even temperature. If a lightbulb is used, the eggs should be protected from the direct rays of the bulb (otherwise the eggs will be cooked by radiation even if the air temperature is correct). Finally, a shallow pan of water is needed to keep a high moisture content in the air. (See figure 19.2.)

It is unlikely that many teachers will be able to build a homemade incubator that will work satisfactorily. It is therefore recommended that a commercial incubator be used. Under no circumstances should someone who is not fully competent to work safely with electrical wiring attempt the project. It is far more complicated than just plugging in a light.

Properly incubated eggs can be checked periodically to examine the stage of development of the growing embryos. Break open the eggs and carefully separate the developing embryo from the rest of the egg. After about 1 week of growth, the embryo will be large enough for the eyes, wings, and legs to be visible.

After about 21 or 22 days of incubation, the chick hatches from its egg. It uses a small ridge on the upper tip of its beak (the *egg tooth*) to break open the shell. The ridge drops off shortly after the chick hatches. Several hours are usually needed, for the chick to pick its way out of the shell. The chick emerges wet and bedraggled, but soon the downlike feathers dry and the chick becomes a soft ball of fluff.

Once the chicks are hatched they can survive a more varied environment than the incubator. As a result, the homemade chick brooder is likely to be more successful than the homemade incubator.

A brooder must provide a warm place for the chicks and some freedom of movement so that they can run and eat. A two-part box, as shown in figure 19.3 is useful. The inside half can provide warmth if heated with a small lightbulb carefully shielded against fire and electrical danger. Be sure that the bulb is out of reach of the chicks.

The other half of the box (the outside half) should be an open screened area to permit free circulation of air and allow easy viewing. Chicks should have food and water available at all times.

If you decide to have chicks in your class, it is important to realize that they do not come without grime and other problems. They require a lot of care in feeding and in keeping their brooder clean. Any neglect in cleaning will quickly attract flies, mites, and other pests. It is probably wise to give them away after a week or so.

Finally, any neglect in heating and feeding will result in death for at least some of the chicks. So let the children enjoy and learn about the eggs and chicks. Then give them away to someone who has the time and ability to care for them.

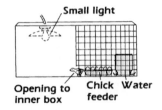

FIGURE 19.3 A chick brooder can be made from a box divided into two parts. Chicks should be able to move freely from the heated half to the open half.

Reptiles

Reptiles are a class of animals that is cold-blooded. They have a backbone and an armored (or scaly) skin. Reptiles breathe air with lungs and usually lay hard- or soft-shelled eggs. There are over six thousand species. Snakes, turtles, lizards, alligators, and crocodiles are some examples.

Event 19-E, What Am I? (#4), highlights the characteristics of reptiles. The mystery animal of this event is the turtle. Many types of reptiles spend most of their lives in the water. Nevertheless, they must breathe air with lungs to survive.

Some sea turtles spend most of their lives in the water and seldom come on land. They have flippers, which help them swim well, but which are poor for walking on land. Other turtles, more properly called tortoises, live mostly on land and occasionally go into the water. Accordingly, they have feet with toes and claws instead of flippers.

Because reptiles are cold-blooded, they depend on their surroundings for their body heat. If the weather gets cold, they slow down and become sluggish. Warm weather is needed for them to function at their best. As a result, there are no turtles in very frigid climates. By contrast, reptiles abound in the tropics.

Turtles can usually survive fairly well if properly cared for. A habitat for a turtle should include some water, a gradual incline from the water to some sand or soil, and perhaps a flat rock. (See figure 19.4.) It should also be fairly warm and have some sunlight, but shade should always be available if the turtle wants it.

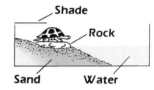

FIGURE 19.4 A habitat for a turtle should include water and a gradual slope to sand or soil. Include also a flat rock and a shelter from the sun.

Turtles can be fed bits of lettuce if they are vegetarians. If they are not, they can be fed bits of hamburger or some insects. Be sure you know the type you have. Commercial turtle food is generally available in pet shops.

There certainly are benefits associated with having a turtle in the classroom. However, there are also problems. According to reports from zoo authorities who present educational programs to schools, many turtles are mishandled in the classroom and die.

Some starve to death because meat-eaters are fed plant food and vice versa. But, more likely, the animal is given too much food. The excess rots and contaminates the container. Still others die from drowning because there is no land to rest on. They are good swimmers, but they cannot swim forever.

The teacher should be fully aware of the benefits and problems in deciding whether to have a turtle in the classroom. Perhaps the best solution for a teacher who would like to have one, is to keep it for a limited period of time. Most of the educational value is gained in several weeks. After that time it is often more humane to release the animal than to keep it.

Amphibians

Amphibians are a class of animals that is somewhat similar to reptiles. Each type is cold-blooded, lives on both land and water, and lays eggs. There is only one major difference. Amphibians have unarmored skin, which may be smooth or bumpy; reptiles have armored, or scaly, skins.

The difference between amphibians and reptiles is highlighted in *Event 19-F, What Am I? (#5).* The animal in the riddle is a frog, and the correct class is amphibian.

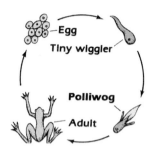

FIGURE 19.5 The life cycle of a frog includes the egg, tiny wiggler, polliwog, and adult.

One additional difference between reptiles and amphibians is that the latter depend on gills during the early stages of their life cycle. However, the adult members of the amphibians are lung-breathers.

The frog is a good example of an animal that goes through a series of major changes in its life cycle. It starts out as an egg that hatches into a tiny tadpole, or polliwog. The tadpole has gills and gets its oxygen just as fish do. They do not breath air with lungs at this point in their development. Slowly, the tadpole grows legs and loses its tail. Finally, the legs are fully grown, the tail is gone, and the frog breathes with lungs. (See figure 19.5.)

Frogs are able to obtain some oxygen from the water through their skins. This allows them to survive the winter months buried in the mud at the bottom of lakes and streams. When the ground and water warm up in the spring, they return to the surface.

Fish

Fish are a class of animals that is cold-blooded, live in water, and are usually covered with scales. There is no known exception to the trait that all fish use gills to extract oxygen from water.

However, there are several kinds of fish, among the thousands of species, that have two methods of getting oxygen. In addition to using gills, they also breathe with a lung.

One of the fish that uses two methods of obtaining oxygen is the lung fish, referred to in *Event 19-G, What Am I? (#6).* (Again, the children should not be expected to identify the specific animal by name.) Children should be able to identify the animal as a fish because only fish use gills to get oxygen from the water during their entire life cycle.

Contrary to some other animals, fish are often fairly easy to keep in the classroom. They do not require as much care as most other animals. Fish such as guppies are ideal for a classroom aquarium. They are inexpensive, reproduce quickly, tolerate a fairly wide range of temperatures, endure crowded conditions well, and are easy to feed.

By adding a few sea snails, the amount of care can be reduced even further. The snails are scavengers, or "garbage collectors." They help keep the aquarium clean; they also eat the algae that often grows in the water even if the aquarium is kept out of direct sunlight, if kept in the sunlight, the algae growth will get out of control.

A few sea plants can improve the aquarium still more. They supply the water with oxygen and remove carbon dioxide. With the right combination of fish, plants, and snails, the aquarium is said to be balanced. That is, the plants and animals work in harmony to balance each other's needs. Such an aquarium seldom needs cleaning. If it has a good filter, it may go all year without cleaning.

Event 19-H, Chordata Database, gives pupils an opportunity to understand how animals are classified. Encourage the use of the database during the "Who Am I?" game. A "big idea" behind the use of a database is for students to develop an appreciation for the ease and speed at which a database can sort tremendous amounts of information.

Adaptations of Nature (Events 19-I through 19-M)

Discrepant Events and Pupil Investigations

Event 19-I. Adaptations of Nature: Feet

What can you tell about animals by just looking at their feet? Ask pupils to determine the characteristics of the birds that are represented by the feet in figure 19.6.

Pupil Investigations (may include the following processes):

1. Comparing the webbing, talons, and placement of toes in the three examples.
2. Inferring that the feet with toes in front and back belong to a perching bird.
3. Inferring that the foot with the sharp talons belongs to a predator such as an owl or hawk.
4. Inferring that the webbed foot belongs to a bird that lives on or near water.

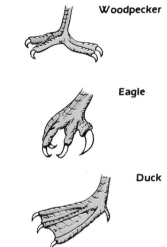

FIGURE 19.6   Can you tell what each of these birds does with its feet?

Event 19-J. Adaptations of Nature: Eyes

What can you tell about animals by just looking at their eyes? Ask pupils to determine the characteristics of the animals that are represented by the eyes in figure 19.7.

Pupil Investigations (may include the following processes):

1. Observing that two animals have eyes located in the front of the head—designed for looking ahead.
2. Observing that two animals have eyes located at the sides of the head—positioned to see in all directions at the same time.
3. Inferring that the position of the eyes is related to the animal's need to gather food and to survive.
4. Generalizing that predators have eyes in front to pursue their food and that the intended victims have eyes on the sides of the head designed to detect the pursuer.

FIGURE 19.7   Can you tell by looking at the eyes which animals do the pursuing and which are the pursued?

Event 19-K. Adaptations of Nature: Beaks

What can you tell about animals by just looking at their beaks? Ask pupils to determine the characteristics of the birds shown in figure 19.8.

Pupil Investigations (may include the following processes):

1. Inferring that the short, pointed beak is adapted for cracking seeds and nuts.
2. Inferring that the large, powerful hooked beak is designed for tearing.
3. Inferring that the long, rounded beak is designed for scooping food out of watery places.

Event 19-L. Radiating Ears

Connect the temperature probe to the computer. Fill containers of different shapes and sizes with equal amounts (250 ml) of warm water (50° C or higher) one at a time. Have the computer collect the change in temperature over a period of 25 minutes for each.

Pupil Investigations (may include the following processes):

1. Observing which container lost heat fastest.
2. Interpreting the different slopes of the graphs generated for each container.
3. Inferring that the larger the surface area of a container the faster the heat is dispersed.
4. Applying the principles of heat radiation to animal adaptation.

Condor

Sparrow

Event 19-M. Match the Animal with Its Food

Write two lists on the chalkboard; the first list of animals, and the second of the foods they eat. Have children match up the animals with the foods:

Animals	Foods
Cow	Fly
Frog	Fish
Hawk	Grass
Hippopotamus	Mouse
Lion	Seaweed
Pelican	Zebra

Duck

FIGURE 9.8 Can you tell what each of these birds does with its beak?

In primary grades, pictures can be used for the animals and foods. (**Note:** It is not important that these animals be the only ones selected. Choose any animals that you can easily find. Also, depending on the grade level, more or fewer animals can be used.)

Pupil Investigations (may include the following processes):

1. Predicting (incorrectly) that big mouths and big teeth are those of animals that are carnivores. (The hippo is a vegetarian).
2. Predicting that sharp teeth or beaks are used for tearing food.
3. Comparing the type of teeth or beak of an animal with the type of food it eats.

Events 19-I through 19-M Explained in Context (Adaptations of Nature)

The earlier exercises in which pupils classified animals were, to some degree, exercises that focused on the various structural differences among animals. Those differences are the end result of millions of years of adaptations and changes to their surroundings. **Adaptation** is the process of making adjustments to enable an organism to be better suited to live and reproduce in its environment.

Fish, which live in water, have adapted breathing organs that allow them to extract oxygen directly from water. Mammals, who maintain a constant body temperature, have hair which helps to insulate them from the effects of extreme cold weather.

In this section we will point, not to the gross adaptations that are the basis of the classification system, but to the lesser adaptations which are not as obvious. Nevertheless, the adaptations are quite useful in teaching children about how animals cope with their surroundings. Those animals that are better able to cope, survive. Those that do not, die out.

In *Event 19-I, Adaptations of Nature: Feet,* we see three types of feet. Each type is designed for special purposes. One type is designed to perch on branches. It has toes in front and back. The sparrow, parakeet, blue jay, and woodpecker are such birds.

Another type is designed for grasping and holding smaller animals. The hawk, owl, and eagle are examples of such birds. The third example is the webbed foot of a marsh or water bird. The webbed foot allows the bird to walk on the muddy bottoms of shallow lakes and marshes.

Another example of specialized adaptation is shown in *Event 19-J, Adaptation of Nature: Eyes.* Notice that the owl and lion have eyes in the front of the head. Those eyes are designed to look ahead. Both of these animals are predators. Their eyes are suited best for pursuing, for looking at something that they are chasing.

The other two animals, however, are the ones being pursued. Their eyes are located on the sides of the head, so that they can detect an enemy that might sneak up from any direction. It is a form of defense that gives them a chance to spot a predator at the earliest possible instant. An instant is sometimes the difference between capture and escape.

Some specialized types of beaks are shown in *Event 19-K, Adaptations of Nature: Beaks.* The predator has a beak that can rip and tear its food. Examples are the eagle, hawk, and condor.

The seed-eating bird has a short pointed beak that can crack open seeds. The sparrow, parakeet, and nuthatch are examples of such birds. The third example is of a water bird such as the duck or goose, which strains seawater through its spoonlike bill or scoops up vegetation from shallow lake bottoms.

Event 19-L, Radiating Ears, demonstrates an important principle of heat radiation. The larger the surface area, like elephant ears, the greater the heat loss. (Jump ahead to see figure 19.10).

Event 19-M, Match the Animal with Its Food, is designed to show how beaks or mouths are adapted to obtain the foods those animals eat. In this event, the cow has a mouth with teeth designed to cut grass easily; the frog has a sticky tongue to pluck the resting fly; the hawk has a sharp beak to tear

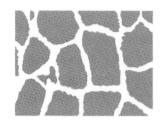

FIGURE 19.9 The giraffe's coat of patches allows the giraffe to blend into its natural surroundings.

FIGURE 19.10 The African elephant uses its ears like radiators to rid itself of excess heat.

apart the mouse; the hippopotamus has a huge mouth to scoop up underwater vegetation; the lion has sharp teeth for tearing its prey (zebra); and the pelican has a huge bill to grab fish.

There are many more adaptations of nature that have developed in animals. Here is a list of a few of them:

1. The camel's feet are big and flat so that it can walk on sand without sinking in. In similar surroundings a horse would sink in and have more difficulty walking.
2. The camel, which survives well in arid regions, has nostrils that permit the breathing of air but keep out blowing sand. It also has very long eyelashes to keep blowing sand out of its eyes.
3. Polar bears are adapted to their environment in a number of ways. They are colored white so that they blend into the background. They have thick fur to protect them from the cold. They even have fur pads on their feet to keep them warm and to give them better traction on the ice.
4. The tiger and giraffe are good examples of animals with protective coloration. (See figure 19.9.) The stripes of the tiger and the patches of the giraffe help the animals blend into their surroundings.
5. The elephant is a huge animal. Yet it can walk through moderately wet and soft ground without getting stuck. Its foot is designed to spread out when stepping down on the ground. When pulling up, however, the foot shrinks, permitting it to be lifted up without getting stuck.
6. An African elephant lives in a very hot climate. Its ears are extremely large and are used for more than hearing: the big, floppy ears are also used like radiators to get rid of excess heat (to cool off). (See figure 19.10.)

Insects (Events 19-N through 19-P)

Discrepant Events and Pupil Investigations

Event 19-N. Classifying Insects and Other Animals

Display a dozen or more pictures of various insects and other animals. Include some spiders and worms. Ask pupils to classify them.

Pupil Investigations (may include the following processes):

1. Analyzing the pictures to find certain traits that are similar in various animals.
2. Classifying the animals into groups.
3. Comparing the groups chosen by the pupils with the official classification system.

Event 19-O. Fruit Fly Metamorphosis

Allow some fruit flies to gather on some very ripe fruit, such as bananas, in an open jar. Then cover the jar with very fine wire or some cotton. Keep the jar in a warm place (room temperature is okay) but out of direct sunlight. Observe for 1 to 2 weeks.

Pupil Investigations (may include the following processes):

1. Observing the fruit fly colony for a period of 1 or 2 weeks.
2. Recording data by drawing diagrams of the stages of development.
3. Predicting the size of the colony for future dates if growth is unhampered.

Event 19-P. Ant Farms

Dig out the center of an ant hill and drop the contents into a tall, narrow, glass-walled container. Cover the outside of one wall of the container with a sheet of dark construction paper. Observe for several weeks.

Pupil Investigations (may include the following processes):

1. Observing that the ants tunnel into the soil.
2. Discovering that the tunnels are more visible behind the covered side than the uncovered side.
3. Inferring that ants prefer to work in dark areas.
4. Identifying different tasks performed by ants and by different parts of the colony.

Events 19-N through 19-P Explained in Context (Insects)

Earlier we discussed several classes of animals with backbones. There are also many types of animals without backbones, with **insects** being the most predominant among that group. In fact, insects have the greatest number of species of all animal groups.

It is estimated that there are between 600,000 and 800,000 species of insects. (A species is a group of related members who can generally reproduce only with other members of that group.) Insects make up about 70% of all the animal species in the world.

There are several characteristics of insects that help us identify them: they have six jointed legs, a three-segment body (**head, thorax,** and **abdomen**), and an **exoskeleton** (a hard outer coat or covering that serves the same purpose as our inner skeleton). (See figure 19.11.)

These characteristics can be observed in *Event 19-N, Classifying Insects and Other Animals.* If there are good pictures of insects available for display, the distinguishing features should be quite visible.

In the beginning of the lesson, let the pupils group the animals according to any system that seems to make sense to them. After they have finished their original groupings, compare their work with the official classification system. Common examples of insects are flies, moths, butterflies, grasshoppers, mosquitoes, bees, and ants.

Be sure to include animals other than insects, such as spiders and worms. Worms differ from insects in exoskeleton, legs, and body parts. Spiders look much like insects and have jointed legs. However, they are different because they have eight legs, two body parts, and no exoskeleton.

Insects have many adaptations suited to their particular needs. For example, they have a good sense of smell and are attracted to food from long distances. You have, no doubt, noticed that they generally can find the food at a picnic.

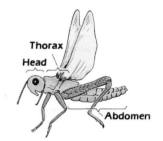

FIGURE 19.11 An insect such as a grasshopper, bee, or ant has six legs, an outer covering, and a three-part body. (A spider has eight legs and two body parts.)

Their sense of smell is quickly confirmed anytime food is left outside a refrigerator or anytime food scraps are discarded into a garbage can. If left uncovered, flies and other insects quickly swarm around a can.

Insects go through great changes, called a **metamorphosis,** during their life cycles. Most insects begin as eggs until the **larvae** hatch. After a period of time in which the larvae constantly eat, a covering such as a **chrysalis** or **cocoon** is formed. Eventually, the **adult** insects emerge.

These four stages of the life cycle are included in *Event 19-O, Fruit Fly Metamorphosis.* Fruit flies are often used in classroom exercises because they grow to full adults in only 8 days. Other insects take much longer.

The only real problem with fruit flies is that they are so small. Be sure that pupils have magnifying glasses available so that they can study the four stages of development inside the jar. The eggs will be especially difficult to see.

Not all insects go through all four stages of development. A grasshopper, for example, has only three stages in its development. It starts as an **egg,** hatches into a **nymph** (which looks like a miniature adult), and grows to an adult.

Some insects live in highly organized societies. Bees, for example, have a society in which some workers are assigned to feed the young, some to gather honey and pollen, others to make wax for the hives, some to tend the queen, some to help regulate the temperature of the hive, and others to guard the hive from intruders.

Ants are somewhat similar to bees. They also live in organized colonies. The ant colony can be observed very easily by placing it into a sealed display frame as suggested in *Event 19-P, Ant Farms.* Gather ants and soil for the ant farm from an anthill.

After gently placing the ants and soil into the display frame, commonly referred to as an "ant farm," seal it tightly so that none escape into the classroom. A typical ant farm is made with two glass panes about 20 to 30 centimeters wide and 15 to 20 centimeters high. The panes are held in a wooden frame that keeps the glass panes about 3 to 4 centimeters apart.

Be sure to keep the soil slightly moist. Otherwise the ants will not be able to tunnel effectively. If the soil is too dry, the tunnels tend to collapse and crumble. On the other hand, do not make the soil too wet. It speeds up the growth of molds and in extreme conditions, the ants could drown.

Place a small container of sugar water inside. That should satisfy their need for food. Ants recognize their own hive members and attack any intruders that might also go for the food.

If you cover the exterior of one side of the glass display case with black construction paper or other opaque material, the ants will build their tunnels right against the face of the glass. Ants avoid daylight, so you will seldom see tunnels in an uncovered part of the ant farm.

The covering can be removed from time to time to observe the ants at work. Often, the tunnels and inner chambers of the colony will be revealed.

Pupils often think that all insects are harmful. That is not true. Children should realize that many insects are beneficial. Honey bees, for example, are extremely beneficial because they produce honey and pollinate flowers and fruits. Without pollination, many flowers, fruits, and crops would disappear from the face of the earth.

If insects would disappear, so would many types of birds. The only birds that could survive would be seed-eaters and plant-eaters. Even those birds might be endangered because many seeds and plants depend on pollination to reproduce.

Insect Cages and Collections

Some insects, such as moths and butterflies, may be collected and mounted for display purposes. Care must be taken so that the brittle parts of the insect are not destroyed.

Insects can be killed in a killing jar. A wide-mouthed jar can be used for this purpose. Soak some cotton with fingernail polish remover (ethyl acetate), and place it at the bottom of the jar. Cover the cotton with a sheet of perforated tinfoil or cardboard. Drop the insect into the jar and cover it for about 20 to 30 minutes.

The insects should be carefully spread out after removal from the jar. Do not attempt to change the positions of the wings and legs after the specimen has dried out. In a day or two they become so brittle that the parts will break if you try to bend or adjust them.

The insects can be pin-mounted on a sheet of styrofoam or other suitable material. After mounting, be sure to label the specimens. Finally, a frame should be built to hold the mounting board, and then a glass or plastic cover installed. In that way the specimens will be protected from damage, yet be easy to view.

Insect cages can be made from wide-mouthed jars with holes punched in the cover. Larger cages can be made with wire screen and aluminum pie plates.

Such cages are good observatories. For example, a caterpillar can be placed inside a wire cage along with the leaves and twigs on which it was found. Fresh leaves should be added to satisfy the caterpillar's food requirements. Eventually, it may spin a cocoon from which a moth or butterfly emerges.

Combining Assessment with Instruction

Art and literature are an excellent way for students to show what they have learned. Provide a list of pictures and names of spiders and insects common to your geographic region for the students to individually select for a project. Students should find books and/or websites about their selected insect or spider. Reading books such as *Over in the Garden* by Jennifer Ward (Scholastic) will encourage children to find other helpful books to read about insects and spiders. After students have gathered information about their insects, have students construct a model making sure that all of the appropriate body parts, number of legs, etc., are included. Provide students with paper bags, craft sticks, clay, egg cartons, or other materials to construct their insect or spider. Older students may want to use thin wire and tissue paper to construct three-dimensional models. Have students label the body parts.

Students should write a short story about their spider or insect that includes the type of environment that is appropriate, preferred temperature range, climate information, habitat, and food sources. As a class, construct a large mural on the bulletin board. Encourage students to brainstorm what should be included—such as rocks, trees, grass, flowers, soil, and dark and sunny areas—so that they might place their model in an appropriate spot on the mural. Display the student's creations on the mural. Some insects and spiders may hang from the ceiling.

Evaluate how well students applied what they've learned about their insect or spider to their designs. Evaluations will differ depending upon grade level but all projects should contain appropriate body parts and number of legs in the model; have sufficient information of preferred living conditions such as climate, food, and predators for the insect or spider in the short story; and be neat.

The following sites may help with this assessment:

www.entsoc.org/education/elem_mid/elem_mid.htm (Entomological Society of America),
www.enchantedlearning.com/crafts/insects,
www.crafts4kids.com/projects/upright_insects.htm

Sites and Software

The following websites and software are appropriate to use with this chapter. Note that computer software and websites change rapidly. This makes it necessary to investigate the stable websites for new links and software catalogs for updates. (Also check chapter 16, Teaching Children about the Oceans.) Visit www.mhhe.com/friedl6e to link to these directly and for study resources.

Sites

Biology Lessons (grades K–8), San Diego State U.	www.biologylessons.sdsu.edu/
Center for Insect Science, U. of Arizona	insected.arizona.edu
Seaworld	www.seaworld.org/ animal-info/index.htm
Kids Corner, U.S. Fish and Wildlife Service	www.fws.gov
National Wildlife Federation Kids	www.nwf.org
Animals A to Zoo: Animal Planet	animal.discovery.com/guides/ atoz/atoz.html
Howstuffworks: "Animals"	www.howstuffworks.com/ category.htm?cat=Anim
Smile Program Biology Index	www.iit.edu/~smile/biolinde.html#b2
Classifying Critters	www.hhmi.org/coolscience/ critters/critters.html

Software

This House Is Bugged! (Video Architects/Sunburst) (2–5)
One Small Square: Backyard (Carolina) (3–7)
Rainforest Explorer (Carolina) (3–7)
SimPark (Discovery) (2–6)
Sammy's Science House (IBM) (K–2)
Rainforest Researchers (Tom Snyder) (5–8)
Learn about Animals (Sunburst) (K–3)
Learn about Insects (Sunburst) (K–3)
Junior Nature Guide Series: Insects (Discovery) (1–6)
Junior Nature Guide Series: Amphibians and Reptiles (Discovery) (1–6)

Key Terms

abdomen, *381*

adaptation, *379*

adult, *382*

amphibians, *375*

bird, *373*

chordata, *371*

chrysalis, *382*

class, *371*

cocoon, *382*

egg, *382*

exoskeleton, *381*

family, *371*

fish, *376*

genus, *371*

head, *381*

insects, *381*

kingdom, *371*

larvae, *382*

mammals, *372*

metamorphosis, *382*

nymph, *382*

order, *371*

phylum, *371*

reptiles, *375*

species, *371*

subspecies, *371*

thorax, *381*

Teaching Children about Nutrition and Health

NATIONAL SCIENCE EDUCATION STANDARDS ALIGNMENT TO EVENTS

The events in this chapter help accomplish several of the NSES for content. The event(s) that align with a given content standard are listed below that standard.

LEVELS K–4

UNIFYING CONCEPTS AND PROCESSES
- Systems, order and organization
  20-J and 20-K
- Change, consistency, measurement
  20-B and 20-C
  20-O
- Evidence, models and explanation
  20-B and 20-C
  20-G through 20-I
  20-P

PHYSICAL SCIENCE
- Properties of objects and materials
  20-D through 20-H

LIFE SCIENCE
- The characteristics of organisms
  20-A through 20-Q
- Organisms and their environments
  20-I through 20-Q

SCIENCE AND TECHNOLOGY
- Abilities of technological design
  20-M and 20-N

- Understanding science and technology
  20-D through 20-F
  20-H and 20-I
  20-L
  20-Q

SCIENCE IN PERSONAL AND SOCIAL PERSPECTIVES
- Personal health
  20-A through 20-Q
- Types of resources
  20-I through 20-Q

LEVELS 5–8

UNIFYING CONCEPTS AND PROCESSES
- Systems, order and organization
  20-J and 20-K
- Change, consistency, measurement
  20-B and 20-C
  20-O
- Evidence, models and explanation
  20-B and 20-C
  20-G through 20-I
  20-P

PHYSICAL SCIENCE
- Properties and changes in properties of matter
  20-D through 20-H
- Transfer of energy
  20-I through 20-Q

LIFE SCIENCE
- Structure and function in living systems
  20-A through 20-Q

SCIENCE AND TECHNOLOGY
- Abilities of technological design
  20-M and 20-N
- Understanding science and technology
  20-D through 20-F
  20-H and 20-I
  20-L
  20-Q

SCIENCE IN PERSONAL AND SOCIAL PERSPECTIVES
- Personal health
  20-A through 20-Q
- Science and technology in society
  20-N

Daily Requirements

The United States Department of Agriculture (USDA) was founded in 1862 to educate the public on agricultural and nutritional issues and to collaborate with agricultural businesses to provide a reliable, consistent food source. In 1894 the first dietary guide, *Farmers' Bulletin* by W.O. Atwater, was published. The guide delineated the need for protein, carbohydrates, fat, and "mineral matter" and gave recommended portions based on an American male. As science became more sophisticated, essential minerals and vitamins such as iron, calcium, and vitamin C were discovered and added to the recommendations.

The USDA's first food guide, *Food for Young Children,* by Caroline Hunt, was published in 1916. It described five food groups: milk and meat, cereals, vegetables and fruits, fats and fatty foods, and sugars and sugary foods. Over the next 10 years the USDA published flyers on amounts of food to purchase on a weekly basis for various family sizes. The economic depression of the 1930s spurred a new form of food recommendations based on cost levels and 12 major food groups.

In 1941, the Food and Nutrition Board of the National Academy of Sciences published the first set of Recommended Dietary Allowances (RDAs), which gave recommendations for caloric and essential nutrient intakes. The nine essential nutrients focused on were protein, iron, calcium, vitamins A & D, thiamin, riboflavin, niacin, and ascorbic acid (vitamin C). The USDA revised its food guide to reflect foods that met the minimum daily essential nutrient requirements as outlined by the RDAs, but it didn't give any caloric guidance. This guide, the Basic Seven food guide, was released in 1943 as a leaflet called the *National Wartime Nutritional Guide.* In 1956 this food guide was revised to the Basic Four, and with only minor revisions to the fat and sugar recommendations in the 1970s, remained the major dietary guideline until the 1990s.

The major problem with the Basic Four and earlier food guides was that they only gave recommendations for the foundation of a healthy diet. The guides did not give advice on caloric intake or proportions needed for optimal health. In the late 1970s research showed that people who consumed high levels of calories, fats, and sodium were at higher risk for diseases such as heart failure and diabetes. The USDA along with the Department of Health and Human Services produced a food guide called *A Pattern for Daily Food Choices* with an illustrative food wheel graphic and was disseminated by the American National Red Cross. This first attempt at a more prescriptive food guide was well received by nutritional experts but not the public. Consumers needed more specific food-related guidance, definition of technical terms, and practical tips for behavior change strategies.

The USDA revised the food wheel to better reflect consumer needs and the food pyramid was created in 1992. The food pyramid has successfully replaced the Basic Four as the major dietary guideline in the United States, but nutritionists and health advocates have some major criticisms of the pyramid. The portions given for foods are inconsistent. Some foods such as grains are given in ½ cup portions while others such as dairy are given in specific measurements based on the minimum or maximum daily recommended nutrients, making it difficult to judge a healthy portion size.

In addition, it does not delineate foods according to their nutritional value within a food group. For example, whole wheat bread has higher nutritional value than corn chips, and fish, because of it's low cholesterol and high lipids, is better for you than red meat.

Finally, the food pyramid does not indicate the glucose load (GL) and index (GI) of foods. Diabetes research shows that foods with high GL and GI quickly raise blood-level sugar causing the body to produce excess insulin. Over time the body becomes resistant to insulin and adult-onset diabetes occurs.

In response to these oversights, Dr. Walter C. Willett, a professor at Harvard's School of Public Health, published a revised food pyramid in his book,

Eat, Drink, and Be Healthy. He lists daily exercise and weight control as the basis and provides modified food categories that reflect the actual nutritional value of grains, meats, vegetables, dairy, and fruits. Dr. Willett's revised food pyramid also takes into account GL and GI of foods by separating out high GI foods such as potatoes and white bread from the base of the USDA's pyramid and placing them at the top to be used sparingly. Additional information can be found in "Dietary Recommendations and How They Changed Over Time" in *America's Eating Habits: Changes and Consequences,* edited by Elizabeth Frazao and published in 1999.

Cell Growth (Event 20-A)

Discrepant Event and Pupil Investigations

Event 20-A. See Cells

An onion is a bulb consisting of many layers. Some of the layers are extremely thin. Remove a piece of this filmlike layer and place it under a microscope to observe the cells.

Obtain a sample of another type of cell by gently scraping your cheek (inside your mouth) with the blunt end of a toothpick. Place the whitish smear on a slide and cover it with a cover plate. Observe it under a microscope. Finally, place a drop of pond water under a microscope and observe.

Pupil Investigations (may include the following processes):

1. Observing that the onion skin is composed of cells.
2. Discovering that the material from inside the mouth also consists of cells.
3. Comparing an onion cell with a cell from inside the mouth.
4. Contrasting one-celled plants and animals found in the sample of pond water.
5. Drawing diagrams of the cells.

Event 20-A Explained in Context (Cell Growth)

Growth in living things takes place in the **cell,** the smallest unit of life. Most cells are too small to be seen without the aid of a good hand lens or a microscope.

Robert Hooke, an English scientist, was the first person to observe cells. He viewed the cells of cork, wood, and other plant specimens. Shortly thereafter, a Dutch scientist, Anton van Leeuwenhoek (*Lay*-venhook), discovered that pond water contained one-celled animal life.

Pupils should be given a chance to observe the structure of several types of cells. They may recall the cell structure of leaves discussed in chapter 18. For this chapter they should review that information if necessary and perform *Event 20-A. See Cells.*

The onion skin is suggested because its skin is thin enough to give a fairly clear image of the cell's structure. However, be sure to use the very thin film from between the layers. Everything else is too thick to use.

A microscope of "100 ×" magnification will give a view of the cells somewhat like those shown in figure 20.1. Any greater magnification tends to blur the image. Sometimes a clearer picture can be obtained if the cells are stained with a dilute iodine solution.

FIGURE 20.1 Microscopic view of onion cells. Note their relatively uniform structure.

The cheek cells scraped from inside the mouth look different. They look like those shown in figure 20.2. Again, 100-power should be the maximum power used to study the cells.

In general, the cheek cell will appear transparent and be hard to see. The cell walls are made of thin nonrigid membranes. Pupils should be led to the conclusion that plant cells have thicker and more rigid cell walls than cells from human tissue. (That is why wood, for example, can be used for building purposes.) Upon close examination you should be able to see the nucleus (the darker spot) at the center of the cell.

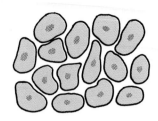

FIGURE 20.2 Microscopic view of cells scraped from inside the cheek.

Growth Rates (Events 20-B and 20-C)

Discrepant Events and Pupil Investigations

Event 20-B. Weight Table
Check the weights of males and females in table 20.1 What conclusions can you draw from the data in the table?

Pupil Investigations (may include the following processes):
1. Observing that up to age 12, boys and girls have the same average weights.
2. Discovering that at the 12 to 15 age period, girls weigh more than boys.
3. Discovering that beyond 15 years of age, males weigh more than females.
4. Inferring that girls mature earlier than boys.

Event 20-C. Height Table
Check the heights of males and females in table 20.2. What conclusions can you draw from the data in the table?

TABLE 20.1

Weight Table

	0–1 Yr	1–3 Yr	3–6 Yr	6–9 Yr	9–12 Yr	12–15 Yr	15–18 Yr	18–35 Yr	35–55 Yr	55–75 Yr
Male	18 lb.	29 lb.	40 lb.	53 lb.	72 lb.	98 lb.	134 lb.	154 lb.	154 lb.	154 lb.
Female	18	29	40	53	72	103	117	128	128	128

TABLE 20.2

Height Table

	1–3 Yr	3–6 Yr	6–9 Yr	9–12 Yr	12–15 Yr	15–18 Yr	18–35 Yr	35–55 Yr	55–75 Yr
Male	34 in.	42 in.	49 in.	55 in.	61 in.	68 in.	69 in.	69 in.	69 in.
Female	34	42	49	55	62	64	64	64	64

Pupil Investigations (may include the following processes):

1. Observing that up to age 12, boys and girls have the same average heights.
2. Discovering that at the 12 to 15 age period, girls are taller than boys.
3. Discovering that adult males are taller than adult females.
4. Inferring that girls mature earlier than boys.

Events 20-B and 20-C Explained in Context (Growth Rates)

Children are interested in the average growth rate of boys and girls. These are shown in *Event 20-B, Weight Table.* Pupils will see that up until 12 years of age, boys and girls are of the same average weights.

Then the girls move ahead of the boys during the next 3 years. The gains by the girls are due mostly to the growth spurt that seems to affect girls earlier than boys. Boys, too, tend to start their growth spurt but, for a few years, lag behind the girls.

The height data, shown in *Event 20-C, Height Table,* confirms the pattern found in the weight table. Again, girls grow taller than boys during the 12 to 15 year age period.

We must realize that the figures are for people of slight to medium build. People with different body builds will have weights and heights that vary from the average. A more complete set of height and weight tables is given in table 20.3.

Another factor that should be emphasized is that some people tend to mature earlier than others. Thus, one person may be at his or her adult

TABLE 20.3

Heights and Weights

Men				Women			
Height	Small (lb)	Medium (lb)	Large (lb)	Height	Small (lb)	Medium (lb)	Large (lb)
5 ft 2 in.	128–134	131–141	138–150	4 ft 10 in.	102–111	109–121	118–131
5 ft 3 in.	130–136	133–143	140–153	4 ft 11 in.	103–113	111–123	120–134
5 ft 4 in.	132–138	135–145	142–156	5 ft 0 in.	104–115	113–126	122–137
5 ft 5 in.	134–140	137–148	144–160	5 ft 1 in.	106–118	115–129	125–140
5 ft 6 in.	136–142	139–151	146–164	5 ft 2 in.	108–121	118–132	128–143
5 ft 7 in.	138–145	142–154	149–168	5 ft 3 in.	111–124	121–135	131–147
5 ft 8 in.	140–148	145–157	152–172	5 ft 4 in.	114–127	124–138	134–151
5 ft 9 in.	142–151	148–160	155–176	5 ft 5 in.	117–130	127–141	137–155
5 ft 10 in.	144–154	151–163	158–180	5 ft 6 in.	120–133	130–144	140–159
5 ft 11 in.	146–157	154–166	161–184	5 ft 7 in.	123–136	133–147	143–163
6 ft 0 in.	149–160	157–170	164–188	5 ft 8 in.	126–139	136–150	146–167
6 ft 1 in.	152–164	160–174	168–192	5 ft 9 in.	129–142	139–153	149–170
6 ft 2 in.	155–168	164–178	172–197	5 ft 10 in.	132–145	142–156	152–173
6 ft 3 in.	158–172	167–182	176–202	5 ft 11 in.	135–148	145–159	155–176
6 ft 4 in.	162–176	171–187	181–207	6 ft 0 in.	138–151	148–162	158–179

Source: Metropolitan Life Insurance Company height and weight tables for ages 25 to 59. Heights include shoes with 1-inch heels. Weights include clothes weighing 5 pounds for men and 3 pounds for women.

height at age 12, while a classmate may not even have started his or her growth spurt. Even members of the same family will often vary in their rates of development.

One final factor that affects the figures shown in the tables is that they change from generation to generation. About 1 inch has been added to the average height of adults every 25 years for the past 100 years. The average weights have increased also. Discuss what may have influenced those figures. Undoubtedly, better nutrition in recent generations has been an important factor.

Food Tests and Tastes (Event 20-D through 20-H)

Discrepant Events and Pupil Investigations

Event 20-D. Testing for Starches

Gather together a variety of food samples. Include such items as rice, oatmeal, honey, puffed wheat, soda crackers, grape juice, meat, peanuts, potatoes, white bread, butter, corn syrup, and fruits. Let the pupils determine which of these foods contain starch.

Pupil Investigations (may include the following processes):

1. Reading to find out how to test for starch.
2. Testing samples with drops of diluted iodine.
3. Classifying the foods according to their starch content.

Event 20-E. Testing for Fats

Use the same group of food samples as was used in Event 20-D and determine if any of them contain fat.

Pupil Investigations (may include the following processes):

1. Reading to find out how to test for fats.
2. Testing samples by rubbing them against paper.
3. Classifying the foods according to their fat content.

Event 20-F. Testing for Sugars

Use the same group of food samples as those used in Event 20-D and determine if they contain sugar.

Pupil Investigations (may include the following processes):

1. Reading to find out how to test for sugar.
2. Testing each food sample with glucose strips or Benedict's solution.
3. Classifying the foods according to their sugar content.

Event 20-G. Testing for Taste

Prepare containers of sugar water, salt water, diluted unsweetened lemon juice, and bitter chocolate. Take a cotton-tipped swab and dip it into one container; then apply it to the tongue. Be sure to move the swab along the front, sides, and back of the tongue. Let the taste linger on your tongue and decide which part seems to be most sensitive to each taste.

After each taste test, it is advisable to drink a small amount of water and swish it around your mouth before swallowing. This tends to clear out the old taste and makes it possible to do each new taste test afresh. (Even so, tastes from a previous test will sometimes interfere.)

(**Caution:** Be sanitary. Each pupil should have a personal set of tiny paper-cup samples. Pupils should not dip their swabs into "community" containers.)

Pupil Investigations (may include the following processes):

1. Testing to see which part of the tongue is most sensitive to each of the tastes.
2. Recording the results of the class investigations.
3. Generalizing that different parts of the tongue are sensitive to different tastes.

Event 20-H. Mixed-Up Tastes

Prepare small slices or cubes of apples, pears, onions, and potatoes. Select several volunteers to be "tasters." The subject must taste the foods with eyes closed and, even more important, *with nose held tightly shut.*

Pick up a sample with a toothpick and place it into the subject's hand. The subject then tastes the food *while continuing to hold the nose tightly shut.* The subject should try to identify the four samples. (Remember, if the nose is released, even for an instant, the event will not work.)

Pupil Investigations (may include the following processes):

1. Observing and recording the taste tests of the subjects.
2. Inferring that the sense of sight affects the sense of taste.
3. Inferring that the sense of smell affects the sense of taste.

Events 20-D through 20-H Explained in Context (Food Tests and Tastes)

Testing Foods

Several common ingredients of foods can be detected by performing rather simple tests. *Event 20-D, Testing for Starches,* is done by placing drops of dilute iodine on the foods to be tested. If the food contains starch, the iodine turns a deep purple or almost a totally black color. If starch is not present, the iodine will not change color.

The fat test, as suggested in *Event 20-E, Testing for Fats,* is even easier to do. All you need to do is rub the sample on paper. For example, what happens if you rub a peanut against some paper? A mark appears: a grease spot. It represents the fat in the peanut. Any food with a substantial fat content will leave a similar mark.

The sugar test, as suggested in *Event 20-F, Testing for Sugar,* is accomplished by using glucose strips. They are available in a drug store. Just follow directions on the box.

In years past, a more complex test was used, but many schools will probably still have available the proper test liquid called Benedict's solution. Benedict's solution is an **indicator.** An indicator solution is a substance that changes color to "indicate" the presence of the test food.

TABLE 20.4

Starches, Sugars, and Fats

Starch	Sugar	Fat
Potato	Corn syrup	Peanut
White bread	Honey	Meat
Oatmeal	Grape juice	Butter
Puffed wheat	Many fruits	
Soda cracker		
Rice		

If the test sample is a liquid, just add a few drops of the solution and heat it. If simple sugars are present, the sample turns red. If the food sample is a solid, it will have to be ground up and mixed with water before testing.

Surprising as it may seem, Benedict's solution will not detect table sugar because it is a complex sugar. Only simple sugars can be identified by this method.

The sample foods listed in the events are shown in table 20.4.

Proteins can be detected also, but the process is the most complex of the tests. First, mix about a teaspoonful of copper sulfate into a half glass of water. Then take several drops of this solution and several drops of household ammonia and mix them in a glass containing the food to be tested. If the food contains protein, the mixture turns purple.

It is easy to test liquid proteins such as milk, but solids must be crushed or ground and then mixed with water. The liquid mixture can than be tested.

The Sense of Taste

Pupils will find that different parts of the tongue are sensitive to different tastes by performing *Event 20-G, Testing for Taste.* In general, the tastes that can best be detected on the parts of the tongue are shown in figure 20.3.

Record the data for the class on the chalkboard to see which tastes tend to be most noticeable on various parts of the tongue. The majority will likely agree with the data in figure 20.3, but some members of the class will probably get different results.

Results are affected by the fact that some people actually do have different taste sensations. However, even with people who have "normal" tongues, it is sometimes difficult to keep the various samples from mixing inside the mouth. As a result, some pupils may not be sure where the sample taste is focused.

After pupils have decided that the tongue is useful for detecting tastes, they may be surprised to discover in *Event 20-H, Mixed-Up Tastes,* that the sense of smell is very important to the sense of taste.

The most important aspect of this taste test is that the subject *must* hold the nose shut. If even a small whiff of onion, for example, gets through, the test is lost. If you can get the pupils to hold their noses, they will have great difficulty detecting the differences between the four samples. It is often the texture or consistency, not the taste, that gives the only clue.

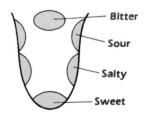

FIGURE 20.3   The tongue is sensitive to different tastes.

It is almost impossible to do the entire set of four foods without at least a slight lapse in nose-holding. As a result, the subjects will often be able to tell what the samples are. If so, ask them if it was easier to tell when not holding the nose. Invariably, they will admit that it was much easier to tell that way. Thus, the event is successful even if some cannot do the entire activity completely right.

One variation of the smell and taste test is to blindfold the subjects but, this time, allow them to smell. Give them a sample food (using toothpicks to hold the food) while holding another sample under their noses. Often the smell of the sample under the nose is strong enough to confuse and over-power the taste being sensed on the tongue.

This event works best if the food on the tongue has a weak smell while the one under the nose has a strong smell (perhaps a potato on the tongue and an onion or an apple under the nose).

Foods and Diets (Events 20-I through 20-Q)

Discrepant Events and Pupil Investigations

Event 20-I. Favorite Foods: Helpful or Harmful?

Ask pupils to list all the foods they would eat for one full day if they could select anything they wanted. The list should include food for meals and any between-meal snacks. When they have finished their lists, analyze them to see if they meet the needs of good nutrition.

Pupil Investigations (may include the following processes):

1. Recording the foods eaten in a day.
2. Comparing the list with good nutrition standards. (Compare with the six food groups given later in this chapter.)
3. Calculating the calorie totals for each pupil if a calorie reference can be obtained.
4. Generalizing that taste is not a reliable guide to good nutrition.

Event 20-J. Classifying Foods # 1

Display a wide variety of food pictures on the bulletin board. Let pupils select foods that fit the six food groups of (1) fats, oils, and sweets; (2) milk, yogurt, and cheese; (3) meat, poultry, fish, etc.; (4) bread, cereal, rice, and pasta; (5) vegetables; and (6) fruits.

An alternative method is to classify the foods without regard to the groups listed here. Just ask the children to fit the foods into any groups that they think might be appropriate.

Pupil Investigations (may include the following processes):

1. Analyzing the types of foods to see where they fit the best.
2. Comparing the selections with the six food groups.
3. Appreciating the importance of good nutrition.

Event 20-K. Classifying Foods # 2

Use the same display of food pictures as was used in the last event. This time ask the pupils to place the foods into the following three groups: (1) fats, (2) carbohydrates, and (3) proteins.

If some foods do not fit very well into any one group, just delete those pictures from the display. Ask student to place the foods into the groups where they fit the best. (**Note:** You will need a nutrition book or some other reference that can supply the information to make the proper classifications. There are far too many possible selections to include them here.)

Pupil Investigations (may include the following processes):

1. Analyzing the types of foods to see where they fit best.
2. Comparing the selections with the three food groups.
3. Appreciating the importance of good nutrition.

Event 20-L. Hidden Calories

Let us assume that you have two items of food, each weighing 100 grams. The label on the first item reports that the food contains 50% proteins and 50% fat. The label on the second item reports 60% proteins and 40% fat. Yet, the second item has more fat than the first item. How is that possible?

Pupil Investigations (may include the following processes):

1. Questioning the data that are given (and being assured that they are reported as stated above).
2. Discovering that there are two ways of measuring the caloric content of foods.
3. Inferring that the fat content of the two items was measured two different ways.

Event 20-M. Sugar: Good or Bad?

The cells in our bodies use glucose for energy. They use nothing else. Every food that your body uses as energy cannot be used until it is changed to glucose. It may enter the body as fat; carbohydrate, or protein; but if it winds up as energy inside the cells, it has been changed to glucose. **Glucose** is sugar.

Here is a question for the class: If sugar is the only thing that the body can use for energy, why not eat it directly—in candies, desserts, and other "goodies"?

Pupil Investigations (may include the following processes):

1. Analyzing the way the body uses sugar.
2. Forming a theory (incorrectly) that eating lots of sugar is good.
3. Generalizing that too much sugar may be harmful.

Event 20-N. Cereal Database

Have each pupil bring to school a different type of dry cereal. Each pupil should research the characteristics of their particular cereal and briefly report it to the class. The class should then determine which fields should be included in the cereal database. The *fields* may include: calories, calories from fat; total fat, cholesterol, sodium, sugar content by percent and by weight, vitamin percentages, fiber content, cost per box, and net weight in grams and ounces. Pupils may also conduct a survey and include the survey results in the database. The survey may involve: rank ordering in a taste test for cereal alone, taste test for milk and cereal, rate at which the cereal was too soggy to enjoy, box appeal, or even "inside box free prize incentives." Have pupils enter the information for their selected cereal into the *file* "Cereal Database."

Pupil Investigations (may include the following processes):

1. Collecting information about nutrition.
2. Designing and conducting a survey.
3. Experimenting with different characteristics of cereal; for example, rate of sogginess.
4. Sorting for a given *field* or characteristic of the cereal, using a database to answer a research question.

Event 20-O. Calorie Counting

How many calories do you need for daily living? Your calorie needs can be found by using the following rule of thumb: Multiply your weight by 12 if you are inactive, by 16 if you are moderately active, and by 20 if you are very active.

Pupil Investigations (may include the following processes):

1. Analyzing one's level of activity.
2. Calculating the figures by using one's correct activity level.
3. Comparing the needs with the intake selected in Event 20-D.
4. Analyzing one's personal weight to see if intake has exceeded use.

Event 20-P. Overweight or Overfat?

Solve the following two puzzles: Suppose two men are both 6 feet tall. One man weighs 220 pounds and the other 175 pounds, but the *lighter* of the two is too fat. How can that be possible?

Suppose a woman is 5 feet 6 inches tall and is weighed at two different times. She weighs 130 pounds both times. When weighed the first time, she was at a recommended weight; but the second time she was considered "too fat." How can that be possible?

Pupil Investigations (may include the following processes):

1. Forming a theory that the proper weight may depend on factors other than height.
2. Discovering that the proper weight changes for a given individual with the passage of time.
3. Inferring that "weight" does not necessarily mean "fat".

Event 20-Q. Supermarket Diets

Collect headlines about diets from the tabloids that line the checkout stands of supermarkets. What are four themes that are found most often in those headlines? How valid are the diets?

Pupil Investigations (may include the following processes):

1. Collecting data on supermarket diets.
2. Classifying the claims according to standards selected by the class.
3. Analyzing whether the claims are reasonable or extravagant.

Events 20-I through 20-Q Explained in Context (Foods and Diets)

We know that food is necessary for health and energy. But do all foods serve these functions equally well, or are some better than others? If there are differences, how can we find those that are better than others from the hundreds that are available?

Food Groups

How can we follow a well-balanced diet? Do we depend only on taste? Find out how reliable your sense of taste is in selecting a good diet. Ask children to do *Event 20-I, Favorite Foods: Helpful or Harmful?*

Most pupils will, no doubt, show a strong preference for sweets. Conversely, they will avoid vegetables, grains, and possibly meats. It is not likely that many pupils will select a well-balanced diet on the basis of their "favorite foods." The activity should make it clear that diets based on taste alone may have serious deficiencies.

What foods should we eat to meet our daily needs? The body requires food for three general purposes: (1) to provide energy, (2) to build and repair cells, and (3) to regulate body processes.

All of these needs will be provided if foods are selected carefully. To make food selection easier, foods have been grouped into six categories by nutrition experts. Compare these groups with those selected by pupils in Event 20-J Classifying Foods #1.

Nutrition experts devised a six-group system that is called the *Food Guide Pyramid* (or more commonly, just "*food pyramid*"). See figure 20.4

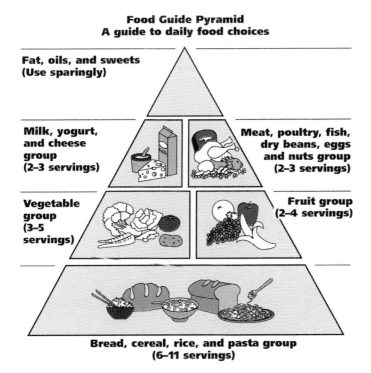

FIGURE 20.4   How does your daily food intake compare with the Food Guide Pyramid published by the U.S. Department of Agriculture?

The Six Food Groups of the Food Pyramid
The Base

Bread, Cereal, Rice, and Pasta Group

(6 to 11 servings daily)
Breads of whole grain (preferred over white bread)
Breakfast cereals of wheat, oats, corn, and rice

The Second Level: Two Subgroups. Eat These Often.

Vegetable Group

(3 to 5 servings daily)
Dark green or deep yellow vegetables

Fruit Group

(2 to 4 servings daily)
Apples, grapes, bananas, etc.

The foods in this level are important for health. It is likely that children will often skimp on the vegetable group. (Remember the phrase children hear often: "Eat your vegetables.")

The Third Level: Two Subgroups. Eat These Less Often.

Dairy Group

(2 to 3 servings daily)
Milk, yogurt, and cheese

Meat, Poultry, Fish, Dry Beans, Eggs and Nuts Group

(2 to 3 servings daily)
Foods listed in group name

Although these foods are also essential for healthy diets, they are often taken in excess. It is important to limit the intake to the number of servings recommended. Children and teenagers need somewhat more than adults.

Amino acids in proteins are needed to build and repair cells. These are readily available in meat, poultry, fish, and eggs. Beans, peas, lentils, and nuts should be eaten in combinations to obtain these necessary amino acids.

The Top Level: Use Sparingly.

Fats, Oils, and Sweets Group

The foods from this group should be used sparingly.

The base of this pyramid includes breads, cereals, rice, and pasta. Six to 11 servings daily are recommended from this group. The next level recommends 2 to 4 servings of fruit and 3 to 5 servings of vegetables. The next level combines the meat and dairy groups. Although essential for life, it is very easy to eat too many from this level. Thus, it occupies a fairly, narrow space on the pyramid.

On top are oils, fats, and sweets. Again, some of these are necessary for good health, but it is very easy to consume too much. The foods on top of the pyramid should be used sparingly.

After pupils have had a chance to study these groups, let them prepare sample meals for a day. Such an exercise should help pupils gain an understanding of good nutrition.

TABLE 20.5

Proteins, Fats, and Carbohydrates

	Proteins	Fats	Carbohydrates
Calories per gram	4	9	4
Will build tissue	Yes	No	No
Will provide energy	Yes	Yes	Yes
Toxic residue	Ammonia	Ketone	None
Excess calories stored as	Fat	Fat	Fat

Protein, Fat, and Carbohydrate

The six food groups listed above have been widely used for many years. However, another way of classifying foods can also be highly beneficial. All foods can be divided into proteins, fats, and carbohydrates. Demonstrating this fact was the purpose of *Event 20-K, Classifying Foods #2*. A summary of data related to the three groups is given in table 20.5.

Protein is absolutely essential for good health. It is the *only* food that can be used to build muscle tissue. Protein is broken down into amino acids, which are the basic building blocks of muscles and connective tissue.

How much protein is needed? Probably less than most people eat. A person needs about 1 to 2 grams of protein per kilogram of body weight. Thus, a person of 60 kilograms (132 pounds) can use a maximum of 120 grams of protein (or 480 calories) per day. That amount is about 20% of a normal diet. What happens when someone eats more than is used for tissue-building? It does *not* go into additional muscle. It is used for energy or stored as fat.

Protein is not a particularly good source of energy. One of the main problems with protein is that, when broken down for energy, ammonia is formed as a toxic by-product. Ammonia needs to be flushed out of the body.

High-protein diets will often show weight loss during the first few days (giving the dieter a false sense of success) because fluids are lost when the body gets rid of the ammonia. Unfortunately, the initial weight loss is not fat, just fluid.

Fats are high-energy foods, packing 9 calories per gram. That is more than twice the calories of proteins and carbohydrates.

A small amount of fat is needed in the diet, but most people consume far more than necessary. The amount of fat consumed daily should be limited to 30% of all calories taken in. The percentages of fat in some typical foods are listed in tables 20.6 and 20.7.

When fat is used for energy, toxic by-products called *ketones* are formed and must be flushed out of the body. Thus, a high-fat diet can actually produce a short-term weight loss. That weight loss, however, is only the loss of water caused by the flushing-out process.

Too much fat harms the body. The most obvious harm is excess weight. In addition, fat clogs the arteries and circulatory system. Fat may also "teach" the body to "desire" excess weight. Once deposited as fat, it does *not* want to leave (as most dieters know only too well).

TABLE 20.6

Percentage of Fat in Foods (grouped by percents)

100%	**60–70%**	**20–30%**
Butter	Eggs	Tomato soup
Corn oil	Potato chips	Crackers
Mayonnaise	Steak	Ice milk
	Chicken thigh	Low-fat yogurt
90–100%		
Cheese dressings	**50–60%**	**10–20%**
Olives	Hamburger	Broccoli
Bacon	Skim cheeses	Corn
Some nuts	Salmon	Egg noodles
	Trout	Cottage cheese
80–90%		Split-pea soup
Avocado	**40–50%**	Red snapper
Some nuts	Biscuits	Lobster
Sour cream	Doughnuts	
Bologna	Whole milk	**0–10%**
	Ice cream	Skim milk
70–80%	Sirloin	Many fruits
Many cheeses		Many vegetables
Some nuts	**30–40%**	Potato
Pork	Granola	Many fish
Hot dogs	Cheese pizza	
	Corn bread	
	Low-fat milk	

How does fat "teach" the body to "desire" excess weight? There is evidence to support the theory that fat upsets the *appestat*, or "set point"—the body's mechanism for regulating its percentage of body fat.

Once the set point (or percentage of body fat) is raised, it seldom comes down again regardless of diets. Thus, as people age, there is a slow but gradual increase in body fat that resists all attempts at reversal. Only one factor is an exception: exercise.

Exercise seems to be the sole way of reversing the set point. It has to be sustained for at least 20 to 30 minutes at a time, and it must be done a minimum of three or four times a week to be effective. Exercise will be discussed in greater detail later in this chapter.

Once students know the importance of limiting the fat intake, they should realize that it is very easy to go over recommended levels without realizing it. It is not just the case of absent-mindedly snacking on nuts and potato chips. Instead, it is easy to underestimate the amount of fat in foods. How? That is the purpose of *Event 20-L, Hidden Calories.* If the first item contains 200 calories of fat and 200 calories of proteins, we can easily see that the total calories are divided evenly between the two components. That is, 50% of the calories come from fat, and 50% come from proteins.

However, if the fat and protein contents are listed by *weight*, then we have an entirely different matter. In our example, the second item reports the

TABLE 20.7

Percentage of Fat in Foods (by food groups)

Vegetables	*Grains*
Nuts—70–90%	Biscuits—40–50%
Tomato soup—20–30%	Doughnuts—40–50%
Broccoli—10–20%	Granola—30–40%
Corn—10–20%	Corn bread—30–40%
Split-pea soup—10–20%	Crackers—20–30%
Potato—0–10%	
Most other vegetables—0%	*Fish*
	Salmon—50–60%
Meats	Trout—50–60%
Bacon—90%	Red snapper—10–20%
Bologna—80–90%	Lobster—10–20%
Pork—70–80%	Most other fish—0–10%
Hot dogs—70–80%	
Steak—60–70%	*Oils*
Chicken thigh—60–70%	Butter—100%
Hamburger—50–70%	Cooking oils—100%
Sirloin—40–50%	Mayonnaise—100%
Dairy	*Other*
Sour cream—80–90%	Potato chips—60–70%
Cheeses—70–80%	Eggs—60–70%
Skim cheeses—50–60%	Egg noodles—10–20%
Whole milk—40–50%	
Ice cream—40–50%	*Fruits*
Cheese pizza—30–40%	Olive—90%
Low-fat milk—30–40%	Avocado—80–90%
Ice milk—20–30%	Most other fruits—0%
Low-fat yogurt—20–30%	
Cottage cheese—10–20%	
Skim milk—0–10%	

contents by weight not by calories. Thus, 40% of fat, by weight, is equal to 40 grams. Since each gram of fat contains 9 calories, you get a total of 360 calories of fat.

The protein weighs 60 grams, but contains only 4 calories per gram for a total of 240 calories. Thus, the second item actually contains 60% of its calories in fat, even though that fat is only 40% of the product's weight. Be sure to read labels carefully when shopping for foods.

The third type of food shown in table 20.5 is called **carbohydrate.** At one time the carbohydrates were considered undesirable foods, often being blamed as the cause of overweight. However, recent evidence shows just the opposite.

Carbohydrates do not produce an excess of calories per gram, and they have many benefit's not found in other foods: First of all, many carbohydrates are rich in vitamins that are needed to regulate body processes.

Second, many carbohydrates, especially the vegetable-fruit group, provide fiber that seems to aid digestion without adding calories. (One medium potato of 100 grams contains only 98 calories; 100 grams of butter, on the other hand, contain 716 calories.)

Third, carbohydrates are excellent energy foods. When digested, they produce no harmful toxins that inhibit bodily functions. In fact, it is well known that carbohydrates are now preferred by endurance athletes, such as marathon runners, who "carbo load" for several days prior to a race.

Sugar

Event 20-M, Sugar: Good or Bad? poses a real discrepancy, at least at first glance. Most pupils know that too much sugar is "bad for you" and that too many sweets should be avoided. Yet they now find out that nothing else can be used in the cells to produce energy. If that is true, why should sugar be bad for you?

The answer is somewhat like saying that water is essential for life, but if you are a nonswimmer and fall into a pool, it could kill you. The big problem with sweets is that they overload the system with sugar.

To understand the danger of too much sugar, let us look first at how the body uses sugar from nonsugary foods. When nonsugars are consumed, they are converted to glucose in a slow, orderly manner. Glucose is released into the bloodstream for an extended period of time. A potato, for example, can release its energy for many hours.

Look at figure 20.5. Normal blood sugar levels are between 60 and 120 milligrams (mg) per deciliter of blood. After eating a meal, the levels go up to the 120 mg mark. It provides the person with lots of energy. Gradually the glucose (and energy) levels decline. After some hours the glucose level reaches 60 mg. This makes one tired (to slow down and preserve energy) and hungry (to replenish energy).

Now, let's see what happens when too much sugar is consumed directly. The sugar enters the bloodstream immediately (even complex sugars are quickly changed to glucose). This quickly raises the blood sugar levels in the body. If the glucose level goes *above* 120 mg, it is toxic and the body's natural defenses quickly go to work to get rid of the excess sugar.

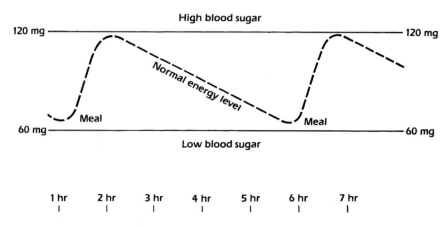

FIGURE 20.5   Normal blood sugar ranges from 60 to 120 milligrams per deciliter of blood.

The **pancreas** dumps insulin into the bloodstream, which purges the excess sugar. But the body is so stressed by the excess sugar that it overcompensates and purges too much sugar from the bloodstream. Thus, after consuming sugar, it is entirely possible that within a short time the bloodstream will have a *shortage* of sugar in it. In other words, sugar may be an energy "pick up," but it is followed by an energy "let down." See figure 20.6.

Overeating sugar is harmful in four ways: (1) it makes you fat; (2) it makes you hungry; (3) it makes you tired; and (4) it might make you sick. Now the details.

How does sugar make you fat? What happens to all those calories that are swept out by the insulin? Most are stored as fat. Thus the fastest way to convert food to fat is to eat too much sugar,

How does sugar make you hungry? When the body overcompensates and removes too much sugar from the bloodstream, the body suddenly has a shortage of energy. A natural response by the body to this shortage is to try to replace the shortage . . . by making you hungry.

How does sugar make you tired? When blood sugar is low, your energy is low. When you have no energy, you get tired. In turn, you tend to slow down, burning fewer calories than normal. As a result, you can actually gain weight while eating less.

How does too much sugar make you sick? There is evidence that too much sugar produces dental caries (cavities) and that excess sugar may be a cause of hypoglycemia (chronic low blood sugar) and diabetes (chronic high blood sugar).

It should be noted that refined sugar is a fairly recent discovery. Several generations ago, people did not know how to make refined sugar. Sweeteners were limited to an occasional raiding of a beehive for honey, Thus, the human body did not have thousands of years of evolutionary experience to condition itself to this substance. The sweetener has been widely available only in fairly recent generations, and overdosing can be a shock to the body.

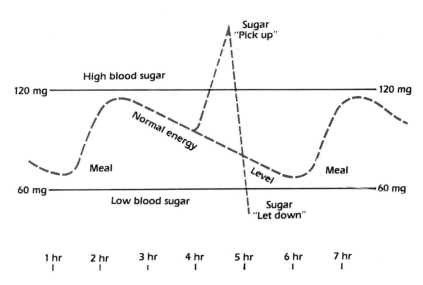

FIGURE 20.6   What happens when too much sugar is eaten? The blood sugar level jumps, then crashes.

TABLE 20.8

Calorie Use by Weight and Activity

Type	Multiply by	80 lb	100 lb	120 lb	140 lb	160 lb
Inactive	12	960	1200	1440	1680	1920
Moderate	16	1280	1600	1920	2240	2560
Very active	20	1600	2000	2400	2800	3200

Event 20-N, Cereal Database, gives pupils an opportunity to understand how to read the nutrition fact label on cereal boxes. Include discussions about the amount of sugar they are consuming early in the morning. Conduct an experiment to determine if and when pupils get hungry and tired during morning classes. Is it the same for students who eat sugar products for breakfast and those who don't? Keep in mind that a "big idea" behind the use of a database is for students to develop an appreciation for the ease and speed at which a database can sort tremendous amounts of information. A database helps scientists make sense of the overwhelming amount of data collected.

Caloric Needs

Event 20-O Calorie Counting, is a good exercise for pupils to gain an understanding of their calorie needs. It is important for them to realize that calorie needs are based on several factors. Most will know that one factor is weight: A big person needs more calories than a small person.

What many do not realize, however, is the effect of activity. They may have some concept that if you work hard or play hard it takes more energy. But often they are amazed that a small active person needs more calories than a larger sedentary person. Check table 20.8 for some sample figures.

As can be seen in the table, a very active 80-pound child will use more energy than an inactive person who is 50% heavier (120 pounds), and a very active 100-pound person will burn more energy than the inactive person of 160 pounds.

Another way to determine caloric needs is to check on the kinds of activities that are performed in a typical day. Let pupils use table 20.9 to calculate their energy needs during a typical day.

It is likely that by using table 20.9 pupils will get higher values than those shown in table 20.8. Pupils tend to evaluate their activity levels higher than they really are.

Pupils may be amused by changes in the meaning of the terms **active** and **sedentary** during the past century. In 1900, a nutrition textbook described a sedentary male as one who worked in an office for 10 hours a day, 6 days a week. He did not sit down but worked at a stand-up desk and walked much of the time.

In addition, he walked an hour each, to and from work, and spent from 1 to 2 more hours daily doing chores round his home. These chores included splitting wood and shoveling coal. There are few "active" men today who expend as much energy as the "sedentary" man of 1900.

Another factor that affects the consumption of energy is the weather. During cold weather, more energy is burned to maintain body temperature than when the weather is warm.

TABLE 20.9

Calorie Use per Activity

Forms of Activity	Calories per Hour	
	Men (per lb)	Women (per lb)
Sleeping	0.4	0.4
Sitting quietly	0.6	0.6
Standing	0.7	0.6
Light exercise	1.1	1.0
Walking slowly	1.3	1.2
Walking moderately fast	2.0	1.8
Swimming	3.3	3.0
Jogging	3.7	3.4
Walking very fast	4.2	3.9

Diets

Counting calories will often lead to a discussion of diets. Even some grade school pupils will have been on a diet, and almost all will have parents or older family members who have been on one.

Who should go on a diet? Someone who is overweight is the quick answer. Who is overweight? Just check the height and weight tables. Refer back to table 20.3 from the Metropolitan Life Insurance Company to see typical values for adults ages 25 to 59. The figures are of people fully clothed and wearing shoes. To find your place on the table, weigh yourself fully clothed. If you measured your height in bare or stocking feet, add 1 inch to find your proper place on the chart.

The table is a good approximation. However, there are many exceptions that pupils should be aware of. Normally, "overweight" means "overfat," but not always. Two exceptions are highlighted in *Event 20-P, Overweight or Overfat?* If two men are both 6 feet tall, how can the 175-pound man be overweight instead of the one who weighs 220 pounds? The answer: When the 220-pound man happens to be an all-star fullback in the National Football League. His extra weight is all muscle.

Athletes who are involved in strength sports like football often engage in intense training to build strength. As a result, many professional athletes gain considerable muscle mass and weight. However, that kind of weight (added muscle) is good, because it allows you to accomplish more work with less fatigue. It is fat that is harmful.

The 175-pound man, however, could be of very slight build and have a percentage of body fat in excess of good health. So, although the tables are a good approximation, there are exceptions to the figures. In summary, being overfat is a greater problem than being overweight.

The second example in Event 20-P is of a woman whose weight did not change from one time to the next. Yet, she was at a proper weight the first time, but "too fat" the next. How can that be? Simple! The weighings were 30 years apart.

Assume that at age 20 the woman was in good health and active in sports. Her weight would include a goodly amount of muscle tissue but very little fat. However, if she was inactive for the thirty years, she would surely lose muscle tissue. Remember that muscles must be exercised to maintain them. Thus, if she is the same weight as originally, the loss of muscle is made up by an increase in fat. As a result, it is quite likely that at the second weighing, she is overfat.

It is quite common for people to lose strength as they grow older. The reason for the loss of strength is lack of the kinds of activity that developed that strength in the first place. Inactivity causes muscles to shrink.

Even if a person maintains the same weight as he or she grows older, the percentage of body fat tends to increase. Unfortunately, the situation is made even worse by the fact that there is often an increase in weight, over and above the shift toward more fat.

How can you tell if you are too fat? In addition to using the weight-height table, there are several other methods that can be used.

1. *Check your belt.* When a person reaches full maturity, the waist size does not change except for fat. Thus, if an adult gains an inch at the waist, it is an inch of fat. (Of course, this method does not work for children who are still growing.)
2. *Use skin-fold calipers.* "Pinch an inch" to see if you are too fat. Fat is deposited just below the skin on many sites of the body. Measuring the thickness of a fold of skin gives an indication of the percentage of body fat. Fairly accurate measurements can be taken by using skin-fold calipers, available from many science supply houses.
3. *Water-displacement method.* This is a method in which a person is weighed twice: once underwater and again out of water. Then the amount of displaced water is compared to the difference in weight to give an accurate body fat measurement. This method is generally available only at research centers.

The final activity, *Event 20-Q, Supermarket Diets,* is useful to call attention to many fad diets that people often try. It is amazing how often a new, spectacular diet is proclaimed in the headlines of the magazines that line the checkout counters of supermarkets.

If the front pages are observed for a month or more, pupils are likely to find at least four major claims promoted in the headlines:

1. It is quick ("Lose a pound a day").
2. It is easy ("Fat melts away" . . . sometimes "while you sleep").
3. You can "eat all you want" ("including candy, cake, steaks, snacks").
4. You can be like a television or movie star.

Why do the magazine publishers make such claims? Probably because those claims help sell the magazines. Why do people fall for those claims? Because they *want* to believe. Unfortunately, many (probably most) of the fad diets that are so highly promoted are worthless. Some may even be harmful.

First of all, look back at table 20.8 to see how many calories you use per day. Then compare that figure with 3500 calories, the amount in 1 pound of fat. Thus, unless you actually need 3500 calories a day, it is quite impossible to "lose a pound a day." In fact, if you are an inactive person of 145 pounds and eat nothing at all, it takes 2 days to lose a pound of fat . . . assuming that only fat is lost!

TABLE 20.10

Composition of Lost Pounds in Various Diets

Type Diet	Fat (%)	Muscle (%)	Fluid (%)
"Sensible" diet, alone	75	10	15
Crash, or starvation diet	50	50	0
Slow diet with exercise	98	−10 (gain)	2

Unfortunately, fat is often *not* the only thing that is lost. If a person goes on a crash diet, the body often "protects the fat" and burns muscle tissue for fuel. (Remember, muscles must be exercised. Otherwise, muscle tissue is lost.) Some details are shown in table 20.10.

The best hope of losing weight is to follow a sensible diet, combined with an exercise program. You should not expect to lose more than 1 or 2 pounds a week. Obviously the diet and exercise program must be maintained for a long time for it to do any good.

Aerobic and Anaerobic Exercise

There are two types of exercise: *aerobic* and *anaerobic.*

Aerobic means "with oxygen." It is the kind of exercise in which the oxygen needs of the body are met by breathing. As a result, aerobic exercises can be maintained for a long time.

Aerobic exercise is excellent for the heart and lungs. It develops endurance (a measure of fitness) but not much strength. A distance runner is a prime example of a person who does aerobic exercise.

Much less strenuous, but just as good for most people, is easy jogging, brisk walking, easy swimming, biking, jazzercise, or any other activity that keeps the heartbeat elevated for 20 to 30 minutes.

Anaerobic means "without oxygen." It means that a muscle performs at a level in which oxygen needs are greater than can be supplied by breathing. The muscle cells can operate that way for a short while.

An example of an anaerobic activity is the 100-meter dash. It is much more strenuous than jogging, but can be performed for only a very short time. Track experts claim that, even in the 100-meter dash, most sprinters cannot maintain their maximum speed for the full distance.

Other examples of anaerobic activity include hitting a golf ball, kicking a football, lifting a heavy weight, jumping, swinging an ax, throwing a discus, and hitting a baseball. Anaerobic exercise develops strength and is the kind of exercise performed by weight lifters and bodybuilders.

Combining Assessment with Instruction

Have students keep a log of their food intake and exercise for one weekend. Provide them with a calorie counter and have them compare their caloric intake and caloric expenditure. Students should report the following:

- What they ate and the approximate portion size.
- All the physical activity performed during the day and the amount of time spent on each activity.

- The number of calories consumed and the number of calories used throughout the weekend.
- Whether their caloric intake and expenditures were about equal for the 2-day weekend.
  In addition, ask students to do the following:
- Sort the foods they ate into the six groups indicated on the food pyramid.
- Write a paragraph about their food choices and portion sizes. Did they make good choices and why? Are portion sizes appropriate? Explain.
- Tell what might have been healthier choices. Explain.
- (For middle school students) Include a pie chart that displays the percent based on calories of each of the six food groups that they ate for the weekend.
- Assume that a friend was coming to visit next weekend and they knew that he or she ate only healthy foods. What would they plan for meals and snacks? Include two recipes of healthy, good-tasting snacks. Be creative.

Evaluate the students on their understanding of portion size and the amount of each food group that a healthy diet comprises. How completely did they answer the questions? How complete is their log? How creative were they with their snack recipes? Do they have an understanding of what foods each of the food groups comprises?

Sites and Software

The following websites and software are appropriate to use with this chapter. Note that computer software and websites change rapidly. This makes it necessary to investigate the stable websites for new links and software catalogs for updates. Visit www.mhhe.com/friedl6e to link to these directly and for study resources.

Sites

Nutrition Education Materials USDA, K–6	www.nal.usda.gov/fnic/pubs/bibs/edu/preschool.html
Get the Facts about Nutrition! Discovery Health	health.discovery.com/centers/nutrition/nutrition.html
Kids Health	kidshealth.org/kid/stay_healthy/food/labels.html
Center for Health and Health Care in Schools	www.healthinschools.org
The Food Pyramid Controversy: What Shape Should Your Diet Take?	www.infoaging.org/feat14.html
USDA Nutrition	www.nutrition.gov/home/index.php3

Software

Health Beats Series (Core Learning) (4–10)
Human Genetics (NeoScience) (6–10)
The Human Body (Sunburst) (K–2)

Key Terms

Teaching Children about Fitness: The Heart, Lungs, and Muscles

NATIONAL SCIENCE EDUCATION STANDARDS ALIGNMENT TO EVENTS

The events in this chapter help accomplish several of the NSES for content. The event(s) that align with a given content standard are listed below that standard.

LEVELS K–4

CONCEPTS AND PROCESSES
- Change, consistency, measurement
  21-A and 21-B
  21-D and 21-E
  21-H and 21-I
  21-Q and 21-R
- Evidence, models and explanation
  21-A through 21-R

LIFE SCIENCE
- The characteristics of organisms
  21-A through 21-R

SCIENCE AND TECHNOLOGY
- Understanding science and technology
  21-D
  21-H and 21-I
  21-R

SCIENCE IN PERSONAL AND SOCIAL PERSPECTIVES
- Personal health
  21-A through 21-R

LEVELS 5–8

CONCEPTS AND PROCESSES
- Change, consistency, measurement
  21-A and 21-B
  21-D and 21-E
  21-H and 21-I
  21-Q and 21-R
- Evidence, models and explanation
  21-A through 21-R

LIFE SCIENCE
- Structure and function in living systems
  21-A through 21-M

SCIENCE AND TECHNOLOGY
- Understanding science and technology
  21-D
  21-H and 21-I
  21-R

SCIENCE IN PERSONAL AND SOCIAL PERSPECTIVES
- Personal health
  21-A through 21-R
- Risks and benefits
  21-P through 21-R
- Science and technology in society
  21-D
  21-H and 21-I
  21-R

What Is Fitness?

Not too many years ago a typical dictionary did not contain an entry on **fitness;** and under the word *fit,* the definitions pertained mostly to an agreement, say, between the size of the shoe and the size of the foot.

In recent years the term has taken on a new meaning—being of sound mind and body. Specifically, fitness means to be able to endure vigorous physical activity for a long period of time.

Programs such as the ACES project and The President's Challenge were formed in the last 30 years to promote physical activity/fitness among school-age children. Physical Education Teacher Len Saunders of New Jersey began project ACES in 1989. The program was designed to show the importance of physical education in school. Each May, on a designated date and time, millions of schoolchildren worldwide simultaneously exercise to show the world that they take being physically fit seriously. Similarly, The President's Challenge motivates students between the ages of 6 and 17 to build strength, endurance, and flexibility as well as maintain a physically active lifestyle.

The Office of Disease Prevention and Health Promotion reported in their 2001 report, *Healthy People 2001*, that physical inactivity contributes to 300,000 preventable deaths a year in the United States. Some 40% of deaths in the United States are caused by behavior patterns that could be modified—such as a sedentary lifestyle. Significant health benefits can be achieved by moderate physical activity such as walking briskly or raking leaves for 30 minutes. This daily activity can reduce substantially the risk of developing or dying from cardiovascular disease, type-2 diabetes, and certain cancers such as colon cancer. Daily physical activity helps to lower blood pressure and cholesterol; helps prevent or retard osteoporosis; and helps reduce obesity, symptoms of anxiety and depression, and symptoms of arthritis.

The report goes on to say that overweight among children and teens has doubled in the past two decades; 13% of children aged 6 to 11 years and 14% of adolescents aged 12 to 19 years were overweight in 1999. School-based interventions have been shown to be successful in increasing physical activity levels. Childhood and adolescence are pivotal times for preventing sedentary behavior among adults by maintaining the habit of physical activity throughout the school years.

Measuring Fitness (Events 21-A and 21-B)

Discrepant Events and Pupil Investigations

Event 21-A. The 1-Mile Run-Walk

This is a strenuous test for most pupils. (Any pupil who has been cleared by a doctor to participate in any school sport is normally cleared for this test.) In this test the pupils finish a mile as fast as they can.

Those in good condition can probably run the entire mile. Others will probably have to do some walking. Let pupils run or walk according to how they feel. Satisfactory times are listed in table 21.1.

Pupil Investigations (may include the following processes):

1. Measuring the time needed to cover 1 mile.
2. Interpreting the figures given in table 21.1.
3. Generalizing about the level of fitness.

Event 21-B. The Sit-Up Test

This is a a test of strength. Pupils try to do as many sit-ups as possible in 1 minute. These sit-ups are done with bent knees, with arms crossed in front of the body, hands on the shoulders. Another person may hold down the ankles during the test. (See figure 21.1.)

Pupil Investigations (may include the following processes):

1. Measuring the number of sit-ups done in 1 minute.
2. Interpreting the figures given in table 21.2.
3. Generalizing about the level of fitness.

TABLE 21.1

1-Mile Run-Walk: Acceptable Times (in minutes)

Age	Male	Female
5	16:00	17:00
6	15:00	16:00
7	14:00	15:00
8	13:00	14:00
9	12:00	13:00
10	11:00	12:00
11	11:00	12:00
12	10:00	12:00
13	9:30	11:30
14 and older	8:30	10:30

Source: Taken from FITNESSGRAM Health Fitness Standards, developed by the Institute for Aerobics Research, 12330 Preston Road, Dallas, Texas 75230, and sponsored by the Campbell Soup Company.

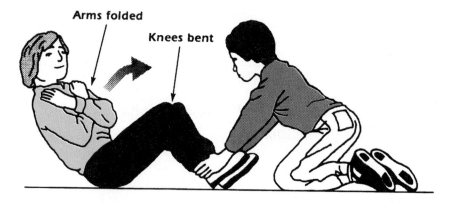

FIGURE 21.1   How many sit-ups can you do in 1 minute?

TABLE 21.2

Sit-Ups: Acceptable Number in 1 Minute

Age	Boys	Girls
5, 6, 7	20	20
8	25	25
9	25	25
10	30	30
11	30	30
12	35	30
13	35	30
14 and older	40	35

Source: Taken from FITNESSGRAM Health Fitness Standards, developed by the Institute for Aerobics Research, 12330 Preston Road, Dallas Texas 75230, and sponsored by the Campbell Soup Company.

Events 21-A through 21-B Explained in Context (Measuring Fitness)

Fitness is achieved by fairly vigorous exercise that is performed at least three times a week for about 25 to 30 minutes each time. Such a program produces a sound heart and lungs (the **cardiovascular system**) as well as strong muscles and bones.

A person who is fit has a cardiovascular system that can process oxygen very well. Those who are not fit cannot process nearly as much. By measuring the body's ability to process oxygen, a person's general fitness can be measured. In a lab, a person can be hooked up to monitoring equipment to check how the heart and lungs function while engaging in strenuous exercise. Such testing produces sophisticated data.

In the absence of such equipment, which is the case in most schools, there are a number of relatively simple tests that can be used to measure the degree of fitness.

Fitness is given in *aerobic capacity* of "ml O_2/kg/min." That means "milliliters of oxygen per kilogram (of body weight) per minute."

A person who is very fit will have the ability to process lots of oxygen, but the person who is not fit will process much less. The highest figures ever reported are of marathon runners—some of whom are able to process up to 80 milliliters of oxygen per kilogram of body weight per minute. In comparison, someone who is in poor physical condition will have a reading in the 20s. Someone who is able to run 5 miles in 1 hour will have a reading of about 45.

Events 21-A, The 1-Mile Run-Walk, and *21-B, The Sit-up Test,* are both "max" tests. That is, they are maximum efforts. What is an acceptable time? It depends on the age and sex of the pupil. Acceptable times are shown in table 21.1.

Another measure of fitness is muscle strength. An especially good test of strength is the sit-up. It measures the strength of the stomach muscles and those muscles involved in keeping the body upright. Weakness there can lead to back problems. How many sit-ups should a pupil be able to do? Again, the answer depends on the age and sex of the pupil. Acceptable fitness levels are given in table 21.2.

The 1-mile test and the sit-up test are good measures of fitness. However they do not cover all areas of fitness. A complete assessment of fitness is beyond the scope of this book.

There are organizations such as the ACES project and The President's Challenge that promote physical activity/fitness for school-age children. Computer fitness calculators and reports can be useful in helping children become more aware of fitness criteria. One such report is the FITNESSGRAM which personalize a fitness report for each pupil. Go to www.americanfitness.net/Fitnessgram.

The Heart and Circulatory System (Events 21-C through 21-F)

Discrepant Events and Pupil Investigations

Event 21-C. Teetering Toothpick

Carefully place a toothpick into the end of a thumbtack (or attach with a drop of glue) and set the thumbtack on the wrist as shown in figure 21.2. Observe

FIGURE 21.2   What makes the thumbtack-toothpick device sway when placed on the correct spot on the wrist?

carefully. Adjust the position of the thumbtack several times until you can see it moving with your pulse. (**Note:** Rest the hand on a table or desk to keep it as steady as possible. If the hand is really steady, any movement caused by the heartbeat is more likely to be noticed.)

Pupil Investigations (may include the following processes):

1. Discovering that when placed in the right spot the thumbtack-toothpick device wobbles.
2. Observing a rhythmic movement.
3. Inferring that the movement is caused by the heartbeat.

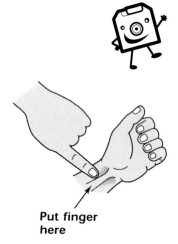

Put finger here

FIGURE 21.3   Place fingers in the hollow along the cord on the thumb side of the wrist and you will feel the pulse.

Event 21-D. Pulse and Exercise

Teach the pupils to take their own pulse. If you tell them to place their fingers on the wrist, they will grab the front, the sides, the back, just about anywhere on the wrist, with very little success. Here is a way that works quite well: Have them make a fist so that the wrist is facing upward. It also helps to rotate the fist slightly upward. In this position the cords pop up on the wrist. See figure 21.3. Then ask them to place two or three fingers into the *hollow* along *the thumb side* of the cord. That is where the pulse can be found. (**Note:** Once the pulse has been located, the hand can be relaxed.)

Have pupils take their pulse. Then have them do a few minutes of brisk exercise and then take their pulse again. Finally, have the pulse taken once more after 5 minutes of rest. (**Caution:** Some teachers like to have pupils climb stairs. Going *upstairs* may be acceptable if supervised. However, *never* let pupils run *down* stairs. It is very dangerous. Why? If you fall while going up, you don't fall very far. If you fall going down, it may be a long tumble before hitting bottom.) Have students also measure their heart rate using a heart rate sensor available with most MBLs or CBLs. With the sensor connected to the computer, clip the sensor to your earlobe. Begin recording data as you rest. Now do the step test as you record the heart rate. Keep recording as you slow to a resting position. Compare the rates gathered by the computer to that of the results you collect by hand as suggested next.

Pupil Investigations (may include the following processes):

1. Recording the pulse rates in each of the instances described above.
2. Charting the pulse rates of the class members before and after exercise.
3. Calculating the class averages before and after exercise.
4. Analyzing the relationship between exercise and pulse rates.
5. Comparing heart rates measured by a computer sensor to rates collected by hand.

Event 21-E. Maximum and Exercise Heart Rates

The maximum heart rate for a newborn infant is 220 beats per minute. The maximum declines by one beat for every year of age. The safe sustained exercise rate for a person beginning an exercise program (assuming that there are no medical problems) is about 70% of the maximum.

Have the pupils figure out their maximum and safe exercise rates. Ask them also to figure those rates for a person 40 years old and another 60 years old.

Pupil Investigations (may include the following processes):

1. Calculating their maximum and safe exercise levels.
2. Inferring that the declining maximum rates reduce physical capacities in older people.
3. Analyzing the relationship between the declining maximum heart rates and the process of aging.

Event 21-F. Hands Up and Down

Look carefully at the back of your hands as you hold them down low. Can you find the raised veins in the back of the hands? Leave the hands down for a minute or two. Is there any change in the veins? Now raise the hands overhead and observe. What happens to the veins?

Pupil Investigations (may include the following processes):

1. Observing that the veins are visible on the back of the hands when they are held low.
2. Discovering that the veins disappear quickly when the hands are held overhead.
3. Inferring that there is a relationship between gravity and the movement of blood in the veins.

Events 21-C through 21-F Explained in Context (The Heart and Circulatory System)

No mechanical pump has ever been devised that is even close to the efficiency of the human heart. Consider the job that it does. For the average person at rest, it pumps about 70 times per minute. At that rate it pumps 4200 times per hour, 100,000 times per day, and over 37,000,000 times per year.

At rest, the heart pumps about 140 grams of blood per stroke. This figure is equal to 10 kilograms of blood per minute, 600 kg per hour, and over 4.5 million kg per year.

In volume, the heart pumps about 8 liters every minute, 480 liters per hour, 11,500 liters per day, and 4 million liters per year.

The stream, of blood that leaves the heart travels at about 100 meters per minute. (That is the length of a football field plus one endzone.) As it branches out into smaller and smaller vessels, the speed decreases: It makes its trip to the lungs, back to the heart again, then out to other body tissues, and finally returns to the heart—all in about 23 seconds.

The figures are given so that pupils can gain an appreciation of the truly astounding job that the heart does. The children should not be expected to memorize those figures.

Blood flows through passages called **arteries** as it moves from the heart to the tissues. While in the main arteries, the beat of the heart can be detected by fingers as well as instruments. A good place to locate the pulse is along the tendon that runs lengthwise near the surface of the wrist. Place two or three fingers into the hollow along the tendon on the *thumb* side of the wrist.

If the right spot is found, the pulse will be strong enough to make the toothpick pulsate with the beat of the heart, as suggested in *Event 21-C,*

Teetering Toothpick. It will actually be possible to count the heart rate by looking at the toothpick.

The movement can also be detected if a tiny mirror is placed on just the right spot of the wrist, and a strong light is reflected from the mirror to a wall. The light will flicker as the mirror moves slightly in response to the pulse beat.

After the pupils have had some practice in taking a pulse, they will be ready for *Event 21-D, Pulse and Exercise.* Pupils will find that there is a great increase in the pulse rate taken right after exercise.

Exercise causes large muscle groups to work. As soon as work is begun, the muscle cells need a greatly increased volume of oxygen. That is why people begin to pant and gasp for air when engaged in very strenuous exercise. The oxygen is carried to the muscles where it is used to burn fuel for energy. The muscle cells also produce waste products, which are carried away from the cells by the blood.

When exercise ends, the muscles soon return to normal. Thus, after 5 minutes, the pulse rate should be back to normal.

Pupils will find that there are many differences in the pulse rates among various members of the class. The differences can be caused by many factors. Some pupils will have worked much harder than others and, as a result, will show higher post-exercise pulse rates.

However, even if all pupils had exercised at exactly the same rate, there would still be differences. One of the major factors affecting the pulse rate is a person's physical condition.

Athletes who are in top physical condition will show a resting heart rate much lower than normal and an exercise rate also much below normal. They have developed such a strong heart that it can do its job at a much slower pace than the normal heart.

Some world-class marathon runners have resting heart rates as low as 35 to 40 beats per minute. Then when they are running a marathon (of more than 26 miles) at a pace of close to 5 minutes per mile, the heart rate is often only about 120 beats per minute. A sedentary person often reaches that rate by climbing a single flight of stairs.

One of the key indicators of fitness is the resting heart rate. To gain an impression of its real benefits, look at some examples of typical heart rates. As stated in *Event 21-E, Maximum and Exercise Heart Rates,* the maximum heart rate decreases at a rate of one beat per year from the 220 rate of a newborn infant. The safe exercise rate is about 70% of the maximum (assuming no medical problems).

Some values for several age groups are shown in table 21.3.

TABLE 21.3

Heart Rates

Age	20	40	60
Maximum rate	200	180	160
Safe exercise rate (70% of max)	140	126	112
Resting heart rate	70	75	80

Look closely at the figures for the three age groups. As the person grows older, the safe range is lower and lower. At the same time, because of a lack of exercise, the resting rate tends to go up slightly. Can you see the narrowing of the safe range as the person grows older? At age 20 the resting rate can double before it exceeds the safe range. At age 60, however, it can only increase by 40%.

Can you see one reason why heart problems tend to occur more in older people than in the young? Of course, there are many other factors that tend to endanger the heart as a person grows older. The safe exercise rate is only one factor.

What happens if a person regularly engages in vigorous exercise? One of the major effects is a *lowering* of the resting heart rate. Look at the effect that might have on the 60-year-old person. It is not unusual to lower the resting heart rate to 60 within 3 months. In rare cases the resting rate can be lowered to 40 beats per minute.

How much of a reserve does the 60-year-old person have after becoming fit? Instead of a reserve of only 40% (the difference between 80 and 112 in table 21.3), it now changes to a reserve of 87% if the resting rate is 60 and to a whopping 180% if the resting rate is 40.

Even those figures are understated, because exercise not only *lowers* the resting heart rate, but it also *raises* the safe heart rate. A person who is very fit can exercise safely at a level at or near the maximum heart rate. Thus, the safe margin jumps to 167 percent for the 60-year-old who has a resting heart rate of 60 and to an astounding 300% safety margin if the resting rate is 40.

In recent years thousands of older people have become active and have gained the benefits of a strong heart. Instead of sitting in a rocking chair, many oldsters now go for a 5-mile jog.

During exercise the flow of blood increases to the working muscles, but decreases to the inactive muscles. Thus, a runner will have a great increase in the flow of blood to the leg muscles. In fact, during a 5-minute race blood flow to the leg muscles increases an amazing 15 times (1500%).

At the same time, the flow of blood to the stomach is sharply reduced. What do you suppose happens to a big meal if you run vigorously right after eating? It just *sits* there! It is obviously not a good idea to eat just before vigorous exercise.

Have you ever noticed that when your hands are down low the veins on the back of the hands are easier to see than if you hold your hands high? The veins are especially visible on middle-aged and older people, but even children can notice them.

If the veins are so clearly visible, why not take the pulse there? Try it? You will feel nothing. There is no pulse in the veins because the blood has made its journey through the tissues and is no longer directly pushed by the pumping heart. The blood is pushed along by the blood that follows and also by the action of muscles.

Therefore, veins in the lower part of the body, the legs, and hands that are held low will fill up with blood. The force of gravity will tend to cause the blood to fill up the veins so they bulge and are easy to see on the back of the hands.

That is what happens in *Event 21-F, Hands Up and Down*. When the hands are held low, gravity causes the blood to fill up the veins before it makes its way back to the heart. When the hands are raised, however, gravity helps push the blood down. The pressure on the veins is reduced, and the veins disappear from view.

The buildup of blood in the veins sometimes causes problems for people who stand for long periods of time. They get swollen legs and feet. The swollen and painful legs are a result of standing, not of walking. During walking, the muscles of the legs gently massage and push the blood back to the heart.

When the heart beats, it sends blood to all parts of the body. Sometimes the arteries become filled with obstructions so that it becomes more and more difficult for the blood to reach the tissues. The heart tries harder and harder to do its job and gradually increases the pressure at which it sends out the blood.

If the pressure gets too high, it becomes dangerous. It can stress the blood vessels just as too much air can stress a balloon. A "normal" safe blood pressure reading is 120/70.

There are two figures in that reading. The high value (called **systolic**) is the maximum pressure during the stroke of the heart. The low value (called **diastolic**) is the value to which the pressure drops between heartbeats. A reading of 140/90 is considered to be "high," and a reading of 160/95 is labeled **hypertension** and should receive medical treatment.

Health authorities have found that aerobic exercise tends to reduce high blood pressure. Aerobic exercise is any activity that is continuous and that pushes the heartbeat to its safe exercise level. Thus, someone who is in poor physical shape can reach his or her exercise level with a brisk walk, but an athlete must run or jog to achieve the same value. Jogging, swimming, aerobic dancing, and biking are examples of aerobic exercises. This topic was discussed in more detail at the end of chapter 20.

Lungs and Respiration (Events 21-G through 21-I)

Discrepant Events and Pupil Investigations

Event 21-G. Cloudy Water

Prepare four or five glasses, each containing a liquid that appears to be water. Unknown to the pupils, however, two of the tumblers should contain limewater instead of tap water. Ask a pupil to stand in front of each glass and exhale through a straw into the liquid. Let them blow through the straws for about a minute. What is observed?

Pupil Investigations (may include the following processes):

1. Observing that the water becomes cloudy in two of the containers.
2. Discovering that with further blowing a chalky precipitate forms in the cloudy water.
3. Inferring that there is something in exhaled breath that causes the water to turn cloudy.

Event 21-H. Measuring Lung Capacity: Inverted Jar

Arrange a jar, water, and tube as shown in figure 21.4. Be sure to start with the inverted jar completely filled with water; then exhale through the tube and see how much air you can exhale.

A jar of about 4 liters is big enough for elementary school pupils and will be sufficient for some adults. However, many adults may need a larger container, as will some mature student athletes. A container of 6 liters will be large enough for everyone.

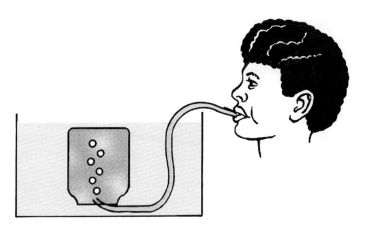

FIGURE 21.4   Measure your lung capacity by blowing through a tube into an inverted water-filled bottle.

Pupil Investigations (may include the following processes):

1. Measuring the lung capacity of all pupils in class.
2. Comparing the lung-volume figures with physical size.
3. Comparing the lung-volume figures with physical fitness.
4. Generalizing that lung-volume is increased by exercise.

Event 21-I. Measuring Lung Capacity: Lung-Volume Bag

Obtain some lung-volume bags from a science supply house (Hubbard Scientific, Cenco, Science Kit, etc.), and measure lung volumes by having pupils exhale into them. (These are more convenient to use than the inverted jar.)

Pupil Investigations (may include the following processes):

1. Measuring the lung capacity of all pupils in class.
2. Comparing the lung-volume figures with physical size.
3. Comparing the lung-volume figures with physical fitness.
4. Generalizing that lung volume is increased by exercise.

Events 21-G through 21-I Explained in Context (Lungs and Respiration)

Respiration means breathing, that is, inhaling and exhaling air. We inhale oxygen and exhale carbon dioxide and excess water. Remember the path that blood takes in its trip through the body's **circulatory system?** The blood picks up oxygen from the lungs and sends it to the cells where it is burned for energy.

The waste products of the cells (mostly carbon dioxide) are collected, carried to the lungs, and exhaled. The cycle is repeated endlessly.

Air that is inhaled contains 79.02% nitrogen, 20.94% oxygen, and 0.04% carbon dioxide. Air that is exhaled contains about 79.2% nitrogen, 16.3% oxygen, and 4.5% carbon dioxide. You will notice that about 4% of the oxygen is removed and 4% of the carbon dioxide is added by the respiration process.

The exchange of oxygen-carbon dioxide in the body is similar to the exchange that occurs during any kind of oxidation. The oxygen is needed to support the "combustion" or "burning of fuel" that takes place. A simplified, unbalanced equation shows the process:

$$CH + O \longrightarrow H_2O + CO_2$$

carbohydrate and oxygen $\qquad\qquad\qquad$ water and carbon dioxide

We can detect the carbon dioxide in exhaled air by blowing into a bottle of limewater as suggested in *Event 21-G, Cloudy Water.* Limewater is used as an indicator to detect carbon dioxide.

The normal breathing rate is about 16 to 24 times per minute. The total air exchange is about 9 or 10 liters per minute. However, the rate of air exchanged increases sharply during exercise because only about one-tenth of the lungs are used when resting.

Smoking reduces the effective air space of the lungs and reduces the efficiency of the oxygen-carbon dioxide exchange process. The lost space and efficiency is generally unnoticed at rest, but becomes quickly apparent during exertion.

The physical **lung capacity** can be measured in several ways. A measuring device called a **spirometer** is used to measure lung volume. However, such a device is often not available in a typical elementary school. As a result, two other methods are described that can be used.

Event 21-H, Measuring Lung Capacity: Inverted Jar, and *Event 21-I, Measuring Lung Capacity: Lung-Volume Bag,* are two methods that can be used in a classroom. The inverted jar is probably the least expensive, assuming that there is a large glass bowl or aquarium available in the classroom. With a gallon jar and a rubber hose, it is possible to measure lung volumes for all pupils.

A number of precautions should be observed. First of all, be sure to keep the mouthpiece of the hose clean. It can be wiped with an alcohol solution after each pupil has used it. Second, use a hose clamp or some other method to keep the air inside the jar long enough to record the results. Otherwise the air will escape as soon as a pupil takes the hose from his or her mouth. Finally, the measurements will be far more accurate if you mark the jar ahead of time with grease pencil or marker to show liters and fractions of liters.

The lung-volume bags are even more convenient. They come with disposable mouthpieces, so it is easy to keep it clean for all pupils. Just inhale as much as possible and then exhale into the bag. When finished, gather up the bag, starting from the mouthpiece, until the trapped air fills up the bag. Read the volume directly from the values marked on the bag. (See figure 21.5.)

What kind of volumes can you expect from pupils or adults? The averages are shown in table 21.4.

A muscle, the **diaphragm,** controls the action of the lungs. When the muscle pulls down, it creates a partial vacuum in the lungs. Air rushes in to fill that vacuum. To exhale, the muscles merely squeeze the lungs together—forcing the air out. The way the lungs work can be demonstrated with a device such as is shown in figure 21.6.

For best results cut off the bottom of a heavy plastic jug, or use an open glass cylinder fitted with a wide one-hole stopper. Securely attach a rubber diaphragm across the big opening with rubber bands or tape.

As you push in on the diaphragm, the balloon (the lung) squeezes together to push out the air (exhales). When you pull out on the diaphragm, the "lung" fills with air (inhales).

FIGURE 21.5 A lung-volume bag. Exhale into the bag and measure your lung volume.

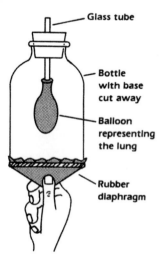

FIGURE 21.6 Pull on the rubber diaphragm and the balloon fills; push in and the balloon empties. This shows the action of the lungs.

TABLE 21.4

Lung Volumes

Age	Male (cc)	Female (cc)	Age	Male (cc)	Female (cc)
4	700	600	18	4200	2800
5	850	800	19	4300	2800
6	1070	980	20	4320	2800
7	1300	1150	21	4320	2800
8	1500	1350	22	4300	2800
9	1700	1550	23	4280	2790
10	1950	1740	24	4250	2780
11	2200	1950	25	4220	2770
12	2540	2150	26–30	4150	2720
13	2900	2350	31–35	3990	2640
14	3250	2480	36–40	3800	2520
15	3600	2700	41–45	3600	2390
16	3900	2700	46–50	3410	2250
17	4100	2750	51–55	3240	2160

Muscles, Bones, and Skin (Events 21-J through 21-M)

Discrepant Events and Pupil Investigations

Event 21-J. Muscle Pairs

Muscles work in pairs. When one muscle contracts, the other must relax. An easy way to examine this principle is to have a pupil stand in front of a counter. Place a hand underneath the counter and then lift. While holding this position, have other pupils feel the working muscle (the biceps) and the resting muscle (the triceps). Then, place the hand on top of the counter and push down. Again, have pupils feel the two muscles.

Pupil Investigations (may include the following processes):

1. Discovering that the working muscle is hard and contracted, but that the other muscle is relaxed.
2. Discovering that when the hand is pushed down, the working and relaxing muscles are reversed.
3. Generalizing that muscles work in pairs; when one muscle contracts, the other relaxes.

Event 21-K. Posture Strains

Stand, leaning forward at the waist. Hold this position for a minute or two. How do you feel?

Pupil Investigations (may include the following processes):

1. Observing that it becomes very tiring to stand this way.
2. Comparing this activity with the strains placed on muscles as a result of bad posture.
3. Inferring that good posture is less tiring than poor posture.

Event 21-L. Touch Test

Have pupils work in pairs. Find out if they can tell by touch if one or two points of a hairpin is touching the skin. One pupil is the experimenter; the other is the subject.

The experimenter takes a hairpin and gently presses one or both points against the skin of the subject. The subject does not look but tries to tell by touch how many points are touching the skin. Try with the points close together and also farther apart. Touch the back of the hand, the fingertip, the neck, and the arm.

Pupil Investigations (may include the following processes):

1. Observing that there are differences in how well the points can be detected on the body.
2. Experimenting to find out how far apart the points of the hairpin can be placed before they can be sensed as separate points.
3. Inferring that those places where the points can be felt the best are areas with the most nerve endings.

Event 21-M. One Nose or Two?

Cross your fingers and close your eyes. Then touch your nose with your crossed fingers. Hold them there for a while and move them around. What do you feel? (This event works best if you cross your fingers, and then use your other hand to "over cross" them.)

Pupil Investigations (may include the following processes):

1. Feeling the sensation of two noses.
2. Comparing the sensation of the fingers crossed and uncrossed.
3. Generalizing that the sense of touch can sometimes give false reformation.

Events 21-J through 21-M Explained in Context (Muscles, Bones, and Skin)

The human body is supported by a framework of bones called the **skeleton.** The skeleton, in turn, is held together by a network of cartilage, ligaments, tendons, and muscle.

Look at pictures of skeletons and bones and note especially how the joints are attached to each other. Examine some chicken bones, observing the hinge joint of the knee and the ball-and-socket joint of the hip.

Perhaps some of the most interesting bones are those of the spine. Each segment is capable of limited movement, so we can bend and twist; yet, strain can damage these bones. It is particularly dangerous to try to lift heavy loads the wrong way. Lift incorrectly, and the inner edges of the vertebrae are pinched while the outer edges are pulled apart. (See figure 21.7.) That could result in a serious back injury.

You should lift by bending your knees, not your back. In figure 21.8, the model is shown in the correct lifting position. Notice that the spine is straight, not bent, and that the lifting is done with the legs, not the back.

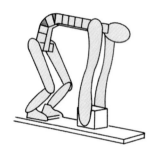

FIGURE 21.7 Lift the wrong way and the spine goes "b-o-i-n-g!"

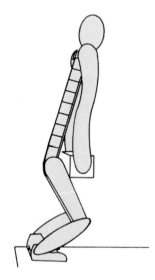

FIGURE 21.8 Lift correctly and the strain is placed on the legs instead of the back.

Almost one-fourth of all disabilities suffered by American workers are caused by improper handling of materials. Correct lifting procedures will help avoid the many assorted strains, sprains, and other injuries that can otherwise occur.

Muscles work in pairs. When you lift your leg and bring the foot forward to take a step, it is the large muscle group in front of the leg (quadriceps) that is contracting. Then when the foot is planted, the muscle group in the back of the leg (hamstring) contracts to push the body ahead

It is important to realize that muscles can only contract or pull. They cannot push. Thus, when you bring your hand up and bend your elbow, your biceps (in front of your upper arm) is contracting while the muscle in back of your upper arm (the triceps) is relaxing. *Event 21-J, Muscle Pairs,* shows this principle very well. It is easy to tell which muscle is contracting and which is relaxing.

If one muscle contracts the other must relax. Otherwise the muscles will be working against each other. Normally, in relaxed use, the muscles work together very well. However, if muscles are overloaded, they will not relax properly. That condition greatly increases the workload of the active muscle and reduces its efficiency.

Where might such overloading occur? One common place to find examples of muscle overloading and inefficiency is at a track meet by runners who have overextended themselves. Have you ever seen a runner "tie up" while straining to finish a race?

The muscles become loaded with waste products and no longer respond. The muscle that should be relaxing remains tense, and the runner struggles along with a bent-knee stride that greatly inhibits the running motion.

One way in which athletes try to avoid "tying up" is to keep muscles limber and flexible with careful stretching exercises. Flexible muscles allow a greater range of motion and are more resistant to the tensions of extreme effort.

Good posture is important to good health and is often a clue to a person's physical condition. It is unlikely that a good athlete will have poor posture. When muscles are strong and in good condition, posture is usually good. In turn, good posture causes very little strain.

Poor posture, however, causes much greater strain. *Event 21-K, Posture Strains,* is a good activity to show the effects of poor posture. It takes only a minute or two for strains to become evident if you try to assume an obviously poor posture. Leaning out of position for even a short time will quickly fatigue muscles that are stressed by the out-of-position body. The event should help pupils realize the benefits of good posture.

Skin

The **skin** that covers your body is sensitive to touch. The degree of sensitivity varies from one place on the body to the next. This sensitivity can be explored by performing *Event 21-L, Touch Test.* Both points of the hairpin can usually be detected by touch in places that have many nerve endings, such as the fingertips.

However, on the back of the hand, the neck, and other parts of the body, there are fewer nerve endings. As a result, it is impossible to tell if one or two points is touching the skin, unless those points are fairly wide apart.

You can try another activity that shows how the sense of touch varies among different sites of the body. For example, pinch the skin at your elbow.

Then pinch the skin on the back of your wrist. Where does it hurt more? For most people, the back of the wrist is far more sensitive.

Another activity that shows how we obtain messages from our sense of touch is demonstrated in *Event 21-M, One Nose or Two?* When you cross your fingers and then touch them to the tip of your nose, you will feel a strange sensation. It almost feels as if you have two noses! The left side of the first finger and the right side of the second finger both feel something, and it gives the impression of two objects.

Four different kinds of sensation can be felt by the skin: pain, pressure, heat, and cold. The events in this section all pertain to the effects of slight pressure on the skin and to how well those pressures can be detected.

Effect of Tobacco and Caffeine on the Body (Events 21-N through 21-R)

One cannot discuss fitness and health without a look at the effects of tobacco on the human body. It is important that this discussion be presented in the elementary school because many pupils begin to smoke during the elementary grades.

One preliminary caution: Be sure to present this topic in such a way that it does not ridicule or degrade adults who smoke. After all, many parents are likely to be smokers. The evidence against smoking is quite strong, and the case can be made without ridiculing adults.

One way to proceed is obvious. Simply tell them, "Be sure *not* to ridicule adults who smoke." Another way is to pretend that there are several sets of "smoking" parents sitting in the back of the room. How would they feel about your presentation? If the lesson is presented correctly, parents who smoke will be your strongest supporters.

Discrepant Events and Pupil Investigations

Event 21-N. Why Adults Smoke

Ask pupils to think of reasons why adults smoke. Pupils always hear reasons why people *should not* smoke, but in this case ask them to think of reasons why adults *do* smoke. Write the reasons on the chalkboard.

Pupil Investigations (may include the following processes):

1. Investigating to find out why adults smoke.
2. Recording data from their parents and other adults about the reasons for smoking.
3. Inferring from the responses that parents who smoke often prefer that their children do *not* smoke.
4. Generalizing that most adults who smoke consider smoking harmful.

Event 21-O. Why Children Smoke

After completing the list of reasons of why adults smoke, ask, "Why do children smoke?" Go over the list of responses given for adults. Do any of them apply to children ("Something to do"; "It tastes good"; "It is relaxing after dinner"; etc.)

The class will likely erupt in laughter when looking at those reasons for smoking. They know that children do not smoke because "it tastes good" or because "it is something to do after dinner"! None of the adult reasons apply. Ask them to think about the real reason why children smoke.

Pupil Investigations (may include the following processes):

1. Comparing the adult reasons for smoking with those that might apply to children.
2. Discovering the major reason that children smoke is peer pressure.
3. Devising a method of resisting peer pressure to smoke.

Event 21-P. Why Adults Quit

Studies have shown that adults quit smoking for three main reasons. Ask children to predict (to vote on) which of the following reasons they think is the most effective: (1) health reasons, (2) example-giving, or (3) mastery (to gain control over the habit).

Pupil Investigations (may include the following processes):

1. Predicting the reasons that adults give for quitting.
2. Recording and placing in rank order the predictions of the class.
3. Comparing their votes with the evidence from health authorities.
4. Inferring that some reasons will be effective and others not.

Event 21-Q. Cigarette Money

Ask the class to spend some cigarette money. However, instead of spending it on cigarettes, how much would there be if it were saved for a month, and for a year. Assume the use of one pack a day at a cost of $3.00 per pack. How much would be saved in a month? In a year?

Then ask them, to take that figure, go to a favorite catalog, and make a list of things they want, equal to the cigarette money that they would save during the month or year.

Pupil Investigations (may include the following processes):

1. Calculating the cost of a pack of cigarettes for a month; for a year.
2. Calculating the cost of goods selected from a catalog or newspaper which equal the cost of the cigarettes.
3. Generalizing that cigarette money goes up in smoke, but that the same money could buy something more useful.

Event 21-R. Hot or Cold Hands

Using a temperature probe connected to the computer, measure the body temperature of a pupil by placing the probe under his armpit until the temperature stabilizes. Record the core body temperature. Now measure the finger temperature of the pupil by having him place the temperature probe between the index finger of one hand and both thumbs. Adjust the position until the temperature stabilizes.

Have the pupil quickly eat a chocolate bar and drink a diet soda. Continue to record the fingertip temperature over a 20-minute period of time in

2-minute intervals. Do you predict his temperature will go up, down, or stay the same after consuming the foods? Why?

Pupil Investigations (may include the following processes):

1. Predicting (incorrectly) that the fingertip temperature will rise.
2. Analyzing the temperature versus time graph.
3. Inferring the reason(s) for the temperature change.
4. Generalizing the effects of what you eat on body functions.

Events 21-N through 21-R Explained in Context (Effects of Tobacco and Caffeine on the Body)

Event 21-N asks *Why do adults smoke?* Most pupils will not have given that question much thought. When you ask it, they will say, "I guess they must like it" or "I suppose it tastes good." Ask children to think of as many reasons as possible and then list the reasons on the chalkboard. The reasons most likely to be given include:

1. It tastes good.
2. It is something to do.
3. It is a habit.
4. They like it.
5. It is relaxing.
6. It helps to keep them from overeating.

After they have given all the reasons that they can think of, focus on the real reason: Adults smoke because *it is too hard to quit!* Add that reason to the list on the chalkboard.

According to a national survey by a major television network, about 70% of all adult smokers have made at least one serious attempt to quit! That means that *most* adult smokers do so because *it is too hard to quit.* Children have a right to know that information.

Follow up by exploring when most adults *started* to smoke. They started before they were adults! Children have a right to know that information also. Surprisingly, the decision to smoke is usually not made by adults. It is made by children. By the time they become adults, most smokers are addicted. Practices and attitudes of adult smokers can be summarized as follows:

1. They began smoking before they were mature adults.
2. They would now prefer to quit.
3. They would feel just as mature if they did not smoke.
4. They strongly prefer that their own children do not smoke.

Have pupils ask their parents (who smoke) about the above attitudes. It is likely that the parents will confirm the findings. Of course, it is again important to present the information and to ask the questions in a way that does not disparage or ridicule adults. If the topic is handled carefully, parents who smoke will be your strongest allies.

Most parents will admit that they started to smoke at an age when they were not yet fully mature. They will admit that it has become a strong habit and that it is too hard to quit. Many pupils will bring back reports that their parents have seriously tried to quit.

Once pupils know the details of why adults smoke, they will be in a better position to resist the peer pressures that so many of them face. However, the next event is even more important.

Event 21-O, Why Children Smoke, is a vital follow up. Ask pupils why children begin to smoke. Then turn to the list about adult smokers that should still be on the chalkboard.

You can say that we already have a list of reasons why people smoke. Are these the reasons why children smoke? The class will likely burst into laughter. They *know* that schoolchildren do not smoke because "it tastes good" or "it's something to do" or any other reason on the adult list.

They will almost always give the right reason. In one form or other they will say: "those kids think they're more grown up"; "they think that they are more important than others"; "they think that they are big shots!" Teachers call it peer pressure; children call it "being cool" or being a "big shot"!

Discuss the reason with the class and then add it to the chalkboard. Use the term "big shot" in discussing the reason. It is important to blunt the attitude of superiority that the child-smoker uses in trying to get others to smoke. Use the term and explore the attitude.

Ask the pupils if they have ever seen one of their classmates smoke. Of course, do not ask for names. If that question is asked in the fourth, fifth, or sixth grade, the answer is almost always "yes." Ask them to analyze the situation. Did the smoker act proud? Did the smoker act as if he or she were superior? Like a big shot? Did the person act as if he or she were more mature or "grown-up?"

The beginning smoker is most likely driven to smoking by peer pressure and a feeling of prestige. They use this feeling as a powerful lever to make a nonsmoking child feel like a "sissy" or immature. It is important that the pressure be blunted.

Ask if a child who sneaks a smoke is really a big shot. Is that child really mature? Do adults try to prove their maturity that way? Children can easily see that only immature children will try to pressure others to smoke. Adults don't act that way.

At this point we should mention that health dangers are *not* very effective in keeping children from smoking. Why not? Just observe how a child might be confronted with the temptation to smoke. Suppose a boy is walking home from school and comes across several of his classmates sneaking a smoke behind some bushes. They call to him to "come on over." They push a lit cigarette toward him and say, "Here, have a smoke." Suppose the child does not want to smoke. How does he avoid the pressure? He might say, "No, thanks. I don't care to smoke." "What's the matter? Are you a sissy?"

One cannot expect the boy to respond, "I am worried about emphysema and hardening of the arteries." So, what can the victim say to blunt that powerful question: "What's the matter? Are you a sissy?"

The victim can say: "What's the matter? Are you a *big shot?*" "Do you think you are *superior?*" "I don't need to smoke to act grown-up."

It is important that a teacher go over the pressures presented to children. Once the topic is fully explored in the classroom, it is quite likely that those who *do* already smoke will tend to avoid the tactic with other pupils in the class.

Why Do Adults Quit?

Event 21-P, Why Adults Quit, presents three reasons why adults have quit smoking. Surprisingly, health is not the main reason. True, most adults realize the health dangers, but the dangers seem far away. They rationalize: "I'm too young to get cancer or emphysema"; or "I don't inhale much"; or "I use filter tips."

One of the most important reasons is that of "example setting." That is why parents have quit—to set an example for their children; why teachers have quit—to set an example for their pupils; and why doctors have quit—to set an example for their patients.

In 1950, more than 60% of all doctors smoked, but by 1965 only about 30% smoked. The trend is even more dramatic among newly graduated doctors. In the late 1990s, less than 4% of newly graduated medical doctors smoked.

Another major reason for quitting is "mastery." Many people have come to realize that smoking has taken over their lives. They decide that they will become the master of the smoking urge, not its victim.

The Cost of Smoking

Children are likely to have heard about "cigarette money." Ask them how much that money can amount to in a year or more. Perform *Event 21-Q, Cigarette Money,* and see how much money is used in a year if a smoker buys one pack of cigarettes a day.

Assume that cigarettes cost $3.00 per pack. That amounts to $90.00 a month (for a 30-day month), and $1095.00 a year. Let the pupils do the calculations themselves. The figures will astound them. Then let them look through a catalog or newspaper ads to see what they could buy with the "cigarette money."

To continue with the exercise, you may ask the pupils to figure the cost of smoking during an entire lifetime. Assume that a person begins smoking at age 15 and continues to age 75. How much is spent during the 60 years, assuming there is no increase in price? The figure is $65,700. Ask them how they would spend that amount of money.

If the money is invested at the end of every year to gain compound interest at 6% a year, the total grows to more than $173,280 in 40 years, $207,600 in 50 years, and $239,040 in 60 years. Those are truly astounding figures. In addition to showing the cost of smoking, the figures are quite effective in showing the power of compound interest.

In *Event 21-R, Hot or Cold Hands,* most pupils predict that the temperature will rise. They state that sugar increases metabolism and that digestion produces heat. Challenge pupils with why you had the person eat a candy bar and *diet* pop if sugar was the substance being tested. Other pupils state the temperature will decrease since you are drinking cold pop. (Make sure the pupil holds the pop can in the opposite hand being measured with the temperature probe. In fact, this experiment surprises most pupils when the temperature decreases. The caffeine in both substances is the culprit. Caffeine restricts the blood vessels allowing less blood, and therefore less heat, to the extremities. This is why doctors encourage people to restrict caffeine intake. It makes the heart work harder. The activity works best with pupils that have a low caffeine intake as a natural eating habit (little chocolate and cola). Many times the fingertip temperature will decrease by 5 degrees or more making the temperature difference between the core body temperature and the finger temperature even greater. Caffeine, like nicotine, is addictive. At about 300 to

600 mg per day (about 5 cups of coffee, or 6 to 7 cans of pop) you start running the risk of caffeine related health problems.

Combining Assessment with Instruction

Suggest to the students that they will be publishing a health and fitness information and tip book. Each small group of students will be responsible for a selected chapter. Brainstorm what chapters should be included. They might want to include such chapters as:

- Benefits of exercise.
- Nutritious food choices.
- Healthy heart.
- Breathing in fresh air (protecting the lungs).
- Summer sunshine and skin (including sunscreen or insect repellent).
- Injury prevention and safety.
- Drug and alcohol prevention.
- Over-the-counter drug safety.
- Muscle power.

Each chapter should have three parts. The first part should summarize the "big ideas" about that topic. It may include such information as the function of a body organ or statistics about health issues related to that topic. Students might discuss summer sun safety and the need for sunblock. They could include statistics about skin cancer and its causes.

The second part should include a list of tips related to the chapter that help maintain healthy habits or prevent disease or other health issues. In keeping with the skin and sun health issues, students might summarize how to care for the skin during the summer- or wintertime to prevent skin damage.

The third section should include a cartoon, drawing, poem, or some other creative entry that illustrates the content of their chapter topic. Three sample illustrations done by a student for a summer sunshine or safety chapter are given in figure 21.9.

Sites and Software

The following websites and software are appropriate to use with this chapter. Note that computer software and websites change rapidly. This makes it necessary to investigate the stable websites for new links and software catalogs for updates. Visit www.mhhe.com/friedl6e to link to these directly and for study resources.

Sites

School Program	www.projectaces.com
Physical Activity Fact Sheet	fitness.gov/physical_activity_fact_sheet.html
Fitness Testing	www.exrx.net/Testing.html
Fitness Center—Discovery Health	health.discovery.com/centers/fitness/fitness.html
Cooper Institute FITNESSGRAM	www.cooperinst.org/ftgmain.asp
Nutrition Education Materials (USDA, K–6)	www.na/usda.gov/fnic/pubs/bibs/edu/preschool.htm

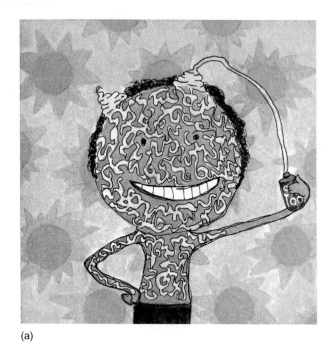

(a)

(b)

(c)

FIGURE 21.9   (a) Remember to use sunscreen; (b) use insect repellant, especially near dusk; and (c) drink plenty of water.

Software

FITNESSGRAM kit and CD Human Kinetics Publishers (1–12)

Key Terms

arteries, *415*

cardiovascular system, *413*

circulatory system, *419*

diaphragm, *420*

diastolic, *418*

fitness, *410*

hypertension, *418*

lung capacity, *420*

respiration, *419*

skeleton, *422*

skin, *423*

spirometer, *420*

systolic, *418*

Glossary

A

Absolute zero. The coldest temperature theoretically possible; point at which all molecular motion stops; 0 degrees Kelvin, minus 273 degrees Celsius, and minus 459.6 degrees Fahrenheit.

Action-reaction. See Law of Motion, third.

Adaptation. Organism's modification in structure, function, or behavior suitable to the environment.

Additive rule (of colors). The color obtained when two or more colored lights are combined; when all colors are combined, they produce white.

Adhesion. An attraction between unlike molecules.

Aerobic. With oxygen; a type of activity in which the body's oxygen needs are met by breathing; it builds endurance.

Aileron. Moveable part on a wing of a plane used to turn or bank the plane.

Airfoil. The curved shape of a propeller or wing.

Air pressure. The pressure of the weight of the atmosphere.

Alpha particles. Weak radiation that can be blocked by a sheet of paper or a few centimeters of air.

Alternating current (AC). A current that goes back and forth; produced by coils and magnets; the type produced by power companies.

Ampere. The rate of current flow; one amp lights one 100-watt bulb.

Amphibian. A class of cold-blooded egg-laying animals that can live on both land and water.

Amplitude. The size of waves.

Anaerobic. Without oxygen; vigorous activity that can only be maintained for a short time; it builds strength.

Angiosperm. Seed of flowing plant.

Angle of incidence. The angle of incoming light rays.

Angle of reflection. The angle of outgoing (reflected) light rays.

Angstrom. Unit of length, used to measure the length of light waves. One million angstroms equal one meter.

Animal. One of the five kingdoms of life forms. They contain no cellulose or chlorophyll, are capable of independent movement, and are capable of feeling and sensation.

Appestat (or "set point"). The body's mechanism for maintaining its percentage of body fat; goes down with regular exercise.

Arteries. The vessels that carry blood from the heart to the cells.

Atom. The smallest part of an element, made of electrons and protons.

Attraction, magnetic. Magnetic forces in which opposite poles are attracted to each other.

B

Barometer. Instrument used to measure the pressure of the atmosphere.

Battery. A combination of two or more cells. The term is often used incorrectly to refer to a single cell.

Bernoulli's principle. When the speed of a liquid or gas is increased, its internal pressure is decreased.

Beta rays. A stream of electrons with weak penetrating powers.

Bird. Warm-blooded animal with two legs and feathers.

Block mountain. Mountain formed when one layer of the earth is pushed up and slides over another layer of the earth.

Boiling point. The temperature at which a liquid changes to a gas.

Bread, cereal, rice and pasta group. Food group from which 6 to 11 servings daily should be selected.

Brownian movement. The haphazard motion of tiny particles suspended in a gas or liquid resulting from bombardment by the fast-moving molecules of gas or liquid.

Buoyancy. The lifting force of water; allows some things to float.

C

Caloric (food). The heat energy value of food, equal to 1000 calories of heat. Also called a kilocalorie.

Calorie (heat). Amount of heat needed to raise the temperature of 1 gram of water by 1 degree Celsius.

Capacitor. An electronic device that can store an electrical charge.

Capillary action. The attraction between two substances within tiny hairlike passages.

Carbohydrate.   An ideal energy food with a value of 4 calories per gram; cannot be used to build tissue.

Cardiovascular system.   Organ system in which blood vessels distribute blood under the pumping action of the heart.

Cell.   Smallest unit that displays the properties of life.

Celsius scale.   A temperature scale with a boiling point of water of 100 degrees and a freezing point of 0 degrees.

Center of gravity.   The point at which all of the weight of a body may be considered to be concentrated.

Centigrade scale.   Celsius scale based on 100 degrees between freezing and boiling points of water.

Charged object.   An object with either a surplus or shortage of electrons.

Chemical change.   The change of a substance into a new substance; i.e., fire, rust.

Chordata.   Group of animals with a backbone.

Chrysalis.   A hard-shelled pupa of a moth or butterfly.

Circuit.   A path for an electrical current.

Circuit, closed.   An electric circuit with the switch turned on.

Circuit, open.   An electric circuit with the switch turned off.

Circuit, parallel.   An arrangement of two or more batteries or bulbs in which two or more paths exist for current flow.

Circuit, series.   An arrangement of two or more batteries or bulbs in which only a single path exists for current flow.

Circuit, short.   A sudden drop in electrical resistance; an abnormal condition of excess current.

Circuit breaker.   A safety device that cuts off the current when it is too large for the wires in that circuit.

Circulatory system.   The body's system of arteries and veins through which blood delivers oxygen and nutrients to the cells and waste products are removed from them.

Classifying matter.   A system of grouping, to bring order out of chaos.

Climate.   The long-term condition of the atmosphere.

Cocoon.   In many insects, a soft, silky covering of the pupa stage of development.

Cohesion.   The attraction between like molecules; it keeps a solid from falling apart.

"Coke-bottle" shape.   The "pinching in" of the fuselage of an airplane in an amount equal to the cross section of the wings. The fuselage looks somewhat like a coke bottle.

Cold-blooded.   Animals whose body temperatures vary with their surroundings.

Cold front.   A large mass of cold air pushing into a mass of warmer air.

Color.   The visible effect produced by certain frequencies of light.

Color, additive.   *See* Additive color.

Color, subtractive.   *See* Subtractive color.

Compass.   A device with a small pivoting magnet that points to the earth's north pole.

Complementary colors.   Two colors that when combined produce white.

Composting.   A process of mixing decaying organic materials with water and oxygen. The result is used to fertilize or condition soil.

Compound.   A substance consisting of two or more kinds of atoms; i.e., water (H_2O) or carbon dioxide (CO_2).

Concave lens.   A lens that spreads light rays apart; it is thinner in the middle than at the edges.

Condenser.   A device in which static charges can be stored.

Conduction.   Transfer of heat from molecules to adjoining molecules.

Conductor (electrical, heat, sound).   A substance that is a good carrier of electricity, heat, sound, respectively.

Conservation.   The wise use of natural resources.

Constructive interference.   When two or more waves combine to increase the size of the resulting wave.

Contraction.   The shrinking of matter when it cools.

Convection current.   The transfer of heat by movement of a liquid or a gas; physical movement of a fluid due to uneven heating and cooling.

Convex lens.   A lens that brings light rays to a point; it is thicker in the middle than at the edges.

Core.   The hot dense center of Earth believed to be made mostly of iron and nickel.

Crust.   The outer most layer of earth 3 to 40 km thick.

Current.   *See* Alternating current; Direct current. Convection current.

Cuttings.   A means of plant propagation in which a leaf or leaf stalk is cut from a plant and placed into soil where the leaf takes root.

D

Decibel.   A unit of sound loudness.

Degree.   A unit used to measure temperature

Density.   Mass per unit volume of a substance.

Destructive interference.   When two waves combine to decrease or eliminate the size of the resulting wave.

Dew point.   The temperature at which moisture in the air condenses to form dew.

Diaphragm.   Dome-shaped horizontal sheet of muscle and connective tissue that divides the thoracic cavity from the abdominal cavity.

Diastolic pressure.   Blood pressure measured at its minimum pressure during a given heartbeat.

Dicotyledon.   A seed divided into two major parts, such as beans and peanuts.

Direct current (DC).   A current going in one direction only; obtained from all sources except electromotive.

Discord. The unpleasant effect of two or more notes sounded together.

Discrepant event. An event or activity with a surprising or unexpected outcome.

Drag. The resistance of air on an airplane in flight. The force on a plane that holds it back.

Dry cell. A chemical cell that does not leak or spill when tipped over.

E

Earthquake. Disturbance of massive blocks of the earth's crust, sending out longitudinal primary waves and transverse secondary waves.

Eclipse, lunar (Eclipse of the moon). The blocking of the sun's light to the moon by the earth; when the earth goes between the moon and the sun.

Eclipse, solar (Eclipse of the sun). The blocking of the sun's light to the earth by the moon; when the moon goes between the sun and the earth.

Egg. A reproductive body or cell produced by a female consisting of food and protective envelopes.

Electrical source of heat. The heat that is generated when an electric current goes through a resistance.

Electromagnet. A magnet made of soft iron and many turns of wire; it can be turned on or off when an electric current is turned on or off.

Electromagnetic spectrum. A range of frequencies that includes radio waves on one end, the visible spectrum in the middle, and cosmic rays at the other end.

Electromotive source of electricity. The current produced with coils and magnets; it produces an alternating current.

Electron. Negatively charged particle in an atom.

Electroscope. A device that can detect a static electrical charge.

Electrothermal source of electricity. The current produced by heating one end of two dissimilar metals and cooling the other end.

Element. A substance made of only one kind of atom cannot be changed by ordinary chemical means into anything else.

Elevators. Moveable parts on the tail of a plane used to control the up and down movement of a plane.

Embryo. Immature development stage that is not recognizable compared to the adult stage.

Energy. Resources in oil, natural gas, coal, hydroelectricity, and the atom; used to produce food, clothing, and shelter and to protect the environment.

Erosion. The wearing away of the surface of the earth.

Evaporation. Change of a liquid to a gas.

Expansion. The enlargement of matter as it warms up.

F

Fahrenheit scale. A temperature scale with a boiling point of 212 degrees and freezing point of 32 degrees.

Farsighted. Defect of the eye that results in blurred near-vision.

Fats. Food with an energy value of 9 calories per gram; used for energy, but cannot be used to build tissue.

Fats, oils, sweets group. Food group from which servings should be used sparingly.

Fire triangle. The three elements needed to sustain a fire: fuel, kindling temperature, and oxygen.

Fission, nuclear. The splitting of the nucleus of an atom that releases an enormous amount of energy; used in commercial power plants.

Fitness. Being of sound mind and body; being able to engage in vigorous physical activity for a long time.

Focus. The point to which light rays converge after being refracted or reflected.

Food groups. Six categories into which foods are divided, and from which various daily servings are recommended.

Food pyramid. An arrangement of foods into a pyramid with the base containing those from which most servings should be selected, to the peak from which fewest servings should be selected.

Force. That which can change the state of rest or motion of a body; a push or pull.

Forced vibrations. Sounds that are made louder when a surface is forced to vibrate at the frequency of the incoming energy.

Freezing point. The temperature at which a substance changes from a liquid to a solid.

Frequency. The number of waves per unit of time.

Friction. The rubbing of one substance against another. It produces heat.

Fulcrum. The point or support on which a lever pivots.

Fungi. One of the five kingdoms of life forms. Fungi need no sunlight to grow, and include molds, yeasts, mushrooms, and lichens.

Fuse. A safety device that cuts off the current when it becomes too large for the wires in the circuit.

Fusion, heat of. The absorption (or release) of heat when a substance thaws (or freezes).

Fusion, nuclear. Two atoms of hydrogen join (or fuse) to make helium, releasing an enormous amount of energy; the energy of the sun and stars; the energy of the hydrogen bomb.

G

Galvanometer. A device that detects tiny electric currents.

Gamma rays. Highly penetrating radiation such as x-rays.

Gas. A substance with no definite shape or volume. It can be held only in an enclosed container.

Gear. A special wheel and axle in which the wheel has teeth.

Geographic poles. The points at the North and South Poles around which the earth rotates.

Grafting. A method of plant propagation in which a part of one plant is joined to another plant.

Gravity. The attraction of the earth for an object; the attraction of the sun and moon for objects.

Grounding. Neutralizing an object with a static charge.

Gymnosperm. Seed of nonflowering plant.

H

Hardness scale. *See* Moh's scale of hardness.

Harmony. The pleasing effect of two or more musical notes sounded together.

Heart rate: maximum. The highest rate at which a heart is capable of beating It is usually about 220 minus your age.

Heart rate: resting. The lowest heart rate achieved while resting.

Heart rate: safe exercise. For a person without medical problems, this is usually listed as from 60 percent to 70 percent of the maximum rate.

Heat. The energy a substance has because of the motion of its molecules; measured in calories, British thermal units, or joules.

Heat of fusion. *See* Fusion, heat of.

Heat of vaporization. *See* Vaporization, heat of.

"High" (weather). An air mass of relatively high atmospheric pressure traveling in a clockwise direction.

Humidity. The amount of moisture in the air.

Hydrogen ion. A hydrogen atom that has lost its electron.

Hydrometer. A device that measures the density of liquids.

Hydronium ion. H_3O^+.

Hydroponics. A method of gardening without the use of soil where nutrients are supplied in the water.

Hydroxide ion. OH^-.

Hypertension. Elevated blood pressure, particularly the diastolic pressure.

I

Ideal mechanical advantage. How much a machine increases the effort input into a job if there is no friction.

Igneous rocks. Rock formed from molten matter.

Illuminated object. An object that is visible by reflected light.

Inclined plane. A slope like a ramp or stairs to make work easier. A simple machine.

Index of expansion. The rate of expansion of a substance per degree rise in temperature.

Indicator. A material that is used to detect (indicate) the presence of a looked-for substance.

Induction, charging by. Inducing an opposite charge in an object by grounding it while holding a charged object nearby.

Inertia. *See* Law of motion, first.

Inquiry. A method of teaching and learning in which pupils learn through active participation in science activities.

Insects. A class of animal with an exoskeleton, three body segments, and three pairs of jointed legs.

Insulator (electrical, heat). Any material that is a poor carrier of electricity, heat.

Interference (light). *See* Constructive interference; Destructive interference.

Inverse-square law. A relationship in which the strength of a quantity decreases as the square of the distance from the source.

Ionizing radiation. Radiation capable of dislodging electrons. The ability to penetrate varies greatly from alpha particles, which can be stopped by a sheet of paper, to gamma rays, which can penetrate heavy layers of metal.

Isostatic adjustment. The settling or rising of the earth's surface due to massive gains or losses in weight.

J

Jet engine. Engine that gets thrust from high-speed exhaust gases.

Joules. The unit of work. Product of one newton of force acting through a distance of one meter.

K

Kelvin scale. A temperature scale with the zero point at absolute zero, the freezing point at 273 degrees, and the boiling point at 373 degrees.

Ketones. Toxic by-products formed when fats are broken down for energy.

Kindling temperature. The temperature at which a substance will burst into flame.

Kingdom. The name given to the five groups into which all life forms are classified. Primary divisions into which natural objects are grouped such as plants, animals, lifeless materials and protists.

L

Land breeze. A breeze (usually at night) going from land to a body of water.

Law of motion, first (Inertia). An object at rest tends to stay at rest, and an object in motion tends to stay in motion.

Law of motion, third. For each action there is an equal and opposite reaction.

Leaves. Manufacturing centers of a plant combining carbon dioxide and water to produce simple sugars and starch.

Lens. *See* Concave lens; Convex lens.

Lever. Rigid bar free to turn about a fixed point called a fulcrum.

Leyden jar. The original device invented to store static electricity.

Lift. The upward force of air exerted on an airplane.

Light. A force of energy in the visible part of the spectrum.

Lightning. A powerful static discharge among storm clouds or between storm clouds and objects on earth.

Lightning rod. A device that protects structures from damage by lightning.

Lines of force. Lines of attraction or repulsion between poles of magnets.

Like charges. Two objects with similar charges. They repel each other.

Like poles (magnetic). When two north poles or two south poles are brought near, they repel each other.

Liquid. A substance with definite volume, but no definite shape; it takes the shape of its container.

Lodestone. A natural magnetic rock used in ancient times as a directional aid on ships.

Longitudinal wave. *See* Wave, longitudinal.

Loudness. The effect of the intensity of sound energy on the ears.

"Low" (weather). An air mass of relatively low atmospheric pressure traveling in a counterclockwise direction.

Luminous object. An object that is visible because it emits its own light.

Lung capacity. Volume of air the lung can hold.

M

Machine. A device that changes the amount, speed, or direction of a force.

Magnet. Iron, nickel, cobalt, and certain alloys with domains in alignment.

Magnet, permanent. A magnet that cannot be turned on or off; it retains its magnetism over time.

Magnet, temporary. *See* Electromagnet.

Magnetic domains. Grouping of atoms into small regions in magnetic substances.

Magnetic field. The region near a magnet through which it extends its force.

Magnetic poles. The concentration of forces at the ends of magnets; the points on the north and south regions of the earth at which the earth's magnetic fields concentrate.

Mammals. A class of warm-blooded animals that possess hair and nurse their young with milk glands.

Mantle. The layer of the earth located between the crust and the core.

Matter. Anything that has mass and takes up space.

"Max" test. A fitness test that is based on maximum effort.

Meat-poultry-fish group. Food group from which two to three servings should be selected daily.

Mechanical source of heat. Heat produced by physical action such as bending, friction, pressure, and striking.

Melody. The tune of a musical composition; the effect of single notes in sequence.

Melting point. The temperature at which a solid changes to a liquid.

Metamorphic rock. Rock that has been changed through the action of heat and pressure.

Metamorphosis. The great change in the life cycle of insects.

Meteorology. The study of atmospheric conditions to understand and predict weather.

Mildew. A fungus that grows on damp and dark non-food items.

Milk-yogurt-cheese group. Food group from which two to three servings should be selected daily.

Millirem. Damage done to human tissue by one thousandth rad of rays.

Mineral. Inorganic matter containing specific elements or combination of elements.

Mixture. Two or more substances that are blended without uniting chemically.

Moderator. Agent used to slow up neutrons in a controlled chain reaction.

Moh's scale (of hardness). A scale used to measure the hardness of rock.

Mold. A fungus that grows on damp and dark food items.

Molecule. The smallest part of a compound that has the properties of the compound.

Monerans. One of the five kingdoms of life forms. They do not manufacture their own food. Bacteria are an example.

Monocotyledon. A seed that is not divided into parts such as rice, corn, and wheat.

Monsoon. A special type of sea breeze that covers a large area of the earth's surface.

Moon phases. *See* Phases of the moon.

Musical tone. Sound produced by regular vibrations in matter.

N

Natural frequency (natural vibrations). The normal, unhampered frequency of an object when struck.

Neap tide. *See* Tide, neap.

Nearsighted. Defect of the eye that results in blurred distant vision.

Negative charge. An object with a surplus of electrons.

Newton's laws of motion. Law 1: Every body continues in its state of rest or motion in a straight line, unless acted upon by another force. Law 2: The acceleration of a body is directly proportional to the net force acting on the body and inversely proportional to the mass of the body. Law 3: To every action force there is an equal and opposite reaction force.

Nonconductor. Any substance that is a poor carrier of electricity, such as plastic, rubber, glass, and paper.

Nuclear energy. The energy released by splitting an atom (fission), or fusing two atoms into one (fusion).

Nucleus. The positively charged center of an atom containing protons and neutrons.

O

Ohm. A unit of electrical resistance; resistance affected by length, thickness, temperature, and composition of the material.

Opaque. A substance through which light cannot pass.

Orbit. The path of a satellite around a heavenly body.

Oxidation. The decomposition of an element by action of oxygen. Examples of fast oxidation are fire and explosion. Examples of slow oxidation are rusting of iron and rotting of organic matter.

P

Pancreas. Internal organ that produces digestive enzymes and the hormones insulin and glucagons.

Parallax. The apparent shift of an observed object because of the difference between two points of view.

Parallel circuit. *See* Circuit, parallel.

Percussion instrument. An instrument played by being struck, includes drums, bells, and piano.

Periodic Table of the Elements. The grouping of all substances in a comprehensive table.

Permeability of soil. The ability of soil to allow water to pass through it.

Persistence of vision. The retention of an image by the eye for a brief instance after the stimulus is gone.

Phases (or states) of matter. The three forms of existence that are common to most all matter: solid, liquid and gas.

Phases of the moon. The change in the appearance of the sunlit part of the moon during its 28-day orbit of the earth; spells out D-O-C.

Photoelectric effect. Electricity produced when light strikes certain substances.

Photometer. A device that can measure light brightness.

Photon. A bundle of light energy.

Photosynthesis. Process in a green plant that combines light, water and carbon dioxide to produce oxygen and carbohydrates like glucose.

Phylum. A major subdivision of the animal kingdom.

Physical change. A change in appearance only, such as tearing paper, breaking glass, or melting butter.

Piezoelectric. Electricity produced by applying pressure or stress to certain crystals.

Pitch. The frequency of sound waves; the highness or lowness of sound.

Pith ball. A substance from inside a corn stalk that is very sensitive to static charges.

Plant Kingdom. One of five kingdoms of life forms. They contain cellulose, can manufacture chlorophyll, and are not capable of independent movement.

Poles (geographic). The North and South extremes of the earth, connected by an axis around which the earth rotates.

Poles (magnetic). Two opposite points of a magnet at which magnetic forces are concentrated.

Positive charge. An object with a shortage of electrons.

Primary colors (of lights). Red, blue, and green; additive; when mixed they make white.

Primary colors (of paints). Magenta, cyan, and yellow; subtractive; when mixed they make black.

Process skills. Skills of investigation such as observing, inferring, recording data, classifying, experimenting, generalizing, measuring, forming theories, comparing, and predicting.

Proteins. A class of foods with an energy value of 4 calories per gram; used for building tissue and for energy.

Protists. One of five kingdoms of life forms. They are one-celled and manufacture their own food. Paramecium and diatoms are examples.

Pulley. A wheel with a groove in its rim in which a rope is placed. A simple machine.

R

Radiation (heat or light). The transfer of energy by waves through space.

Radiation (nuclear). Ionizing rays that penetrate matter and knock off electrons from atoms.

Reflection, even. Light bouncing off a smooth surface; image is visible on surface.

Reflection, uneven. Light bouncing off a nonsmooth surface; no image visible.

Refraction. The bending of light as it passes from one medium into another at an angle.

Relative humidity. The amount of moisture in the air compared to the amount it is able to hold.

Reptiles. A class of cold-blooded animals with a backbone and an armored or scaly skin.

Resistance (electrical). Opposition of a substance to an electrical current passing through it.

Resolving power (of lenses). The useful magnification of lenses, limited by the wavelength of light.

Resonance. Sounds that are made louder when an object absorbs energy at its own natural frequency.

Respiration. Breathing; inhaling and exhaling air.

Rheostat. A control device that can raise or lower the current in a circuit.

Rhythm.   The timing pattern of music; also called tempo.

Rock.   A piece of the hard part of Earth consisting of a single mineral or mixture of minerals.

Root.   Part of a plant that anchors the plant and gathers water and minerals.

Rudder.   Moveable part in the back of a plane used to move the nose of a plane right or left.

Runners.   A means of plant reproduction in which growth spreads out from a plant stem and takes root.

S

Salinity.   The amount of salt dissolved in seawater given in percentages or parts per million.

Satellite.   A natural or artificial body that orbits around a larger heavenly body.

Screw.   An inclined plane wrapped around a cylinder; a simple machine.

Sea breeze.   The breeze formed on a hot day, going from a body of water toward land.

Season.   One of four equal periods of a year (spring, summer, fall, winter).

Sedimentary rocks.   Rocks formed by the action of water in which matter is laid down in layers.

Series circuit.   *See* Circuit, series.

Set point.   *See* Appestat.

Short circuit.   A sudden and massive drop in resistance in an electrical circuit.

Simple machine.   Mechanical machines that convert one kind of motion in to another.

Siphon.   An inverted "U" shaped tube, with legs of unequal length. Uses air pressure to transfer liquids from an upper level, over an obstruction, to a lower level.

Solar system.   The sun plus the planets and other heavenly bodies that orbit around it.

Solid.   A substance with definite volume and definite shape.

Sonic.   At the speed of sound.

Sonic boom.   The sound heard on the ground of the pressure wave formed by an airplane traveling at supersonic speed.

Sound.   A form of energy caused by vibrating matter.

Sound, speed of.   Three-hundred-thirty meters per second at 0 degrees Celsius.

Species.   Any group of related plants or animals that can generally reproduce only with other members of that group.

Spectrum, color.   All the colors that make up visible light.

Spectrum, electromagnetic.   *See* Electromagnetic spectrum.

Spiders.   A class of animals with a body of two segments and four pair of jointed legs.

Spirometer.   Instrument used to measure lung capacity.

Spring tide.   *See* Tide, spring.

Staging.   A technique of spaceflight where one or more smaller vehicles hitch a ride, piggyback style, on a large space vehicle.

Stalactites.   Rocks hanging from the ceiling of a cave; formed by dripping mineral-laden water.

Stalagmites.   Rocks built up from the floor of a cave; formed by dripping mineral-laden water.

Starch.   A carbohydrate form of food stored in plants.

States of matter.   *See* Phases of matter.

Static electricity.   The buildup of positive or negative charges on an object.

Steam.   Invisible gaseous state of water.

Stem.   Part of the plant that carries water and nutrients to the leaves.

Stoma.   Tiny openings in the underside of leaves through which gases are exchanged with the air.

Stringed instrument.   An instrument on which a string is set in motion by plucking or bowing, includes violin, banjo, and guitar.

Sublimation.   The change of a substance from a solid to a gas without going through the liquid state.

Sub-max test.   A test of physical fitness that does not require a maximum effort.

Subtractive rule (of colors).   The color obtained when two or more paints are combined; when all colors are combined, they produce black.

Supersonic.   Faster than the speed of sound.

Surface tension.   A form of cohesion that occurs on the surface of a liquid.

Switch.   An electrical device that opens or closes a circuit.

Systolic pressure.   Blood measured at its maximum pressure during a given heartbeat.

T

Temperature.   The average motion of molecules; how hot or cold something is, measured in degrees.

Tempo.   The timing pattern of music; also called rhythm.

Thermometer.   A device that measures temperature in degrees.

Three-way switch.   An arrangement of three wires (three ways) in which a light (or an appliance) can be controlled from two places, such as a light switch at each end of a halfway.

Thrust.   A force that pushed an airplane or space vehicle ahead.

Tidal wave.   *See* tsunami.

Tide, neap.   The effect on the tide when the sun and moon are at right angles to each other; low tide.

Tide, spring.   The effect on the tide when the sun and moon are in line; high tide.

Tornado.   A localized violent twisting air mass that has very low internal pressure.

Trajectory.   The path of a thrown (or propelled) object, affected only by inertia and gravity.

Translucent.   A substance such as frosted or stained glass that permits light to pass through, but through which objects cannot be seen clearly.

Transparent.   A substance through which objects can be seen clearly.

Transverse wave.   Wave at which the particles vibrate at right angles to the direction the wave travels.

Tsunami (tidal wave).   A great water wave caused by a major underwater disturbance.

U

Uncharged object.   An object that has no surplus or shortage of electrons.

Unlike charges.   Two objects that have opposite charges. They are attracted to each other.

Unlike poles (magnetic).   The north and south poles of a magnet. That attract each other.

V

Vacuum.   A space with nothing in it; absence of matter.

Vaporization, heat of.   The absorption (or release) of heat when a substance boils (or condenses).

Vegetables-fruit group.   Food group from which three to five servings should be selected daily.

Veins.   Vessels that carry blood from the cells back to the heart.

Vibration.   The back and forth movement of an object or substance.

Volt.   A unit of potential difference; or unit of electrical pressure.

Volume (loudness).   The size (amplitude) of a sound's frequency.

VPS.   Vibrations per second (frequency).

W

Warm-blooded.   Animals whose body temperature remains stable.

Warm front.   A mass of warm air driven into a mass of colder air by a large weather system.

Water cycle.   The path of water in the atmosphere, from evaporation to clouds to rain.

Wave, longitudinal.   A push-pull motion of matter that carries energy.

Wave, primary.   Earthquake wave that travels through solids, liquids, and gases.

Wave, transverse.   A side-to-side or snakelike motion of matter that carries energy.

Weather.   A short-term condition of the atmosphere.

Weathering.   The gradual physical and chemical wearing away of rocks.

Wedge.   Double inclined plane used to split or separate objects.

Wet cell.   A chemical cell that produces direct current form dissimilar materials and a conducting liquid.

Wheel and axle.   Simple machine consisting of a large wheel rigidly attached to a smaller one.

Wind instrument.   An instrument in which an air column is used to make the sound, includes reeds, flutes, and horns.

Work.   The result of a force moving an object a certain distance. It is determined by multiplying the force by the distance through which the force acts.

Y

Yeast.   A fungus plant used in bread-making and in the production of alcohol.

Index